SPOILS
OF POWER

To Don

Best regards

Jeffrey Archer

JEFFREY SIMPSON

SPOILS OF POWER

THE POLITICS OF PATRONAGE

COLLINS TORONTO

First published 1988
by Collins Publishers
100 Lesmill Road, Don Mills, Ontario

Canadian Cataloguing in Publication Data
Simpson, Jeffrey, 1949–
Spoils of power

Includes index.
ISBN 0-00-217759-5

1. Patronage, Political—Canada—History.
2. Corruption (in politics)—Canada—History.
I. Title.

JL86.C67S55 1988   324.2'040971   C88-094489-7

Printed and bound in Canada

1st printing

"Patronage is the outward and visible sign of an inward and spiritual grace, and that is Power."
BENJAMIN DISRAELI.

CONTENTS

Foreword   1
Introduction   6

Part I: The Origins of Patronage

1 Mulroney 1984 – *Dividing the Spoils*   17
2 Responsible Government – *The British Legacy*   35
3 Sir John A. Macdonald – *The Great Bestower*   65
4 Sir Wilfrid Laurier – *Grits on High*   98
5 Patronage in Transition – *Borden, King and St. Laurent*   123

Part II: Provincial Patronage

6 Newfoundland   146
7 Prince Edward Island   161
8 Nova Scotia   168
9 New Brunswick   185
10 Quebec   195
11 Ontario   217
12 Manitoba   240
13 Saskatchewan   256
14 Alberta   272
15 British Columbia   282

Part III: Velvet Robes

16 Judges, Lawyers and Lieutenant Governors   300
17 The Senate   311

Part IV: The New Face of Patronage

18 Trudeau – *Return to Grit Heaven*   331
19 Mulroney 1988 – *Power Despoiled*   355

Notes   379
Appendix   404
Index   406

For Robert and Eve

FOREWORD

SYMPATHETIC FRIENDS, when alerted to my intentions for this book, wondered how many volumes I intended to write on political patronage in Canada. Their commiseration reflected the commonly held but not misplaced view that since patronage has always been so central to Canadian politics, once a writer got going on the subject, the most difficult problem would be knowing when to stop. Demands of commerce and common sense dictated one manageable volume, but I am acutely aware that a multitude of descriptive and theoretical observations about political patronage could have been added.

Writers by nature are a presumptuous lot in assuming that they have something worthwhile to say. Deciding what to say and, more important, how to say it and to whom adds to presumption, because different readers will have different needs and expectations. My own presumption is total since this book was conceived for specialists and the "ordinary reader" alike. Whether what follows throws a bridge between the two audiences remains for them to decide. A writer can only live in hope.

Spoils of Power is about one aspect of Canada's political culture and its provincial variants. There are elusive qualities about political culture that perhaps explain its fascination for social scientists and journalists—just when things seem easy to nail down, events and personalities change, altering or even shattering perceptions.

1

I like to think of a country's political culture as a prism subjected to a variety of beams of light which represent social, economic, political and cultural forces. These beams are then refracted by the prism to produce policy decisions, election results, new personalities, the ongoing warp and woof of the nation's political life. An essay about patronage, then, can be thought of as an attempt to trace one of those beams through the prism.

I make this point to avoid misunderstanding. I am not suggesting that Canada's political culture has been shaped only by patronage. Nor do I think that only the hunt for spoils and the power to distribute them are all that motivate those who participate in the nation's political life. Unidimensional explanations of individual or collective political behaviour are best left to ideologues and zealots.

Although many writers have insisted on the importance of patronage to understanding Canadian political culture, curiously few have written extensively about it. Pieces of the story have been analysed, sometimes with considerable discernment, occasionally with mirth, but nobody as yet has hazarded pulling the thread of patronage through the whole broad cloth of Canada's political experience. Such a job has imposed mighty burdens of selection and a certain unwelcome discipline. Some readers will note the omission of comparative context — the origins and practice of patronage in Canada compared with the United States, western Europe, and even the developing countries. I can only plead guilty that, having read a chunk of the voluminous literature on comparative patronage, I decided in the interests of disciplining an already sprawling essay to leave to others the task of fitting patronage in Canada into a comparative context. Fortunately, an outstanding start has already been made by Gordon Stewart, whose *Origins of Canadian Politics* influenced those sections of this book that deal with the eighteenth and nineteenth centuries. I gladly acknowledge my intellectual debt to him.

Political patronage in Canada has been so colourful and ubiquitous that I was constantly forced to deal cursorily with events that I knew could have borne a more detailed and searching description. That partly explains why I opted for footnotes — to show the trails that I followed and that others with more time or discernment might wish to explore. I could have added heaps of additional references, but opted for a balance between indicating the trails and not getting lost in the forest of academic conventions. The footnotes are thus a surrogate bibliography. I also translated French quotations into English, a practice frowned upon by the scholastically pure but usually welcomed by the rest. Bilingualism, after all, has its limits.

In the pages that follow I tried to keep my own opinions slightly in the background, preferring to let readers draw their own conclusions. But perhaps it is worth stating here that my views of patronage did change somewhat. I started out from the fashionable position of outrage, but shifted, upon reflection and research, to what I hope is a more balanced position.

I still do not find patronage terribly tasteful. I find that as a practical matter it brings out some of the worst aspects of our political system. I deplore those instances in which political loyalty or longevity outweigh merit. I do not think, for example, that we have been served by the Senate. Even if it were to continue to be an appointed body, it could function better as a chamber of sober second thought if the best-qualified people, as opposed to the most acceptable partisans, were appointed. The same observation could be made about citizenship courts and many boards, agencies and commissions. And I am on the side of the angels in deploring those kinds of patronage that spill over into corruption, graft and influence-peddling.

I also worry that in administering patronage we Canadians may have discovered the worst of two possible worlds. The American political system sees thousands of persons change with each administration, and a safety valve exists in that most of these individuals—Supreme Court justices being an obvious exception—leave with the arrival of a new president. In Britain, titles and appointments to the House of Lords are relatively harmless manifestations of patronage. In our system, however, people stay on for long periods in appointed positions that do influence Canadian affairs in an important way, and the remuneration they receive from the state is often considerable. What to do with them when our governments change causes endemic headaches.

About the more benign forms of patronage, especially those involving appointments, I am now more sanguine. It strikes me as normal, even desirable, that the party in power can encourage change partly by appointing new people to administer parts of the governmental apparatus. There is something, too, to the argument that if the politicians did not make the choices, the bureaucrats would, for there is something called bureaucratic patronage, evidence of which is not so easily apparent but nevertheless exists.

I suppose I wish there were a little more frankness and a touch less hypocrisy in making appointments and favouring friends. I wish politicians would use their patronage powers with more care, seeking a blend of merit and partisanship. I wish they would explain the positive reasons for patronage, and that the media, while remaining vigilant about excesses, would accept some of those reasons. I wish, too, that the Opposition parties would outline how they would proceed in similar circumstances. But I am not waiting with bated breath for any of this to happen. Patronage remains with us and always will as long as governing means making choices and exercising discretion. An alert, well-informed public is the best check I can think of against the abuses of patronage.

There were times — indeed, more times than I care to remember — when I despaired of ever finishing this book. A daily political columnist is a journalistic Prometheus, chained by sins of self-delusion and intellectual masochism to a computer rather than a rock. Launching this project while also trying to catch the quicksilver of daily events was only for the foolhardy or preposterously ambitious which may have amounted to the same thing. In any event, with my other obligations, *Spoils of Power* could never have been completed without considerable help from others.

The Parliamentary Library is a treasure for everyone lucky enough to be permitted its use. I know I drove some of the staff there to distraction, and richly earned the reputation of its most bothersome user. The mere sight of me coming with yet another list of requests for long-forgotten theses and inter-library loans sank many a heart. But they smiled through it all, provided their usual superb service, and can take some solace that, despite their doubts, this book was eventually published. To the staff and chief librarian Eric Spicer, a heartfelt thank-you. Provincial archivists in Nova Scotia, New Brunswick, Ontario, Manitoba, Saskatchewan and British Columbia also deserve my thanks.

Scholars and friends critically read parts of the manuscript, thus saving me from assorted bloopers, sharpening my perspectives and clarifying my obscurities. Whatever errors of fact or intepretation remain are manifestly my own. They are all busy people, and I thank them for their time and wisdom. They include Graham Fraser, and Professors J.A.W. Gunn, George Rawlyk, Ed Rea, Gerry Friesen, William Brennan, George Hulmes, David Elkins, Donald Blake, Ramsay Cook and Peter Waite.

Norman Webster, my editor-in-chief at *The Globe and Mail*, must occasionally wonder if he presides over a publishing house rather than a newspaper, but he swallowed hard and allowed me to be absent from the bottom left-hand corner of the editorial page for two months. (That absence may have cheered more readers of the page than I care to contemplate.) Those two months I spent as Skelton-Clark Fellow in the stimulating environment of the Queen's University department of political studies. I am grateful to my alma mater for the Fellowship and the fellowship. So, too, I thank the Canada Council for a grant that financed some of the research. The discriminating eye and sound judgement of my editor at Collins, Chuck Macli, helped to pound a morass of words into a book. Various people granted me interviews on sensitive contemporary subjects. They asked for and require anonymity, but they know who they are and how much I owe them.

Wendy may not know how much I owe her, but she still remains *sine qua non*.

Ottawa,
Kingston,
Thompson's Point, Charlotte, Vermont
1985–1988

INTRODUCTION

PATRONAGE is the pornography of politics, enticing to some, repulsive to others, justified as inevitable, condemned as immoral, a practice seldom considered a fit subject for polite discussion. Like pornography, patronage stirs the most basic human passions and sparks the most emotional of responses. Those who fulminate against patronage as a secular sin against the body politic have themselves often become mighty sinners when given the chance. Attempts to eradicate political patronage have failed as utterly as all efforts to eliminate sexually explicit material from society, partly because the judgment about the utility and desirability of patronage depends, like the judgment about pornography, on the eye of the beholder. Some people insist that patronage is indispensable to the art of politics; others declaim it as a perversion of acceptable standards of political behaviour.

Countries move through stages of development, and the judgment about the acceptability of patronage changes with each stage. In democratic societies, political parties pass through stages during which loyalties are secured and participation is mobilized by different means. In the early stages, political loyalties emerge from traditional patterns of deference to local figures of authority. Later, as electoral competition heats up and the franchise widens, material benefits are increasingly required to bind men to parties, because the automatic authority of traditional patrons can no longer be taken for granted. Still later, new loyalties emerge based on occupational ties, and inducements for political support shift from material ones to those of policy, ideology and, especially in the television age, the personality, attitudes and values of political leaders.[1]

The history of political patronage in Canada can be seen in the evolution of the parties through these stages of development, and in the interplay between the parties and the general public. What a British governor needed to secure support, what Prime Ministers John A. Macdonald and Wilfrid Laurier required to build national parties, how recent party leaders won electoral success and secured political loyalty, depended partly upon the stage of political development, and therefore the political culture, at various times in Canadian history.

Patronage has always preoccupied Canadian governments. Every government, federal or provincial, had to develop a procedure for filling the positions and allocating the preferments at its disposal, from the apex of the patronage system, the Canadian Senate, to part-time, low-paying jobs. The long march towards responsible government in British North America was largely the story of the elected representatives' struggle to wrest the right to dispense patronage from the British governors and their supportive cliques. The reformers' fight transposed to Canada a century-long struggle in Britain to transfer the King's patronage powers to the prime minister and the cabinet.

Responsible government transferred patronage but did not bring stability. The prize had been won, yet no one could capitalize upon it to build a stable party. This was the particular contribution of Sir John A. Macdonald who, with a variety of tools including patronage, built a national party rooted in the constituencies, capable of integrating a widely scattered and heterogeneous population into a national and political whole. This second phase of Canada's political development, beginning with Confederation, drew to an end around World War I, by which time the Liberals under Sir Wilfrid Laurier had come to emulate Macdonald's formula for political success, including his use of patronage. The third stage was the long period of Liberal domination under Mackenzie King and Louis St. Laurent, during which patronage remained central to party management but suffered periodic setbacks. The crucial change separated the party in power from the civil service, since in the Macdonald and Laurier periods the civil service had been a political extension of the party in power. This third phase represented the heyday of brokerage politics, in which the distribution of benefits was deemed essential for keeping all regions content. But that system began slowly crumbling in the 1960s as Canadian politics entered the modern, and fourth, phase of its development, a phase through which we are still passing and which has been altering, more fundamentally than did the previous three, the assumptions and practices of patronage. In ways the recent prime ministers — Pierre Trudeau, Joe Clark, John Turner and Brian Mulroney — have dimly understood at best, or completely misunderstood at worst, new forms of political mobilization and participation were required to replace the old materially driven ones. And so this fourth phase was marked — and still is — by an uncomfortable co-existence of traditional methods of political mobilization, including patronage, with tentative, new models developed for a public grown less tolerant of the traditional methods.[2]

Contemporary Canadian political debates abound with charges and countercharges about patronage, but many of the exchanges lack agreement about what constitutes a suitable definition. For exampe, when Brian Mulroney appointed Jean Drapeau as Canadian ambassador to the United Nations Educational, Social and Cultural Organization in Paris, various newspapers and Opposition politicians immediately cried "patronage." A dubious appointment it may have been — Drapeau was too ill to continue as mayor of Montreal — but patronage it was not. Drapeau had never rendered any partisan service to the Conservative party, nor would he after accepting the appointment. Similarly, allegations of patronage often suffuse discussions about political fund-raising, although seldom can critics point to a specific *quid pro quo*: money in return for favours.

But what is political patronage? Even some excellent academic treatments differ in defining the practice. Almost every writer agrees that patronage involves the giving of full- or part-time employment or contracts to supporters of the government.[3] But what of honorific favours? And does patronage necessarily require a monetary or tangible reward? Many writers think the definition of patronage should move beyond employment or contracts to include all forms of material benefits.[4] Once again, this definition seems to preclude honorific favours, but it does expand patronage to encompass — perhaps unintentionally — such practices as vote-buying and "treating" (the payment for votes with liquor). Still others prefer an even wider definition, to include not only material benefits but grants of extraordinary treatment.[5] For example, the longstanding tradition in Canadian provincial politics of paving roads in front of supporters' houses, while leaving as dirt and gravel the roads in front of opponents' houses, was clearly political favouritism based on government discretion, although the practice did not bestow employment, contracts or any material benefit directly upon those with the paved road.

By opting as this book does for a broad definition of patronage as appointments, contracts and other measurable forms of preferment, an immediate distinction is upon us. A great deal of what is properly called patronage has nothing whatever to do with criminality, or even dubious morality. Patronage is both more and less than criminality: more in that it encompasses many more examples of partisan favouritism than criminal activity such as bribery to secure votes or preferment; less in that patronage usually breaks no laws and merely raises questions about ethical conduct in government, the acceptability of which often has as much to do with the eye of the beholder, conditioned by the political culture of the country or province, as it does with the acts in question.

In Canada, today as yesterday, there are significant regional differences in public attitudes towards all forms of political patronage short of criminality, with tolerance towards patronage more readily found, say, in rural New Brunswick than in the urban centres of Western Canada. And for a variety of reasons — including modernization, urbanization, improved communications, better education, expanded bureaucratization, new emphasis on the personalities of political leaders — Canadian attitudes towards patronage have changed, so that practices once greeted with shrugs now provoke roars of disapproval.

Patronage, then, can be criminal activity (vote-buying, graft, bribery), but it is more commonly divorced from criminality. Even some of the criminal varieties of patronage, which would now be universally condemned, were once so conventional in Canadian politics that the perpetrators tried, wherever possible or expedient, not to make a fuss about similar practices of their opponents on the theory that both parties could point fingers with equal verity and passion. Thus, widespread vote-buying in the last century and early part of this century produced not only controverted elections, whose results were thrown out by the courts, but also private arrangements between the parties to "saw off" some disputed ridings; that is, agreement not to seek to overturn the election result in one riding in exchange for similar restraint by the other party in another riding.[6] The tollgating of liquor companies by provincial governments — payments to the governing party in exchange for listing the companies' products in government-run liquor stores — was widely practised by both Liberals and Conservatives. But neither party blew the whistle. Indeed, when a party finally got caught, its defence — sound in politics, weak in law — was that the other party had always nicked the liquor companies, too.

Apart from the distinction between criminal and non-criminal forms of patronage, another distinction is always worth bearing in mind. Patronage is frequently considered corrupt political activity, especially by people who regard its practise as an offence against good government, proper ethics, sound morality, efficient delivery of services, or whatever. Lord Acton's dictum about the corrupting temptations of excessive power is often trotted out by critics when a prime minister makes a bevy of patronage appointments. These exemplify, in the minds of editorial writers or Opposition politicians, the arrogance, venality and corruption of the prime minister in question.

Political corruption, strictly speaking, can be simply defined as "private gain at public expense."[7] Like patronage, the judgment as to the utility and desirability of corruption depends, in part, upon the political culture of the time. By political culture, we mean customary and approved aspects of political life which reflect the expectations, goals and laws the public uses to judge political behaviour. Absolute monarchs, for example, sold offices, including many needless ones, because they were broke. French kings of the seventeenth century perfected the *vénalité des offices*, selling practically all real offices and creating *offices imaginaires*, or positions without responsibilities. The sale of offices and creation of sinecures produced a vast bureaucracy that drained the treasury and made monarchs even more anxious for easy money. This seemed corrupt all right, yet the French philosopher Charles-Louis Montesquieu thought the practice acceptable because it created contending centres of authority. Nor is it always a simple business to equate corruption with inefficiency or dysfunctional behaviour. Corruption may get things done, as it frequently does in developing countries, whereas what we might consider correct behaviour produces wheel-spinning. Mexico runs on *la mordida* — the bite — and Nigeria on the "dash." Both systems of bribery are practised at every level of society, yet such practices are tolerated because they distribute money throughout the country and induce officials to take decisions they might otherwise prefer to delay.

Corruption permeated the urban political machines in the United States. People were on the take up and down the chains of command, but the machines did integrate into the social and political life of large American cities ethnic groups which might have longer remained on the fringes of society. The machines threw down ladders to the groups at the bottom, some of whose members rose up to positions of prominence. The urban reform clubs, the anti-corruption leagues, the muckraking journalists who swore eternal enmity against the big-city machines were almost all dominated by white middle-class reformers who did not need the machines for social advancement. They had it made already, either by their upbringing, education or economic status. But for the people who depended on the machine — and its corrupt practices — the reward network with its particularistic, concrete benefits meant social advancement, participation of a sort, delivery of services, and perhaps a bit of loose change.[8]

The boundary, therefore, between patronage and corruption is a subtle one. Patronage may not be a corruption at all—"private gain at public expense" — nor is all corruption necessarily criminal.[9] The appointment of party supporters to government positions does involve private gain, for the office-holders are remunerated for their work, but this is hardly at the public expense in the sense of costing the treasury money. The positions must be filled; somebody must run the Crown corporations, government departments, or plow the snow and haul the gravel. But clearly some aspects of patronage do involve corrupt activity, even when this activity falls short of criminality. For example, some Canadian provinces used to insist that empty liquor and beer bottles be returned to designated agents, who bought the bottles for a fixed price, then resold them at a higher price to the government liquor and beer stores. There was nothing criminal about these "bottle exchanges"; every government had its own agents, who changed after the other party took power. But the system was corrupt in the sense that individuals made private gains at the public expense, since the whole system of returning empties could have been organized more cheaply and efficiently. To take another example, it can be considered a corrupt form of patronage, although not necessarily a criminal one, to arrange public tendering in such a way that only firms favourable to the government get on the list, or to select from an openly tendered competition a politically favoured firm which did not submit the lowest bid, even if such discretion is allowed by statute.

The problem of distinguishing corruption from patronage, and of placing both in the context of a certain stage of political development, is compounded when, as in Canada, there are diverse ethnic groups and different regional political cultures, each one varying from the others in its practices and assumptions.[10] Broadly speaking, the further west one moves in Canada, the less prevalent patronage becomes and the less tolerant provincial electorates are of its manifestations. But even this generalization demands substantial caution. Quebec, for example, has grown increasingly intolerant of patronage in the last decade or so, whereas Alberta and Saskatchewan have brought back certain forms with a vengeance.

Without stretching the point, parties can be viewed as the enemies of corruption. In societies where the interests of the individual, the family, the clique, or the tribe are paramount, political institutions have little legitimacy with the people as a whole. Political institutions are valued, if at all, by particular groups for what they can deliver to individuals or their families. No sense of the common weal intercedes and no compromises are forced by the requirement to associate with others in the quest for power. These societies offer the widest scope for corruption, since the regime's legitimacy is based solely on what can be extracted from them by fair means or foul. Compared with the endemic corruption of these societies, the political patronage of typical organized parties in modern societies seems benign. National parties demand the transcending of individual or familial desires, or at least marrying them to the desires of others. As such, parties engender stability, which is the enemy of the disorganized, anomic, amoral, individualistic political community within which corruption in less developed countries thrives. Moreover, patronage has been a tool — one might even say the principal tool — by which parties became institutions for national integration in Canada, the United States and, to a lesser extent, Great Britain.[11]

For there to be patronage, there must be a patron and a client. Many of the greatest works in the history of art and music flowed indirectly from the patronage extended the artists by wealthy individuals — kings, princes, nobles, merchants. In each case, the exchange was reciprocal: the patron received a work of art to beautify his home or estate, lift his spirits, or demonstrate his power to subjects or fellow-citizens; the artist received the necessary financial support to create his work and the opportunity to display it. But their exchange was also one of dependence: because the patron held the means and the power to reward the artist. The canon law of the Catholic Church sanctioned patronage, defining a patron as one who financed the construction of a church in exchange for the privilege of controlling the lives of the congregation and, sometimes, the right to appoint lower officers of the clergy.[12] The Romans created a class of free men — not citizens — who attached themselves to patrons.

In this core relationship between patron and client appear the indispensable elements of reciprocity, dependence and discretion, subtle concepts that may vary from one patronage relationship to another.[13] Reciprocity means that both patron and client expect something from their arrangement. The patron gets services or allegiances; the client gets benefits he might not otherwise receive. The reciprocity can be based either on past performance or on expectations of future behaviour; in other words, patronage can be a reward or an inducement. Dependence illustrates that the patron ultimately possesses the resources, including statutory authority, which place him in a position of superiority over the client. But dependence can subtly turn into a symmetrical power relationship if the client, by withdrawing or shifting his support, can cause the patron to lose power. Discretion refers to the patron's option of granting or not granting rewards, depending on his satisfaction or dissatisfaction with the client's loyalty. Thus, while discretion, or favouritism, enhances the patron's power in competition with would-be patrons, it can also give some power to the client, who can exercise discretion by switching his loyalty to another patron in the hope of receiving better rewards. Discretion, however, brings greater headaches to the patron than to the client, since the mere possession of power does not guarantee an effective use of patronage. The history of Canadian politics shows that the use of patronage, rather than the mere possession of the resources to dispense it, is a litmus test of political success. Some prime ministers—Macdonald, Laurier, King—have used it with subtlety and a sure sense of purpose. Other prime ministers—Mackenzie and Mulroney—have misunderstood its exacting requirements.

In politics the politician is the patron, the voter the client. Prime ministers and premiers are the ultimate patrons, since they possess more resources for rewarding cabinet and caucus members, party supporters, and communities or regions. To them are beholden the mini-patrons, or brokers, who execute their instructions. Indeed, the notion of patronage, in essence a one-to-one relationship between patron and client, can be widened to include porkbarrelling, whereby political patrons may grant discretionary benefits to whole communities or regions as an inducement or reward for political support. Patronage is individualistic; porkbarrelling is communal. Put another way, porkbarrelling is patronage writ large, the exercise of political discretion to favour communities or regions on the basis of partisan considerations.[14]

Perhaps it is fair to observe that patronage is endemic to organized human society because everyone naturally prefers and trusts the company of friends to that of adversaries. The problem for political practitioners and observers has always been finding the point at which preference injures the public interest, a shifting and uncertain notion.

Some analysts have argued that patronage, and especially its corrupt forms, springs from basic human weaknesses.[15] Put metaphorically, corruption is attributable to rotten apples in the political barrel, or to psychological abnormalities in elected politicians, whereas more benign forms of patronage arise from normal desires to reward friends and discomfort enemies. Following this line of analysis, the scandals during John A. Macdonald's and Mackenzie King's governments flowed from the psychological makeups of these prime ministers.

Other analysts believe that institutions create imperatives for corruption and patronage that lure basically upright political leaders down paths they would not otherwise travel. If only political institutions were properly adjusted, if only sufficient checks and balances were instituted, if only wise laws were passed, then corruption and patronage would end. Rotten barrels, rather than rotten apples, cause the problems. This institutional explanation suggests that there would never

have been a Pacific Scandal if proper laws governing political fund-
raising had existed; nor would King have been able to load the Senate
with Liberals if the Fathers of Confederation had opted for the pre-
Confederation model of an elected upper chamber.

Still other analysts believe that patronage and corruption arise
from the broad pressures brought on governments by diverse elements
of society. The market for apples, rather than rotten barrels or rotten
apples, causes the problems. There would never have been a Pacific
Scandal, following the systemic analysis, if railroad promoters had not
rained down so many pressures upon governments; nor would King
have loaded the Senate with Liberals if so many party supporters had
not importuned him with requests for preferment.

None of the foregoing analyses explains the roots of patronage;
they all contribute in different measure to the explanation, and all will
recur throughout this book. Nor can any one approach definitively
answer the question of who initiates the dynamics of patronage — the
patron or client, or both — perhaps because the instances and means
of patronage are so varied that no single analytical framework could
ever suffice. Nor does any one framework fully explain a patron's
headaches when confronted by competing clients. In modern Canadian
politics, for example, political leaders are now caught between the need
to satisfy their own supporters, who demand rewards and preferments,
and the voters as a whole, many of whom believe that the traditional
ways of rewarding partisan supporters smack of unacceptable favouritism, cronyism and flawed ethical behaviour. The demands of party
management now increasingly conflict with the demands of electoral
appeal because the political expectations of party supporters no longer
in all cases reflect the political culture of their society.

Similarly, the time-honoured dilemma of porkbarrelling for any
national party is that the application of communal patronage to one
region immediately sparks demands for equal treatment elsewhere.
From these pressures springs the inherently inflationary aspect of
patronage and porkbarrelling: a reward in one quarter enlarges expectations elsewhere, which, persistently pressed, force a political leader
tangibly to meet them or risk the withdrawal of client support.

The inflationary pressures of patronage cannot be met by any but
the wealthiest of patrons; even absolutist monarchs were forced to sell
offices to raise revenues to meet their own extravagances, the financial
needs of the state, and the demand for places and preferments. Once
elected officials became the patrons, the state became the patrons' treasure. Democratization also increased the number of clients.[16] These new
clients could bargain for preferential treatment in the coin of individual
or communal votes, and patrons invariably discovered that the

demands exceeded the available supply. When parties emerged from informal groupings of individual legislators, they became the principal vehicles for satisfying clients' demands. The clients, thanks to modern communications and better education, could readily measure their rewards against those of others, compounding still further the demands on the political patrons. The historical landscape of Canadian politics is littered with corpses of leaders who attempted to explain to the voters that the treasury could sustain no further demands and who despaired of ever finding sufficient preferments to satisfy surplus demands. The inflationary expectations of patronage push up the costs for any political patron trying to keep his clientele happy. The arrival of deficit financing as an intellectually approved method of arranging a nation's finances further widened the patron's opportunities for porkbarrelling. Yet soon the Canadian political patron and his party were caught again in the swirl of the revolution of rising expectations, wherein preferments, especially communal ones, were no longer considered to be favours given at the discretion of hard-pressed patrons, but services, payments and other forms of spending perceived by recipients as rights of citizenship. What bedevils contemporary Canada is that because the demands of clients are unremitting, the patrons' desperation to respond never slackens, not because there is widespread evidence that discretionary spending will buy them political benefits — for bushels of evidence suggest the contrary — but because there is fear of political reprisal if their answer is no.

Still, patronage remains a fixture of Canadian politics because the political patrons consider at least some of its putative benefits indispensable. Faced with the demand for rewards from supporters, political patrons believe patronage to be essential, or at least important, for maintaining an active party organization. Commenting on the same problem in the United States, Walter Lippmann wrote in 1930, "It is, I think, literally true that if the exchange of favors were suddenly and miraculously abolished, there would be a wholesale voluntary retirement of petty politicians to private life, for they would lack then the incentive to stay in politics and the very means by which they maintain their political influence."[17] This sweeping and somewhat cynical interpretation of political motivation goes too far, since the reasons for political participation do extend beyond the receipt of favours; but some participants are indeed motivated by the anticipation of reward. To deny it would be as naive as to suggest that only the expectation of favour lures men and women into politics. Suffice it to say that the expectation of favour, a core element of patronage, is among those motivations for political participation that party leaders cannot ignore.

Patronage, perhaps more obviously, is designed to secure votes and supporters for the patron. Generations of political leaders in Canada reckoned this to be its principal benefit. Whether patronage still delivers these benefits to the political patron is increasingly dubious, but in earlier stages of Canada's political development party leaders relied on patronage at least as much as any other political tool for creating national parties and garnering public support.

Patronage also financed politics, at first quite directly because parties did return favours for the money they received from benefactors, later indirectly because campaigns became publicly financed and contributions were opened to public scrutiny. Even so, parties now organize clubs for major contributors, who receive privileged access to cabinet ministers at specially organized events.

Finally, patronage induces discipline within parties, because members are beholden to the leadership for actual or anticipated rewards. Patronage can buy off the disaffected; its withdrawal can punish the disloyal. Its utility as an integrating force in the building of national parties has been demonstrated. Patronage, by offering benefits to people in all regions, has helped to steer Canada away from parties based on race, religion or region, which would have led to unstable coalition governments. Patronage, whatever its costs, has done its bit for national integration and political stability.

There is probably less frank discussion of patronage today than fifty or a hundred years ago, when party leaders freely acknowledged why and how they were using it. Macdonald even publicly elevated patronage to a constitutional principle — only the supporters of the government had the right to government positions. These days, shrill rhetoric and secretive conversations have largely supplanted all reasonable discussion of patronage, and guilt has become its handmaiden. Confined to the shade, illuminated only occasionally by shafts of common sense, the mere mention of patronage conjures an army of dark spirits that spread everywhere, angering clients, weakening patrons and disturbing the voting public. A case in point is the trouble that befell Prime Minister Brian Mulroney.

PART I

THE ORIGINS OF PATRONAGE

CHAPTER 1

MULRONEY 1984
DIVIDING THE SPOILS

"First, this great and glorious country was built up by
the political parties; second, parties can't hold together
if their workers don't get the offices when they win;
third, if the parties go to pieces, the governments they
build up must go to pieces; fourth, then there will be
hell to pay."
George Washington Plunkitt of Tammany Hall.

"It's something right out of an Edward G. Robinson
movie — the boys cutting up the cash. A little hold-up
and then you're dividing the cash at night. I think that
this is absolutely scandalous . . . There's not a Grit left
in this town; they're all gone to Grit heaven. I think
that this is going to require a great gesture by the new
prime minister and I undertake today that all political
appointments will be of the highest unimpeachable
quality. I'm going to send out a dramatic signal of
renewal in this area of Canadian life."
Brian Mulroney, July 9, 1984.

ON SUNDAY MORNING, September 16, 1984, the day before Brian
Mulroney became Prime Minister of Canada, a group of Conservatives
drawn from every province gathered in the Governor-General's suite
of Ottawa's Westin Hotel, their presence a testament to how meticulously and eagerly Mulroney approached the spoils of power. Most of
those attending had spent years, even decades, working as fund-raisers,
campaign managers or members of Parliament, and had been personally selected by Mulroney for their knowledge of the Conservative
party. They had been summoned by the prime minister-in-waiting to
assume responsibility for co-ordinating from coast to coast the new
Conservative government's patronage. The timing of the meeting
inadvertently revealed the government's priorities. Mulroney did not
unveil his cabinet until the next day, by which time the lynchpins of his
patronage machine had already clicked into place.

Many of those assembled had worked actively for Mulroney in
the leadership campaign, but what characterized them all more than
anything else was length of service to the Conservative party. British

Columbia's Jim Macaulay, now a Vancouver lawyer, had started as executive assistant to Davie Fulton, a senior minister in John Diefenbaker's government. A Mulroney supporter in 1983, Macaulay had signed on as Conservative campaign chairman for British Columbia in the 1984 election. Peter Bawden, a wealthy Alberta oilman, had served two terms in Parliament during the 1970s. Will Klein had helped to build up the Saskatchewan Conservative party as the free enterprise alternative to the New Democrats in that province. He ran Pioneer Trust, remained close to Premier Grant Devine, and had supported Mulroney in 1983. From Manitoba came Arni Thorsteinson, president of Shelter Corporation, a development company. Thorsteinson had been a wheel in Conservative circles for decades, a fund-raiser for both the federal and provincial parties.

Michael Meighen from Ontario and Bernard Roy from Quebec were among Mulroney's oldest friends. Meighen, the grandson of a Conservative prime minister, was a transplanted Quebecker and, as such, an odd choice perhaps for Ontario's representative at the meeting. But no one had Mulroney's trust more than Meighen, except perhaps Bernard Roy, Mulroney's law school classmate at Laval University, friend and counsellor thereafter, organizer of the immensely successful Conservative campaign in Quebec in 1984, and Mulroney's choice to be principal secretary in the Prime Minister's Office.

Everybody in the Conservative party in Nova Scotia knew Ken Matthews, a lawyer from Truro; he'd been around since Robert Stanfield's premiership, filling a variety of party positions, including president of the provincial party and member of the national campaign committee when Stanfield became federal leader. Like Matthews, Alan Scales, a lawyer from Charlottetown, had been provincial party president. It was not exceptionally difficult to know every Conservative of consequence in Prince Edward Island, but it was important because by tradition on the Island the spoils of power represent deadly serious business. Jim Ross, a Fredericton developer, was a chum of Dalton Camp and Norman Atkins, the New Brunswick mafia who advised Premier Richard Hatfield. Of perhaps more importance, Ross knew Finlay MacDonald, the backroom Conservative who more than any man besides Mulroney drew these men together. John Lundrigan of Newfoundland, a fiery member of Parliament in the 1970s and now a businessman, rounded out the group.

These men, then, had been assembled in Ottawa by Mulroney for an assignment Conservatives had muffed before, but were determined this time to get right.

Mulroney had unseated Joe Clark by fanning the flames of Conservative frustration at the party's chronic inability to win and retain power. The vast majority of the Conservative front bench, the pillars of the party establishment, had supported Clark. But Mulroney had triumphed among the rank and file, to whom he had pitched his political appeal. Those months on the road cajoling delegates, those endless telephone calls from his exile in Montreal, those years of turning the conspiratorial world of Quebec Conservative politics to his advantage had sharpened Mulroney's already acute intuitive ability to say what his listeners wanted to hear. He appeared to lead, at least in those years, by keeping his nose trained on the aroma of discontent. Everything he heard and sensed instructed him that the next time the Conservatives governed—whenever that unlikely eventuality arrived—the rank and file would not tolerate shilly-shallying. They would demand rewards, and he would provide them.

By mid-campaign in 1984, a Conservative landslide beckoned. Mulroney would have to be ready to deal immediately with the unrequited ambitions of the rank and file, not in six months or a year, as Joe Clark had done, but quickly. Mulroney's debt to them explained why a vast and co-ordinated Conservative patronage plan had already been prepared for those whom he assembled that Sunday morning to receive their marching orders.

Canadian prime ministers have always understood that, properly applied, patronage helps to build and maintain broadly based national parties, turning Canada away from the patchwork coalitions of religious, ethnic or regional parties in some Western European countries. Patronage provided a mirror the party in power could hold up for the whole country, beckoning individuals, groups and regions to see some of their own reflected in it and be reassured or dismayed, depending upon the effectiveness of patronage, about the accuracy of the party's claim to represent the whole damnable complexity of Canada. In recent years the traditional reflections in the patronage mirror — partisan, religious, linguistic and regional interests — are no longer sufficient proof of the broadness of a political party. Now the mirror must also reflect the interests of women, native peoples, young Canadians, old Canadians and various multicultural groups. Their understandable desire for recognition accentuates a political leader's frustration at the gap between the demands for reward or recognition and the supply of positions or preferment.

The Liberals, in power for so long, had never underestimated the importance of patronage. They used it remorselessly, sometimes shamelessly. Mulroney intended to follow their example—indeed, the example of every Canadian prime minister, starting with the past master of political patronage, Sir John A. Macdonald. Mulroney would use the spoils of power to widen the Conservatives' political appeal, requite the ambitions of the faithful, and secure within the far-flung institutions of the federal government a readier acceptance of the aims of the Conservative party. Above all Mulroney understood that the party would not tolerate a repeat of Joe Clark's patronage performance.

When Clark led the Conservatives to a minority triumph in 1979, party faithful throughout Canada waited for their share of the spoils. But Clark and his ministers buried themselves in other priorities; they assumed that a run of perhaps two years in power awaited them. So the Clark team took their sweet time rewarding friends, partly because in their spectacular and touching naiveté, they had given no systematic thought to distributing the spoils of power.

Clark asked defeated Conservative candidate and former member of Parliament Jean Piggot to organize a system for collecting information on available order-in-council appointments and suitable Conservatives to fill them. While Piggot beavered away at her assignment, ministers proceeded at their own pace and followed their own devices, some making the necessary appointments quickly, others dithering from indecision or the crushing burden of other business. Alas for Clark, Piggot's system, a computerized matching-list of appointments and candidates, was ready at about the time his government collapsed. To Clark's credit in history, but to his detriment as party leader, the prime minister left one hundred and eighty-one recommendations for appointments unsigned on his desk after the Commons defeated the John Crosbie budget. Clark believed the making of such appointments by a defeated prime minister would offend the spirit of political fair play. He would make them after the Conservatives returned with a majority government.

Clark struggled to retain his leadership for three years after the debacle. Many were the reasons for his failure, but in the hushed conversations that sealed his fate there echoed a soft but insistent refrain: Clark had let the party down. Anyone who did not understand that power meant rewarding friends and discomforting foes was weak, wimpish and not to be entrusted again with the faithful's confidence.

Brian Mulroney was determined to avoid Clark's mistakes. Although a newcomer to elected politics, Mulroney had studied with envy and admiration how the Liberals' patronage machine and huge dollops of federal spending contributed to the party's dominance in Quebec. Mulroney observed how the allure of power and the anticipation of reward helped to attract the best and the brightest of federalist Quebeckers to the Liberal party, leaving the Conservatives with a freakish assortment of malcontents, conspirators and *Union Nationale* hangovers. Liberal patronage extended so widely in Quebec that every contractor, lawyer, architect, ad man — in short, anyone with substance or prospects — understood to which party money should be channelled and votes directed.

The federal Liberal party in Quebec, like the provincial Conservative party in Ontario until 1985, was broadly based, reflecting almost all segments of society. This was the model Brian Mulroney desired for a Conservative government, but before he could lead that government, he had to transform the frustrations of enough rank-and-file Conservatives into votes at the leadership convention. He knew his audience. Liberals and New Democrats would get appointments, he told Conservative delegates, but only after "I've been prime minister for fifteen years and I can't find a single living, breathing Tory to appoint." Civil servants, the favourite targets of disgruntled Conservatives, would receive their "pink slips and running shoes." Who would replace the departing civil servants remained an open question, but Conservatives assumed they knew the answer.

The 1984 election campaign presented Mulroney with a surprise and an opportunity. Patronage had seldom figured prominently in Canadian election campaigns, apart from the fall-out from the Pacific Scandal that covered John A. Macdonald. Even when prime ministers had rewarded a flock of supporters on the eve of a campaign, the voters had seemed unmoved. Occasionally in campaigns politicians had fulminated about the other side's abuse of patronage, but few voters had taken this rhetoric seriously, except perhaps party workers who resented those of a different political persuasion lining up at the trough. The cry of patronage rallied the faithful, galvanized the foe, and left everyone else unimpressed. Probably, voters knew from history that what the outs decried they would practise if they got in.

Yet the 1984 campaign shattered all the conventional assumptions. Suddenly, patronage became an issue in the sense that it was noticed and extensively discussed outside the political parties. Prime Minister Pierre Trudeau had departed politics by handing thirteen of his members of Parliament positions in the Senate, the judiciary, and on government boards and agencies. Former cabinet minister Bryce Mackasey received his second patronage plum — he had once been appointed chairman of Air Canada—in the form of an ambassadorial post in Portugal. Trudeau's cabinet had also approved dozens of order-in-council appointments, most of them to Grits, including the wife of Trudeau's pollster, Martin Goldfarb. John Turner, Trudeau's successor, had been foolish enough to sanction this orgy, inextricably associating himself with all the cynicism and arrogance that accompanied Trudeau's final, defiant finger pointed at the Canadian public. The orgy confirmed what many Canadians already suspected: Liberals were pretty much of a piece, greedy, smug, more concerned with their own interests than with the national interest, oblivious to outrage, deaf to dissent.

In the days before the orgy, Liberals in Ottawa chuckled proudly at the prospect of so many of their own being cared for in one grand manoeuvre. It would be so Trudeauesque, so daring, so comprehensive, so clever. Never did they believe that, apart from a few sanctimonious editorials and partisan barbs from Mulroney, the orgy would assume a political life of its own, wounding all who had instigated or sanctioned it. Nor did Mulroney, as opportunistic as the next politician and more opportunistic than most, contemplate scoring many political points from the affair. A few funny partisan cracks would suffice for public consumption before the issue died. Extended criticism might only remind the country of his own extravagant promises about patronage to the Conservative faithful during the leadership campaign.

On the Conservative campaign trail, Mulroney let down his guard long enough to ventilate his true feelings. Speaking of his old friend Bryce Mackasey, Mulroney cracked, "I've always said there's no whore like an old whore." He continued, "If I'd been in Bryce's position, I'd have been right in there with my nose in the public trough like the rest of them." Mulroney's advisers immediately recognized a blooper. Public debate about the orgy was not evaporating; like a bad smell, the memory of the orgy was worsening with age. Mulroney had ripped open the cellophane wrapper in which he intended to spend most of the campaign. Campaign manager Norman Atkins told Mulroney to apologize, publicly and fast.

A Canadian election campaign stumbles on for eight weeks. The length of the marathon militates against any party sustaining all but a few issues throughout the campaign. Liberal patronage, so thoroughly aired in the opening stages, might well have faded as a subject for daily repartee, its corrosive work already done. But John Turner got carried away.

Turner had structured his campaign like a three-ringed circus in which acrobats kept falling off the highwire, clowns forgot their makeup, flame-eaters scorched themselves, and the master of ceremonies muffed his lines. Turner's shambolic campaign organization precisely reflected his own uncertainties, the furious factionalism around him, and an inability to define the Liberal idea of Canada in the post-Trudeau period. Bickering attended every strategic and tactical decision of the Liberal campaign, so it was hardly surprising that in the minutes before entering the television studio for his debate in English with Mulroney and New Democratic Party leader Ed Broadbent, two advisers badgered Turner with contradictory advice. Senator Keith

Davey urged Turner to rough up his slick Conservative opponent; Bill Lee, Turner's leadership and election campaign manager, insisted Turner avoid personal attacks and present instead a prime ministerial image. Turner, torn as he was throughout the campaign, entered the studio uncertain about tactics. He held a dim view of Mulroney, calling him in private a lightweight and a clever charmer. Polls early in the campaign had reinforced Turner's conviction that nothing could arrest his march of destiny to 24 Sussex Drive.

None of Turner's advisers knew later why he had done it. They might have disagreed on everything else, but they rallied behind one recommendation—avoid, if possible, any discussion of patronage. The subject could only place Turner on the defensive; if it were raised, he should bob, weave, shuffle and get on to the next subject. When patronage popped up early in the debate, Liberal strategists held their breath, but the debate quickly veered in another direction. The worst was over, or so they believed.

Yet there he was, seizing the initiative, wading into Mulroney for promising patronage to Conservatives. "The style you've been preaching to your own party reminds me of the old *Union Nationale*," Turner charged. "It reminds me of patronage at its best." Mulroney, wide-eyed at his good fortune, immediately reminded the nation of the Trudeau orgy sanctioned by Turner. "You owe the Canadian people a deep apology for having indulged in that kind of practice with those kinds of appointments," Mulroney fired back. Turner, obviously flustered, replied, "I had no option." Mulroney, an exposed chin appearing within his range, unloaded: "You had an option. You could have said, 'I'm not going to do it. This is wrong for Canada, and I am not going to ask Canadians to pay the price.' You chose to say yes to the old attitudes and the old stories of the Liberal party." Turner began mumbling his "I had no option" line, but Mulroney cut him off. "That is an avowal of failure. That is a confession of non-leadership and this country needs leadership. You had an option, sir. You could have done better."

In television monitoring booths across Canada, news producers rubbed their hands in glee. They had found their "clip", the ten-second snippet of film to encapsulate the debate. Whenever television referred to the debate, viewers saw the thrusting jaw, the accusatory finger, the furrowed brow and the feigned outrage of Brian Mulroney cornering a wimpering John Turner.

Mulroney, savouring his television triumph upon returning to the campaign trail, poured on the scorn. "We don't have to be the victims of a paralysis of old attitudes and old ideas," he cried, "and of a prime minister who stands before a national television audience and says 'I had no option, the devil made me do it.'" The last phrase belied the ham in Mulroney, and when the laughter subsided, he knitted his brow, dropped his voice an octave, assumed a grave air and concluded, "He could have said no to the base instincts of the Liberal party. He could have said yes to Canada."

As political theater, little could top it; as political hypocrisy, nothing could beat it.

Mulroney certainly did intend to do "better," but not in the high-minded, moral fashion he suggested during the television debate. While he hammered the Liberals throughout the campaign for abusing public trust through gross patronage, Mulroney was quietly putting the finishing touches to his own party's assault on the spoils of power, an assault that began shortly after he captured the party leadership in 1983.

About two weeks after becoming leader, Mulroney called Finlay MacDonald, a veteran strategist in the backrooms of the Conservative party and a Clark partisan in the leadership struggle. Mulroney asked MacDonald to prepare some preliminary thoughts about the proper organization of a transition team should the Conservatives win the election. MacDonald duly reviewed the work of Clark's transition team and the reports Clark had commissioned in 1982 about the problems of planning the early months of a government.

Mulroney was campaigning for a Commons seat in the Central Nova by-election in the summer of 1983 when MacDonald delivered his preliminary report on the transition to Mulroney's temporary apartment in New Glasgow. During his flip-card presentation to Mulroney and advisers Charles McMillan and Fred Doucet, MacDonald recommended the establishment of four committees: policy co-ordination, machinery of government, staffing of ministerial offices, and appointments. MacDonald nominated himself, and Mulroney accepted, to head up the appointments committee and lead an informal group of the heads of all the committees. His organizational charts looked impressive enough on paper; they neglected only the prickly sensitivities of the elected politician. When MacDonald subsequently unveiled his plans to the Conservative caucus, MPs complained that such a critical matter as the preparation for government, including patronage, should not be left in the hands, however capable, of a backroom boy. MPs wanted one of their own in charge, someone who understood the prerequisites and vicissitudes of caucus and Commons, in short, a peer. MacDonald heeded the caucus' complaints. Erik Nielsen, the Conservative House leader, became head of the transition team, a task he tackled with customary seriousness.

MacDonald's particular responsibility, government appointments, had always preoccupied Canadian political parties. Every government, federal and provincial, had to develop a procedure for filling the positions at its disposal, from the apex of the patronage system, the Canadian Senate, to part-time, low-paying jobs. Indeed, part of the political history of Canada could be cast as an endless struggle for patronage. The fight for responsible government in British North America had been largely about wresting the right to dispense patronage from the British governors and their supportive cliques. The reformers' fight transposed to Canada a century-long struggle in Britain to transfer the king's patronage powers to the prime minister and his cabinet. First in Britain, then in Canada, non-elected patrons — king, governor or noble — yielded up their patronage power to elected officials, who needed it to knit together parliamentary majorities. Later still, party organizations — rather than loose, informal networks of the leader's friends — provided channels for binding together leaders and followers, or patrons and clients, through patronage.

The amount and kind of political patronage changed over the decades. The demands of efficiency gradually eroded the idea that those who worked for government owed their jobs to the party in power. Merit, always mentioned but seldom valued by those who defended the rewarding of friends, was gradually accepted as the indispensable criterion for deciding appointments to the bulk of civil service positions, rather than as an objective to which only lip service need be paid. Major crises helpfully illuminated the inefficiencies of patronage at the fulcrum of government decision-making. The French wars and the American War of Independence exposed the appalling inadequacies of Britain's public service. The unhappy, even tragic, experiences of Canadian soldiers in World War I — leaky boots, rotten potatoes, faulty rifles, incompetent officers — produced a clamour for reform. As government grew throughout the twentieth century, it touched the daily lives of more citizens, so that people could judge for themselves the waste and inefficiency associated with patronage. More widespread education, fewer fiercely partisan newspapers, an urbanized and therefore more impersonal society, the growth of the electronic media — these were among the developments that whittled down patronage at the core of the public service.

Yet, as the Conservatives discovered when they studied the list of governor-in-council appointments, the explosion of government activities had opened up additional opportunities for patronage in a plethora of Crown corporations, boards, agencies, commissions. When Finlay MacDonald started his work on appointments, nobody could tell him precisely how many positions the federal government needed to fill. The Privy Council Office had a list, but MacDonald found it incomplete. Individual ministries knew what appointments they could make, but no central registry of all government appointments satisfied the Conservatives' needs.

MacDonald handed the task of assembling a data base about the number, type and termination date of all order-in-council appointments to David Dyer at Conservative party headquarters. To those who had known Dyer in his adolescence and university days, his political interest seemed incredible because he had hated politics and believed the worst of anyone associated with it. But he had caught the political bug in his late twenties, and signed on in the 1979 and 1980 elections as a Conservative field worker in southwestern Ontario, where he met hundreds of Conservative loyalists, some of whom would be hunting for rewards if the party won.

The Clark government had compiled its data base *after* the 1979 victory; Mulroney wanted his in place *before* the 1984 campaign. So the laborious work of compilation and codification continued in the latter part of 1983 and first half of 1984, until the computer at Conservative headquarters could spit out some three thousand, five hundred order-in-council positions, with the name of the incumbent, a brief description of the position's responsibilities, and the duration and expiration date for the term. The data base, which the Conservatives simply placed in the Privy Council computers after the 1984 election, enabled the party to know month by month how many positions fell vacant, the salary level, and the probable regional, linguistic or occupational background of the required replacements. The Conservatives could tell with the push of a button that, say, a position on the Freshwater Fish Marketing Board would come vacant in three months, that the position required attendance at four board meetings a year, that the per diem rate was two hundred and fifty dollars plus expenses, that the term ran for four years, and that the incumbent (usually a Liberal) came from New Brunswick.

The Conservatives' data base did not provide information about those appointments historically considered the prerogative of the prime minister — Senate seats, judicial positions, diplomatic posts. These — and cabinet places — had always formed a prime minister's personal patronage, the strings by which he could bind his party to him, reinforce unity or punish dissidence, and enhance its electoral appeal. For roughly the first six decades after Confederation, prime ministers took a direct hand in most, if not all, government patronage. "The patronage." That was how everyone in political circles described the prime minister's, and the government's, unfettered authority to make appointments, including those within the public service. The definite article connoted the formidable sway of this exclusive power.

John A. Macdonald was the first Canadian politician to understand the dynamic potential of patronage. Politicians in pre-Confederation Ontario considered "the patronage" to be a vehicle for wresting power from the Family Compact so that they could reward their supporters and consolidate their own standing or that of their party. Macdonald, however, appreciated that patronage, properly applied, could widen his party's appeal. In so using it, he set the mould for broadly based, non-ideological political parties that spanned religious, linguistic and regional divisions linked by shares of federal largesse and the distribution of rewards. Like all who followed him in high political office, Macdonald occasionally despaired of the toll patronage demanded of his energies and ingenuity. But he shrewdly acknowledged that the energy expended on patronage paid substantial dividends, even if, as was often the case, he could satisfy only some of the thousands of solicitations and recommendations he received for places and preferments.

This most human of prime ministers remained almost unfettered by the scruples of other public men concerning the harmful effects of patronage. He knew, for example, that election campaigns were saturated with dubious, if not corrupt, practices; indeed, in his own campaigns he had had two close scrapes with the laws against electoral corruption. Parties were beholden for money to wealthy men and corporations; he had himself been caught out in the Pacific Scandal. But Macdonald took men as they were, rather than as he hoped they might become. He accepted their greed, follies, and ambitions, and tried to marry them to his party's cause.

Sir Wilfrid Laurier adopted Macdonald's political *modus vivendi*, and by so doing supplanted Conservatives with Liberals as the predominant political party of Canada. A statesman, to be sure, Laurier never neglected the minutiae of patronage underpinning the political organization that sustained him in office. Like Macdonald, Laurier delegated responsibility to kingpins in each province — Clifford Sifton on the prairies comes to mind — but by contemporary standards Laurier retained an astonishing degree of patronage power.

Only later, with the development of party organizations in the era of Mackenzie King, could prime ministers partially disentangle themselves from political fund-raising and ubiquitous patronage requests. When King insisted after the Beauharnois campaign-contribution scandal that he had known nothing of the contribution, he may or may not have been telling the truth, but his denial did acknowledge a fact of political life — in comparison to his predecessors, King had extricated himself from some of the grinding details of patronage. Not that he wished complete disengagement. King was, after all, the consummate brokerage politician. His skill as a power broker, coupled with his acute personal sensitivities, made him the prototype of a politician profoundly fascinated by patronage's intricate possibilities and exacting subtleties.

King's successors showed varying interest in patronage; they all organized their governments differently for administering it. None of them enjoyed talking publicly about patronage or deflecting personal criticism from Parliament and the media, for by the latter half of the twentieth century, patronage had acquired a widespread opprobrium. Vital though political practitioners consider patronage to be, it now strikes an increasing number of ordinary citizens as a remnant of a less sophisticated age when people relied for government services on the discretion of politicians, not computerized bureaucracy and detailed laws and regulations. The merit principle had been well established in the public service, the programs of social welfare codified, election fund-raising removed from the exclusive confines of corporate boardrooms.

Self-styled statesmen such as Lester Pearson and Pierre Trudeau, neither of whom grew up in the Liberal party, hated discussing patronage and always sounded defiantly defensive when forced to do so. The whole subject offended their *amour-propre* and, in Trudeau's case, the distribution of patronage could scarcely be reconciled with his withering attacks on the practices of Quebec's Premier Maurice Duplessis. But Pearson and Trudeau were party leaders as well as prime ministers, and they had no choice but to render unto their party what its members considered their due. Often, subalterns did the rendering. But the prime minister has his personal patronage prerogatives, and neither Pearson nor Trudeau ever shied from exercising them.

Nor would Mulroney. No purpose was therefore to be served by including in the data base the positions of prime ministerial prerogative. But Mulroney understood enough about Canadian politics and the aspirations of his party to know that the Conservatives had better deliver more promptly and thoroughly than Joe Clark. So, in the middle of the campaign, having dazzled the public with attacks upon Liberal patronage, Mulroney sat down to design his own patronage machine.

Of course, the vast discrepancy between Mulroney's public outrage and private planning reeked of hypocrisy, confirming what critics had long suspected or known of him. But patronage always seemed to breed hypocrisy. Its practice was usually wrapped, with varying degrees of justice, in the cloth of the national interest, either because it integrated disaffected individuals, groups or regions into the political system, or because no democratic government should ignore the willingness of talented men and women to serve their country. Rarely was patronage explained as an intrinsic virtue; it almost always required a covering explanation. And this constant desire of political leaders to paint patronage in colours other than its own led to widespread misunderstandings in the minds of the people, hypocrisy in politicians, and cynicism in both.

Mulroney insisted on only one prerequisite for his machine. There were to be no political ministers. Under Trudeau, ministers from each province gathered regularly to discuss appointments, contracts and other forms of patronage in their area. A designated political minister for each province chaired these meetings, received suggestions from interested caucus members, and provided a conduit for the party rank and file. In Quebec, for example, Marc Lalonde acted as political minister, André Ouellet as fixer. Ouellet, with less onerous ministerial duties than Lalonde's, did the spade work. He contacted Quebec Liberals, listened to their demands, arranged the deals, soothed the egos, suggested the opportunities. In the course of his work, Ouellet acquired such a negative reputation outside the Liberal party and even among some high-minded Liberals that Mulroney laid down the law to his advisers: no André Ouellets. Mulroney changed his mind in the midterm overhaul of his government, but in 1984 his message was inflexible.

MacDonald, Dyer and those they consulted needed to design another kind of system, one that would be more "democratic," meaning that more party members would get an opportunity to plug into the system of appointments, contracts and preferments. Their challenge was hardly unique. Every government since Confederation had devised a system for dispensing patronage and quelling complaints from the rank and file that their political patrons in Ottawa were ignoring local needs. For example, fierce in-fighting erupted within the Liberal party in the 1960s when party officials in Ottawa—such as Keith Davey and Richard Stanbury, both of whom were later rewarded with seats in the Senate—tried to reduce the powers, including patronage, of the provincial wings of the Liberal party. How to reconcile the apparently endemic tensions between centre and region; how to construct a system without political ministers — these were the Mulroney-inspired challenges.

MacDonald's and Dyer's system, approved by Mulroney and Nielsen, involved the creation in each province of provincial advisory committees, or PACs. Each committee, composed of a cross-section of Conservatives, would receive notice from the Privy Council data base three months before an appointment requiring a nominee from that province. The PAC, or so the theory ran, would consult widely with Conservatives in the province, then recommend a suitable candidate, suitability being defined as competence and Conservative credentials.

One or two caucus members—the number depended on the size of the province—would sit on the committee, then funnel back the names of candidates nominated by Conservative MPs for federal positions. The PAC recommendations had to be approved by the minister responsible to Parliament for the board, agency, commission or whatever. The whole PAC system would be co-ordinated by a senior adviser in the Prime Minister's Office. Dyer naturally hoped he might become that adviser; Mulroney instead chose an old friend, Peter White, who had failed to win a Conservative nomination in London, Ontario.

The PACs would handle the bulk of order-in-council appointments, the ones requiring appropriate regional representation, but they were clearly inadequate as a mechanism for filling major national positions, such as chairmen of Crown corporations and major nation-wide agencies. These positions would be considered by a national advisory committee, or NAC, chaired by the deputy prime minister and including such key figures as the party president, the party secretary, the campaign chairman, the caucus chairman, and the prime minister's principal secretary.

The PAC chairmen played a critical role in the system, because to them fell responsibility for selecting the members of their respective committees. Each chairman had to be known and respected by the Conservative enthusiasts provincially, utterly trustworthy and discreet, devoted to the party and, in particular, acceptable to a prime minister who set great store in the importance of patronage.

In mid-campaign, not long after his televised exchange with Turner over patronage, Mulroney sat down with short lists of nominees to head up the PACs. MacDonald, a Nova Scotian, had drafted the short lists for the four Atlantic provinces, Ontario and British Columbia. Nielsen had drawn up lists for the prairie provinces and the territories. Jean Bazin and Bernard Roy, two close friends of Mulroney, had offered suggestions for Quebec. In the strictest confidence, Mulroney made his selections. Nielsen then contacted each of Mulroney's choices, conveying Mulroney's hope that the recipient would agree to chair the committee. If the chairman–designate accepted, Nielsen continued, would he please attend a meeting in Ottawa after the election? Nielsen, for whom secrecy represented a high calling, instructed everyone not to breathe a word of their communication to anyone.

And so, on September 16, 1984 — one day before the cabinet's swearing-in ceremony and the joyous Conservative victory bash at the National Arts Center — the PAC chairmen gathered. Arriving at the Governor-General's suite, the men summoned to co-ordinate Conservative patronage showed all the delight of buddies at a high school reunion. Nielsen, always consumed by the fear of leaks, had deliberately withheld from each PAC chairman the identity of his counterparts in the other provinces. When they entered the room, it was the first time the respective partners in this partisan mission knew who their counterparts would be.

Nielsen delivered introductory remarks as titular head of the transition committee, then departed, leaving MacDonald in the chair. MacDonald spent the rest of the morning explaining the extensive briefing materials he and his team had prepared. He began by reviewing in detail how the PAC system would work, in particular the chairmen's responsibilities for selecting the other members of their committees and for staying in close touch with the party rank and file throughout their provinces. MacDonald outlined the distinction between the PAC's role in governor-in-council appointments and ministerial appointments which, in the case of large departments such as regional industrial expansion, could run into the many dozens. Don't worry about a paucity of appointments, MacDonald joked. There'll be plenty of them to keep you busy—some three thousand, five hundred. In a memorandum entitled "Breakdown of Appointments to Expire in 1985," the MacDonald group projected a "total of 367 appointments to expire sometime in 1985; 70 of which are full-time; 297 of which are part-time." The memo offered a month-by-month breakdown of the positions coming vacant in 1985: nine in January, thirty-five in February, fifty-nine in March, thirty in April, and so on.

This number of appointments should have satisfied PAC ambitions, but it did not. The list highlighted the enduring frustration of patronage dispensers, who had always to reconcile the limited number of available positions with the greater number of aspirants. In eighteenth-century Britain the Crown's administrators had lamented that demand exceeded supply, and the same lament has wound itself through the whole political history of Canada. As politicians could testify, each appointment, once made, risked alienating all the disappointed supplicants.

Not only did the supply-demand gap frustrate dispensers and supplicants, but struggles frequently erupted within organizations responsible for patronage over who should make or contribute to final decisions. In Britain, the Crown's ministers and personal advisers jockeyed constantly for the largest field of manoeuvre, importuning their regent on behalf of friends and supporters. Canadian prime ministers, starting with John A. Macdonald, partially coped with the avalanche of patronage requests by relying on the advice of regional ministers, bishops, caucus members, party kingpins, newspaper editors, businessmen—in short, anyone who could be useful and whose opinions, once given, would make the giver feel important. For often the psychological rewards of the game are sufficient unto themselves. Just to have been consulted boosts one's ego, enhances one's stature, sends out the right signals to friends and enemies.

Opinions sought outside formal party ranks influenced the decisions of prime ministers to varying degrees. When consulted, non-party advisers could only offer their wisest counsel, then wait to see what the prime minister would do with it. These men had influence, perhaps, but not power, either direct or derived. They were given no role to play in the execution of policies, though they may have played some role in shaping them.

Yet, historically, the hope of influencing the outcome of prime ministerial decisions has often persuaded men to submit themselves to the indignities and rigours of political life. The mere possibility of exercising influence, whether great or small, opens their hearts to the complaints and hurts of people whose ambitions can never be realized without benefit of patronage.

Once inside the party structure, derivative power might flow to men who outside it were merely influential; they might be given responsibility for executing the prime minister's decisions, or even enough latitude to exercise their own discretion in matters of patronage. If so, the psychological satisfactions associated with the exercise of derivative power were sure to be greater than those associated with the more ambiguous game of influence.

Just as big-city political machines in the United States by tradition delivered varying degrees of derivative power from level to level through the hierarchy — from mayor to councillor to precinct boss to ward captain to block representative — so too Canadian political parties by tradition created mini-patrons in each province. It suited the diversity of the country. Predictably, these mini-patrons aped all mini-patrons past and present by struggling ceaselessly to enhance their freedom to manoeuvre.

As for the elaborate scheme devised for the Mulroney government by Finlay MacDonald and David Dyer, it would have been perfect had it only reflected an historical appreciation of how the dynamics of patronage systems manifest themselves in Canada, Britain and the United States. But it did not. The system they presented to their mini-patron designates at that fateful Sunday meeting invited a revolt, and one soon developed.

After the luncheon break, the meeting resumed to the rumbling discontent of British Columbia's Jim Macaulay. "I did not come here to play patball," he announced. MacDonald's mechanism, charged Macaulay, would leave PAC chairmen open to ridicule in their provinces. The party rank and file would assume that these chairmen, personally selected by the prime minister, could recommend candidates for all positions, yet this MacDonald-Dyer scheme excluded ministerial appointments. It kept PAC chairmen from recommending party members for major storehouses of political patronage — legal work, architectural and engineering contracts, construction projects. "Patball", in Macaulay's bizarre yet felicitous phrase, meant offering PAC chairmen only some of the patronage rather than most of it. Furthermore, Macaulay asked rhetorically, who among the rank and file would believe the influence, let alone the derivative power, of PAC chairmen in a system that denied them practical access to cabinet ministers?

From around the table spilled declarations of support for Macaulay's criticism. The most emphatic support came from PAC chairmen in the smaller provinces — Lundrigan of Newfoundland was particularly outspoken — where patronage still animated political behaviour and where government decisions affected, in ways unknown in more affluent parts of Canada, the livelihoods of individuals and the well-being of whole communities. The importance of a mini-patron in rural Nova Scotia, outport Newfoundland, or small-town New Brunswick had changed less than the importance of a patron in a wealthy, urban part of Canada. True, the social welfare state and the increased bureaucratization of government had ripped some discretionary powers away from politicians and mini-patrons. Decisions on the awarding of benefits could no longer be entirely dependent on the political loyalty of the supplicants. Improved communications and education had nibbled at the intimate dependency of the patron-client relationship. But no one familiar with politics in Atlantic Canada could deny the still enormously important role of patronage, especially that expensive, largely community-directed embellishment known as porkbarrelling.

The dissent gathered steam. Go back to the drawing boards, the PAC chairmen instructed MacDonald.

Taken aback by the criticism, MacDonald explained again that the prime minister wanted this kind of system. But his arguments banged against the chairmen's insistence that half a loaf simply would not do. They demanded a say in more appointments, a direct link to ministers, and authority to recommend suitable party members for patronage other than appointments. With the afternoon wearing on and no end to the stalemate in sight, MacDonald adjourned the meeting until the next morning. In the meantime, he promised to have a word with Erik Nielsen and to sleep on their criticisms.

MacDonald and Dyer reflected morosely on the wreckage of their hopes. All the enduring tensions surrounding patronage had conspired against them — mini-patrons attempting to expand their power; distrust by the regions of centralized administration; the gap between available rewards and overwhelming demand; the differing regional perspectives about patronage. MacDonald, frustrated and flummoxed, called Nielsen and told the deputy prime minister that the two must meet the next morning. Dyer went home for dinner.

That night, as he pondered what had happened and toyed with ways of rescuing the situation, Dyer struck upon a potential solution. Why not meet the PAC chairmen's demand for direct access to ministers by appointing, not political ministers as such, because Mulroney had ruled them out, but PAC ministers? Each province would contribute a cabinet minister to the PAC committee, not to lead the committee, but to be its conduit to the ministry as a whole. And why not get Nielsen to agree that the PAC chairmen could tender advice on appointments that were strictly speaking out of their hands? He called MacDonald, batted around these ideas, hurried to his office, and drafted a two-page memorandum summarizing these structural and procedural changes.

The next morning, Dyer and MacDonald waited on Nielsen and his assistant Peter Harder in the lobby of the Westin while the PAC chairmen cooled their heels upstairs in the suite. Dyer quickly sketched out his ideas for Nielsen, who said they sounded reasonable enough but that only Mulroney could approve them. With that, the quartet joined the PAC chairmen.

Nielsen, who with his colleagues was preparing for the cabinet's swearing-in ceremony, said he had heard about the previous day's trouble. But a possible solution appeared at hand, provided it met the approval of the PAC chairmen and that of the prime minister. He asked Finlay MacDonald to outline it, which MacDonald proceeded to do after Dyer shoved the memorandum in front of him. The chairmen would receive a wider scope for patronage recommendations, and they'd get their required ministerial contacts. Their roles would be enhanced. Did this sound satisfactory, MacDonald asked? Yes, replied Jim Macaulay and others, that sounded reasonable.

The mini-patrons were content. The Conservatives' patronage machine, meticulously constructed, subsequently refined, was now ready for the assault on the spoils of power, an assault the party had so eagerly awaited and the leader had so carefully planned, an assault that would contribute, as no one in the room foresaw, to staggering setbacks for their party and its leader.

CHAPTER 2

RESPONSIBLE GOVERNMENT
THE BRITISH LEGACY

"Patronage is power"
Letter from supporter to Robert Baldwin.

THE STRUGGLE FOR RESPONSIBLE GOVERNMENT in the British North American colonies, although presented by proponents as a matter of fixed and lofty principle, fooled no one who might lose or gain from its achievement. Responsible government meant, above all, the transfer of patronage power from those who wielded it to those who wanted it. Naturally, the struggle swept up not only those in positions of authority and consequence, but also their active supporters throughout the colonies whose livelihoods depended on the outcome of the struggle. Beyond the supporters spread the legions who, although unlikely to be touched directly by the outcome, nevertheless saw in the struggle the hope of advancement or the fear of decline for their religious creed, economic group or linguistic community.

Patronage, in that period from the Conquest to the winning of responsible government, was not an ancillary consequence of political manoeuvring; it was, in many respects, the motor for those manoeuvres. Personal ambition and the jostling of groups for advancement, the demands of original settlers and recent immigrants, the tensions among English, Irish, Scots and French Canadians, the rivalries among religious denominations, the clash of the enduring attachment to Britain and the siren songs of American democracy, the imperial attitudes towards colonial government and the colonial attitudes towards imperious government—all of these conflicting forces and ideas manifested

35

the centrality of patronage in the political life of the colonies. What emerged from those turbulent times — responsible government and a nascent party system — produced attitudes and practices for the post-Confederation political system, some of which are still with us.

The British, not merely victorious in war but profoundly persuaded of their superiority in peace, naturally established a system in British North America that reflected what they believed worked at home. In this, they miscalculated, although the extent of their miscalculation would take decades to become apparent. Military security seemed to them of paramount importance. The loyalty of French Canadians was decidedly suspect; the presence of the American republic evident and worrisome, especially when cries of annexation echoed through Lower Canada or when radicals in Upper Canada demanded American-style institutions.

Military men, then, arrived in British North America as governors; civilian governors came much later. The early governors varied in personal talents, though not in obduracy, when confronting demands to yield or share their power, including patronage. Whatever their personal inclinations, the governors did operate under instructions from London, although in an era of painfully slow communications necessity frequently forced them to apply general instructions to shifting and sometimes fast-moving events. They were well-paid quasi-monarchs, presiding over colonies where the majority of people struggled to earn a decent living. People might accept the governor's splendid circumstances; he was, after all, the Crown's representative. But the salaries and preferments of other office-holders imported from Britain and those indigenous luminaries who supported the governor irritated some local citizens, alienated others, and hardened the resolve of many to win for themselves the preferments or others.

Some of the governors sent to British North America had previously served time in those unhappy years of the American Revolution. Governor John Wentworth, who arrived in Nova Scotia in 1792, had been New Hampshire's last British governor. The early governors of Quebec had either fought in the Seven Years' War or had lived through the traumatic loss of the Americans colonies. The passing of time did not improve British attitudes towards the United States. War between the two countries erupted in 1812, but the restoration of peace still left supporters of the British Crown looking with horror upon the bustling, apparently uncouth, undeniably corrupt and superficially anarchic political system of the United States. Whereas the British assumed government worked best with centralized authority—the Crown's authority through cabinet in Parliament — the Americans decentralized authority. Not only did American states possess impressive constitutional powers, even the national government's authority was divided between the executive and legislative branches. There was also this bizarre and dangerous business of a written Constitution.

The whole American experiment confused and upset the British cast of mind, for the Americans had essentially designed a political system inspired by some important strains of British political thought and practice in the seventeenth and early eighteenth centuries. There had been, after all, decades of political controveries in Britain between the forces of "country" and "court," controversies that played themselves out in struggles between shifting coalitions conveniently and loosely called Tories and Whigs.[1] The forces of "country," originally found among the Whigs, later among the Tories, opposed the monarchy's absolutist pretensions in the late seventeenth century. The rural grandees of the "country" persuasion resented slights, real or imagined, against their hereditary privileges, and pointed with alarm at Bourbon France where the monarch was unchecked by Parliament.

Decades of political instability followed the Glorious Revolution of 1688, but gradually the forces of "court" prevailed. Actual or impending wars animated British foreign policy throughout the eighteenth century. The necessity for military action and the money to pay for it reinforced those of the "court" persuasion favouring a strong central government. When, in the later part of the eighteenth century, politicians acting in their own interests supplanted the Crown's own agents in the assembling of parliamentary majorities, the rout of the "country" forces was complete. The members of the artistocratic oligarchy and thrusting merchant class that comprised political Britain understood that advancement and preferment could best be achieved through gaining control of, rather than resisting, a strong central authority. Tories, after witnessing the anarchy of the French Revolution, became the stoutest defenders of constitutional monarchy checked by a landed aristocracy in Parliaments of limited suffrage, deference to established privileges, and manipulations based on the enticements of money and the influence of "place."

This British centralization of authority proved to be anathema in governing the Americans. Yet the success of the American Revolution merely convinced the British that they had lost the American colonies because their authority had not been centralized enough. Bewildered governors had assumed a compatibility between the socio-economic conditions and political conventions of Britain and America. But too many powerful interest groups—from southern plantation owners to northeastern merchants—shared authority and commanded loyalty in the American colonies for a centralized system to work. Too many Americans felt excluded from the cliques through which British governors attempted to rule; too many traced their ancestry to pilgrims who had arrived with charters or guarantees of religious freedom. They rebelled against British centralism and arrogance, and designed a political system with diffuse power. In America, "country" triumphed over "court."

The British resolved not to repeat in their remaining North American colonies the mistake they reckoned had been made in the Thirteen Colonies. The American Revolution placed a new and vigorous country on the doorsteps of British North America, a geographic imperative that gave a military thrust to early British rule. There were also the dark motives—or so they seemed to certain governors—of the French Canadians. And after the Revolution, loyalists fleeing the American republic streamed north convinced that the traitorous behaviour of American revolutionaries should never be permitted in their new surroundings. British centralized rule, demanded by London and generally supported by the local population, would prevail in British North America. When the Catholic Church in Quebec threw in its lot with the British authorities—in exchange for British guarantees for church prerogatives — the only local institution with the public support to challenge British power became instead the indispensable bulwark for the political institutions the British erected.

Paradoxically, the British assumed they were building in their remaining North American colonies a political system whose centralized pattern mirrored authority at home, whereas in important and destabilizing ways the differences were profound. Into this chasm between conception and practice flowed the agitations, misunderstandings and turmoil of more than half a century. The relationship between the executive and popularly elected representatives of the people, a relationship the British believed they had happily resolved, never ceased to agitate certain colonial minds, especially when the colonists became more familiar with the workings of the *Quebec Act* of 1791 and as the socio-economic and demographic profiles of the colonies changed.

Central to the vexing debates about that relationship and the legitimacy of government authority were questions of political patronage. Who had the right and under what circumstances to spend public money to influence behaviour or secure loyalty? Who could use the power of appointment and for what purposes? More than half a century passed before in all the colonies of British North America, the people's representatives took the unfettered power of patronage from the governor. But in winning this crucial power for themselves, the people's representatives did not break up centralized authority, as had the Americans. They merely claimed it for themselves and, in so doing, discovered a motherlode of patronage with which to build political parties.

From the restoration of civilian rule in 1764 to the *Quebec Act* of 1791, the British governed Canada with a "court" philosophy one step removed from absolutism. The lack of a democratically elected assembly left the governor free from institutional criticism. A 1774 law sanctioned the collection of revenues by the governor and the executive council he appointed. All patronage—from little favours to important posts—rested exclusively with him. No mass manifestations of unhappiness challenged his authority. The Catholic Church's support, offered in the 1760s, was secured with the *Quebec Act* of 1774 which gave secular approval to church customs and the civil law. And the peasantry, the bulk of the Canadian population, had never known anything but absolutism either from their French governors or their *seigneurs*, the landowners. Hierarchy, the peasants presumed, reflected the natural order of things; government from above seemed a predestined state of affairs. With the British came a foreign language, but also respect for local laws, peace, freedom from military duty, and a modicum of prosperity that accompanied Canadian access to the British market.

Like good aristocrats, the governors searched for people in the new society most like themselves, or at least most wedded to the existing order, and found them in the seigneurs. Governors and seigneurs quickly embraced as defenders of the status quo. To the seigneurs the governors gave their patronage in exchange for support for British rule, support the governors assumed the seigneurs could transmit to their peasants across the breadth of Quebec. However understandable the mutual attraction, the marriage of convenience proved to be a mistake for the governors. It could not long obscure the declining state of the seigneurial system. Many of the old, established seigneurs of the French regime were dying off; others lived improvidently. The practice of subdividing estates among male heirs reduced their revenues and prestige.[2] Many lived in the cities, disdaining any abiding interest in the hands-on management of estates. Their economic positions made precarious, their pretensions of leadership shattered by the break with France, the seigneurs struggled to maintain their standing by scrambling after such patronage as the governor could give them.[3]

Against this marriage of convenience railed, of all groups, the English, who might otherwise have been thought delighted with life under the British Crown. So they were, but not without representative institutions, an Englishman's birthright. From them and from such French-Canadian members of the bourgeoisie as a small, poor colony could produce came the first demands for an elected assembly. The two groups intensified their efforts in the mid-1780s, each driven towards the same goal of an elected assembly by different assumptions. The British reckoned they could dominate the assembly by increasing the number of English-speaking counties; the French Canadians figured they could dominate by the sheer force of their numbers.[4]

The *Quebec Act* of 1791 deceived both of them, although it took awhile for the deception to sink in. The Act granted an elected assembly all right, but it was a talking shop. The governor retained the power to appoint his executive councillors, kept control of all the patronage, and even extended his sway by the creation of an upper house — a legislative council — whose members only he appointed. These legislative councillors, the British assumed, would form the embryo of a hereditary aristocracy whose charter members would recreate the House of Lords.

The assumptions of the *Quebec Act* — aristocratic, imperial and conservative — naturally pleased the seigneurs and, in time, the English-speaking population. The seigneurs believed the Act buttressed their standing; but the English began to receive tangibly greater benefits in places and preferments. Substantially outnumbered by French Canadians, the English-speakers nevertheless received more patronage appointments.[5] From 1790 to 1812, French Canadians comprised ninety percent of the population but received only forty percent of the government jobs. English-speakers also enjoyed higher salaries and pensions than French Canadians. These inequities undermined for some French Canadians the purposes of an elected assembly — to give the majority a forum for expression and a fair share of the spoils. For them, the *Quebec Act* was a fraud, or at least a severe disappointment, and from that early disappointment grew irritation, agitation and, later, attempted rebellion by the especially disgruntled.

The clamour for a more representative government grew steadily in the first decade of the nineteenth century. The leaders of the movement formed what might loosely be called a party, *le parti Canadien*, to organize for electoral success, and established a newspaper, *Le Canadien*, to publicize their cause. The reformers achieved sufficiently palpable success in influencing public opinion that in 1809 Sir James Craig threw himself into an election campaign, the first of many instances when British governors intervened to secure a desirable election result. Governor Craig failed, because *le parti Canadien* won the election, a victory that merely exacerbated his irritation. The next year, he closed *Le Canadien*, threw some of the party's leaders in jail, and waged an inflammatory campaign to no avail. *Le parti Canadien* won again.

Governor Craig could not understand the agitation. All the elements were present, or so he and other governors believed, for the recreation in North America of the British system — a popularly elected assembly with restricted suffrage to air the views of the articulate; an appointed upper house (legislative council) to balance popular opinion with the considered judgment of the aristocracy; executive council members to carry out the Crown's agenda (that is, the governor's); and an established church. This edifice would be held together, as at Westminster, by the judicious and pervasive use of patronage and preferment. The "court" philosophy, triumphant in Britain, would prevail in the remaining colonies of North America, ensuring no repetition of the American debacle north of the border.

Yet, in at least three crucial respects, the re-creation of British government in Canada failed. The privileges of the established church rankled people of different religious persuasions. In Lower Canada, the limited patronage given French Canadians exacerbated ethnic tensions. And, most importantly, the failure to make the Crown's advisers —the executive council—responsible to the assembly produced resentment and instability. For that truly was the genius of the British system: the executive in Parliament, doing the king's business as the executive saw fit, with the support of a majority in the Commons.

Effective political power in the colonies lay with the executive council—the heads of departments and the governor's advisers, nominated exclusively by the governor and responsible only to him. This arrangement was supposed to produce a felicitous harmony and stability among all elements of the population. Instead, it produced tension. The members of the executive council tended to be manifestly unrepresentative of the population. They reserved privileges and patronage for themselves, their relatives and members of other established families. In Lower Canada, they were popularly known as the *Chateau Clique*, in Upper Canada as the Family Compact, in the Maritime colonies simply as the governor's cliques.

Since so much Crown business required patronage to manage the assembly, it was inevitable in the North American colonies that the elected representatives' failure to share the benefits and use of patronage produced discord.[6] The struggle for control of patronage took many forms, but revealed itself most clearly in debates about the Civil List. Those on the List represented the officials of government, former officials receiving pensions, and assorted others who, by influence and preferment, had somehow won the governor's favour. Governor Dalhouse's List, for example, contained payments for people completely unrelated to Lower Canada, including the widow of the former governor of Detroit.[7] Governors knew the practical and symbolic importance of the Civil List. It gave them an indispensable tool for enticement and discipline, and the assembly's inability to regulate the names, salaries and pensions on the List illustrated that body's essential subservience to the governor. As Governor Craig correctly observed, control of the

Civil List allowed him "to exercise . . . a complete ascendancy over the country."[8]

For many years, governors depended upon revenues either from Britain or from local taxes raised without reference to the assembly, practices infuriating to reformers who demanded the right to control revenues and expenses, to vote annually on subsidies, and to examine in detail every item on the Civil List. The ensuing struggle—governors standing on their prerogatives, assemblies on their aspirations—produced intense parliamentary manoeuverings and equally intense frustration. Some measure of compromise followed the Napoleonic Wars. The imperial government imposed economies on spending, which in turn forced the governor to borrow money from the assembly's surpluses, accumulated from provincial revenue-raising statutes. In 1818 the governor, Sir John Sherbrooke, placed the entire Civil List before the assembly and asked for the sums required to pay the bill. Although this gesture responded to only one of the reformers' demands, it did represent a step towards a goal that would take longer than three decades more to achieve.

The departure of Governor Craig, a Francophobe, signalled a more conciliatory approach in administering patronage. The next governor, Sir George Prevost, was a discerning and experienced cynic who correctly figured that behind the protestations of principle from leaders of *le parti Canadien* lay "the hope of obtaining employment . . ."[9] He accordingly appointed French Canadians to senior posts, including the legislative council. He even gave Louis-Joseph Papineau, acknowledged leader of the *Canadien* radicals, the modest rank of captain. But the power of appointment and preferment remained firmly in the governor's hands. The squabbling over the Civil List continued unchecked. The assembly demanded control of the List, or at least some economies, especially in the matter of sinecures and pensions. Finally, in 1828, the House of Commons agreed that the assembly should control all revenues, but that the salaries of the governor, executive councillors and judges should remain independent of the assembly's annual votes. Three years later, with the Whigs in office at Westminster, the British government gave the assembly "entire control of Crown revenues in return for a Civil List equivalent to half the revenues granted. The following year it modified this position, offering to limit the Civil List to the sum of the salaries of the five principal personages of the colonial government."[10]

This stop-and-start British policy, a mixture of conciliation and retrenchment, seemed to end with Lord John Russell's *Ten Resolutions* placed before Commons in 1837. These resolutions touched off a firestorm of protest in Lower Canada because Russell rejected *in toto* demands of the *patriotes* for control of appointments and the public purse. He recommended instead that the governor seize whatever funds were required to pay arrears in civil service salaries without consulting the assembly. It took a rebellion, Lord Durham's *Report* and the passing of another decade before British practice and colonial demands concerning control of patronage and the purse were brought into alignment.

Meanwhile, in the fledgling colony of Upper Canada, the same issues provoked similar tensions. Governors such as the rambunctious Sir John Graves Simcoe, the fossilized Sir Peregrine Maitland, and the severe Sir John Colborne ill-concealed their contempt for the idea of an elected assembly, demanded by the loyalists. Upper Canada, to a greater extent than Lower Canada, was a pioneer society of farmers and labourers, many recently arrived and struggling to carve a living, let alone prosperity, from a stubborn land. Religion, more than race, excited envy because Methodists and other denominations resented the established privileges of the Anglican Church, including the Clergy Reserves, and the ties the church enjoyed with those small but powerful groups of Tories that became known as the Family Compact.

This phrase represented an epithet for critics and a convenience for everyone, whatever its limitations as a precise definition for the collection of entrenched office-holders.[11] In practice, the Compact was never quite as tight as its many detractors suggested, but the people who clustered around the governor did share a certain cast of mind. They often came from what passed for established families, and they certainly saw in themselves the beginnings of a local aristocracy which, vigorously defended, would provide the kind of stability British institutions required. The salaries they received, the privileges they enjoyed, the preferments they bestowed all reflected what they assumed to be the natural order of things. Anyone who objected either did not understand the dynamics producing harmony and balance in a properly functioning British system or, worse still, wished to transform that system into something akin to the dreaded American democracy. Loyalty to Britain, or at least to their idea of what Britain represented, was inseparable in their minds from their own privileges.

Anglicans all, they believed profoundly in an established church. They therefore passed over people of other denominations for preferment and favour. Passionately fond of the British connection, they saw themselves as its only true defenders in a country where a large number of inhabitants had either arrived from the United States or referred admiringly to that distressing place. Any attack upon the governor, from whose munificence their blessings flowed, they understood to be an attack upon themselves. Some dimly, others acutely, understood what their replacement as dispensers of patronage would bring. "A new species of responsibility," wrote Chief Justice John Beverley Robinson after Lord Durham's *Report*, "would be nothing more or less than a servile and corrupting dependence upon party."[12]

High salaries, generous pensions, fixed opinions, assertive loyalty to all things British, a self-imposed burden of aristocratic obligation, a common religion — these characteristics bound together the group that enjoyed the governor's favour and did his bidding. Governor and supporters were locked in an incessant and insistent embrace, and invited to join their affair only persons whose discretion and fidelity could be guaranteed, such as a few late arrivals from the proper circles in Britain. Like the cliques in Lower Canada who governed by favour, they justified their preferments by what to them seemed the obvious inadequacies of the rough-hewn, struggling, often illiterate farmers and tradesmen who comprised the bulk of the population. And like their contemporaries in Lower Canada, they initially discounted, then feared, the rising intention of the middle classes to usurp the powers of purse and patronage and use them for their own purposes.

In a pioneer society with an expanding government, a governor could quickly build an impressive network of supporters, using patronage to cement his own authority. Aileen Dunham has described the network:

> "He virtually appointed the executive and legislative councillors, the judges of King's Bench, and the heads of executive departments. He appointed all the officers of the legislative council and assembly, except for the speaker of the assembly. He appointed a sheriff in each district, justices of the peace, registrars of the counties, clerks of the peace, and commissioners of customs. Immigration officers in the various districts were his nominees. After 1828, the whole of the Indian establishment was at his command. As head of the provincial militia he appointed one thousand, five hundred officers . . . the Crown Reserves were at his command for pensions, aid to churches etc. After the foundation of King's College and Upper Canada College the governor selected their staffs. He also appointed district boards of education."[13]

By the late 1820s, the British were applying in Upper Canada the same stop-and-start policy of concession and retrenchment in the face of popular demands for control of purse and patronage. Sir Peregrine Maitland, whose ten-year rule ended in 1828, obdurately resisted any compromises and surrounded himself only with the clique at York. Sir John Colborne, Maitland's successor, took an equally dim view of popular pretensions, but he was willing to expand the membership of the legislative council beyond the York clique. What the Whigs at Westminster gave Lower Canada, they also offered Upper Canada: assembly control of Crown revenues in exchange for a Civil List of £10,800, which the assembly whittled down to £6,500.[14] Under instructions from London, Colborne also assented to restricting the number of office-holders sitting in the assembly, a tradition much in evidence in eighteenth-century Britain.

These measures were only palliatives. The executive, with all its powers of patronage, remained responsible to the governor, not to the elected representatives. And the governor's responsibility ultimately flowed to the government in London, not to the assembly at York. As in Lower Canada, reformers fighting the entrenched oligarchy did not espouse a "country" philosophy of decentralized power and limited government. They sought less costly government, and pointed to waste caused by high salaries, generous pensions and superfluous positions. But they wished to take over the existing system through responsible government rather than to change the basic institutions of government. In 1834, an assembly controlled by reformers sent an address to the governor urging, among other changes, that "the favours and patronage of his Majesty [be] indiscriminately bestowed on persons of worth and talent, who enjoy the confidence of the people, without regard to their political opinions."

Other reformers adopted a less respectful tone, notably William Lyon Mackenzie. His *Colonial Advocate* planted burrs under every establishment fanny, but his own irascibility and unpredictability, to say nothing of his periodic expressions of enthusiasm for things American, made him the least constant of allies. Indeed, critics like Mackenzie who praised things American set themselves up as easy targets for governors, executive councillors and others of the Tory persuasion who sought to alarm the populace about the pressing dangers of American ideas. Partly to justify their own prerogatives, they heaped scorn on the American spoils system in the post-Andrew Jackson age, when a scramble for office attended every change of government. Such behaviour struck the ruling cliques as not only unseemly, but it also prohibited entrenched hierarchies, rendered efficient government less probable, encouraged the dreaded bacillus of faction and party, and summoned forth the basest human instincts. Far better, they assumed implicitly, for privileges to remain tied to established institutions and the aristocratic groups that ran them.

Mackenzie, of course, railed against such patently undemocratic ideas. In his *Seventh Report on Grievances*, a passionate diatribe based on scouring the record of appointments, Mackenzie highlighted "the almost unlimited extent of the patronage of the Crown — or rather of the colonial minister for the time being and his advisers here — together with the abuse of that patronage."[15] His anger, though fiercely personal, was constitutional in origin. And therein lay his problem. Mackenzie was among those on the fringe of political life in the Canadas who might justifiably be described as having shared some "country" assumptions. So iniquitous did he find the concentration of power that he proposed checks on that power, including an extension of the democratic principle to the upper house. Papineau, too, had preached the virtues of an elected legislative council because he believed it would prevent the administration from monopolizing the fruits of office.[16] More generally, the whole democratic thrust of American institutions — election of judges and Senators, the rotation of the spoils, the lack of hereditary privilege, the wider franchise — struck responsive chords in Mackenzie, Papineau and their followers. But when their pinprick rebellions collapsed, it showed not only the hopeless inferiority of their military means but also their lack of popular support. Certainly the majority working for constitutional reform did not share their views. For them, the prize was the transfer of government to themselves with its powers of patronage intact.

Lord Durham, dispatched to analyse the Canadian problem in the wake of the 1837 rebellions, certainly misread the determination of French Canadians to preserve their race, an error that has justifiably encouraged all subsequent generations of French Canadians to consign him to their first circle of demons. "Radical Jack," however incorrect his prediction of French Canada's demise, did analyse correctly that political instability was caused by the discrepancy between how British institutions operated at home and how British statesmen thought they worked in Canada. Egged on by colonial reformers Edward Wakefield and Charles Buller, and influenced by conversations with the Robert Baldwins (father and son) of Upper Canada, Durham recommended what the reformers demanded: responsible government. And he easily perceived, being familiar with the British experience, the centrality of patronage to the effective exercise of responsible government. He wrote with eloquence and prescience:

> "The slightest acquaintance with these Colonies proves the fallacy of the common notion, that any considerable amount of patronage in them is distributed among strangers from the mother country. Whatever inconvenience a consequent frequency of changes among the holders of office may produce, is a necessary disadvantage of free government, which will be amply compensated by the perpetual harmony which the system must produce between the people and its rulers. Nor do I fear that the character of public servants will, in any respect, suffer from a more popular tenure of office. For I can conceive no system so calculated to fill important posts with inefficient persons

as the present, in which public opinion is too little consulted in the original appointment, and in which it is almost impossible to remove those who disappoint the expectations of their usefulness, without inflicting a kind of brand on their capacity or intelligence."[17]

A foe of Tories at home, Lord Durham naturally found distasteful the "family compact," placing the words in quotation because he understood its members were not related by blood but by a common cast of mind. After describing their grip on "almost all the highest public offices," he concluded that a "monopoly of power so extensive and so lasting could not fail, in the process of time, to excite envy, create dissatisfaction, and ultimately provoke attack." The same situation prevailed in Lower Canada where "such was the limitation on the authority of the Assembly of Lower Canada [that] it might refuse or pass laws, vote or withhold supplies, but it could exercise no influence on the nominations of a single servant of the Crown."

Durham was slightly ahead of his time, or at least of the British government. Westminster accepted his recommendation for a union of the Canadian colonies, but it rejected responsible government. The British would tinker with but not fundamentally alter the existing system. The failure of British assumptions to correspond to colonial reality, identified by Durham, would continue to create instability in the united assembly of the Canadas.

Elsewhere in British North America, the same failure motivated the struggle for responsible government, even in the tiny colony of Prince Edward Island. That colony, after all, had been conceived in patronage. In 1767, the Island was divided into sixty-seven parcels of land, and each parcel was handed to a favourite of the British court. For more than a hundred years thereafter these absentee landlords retarded economic development because the bulk of them took little, if any, interest in their distant estates. Naturally, the struggle to recapture control of this property dominated Prince Edward Island's political life.

Organized government on P.E.I. brought scandal and corruption. Walter Patterson, the first governor, was accused of misappropriating £13,000, benefiting personally from the sale of lands and having an affair with the wife of the chief justice. The Island's elected representatives quickly broke into pro- and anti-Patterson forces, with the chief justice robustly supporting the antis. To this quarrelling Patterson responded as Craig had in Lower Canada, although with more success. He dissolved the assembly, fired the chief justice, spent £2,000 on the campaign, and secured an assembly more to his liking. As one writer wryly put it: "Election campaigns had come into their own in P.E.I.

That style of campaign would continue over the next two centuries."[18] Subsequent governors in the early nineteenth century bore the marks of bottom-of-the-barrel choices, dregs desperate for the patronage crumbs of the British government, a category which decidedly included the governorship of a tiny, frigid, distant backwater. The governor who arrived in 1805 was over eighty years of age and more than ninety when he left. His successor "left the government in a state of chaos." His replacement "proved to be the worst governor in the history of the province."[19]

These dullards, having won their jobs through pull back home, saw nothing wrong in Prince Edward Island with appointing sons and other relatives to positions. By the 1830s and 1840s, the patronage of Prince Edward Island, as elsewhere in British North America, remained in the hands of the governor and a clique surrounding him. What differentiated the Island's clique was its tiny size. Nearly all members of the executive council were related. Jobs were passed from generation to generation. Members of the clique held more than one job, and sometimes as many as five. Resistance mounted, and the two targets identified by reformers were the clique and the absentee landlords. The struggle against the first target lasted nearly four decades and was resolved before the problem of the absentee landlords.

In 1810, the first rumblings of discontent echoed throughout the Island with the formation of the Club of Loyal Electors, whose members aimed to break the landlords' grip and master the assembly "for controlling . . . the appointments of public offices."[20] The reformers of Prince Edward Island, like their counterparts in the other colonies, keenly resented being excluded from government patronage and resolved to wrest it from the governor and the clique by means of responsible government. Before the British granted responsible government in 1851, the reform majority in the assembly and the Colonial Office had been stalemated for nearly three years in a dispute over the Civil List. The assembly had been insisting upon responsible government first, after which it would assume the burden of the Civil List's salaries. Britain stood the demand on its head: Pay the Civil List first, then negotiate greater political powers. After elections produced a thumping three-to-one majority for the reformers, the British yielded to demands for responsible government and the patronage that accompanied it.[21]

In Nova Scotia, too, the struggle for responsible government turned on control of the spoils of power. High-minded and vital principles certainly inspired Joseph Howe and others struggling for responsible government, but they did not forget that with responsible government went the patronage of the governor and his clique.

The governor had plenty of patronage all right, but not quite as much as he would have liked. British ministers, especially secretaries of state for the colonies, had supporters to care for, and some of them wound up in Nova Scotia (and elsewhere) without the blessing or support of the governor. The governor could always make recommendations in favour of his own friends — and frequently did — to his superiors in London. Governor John Wentworth, for example, suffered only a few rejections among the many suggestions he sent over the ocean, partly because he was so well regarded at home. Wentworth, appointed governor in 1792, knew colonial service well. He had served as Britain's last governor in New Hampshire, and the experience coloured all his subsequent actions. Having witnessed the loss of one colony, he was not about to relive the experience. Treachery, even treason, could rear its head at any time, but he reckoned that no such inclinations lurked in the hearts of loyalists who, often at enormous personal sacrifice, had fled north before and after the American War of Independence. Wentworth therefore favoured Loyalists for senior posts, although he did bestow many of the lesser appointments on pre-Loyalists.[22]

Wentworth's policy, unwittingly no doubt, exemplified the integrative function of patronage. The loyalists arrived unsure of their position, immigrants under a familiar flag in a strange land, demanding to play a role in such political life as existed in eighteenth-century Nova Scotia. Once they knew that under Wentworth they would share in the patronage and become political players, they accepted their new home and became staunch supporters of the governor.

Wentworth's policy of appointing friends meant that by 1803 he had a council entirely to his liking; that is, prepared to defend his every decision. Wentworth stood against the assembly three times before he departed in 1808; three times the council supported him.[23] Nepotism flourished: Wentworth appointed his brother-in-law treasurer, councillor, registrar and clerk of council; Wentworth's son received a councillorship in 1801 and his father's recommendation for three positions that fell vacant after the death of another relative in 1809.

A compliant assembly meant Wentworth need not bother much with patronage for keeping the assemblymen in line. Instead, he paid more attention to the council, whose membership he determined and counted upon to quell the assembly's occasional grumpiness. Subsequent governors, however, discovered how useful patronage could be to discipline assemblymen — in granting contracts, influencing appointments, and especially in building roads and bridges, the axis around which so many political debates turned. Everyone in or around the political life of early nineteenth-century Nova Scotia understood that dissent ended hope of advancement and preferment, or "place." The power to appoint justices of the peace and commissioners of schools, to award contracts for the Halifax military and naval establishments, to make extensive grants of land—these all rested with the governor and his clique. But benefits could be scattered in the direction of compliant assemblymen whose abiding preoccupation was the issue that invariably determined their political fate; namely an appropriation for a road or bridge.

The system nourished the seeds of its own destruction, not only because such profoundly undemocratic institutions stirred up resentment among groups who wanted the spoils of power for themselves, but because it was expensive and inefficient. Offices took on vested rights, such as setting fees for services and holding positions for life, so that "to even the ordinary onlooker, the provincial civil service must have appeared to be what, in fact, it was: 'a crowd of rapacious . . . men, supposedly carrying on their work under the governor, but really dependent on their own efforts for the lining of their pocket books.' "[24]

The struggle for responsible government accordingly featured repeated attacks on the inefficiencies of the civil service and the unfairness of the appointments procedures. Amid all the lofty talk of high principles, reformers and conservatives alike understood the stakes. The executive councillors, whom the writer Thomas Haliburton (Sam Slick's creator) wickedly called the "twelve old ladies," warned that responsible government would not reward people of good standing in the community and good breeding in their bones, but an unreliable rabble swept into offices on friendship and political fidelity alone. Their protracted defence of entrenched privilege continued even after the first Reform ministry in 1848, when conservatives tried to protect the vested rights of office-holders, or at least secure handsome settlements for them.[25]

In the end, some officers did receive full compensation when the Reformers swept them out. Others got partial compensation. But everyone appointed by the Tories in spite of the Reformers' prior warnings got what, at a much later time and in different circumstances, a campaigning Conservative party leader named Brian Mulroney called "pink slips and running shoes."

Joseph Howe—like William Lyon Mackenzie, Louis-Joseph Papineau, Robert Baldwin, Louis-Hippolyte LaFontaine and other Canadian reformers — knew that with responsible government went the patronage. At times, Howe seemed ambivalent about its utility and desirability. In the first Reform ministry, he urged generous treatment for certain deposed officials; more vengeful Reform members several times reduced the payments he suggested. Howe wrote to a supporter who wanted to drive opponents off the local school board: "If you were my brother, I would not permit your interest to weigh [a] feather against a trust so sacred as I believe our public school system to be."[26] These sentiments were a mild antidote to his prevailing belief that the representatives of the people should have the patronage and never shrink from using it.

In Howe's letters to Lord John Russell, the Nova Scotian's desire for control of the patronage equalled his desire to get rid of the clique "who are remarkable for nothing above their neighbors in the colony, except perhaps the enjoyment of offices too richly endowed; or their zealous efforts to annoy, by the distribution of patronage and the management of public affairs, the great body of the inhabitants."[27] Howe pleaded with the British minister to apply British standards of government and patronage to Nova Scotia: "For the honour of the British name . . . let us manage our own affairs, pay our own officers, and distribute a patronage altogether beneath your notice among those who command your esteem."[28] In this way, Nova Scotians' attachment to Britain would be enhanced.

When responsible government finally arrived, Howe tried occasionally to curb the worst excesses of the Reformers' hunger for patronage. But he succinctly stated his true convictions in a letter to a friend: "Our Deities of the older time . . . were immovable on their pedestals. Now we can bowl them out like ninepins."[29] By the 1850s, Conservatives and Liberals battled together in each election, both factions bent on transforming the council from a repository for representatives of the upper class into one for party supporters. The period 1857–1863 featured frequent changes of government and implantation of an American-style spoils system. The Conservatives dismissed thirty officials from 1857 to 1860, the Liberals eighty-two from 1860 to 1863, and the Conservatives sixty in the six months after returning to office in 1863.[30] By 1862, the lieutenant-governor could cable home: "There is now no political question which divides them, and which should keep them in perpetual antagonism to one another. The matter in dispute is now simply one of men, not measures."[31] Such a description would fairly apply to the politics of Nova Scotia for the next century and a quarter.

Neighbouring New Brunswick arrived at responsible government later than the other colonies and by a completely different route. New Brunswick boasted not one but two Compacts, and an assembly reminiscent of the American colonies before Independence, eagerly voting large sums of money in equal disregard for the availability of revenues and the governor's approval. Long before the other colonies, New Brunswick demonstrated some aspects of responsible government; long after the other colonies, it finally accepted, with no discernible enthusiasm, the entire edifice of responsible government. But throughout the twisting political history of early New Brunswick, patronage remained central.

New Brunswick's early years followed the familiar pattern: governor and council perpetually battling over appointments, the Civil List and the raising of revenues. Four-fifths of the colony's acreage was locked in Crown lands, and the management of this domain produced the vast majority of political conflicts and grievances.[32] New Brunswick's economy, then as now, depended heavily on the timber trade. Its ups and downs reflected the needs and policies of the mother country: The Napoleonic wars brought boom, peace brought bust; preferential tariffs assured markets, free trade imperilled them. By definition, lumbering was seasonal work which every year threw upon the market men looking for additional part-time employment. The timber trade also tied men to corporate concerns controlled by a few capitalists who, in turn, either exercised political influence directly or through agents. The commanding heights of the New Brunswick economy lay securely in the hands of an oligarchy. An army of dependent men, scattered widely in isolated settlements and small towns, provided fertile ground for the emergence of a deeply rooted, parochial system of patronage.

In 1819, the executive council placed a duty of one shilling per ton on timber cut on Crown lands, a levy that yielded a splendid bounty of £20,000 by 1824, every bit of which remained beyond the purview of the assembly. Over this bounty, indeed over all aspects of the timber trade, presided Thomas Baillie, a self-assured Englishman appointed commissioner of Crown lands and surveyor-general of New Brunswick, positions with nearly dictatorial powers and princely salaries. In 1833, he further secured his power by marrying the daughter of William Odell, the provincial secretary. From this duo stretched long lines of influence and patronage. The concessions their heirs arranged and the appointments they sanctioned had as an abiding purpose the reaffirmation of their own power. Around them in the executive council and, to a lesser extent in the assembly, were grouped their supporters, too disparate to be called a party but bound nonetheless by personal ties to Baillie and Odell. This group was called, a bit unfairly, the Family Compact; a label imported from Upper Canada could more properly have been pinned on their opponents, the timber barons and Saint John merchants who formed a majority in the assembly. These men resented the dictatorial assumptions of Baillie. They chafed at his regulations as commissioner of Crown lands and surveyor-general. But most of all, they coveted the vast patronage and considerable revenues that the timber trade poured into the colony's coffers.

Not that the assembly lacked its own revenues. Other monies came from statutes which the assemblymen, in the finest traditions of the British Parliament before Queen Anne and of the American assemblies before Independence, had voted for their own purposes. Their purposes invariably turned out to be a dizzying variety of local improvements, roads and bridges mostly, which were not approved by the governor, but by the appropriations committee of the assembly, whose criteria for spending money were the presumed needs of their districts and their own need to assure continuing political support. No assembly in British North America ever practised log-rolling more systematically than did the assembly of New Brunswick.[33] Still, the assemblymen could not be fully satisfied until they controlled all of Baillie's swollen treasury.

By his own arrogance, abuse of patronage, antipathy towards Loyalists, and vice-regal remuneration, Baillie alienated just about everyone who counted in New Brunswick. Twice assembly delegations travelled to Britain, pouring out their grievances against Baillie and the system he administered. They charged him with mismanaging funds. They claimed his agents, or "harpies," had committed fraud. Each time, British authorities demanded that in return for clipping Baillie's authority the assembly must defray the costs of the Civil List. Finally, the assemblymen got sympathy from Lord Glenelg, whom they called their "fairy godfather." He agreed in 1835 to turn over control of Crown lands and revenues to the assembly, and, as an additional bonus, £170,000 accumulated by Baillie, in exchange for a guarantee that the Civil List would protect the rights of existing civil servants. The guarantee of protection bought off objections from many in entrenched positions, but nothing could cool the smouldering anger of Baillie and Odell, who subsequently founded their own newspaper and agitated ceaselessly against the spendthrift ways of the assembly. The assemblymen knew a good man when they found one; they gratefully purchased and hung in the assembly building a full-length oil portrait of Lord Glenelg, resplendent in uniform.

Baillie had a point. He had husbanded a nest egg of such proportions that when it fell into the assembly's hands, the government of New Brunswick found itself in the extraordinary position of being able to lend money to commercial banks.[34] In the other colonies, assemblies still struggled for control of patronage and the purse; in New Brunswick, the assembly had triumphed. The executive council was pathetically weak, its members chosen almost entirely from the assembly. Responsible government of a certain kind had arrived, and New Brunswickers looked with consternation at the rebellions that momentarily shook the Canadas. The assembly even sent the militia to assist in squelching the rebellion in Lower Canada. Lord Durham's *Report*, the subject of excited discussion in all the other colonies, barely rippled the placid waters of New Brunswick. The Age of Smoothery, as one New Brunswick paper described the period, had arrived.

The assembly triumphant meant the abdication of all executive authority. It was both legislature and executive, without so much as a first minister, a cabinet, a treasurer, in short, any co-ordinated group to propose measures or ensure a balance between revenues and expenditures. This was a kind of American system without a president, since the governor, as successive ones discovered, was guaranteed his salary and not much else. Stripped of patronage and unable to influence the purse, the governor had no choice but to accede meekly to whatever the assembly triumphant desired. Sir John Harvey, who arrived in 1837, was ultimately undone by the Maine boundary dispute, but until then his popularity remained unsullied, largely because he smiled a great deal and let the assembly do what it wished. Lord Sydenham may have accurately described New Brunswick's system as "abominable," but that was fine for him to say. Harvey could do little about it, especially with provincial coffers overflowing. The path of least resistance, a merry acquiescence, seemed sensible and profitable, especially since the assembly, which seemed to have money for everything else, supplemented his salary with an additional stipend and voted £9,000 for improvements to Government House.

Harvey's successor, Sir William Colebrook, arrived to find the colony's accounts sliding ominously into the red. He resolved to put matters right, first by refusing to sign warrants for road construction, then by dissolving the assembly in 1843 and intervening vigorously in the campaign. The efforts shattered his lances. No one of consequence in New Brunswick wished to end the assembly's profligate ways because then, as now, the political seductions of spending overwhelmed the requirement of economic restraint. A balanced budget, whatever its intellectual attractions, meant less patronage for assemblymen, fewer roads for their people, and reduced part-time employment for loggers, sawmill labourers, farmers and fishermen. Colebrook, suitably chastened, retreated to the acquiescent policy of his predecessor. When Colebrook yielded his position to the worldly and wise Sir Edmund Walker Head, the new governor could write: "A great deal has been said in these provinces on the question of Responsible Government, but the one peculiar subject on which the Executive Government ought to be responsible to the representatives of the people—the relation of expenditure to revenue—is practically conducted to exclude all responsibility."[35]

Head went on to offer a characteristically vituperative description of the assembly — "a scene of jobbery of the grossest kind." No sense of colony-wide obligations impinged upon the parochial concerns of the assemblymen. Their abiding purpose was to squeeze whatever revenues they could from the treasury for local improvements. They consistently rejected proposals for a geological survey, a training school for teachers and an asylum for the mentally ill, because such expenditures for the common good would have reduced available disbursements for their constituencies. Private members bills, rather than government measures, dominated assembly debate. With the locus of genuine power in the appropriations committee, which included one member from each county, the assembly could spend with scarcely any regard for the province's ability to pay.

The system made assemblymen little tyrants in their districts. They got the money from Fredericton, determined which projects would proceed, allocated the contracts to their friends, relatives and supporters, and so instituted the kind of patronage system classicaly found in underdeveloped countries, where government services depend exclusively upon the discretion of the local patron. In a colony of scattered settlements and concentrated wealth, the patronage system reinforced the power of local magnates because they usually doubled as assembly representatives. Such circumstances militated against the creation of parties, the prerequisite of truly responsible government; assemblymen acted like prime ministers and treasurers, but did not bother themselves about the general interest.

It took external events to shock the colony out of its provincial lassitude — the ending of British navigation laws and the triumph of free trade. In 1847 and 1848 protest meetings against these British policies took place throughout New Brunswick, reflecting a sense of impending doom that bordered on panic. The threat to a colony so reliant on mercantilism was overwhelming. Under such circumstances, the scattered voices calling for true responsible government in New Brunswick received a more attentive hearing. As well, by that time responsible government had been adopted by the newly created United Province of Canada, furnishing New Brunswick reformers with a ready example. As colonial secretary in 1847 Earl Grey established a policy of appointing to the executive council only men who commanded the support of the national assembly — a policy that seemed to presage party government.

So when Sir Edward Head was sent to New Brunswick in 1848 to take up the post of governor, the old New Brunswick system was showing the embarrassing strains of profligacy. His instructions from

London were clear: to move the government toward greater account-ability. Thus, new assemblymen were able to take advantage of liberal political sentiments abroad and economic hard times at home to challenge the supremacy of the established families. They took the designation of "Liberals," although their opponents called them "Smashers," and, through two elections and a parliamentary deadlock, emerged in 1854 as New Brunswick's dominant political force. The Liberals held provincial sway until Confederation, acting with as much discipline as could be expected to exclude independent assemblymen from the patronage and use this tool to the advantage of party. With the change of government went a slaughter of the innocents. "Office-holders who opposed the Smashers at election time were ruthlessly stripped of their places. Friends of the Smashers stepped into them."[36] Responsible government, with all its implications, had come to New Brunswick.

The contract between New Brunswick and the Canadas could not have been sharper. In the Maritime colony, responsible government came late, not through prolonged internal agitation, extensive entreaties to British authorities, or political instability, but rather through a combination of external shocks and decisions of the mother country. By contrast, in the Canadas the aftermath of the Durham *Report* produced deadlock and recrimination when men of steely purpose clashed over how best to organize government. At the centre of their clash was the power of patronage. The supreme question was whether all the manifestations of state power should be assumed by a party capable of mustering the confidence of the assembly, or by men beholden to the governor who would demonstrate responsibility by rising above the intrigues and ambitions of faction and party.

The Reformers of Canada East and Canada West, as the colonies became known after the 1841 *Act of Union*, took the patronage question seriously. By patronage, those who had been denied preferment by the ruling cliques and their Tory supporters in the assembly would be given slices of largesse. Robert Baldwin set forth most eloquently the doctrine of responsible government: The provincial assemblies should be given control over local affairs; parties should become the vehicle for expressing the assemblies' will; and appointments should be made only on the recommendation of the party commanding a majority in the assembly. In these enunciations of high principle, Baldwin never forgot the counsel contained in a letter from a Reform associate: "Patronage is power."[37]

For nearly a decade, British authorities had been aware of the unhappiness in the Canadas over the disposition of patronage. The Colonial Office believed this unhappiness could be mitigated by instructing governors to widen the recruitment for the executive council, thus encouraging some patronage recommendations from outside the closed circle around the governor. Sir Francis Bond Head, arriving after Mackenzie's *Seventh Report on Grievances* in 1835, was instructed by Lord Gosford that "in the selection of persons to execute Public Trusts you will be guided exclusively by the Comparison of the claims which the different candidates may derive from past Services, or from personal qualifications." Bond Head was told to reduce the political partiality of magistrates by making appointments without "any political consideration."[38]

The same forlorn hopes inspired the four governors who shuffled through the Canadas from 1840 to 1845, namely that by widening his circle of advisers, the governor could safeguard his authority and confirm his patronage powers. Although Bond Head paid scant regard to his instructions, Governors George Prevost, Charles Bagot and Charles Metcalfe did pay them heed. Bagot and Metcalfe even invited Baldwin and LaFontaine to join the executive council. They all attempted, in their different ways, to practise Lord John Russell's doctrine of 1839, which ended appointments for life except for judges and those titles not affecting the "character and policy of the government." The body of other officers should reflect the temper of the assembly, wrote Lord Russell, but they most emphatically should not be responsible to the assembly. They would be representative of the assembly but responsible only to the governor, and this priority would bring about, or so the Colonial Office believed, the happy state of balance and harmony that characterized the British Constitution.

The trick was to secure an assembly whose views could be made compatible with the governor's. Placing Reformers on the executive council *might* help reduce friction, but a compliant assembly certainly *would*. Thus, the governors of the Canadas strode down the dead-end trail blazed by the likes of Governors Craig and Dalhousie of Lower Canada and Governor Patterson of Prince Edward Island: They threw the full force of their office into the electoral fray. Their short-term successes masked the doleful long-term effects on both the authority of their office and the emerging traditions of Canadian politics.

Bond Head did his best to disenfranchise Reform voters before the *Act of Union*. Lord Sydenham conveniently gerrymandered seats in Canada East after the *Act of Union*, aiming to break up the French Canadian Reformers' solid block under Louis-Hippolyte LaFontaine and so deal with French Canadian assemblymen as individuals subject to the governor's patronage and flatteries. By royal proclamation, Sydenham changed the electoral boundaries to favour English and urban constituencies he thought likely to return candidates favourable to his administration. Throughout the Canadas "the use of patronage, of gerrymander, the sending of troops to the right constituencies, the issuing of land patents when needed to enfranchise new voters — all played a part in the governor's tactics . . . So did the directed voting of those who held places in the government's services."[39] Sydenham's campaign was a hands-on affair. "The governor plans and talks of nothing else," wrote his civil secretary. Confided Sydenham proudly: "I fought the whole battle myself."[40]

"Battle" correctly described what often transpired. Canadian elections were usually tempestuous affairs featuring public voting, bribery, thuggery and intimidation. Governor Sydenham's intervention rendered white-hot the passions of the first campaign following the *Act of Union*, when every political group struggled for an important place in the new Parliament. Police and returning officers seemed helpless against the hordes of supporters—some paid, others drunk, all determined — who surrounded the hustings where electors declared their voting intentions and crowded the inns where liquor flowed freely and cash greased open palms. In Quebec, rioting and violence among French Canadians, Irish and Scots disturbed many polling locations. In LaFontaine's overwhelmingly French Canadian riding, the governor's forces put the voting place in a tiny English-speaking hamlet. "As the voting opened, he [LaFontaine] marched through the woods into New Glasgow with over eight hundred men of his own, armed with clubs and pitchforks—only to find a better-armed enemy, some six- or seven-hundred strong and including two hundred bully boys, drawn up strategically in full possession of the polling place."[41] LaFontaine appealed for troops. When none came, he conceded the election. Riots also broke out in Canada West, and men were killed at polling places in Halton West, Durham and Toronto.

The corruption, if not the violence and intimidation, of electoral practices in Lower Canada did not begin with Sydenham's intervention. Assembly elections in Lower Canada had often been accompanied by the full panoply of skullduggery, bribery, treating, personation and other malpractices to test the wits of men. Everyone engaged in these practices, and guilt was sufficiently widespread that members conspired to frustrate subsequent investigations. No election was ever investigated during the assembly's first fifteen years. Of all the petitions thereafter presented to the assembly to controvert election results, only twenty-eight percent were examined, eight percent were dismissed and sixty-four percent were never concluded. French Canadians, who had never known democratic elections, received this precious gift from their British conquerors, only to watch governors such as Craig and Dalhousie pervert the results. Dalhousie, for example, dismissed all officers of the militia opposed to the administration prior to the 1827 election. He ordered all those on the government payroll to support the administration's favoured candidates. No wonder French Canadians adopted the political mores of the English. "The English officials and electors of Lower Canada had a duty to introduce an alien people to the best traditions of representative government; instead they showed the French Canadians that the franchise was merchandise to be bought and sold, that controverted election laws were to be circumvented, that electoral honesty meant political failure and electoral dishonesty success, public office and power."[42] Against this background, French Canadian Reformers demanded nothing less than full control of the electoral machinery that responsible government would bring.

Upper Canada had been spared many of the worst electoral abuses of Lower Canada. Laws passed in the 1820s standardized procedures for investigating petitions; nearly ninety percent of them were determined, and seventy percent were sustained. But, once again, the intervention of the governor in the 1836 election produced "as widespread and contentious an attempt to subvert the franchise as any colonial administration had up to that moment engaged in."[43] The *Act of Union* carried forward Upper Canadian laws for investigating election petitions, but the assembly committee discharging these statutory responsibilities soon became ensnarled in the partisan manoeuverings of the shifting coalitions that jockeyed for power. On one occasion, when it appeared the Conservatives would lose a seat — and so a majority in the assembly — because an investigating committee would render an unfavourable verdict, the Conservatives neutralized the committee by successfully offering a Reform member three patronage posts in Prince Edward County in exchange for his resignation from the assembly.[44]

In Canada West, then, as in Canada East, Reformers understood from their practical experiences that only the patronage of controlling the militia, nominating returning officers and the Speaker of the assembly, and the offering of inducements to wavering assembly members could give their party a chance to consolidate power at election time. In this eminently practical way, they appreciated that "patronage is power."

The governors certainly fought hard to conserve their power, and in so doing persuaded themselves that they were fulfilling Lord Durham's recommendations for responsible government. After all, had not Durham insisted upon a strong executive, which meant preserving the Crown's prerogative? And was not Metcalfe, the governor who precipitated the final crisis, in receipt of instructions from the colonial secretary to consult his councillors but to remember that "you yourself[are] the head of your administration, not even bound to accept their advice, but always bound to receive it."[45]

If Metcalfe yielded the power of patronage, he would abandon the Crown's prerogative which, in his eyes and in the eyes of many influential Canadian citizens, remained the cornerstone of British liberty, the ultimate check against arbitrary authority. By selecting councillors from a cross-section of the community, by listening to their advice, but by retaining the ultimate authority, Metcalfe convinced himself that he was safeguarding the Crown's prerogative, ensuring a strong executive and delivering responsible government. His arguments carried particular weight in Canada West where a Yankee brush could easily tar his opponents, especially those in the western parts of the province where the American influence was greatest. Among Tories, some of whom had formed part of the Family Compact, Metcalfe's argument about prerogative both confirmed their intellectual beliefs, or gut instincts, and reinforced their own positions of influence. Even in Canada East, a minority supported the governor's views, either because they shared his distaste for the Reformers or because they felt the Crown's prerogative better protected French Canadian interests. They remembered that the Crown had pardoned those who had rebelled in 1837; they doubted whether their political opponents would have shown the same mercy.

So Metcalfe was not without allies when the great crisis of 1843–44 erupted—over patronage.[46] Metcalfe, following his own definition of responsible government, had invited LaFontaine and Baldwin to sit on the executive council. LaFontaine, in particular, had used his position to distribute the limited patronage that accompanied it to his supporters in Canada East. This distribution certainly reflected the partisan purpose of binding his people to *le parti Canadien*, but the patronage also served LaFontaine's broader purpose of persuading French Canadians that the union of the Canadas, if properly organized under responsible government, could better ensure their rights and prosperity than the enticements of an independent state. His supporters included many of the French Canadian bourgeoisie who had hungered since the *Act of Union* for a fuller recognition of their importance through the dispensation of government largesse. They expected of him what he delivered within his limited capacity as a councillor: the spoils of power. Not for the last time in the history of Canadian affairs, then, patronage would be used as an indispensable tool of political integration, bidding those who might otherwise have felt excluded or alienated from the mainstream to consider that they could properly share in the benefits of a wider community. Jacques Monet has described LaFontaine's approach:

". . . despite his own personal and gradually increasing disgust at the need for such methods, LaFontaine knew that 'patronage is power.' Accordingly, within six weeks he had appointed at least one judge, commissioners of all kinds, clerks for post offices, and an endless number of special magistrates empowered and paid to issue marriage licences. He also wrote to the *Canadien* members who had returned to their ridings and asked them to suggest candidates for posts as clerks, registrars, inspectors of potash, school commissioners, magistrates, customs inspectors, immigration doctors, justices of the peace . . . LaFontaine could not afford to forgo this opportunity . . . Since he could not make the Union loveable, he at least would make it profitable. Also by letting the flatteries and salaries of office percolate down to all classes of society—from merchants who wanted seats on the legislative council, through the poor professionals who could not earn a living without some government appointment, to the impoverished habitants of the crowded seigneuries—he gave the *Canadiens* the best proof that the government of the Union was their own, that it served their interests. He created among them, if not attachment to the new order, at least a psychology of consent."[47]

This imperative of patronage, which has guided many French Canadian federalists ever since, drove LaFontaine towards the final confrontation with Metcalfe. The two had quarrelled before over appointments, their views of responsible government colliding. Similar arguments pitted Metcalfe against Baldwin, who insisted that the Reform majority in the assembly gave him and LaFontaine the right to make appointments unfettered by the governor's preferences. An uneasy truce preceded the final rupture, which attended the fever over Baldwin's Secret Societies Bill aimed at curbing the political influence of the Orange Order, a hotbed of unreconstructed Tories.

Suddenly, the crisis burst into the open. The gap that had yawned since the *Quebec Act* of 1791 drew both sides to the precipice. Metcalfe appointed one of his own supporters clerk of the peace for the Dalhousie district, a position Baldwin desired for one of his own men. Metcalfe doubled the insult by offering the position of Speaker of the legislative council to an opponent of the Reformers. He informed Baldwin of neither move. LaFontaine and Baldwin promptly asked the governor not to make any appointments without consulting them. When Metcalfe refused, they resigned, taking with them all but one member of the executive council. Both sides understood the stakes: for LaFontaine and Baldwin, nothing less than the full application of responsible government; for Metcalfe, the avoidance of the evils of partyism, or, as he put it, whether "the patronage of the Crown should be surrendered to the assembly for the purchase of parliamentary support."[48] The Reformers perceived the conflict as one of profound principle, Metcalfe as one of sordid opportunism.

Metcalfe, undaunted, slowly knit together another ministry, a collection mostly of Tories in Canada West and an unlikely assortment in Canada East of old nationalists, Crown supporters, and English-speaking Tories in Montreal. The ministry limped on for nine months before Metcalfe called elections, into which he threw, in the tradition of some previous governors, the entire arsenal of his considerable influence. In Canada East, Metcalfe could make little headway against LaFontaine's faithful bloc, but the governor's men won just enough support in Canada West to form a government. There the American bogey, the fury of the Orange Order at the Secret Societies Bill, the charges of blatant partisan opportunism — all were hurled against Baldwin's Reformers with telling effect. The governor's views of the Crown's prerogative still carried weight. Its demolition, cried his defenders, would lead to a "practical declaration of independence" from Britain.

The Reformers, despite LaFontaine's grip on Canada East, lost sufficient ground in Canada West to allow Metcalfe a narrow victory. The new ministry, led by William Draper and Denis-Benjamin Viger, lasted somewhat longer than Metcalfe, who was slowly dying of a cancer on his face. Yet his victory for the Crown's prerogative against the forces of partyism in the dispensation of patronage was utterly pyrrhic. Having campaigned so hard for an assembly favourable to his interests, Metcalfe, his health ebbing away, could only acquiesce in the decisions and recommendations of men with the assembly's confidence, including in matters of patronage. "The final irony of the Metcalfe regime was that, by its end, government was operating on much the same basis that Metcalfe had originally set out to oppose."[49] The gap, which Metcalfe and all his predecessors had laboured to maintain, was suddenly narrowed by the very local forces he counted on to preserve it. The triumph of party over prerogative, repeatedly crystallized in the struggle over patronage, was now at hand.

Lord Elgin, Durham's son-in-law, replaced Metcalfe, and his instructions were to seal the gap. The colonial secretary, Earl Grey, had already instructed the lieutenant-governor of Nova Scotia to recognize the executive's responsibility to the assembly, the culmination of Joseph Howe's long campaign. To Elgin, Grey gave the same mission in the Canadas. Elgin understood completely his task and its consequences. He wrote to the colonial secretary that he intended "to establish a moral influence in the province which will go far to compensate for the loss of power consequent on the surrender of patronage to an executive responsible to a local parliament."[50] He quickly saw the importance all politicians attached to patronage, and feared for the worst. After the Reformers won their first election under responsible government, he wrote: "On one point I apprehend some difficulty —

There will be an attempt I fear to deal harshly, Yankee fashion, in some instances with subordinate officials, for the twofold purpose of punishing political opponents and providing places for political friends."[51]

Elgin's concerns were slightly exaggerated. The mid-winter elections of 1847–1848 swept the Reformers to office, but no slaughter of the innocents followed. The Reformers allowed some Conservatives to remain in their posts, provided they agreed not to take part in partisan activity. One study suggests the Reformers in 1848–51 appointed approximately the same number of people as the Conservatives from 1845–1848. But the principles and practices of responsible government, inadvertently sanctioned by Metcalfe for the Conservatives and officially authorized by Elgin for the Reformers, opened up new possibilities in Canadian politics.

Parties now completely controlled political patronage. Political leaders needed patronage in the shifting sands of parliamentary manoeuverings to anchor independent or wavering members. They required it to satisfy the demands of their supporters in the country. They used it to lure people into political parties, just as they used its more corrupt forms at election time to secure votes. They exploited its important symbolic value for demonstrating that elements of Canadian society previously excluded from the spoils of power could find a welcome home within the system. They wielded it as a sword of revenge against their political foes. They withdrew it as a penalty for disloyalty bordering on treason, the retribution imposed on dissidents in Canada East who in 1849 supported annexation to the United States. They displayed it everywhere so that everyone who sought government action or political favour understood that the road led directly to the party in power. Most of all, they employed patronage to build a network of loyalty and obligation throughout the scattered communities of a vast land, binding people together through party, making individuals feel part of an entity that transcended local circumstances.

Partisanship permeated everything in Canada, from the great issues of state to public support for private business projects, down to the smallest matters of parochial concern. From big businessmen to seasonal workers, so many citizens depended upon government that British observers, comfortably if arrogantly reflecting upon their own country's politics, evinced amazement and dismay at the ubiquity of political partisanship in Canada. A description of the victorious LaFontaine might easily be applied to many who subsequently shouldered the burden of Canadian political leadership: "For years he spent every day . . . selecting from among the endless stream of favour-seekers a long list of judges, Queen's Counsels, justices of the peace, medical examiners, school inspectors, militia captains, postal clerks, mail conductors, census commissioners, and so on."[52] The triumph of party chained a party leader to the rock of patronage.

The tortuous struggle for responsible government throughout the British North American colonies ended with the triumph of "court" more than half a century after its triumph in Britain. A strong executive —the singular goal of colonial secretaries, governors, and even colonial reformers in Britain — retained its overwhelming power, transmuted from the Crown's prerogative to party government in legislatures. The Tories had seen party coming, fought against it, lamented its arrival, but in defence of their own privilege and prerogative, had ultimately set themselves up both as targets and active agents in the hunt for spoils. Indeed, the Tories had frequently been the strongest boosters of an activist government, prepared to excuse its excesses against the Reformers' complaints about waste and inefficiency. Active government meant expanding government, which in turn provided new opportunities for patronage. The customs branch and the post office both came under Canadian control in the early 1850s, departments that remained for decades among the most hardened enclaves of ministerial patronage. The bureau of agriculture, the Crown law office, the militia and Indian affairs departments, the vast expansion of the public works department—all offered resting places for the politically faithful.

What remained, in the aftermath of responsible government, was a great executive power anchored by patronage, but without stable parties capable of effectively harnessing that power. The coalitions of the responsible-government period splintered, in Canada West and Canada East, under the pressure of new economic and social forces. Governments came and went in merry profusion; political actors moved in and out of coalitions like passengers trapped on a ferry boat. It took someone with a masterful political understanding and a rare combination of personal talents to marry this great executive power to one political party, and to maintain the union by patronage.

CHAPTER 3

SIR JOHN A. MACDONALD
THE GREAT BESTOWER

"He always cared for his wounded birds' "
Sir Joseph Pope,
secretary to Sir John A. Macdonald.

JOHN A. MACDONALD had been active in politics for twenty-four years before Confederation in 1867: as alderman in Kingston, member of the assembly of the Province of Canada, leader of the Canada West (later Ontario) wing of his party and, at times, Canada West leader of the government. His career had straddled the period from before responsible government to the emergence of a new country, long enough to satisfy or demoralize most men, but less than half the length, as things turned out, of what would become a political life spanning five decades.

Macdonald thought many times before Confederation, and a few thereafter, of giving up the political game, returning to his law practice and devoting his full energies to the various business projects and investments he continued to make throughout part of his political career. "I thoroughly understand that business," he bragged to a friend about his work for a British company investing in Canadian real estate, "and can invest without risk of loss."[1] The grinding toil of politics sometimes wearied him, and occasionally drove him to drink—"John A. was ill," the papers would report, using the euphemism of the day to explain his absences. But the call of politics usually animated him, summoning the particular blend of talents and enthusiasms that made Macdonald the supreme practitioner of his craft through the formative years of Canada's political culture.

Macdonald was better than any of his contemporaries at politics. Some were intellectually more rigorous—Edward Blake, for example; some more eloquent in discourse — Wilfrid Laurier; some more discerning in economics — Richard Cartwright, to be sure; others possessed of a more fiery passion—George-Etienne Cartier in his prime; still others guided by a stronger moral sense—Alexander Mackenzie, to a political fault in those years of flexible standards. None, however, displayed Macdonald's painstaking attention to things political or drew on a deeper store of experience; and none better appreciated the motivations, egotistic or altruistic or pecuniary, that made men politically loyal. Partly, Macdonald was better at politics than any of his contemporaries because he worked harder at it. To a degree politicians of a later age would have found simply unbelievable, Macdonald immersed himself in political organization, fund-raising and tactics. His letters, laboriously written in his own hand or dictated to secretaries, brim with attention to a thousand details of politics. But scrupulous attention to detail alone did not guarantee success. The details had to be bound together in a common design. Person by person, group by group, institution by institution, he assembled the building blocks of a national party and structured them to maintain his party in power—and, as a corollary, bring stability to what had been an unstable, factious political system.

Macdonald's genius, and an important reason why he stood above all his contemporaries, lay in understanding the root causes for the instability that characterized Canadian political affairs before and for about two decades following the achievement of responsible government. His solution — the binding together of "moderate men" in the French- and English-speaking communities of Canada — required a cohesive political party, directed by the leadership but anchored in the constituencies, which could effectively wield the centralized executive power surrendered by the British governors. The shifting coalitions of the 1850s and early 1860s, with their "double majorities," "double shuffles," frequent elections and revolving-door cabinets, had been unable to use that power coherently. Macdonald's abiding purpose, the whip that focused his attention on political details, was to play the "long game" of building a national party, the achievement of which, he gleaned from his insights into the human character and the Canadian political tradition, required the judicious and ceaseless use of patronage.

Macdonald came to political maturity when politicians considered patronage normal and necessary. Political men of the nineteenth century described it as "the patronage," and thought it as natural an outgrowth of politics as laws, regulations and dissolutions of Parliament.

Adversaries condemned one another's abuses of patronage, but these charges and countercharges evanesced into political insignificance because everyone in politics knew that the "outs" frequently spoke from envy rather than genuine anger. Out there in the country, everyone seemed to desire "the patronage," as any politician could tell from his mailbag. The allure of patronage enticed men into politics; its dispensation strengthened their loyalty. Even some of patronage's more corrupt forms — conflicts of interest, "treating" at election time — were either ignored entirely or penalized by the mildest sanctions. Bribery of voters, of course, was illegal although universally practised, and dozens of elections were controverted on those grounds.

Politicians, including Macdonald, drew the line at bribery of elected officials. Even Macdonald's most remorseless critics, who accused him of perverting every other acceptable standard of political behaviour, conceded that he had never indulged in corrupt practices for personal gain. He so stiffly dismissed an offer of a thousand dollars a year for four years in a letter from a supplicant in Sarnia, who desired the position of county registrar for his son, that the chastened supplicant wrote back five days later (the post office worked fast in those days), "I assure you it was in an unguarded moment that I wrote my letter . . . [and] I beg humbly of you to forgive the error I have fallen into. Depend on it, it will never happen again."[2]

Macdonald accepted the political mores of his time; indeed, he did more than anyone else to establish them. His standards and practices drove opponents (and occasionally supporters) to distraction, but his opponents became successful only after adopting them. Moralizing was foreign to his makeup. He accepted men as he found them, and used their weaknesses and their talents to promote his party's objectives. Alexander Mackenzie and Oliver Mowat might insist that politics should be tinged with the precepts of a higher calling; Macdonald considered them foolish for so believing. He was a political man to the tips of his fingers.

Macdonald was also a businessman, in an age in which the politics of business enjoined the business of politics. Kingston was his home and political bedrock, a solid if pretentious town that never got over losing the designation of capital of the Province of Canada and the emergence of Toronto as the economic centre of Canada West. Still, Kingston did boast a thriving business community, into which Macdonald fitted before Confederation as a corporate lawyer, land speculator, investor and politician.[3] As a businessman he dealt in railways, steamships, road construction companies, land speculation and land development. Macdonald was a director or promoter of some of Kingston's largest incorporated companies, a fact that was not alarming or even surprising because many other Kingston businessmen also participated in politics. Once elected to the assembly as member for Kingston, Macdonald openly pressed the causes of the companies with which he was associated either by presenting bills for their incorporation or seeking amendments to their charters. He was director of and solicitor for the Commercial Bank and the Trust and Loan Company, and intervened repeatedly in the assembly on behalf of these companies. That his respective business and political interests might conflict never seemed to bother him, for political men considered this kind of interplay between business and politics perfectly acceptable.

Macdonald did more than represent Kingston business interests; he brought tangible benefits to the city in the form of public works. In the 1850s, Kingston could boast the construction of a post office, a court house and jail, a customs building and an insane asylum — a record other communities could only envy. He learned from his early political years in Kingston that political success never lies in promising less.

Macdonald dealt extensively in real estate beyond Kingston, speculating in land for the first time by buying farm lots for subdivisions. Alone or in partnership, he bought land and buildings throughout the province — in Toronto, Guelph, Napanee, Owen Sound, Peterborough, Sarnia, Madoc, Gananoque—sometimes turning a profit, sometimes not. He assumed the presidency of a British company operating in Canada, the St. Lawrence Warehouse, Dock and Wharfage Company of Quebec City, and remained associated with it for twenty-five years. He also served on the board of a British insurance company. Through these dealings, Macdonald became good friends with many leading Canadian business magnates. Some, such as Alexander Galt and Luther Holton, were also politicians. He even knew some American and British magnates.

Curiously, perhaps, Macdonald showed only passing interest in railway investment, although many of his important political contemporaries did. "All my politics are Railroads, and I will support whoever supports Railroads," harrumphed that crusty Upper Canadian Tory, Sir Allan Napier MacNab. No wonder. MacNab served as president of the Great Western Railway and chairman of the Canadian legislature's standing committee on railways and telegraphs. In 1854, a leading Canadian minister, Francis Hincks, was caught participating with the Mayor of Toronto in an insider's deal that gave the minister a £10,000 profit in debentures for the Northern Railway—a bit of overt corruption that sent Hincks into exile for fifteen years as governor of Barbados and British Guyana. Alexander Galt was the Grand Trunk's man. So, too, was George-Etienne Cartier, who acted as solicitor for the Grand Trunk and was the company's principal political spokesman for most of the 1850s and 1860s. Cartier also served as chairman of the legislature's railway committee for fourteen years, always equating the interests of the Grand Trunk, headquartered in Montreal, with that city's vocation as the commercial centre of Canada.

Given such links during the formative period of the Canadian political culture, a Canadian Pacific Scandal was waiting to happen. Railways meant development, expansion, contracts and patronage. Favours passed between politicians and railway magnates in many forms — free passes; transportation for voters, shipped surreptitiously to the Canadian polls from across the American border; contributions to political campaigns, and jobs for political friends. Sir Sandford Fleming, Canada's foremost civil engineer and creator of the Intercolonial, was not alone among railway executives in complaining periodically about the men foisted upon him for political reasons. The tracks the railwaymen laid carried gravy trains, and the politicians climbed aboard. An English lobbyist for the Grand Trunk described his experience in Canada: "My work was almost exclusively 'lobbying' to get a Grand Trunk bill through the House of Representatives [sic] . . . It was clear that some twenty-five members, contractors etc. were simply waiting to be squared either by promise of contracts or money. As I had no authority to bribe, they simply abstained from voting and the bill was thrown out. £25,000 would have bought the lot but I would rather that someone else had the job than myself . . . Upon my word, I do not think that there is much to be said for Canadians over Turks when contracts, places, free tickets or railways or even cash was in question."[4]

The symbiosis between businessmen and politicians was fundamental to the political culture in which Macdonald operated, and as politician and businessman he helped maintain it. Politicians were poorly paid. They either entered politics wealthy or tried to use their political influence to get wealthy; or, like Macdonald, they engaged in business perhaps hoping to strike it rich, but more likely to supplement meagre political remuneration. Parties could not be financed without the help of the business community. The franchise was more widely available in Canada than in Britain, the costs of communication greater. If a party was to be anchored in the constituencies, the way Macdonald knew it must, then this anchor carried a price tag, and such moral scruples as might have troubled more delicate souls never disturbed his nor, in fairness, most of his contemporaries'. In the interplay of politics and business lay reciprocal obligations all right, but it was not always clear who was patron and who was client. Each had power over the other, and the discretion to use it to punish or reward. Businessmen and politicians exploited one another's vulnerability, businessmen trying to lever politicians requiring cash for their erstwhile supporters, politicians trading implicitly, and sometimes explicitly, on the political power that would be theirs after the election if enough money was spent in the right places.

Macdonald could see the political requirements that commended themselves, given the instability of the period following responsible government. He emerged as leader of the Ontario Conservatives, but these represented only one of four groups in the coalition called Liberal-Conservative. Reformers, having won responsible government, soon drifted apart. Convinced they had accomplished the great task of their generation, Baldwin and LaFontaine retired, thus dissolving a bond between French- and English-speaking factions. Reformers in Canada West, too, began splitting apart. A new group, called the Clear Grits and based in the rapidly growing area west of Toronto, took up the cry of representation by population. It was a sure-fire way of alienating the French of Canada East. With their population growing less rapidly than that of the sister province, they insisted upon equality of representation for both provinces in the assembly.

The Clear Grits' new organ, *The Globe* under George Brown, pounded away at Grit refrains — thrifty government, free trade, the damnable grip of the Montreal-based Grand Trunk and, more broadly, the domination of Montreal commercial interests over those of Toronto. Righteously clothing their sectional interests in the language of high principle, Clear Grits shattered the Reform coalition. Reformers east of Toronto were torn between the commercial interests of Montreal and Toronto.

In the years preceding and following Confederation, Macdonald systematically lured reformers from eastern Ontario and elsewhere away from the Clear Grits. Their pact required a common purpose and suitable local arrangements, including Macdonald's agreement to turn over a share of the patronage to sympathetic Reformers. Sir Joseph Pope, Macdonald's faithful private secretary, described the reaction in the immediate pre-Confederation period:

> "To be large-minded is not given to many; people, as a rule, are local, and the Conservatives living in the constituencies represented by [the Reformers] . . . were no exception to the general rule. They had supported John A. for twenty years; had helped him into power, and had gone with him into Opposition. John A. was in office now — was head of the Government — yet every position in the constituency fell to their political opponents; to men who in the past had devoted their energies to put it out of Mr. Macdonald's power to have any offices to bestow. This condition of things was intolerable."[5]

Macdonald appointed W.P. Howland, a leading Reformer who had joined his coalition, lieutenant-governor of Ontario, a prize patronage plum. Macdonald even allowed the Reformers to select the governor-general of the North-West Territory, a decision he told Howland had "caused more dissatisfaction among my Conservative friends than any other."[6] For all his efforts, Macdonald could not dislodge the Clear Grits from their Ontario bastions. In four elections from 1854 to 1867, Macdonald's Liberal-Conservatives only once won a majority of Canada West seats.

Reformers in French Canada looked askance at the Clear Grit demands. Not for them, given the traditions of Quebec, the excessively democratic spirit of the Clear Grits. Nor could they countenance an attack on the supremacy of Montreal, the great gathering point for goods and services, the nexus between far-away markets and the Canadian hinterland. Into this fractured picture fitted Macdonald's coalition: old Upper Canadian Tories, heirs of the Family Compact, whose influence waned with each passing year; Macdonald's own Conservatives, augmented by moderate Reformers who could not stomach the Clear Grits; the English-Canadian merchant class of Montreal; and the increasingly powerful French-Canadian *bleus* led by Cartier, who responded to the influence of the Clear Grits in Ontario by pulling many French Canadians away from the radical faction in the *bleus* and into an alliance with Macdonald's "moderate men" of Canada West.

On paper, the coalition looked formidable. In practice, it creaked. Macdonald understood — this was part of his genius and his legacy — that to be successful he had to rely on the "sheet anchor" of the French-Canadian vote. Opponents and supporters alike often accused Macdonald of toadying excessively to the French, but he knew no party could endure without being "Frenchified." The French Canadians had stood united behind LaFontaine during the fight for responsible government; sensibly led, they would stand united again. That meant finding the right lieutenants, a ticklish problem after Cartier's death, and attaching the party to the powerful interests of church and commerce. It also meant dispensing vast quantities of political patronage to convince French Canadians, as LaFontaine had done, that their interests could best be protected in a wider union, especially if they voted the correct way. But Macdonald needed more than the French-Canadian "sheet anchor"; he had to build up the party in Canada West, a task rendered exceedingly difficult by the Clear Grits and by the limited horizons of some of his own supporters.

The old Tories were as much a burden as a help. Their Orangeism scared off other denominations, and their static vision of society annoyed the middle classes. Their understanding of patronage, epito-

mized by Macdonald's predecessor William Draper, typified the problem. The old Tories took a cloistered view of patronage. They used it
only to reward friends, who tended to constitute a narrow circle. They
did not seem to understand, as Macdonald clearly did, that patronage
could entice new men and groups into the party. Like them, Macdonald
would always use patronage to reward friends, but he cultivated a much
wider circle of friends. Nor did the old Tories fully appreciate that
future political success would require constituency organizations and
the ability to prevail in the hurly-burly of election campaigns. Perhaps
they were too tired, undoubtedly they were blinkered; they failed to
realize the dynamic advantages of patronage.[7] Patronage, in patient
and skilled hands, could co-opt enemies and contribute to a wider,
more stable party.

"Pray save the county and let there be no split," Macdonald wrote
a friend in 1858, ". . . The only question should be, Who will get the
most votes?"[8] That sentiment was often more easily expressed than
achieved. Macdonald may have been the leader, but of what? A collection of like-minded men might be the best description, except they
were not like-minded on everything. They lacked the cohesion brought
about later by the development of rigid parliamentary parties. The
cause they fought for was usually themselves, and they were not easily
disciplined by anyone. Only when the members turned up at the assembly after an election and began voting did anyone truly know the state
of parliamentary opinion. Election results, unless overwhelming, usually provided only a rough guide. So Macdonald, presiding over a
coalition, deplored a split—"[it]discourages our friends and strengthens our foes"—meaning, the appearance of two or more candidates in
an election professing fidelity to the Conservative cause. Before Confederation, his was the "Liberal-Conservative party," a fusion of Tories
and Reformers that sometimes made avoiding a split exceedingly difficult. But Macdonald would go to extreme lengths to do it, for little
offended his political instincts more. "You might have bought him off,"
he wrote a friend, expressing his exasperation at a candidacy that por-
tended a split. Macdonald took matters in his own hands. "I have taken
the desperate course of using the telegraph today to buy off Nassau at
any price, but I fear it is too late."[9] If a buy-out succeeded, fine; if not,
there was always patronage, a post eagerly sought and willingly dispensed in exchange for the withdrawal of a candidacy.

Splits reflected the apparently endemic instability of pre-Confederation politics. Parties rooted in the constituencies required a degree
of centralized control, a requirement that imposed on Macdonald the
burdens of party organization. Through thousands of letters, messages

conveyed by third parties, and personal contacts, Macdonald began knitting together a party with loyalty to the leader as a paramount virtue. To a degree later party leaders would find astonishing, Macdonald immersed himself in the political minutiae of Canada West and, subsequently, of all the provinces of English-speaking Canada. In Canada East—and later in Quebec—his sway ran through lieutenants.

Decades of leadership increased Macdonald's moral authority over the party, not his sense of morality. Not only did Macdonald deliver more victories for the Conservative cause than anyone else, he also knew more people in the party. But moral authority alone could not guarantee enduring success; party loyalty had to be secured by the tangible satisfaction of self-interest. Partisan spirit animated almost every aspect of nineteenth-century Canadian political culture, and as parties developed they became extended social clubs, touchstones for personal identity. Their organized events, such as the summer political picnics, added spice to community life; their newspapers fed the faithful a steady diet of colourful comment; their grip on the levers of power provided jobs, contracts and opportunities for advancement. Lord Dufferin, the governor-general, wrote despairingly about partisanship shortly after arriving in Canada in 1874. "Amongst the other men of eminence and ability in the Dominion . . ." he informed his superiors in London, "They are partisans of the one side or the other, and utterly committed to their respective parties, both by their votes, and the habitual violence of their language."[10]

A child of this bruising partisanship, Macdonald became its supreme practitioner. He understood that, by fair means or foul, he must build a party capable of harnessing the immense executive power of the national government, a task requiring decades of devotion. Indeed, even in the first Parliaments following Confederation, "loose fish," or "ministerialists," sat in the House of Commons, willing to trade their votes for personal advantages or benefits to their constituents. Not until the late 1870s and 1880s could Macdonald fairly say that he had created loyalty to the national party in all regions.

Confederation offered Macdonald an extraordinary opportunity to sink the roots of the Conservative party in Nova Scotia and New Brunswick. When British Columbia, Manitoba and Prince Edward Island subsequently joined the new nation, there was the Conservative party — ready to reward supporters, to take command of important political positions and, more generally, to indicate to voters that benefits flowed exclusively from fidelity to the Conservatives. It was not coincidental, therefore, that the Conservatives were the preferred party in every province, save Nova Scotia, at the time of their respective entries into Confederation.*

In Nova Scotia, the Confederates, almost to a man identified with the national Conservative party, were soundly defeated in the first election after the Confederation agreement, but Macdonald's beneficence softened the sting of their defeat. Many wound up as judges, Senators and members of the public service.[11] This beneficence, however, offered nothing extraordinary in the highly charged partisan world of Canadian politics. What more tellingly displayed Macdonald's subtle and sure sense of tactics was his way of treating opponents of Confederation, notably Nova Scotia's tribune, Joseph Howe.

Howe had struggled against Confederation with customary vigour, inveighing against the loss of Nova Scotia's precious sovereignty. For years, Howe's fiercest opponent had been the redoubtable Conservative Sir Charles Tupper, Macdonald's right-hand man in Nova Scotia and the leader of the Confederate forces. Their mutual antipathy can perhaps best be illustrated by Howe's newspaper, *The Chronicle*, which once described Tupper as being "like a bayou, stagnant and full of crocodiles, alligators and lizards, and creeping slimy reptiles, burying themselves in oozy mud, breathing nephretic gases, fatal to all living creatures."[12] A working relationship would not easily develop from such remorseless antipathy, yet Macdonald eventually succeeded in bringing Howe and Tupper together in the same national cabinet.

Confederation rendered the communal soul of Howe and the anti-Confederates open to all the furies. They agitated, editorialized, made representations to London. They had roundly defeated the Confederates, yet the awful fact of Confederation remained. While Howe inveighed against the dreadful deed, Macdonald in Canada West began swinging the lariat that eventually pulled Howe to his side. Once it became clear that the British authorities would not undo the Confederation agreement, Macdonald reckoned that with the proper inducement Howe might abandon the anti-Confederate position. Macdonald wrote Howe four times, offering him a determining voice in dispensing federal patronage appointments to Nova Scotians. Macdonald offered to hold open posts such as Senate seats, commissioners, prison officials, and positions on the railway board until Howe recommended suitable candidates.

Withholding appointments until Joseph Howe's change of heart

The first governments in British Columbia and Manitoba were led by coalitions, not parties. Their leaders, however, were favourable to Macdonald.

typified one of Macdonald's most enduring strategies. So frequent were his tactical delays that he can be fairly described as the first Canadian politician of consequence to appreciate what all experienced leaders eventually acknowledge—that the hint of a patronage position pleases many, but the granting of it pleases only one. Newspapers dubbed him "Old Tomorrow." Lord Tomorrow, he joked, is what he would call himself if granted a peerage.[13]

In enticing Joseph Howe into the Confederates' camp with patronage powers, Old Tomorrow was playing the long game, much to the consternation of Nova Scotia Conservatives who clamoured for the positions. "Now, my dear Doctor," Macdonald wrote an agitated Tupper, "if I appointed a Union man to office now, it would be a breach of faith on my part, would give Howe an opportunity of throwing himself back again into the arms of the violent antis."[14]

Howe, rebuffed in London, agreed to meet Macdonald, also the federal finance minister, to discuss "better terms" for Nova Scotia and a decisive say in the awarding of federal patronage. "It was unwise," Howe conceded (or rationalized), "to continue the system of giving all places to a minority of the population."[15] He agreed to join Macdonald's cabinet as president of the council and to seek a Conservative seat in a Nova Scotia by-election. The anti-Confederates, roused to renewed fury by the treachery of their former ally, threw everything they could against Howe. But Macdonald's new ally boasted that if the Halifax merchants poured money into the riding to defeat him, he could "send a telegram which would bring me two pounds—for every one that they can raise." Macdonald, wincing at the indiscretion, nevertheless conceded, "we must try to justify his statement."

Macdonald raided the government's secret service fund for $11,575, forced ministers to raise money to aid Howe, and cajoled them into contributing personally. Elected by a small majority, Howe arrived in Ottawa to execute Macdonald's plan: the political pacification of Nova Scotia with money and positions. In particular, Howe and Macdonald broke the prevailing rule whereby defeated Conservative candidates or party organizers in seats held by Opposition MPs determined all the local patronage. Anti-Confederate MPs were wooed with offers of consultation on patronage, and supporters back home received their share. Typical of Macdonald's approach was his question to Howe about the possible appointment of a prominent anti-Confederate to the bench. Would he "take the shilling" and agree "to play our game here" Macdonald wondered?[16]

The sound of anti-Confederate tents folding echoed throughout Nova Scotia by the second election. Macdonald had accomplished his task. Some anti-Confederates had taken the shilling; others had simply resigned themselves to the apparently unalterable fact of Confederation. Anti-Confederate papers advised voters to support the Liberals. Howe, personally re-elected, worried in Ottawa about the defeated Conservatives from Nova Scotia and offered most of them posts. These were the last acts of an enfeebled man in a government heading for the political abyss. Howe had not been well during the campaign—he had spent it in the United States—and soon departed for a patronage job of his own. Macdonald named Howe lieutenant-governor of Nova Scotia, a position he occupied until his death a month later.

Macdonald's daring plan delivered every intended result. Within a decade of the anti-Confederates' triumph, the Conservatives were competitive in Nova Scotia politics. Eleven years after Confederation, the Conservatives took power. Nova Scotia had accepted Confederation, although repeal agitation would shake the province's politics again in the 1880s. Macdonald had not accomplished all these objectives by patronage alone, but he could not have accomplished any of them without it. Patronage was crucial to his long game in Nova Scotia. It was always central to his conception of power, party-building and, ultimately, nation-building. His subtle but pervasive use of patronage to woo Nova Scotians offered a clear example of the integrative function of patronage in Canada. Patronage assuaged hurt feelings; it gradually induced recipients to transfer loyalties and made them feel part of a larger whole, not necessarily by broadening their horizons and forcing them to abandon local loyalties, but by encouraging them to see that those loyalties could be supplemented by additional ones. Patronage created a new set of mini-patrons, regional representatives of the national party, and invited clients—that is the voters—to understand that Confederation widened the available resources against which the clients could make their claims. Later, as the nation expanded geographically, new departments were created (agriculture, fisheries, interior) for grappling with the particular problems of the newly incorporated areas. The new bureaucracies, usually staffed by partisans, further extended the party's reach. In Nova Scotia's wooing, Macdonald established a pattern of dovetailing the national interest of Canadian unity with that of his party. It was a pattern that was to periodically resurface throughout the history of Canada — even in recent times, in Prime Minister Pierre Trudeau's struggle to secure the Canadian federation through the defeat of Quebec secessionists.

Broadening the base of his party of "moderate men" required Macdonald to pay scrupulous heed to religious divisions, especially between Protestants and Catholics. The Conservatives of Canada West had frequently been perceived as the Anglican party, a perception bound to restrict the party's political growth. Macdonald rightly boasted that he had appointed more Catholics than any previous political leader. Such appointments not only sent the proper signals to his "sheet anchor," Quebec, but brought support from Catholics elsewhere. Nowadays, religious considerations colour only the occasional appointments, such as senior posts in Prince Edward Island. Macdonald, whose own religious convictions were not particularly deep, profoundly understood the influence of religion on political behaviour in the nineteenth century and always sought the views of bishops and other senior religious officers.

Macdonald prized loyalty above all else. Those who stood with him in the cauldron of politics deserved his gratitude. If defeated, they could expect a just reward because, as Sir Joseph Pope noted, Macdonald always cared for his "wounded birds."[17] Thomas D'Arcy McGee, to cite just one example among many, wished to leave politics. Macdonald gave him the post of commissioner of patents at a salary of $3,200 a year. "This office would have been in great measure a sinecure," Macdonald conceded to the archbishop of Halifax.[18] Macdonald remained for so long at the pinnacle of Canadian politics that upon his death dozens of his closest comrades and hundreds of other political acquaintances were settled in positions from the Senate to the judiciary, from the upper reaches of the public service to customs offices, from militia posts to lieutenant-governorships. "I never desert a friend," Macdonald once asserted.[19] Sometimes political circumstances prevented Macdonald from rewarding loyalty as rapidly as he might otherwise have wanted. He was not nicknamed Old Tomorrow for nothing. But, as he told one impatient office-seeker, "my plan thro' life is never to give up. If I don't carry a thing this year, I will next." Again, the long game.

The call of loyalty and the demands of party required a chain of authority, for although Macdonald immersed himself in the exacting details of politics and patronage, he could not do everything himself. There was no sense whatever in demanding the loyalty of his followers in the House of Commons if they could not become mini-patrons with slices of patronage to pass out in their constituencies as they saw fit. A tradition carried over from pre-Confederation days hardened into an operating rule under Macdonald: no appointments in any constituency without the approval of the local Conservative MP. Where none existed, the responsibility fell upon the defeated Conservative candidate, party organizers in the riding, or Conservative MPs from neighboring constituencies. This operating rule has remained a fixture of Canadian politics ever since. When broken, for whatever political reason, the MP considered himself hard done by, fearful of being made a laughing stock at home. In a showdown, the MP could issue the ultimate threat: "My only alternative will be," wrote one aggrieved Conservative MP to Macdonald, "to resign my seat. . . . Review the whole matter . . . for my sake and for the old friendship existing between us and also for the sake of those friends who worked night and day for me."[20]

Cabinet ministers formed the general staff of the patronage system. Although thousands of clients directed their entreaties to Macdonald personally, he consulted widely before making decisions and, more often than not, delegated the decision to appropriate regional ministers. They often knew local conditions better than he did, since they directed departments whose employees were better known to them than to him. The enhancing of their local political authority required that they be seen as dispensers of largesse, as powerful operators on the national scene. So, too, Macdonald relied heavily on advice from Conservative provincial premiers because the federal and provincial parties, although led by different sets of men, were organically linked. Only decades later did provincial premiers dream of distancing themselves from federal parties, even to the point of creating entirely separate party organizations. To consult a provincial premier, and frequently to abide by his advice on matters of patronage, was as natural in the nineteenth century as for one brother to consult another in an important family matter.

For example, some of Macdonald's most difficult decisions of internal party management revolved around selecting the acknowledged Quebec lieutenant for the Conservative party, one who could rally the various factions that sometimes tore at each other with surprising bitterness. Cartier clearly filled this role throughout his career at Macdonald's side, but his death created a vacuum that no subsequent Quebec Conservative ever adequately filled. Ministers Hector-Louis Langevin and Joseph-Adolphe Chapleau quarrelled so incessantly over patronage that Macdonald divided the province between them. Chapleau insisted on a primary role in the Montreal region; Langevin took the rest.

What had been standard patronage practice Macdonald elevated to a constitutional principle: Only the supporters of the government had the right to make appointments and to receive them. "In the distribution of government patronage," Macdonald explained, "we carry out the true constitutional principle [that] whenever an office is vacant it belongs to the party supporting the government."[21] This principle he elaborated upon in a debate with Luther Holton, Liberal MP for Chateauguay, who complained about the failure to appoint a collector of customs in Toronto and insisted that he had "as much interest and as much right to make his voice heard" as Conservative MPs from Toronto. On the contrary, replied Macdonald, Holton "from a constitutional point of view . . . had no right at all to the exercise of the patronage alluded to." Holton was neither a Conservative nor a Toronto MP. Constitutionally, therefore, Holton was disqualified on two counts.[22] At least Macdonald was consistent. He upheld the same principle in Opposition.

Macdonald's "true constitutional principle," that only supporters of the government should make appointments, applied equally to the issue of who should receive them. The civil service was *the* motherlode of patronage, and no matter how many reports condemned the nefarious influence of patronage on the civil service, Macdonald never eschewed what he considered an indispensable means of fusing his party to the vast executive power of the national government. After all, what had the fight for responsible government been about if not to transfer to elected representatives the unfettered right to make government appointments? The idea of a politically neutral civil service was as far-fetched, Macdonald said, as "trying to put Canada back to the age of Adam and Eve, before the apple."[23]

Macdonald had never been among the critics of sweeping federal authority. Indeed, he had argued strongly but fruitlessly in the pre-Confederation period for a legislative union. He preferred an even stronger national authority, and intended to use it to build a nation from sea to sea and a party reaching down into every nook and cranny of Canada. He was a Hamiltonian in Canadian clothes, a Conservative who understood that the state need not be feared, but vigorously used to promote business interests, economic development and political longevity. Assertive provinces offended his sense of Canada's future. They also competed for political loyalty. Nowhere did Macdonald sense the threat more acutely than in Liberal Premier Oliver Mowat's expansion of the civil service in Ontario. Mowat threw off the old Clear Grit ideas of limited government; he thrust the state, and therefore the provincial Liberal Party, into new areas of economic life, setting up an intense political struggle with Macdonald that ran from constitutional disputes down to local tussles over patronage.*

Richard Cartwright, a leading member of the first post-Confederation Liberal cabinet, described what his team encountered upon taking office. "We very soon found that we lived in a glass hive. Hardly a question could be discussed in Council, and certainly no resolution arrived at, which was not known at once to our opponents. Nay, it was quite a common case for us to find that measures which had not been submitted to Council were known to our enemies long before they

---

*For Mowat's use of patronage, see chapter 11.

were considered by the majority of Cabinet. The fact was that not only almost all the higher offices in the Civil Service, but practically all the subordinate places, were filled with more or less zealous partisans of our opponents."[24] Even allowing for Cartwright's lusty partisanship, he mounted an impressive case, one buttressed by a series of inquiries into the civil service.[25] Entry into the service depended more on the applicant's connections than his merits. If by chance the applicant had talent, that was a bonus; his political connections counted for more.

An 1877 inquiry laid bare the corrosive effects of patronage. "Employees remain as a rule in the positions to which they are first nominated, vacancies being filled by new appointments from outside the service, made, as usual, by political influence." The committee offered other sweeping criticisms. "Generally speaking, political influence has been found to interfere more or less in the working of all branches of the Service, and always with bad effect. . . . The condition of the Civil Service has not been, and is not satisfactory. . . . The Service should be looked upon merely as an organization for conducting the public business, and not as a means of rewarding personal political friends."

Four years later, another commission examined the civil service and discovered the familiar political habits: appointments and promotions based largely on patronage, and a public that expected nothing less. The commissioners ascribed most of the civil service's inefficiencies and morale problems to a single source:

"While there exists in the public mind a very general belief that the Civil Service is defective and inefficient, and that the true remedy is the abolition of political patronage and personal favouritism in making appointments to public offices, there is on the other hand an impression that it is difficult and almost impracticable to apply the remedy and that those who possess the power of patronage will continue to exercise it. . . . [Patronage also] embarrasses Ministers in providing an efficient public service, and it causes great and often irresistible pressure to be brought on Members of Parliament to force their consent to the nomination and appointment of unfit persons. It has, we think, a mischievous effect on the public mind in making the desire for offices too strong an impulse in political conduct; for while the higher offices of State are the laudable and legitimate objects of the ambition of statesmen, the scramble for paltry patronage and for the smaller offices of the Service, cannot but have a bad effect alike on those who exercise and those who enjoy such patronage."

The commission recommended open competitive examinations to replace the perfunctory ones then in use, a recommendation perhaps inspired by American civil service reformers scandalized by the spoils system in their country.[26]

The commission's report gave rise to the *Civil Service Act* of 1882, which required examinations for candidates entering the service and those seeking promotions. Unfortunately, a series of amendments subsequently watered down the Act, so that yet another commission, this one in 1892, could report that "the amendments in general have tended in the direction of the relaxation of the provisions of the original Act, and the consequent prevention of its intention from being carried out." Like weary carollers, the commission members took up the familiar refrain of open examinations and promotions based on merit. But they had seen enough to resist predicting success. "It is possible that public sentiment in Canada may not as yet be ripe for open competition generally," they wrote, "and it may not be possible as yet to eliminate altogether the power of politics in making appointments."

Whatever their insight into public sentiment, they had read Macdonald correctly. The old man was not about to throw over a lifetime's conviction when it had proved so advantageous to his party and so precisely corresponded with his insights into the human character. Macdonald had seen all the reforms, beginning with the 1857 *Civil Service Act* which created the civil service examining board; indeed, he had been forced against his better judgment to introduce a few of them himself. But the reforms were always piecemeal, easily bypassed, more impressive on paper than in practise, sops to periodic criticism, impediments to the "true constitutional principle" and the rooting of the Conservative party throughout Canada. The civil service was too handy, too necessary for his grand designs.

There could be no patronage without electoral victory. Whatever means, short of physical violence, that might enhance Conservative prospects were fair game, regardless of what the law said. Only one cardinal rule applied—the leader must not know, or at least be able to plead that he had not known, of illegal or dubious practices, a rule passed down from generation to generation of Canadian politicians, the last hardy line of defence against the Opposition, the newspapers, the police and the courts. This rule, strictly applied, twice saved Macdonald's career.

In 1874, the Conservatives warmed the cold benches of the Opposition for the first time since Confederation, their unaccustomed location a consequence of the Canadian Pacific Scandal. The election of January had returned Macdonald in Kingston with a majority of only thirty votes—830 to 801.[27] The victory had obviously been bought for a price, a common occurrence in those years. Nevertheless, the defeated Liberal candidate thought John A.'s narrow win merited a petition to the courts. The Liberals duly received their day in court — by 1874, judges decided controverted election cases rather than parliamentary committees — under the personal supervision of William Richards, chief justice of Ontario. The evidence overwhelmingly demonstrated that Macdonald's agents had paid inflated prices to innkeepers and publicans to secure their support. They had also distributed money as bribes and "treated" voters to free drinks on voting day. The question remained: What did Macdonald know? Macdonald testified that he had left the practical arrangements of his campaign in the hands of trusted comrades, including his lifelong friend (and future cabinet colleague) Alexander Campbell. He assumed that they knew the law, but to be sure he had reminded them of it. Taverns, he told the court, were normal places to hold political events and to influence voters. If "treating" had occured, if inflated prices had been paid to owners of such establishments, these acts had occurred without his knowledge. Yes, Macdonald said, he had contributed four thousand dollars towards his own election expenses, but this sum had been turned over to Campbell.

The defence of ignorance, so handy and so strained, sufficed because Canadian law, unlike the British *Corrupt Practices Act* of 1854, did not make candidates liable for the acts of their agents. Chief Justice Richards therefore accepted Macdonald's testimony that "he did not, directly or indirectly, authorize or approve of or sanction the expenditure of any money for bribery or promise of any such purpose. . . ." That bribery and other corrupt practices had sullied the election, the chief justice left no doubt. Campbell, he wrote, "showed an indifference as to whether the law of the land was violated or not." He continued: "A great deal of money was admittedly spent in corrupt purposes, some in direct bribery, and in treating, to the extent of avoiding the election; and some of the parties who made this improper use of the money, in giving their evidence, spoke of it in a way which might induce those who heard them to suppose that they rather took pride in having violated the law. . . ." Reading between the lines of his decision, it seems clear the chief justice knew perfectly well how the electoral game was structured to offer the candidates an implausible but unassailable defence. Confessing himself "much embarrassed in coming to a conclusion," he praised the petitioner for being "well warranted in continuing the inquiry as to the personal complicity of the respondent [Macdonald]." Given the testimony, the chief justice had to exonerate Macdonald, but his decision to award the petitioner full costs and Macdonald nothing indicates what he really thought of Macdonald's claim of ignorance. The evidence of bribery and other corrupt practices, however, voided the election. A subsequent by-election returned Macdonald with a reduced majority of seventeen votes. A letter from Campbell written shortly after the election, listing the campaign funds received, perfectly illustrated how organizers protected politicians.

"Shall I send you a memo of the payments," wrote Campbell, "or would you rather not know just yet?"[28]

Macdonald's corrupt methods, or legally speaking those of his agents, were the conventional ones. Other methods, as recorded in decisions of other controverted elections, were more imaginative. It was not uncommon for parties to slip voters across the American border by train or boat, then hustle them back before nightfall. In one case, a judge reported that two agents had plied voter M with whiskey, then taken him to an island. "One of the agents then left, and the other sent M to another part of the island for their coats. During M's absence, the latter agent left the island with the boat, but M got back in time to vote, being sent for by the opposite party."

The definition of treating often taxed judicial wits. When was a drink offered to influence voting behavior? When did imbibing reflect only friendship? One judge wrote: "When the object of an agent in treating is to gain popularity for himself, and not with any view of advancing the interest of his employer, such treating is not bribery." Another reasoned: "Treating, when done in compliance with a custom prevalent in the country and without any corrupt intent, will not void an election." So treating, a legal offence, could result in the voiding of an election, but the practice was so widespread, the social opprobrium attached to it so small, and the difficulty of proving motive behind such an everyday offence as drinking so problematic, that judges turned, if not a blind eye, then at least a half-shut one, to the practice, as did the public. As one Canadian authority has written: "There is considerable evidence to suggest that a large portion of the history of Canadian politics could be written in terms of its alcoholic content."[29]

Bribery was unquestionably illegal, and the trick in its administering was to avoid being caught, or to ensure that the candidate could not be directly traced to the bribe. Even when caught, candidates minimized the damage by pleading guilty on one count, frustrating their opponents who had other evidence to present. In the four years following the 1874 statute requiring judicial determination of petitions against controverted elections, sixty-five elections results were contested, affecting more than one-third of the House. Forty-nine of these were upheld, although the cardinal rule of ignorance meant that judges implicated members in only three cases. The shocking number of successful petitions under the *Controverted Elections Act* of 1874 made the politicians crafty. Petitioners against alleged corrupt electoral practices c̦ u̦ not have to reside in the constituency where the offences occurred. So parties could launch petitions in a number of constituencies, hoping for the "saw-off," a backroom deal, arranged by the leading members of each party, whereby one side would drop various petitions in exchange for reciprocal generosity from the other side.[30] Or both sides simply agreed not to proceed with petitions, an arrangement satisfactory to overworked judges and to everyone worried about judges being dragged into incessant political warfare.

Macdonald, whatever his testimony in 1874, knew all about the corrupt variations of patronage. In 1882, he found himself once again in the dock. This time, the redoubtable Liberal Richard Cartwright brought the petition against Macdonald's election in Lennox.[31] Cartwright and local Liberals spared no effort in collecting evidence; the petition contained one hundred and thirty-two allegations of bribery and other offences, including thirteen against Macdonald himself. On the first day of the trial, twenty-four of thirty bribery charges were proven against Macdonald's agents. Macdonald's lawyer quickly threw in the towel, admitting that it was "impossible to resist this evidence," but suggesting that the personal charges against Macdonald be dropped. The judge and lawyers for the petitioner agreed, and the election was declared void. Years later, Cartwright lamented the "misplaced generosity" of local Liberals. As for Macdonald, he had taken out an insurance policy — simultaneously running, as the law then allowed, in the Conservative bailiwick of Carleton, which returned him with a comfortable majority.

Perhaps the last word should be given to Judge John Douglas Armour, who presided over the trial and later became chief justice of Ontario. He asked in 1884: "Is not bribery the cornerstone of party government? Men are party men for the spoils; they support the government of the day for the spoils." Realistic this assessment undoubtedly was, and who better to know than Armour? He had been a Conservative crony of Macdonald's since 1863 and was corresponding with him about political matters in the weeks preceding the trial. Four years after the Lennox case, Macdonald offered Armour a knighthood, then appointed him chief justice of Ontario. As one writer has wryly noted, the Macdonald-Armour relationship showed why "it pays to have friends at court."[32]

Every manner of corruption permeated electoral politics at the constituency level, but what Macdonald called "his greatest triumph" involved the entire electoral machinery of federal politics. The *Franchise Act* of 1885 sparked the longest and most acrimonious parliamentary debates since Confederation, because for all the high principles invoked to defend or attack the Act, Liberals and Conservatives alike understood the stakes. It was, put bluntly, Macdonald's most brazen exercise of patronage.[33] Until 1885, the laws governing the franchise — who could vote, the arrangements for voting, and the appointments of returning officers — had been provincial laws, elements of the *status quo ante* that the Fathers of Confederation decided to leave intact in the 1867 agreement. For Macdonald, provincial control of the franchise arrangements left too many hostages to fortune, especially his Conservative forces in provinces dominated by Liberal governments such as Ontario's. Controlling the franchise laws would deliver to the federal government, and therefore to the Conservative party, an enormous capacity to influence the results of elections, which in those days were frequently decided by a few handfuls of votes. The Act also gave Macdonald a huge reservoir of positions to be filled by the party faithful. Naturally, the Conservatives advanced other perfectly defensible motives, including that a federal franchise law would enhance national unity and bring order to the patchwork provincial requirements. The Liberals insisted that differing provincial regulations met the spirit of a federal country. But they more frequently insisted that the *Franchise Act* fitted snugly with Macdonald's designs for a monopoly on political power, evidence of which they had also noted in Macdonald's famous gerrymander of constituencies in 1882. And although the Liberals could not say so publicly, the existing laws suited their own political purposes, especially in Ontario, and even in Quebec, where the Conservatives were heading towards defeat at the hands of the Liberals, led by Honoré Mercier.

The Conservative majority carried the day, a political triumph that obscured the intellectual inconsistency of their approach. Macdonald had defended his bill on the grounds that provincial control produced a patchwork of laws. But his own was a "nightmare of complexity," featuring a hodgepodge of standards that treated unequally different regions, classes and individuals.[34] Nor could the federal government guarantee effective administration of the Act. Inquiries flooded into Ottawa, overwhelming officials; printing errors marred almost every list; citizens everywhere displayed confusion. Names of eligible voters were omitted; names of the deceased or ineligible turned up repeatedly.

The task of sorting out these difficulties at the constituency level fell to those filling the newly created position of revising officer. Macdonald scoured the country for the appropriate barristers and country judges, preferably with Conservative credentials, to become revising officers. He had to show some caution, lest the patronage be so brazen that it would support the Opposition's charges of a power grab. But the vast majority of his selections for these patronage plums were faithful Conservatives who, in their adjudications and interpretations of the Act, could be counted upon to assist the cause. Naturally, the confusion caused by the poor administration of the *Franchise Act* invited massive fraud. Personation ran rampant at election time; importation of outside voters placed an additional burden on railways. Parties rented special trains and gave voters free tickets to come from other parts of Canada, or even the United States, to the constituencies whose lists sported their names. The Liberals apparently ran up 338,413 person-miles on the Grand Trunk bringing voters to the constituencies. The Canadian Pacific transported voters for the Conservatives.[35]

The Liberals handed responsibility for franchise laws back to the provinces in 1898 (Ottawa retrieved it in 1917), but Macdonald had achieved his objective for his remaining years in politics—that of conferring on his party a significant advantage in shaping electoral laws and providing opportunities for the faithful. It was his bill—nudged by him through the Commons, administered by his appointees, inspired by his sense of the national interest—that put the federal government's vast executive power at the disposal of the Conservative party. It was, as he described it, his "greatest triumph," a crystalline demonstration of patronage.

Election campaigns focused political debate, but the daily stream of discussion about the nation's affairs flowed through newspapers, the principle source of information for scattered communities strung out across a vast country. Newspapers, reflecting their environments, were parochial and partisan. They were also surprisingly numerous. Nine years before Confederation, Canada boasted a population of two million people who were served by twenty daily newspapers, eighteen tri-weeklies, fifteen semi-weeklies and one hundred and fifty-six weeklies.[36] By 1892, Ontario alone had forty-two daily newspapers published in twenty centres, of which thirty-six were clearly partisan.[37] So many papers competing in limited markets imposed severe pressures on proprietors, who in turn looked to their political friends for assistance. The imperatives of survival drove newspapers and politicians together. Proprietors needed government advertising or printing contracts to improve balance sheets. Politicians needed editorial support and, more important, slanted news coverage to convey their message to the population. The loss of a Conservative organ rendered a telling blow to the party, and the defeat of the Conservative party cost a supportive newspaper dearly.

In the major population centres, Conservative and Liberal papers competed with a frenzied intensity. Editorials frequently attacked the competitor. The metropolitan dailies covered parliamentary debates extensively, always alert to the most favourable interpretations for their political friends and ever eager to portray foes in the worst possible light. Parliamentary correspondents understood these responsibilities; failure to comprehend meant a quick recall to the dungeons of the city desk.[38] The smaller papers, of course, could not afford their own parliamentary correspondents, but they did have editors with pens a'ready to strike blows for the proper political cause.

No politician could be immune from the knowledge that newspapers, despite all the nostrums about freedom of the press, were *de facto* extensions of political parties, tied not in a structural sense, but through a series of mutual obligations. So the maintenance of friendly newspapers became one of a political leader's enduring responsibilities, carried out by flatteries and more important, by patronage. The means of patronizing a newspaper were many: government advertising, purchase of subscriptions, direct payment to journalists, places and pensions for journalists. When in 1877 the Speaker was discovered to be holding a printing contract, thus rendering himself ineligible to sit in Parliament, his defence was that "everybody did it."[39]*

Macdonald corresponded frequently with newspaper proprietors and editors, exchanging political gossip, discussing their requests for government advertising and contracts, and occasionally chiding them for insufficiently supporting the government. He flattered their vanity and fattened their pocketbooks; they furthered his career. No proprietor, no matter how small the paper, was above pressing his commerical claims. "Would you kindly interest yourself in [sic] my behalf by requesting the Returning Officer for South Huron for the printing required for election purposes?" wrote the owner of *The Seaforth Sun* in the aftermath of the *Franchise Act*. "Heretofore, the printing went to the Grit office, and I am certain that were you to request the change it would be given to *The Sun* — a supporter of youself. I need the printing as it is a difficult matter to fight the Grits of South Huron."[40] Owners were easily offended by largesse they considered unfairly distributed elsewhere. "We find that *The Ottawa Citizen* has received work to about twelve thousand dollars; we seem to have had five dollars worth," wrote the managing director of *The Hamilton Spectator*. "We will thank you very much if you will give instructions that we receive a fair share of patronage."[41] Newspaper proprietors, like other businessmen, struggled to get their companies on approved government lists for contracts. If they failed despite impeccable Conserv-

---

*Lord Dufferin wrote to London about this affair that "when public attention was once drawn to the circumstances, it was discovered that dozens of other members, including leading personages both on the government and the Opposition benches, were in the same predicament. Almost all our members of Parliament are connected with important firms of different sorts, and as a consequence have supplied the Government from time to time with timber, stone, iron, furniture, legal advice and other commodities."

ative credentials, they assumed oversight rather than malice. "I enclose a slip showing the amount of money paid by the government for extra printing and would draw your attention to the face that *The News* is not represented," complained the owner of a Kingston paper. "Surely when the *St. John Sun* gets over $9,000 and *The Moncton Times* over $7,000, you can give something for the support of the paper which advocates your cause in your own constituency."[42] The lists, after all, determined the patronage. In Halifax, the Conservative organ *The Herald* received more than ninety percent of all federal government advertising from 1884 to 1894, with piddling sums going to the Liberal paper, *The Chronicle*.[43] In Toronto, the Conservatives became so upset with their organ, *The Mail*, that they established another paper, *The Empire*. Before their pique, they gave *The Mail* the bulk of government advertising, offering only crumbs to *The Globe*.[44]

The rooting of the Conservative party required money, and an expanding national government provided a means to get it. Not only were businessmen frequently dependent upon government decisions for the success of their ventures, they eagerly spied opportunities for profit in public works projects, government supplies and other government services.[45] Getting on the party-approved lists of eligible suppliers produced an avalanche of requests, some fawning, others indignant, all insistent. Contracts were especially enticing because cost overruns, then as now, were endemic to doing business with the government. Carefully disguised, overruns could produce an even larger return. Even contracts ostensibly awarded through competitive bidding could be tailored to further the political objectives of the Conservative party. Naturally, the public works department provided the widest opportunities for patronage, so it is not surprising that Macdonald's long-time public works minister, Hector Langevin, should have been so intimately involved in patronage and corruption. Indeed, some of Langevin's friends — the ones who connived with him in an elaborate scheme which eventually forced Langevin out of politics — availed themselves of the largesse of his department even before Confederation, during the construction of Canada's Parliament Buildings.[46]

In 1859, the government let contracts for the construction of a massive neo-Gothic building on the hill overlooking the Ottawa River. The department of public works insisted that the cost of the main building would be no higher than three hundred thousand dollars, and that of both departmental buildings two hundred and forty thousand. Thomas McGreevy of Quebec City, an engineer, won the construction contract, a victory not exclusively based on his bid. McGreevy was an important Conservative fund–raiser and a strong supporter of Joseph

Cauchon, the minister assigned to the department in 1861. McGreevy won the bidding despite a tender which neglected to include an itemized list of prices, as required by law. This he submitted sometime later. There is evidence that departmental officials, presumably acting on instructions from the minister or on assumptions about his preference, added to McGreevy's schedule of prices some of the items listed by losing bidders. From first conception to final execution, the construction of the Parliament Buildings constituted a major scandal. Cost overruns hit every aspect of the project; indeed, some of the suppliers later admitted they had assumed there would be overruns and that the government would foot the bill. The initial plans contained no provision for heating the buildings, an extraordinary omission for anyone remotely familiar with the delights of an Ottawa winter. Departmental officials were negligent, Cauchon at fault, and the whole sorry mess compounded by the patronage appointment of a Clerk of the Works around whom McGreevy ran circles. The tangled tale of incompetence and patronage was never fully sorted out, despite official inquiries. By 1867, the Parliament Buildings had already cost $1,419,355, and they were still incomplete. McGreevy, however, remained on the job.

The granting of contracts to friends of the Conservative party continued throughout all of Macdonald's post-Confederation leadership. Those on the "list," those fortunate enough to win contracts, were expected to support financially the Conservative party. This they did voluntarily, knowing that failure to oblige might bring regrettable commerical consequences, or because they had no choice. Tollgating, the mandatory return of a percentage of the value of government contracts to the governing party, became standard practice. It was, as always, a difficult form of patronage to prove, because the arrangements were made secretly. Occasionally the scam burst into the public domain, ruining careers but apparently not provoking voters to turf the rascals out.

Hector-Louis Langevin was a Father of Confederation who assumed, upon George-Etienne Cartier's death, the mantle of Macdonald's chief French-Canadian lieutenant, a mantle frequently contested by other French-Canadian Conservatives.[47] Langevin began his ministerial career in the first post-Confederation cabinet as secretary of state, and two and a half years later he moved to the department of public works, the greatest single source of government patronage. But the Pacific Scandal fell about his head. Langevin received thirty-two thousand dollars after Macdonald's desperate request of funds from Sir Hugh Allan of the Canadian Pacific Railway. He did not run in the subsequent election called by the Liberals following Macdonald's resignation. Instead, he bided his time, waiting for memories of the Pacific

Scandal to wane before contesting a by-election in Charlevoix, where the misfortune of being caught plagued him again. The *Controverted Elections Act* defined "undue influence" as grounds for annulling an election, words with special political meaning in Quebec, where anti-clerical Liberals insisted curés systematically campaigned for the Conservatives. That the curés of Charlevoix county preached the Conservative cause from their pulpits was not in doubt, but did such preaching constitute "undue influence"? The lower court judge, an old friend of Langevin's who heard the petition of the defeated Liberals, said no. The Supreme Court disagreed, annulling the election and levying six thousand dollars in costs against Langevin. An old friend and political ally assumed the debts—Thomas McGreevy.

Langevin ran successfully in the second by-election. That result, too, was contested, but the courts dismissed the petitions. When the Conservatives returned to office in 1878, Langevin resumed his ministerial career in the department of public works. There he presided amiably — his tranquility was shaken by other matters, notably the ambitions of other French-Canadian Conservatives to supplant him as Quebec lieutenant — ensuring that Conservatives good and true got their share of the contracts. The patronage of appointments Langevin considered the natural order of things. "I have no doubt there will always be politics connected with appointments made by any government," he told the Commons. "I have yet to see a government which will appoint its opponents to office. As a rule the government appoints its friends." Meanwhile, in Quebec, a major tollgating operation, sanctioned by Langevin and executed by McGreevy, raked in money for the Conservative party. This tidy operation might well have gone unnoticed by the general public but for what a French-Canadian writer has called "the Canadian and modern version of the fratricide of Cain."[48]

Robert McGreevy had taken over from his brother Thomas McGreevy the last stages of construction of the Parliament Buildings. He had then become a silent partner in an immensely successful construction firm in Quebec City, his role there being largely to use his influence with Thomas and Langevin to secure contracts. Whether through Robert's efforts or other pull, the company received a long string of contracts from Langevin's department, although the firm seldom submitted the lowest bid. Suddenly, for reasons that still remain fuzzy, Robert and Thomas became involved in a nasty lawsuit over a division of profits, and from that fratricidal dispute leaked out the information that brought Langevin down.

The *agent provocateur* in the drama was Joseph Israel Tarte, news-

paperman, political chameleon, notorious rabble-rouser, party organizer, in short, Quebec's leading authority on closeted skeletons.[49] Tarte
began dribbling out the information in his powerful newspaper, *Le
Canadien*, alleging that Langevin had passed on insider information to
the McGreevy brothers so that their firm would win contracts. There
were suggestions of kickbacks to the Conservative party, bribes to Langevin and, by inference, a systematic tollgating of contractors. Tarte
stood successfully for Parliament in 1891 as a Liberal—he had once
been an ultramontane and a Conservative—and promptly brought his
accusations to the floor of the House of Commons. He alleged "that
from the year 1883 to 1890, both inclusive, the said Thomas McGreevy
received from Larkin, Connolly and Co. (the construction company)
and from his brother R.H. McGreevy, for the consideration above
indicated, a sum of $200,000. . . . That certain members of the firm
of Larkin, Connolly and Co. paid and caused to be paid large sums of
money to the Hon. Minister of Public Works out of the proceeds of
the said contracts." The details of the parliamentary inquiry, at which
Langevin denied all wrongdoing, need not concern us—the Conservative majority produced the expected whitewash. The evidence, seen
in the light of history and acknowledged by everyone apart from the
Conservatives, demonstrated that the McGreevys had traded on their
influence, secured excessive profits for their firm, and sent back contributions to the Conservative party. Thomas McGreevy had obviously
raised money using the minister's name with Langevin's knowledge,
and perhaps encouragement. Langevin submitted his resignation as
minister, while disclaiming wrongdoing, in exchange for the whitewashed report. He died fifteen years after his retirement "with his name
a byword for corruption,"[50] and with the Ottawa building that houses
the Prime Minister's Office named for him.

Macdonald could distance himself from the McGreevy-Langevin
scandal because of his poor health (although he had done nothing when
Tarte brought the incriminating information to him privately), and he
died before Langevin's resignation. He also remained aloof from the
other, less spectacular scandals involving construction of the Baie des
Chaleurs Railway and the unsavoury activities of Conservative MP J.C.
Rykert, caught speculating in land through the department of the interior, an affair that touched but did not wound Macdonald.[51] He was
dead when another scandal from his later years unfolded: allegations
that a cabinet minister, Sir A.P. Caron, took a portion of government
subsidies awarded to a Quebec railway and funnelled the money
through Thomas McGreevy into twenty-two Quebec ridings.[52] Two
years after his death, the party was hit by further allegations of corruption, this time over construction of a bridge at Lachine. These scan-

dals were all part of Macdonald's legacy, of the political culture he had done so much to shape, but he was beyond mortal reach when they were unearthed. In any event, none of them unduly alarmed the public. The Conservatives from 1891 to 1896, when the party's string ran out, won sixty-two of eighty-three by-elections.[53]

There had been one scandal, the most spectacular of all, from which Macdonald could not hide. The Pacific Scandal ignited such a firestorm of protest that Macdonald, despite the contrived brilliance of his parliamentary defence, could not withstand the inevitable: the only Conservative electoral defeat under his leadership.[54] The deal was sweet and straight, an unalloyed example of patronage of the grossest kind, an advantage given Sir Hugh Allan in exchange for sizeable campaign contributions. The evidence could not have been more damning — a letter from Cartier explaining how the contributions were to be apportioned among leading Conservatives, and most damaging of all, Macdonald's desperate telegram in the dying days of the campaign: "I must have another ten thousand; will be the last time of calling; do not fail me; answer today." Nineteen lethal words, it seemed, spelled the end of a political career, especially when added to those Macdonald scribbled on a note Cartier had earlier handed Allan: "I authorize you to assure Allan that the influence of the government will be exercised to secure him the position of president."

Macdonald pleaded extenuating circumstances, specifically the vast patronage arsenal thrown against the Conservatives by the provincial Liberals of Ontario. "Every member of the Ontario government went into the field, either as a candidate or a political agent, and its whole power was used to defeat my friends," he told Parliament in explaining the desperate telegram to Allan. "As the provincial government has all the local and county patronage of every kind, and the whole control of the sale and disposal of the public lands, timber and mines, you may easily fancy the extent of the power they can exercise. Every manufacturer of lumber who wished to get an area of country for lumbering purposes, and every person having got, or wishing to obtain, or retain, a mining licence, was transformed into an electioneering agent. I had, of course, cries for help from all sections, and redoubled my exertions to procure it from every available source."[55]

These "cries for help" were indeed directed at Macdonald, for party leaders were also chief organizers and political fund-raisers. Six decades later, Prime Minister Mackenzie King could insist amid the Beauharnois fund-raising scandal that he had known nothing of what transpired, but such a defence, whatever its merits, could not be sustained in the nineteenth century. Macdonald, as his correspondence shows, was deeply involved in raising money, allocating it to the constituencies, encouraging promising candidates into the political field with intimations of financial gain. He had neither a Carleton Club nor a party organization divorced from his own office to raise money. He was not wealthy. He could not pour his personal treasure into the Conservative party, as party leader R.B. Bennett subsequently did. He had to wring the money out of others to keep the party going.

Macdonald was both child and architect of the political culture he described in his own defence. Within it patronage not only flourished but provided, in all of its manifestations, the grease that ran election machines and the glue that held political parties together. He had done nothing wrong, except get caught. Nor did he lament the close ties between his party and railroad interests, because "the Conservative Party in England does not repudiate the actions of the brewers and distillers and the Association of Licensed Victuallers in electing candidates in their interests, and we did not repudiate or reject the influence of the railway interest."[56] The Pacific Scandal, with its offensive assumptions, could not be divorced from the environment from which it arose. The mutual dependence of business and government, the close personal relationships between prominent politicians and leading businessmen, the parties' need to expand their reach into the constituencies, the belief in the necessity of patronage in politics, the prevalent corruption in electioneering, the tiny majorities in so many constituencies — all these factors made it likely, perhaps inevitable, that a massive scandal would break over Macdonald's head. And nothing better testified to his resilience — and the electorate's live-and-let-live attitude towards most forms of patronage, benign and corrupt — than Macdonald's re-emergence as prime minister six years after his government's humiliating resignation.

Nor did the Pacific Scandal sever the links between the Conservative party and the Canadian Pacific Railway, it just made their relations a bit more circumspect. Macdonald, returned to office, accelerated construction and demonstrated his *bona fides* towards British Columbia, ensuring that the CPR would continue to provide job opportunities for Conservatives. This obligation, he explained to CPR executives George Stephen and William Van Horne, was made so clearly "that by 1884 Macdonald was able to assert that the CPR had no one working on the line who was not—he used Van Horne's pithy phrase — a fully circumcized Conservative."[57] The CPR contributed critically to Macdonald's nation-building plans. He could not let it go, and he was manifestly right in his convictions. His party had always been wedded to large commerical enterprises, based in Montreal and Toronto, through which the nation would develop. Perhaps he understood the warning of John Henry Pope: "The day the Canadian Pacific busts, the Conservative party busts the day after."[58] At the service of these commercial interests he placed the Conservative party, expecting in return their gratitude and support for his political purposes.

His plans and theirs coincided. Both wanted a strong central government to push the railroad west, oversee the expansion of the nation, protect the manufacturing sector of the economy with the National Policy, and consolidate a British country to face all challenges to Canadian sovereignty from the Americans. From the earliest days, Canada lacked a capitalist class sufficiently large and powerful to build the infrastructure required by so young and vast a country. It could be built only with government assistance, or by government itself. And from these imperatives of size and distance sprang the conventional symbiosis of business and government, of businessmen and politicians, of commercial gain and political profit, which so utterly characterized Canada's political culture and economic development. Macdonald's Liberal critics frequently questioned the symbiosis on grounds of favouritism, patronage, corruption, excessive cost and the thwarting of democratic control, but that was all. Only when they, too, adopted the same conventions did their party prosper.

The national government in Canada, unlike that in the United States, did not merely set the rules under which dynamic capitalists carved out a country; it immersed itself in all aspects of economic activity, from underwriting railway loans to financing hundreds of local improvements. The Canadian capitalist class was paltry compared to its American counterpart. It could not easily prosper without the state's support, and that meant the political elite became the country's most important elite with the power of the national government at its disposal. Almost every economic project contained some degree of political involvement, a condition that led, then as now, to rapid politicization of government economic decisions. This condition became especially evident when the interests of the regions were pitted against each other, It was part of Macdonald's genius as a political juggler—and his legacy to all subsequent prime ministers—to establish the convention that the grant of a concession to one region had to be matched by a concession to another. When, for example, Macdonald pushed through the CPR's 1884 loan, the premier of Quebec immediately demanded federal assistance for a railway in his province. Macdonald could not brush him off. The premier's political whip was the votes of Quebec Conservative MPs who dared not return home without money for their railway. Macdonald delayed, then negotiated, and the premier got his money.[59] It was political blackmail. It was Canadian.

That Macdonald's Canada was a rural country—eighty-one percent of the population in 1881 lived in rural areas—represented one element of the intense regionalism that pervaded Canadian life, an intensity noted by foreign observers. The majority of citizens remained rooted where their forebears had settled, if not precisely on the same farm or in the same village, then not far away. The prejudices, beliefs and aspirations of one generation were easily transmitted to another. So were political affiliations, in a country where politics seemed to touch everything and partisanship was necessary to influence government. Language and religion cemented the parochialism of Canadian life.

Indeed, the only bridges across the national divide between English and French Canadians were thrown up by the political parties. In this parochial environment, or rather series of parochial environments, patronage could only flourish. The viability of many regions, especially the more rural ones, depended to varying degrees upon government action. The people themselves, often struggling to make ends meet, looked to government to improve their lot. Government jobs, full-time or even part-time, provided security of employment (at least until a change of government), perhaps a certain standing in the community, and most important, a salary that often eclipsed what they might otherwise make. For the most part, MPs survived on what they could secure for their local electors. They were the intermediaries between the federal treasury and local needs. They were valued less for the good they might do for their country than for the goods they delivered to their constituencies. In the party structure, they represented the link between constituency organizations and Macdonald.

Invariably, the important patronage went to the professionals: accountants, architects, contractors, lawyers.* The patronage fortified their standing in the community, and it confirmed their partisanship. It also augmented middle class individuals throughout Canada who, like the large commercial concerns, saw their interests inextricably influenced by political decisions. They became, for they had little choice, part of the political network. This was especially important in a country with a piddling commerical class and a weak industrial sector, and it was most important of all in Quebec. There, the French Canadians had been largely shut out of the Montreal business community. The emerging French-Canadian bourgeoisie in the pre-Confederation years had taken the shilling of government largesse offered by LaFontaine, and they had never stopped expecting rewards. With the economy in English hands, the French Canadians turned to politics

---

*Macdonald took the justice portfolio in the first cabinet after Confederation, and always paid scrupulous attention to legal patronage of judgeships, casework and Queen's Counsels. Macdonald's use of legal patronage is described more fully in chapter 16.

either as direct participants or hopeful beneficiaries. The French Canadians, Macdonald's "sheet anchor" in pre-Confederation days,
remained his surest guarantee of political longevity. He consistently
faced more acute political competition elsewhere, especially in his home
province of Ontario. Some of his most ticklish political decisions
involved satisfying the clashing ambitions of would-be Quebec chieftains, who often personified the enduring rivalry between Montreal
and Quebec City. By the end of the nineteenth century, LaFontaine's
dream had been realized through Macdonald: the French-Canadian
middle class, the professionals, had become "*la classe dirigeante*" in all
but the large commercial enterprises. They were the darlings of the
state, requiting their suitors, working the system. They were, in a
Quebec writer's telling phrase, "the professional nobility."[60]

The fulminations of Macdonald's opponents, in and out of politics, against his use of patronage rolled off his back and apparently left
the electorate profoundly unimpressed. Richard Cartwright, an acerbic
Liberal and a penetrating critic, described what his party confronted.
"In Ontario," he said, "there was scarcely a riding in which Sir John
could not count on a score of men occupying more or less influential
positions, [all] of whom either owed their appointments to him, or had
been under obligations to him of one sort or another, or of whom he
knew something they would not care to have made public." For all
Macdonald's sins, and Cartwright considered them to be many, "he
had one considerable merit in that he rarely canted about the purity of
his motives or made much pretence of being better than he was."[61]
Upon Macdonald's death, Sir Daniel Wilson, then president of the
University of Toronto, described him as a "clever, most unprincipled
party leader [who] had developed a system of political corruption that
has demoralized the country. Its evils will long survive him . . . Nevertheless he had undoubtedly a fascinating power of conciliation, which,
superadded to his unscrupulous use of patronage, and systematic bribery in every form, has enabled him to play off province against province
and hold his own against every enemy but the invincible last
antagonist."[62]

Goldwin Smith, the quite brilliant if headstrong political com-
mentator, roared from his Toronto lair:

> "The task of his (Macdonald's) political life has been to hold together
> a set of elements, national, religious, sectional and personal, as motley
> as the component patches of any 'crazy quilt,' and actuated, each of
> them, by paramount regard for his own interest. This task he has so
> far accomplished by his consummate address, by his assiduous study
> of the weaker points of character, and where corruption was indis-
> pensable, by corruption. It is more than doubtful whether anybody
> could have done it better than he has done . . . By giving the public

the full benefit of his tact, knowledge and strategy, he has probably done the work for us as cheaply as it was possible to do it. Let it be written on his tomb, that he held out for the country against the blackmailers until the second bell had rung."[63]

Amid the relentless pressures of such a heterogeneous society, profoundly parochial and intensely partisan, the supreme balancer, mediator and tactician built his political party contact by contact, letter by letter, speech by speech, appointment by appointment, reward by reward, dollar by dollar, promise by promise, a party rooted in the constituencies, present in all regions, representative of most groups, an organization dependent upon the intuitive understanding of political motivation and vast experience of one man: himself. Macdonald's sense of the country sometimes failed—the hanging of Louis Riel comes to mind. But he succeeded, where all his predecessors and adversaries had failed, in marrying his party—for it truly was *his* party—to the state, a marriage sealed by the constant application of patronage in all its forms, benign and corrupt.

Macdonald's formula for governing would endure, but through misfortune or stunted vision, none of his immediate Conservative successors applied the formula with the required finesse. It took a Liberal, wise in the ways of men and astute in his reading of the country, to apply the formula and, by so doing, replace Macdonald's party with his own for nearly five generations as the natural governing party of Canada.

CHAPTER 4

SIR WILFRID LAURIER
GRITS ON HIGH

"Remember this, that in politics, the question seldom
arises to do the ideal right. The best that is generally to
be expected, is to attain a certain object, and for the
accomplishment of this object, many things have to be
done which are questionable, and many things have to
be submitted to which, if rigorously investigated, could
not be approved of."
Sir Wilfrid Laurier, 1904, writing to a friend.

WHEN THE FRENCHMAN ANDRÉ SIEGFRIED visited Canada in the first
decade of the twentieth century, the precarious, testy relations between
English and French Canadians struck him as the key to understanding
the country, including its politics. "A land of fears and jealousies and
conflicts," he wrote of Canada in 1907.[1] Wise politicians understood
that fierce ethnic and religious rivalries lurked just below the surface
of Canadian life, capable of bubbling up at a moment's notice. "They
exert themselves, therefore, to prevent the formation of homogeneous
parties, divided according to creed or race or class," Siegfried thought.
"The purity of political life suffers from this, but perhaps the very
existence of the Federation is the price."

Political parties tried, said Siegfried, to keep these rivalries under
control by removing "ideas and doctrines" from the political arena.
"The consequence is that rival candidates commit themselves to identical promises moved by an identical determination to win," he wrote.
"Whichever side succeeds, the country it is well known will be governed
in just the same way: the only difference will be in the *personnel* of the
government." Parties tended "to become mere associations for the
securing of power, their doctrines serving merely as weapons, dulled
or sharpened, grasped as the occasion arises for use in the fight." Parties
made "extraordinary compromises" within themselves to keep together
"heterogeneous elements," and by these internal compromises the par-

ties "have come to regard each other without alarm; they know each other too well, and resemble each other too closely."

To a shrewd outsider, it may have appeared that nothing distinguished Conservatives and Liberals, but to the members of the two parties, their differences provided the stuff of daily political combat. Election campaigns remained raw-boned affairs, replete with widespread chicanery, flaming rhetoric, and elaborate promises. "There [can] be few countries in the world in which elections rouse more fury and enthusiasm than in Canada," Siegfried thought, echoing observations made by a variety of nineteenth-century British governors. Siegfried also noted that "public works are what Colonials demand most of all . . . thus provinces, *communes* and individuals are all united in soliciting from the Government as much in the way of public works as possible." In the House of Commons, debates rumbled into the wee hours of the morning, and committee meetings often featured one side attempting to pin charges of corruption, waste or extravagance on the other. In the Commons public accounts committee from 1896 to 1905, for example, thirty-seven of the forty substantive reports were "frank attempts by one political party to unearth and publicize evidence that would embarrass the other."[2] At the turn of the century, the Liberals and Conservatives were like two rival tribes, membership in which was often fixed at birth, although alterable by appeals to ethnicity, policy or personal self-interest, facilitated by the judicious application of patronage.

When Siegfried's book appeared in 1907, the Liberals had been in office for eleven years under the leadership of Prime Minister Wilfrid Laurier. By 1907, the first French-Canadian leader of a national party had broadened the coalition of the Liberal party. He had succeeded in turning Quebec from its Conservative traditions into a Liberal bastion. Using the advantages of office, he had created Liberal strongholds in the new provinces of Saskatchewan and Alberta, while retaining sufficient strength in the other western provinces, Ontario and the Maritimes to produce the election victories that had allowed the Liberals to supplant the Conservatives as the dominant party of Canada. In the process, Laurier had weaned the Liberals from some of the Clear Grit traditions that had inspired and plagued his predecessors, Edward Blake and Alexander Mackenzie. He had also transformed — and this was perhaps his most lasting contribution — the Liberals in Quebec from a collection of anti-clerical *rouges* into a broadly based coalition. Laurier made the Liberal party acceptable to the clergy, welcoming to Conservatives repelled by intolerant ultramontanism, open to all French-speaking Quebeckers resentful of the Conservatives' handling of the Riel and Manitoba Schools questions, and prepared to extend the helping hand of government to the English-speaking capitalists of Montreal.[3] This transformation changed the dynamics of Canadian politics for nearly a century. Laurier had adopted Macdonald's formula for political success, both its transcending vision and particular tactics, and demonstrated again that imitation in politics, as in life, can be the highest form of flattery.

Laurier has come down to us as one of our most virtuous prime ministers, and indeed he did not lack for virtues. Kindly of spirit, benevolent by disposition, Laurier made friends easily. He forged loyalties that withstood lacerating linguistic and ethnic divisions, until the fiercest ethnic division of Canada's history — conscription — shattered his party. Even then, a rump of English-speaking Liberals remained faithful to this extraordinary man, despite the self-evident political risks they ran in their inflamed constituencies. Like Macdonald, Laurier had an uncanny ability to let men down easily, to remember that the game of politics never stops, and that today's foe might become tomorrow's ally. He had principles, and strong ones at that, but principles that could always be tempered for partisan advantage or national unity. In matters of patronage — still embedded in the heart and soul of Canadian politics — Laurier displayed a finesse and an attention to detail that would have done Macdonald proud. Laurier had no choice because, as his biographer Oscar Douglas Skelton wrote, "the distribution of patronage was the most important single function of the government."[4] Laurier appreciated the importance of patronage and meticulously attended its demands. In the words of Sir John Willison, editor of The Globe and a long-time friend, Laurier displayed "a large toleration for patronage."[5]

Laurier's toleration arose partly from his background. In Quebec, political patronage was woven deeply into the texture of society. But his Quebec upbringing alone could not have shaped his views, for patronage suffused the politics of other parts of Canada. Laurier's ambition played a part. Like Lester Pearson half a century later, Laurier cloaked his driving ambition with self-effacement, combining the charade of Sir Galahad with the cunning of Prince Machiavelli, as newspaper editor John Dafoe wrote. The requiting of political ambition required paying due heed to patronage. Successful party management demanded it and the country expected it. Laurier, after all, had been vanquished by John A. Macdonald, and the lessons of the master were not lost on him. Laurier's personality also made for "toleration." Like Macdonald, he took men as they were, and left their moral perfection to churchmen. He was a politician, and to be a successful politician in the political culture of the period meant to dispense favours so as to ally the interests of ambitious men with the interests of the Liberal party.

In many ways, the Laurier years marked a continuation of the electoral and patronage practices during the Macdonald years. Most, if not all, of the campaign irregularities and illegalities that had sullied elections in the Macdonald era resurfaced in Laurier's. Nearly ninety controverted election cases were heard from 1897 to 1911. This number represented a decline from an earlier period — over eighty constituencies were contested in the 1891 election alone! — not because electoral conduct had improved, but because politicians on both sides increasingly used that old device, the "saw-off." In other matters as well, the Laurier Liberals preferred to imitate the dubious morality of Sir John A. rather than the dismal rectitude of previous Liberal leaders, Alexander Mackenzie and Edward Blake. They had been men of high moral principle, but they also projected a more stunted vision of the nation than had Macdonald. Heirs of Ontario's Clear Grit ethic, they had preached expenditure restraint, attacked waste in government, questioned massive outlays for such public works as the Canadian Pacific Railway, flailed at the cozy relations between the Conservative party and powerful capitalists, and generally lamented the decline in political morality. Neither one had understood Quebec politics and had not found anyone to interpret its intricacies correctly. They were admirable men in their ways, but prickly and rigid, more inclined than others to believe in their own special gifts. Goldwin Smith may have been too harsh, but he came close to the truth: If Mackenzie's virtue as prime minister resided in once having been a stone mason, his liability lay in remaining one.[6]

Clever politicians learn from their opponents' virtues; unwise ones concentrate on their opponents' faults. To Mackenzie, Macdonald had perverted sound government through his profligate spending and had debased political morality through his flagrant favouritism. The mobs of Conservative office-seekers, contractors and partisan hangers-on of the first Macdonald governments appalled Mackenzie, who never tired of furiously denouncing their apparent influence on the Conservative government. The Pacific Scandal confirmed Mackenzie's beliefs: Macdonald ran a government whose partisanship, corruption and brazen illegalities shocked a nation which he felt cried out for higher standards at the top. In this refrain, Mackenzie echoed the Clear Grits, and if he doubted for a moment that the country agreed, he needed only to glance through the Liberal bible, *The Globe*, whose editorial on the eve of the 1874 election proclaimed: "The poll tomorrow is the Thermopylae of Canadian political virtue."[7]

Prime Minister Mackenzie made himself minister of public works, the portfolio with the most obvious opportunities for porkbarrelling and one of the most alluring for patronage. Mackenzie reckoned that by controlling this portfolio, he could bring his own standards to bear on the principle repository of waste and corruption. Instead, the portfolio controlled him. It crushed his spirit, burdened him with a thousand details, and made him the lightning rod for complaints from the Liberals' own mob of office-seekers, contractors and partisan hangers-on. Smith's crack about Mackenzie the stone mason captured his essence in office: Mackenzie chiselled dutifully away, trying to shape each piece of the political edifice according to his own exacting standards, but forgetting about the grand design of broadening the base of his political party. He could not take men as he found them. He insisted upon trying to remake them, and when he repeatedly failed, his isolation and frustration increased. Nor could he effectively delegate responsibility, as Macdonald did and as Laurier would do. Of course, prime ministers in the nineteenth century were expected to immerse themselves in a myriad of patronage details later generations of political leaders could leave to trusted lieutenants. But there came a point, even then, when prime ministers had no choice but to delegate responsibility or be submerged by the avalanche of requests that poured across their desks. Mackenzie, however, never grasped that point, perhaps because he knew he could not trust his colleagues to live by the same standards he set for himself.

The clash between political reality and Mackenzie's values bedevilled his government. In practice, Mackenzie turned out to be less virtuous in matters of patronage than he might like to have been. Having set high standards, he suffered the humiliation of being unable to meet them. His "toleration" for patronage and porkbarrelling never came naturally, but from an always grudging acquiescence to irresistible pressures from party members.

Mackenzie's Scottish sense of economy recoiled as demands for spending poured into Ottawa. He soon discovered that keeping the promises he made while Opposition leader was earning his administration rampant disfavour and probable defeat. The business interests, in particular, counted on government contracts to flow from a robust program of public works. They favoured restraint all right, except when it involved their own commercial interests. And in the constituencies, the clamour for improvements never abated, especially in the far-flung reaches of the Dominion, where grievances had already accumulated against the insensitivity and greed of Central Canada. Coastal communities demanded better harbours. Cities screamed for new federal buildings, especially post offices. Every hamlet desired if not a main railway then at least a branch line.

The pressures for federal spending—and for preferment and place —rained down upon Mackenzie from within his own political formation, itself an uncongealed coalition of interests, not yet a national party. "I have no sinecure," he wrote to his brother, his pen rushing past the required points of punctuation, "in trying to keep together a crowd of French Liberals Irish Catholics Methodists Free Traders Protectionists Eastern Province men Western men Central Canada men Columbians Manitobans all jealous of each other and striving to obtain some advantage or concession. I always knew it was very hard to keep liberals together but my experience has been far in excess of my utmost belief."[8]

Mackenzie arrived in office to find the civil service packed with Conservatives and the Senate with a lopsided Conservative majority. Even in defeat, Macdonald had tried to shoehorn a few more Conservatives into office. In the three weeks before the Mackenzie government took office, Macdonald appointed dozens of his supporters to various positions. On the day John A. resigned, he announced appointments for four former MPs and ministers. The Liberals, naturally enough, cried foul and cancelled most of the last-minute Macdonald appointments.[9] But Mackenzie would not go further, despite his supporters' howls that he dismiss Conservatives from the public service.

Wholesale dismissals marked changes of government in the United States, where the spoils system had been accepted in politics since the presidency of Andrew Jackson. Mackenzie's Liberals, however, had attracted many Conservative voters; a wholesale purge might alienate some recent converts. A purge would also have offended Mackenzie's own sense of fair play and the higher standards of political conduct he set for his government. Despite his cryptic comment that "all the offices are crammed with hostile people so that we can trust no one," Mackenzie retained the vast majority of public servants. "We have not superannuated one man," he wrote, "except where it was urgently sought, and ample reasons were given — and these cases were three in all, I think."[10] Despite what he called "hordes" of spies around him, Mackenzie stood firm. "My object will be . . . justice for all, let the consequences be what they may."[11]

The consequences for internal party harmony were entirely baleful. Mackenzie's government represented the first chance since Confederation for Liberals, or Reformers as some still called themselves, to seize the spoils of power. Mackenzie's rectitude immediately confronted political reality. Office-seekers camped in his waiting rooms. Liberal MPs demanded positions for their supporters. A walk from his office to the Commons chamber often meant listening to importuning advice from a host who had been waiting for a chance to fill his ear.

And the mail! Dozens of letters arrived daily, some burdening his conscience, all demanding his personal attention. Several weeks into the job, he wrote to his daughter: "I devote an hour of this peaceful, beautiful Sabbath morning to the pleasant duty [of letter-writing]. Today, the great army of contractors and office-seekers are shut out and the very office has a Sabbath look."[12] He tried to reward Liberals, as he explained in his bulky correspondence, where everything else was equal. But therein lay the problem, because for almost every Liberal nothing else equalled partisanship. To be a Liberal was to be qualified.

Alfred Jones, Liberal MP from Halifax, whom Mackenzie frequently consulted on patronage, insisted that an insufficient number of Liberals had found jobs on the railway. "It is impossible to fill the Railway offices on political grounds," Mackenzie fumed. "They must have experience, and if we cannot get experienced men among our friends we must take them elsewhere just as you would in a private company or in your own office . . . Don't ask me to do a thing you would not freely do in my place."[13] Mackenzie utterly missed the point: Jones spoke as a politician, not a businessman. Mackenzie poured his special frustrations about the patronage deluge from the Maritimes into another letter to Jones, "I am in receipt of your extraordinary letter about railway and other appointments, and I confess nothing has been written to me for months that has astonished me more. It is really too bad. Half my time is taken up with this question of patronage in Nova Scotia and Prince Edward Island. My life has become a torment to me about it."[14]

Mackenzie, unlike Macdonald and Laurier, could not let disappointed supplicants down gracefully. He made supplicants feel insignificant, angry or rejected. As a device for weeding out the unqualified, he took to administering impromptu examinations for competence to everyone who entered his office looking for a job, hoping to make supplicants realize their unsuitability. He also instructed his secretary to administer the same examinations, and to send in only those who had passed. He wrote George Brown of *The Globe*: "At this point there is a little soreness in several quarters at me simply because the public interest forced me to stand between them and some cherished but improper object."[15] As a wag put it, Macdonald could say no with more grace than Mackenzie could say yes.

The onset of recession heightened Mackenzie's frustration because it threw up more office-seekers and forced the government to curtail expenditures. In 1875, he wrote to a fellow Liberal: "Friends expect to be benefited by offices they are unfit for, by contracts they are not entitled to, by advances they have not earned. Enemies ally themselves with friends and push friends to the front. Some dig trenches at a distance and approach in regular seige form. A weak Minister would ruin the party in a month and the country very soon . . ."[16] A resolute prime minister, as things turned out, was ruining his party. The country survived.

If Mackenzie could do little about the patronage of appointments and contracts, apart from setting his face against it wherever possible, his government did reflect the Liberals' reforming spirit by changing the laws governing elections. One bill replaced staggered polling days —which had been spaced over six weeks in the 1867 election and over eleven weeks in the 1872 election—with a single polling period in a few far-flung constituencies. Another statute gave the courts a role in determining controverted elections, although this reform looked better on paper than in application since the Commons often failed to act on judicial findings.[17]

Mackenzie, for all his moral outrage, saw nothing wrong in rewarding senior party stalwarts, because it neither compromised government efficiency nor wasted money. A long list of ministers received appointments, including Justice Minister Antoine-Aimé Dorion, chief justice of the court of Queen's Bench for Quebec; Minister of the Interior David Laird, lieutenant-governor of the North–West Territory; and Secretary of State David Christie, Speaker of the Senate.

Recession, however, laid its dead hand upon the country during Mackenzie's government and as economic conditions worsened, internal party bickering increased. Liberals seemed disgruntled, every region discontented with its slice of the spoils. An allegation that his brother's company unfairly won a government contract—an allegation he successfully rebuffed—wounded him personally and sent critics snickering about his holier-than-thou double standard. His habitual dourness mirrored the country's mood; perhaps the majority of Canadians did prefer John A. drunk to Mackenzie sober.

Defeated at the polls, Mackenzie underlined his difference from Macdonald. He refused, despite the strongest pleas from Liberal colleagues, to appoint more than a handful of people. "I can quite understand," he wrote to a supplicant, "you have considered me omnipotent in such matters. There could not be a greater mistake. It's all over now. I have no power to make appointments." To another, he explained his motives, "As the election went against us, I could not do in the matter as I intended. It would be creating a new office, and this would be contrary to our own avowal of principle and our convictions. My doctrine was that I was bound as the trustee and guardian of the Liberal party to do nothing that could be held up as a reproach against us, in short, to go out clean."[18] He left, if not necessarily clean, then cleaner certainly than John A. and, for that matter, cleaner than most subsequent prime ministers. He remained to the end a Clear Grit, admirable in his way, standing for important principles, but a prisoner of a limited view of government and a poor practitioner of the arts of patronage. He never shared Macdonald's understanding of patronage as a tool for widening coalitions, meeting the party's financial needs, buying off the disaffected, rewarding the contented. Patronage was a burden, nothing more. That it could also be an opportunity apparently never occurred to him.

It certainly did occur to Laurier. He had been leader of the Opposition for nine years and a member of Parliament for twenty-two years before becoming prime minister in 1896, so he was steeped in the political culture of his time. If he only observed the pressures for patronage before 1896, he felt them directly as soon as he moved into the Prime Minister's Office. They bore down with the arrival of every mailbag, each letter staking out a claim on preferment.

Prime Minister Charles Tupper, following the path blazed by Macdonald, had attempted after his defeat in 1896, but before the Liberals took power, to pad the civil service with Conservatives and to pay off some prominent party stalwarts. The governor-general, Lord Aberdeen, blocked the outgoing prime minister's designs on the grounds of constitutional impropriety. But the padding of the public service had actually begun months before the election call, which rendered Laurier's patronage problems more acute since the Liberals, as was their wont, had campaigned on economy in government. Whatever the merits of economy, Liberal MPs and ministers soon grated against its constraints. "This policy of economy, of being penny-wise and pound-foolish," complained MP Albert Malouin, "is a policy from which the government does not benefit and which hurts the party."[19] Laurier, pestered by Montreal Liberals about why an insufficient number of partisans (including a certain Mr. Nugent) had been not appointed to the main city post office — one of Montreal's patronage plums since the days of Cartier — received this revealing explanation from Postmaster-General William Mulock: "The late Government in the last year or so of their tenure of office appointed a large number of persons temporarily to the service, the Montreal post-office having been specially favoured in this respect, and when I came to look into the condition of affairs there I found the staff vastly in excess of the needs of the service, and there were a large number of temporaries drawing pay without the knowledge of Parliament, and for whose pay Parliament had voted no money, they having been paid illegally out of the appropriation for the succeeding year . . . If I could get the number reduced to what is required, then when vacancies arise appointments could be made, and that would afford an opportunity for Mr. Nugent's appointment if he were recommended by our friends having the patronage."[20]

Never tortured by the exigencies of patronage, Laurier did occasionally give vent to a weary frustration. "If you were sitting in the chair from which I now write," he confided to John Willison, "being beseiged from all sides and having to determine in every case for the best interest of the party, to conciliate, to appreciate, and to smooth difficulties, you would realize how difficult a task it is, though how much more agreeable it would be to follow one's own inclinations in all such matters."[21] Like Macdonald, Laurier could "smooth difficulties" in matters of policy and patronage. He clothed his negative replies in velvet, never making the supplicant feel quilty or inadequate for having bothered the prime minister. He often replied briefly, using a form letter to brush aside requests, but even this letter contained graceful turns of phrase.

Under Laurier a formal system for handling patronage soon developed, the same one, with a notable variation, that Macdonald had successfully employed. Each Liberal constituency association, or regional association, established a patronage committee, sometimes comprising just the MP or defeated candidate and a handful of local notables. These committees' recommendations were heeded by ministers and the prime minister. As Laurier wrote in 1898 to an office-seeker, "Government patronage in each locality is distributed on the recommendation of the member for that locality."[22] Local patronage constituted a government MP's principal tool of political discretion. Proper use of this tool could maintain harmony within the local association, or tear it apart. Appointments of a city-wide or regional nature were made on the basis of recommendations from MPs and ministers, a practice that endures today. Departmental patronage lists for the ordering of supplies and services also followed recommendations of Liberal MPs and defeated candidates. So did the lists of authorized local newspapers receiving government advertising and printing contracts, although ministers kept an alert eye on the major metropolitan dailies. Appointments of province-wide or national importance could be made only after advice from the appropriate regional ministers, except in Quebec where Laurier decided. Laurier replied to a senior member of the Ontario cabinet who wrote recommending the appointment of an organizer, "I have made it a rule not to dispose of any patronage in any Province, except after previous consultation with my colleagues from that Province. You know, as well as I do, that this is the only safe course to follow, and any deviation from it, would be bad tactics."[23]

Macdonald, an Upper Canadian, had delegated Quebec patronage to lieutenants, since his own grasp of politics in that province could never equal his detailed knowledge of conditions in Ontario. Laurier turned Macdonald's formula on its head. He needed lieutenants elsewhere; in Quebec, Laurier would be supreme. It was, after all, Laurier's abiding preoccupation and singular accomplishment to secure Quebec for the Liberal party. This accomplishment, which subsequent generations of federal Liberals took for granted, ranks as among the most important in the political history of Canada. It altered fundamentally the dynamics of Canadian politics, making Quebec a "sheet anchor," to use Macdonald's phrase, for the Liberals rather than for the Conservatives.[24] The political transformation of Quebec, which took the better part of two decades, required the establishment of a *modus vivendi* between the Catholic Church and the Liberal party. Laurier, having played a critical role in establishing that *modus vivendi*, naturally paid careful attention to the views of bishops, as Macdonald had done, hoping at least to win from them political neutrality if not overt support. He took care, therefore, not to appoint prominent anti-clerical *rouges* to any positions that might rile the bishops, induced the Vatican to admit publicly the difference between political liberalism and religious deviance, and tried, wherever possible as prime minister, to keep the bishops out of politics by giving them no cause for complaint.

Laurier's relations with the Catholic Church formed part of a broader plan to extend the Liberal coalition in Quebec. In this, the Conservatives immeasurably assisted Laurier, for in the 1890s they presented an increasingly sorry spectacle of factionalism. The ultramontane group, nicknamed Castors—the pseudonym of a pamphleteer who brilliantly expressed their views—attacked Conservative party members suspected of deviation from church views on politics. Personal rivalries aggravated the divisions; splits over the Manitoba Schools question and railway policies exacerbated them. The precarious state of Quebec's provincial finances, Premier Honoré Mercier's nationalist attacks on Ottawa, the aftermath of the Riel affair — all these factors ate away at the Conservatives' standing in Quebec. In Ottawa, none of the Conservative leaders who succeeded Macdonald used sufficient finesse in dealing with the Quebec wing of the party. Laurier—a French Canadian, a champion of provincial rights, a Liberal acceptable to, if not the first choice of, many clerics — began exploiting the developing fissures within the Conservative ranks, gradually gathering up prominent Conservatives, persuading others to remain neutral, and slowly reducing the Conservative party to what the Liberal party had once been: a doctrinal rump representing only a minority of Quebec opinion.

This transformation, however, spread over many years. By Laurier's second term Quebec was a solidly Liberal province, a bastion that testified to Laurier's skilful party management during his first term, a shift accomplished partly by his use of patronage. In selecting cabinet ministers from Quebec, Laurier all but ignored the *rouge* faction, also known as the "old Liberals," appointing instead Liberals of more recent standing. "No man who had hitherto filled the post of first minister has cared so little for those who were his colleagues in Opposition," grumbled a frustrated aspirant.[25] That statement did not amount to much, there having been only six previous prime ministers, but it did reflect a potential danger. The *rouge* elements could reasonably have demanded more. Laurier smothered their incipient objections with patronage. One with a substantial claim became Speaker of the Senate, another received a written assurance that he would become lieutenant-governor of Quebec, and still another wound up a judge.

The flip side of forestalling trouble from the "old Liberals" was wooing disaffected Conservatives, the "school of Cartier." Laurier's handling of J.A. Chapleau, symbol for the disaffected Conservatives, exemplified the prime minister's sure touch. Chapleau, a lieutenant-governor appointed by the Conservatives, had nonetheless subtly favoured the Liberals in the 1896 election. Chapleau's term was coming to an end in December 1897, and the possibility arose in correspondence between Laurier and Chapleau that he might be appointed for a second term. That possibility outraged the "old Liberals," especially François Langelier, who had been promised the position in writing by Laurier. From this predicament Laurier extracted himself with customary aplomb. He carefully explained his problem to an understanding Chapleau, but allowed Chapleau to serve out his term. He then appointed a Liberal acceptable to the clergy as lieutenant-governor and sent Langelier to the bench, where he continued to receive promotions until Laurier appointed him lieutenant-governor in 1911.

Arthur "Boss" Dansereau was another disaffected Conservative, the nickname appropriately awarded for his control of patronage while the Conservatives dominated Quebec. Dansereau reigned as postmaster of Montreal, a position with considerable patronage possibilities. He had gradually fallen out of favour with elements of the Conservative party and, like Chapleau, yearned for a Quebec united behind a French-speaking leader. Powerful in politics, Dansereau cared little for administration, a weakness that so appalled Postmaster-General William Mulock that he put Dansereau on a leave of absence "pending final action."[26] When Laurier heard of Mulock's action, he immediately restrained his stern colleague and ordered him to write a letter of apology. "For reasons which I deem paramount, knowing the situation in Quebec perfectly, I expect that you will at once re-instate Dansereau in his position." Laurier's treatment of Dansereau paid off handsomely. Dansereau subsequently became editor of *La Presse* and dismayed the Conservatives by turning the paper into a sympathetic organ for Laurier and the Liberal party.

The winning over of newspaperman and Conservative politician Joseph Israel Tarte, however, was Laurier's most stunning coup. Here was a man, more mercurial than any, more dogged than most, who had excoriated the Liberal party during an earlier, ultramontane phase of his career. For him to be enlisted in the Liberal cause, let alone to receive such a prominent portfolio as public works, struck some "old Liberals" as certainly dangerous and possibly politically traitorous. Throughout Tarte's six years as a Laurier minister, elements in the Liberal party waged a relentless campaign against him. But they gained nothing, apart from a higher level of personal frustration, since Laurier always stood behind his sometimes impetuous ally.[27]

Tarte's appointment as minister of public works carried a certain irony. After all, as a newspaper editor and member of Parliament Tarte had been responsible for breaking the McGreevy Scandal which disgraced the Conservative minister of public works, Hector Langevin. That scandal exposed the brazen kickbacks from contractors and the ceaseless application of favouritism that characterized the Conservatives' fund–raising and other political activities in Quebec. Now Tarte entered the temple from which he had chased a previous gang of money-changers and replaced them with another. He used the public works portfolio in the traditional manner, as an extensive slush fund for the Liberal party and its friends, relentlessly spending public funds in a systematic porkbarrelling campaign. Temporary employees on public works projects were preferred to employees on full-time contracts, since their loyalty would be to their political boss rather than their business boss. He had no patience with ministers who did not pay sufficient attention to patronage, and sometimes infuriated them by intervening in their departments. Tarte's constant efforts to secure public works for Montreal, especially the city's port, irritated fellow ministers, and his disregard for the sacred Liberal principle of economy in government scandalized party greybeards such as Richard Cartwright and William Mulock. "We are entering a new era; it is no use being afraid to spend more money," Tarte told the House, speaking as much to his colleagues as to the Conservative Opposition.[28] He did draw the line at wholesale firings of public servants after the 1896 election, a decision that merely incurred the wrath of some "old Liberals" in Quebec, who accused him of shielding his Conservative friends.[29]

Tarte, having once been deeply involved in political organization for the Conservative party, knew how to win elections. In 1893, he spoke some of the most famous words in the history of Canadian patronage, "I was treasurer of the Conservative party for three elections and I must say that we didn't win elections with prayers." Those words, slightly amended (*les éléctions ne se font pas avec des prières*, or elections are not won by prayers), became a telltale phrase for critics of the corruption and patronage that characterized Quebec's political life. But the words rang true. Elections in Quebec, including those involving Laurier, remained struggles of lofty rhetoric and lined pockets.

Tarte transferred his organizational talents to the Liberals when Laurier made him chief organizer in Quebec. He became to Laurier what André Ouellet would later become to Trudeau, a political fixer in the prime minister's backyard, especially in Montreal. (Agriculture minister Sydney Fisher looked after the Eastern Townships; Laurier and minister without portfolio R.R. Dobell, a former Conservative recruited by Laurier, oversaw the Quebec City region.) With Laurier's blessing, Tarte organized constituencies for elections, selected candidates, paid the right people, stayed in close touch with local notables, passed on political gossip, steered contracts in the proper political direction, and recommended patronage appointees. He often ran afoul of fellow Liberals, since tact did not figure prominently in his character, nor did modesty disturb his soul. Yet Laurier stood behind him while always reserving the right to mediate disputes caused or left unresolved by Tarte. If Tarte occasionally required a harness, Laurier would apply it in private. "Don't forget," Laurier wrote a prominent Quebec Liberal, "Tarte is my colleague, and as much through friendship as tactics, my intention is not only to prevent him being attacked, but even to defend him in all times and in all places, without examining whether he is wrong or right."[30]

While Tarte looked after the particulars of federal organization and patronage, Laurier kept up close, friendly relations with the provincial Liberal governments. The federal and provincial Liberals shared workers, sources of money, and a common foe. Laurier is thought to have played an important behind-the-scenes role in the selection of S.N. Parent as leader of the Liberals and premier of Quebec. A strict acknowledgement of each other's patronage terrain, however, characterized relations between the federal and provincial parties, not only in Quebec but across the country. "Provincial patronage is distributed upon the recommendation of supporters of the provincial government in the Legislative Assembly, or of its friends in the riding where it has to be exercised," Laurier wrote a supplicant for a provincial position. "Their full knowledge of all the local circumstances and of what would there serve the best interest of the party, gives to their recommendations a preponderance to which mine was and never will be entitled."[31]

By the time Tarte resigned in 1902, over a dispute about the tariff, he and Laurier had built a mighty political machine in Quebec. Of course, the skilful use of political patronage was only one reason for the Liberals' success, but without it Liberal gains would have come more slowly. Laurier used patronage in Quebec, as Macdonald had across the country, as a tool for enticing political opponents into the fold, rather than exclusively as a system of rewards for the faithful.

Laurier assembled in 1896 one of the most impressive cabinets in Canadian history; friendly commentators called it the "ministry of all the talents." Nova Scotia's W.S. Fielding and Ontario's Oliver Mowat had been lured to federal politics after highly successful careers as premiers. Andrew Blair of New Brunswick, Richard Cartwright and William Mulock of Ontario, and Clifford Sifton of Manitoba were among the other cabinet heavyweights. In English Canada, patronage necessarily flowed through these regional chieftains. Laurier could occasionally intervene to mediate factional disputes in English-Canadian provinces, but wherever possible he gave ministers the discretion of patronage. After 1901, Ontario ministers set up a patronage committee to review appointments for the Senate and judiciary, thus initiating a strategy that became a fixture in federal cabinets. First Mowat, then Mulock, and finally Allan Aylesworth were Laurier's Ontario lieutenants, the main conduits through whom federal Liberals maintained links with their provincial cousins.[32] When Laurier in 1907 wrote suggesting the name of a possible Senator from Ontario, Cartwright, never one to mince words, harrumphed that the prime minister was being "highly impolitic."[33]

Nowhere was the decentralization of patronage authority under Laurier clearer than in Clifford Sifton's empire as federal minister of the interior. Sifton had displayed his talents as an administrator and partisan brawler in the provincial government of Manitoba, where he served as attorney-general during the Greenway Administration. He had organized constituencies and election campaigns with eyes deliberately averted from pervasive bribery, chicanery and skulduggery. He had slipped through changes to the *Election Act* to benefit the Manitoba Liberal government by changing the appointed hour for debate without informing the Opposition.[34]

There were, to be sure, the pious — Mulock, Cartwright and Mowat — in the federal Liberal party. Touched by that sanctimony special to Upper Canadian Reformers, they looked askance at the more brazen partisan activities of their cabinet colleagues, occasionally even troubling the prime minister with their views on ethical conduct. The Ontario Liberal party, over which Mowat presided and to which they were all linked, had evolved into one of the country's most effective political machines, with all its implications for patronage, favouritism, electoral irregularities and occasional corruption. Yet, as O.D. Skelton wryly remarked, "Ontario . . . was frequently too busy saving the souls of the other eight provinces to have time for its own."[35] Sifton, however, remained untouched by the Ontario brand of piety. For him, "politics was a continuous war. The Conservative party was, simply, 'the enemy.' Each battle or squirmish required serious preparation. Independence and idealism therefore had little place among the troops."[36] As minister of the interior and Liberal party organizer for the entire Canadian West, Sifton held sway over a territory stretching from the Ontario border to the Pacific Ocean, and from the American border to the northern-most outposts of civilization in North America. His ministry's regulation of the North-West Territory and the Yukon included homesteading and settlement, immigration, schools, forestry, mineral rights, grazing, railways and national parks. No Canadian politician, before or since, ever ruled such a vast geographic territory.

Sifton harboured equally vast ambitions, for the territory, the Liberal party and himself. Crude though his methods may often have been, Sifton fulfilled almost all of those ambitions, as testified by the territory's population expansion, the Liberal preference of the majority of its inhabitants, and his own personal fortune. Like the Conservatives, Sifton used the authority of the interior ministry for partisan purposes. But what made the political consequences of his tenure so durable was the coincident rapid expansion of the prairies and the subsequent grant of provincial status to Alberta and Saskatchewan, so that for several decades thereafter the Liberal party's imprint remained fixed on the new provinces. Within a year of assuming office, he had placed his own men in positions of authority within the immigration section of the ministry. When the Klondike gold rush opened up the Yukon, most of the officials sent to bring a semblance of order to the unruly territory were Liberals. The homestead agents who fanned out across the prairies — spear carriers in "Sifton's army" — were often the first personal contacts immigrants systematically experienced with Canadians. Immigrants tended to remember that they had arrived under a Liberal government, and government officials constantly refreshed their memory. Similarly, newspapers published in their native languages were subsidized by Liberal governments or owned by Liberal proprietors. By 1904, thirty-five papers in Manitoba, twenty-two in the North-West Territory, and sixteen in British Columbia were on the Liberal government's patronage list.[37] Once again, patronage was being used to integrate newcomers to a political party, in the same way municipal political machines in the United States secured the loyalties of ethnic groups who huddled in the great American cities of the Northeast and Midwest.

The civil service, padded with Conservatives, quickly felt the Sifton whip. Civil servants who had worked actively for the Conservative party received their dismissal notices; others of suspect political sympathies found themselves superannuated, demoted, transferred, denied salary increases, and otherwise made sufficiently miserable that departure seemed preferable to endurance. The deputy minister of the interior and the deputy superintendent-general of Indian affairs both got the chop.[38]

The North-West Territory had its own council, on which the conventional wisdom suggested that non-partisanship could maximize the Territory's leverage on the federal government. (This attitude changed in 1905 when the Laurier government ensured a Liberal cast to the first provincial administrations.) But Ottawa directly administered the Yukon through a commissioner and other officials appointed by the minister of the interior, Clifford Sifton. Once installed in a place so far removed from Ottawa, officials sometimes got too big for their britches, or at least too independent for Sifton. When Commissioner William Ogilvie appointed several known Conservatives, Sifton upbraided him with a lesson in Canadian political reality, "Under our system of government we cannot appoint our opponents to office, and while you are an Administrator under a party government you will have to be guided by that rule."[39] Superintendent Sam Steele, the popular officer in charge of the Yukon constabulary, also resisted the patronage system by appointing several officers without due regard to partisanship. Sifton transferred him to Fort MacLeod. Mining permits were issued with an eye to party affiliation; liquor permits went to party supporters; civil servants held their jobs through patronage; the whole governance of this raw Territory exhibited the full panoply of corruption, from kickbacks to all sorts of under-the-table deals.

Governor-General Lord Minto, a stern critic of Sifton, wrote after returning from a Yukon tour, "The Dominion government seem to have looked upon the Yukon as a source of revenue, as a place to make as much out of as they could, and have used the proceeds largely for political corruption instead of the development of the country, and in so doing are in a fair way to kill the goose that laid the golden egg."[40] Sifton's biographer noted that elections featured attempts to rig the voting lists and also enormous government slush funds, "possibly as much as $10 for every voter in the Yukon. There was a corps of prostitutes and dance-hall girls, paid to keep Opposition voters occupied on election day, but otherwise usually in tow to government officials and businessmen. A small army of unemployed miners was paid just before elections for constructing roads and other works which they never saw. There was a reserve force of aliens (mostly American) who were paid and voted illegally at distant polling stations on the creeks."[41] Perhaps Sifton and Laurier were unaware of all the sordid details of these campaigns, but to suggest their total innocence is to accept that piano players in whorehouses are ignorant of what transpires upstairs.

Sifton scored a major commerical and political coup in securing control of *The Manitoba Free Press* in 1898. The paper, formerly a Conservative organ, immediately became the principal propagator of the Liberal gospel in Western Canada — and an eloquent and skilful one when John Dafoe assumed the editor's chair. Sifton's ownership of the paper, and the attention he paid to its commercial success and editorial slant, reflected the continuing interest leading politicians of the Laurier era took in the newspaper business. Sifton and the Liberal premiers of Alberta and Saskatchewan after 1905 encouraged the creation and commercial profitability of numerous papers throughout Western Canada in the mother tongues of the newly arrived ethnic groups. This they accomplished by the then-conventional methods of steering government advertising and letting printing contracts to friendly papers capable of handling the work, taking out a large number of subscriptions and paying for them with government funds, and, if necessary, finding financial resources among party supporters to keep marginal enterprises alive.

Laurier, too, had always keenly appreciated the need for party organs. As early as 1882, he had written to Edward Blake about the situation in Quebec, "It stands to reason that as our adversaries have 21 papers to our 5, we must forever remain in the minority, no matter what may take place in the political world."[42] Laurier's prime ministerial instructions to Mulock about withdrawing a dismissal notice to Arthur "Boss" Dansereau arose, in part, because Laurier knew Dansereau had been offered the editorship at *La Presse*. Laurier remained in close touch with leading editors of Liberal papers, especially John Willison at *The Globe* and Ernest Pacaud at *Le Soleil* in Quebec City. And he expected Liberal organs to follow the party line closely, since he applied to them his first commandment of politics—loyalty. Laurier owned shares in *Le Soleil* which he sold to Premier Jean-Lomer Gouin in 1907 to satisy Gouin's gripes that supporters of his old provincial Liberal rival, Simon-Napolean Parent, had infiltrated the paper. The agreement stipulated that Laurier would continue to oversee the reselling of the shares and to control completely the paper's editorial approach to federal politics.[43] The Liberals, like the Conservatives under Macdonald, drew up a list of newspapers authorized to receive federal advertising and printing contracts. No sooner had the Liberals won in 1896, for example, than *The Mail* in Toronto ceased receiving government advertising (to be fair, *The Mail* received five dollars of advertising in 1898-1899 and five more in 1899-1900), whereas *The Globe*, which had been all but shut out by the Conservatives, began receiving several thousand dollars a year.[44]

That Sifton bent his part of the civil service for partisan purposes simply reflected the well-established practices of his time. Some firings usually attended a change of government. After the Laurier government took office in 1896, four hundred and seventy-three employees lost their jobs, of whom one hundred and ninety-six — only two percent of the entire federal civil service — were fired for "offensive political partisanship."[45] New civil servants, especially field workers in the so-called "outside service," were hired for partisan reasons, competence being a desirable but not necessary side benefit. The civil service remained small, since Laurier's economic views were those of a nineteenth-century British laissez-faire liberal, and the demands for social-policy reforms from isolated groups and nascent trade unions had not yet gained sufficient public support to warrant a government response. To a large extent, the civil service represented an extension of the party in power.

The federal government had essentially borrowed elements from colonial civil services existing at the time of Confederation to create the new federal civil service. One year into the Confederation experiment, a royal commission began investigating the state of the civil service. Its report heralded a series of subsequent investigations — by royal commissions in 1880-81 and 1891-92, as well as by special committees — all of which underlined the deleterious effects of patronage on internal morale and efficiency. The Liberals, with dreary predictability, had attacked the Conservatives for larding up the civil service with their political friends, but once elected in 1896, the Liberals found patronage in the civil service too enticing a means of consolidating power to act on their previous criticisms. The outside service, in particular, offered a range of part-time or seasonal positions which, allocated by the proper MPs, brought political benefits in the constituencies, notwithstanding periodic headaches caused by the inevitable small-supply, large-demand dilemma. Reforms measures had been implemented, in particular, a board of examiners to administer tests and screen prospective candidates. But the dictates of patronage frequently overrode such fine intentions. Positions were simply listed as not requiring entrance by examination, or the results of examinations were disregarded by politicians more interested in satisfying the needs of supporters than in bowing to the merit principle.

Yet, as the Laurier years stretched on, the prime minister confronted a series of pressures for civil-service reforms which he found difficult to ignore. His predilection had always been to short-circuit critics of civil-service patronage. He wrote his friend John Willison, one such critic of pervasive patronage, "Reforms are for Oppositions. It is the business of Governments to stay in office."[46] Reflecting years later on Laurier's attitude, Willison wrote:

> "When eager civil service reformers confessed their desire to relieve him of the 'incubus of patronage' there crept into his eyes a look of humorous wisdom which would have cooled their ardour if they had understood its significance. He believed there was far more of gain than of loss to governments and parties through control over appointments to office and distribution of government contracts. He knew that 'friends' were necessary to organize constituencies and carry elections and seldom was anxious to discover the sources of their contributions."[47]

If, as O.D. Skelton justly wrote of Laurier and patronage, "no other subject bulked so large in correspondence; no other purpose brought so many visitors to Ottawa," then in Laurier's eyes, so be it. This was the political system he understood, the one with which he felt comfortable and from which he believed indispensable political benefits flowed. But by the turn of the century, American critics had begun to flail at the spoils system in their country. Some of that criticism influenced assorted social reformers, academics and writers in Canada, who urged, often in highly moralistic tones, improvements in various walks of life, including the elimination of patronage from the civil service. The British example continued to inspire those who defined Canada as part of the glorious Empire.[48] All the speeches from Canadian politicians pledging undying fidelity to things British, especially to the traditions of the Mother of Parliaments, rang hollow when critics compared the extent of patronage in the British public service with that in the Canadian. In Quebec, nationalist critics such as Henri Bourassa chastised Laurier for a variety of sins, including the abuse of patronage.

More important still in the growing pressures for reform were the scandals, real and alleged, that beset the Laurier Government in 1906, 1907 and 1908, many of them involving Sifton's previous administration of the Interior department. The Conservatives charged—and they presented compelling evidence — that the advertising of timber limits had been manipulated to favour Liberal friends, and that the system of sealed bids for timber rights had been corrupted.[49] The Commons expended enormous energies debating a series of charges and counter-charges about malpractices in government. The battles raged with special ferocity in the public accounts committee, wherein Conservatives

charged Liberals with favouritism, disregard for due process in awarding contracts, and other forms of costly patronage, to which the
Liberals frequently replied by dredging up similar practices by Conservatives.[50] Serious charges were also brought against Minister of Militia and Defence Sir Frederick Borden and against Minister of Railways
Henry R. Emmerson, forcing him to resign. Minister of Public Works
Charles Hyman left the cabinet over charges of electoral corruption,
including bribery in his London constituency. Allegations against the
administration of the department of marine and fisheries sparked so
much controversy that Laurier ordered a judicial inquiry, whose report
led to the suspension of three civil servants and the resignation of the
deputy minister. He also agreed to yet another royal commission into
the civil service.

The commissioners picked up where their predecessors of 1892
had left off, lamenting widespread patronage. True, the commissioners
acknowledged, the *Civil Service Act* remained on the statute books,
but "the Act has been so amended, re-amended, and whittled down,
that the public service, the Commissioners believe, not only at Ottawa
but elsewhere throughout the Dominion, has fallen back the last fifteen
years."[51] Some genuflections towards the merit principle accompanied
appointments to the "inside service," but "as a rule your Commissioners
found in the outside service that politics enter into every appointment,
and politicians on the spot interest themselves not only in the appointments but in subsequent promotions of officers." The results of examinations were easily circumvented by creating new classifications for
prospective appointees other than those listed in the *Civil Service Act*,
or by hiring people who failed the exams as temporary staff, then
indefinitely extending their term of service. The commissioners recommended a civil service commission, a revamped system of classification, examinations for civil service posts, and respect for the merit
system.

Even Clifford Sifton, of all people, welcomed the recommendations. By now a private member — he had left the cabinet in 1905 in a
dispute over state funding for Catholic schools — Sifton called patronage "the greatest nuisance in public life" and asked that the civil service
be placed on a "higher plane." Across the aisle, Conservatives sat
dumbfounded by Sifton's gall, but he repeated his support for civil
service reform so frequently that even some skeptics admitted that
maybe, just maybe, he believed his own words. As for the Conservatives, their leader Robert Borden was nudging his party towards civil
service reform. So Laurier, with no evident enthusiasm, presented the
Civil Service Amendment Act which, among other changes, established
the civil service commission. The reform looked impressive on paper,

but in reality the mere existence of a commission could not shake politicians from their old habits, especially the use of patronage to fill positions in the "outside service."[52] Laurier, then, left the system of patronage in the civil service he had inherited fundamentally intact. Circumstances forced him to make cosmetic reforms, but the Laurier era represented the continuation of the old ways of patronage rather than the beginning of a new approach.

Laurier also carried forward the Macdonald tradition in dealing with the private sector, transforming his own party in the process. The Grits of Ontario, who formed the largest group in the Liberal coalition when Laurier became leader, had always been Jeffersonians in the Canadian context, suspicious of expanding government, spokesmen for small farmers and merchants. The tariff, indeed Macdonald's entire National Policy, vexed them, because to leading Liberals such as Richard Cartwright it meant the triumph of economically inefficient but politically powerful manufacturing interests over economically efficient but politically weak agrarian and small-business interests. The tariff question periodically gnawed at the party — Tarte left over it, eighteen prominent Toronto Liberals bolted over the issue of reciprocity in 1911, an issue that contributed to the Party's defeat in the election of that year. Until 1911, despite his own free-trade inclinations, Laurier always bore in mind the protectionist preferences of the large commercial interests. In Quebec, peace with those interests dovetailed with his own long game of expanding the base of the Liberal party, especially forging stronger ties with the English-speaking community of Montreal, which had largely supported the Conservatives under Macdonald. The Liberals, once so critical of the Canadian Pacific's links with the Conservative party, even entered the railway sweepstakes themselves, authorizing a second transcontinental line and riding the turn-of-the-century railway boom to establish bonds with the banks and the construction companies that were actively promoting this development. Although flickers of the old Jeffersonian values occasionally disturbed the party, Laurier's Liberals became almost as Hamiltonian in their approach to economic policy as the Macdonald Conservatives.[53]

Laurier's tenure coincided with Canada's first prolonged economic boom since Confederation, a boom that populated the prairies, fleshed out the cities, created the first stirrings of organized labour, galvanized the efforts of social reformers, and set the Laurier government afloat on a sea of buoyant revenues. In such circumstances, money sloshed back and forth between the political and commercial worlds. Some of the uproar that plagued Laurier's governments arose from comfortable relationships of favouritism, which none of the institutions of Parliament—including the auditor-general and the public accounts commit-tee — could control, even if occasionally they could shed light on the darker corners of political practice.

The royal commission into the civil service of 1908, to take just one example, highlighted the widespread practice of padding purchase prices to include payments for patronage. The looseness of control procedures and the prevalence of the assumption that political favour-itism should count in government were fixtures of the Laurier period, just as they had been through Macdonald's long years of power.

The need for a physical infrastructure to unify so vast an expanse of territory, the habitual clamour for public works improvements, and the limited size of the Canadian market continued to make business heavily dependent upon government. Even before Confederation, but certainly during the Macdonald and Laurier eras, the symbiotic rela-tionship between the governing party and commercial interests politi-cized economic decision–making, and tempted both entities into using such leverage as they could muster to extract benefits from one another. Thus, during the Laurier years, corporations and their wealthy owners continued to be the politicians' major sources of money for campaigns.

Elections still drained cash from the pockets of candidates and wealthy supporters in part because election days still featured wide-spread treating and bribery. Party propaganda was also costly, since Liberal party organizers such as Tarte believed in saturating a constit-uency with political pamphlets during the campaign. As one member of Parliament told the House in 1903, "So long as the candidates agree to suspend all ideas of morality during an election and go in for a general picnic, we shall continue to have all the expenditure of money that we have at the present time. Down in my part of the country we have the most moral people to be found in the world; but when an election comes around, they regard it as a splendid holiday. . . . They size up each candidate for what they can get out of him, and they generally run it up to the limit." Under these circumstances, any party needed hooks into the business community for funds.

Canada remained a rural country despite the economic boom of the Laurier period. When Laurier left office in 1911, slightly more than three-quarters of the population still lived in small-town or rural con-ditions, a slight percentage decline from 1881, when the figure was eight-one percent. Manufacturing and banking grew apace in some of the large urban centers of Ontario and Quebec, but much of the Laurier boom resulted from the opening of Western Canada, an opening that confirmed the essentially rural nature of Canadian society. Localism pervaded politics, and conditons were rife for the politics of patronage.[54] Parties pitched for the loyalty of voters through partisan media outlets; they built competing networks of local notables in hundreds of communities across the country through the granting of favours, preferment and place. Invariably, these advantages went to local businessmen or members of the professional middle classes, lawyers especially, so the patronage that glued parties together also contributed to the middle-class essence of political leadership. James Bryce, the acute if snobbish British observer of American democracy, wrote of Canada a decade after Laurier's defeat that politics was "a game played over material interest between ministers, constituencies and their representatives, railway companies and private speculators [which] is not only demoralizing to all concerned, but interferes with the consideration of the great issues of policy."[55] The words belonged to Bryce, the echoes to André Siegfried.

And yet, perhaps these foreign observers had missed what the politics of patronage and the economics of porkbarrelling had achieved. They were the tools that had allowed Laurier to expand the base of his party, making it fully competitive with the Conservative party—as Canadian political history unfolded, more than competitive. If the twentieth century did not belong to Canada, as Laurier had predicted, most of the twentieth century in Canadian politics belonged to the Liberals. Adopting the Macdonald model, Laurier knit together disparate ethnic and linguistic groups, diverse regions, men of different religions, and proponents of varying economic ideas into a political blanket that covered the country.

There could have been other models, based on region or religion or language or class — a French party and an English one; a Catholic party and a Protestant one; a Western Canada party and a Maritimers' Rights party and so on — all sending representatives to Ottawa, there to form ever-shifting coalitions in unstable governments of the kind known in pre-Confederation Canada. Instead the two national parties, the Conservatives under Macdonald and the Liberals under Laurier, held out the hope of rewards to all regions and all electors, whatever their race, religion, or class. In so doing, they brought stability to the governance of the country and legitimacy to its political institutions, both so sorely lacking during the tumultuous decades before Confederation. And patronage, around which so many things political turned, encouraged loyalties to national causes as well as national parties, and helped Canadians conceptualize the national interest.

The centrality of patronage to Canada's developing political culture could not endure throughout the twentieth century in the face of new social and economic presures, especially pressures stemming from the emergence of the mass media and welfare state. But rather than disappearing, patronage took on new and more subtle forms because patrons and clients continued to feel it satisfied not only certain conditions crucial to effective political management in Canada, but also, as Laurier once observed, a basic human need.

CHAPTER 5

PATRONAGE IN TRANSITION

BORDEN, KING AND ST. LAURENT

"I then spoke of appointments and patronage.
Said I loathed the partisan side of politics and was
not prepared to countenance it,"
From Mackenzie King's diary, September, 14, 1939.

WHEN THE LAMPS went out in Europe and a generation began sacrificing its blood and treasure during World War I, Canadians by the tens of thousands laid themselves upon the altar. A few discerning souls may have glimpsed the future; for many, however, the "war to end all wars" appeared to provide the chance to win spurs, even glory, in a quick and mighty affirmation of all that was good. From around the outports of Newfoundland, and from across Canada, the units formed and the men set sail, few, if any, having heard of Beaumont Hamel, the Somme, Passchendaele and Vimy Ridge.

In Ottawa, the Conservatives under Robert Borden, in office since 1911, presided over mobilization, their commitment to the war effort supported by the leader of the Opposition, Sir Wilfrid Laurier. When Sir Wilfrid declared a "truce to party strife" in August 1914, the nation's political unity was assured. Even in Quebec, editorialists supported the war, while sparing their readers the swagger of the English-Canadian newspapers. And then the notices began appearing, newspaper pages framed in black, listing the dead or "missing in action," lists that rent the heart and seared the soul. The "war to end all wars" seemed like a war without end. As the casualties mounted, defiant passions flared in English-speaking Canada and defensive ones burned in French-speaking Quebec. Political rivalries resurfaced under pressures, from within and without the parties, to prosecute better the war effort.

The longer the war dragged on, the more it upset conventional assumptions and practices at home. Conservatives assumed at the beginning, despite Laurier's political truce, that politics would quite literally be business as usual. The war effort demanded a new range of products: uniforms, boots, rifles, munitions, transportation vehicles, rations. And these products, the Conservatives believed, would be provided, as they had always been, by friends of the government. Similarly, all senior appointments, including to the militia, would go to Conservatives. For awhile, everything proceeded along conventional lines, but as the blood began to flow and the country searched for explanations and scapegoats, the old ways were increasingly held responsible for confusion, inefficiency and even deaths. Of patronage much had always been forgiven and forgotten; in war, nothing was forgiven and everything was remembered.

Canada had not fought a full-scale war since Confederation, and it was therefore ill-prepared when one arrived. For more than four decades, a succession of British commanding officers had struggled to squeeze political patronage from the militia, but they confronted entrenched opposition from parliamentarians of every stripe. In the early post–Confederation Parliaments, the "militia lobby,"—members identified with the militia — comprised about one-fifth of the entire Commons; by the early 1890s, the lobby still comprised about one-tenth.[1] Every MP, whatever his personal ties with the militia, understood the importance of the institution in his constituency. The minister of the militia directed a portfolio universally acknowledged to rival public works and the post office in patronage opportunities. Most of the administrative and military appointments to the militia were dictated by partisanship. So were the contracts for supplies. When the militia trooped west to put down the Riel Rebellion, Conservative ministers in Ottawa ensured that friendly suppliers in Winnipeg and elsewhere provided what the men required.

Whatever the military purposes of the militia, it provided a bit of psychological patronage in the form of social prestige for officers. British commanding officers might heap scorn upon pervasive political favouritism, but however much they might complain about unearned allowances, padded pay lists and unqualified Canadian officers, ministers of the militia appreciated that keeping the militia happy paid political dividends at election time. The tussle, then, between military efficiency and political expediency never abated, and flare-ups frequently characterized personal relationships between British military men and their Canadian ministers.[2] Prior to the 1896 election, the Liberals had regularly attacked Conservative patronage abuses in the militia. Once in power, the Liberals placed their own in positions of authority. The social-prestige side of militia appointments reflected itself in the contingent sent to represent Canada at Queen Victoria's Diamond Jubilee in 1897. Twenty-six officers and men were invited; two hundred sailed, the number having been inflated by relentless political wire-pulling of the kind that even today attends the preparation of invitations to state dinners, sent out by the Prime Minister's Office to dozens if not hundreds of party worthies.

When the Conservatives replaced the Liberals in 1911, some of the partisanship had been wrung out of the militia and the Canadian military, but much remained. And none of the partisanship had been squeezed from Canadian politics: Liberals and Conservatives still hammered each other from towns and villages all the way to the Commons chamber. Borden replied to Laurier's offer of a political truce to facilitate prosecution of the war effort by pledging to end party interference in purchasing supplies and making appointments. But Borden, in this as in other ways, misread those of his colleagues for whom the traditional ways of politics were all they knew and could support.

In Toronto, for example, after 1911 local Conservatives had grouped themselves into the Liberal-Conservative Association of Toronto, which consisted of area MPs, Conservative candidates defeated in the last federal and provincial elections, executives from the riding organizations, and representatives of the Toronto Young Men's Liberal-Conservative Association. The association's advisory committee was, in effect, the Conservative party's patronage committee in Toronto, and its secretary, Toronto MP and businessman Edmund Bristol, was the principal conduit for patronage advice to and from MPs. Such a decision-making apparatus for handling appointments, contracts, immigration cases and even licences to sell stamps was quite normal in Canadian politics. The needs of war, however, brought forth dozens of hungry Conservative contractors, who pressed their claims for preferment. Within months of the declaration of war, Toronto contractors began complaining volubly that they were not receiving their fair share of contracts. By October, 1914, barely two months after the outbreak of war, the Conservatives had established a three-member cabinet committee to dispense the patronage arising from defence needs.[3] In Sam Hughes—the minister responsible for the militia and procurement—Conservative contractors and middlemen found a friend at court. He liked their company, shared their enthusiasm for the war effort (and himself), and agreed with their politics.

Hundreds of contract-seekers, job-hounds and Conservative worthies flooded Ottawa with requests for preferment, and from Sam Hughes and his fellow cabinet minister Robert Rogers they got a receptive hearing.[4] Hughes ran the Militia department like an autocrat, oblivious to courtesy, deaf to criticism, immune to all thoughts but that he knew best. Within a year, complaints about leaky boots, faulty rifles, inferior equipment and speculative profits swirled through Ottawa, where they were at first dismissed as the usual partisan scandal-mongering. But they were taken more seriously when letters of complaint from the front and growing lists of the dead and wounded furnished documentation that could not be ignored. Even the first men stationed in Britain complained that the incessant rain exposed the inadequacies of their clothing and the unreliability of their tents. Scandalous stories mounted, breaking into the public domain with charges that two Conservative MPs, William Garland and Arthur Foster, were implicated in shady purchasing deals. For this, Borden read them out of the party.

By mid-May, 1915, with reports of staggering losses arriving with depressing frequency, Borden could write in his diary, "This war is the suicide of civilization."[5] Stories appeared in the press about gross abuses of patronage, especially the profits made by contractor-cronies of Hughes'. The Liberal Opposition, having listened to Borden's promises of an end to preferments in appointments and contracts, set up a full howl in Parliament. The criticisms stirred Borden's own aversion to the sordidness of political life. He had given his word on behalf of the government; now senior ministers were breaking it. He had been promising for nearly a decade to root out patronage from the federal government, without ever having done much about it. Now the combination of his own instincts, the cry for efficient prosecution of the war effort, the grim news from the front, the publicized misdeeds of his own supporters, and the whole unseemly rush for spoils galvanized him into action. In April, 1915, the government established the war purchasing commission, the first step towards a more far-reaching reform. A year later, with blood drenching the western front, the country soured on Sam Hughes. He had become a complete political liability, unpopular with his cabinet colleagues, the favourite target of Opposition MPs and irate editorialists. The veteran Conservative minister Sir George Foster lacerated Hughes in cabinet and denounced patronage in the Commons, which drew an acid entry in Borden's diary: "Foster has no more political sense than a turnip. . . . His speech about patronage was eloquent mouthing; in every day practice no one is keener about petty patronage than he is."[6] In mid-1916 Hughes left the cabinet in disgrace with most Canadians, a fall from power as spectacular as any in Canadian political history. Some measure of the open-arms patronage that marked the early war years vanished with his departure.

The next year brought a change of profound significance in the whole history of Canadian patronage, indeed, in the whole history of

Canadian party politics. The *Civil Service Act* of 1917, a temporary measure (hardened into a durable statute in 1918) had been promised by Borden for a decade and demanded by certain reformers for longer than that. It is likely that changing economic and social forces would have produced similar legislation at some later point; that it was enacted in 1917 had everything to do with the war and the advent of the Union government, a coalition of Conservatives and pro-conscription Liberals determined to work together, however temporarily, for a common purpose. A fierce rear–guard action by disgruntled Conservatives dogged the implementation of the Act in its early years, but once in place, the institutions, regulations, practices and assumptions of the Act could not be overturned, even if they might occasionally be bent for partisan advantage.

The last half of Sir Wilfrid Laurier's fifteen years in power had featured repeated allegations of patronage and corruption, all eagerly pounced upon by Conservatives who thought, wrongly as the election results showed in 1908, that public tolerance had reached its limits. In a major speech in Halifax in 1907, Borden listed sixteen points for reform, including three promising to curtail, and in certain areas, end, political patronage. The Conservative leader, who said his speech represented the party platform for the coming election, promised the "appointment of public officials upon considerations of capacity and personal character and not of party service alone."[7] He pledged new laws to punish bribery and fraud at elections, to publicize campaign contributions, and to in every way facilitate speedy prosecution against individuals guilty of electoral corruption. And he promised "a thorough and complete reform of the laws relating to the civil service so that future appointments shall be made by an independent commission acting upon the report of examiners after competitive examination." After listing his promises, Borden added a personal credo, "Three-fourths of the time of members supporting a government is occupied with matters of patronage. Party patronage and party service have more weight than character and capacity. The public service is cumbered with useless officials. I am convinced that we shall perform a great public duty by establishing in this country that system which prevails in Great Britain, under which a member of Parliament has practically no voice in or control over any appointment to the civil service."

These views of Borden's were bold for a party leader in the first decade of the twentieth century, too bold indeed for many members of his own party, but he held them sincerely. The Conservative leader could never be considered a crusader. He accepted the economic and social system of capitalist Canada; he just wanted it to work better. Increasingly, businessmen shared his thoughts, or rather he shared theirs, for the country was changing and the big industrial concerns wanted consistency from government and a civil service that could help them to open up new business opportunities overseas.[8] Like the businessmen, Borden tended to be glassy-eyed about Canada's economic future if only higher standards of morality and technical efficiency could be brought to bear upon the state. And like theirs, Borden's ideas for reform were top-down—the state, by example and function, would help the private sector get on with doing what it did best: making money and bringing overall prosperity. Public commissions for oversight of railways, tariffs and utilities would neutralize partisanship; politicians, freed from the odious encumbrances of patronage, would consider the national interest; civil servants would be technically skilled and rise in the ranks on their merits, not their connections.

Borden's ends may not have opened the millenium in the minds of more visionary social reformers, but his means were certainly acceptable to them. Even before leading businessmen demanded civil service reform, leading churchmen, unionists, and academics had made it a prominent rallying cry. Their causes—women's suffrage, better working conditions, improved education, restrictions on alcohol — all required state action. Like Borden and the businessmen, social reformers of the latter type united people along occupational lines, but also along moral and sexual lines, thus helping to break down entrenched localism in the political life of the nation. In the United States, too, social activists, in particular urban Progressives and muckraking journalists, had been clamouring for the curtailment of patronage in the civil service. Their message had carried across the border, helping to inspire like-minded Canadian reformers.[9]

Borden, an aloof and dignified man, knew all about patronage. As party leader, he could not be immune from its pressures, but he found everything associated with it intensely distasteful. He grumbled about it privately, and spoke against it publicly, even before his Halifax speech of 1907. He also held an exceedingly dim view of many Conservative backbenchers in Ottawa in large part because, as he said in that Halifax speech, MPs expended most of their political energies worrying about the details of patronage and responding to the nagging demands of their constituents rather than focusing on larger questions of national concern. A memorandum from the clerk of the Privy Council about demands on the prime ministers' time perfectly echoed Borden's persistent complaint. It read, in part, "When he attends to correspondence and interviews on patronage matters or other questions of personal or selfish interest to individuals, his time and energy are taken up unwisely and unnecessarily and to the detriment of the large questions which it is primarily his duty to consider and determine."[10]

If Canada were ever to develop economically, if it were ever to achieve international stature, then somehow Canadian politics had to be purged of the localized, parochial, jealousy-laden, back-scratching, patronage-oriented perspectives of so many politicians. Noble, even advanced, these views undoubtedly were for their time, but giving effect to them would not be easy, especially for a leader who had twice led his party to defeat, in 1904 and 1908. Indeed, the entire period of Borden's leadership of the Conservative party can be viewed as a transition time in the history of Canadian patronage, less dramatic to be sure than the transition to responsible government, less sweeping than the transition to two competing national parties rooted everywhere by patronage, less subtle than the transition through which Canadian politics is now passing, but important nonetheless. The transition that Borden superintended left certain legacies, the most significant of which remains with us today: a politically neutral civil service.

In politics, the shortest distance between two points cannot be measured by a straight line. The drive towards the *Civil Service Act* took a variety of twists and turns. Along the way it suffered substantial defeats, the war-time rush for spoils being only one, and threats from a Conservative rear guard who rejected the merit principle and resented its application. Nor were the means always as desirable as the ends. Borden, despairing of his own troops in Parliament and sensing that he could only refurbish the Conservative party along his lines by reaching beyond its ranks, initiated a flanking action against dissidents in his own party.

For this purpose, he embraced powerful Conservative premiers, in British Columbia, Manitoba, Ontario and New Brunswick, largely entrusting to their machines the federal party's political fate. He campaigned with them repeatedly in 1908 and again in 1911, in part because only the provincial arsenals of patronage equalled what the governing Liberals in Ottawa could throw into an election.[11] Happy as they were to oblige, the premiers did not necessarily subscribe to applying in their own domains Borden's preachments for the federal. Among them, only Ontario Premier James Whitney could be counted on to practise what Borden had in mind. Premiers Richard McBride of British Columbia and Rodmond Roblin of Manitoba presided over two of the country's most efficient political machines. They were not about to alter strategies that brought so much political success. And as head man in New Brunswick, Premier J.D. Hazen would not abandon patronage for all the potatoes in the Saint John River Valley.

To the premiers' support in the election of 1911 Borden added that of prominent Toronto businessmen. This group, many associated with the Canadian Northern Railway project, had broken with the

Liberal party over fears that reciprocity would injure their economic interests. The group, which became known as the Toronto Eighteen, put out feelers to Borden through Clifford Sifton, by then a publicly repentant patronage sinner, desiring to know if Borden agreed with their demands, including three relating to patronage:

> "1. That the future Government, while giving proper representation to Quebec and to the Roman Catholic element, should not be subservient to Roman Catholic influences in public policy or in the administration of patronage;
> 2. That Mr. Borden should pledge himself to place the outside civil service under control of the Civil Service Commission;
> 3. That Mr. Borden should agree to reorganize the Department of Trade and Commerce, place the Department in charge of a strong Minister without undue regard to party considerations, and establish a commercial consular service in order to protect Canadian interests and extend Canadian trade."[12]

The concern about French Canadians may have reflected latent racism; it also spoke to the impression that French Canadians, shut out of financial circles, looked disproportionately to government for rewards. The statements about the civil service and the expansion of the department of trade and commerce underlined the businessmen's belief that the economic destiny of Canada could be enhanced by improved administrative efficiency and new export markets other than the United States. Once elected in 1911, Borden began moving to fulfil his commitments. He appointed Sir George Murray, a former British treasury official, to recommend ways of reorganizing the civil service. Using the British model as his inspiration, Murray recommended that the civil service commission, grudgingly established by Laurier, be empowered to control all civil service positions; that civil servants be given more job security; that temporary employees be curtailed and that ministers "direct" not "administer" policy."[13] The report should have galvanized Borden into action, but instead it gathered dust. Its recommendations were aborted by the Conservative party, still heavy-laden with ministers and backbenchers utterly resistant to any fettering of their powers of patronage. The Conservatives did not slaughter the Liberal innocents en masse upon arriving in power; neither did they shy from favouring their own when positions became available or contracts beckoned.[14] They were simply not prepared to sacrifice what they and their predecessors had considered indispensable tools of political mobilization, no matter what Borden had promised and Sir George Murray recommended.

It took the carnage of war, the scandals of the early years and, most important, the creation of the Union government after the 1917 election to make good Borden's commitment in Halifax in 1907 and the demands of the Toronto Eighteen in 1911, and thereby silence the clamour among civil service reformers. The Union government, by definition, altered traditional political conflict, creating new ground rules for co-operation. Part of the negotiations at the creation of the Union coalition concerned patronage: There would be a sharing of the spoils. Liberals who joined the government — such as the powerful James Calder of Saskatchewan, Frank Carvell of New Brunswick and A.K. Maclean of Nova Scotia — were assured a measure of the government's patronage. But everywhere in the country, supporters of the war demanded more efficient prosecution of the war effort. "Efficiency" became one of the rallying cries of the hour, and the Union program for the 1917 election echoed the cry, promising "to make appointments upon the sole standard of merit."[15] In February, 1918, the government passed an order-in-council under the *War Measures Act* bringing the outside service, itself almost wholly given over to patronage, under the jurisdiction of the civil service commission. Soon thereafter, the government introduced the *Civil Service Act*. The details of the Act contained several important loopholes through which government could wiggle patronage appointments, but its broad effect was to establish merit as the principle criterion for recruitment and advancement.[16]

The *Civil Service Act* represented a triumph for some, a defeat for others. Within the Conservative party, devotees of traditional patronage cried foul, and kept on crying for several years. As the Borden years wore on, Conservative provincial governments fell, so that towards the end of his years, Conservatives observed federal Liberals wielding some patronage in Ottawa and all the patronage in most of the provinces. The disintegration of the Union government and the restoration of traditional two-party conflict made some Conservative MPs all the more determined to resist any curtailment of their patronage powers in the face of powerful Liberal governments. Some diehards, such as Manitoba's Robert Rogers, spoke publicly against the reforms; others, such as Arthur Meighen, (the future prime minister), simply lamented them. "I am down here pretty much alone. . . ." Meighen wrote. "I cannot take the course that a minister could take under the old conditions, and consequently I cannot engage the party support which it has all along been possible to engage."[17] After the war, the government introduced a bill creating a purchasing commission to make permanent the functions of the war purchasing commission across a wider range of purchases, but the opposition was so fierce that the government decided not to proceed.[18]

The complete reclassification of civil service positions in 1919 produced an uproar from civil servants which, in turn, gave ammunition to critics of reform. The uproar, combined with mistakes made by the civil service commissioners, reconfirmed critics in their belief that the new-fangled system delivered the reverse of efficiency and fairness. It brought the very kind of bureaucratic nightmares they had always warned would ensue if patronage were replaced. The so-called Spinney Bill of 1921, named after its sponsor, proposed removing a large number of positions from the jurisdiction of the civil service commission, a tangible example of the resentment still acutely felt in certain quarters of the Conservative party. Exemptions were subsequently widened, giving a somewhat freer rein to patronage. And Prime Minister Mackenzie King, elected in 1921, promptly appointed two Liberal commissioners whose rulings allowed departments, and therefore ministers, greater latitude in selecting employees.

So civil service reform took more than a decade from commitment to legislation, and more years still before it sank roots into the Canadian body politic. But despite the attacks and setbacks, the Act did curtail, more than any reform since Confederation, the use of patronage in what had been one of the most wide-open arenas for politicians. Debates continued at the margin on the issue of a meritocratic civil service; the essence of the idea survived. In national terms, the curtailment of federal patronage paralleled the rise of provincial power where no limitations restricted the use of patronage, apart from the infrequent and inadequate gestures of scattered high-minded politicians. The post-war decades saw the strengthening of provincial governments, with their constitutional responsibilities for highways, resource development and social legislation. To them the contractors rushed and the job-seekers flocked, and national parties found themselves scrambling for money and increasingly dependent upon their provincial cousins for electoral help. The strength of provincial governments, the appearance of protest movements in the West, and the dilution of the integrative function of patronage through civil service reform set the stage for the full blossoming of brokerage politics, an approach to governing perfectly suited to the temperment, style and convictions of Prime Minister Mackenzie King.

Prudish, fussy and physically unprepossessing, King turned out to be Canada's most durable federal politician. He was a coalition-builder *par excellence*, cautious, intuitive, suspicious, an intensely private man in a relentlessly public job.[19] A compromiser by instinct and intellect, King nonetheless considered himself a stirring intellectual force, an insight more apparent to himself than to anyone else. He moved most dramatically when political danger threatened, notably after a brief surge in support for the Co–operative Commonwealth Federation (CCF) in 1942-43 prodded his government into a series of social policy promises and reforms. Otherwise, he preferred incremental change coated in the balm of opaque rhetoric. Few, if any, politicians ever sensed danger more acutely, and this particular clairvoyance stood him in excellent stead, for he wrote the textbook on the first rule of Canadian politics: Governments defeat themselves.

King possessed many skills, some of them severely underrated, but among his best was party leadership. Keeping the Liberal party united and active demanded persistent attention, for in the inter-war years new demands were felt by federal parties. Provinces had gained in importance, and it could not be taken for granted that federal and provincial parties of the same stripe always stood shoulder to shoulder. New political formations in Western Canada—Progressives, Farmer-Labour, United Farmers, Social Credit—beckoned voters away from traditional voting patterns.

The mercurial Liberal premier of Ontario, Mitch Hepburn, brought King more trouble than any other premier. Given these pressures, and his own instincts, King was not about to throw away the tool of patronage for mobilizing support and keeping his troops together. His years in office, and those of his successor Louis St. Laurent, featured no significant reform in the entire field of political patronage. Even the two major scandals of the period—the Customs scandal of 1926, which exposed malfeasance by officials and neglect by a minister, and the Beauharnois fund–raising scandal of 1930—brought only fulminations and partisan rhetoric. Happily, however, the *Civil Service Act* did sink deep roots after the setbacks of the 1920s, so that by the time King returned to office after five years in Opposition, from 1930 to 1935, it was widely acknowledged that partisan considerations should be removed as criteria for filling the bulk of civil service positions. There remained, however, many full- and part-time positions outside the purview of the civil service commission, and these the Liberals used systematically to reward their friends.

The kind of brokerage politics we now associate with King did not begin with him, although he refined it to an art form. In the cabinets of Macdonald and Laurier, the prime minister's sway extended through powerful regional ministers whose views about local matters often carried the day. This was especially so in matters of patronage, and it remained the operating principle under King. Where possible, his cabinets were structured with powerful regional representatives: Ernest Lapointe from Quebec, James Garfield ("Jimmy") Gardiner from Saskatchewan, James Lorimer Ilsley from the Maritimes, and later on men such as Brian Brooke Claxton from Montreal, and Clarence Decatur

(C.D.) Howe from the Lakehead. These men, directly or through agents, controlled Liberal patronage in their areas. King himself tended to make the appointments of national importance, such as seats in the Senate, lieutenant-governorships and diplomatic posts abroad. In the upper reaches of the civil service, King was responsible for bringing men of outstanding ability to Ottawa; the war summoned "dollar-a-year" men from the private sector, so that the senior mandarinate in the post-war years boasted a coterie of immensely talented and dedicated English Canadians — the Toronto Eighteen would have smiled to see how marginal French Canadians had become in the public service — whose commitment was to public service rather than the Liberal party. If anything, they had as much influence on the Liberal party as the ministers had on the government.[20]

The *Civil Service Act*, while removing from partisan control many appointments, still left important patronage for ministerial discretion. A minister such as Jimmy Gardiner knew how to use it. Gardiner had been premier of Saskatchewan, and for years before that, a key cog in a provincial Liberal machine greased by patronage. He therefore arrived in Ottawa as King's minister of agriculture in 1935 already a skilled and experienced user of patronage. And for all the years he remained in Ottawa, nothing of consequence in Saskatchewan and, more generally, in Western Canada passed through cabinet without his input. "His authority was not absolute," wrote the leading student of Gardiner, "but his influence was enormous."[21] Postmasters whose office's annual revenues fell below a statutory limit were not covered by the *Civil Service Act*. Nor were casual employees in the post office, labourers in the national parks, inspectors for agricultural relief programs, caretakers, census enumerators; and when World War II "created the necessity for repatriating the bodies of Canadians, the patronage began to include undertakers."[22]

Gardiner stated his credo simply: "No one should be appointed unless he is known to be a lifelong Liberal."[23] That credo certainly applied to the federal agencies such as the Prairie Farm Rehabilitation Agency (PRFA), whose men on the ground and directors all tended to be Liberals, including defeated candidates. The power to appoint partisans arose from the section of the *Civil Service Act* that read, "The Minister may appoint such temporary, technical, professional and other officers and employees as he may deem necessary and expedient for the carrying out of the provisions of this Act and the salaries and expenses of such officers shall be fixed by the Governor-in-Council." That Act and the 1939 *Prairie Farm Assistance Act* gave Gardiner complete discretion to staff new government agencies; and even after 1951 when many full-time headquarters staff became civil servants fully protected by the *Civil Service Act*, there were still dozens of field workers who, like "Sifton's army" of homestead inspectors, fanned out across the prairies, doing their jobs and showing the Liberal colours. One CCF MP observed in the Commons, "The PFRA is doing much in the prairie provinces, yet I wonder how at every election these PFRA trucks can run around working for Liberal candidates."[24]

Whereas the Prairie Farm Rehabilitation Agency and the *Prairie Farm Assistance Act* exemplified the fresh opportunities for patronage in the federal government, old reliables such as harbour commissions and port authorities offered traditional opportunities. The Montreal Harbour Commission and the Quebec Harbour Commission were classic examples of the old reliables. The elections of 1921, 1930 and 1935, which featured changes of government, witnessed wholesale replacement of employees at the Quebec Harbour Commission. In the 1920s, the commission employed up to three thousand temporary employees, an extraordinary patronage opportunity. All the hiring was done according to a formula that allocated a fixed percentage of positions to the constituencies in and around Quebec City.[25] In matters pertaining to the Quebec City region, relations between Premier Alexandre Taschereau's Liberal government and King's government ran nominally through federal minister Ernest Lapointe, but in practice through Charles "Chubby" Power, the federal Liberals' *organisateur-en-chef*. Power had taken over that responsibility from Philippe Paradis, who had shouldered it from 1912 to 1931.[26] In Montreal, the Liberal machine was supervised by the minister P.J.A. Cardin and directed on the ground by Elie Beauregard. (Paradis and Beauregard both received their own patronage posts from King: seats in the Senate.) The links were crucial to maintain, because the provincial party was awash with money contributed by contractors and industrialists, and some of this money flowed to the federal party. Chubby Power once recalled telling Taschereau that the federal party needed money for a by-election, then watching the premier open a safe in his office and hand over twenty-five thousand dollars with a suggestion to return if more were needed.[27]

Patronage, therefore, tended to be durable and decentralized, although somewhat less ubiquitous than in the pre-World War I era. A new element, however, began to intrude in the organization of patronage under King, an element that began innocuously enough but then continued for many years to be a source of friction among powerful ministers, and eventually became a fixture of Canadian political parties: the national party office.[28] For slightly more than half a century after Confederation, party organization was largely left to parliamentarians. Though every prime minister had a small personal staff, as did cabinet ministers, the parties *per se* used no full-time, paid employees.

Under these circumstances, political patronage, fund-raising, electoral readiness and campaigns themselves were all organized by MPs and their followers. MPs had local patronage committees to advise them, and friends who helped them during campaigns. And, of course, Senators could be exceedingly useful as organizers and fund-raisers.

Andrew Haydon was perhaps the first of what we now call a full-time political organizer. King appointed him national organizer and secretary of the national committee in 1919, when the party desperately needed to be knit together after the rifts that had developed during the later war years. Haydon, a faithful political soldier if ever one existed, suffered through King's interminable grumbling about lack of money, election preparedness and the laziness of those about him. Haydon quit his posts in 1922, fed up with the lack of money and authority.[29] King appointed him to the Senate in 1924, and Haydon continued to be King's chief organizer, in fact if not in formal title, through the 1930 campaign. Through the 1920s, Haydon personally represented the germ of the idea that a political party needed full-time staff to mobilize money and resources for the parliamentary party. Inevitably, the question arose of what role, if any, men such as Haydon would play in dispensing patronage or offering preferments. Indeed, the question is alive today, in an even more acute form among the plethora of non-elected officials on the staffs of the prime minister, cabinet ministers, and the party office, as well as among friends of the party in power with special access. Today's Ottawa is awash with the heirs of Andrew Haydon, conduits for access to elected officials, consultants on how best to raise money from the private sector, advisers on keeping up the morale of the extra-parliamentary party, experts at organizing election campaigns. It is to Haydon's heirs that seekers of preferments or positions now direct some of their entreaties.

Haydon, unfortunately, became centrally implicated in the most serious scandal of the King years—the Beauharnois affair, which broke after the Liberals lost the 1930 election and which King called his party's "valley of humiliation."[30] The pivot of the affair was an order-in-council approved by the King cabinet in 1929, authorizing the diversion of water for the Beauharnois Canal. The authorization might have simply passed for another government concession to a powerful business group, but for revelations of huge payments to important members of the Liberal party and to the party itself. Special committees of the House and Senate heard evidence that Senator W.L. McDougald, a friend of King's, had doubled as a member of a national advisory committee on the desirability of the project and chairman of the board of the Beauharnois Power Corporation. More damaging still were revelations that a company McDougald established to investigate water-power sites in the Beauharnois area had been purchased by the corporation for a grossly inflated price, the clear inference being that the sum represented payment for future favours. So, too, the syndicate paid an annual $15,000 retainer to Andrew Haydon's law firm and an *ex gratia* payment of $50,000 contingent upon passage of the 1929 order-in-council. It also transpired that McDougald had defrayed King's bills during a Bermuda holiday, then wrote the charges off against the syndicate.

Most spectacular of all, however, was the testimony of Robert Sweezey, the Beauharnois project's chief promoter. He told the Commons committee that he had paid "somewhere around $600,000 to $700,000" to the Liberal party during the 1930 campaign, a staggering sum by the standards of those days, indeed even of these days. "Gratefulness," Sweezey explained, "was always regarded as an important factor in dealing with democratic governments."[31] Sweezey also admitted giving $125,000 to someone he believed represented the Ontario Conservative party, and small sums to be variety of MPs.

The combination of damaging evidence — huge profits for King's friend, payments to King's organizer, defrayed expenses for King's holiday, an enormous contribution from a grateful company — placed King in the worst crisis of his political career. *Prima facie* the evidence might have spelled the end; in fact, King wiggled out of difficulty. The Commons committee "strongly condemned" Haydon and McDougald, but left punitive action to the Senate. King urged McDougald to resign, but McDougald refused, then acquiesced when the Senate committee censured him. Haydon died shortly after the Senate's report, but his spirit periodically reappeared in King's dreams, as the prime minister recorded in his diary. King summoned every ounce of political ingenuity and personal sanctimony to extricate himself, insisting he had known nothing about the defrayed expenses or the Sweezey contribution, calling for a royal commission into party fund-raising, admitting that Beauharnois plunged the Liberals into a "valley of humiliation," and defending the wisdom of the 1929 order-in-council. To this day, the argument rages among historians about just how much King knew and when; in his day, the argument prevailed that he knew nothing until the story broke.

The plea of ignorance contrasted sharply with the treatment John A. Macdonald received for his 'valley of humiliation,' the Canadian Pacific Scandal, which directly and properly implicated Sir John for the sufficient reason that as party leader he had personally solicited the funds. The contrast between the two scandals neatly revealed the way party leaders by the 1930s had at least partially removed themselves from direct solicitation of funds. They now had agents, or paid party staff, to find the money to bankroll the party. The transaction of contributions for favours or influence was now at arm's length from the party leader, and strained though the plea of ignorance often seemed on its face, it continued to serve future party leaders, federal and provincial, when they found themselves in difficulty. Whatever the sordid appearances of Beauharnois, whatever the inference others drew about his conduct, King remained convinced of his own incorruptibility. When King asked McDougald to resign from the Senate, he also returned fifteen thousand dollars McDougald had contributed to the fund for renovating Laurier House, where King lived. That fund, organized by Salada Tea magnate Peter Larkin, was one of two from which King benefited, but neither troubled his conscience. King had been launched into politics with a trust fund sponsored by Larkin and other wealthy businessmen.[32] King was not the first party leader to receive supplementary income—Laurier also had received funds from wealthy friends—nor would he be the last. King's successor, Louis St. Laurent, received financial help from wealthy friends to remain in politics. Gifts in kind, such as Pierre Trudeau's swimming pool at 24 Sussex Drive, or salary supplements such as those received by premiers Gerald Regan of Nova Scotia and Richard Hatfield of New Brunswick and Liberal leader Clyde Wells of Newfoundland testify today to the use of this form of potential influence. At least King provided a clear *quid pro quo*: He appointed Larkin Canadian high commissioner in London, the same post later occupied by another King friend and benefactor, Vincent Massey.

King groused continually throughout the 1920s—indeed until he retired as leader in 1948—about the state of party organization and finance. He had not wished to become directly involved in fund-raising, and the Beauharnois scandal drove home the need to create some kind of arm's length structure and pass on responsibility for this requirement. King, acting on Massey's suggestion in the wake of Beauharnois, appointed Norman Lambert secretary of the National Liberal Federation, and from that appointment forward the Federation assumed a much larger role in matters of party organization, fund-raising and patronage. It took many years for the Federation to expand in size and influence, and its influence waned later when the prime minister's staff and admen proliferated and the tax system supported parties. But from the 1930s until well on into the 1960s, this body at arm's length from the leader's office added an important new dimension to Canadian politics. John A. Macdonald once lamented that although British prime ministers had their Carleton Clubs or Reform Clubs to raise funds, he had to do the work himself. In Laurier's day, the prime minister did some personal solicitation, but counted more heavily on Liberal big-shots in Ontario and Quebec, or on wealthy contributors. Prime min-isters from King onwards would perform where necessary — they attended fund–raising dinners or picnics, wrote letters of thanks, sug-gested that certain individuals be approached — but they could isolate themselves from the grubby business of shaking cash from supporters' pockets, leaving such matters instead to organizers or apparatchiks appointed by the party leader. The Senate, in King's day as before and after, was an invaluable source of fund-raisers, since the place abounded with wealthy supporters who would contribute their own money or put the squeeze on friends in the financial communities of Montreal and Toronto.

Once King enhanced the Federation's status after 1932, an obvious question arose: What specific role would it play in fund-raising and patronage? The question moved from moot to practical after the Liberals returned to office in 1935 and, in the words of one author, "Lambert realized that it [the Federation] would have to have some influence over patronage if it were going to exercise any real power."[33] This immediately set up the classic conflict between two would-be patrons: Lambert and others at the Federation who saw themselves as a "gateway to departmental favours," and cabinet ministers who believed that only they, as elected politicians, understood the subtleties and exigencies of patronage. (The conflicts seldom perturbed relations with Quebec Liberals, who ran their own show in everything from fund-raising to organization to patronage.) In a sense, this conflict over the organization of patronage became endemic to all the parties. It showed up throughout the King–St. Laurent years, flared noticeably between the new party organizers in Ottawa and Liberal kingpins in the provinces during the Pearson years, generated clashes between some cabinet ministers and the prime ministerial entourage during the Tru-deau years and figured in the early tensions between those who for-mulated Prime Minister Brian Mulroney's plans for patronage and those who were charged with administering the plans.

Ministers with the clout of C.D. Howe and Jimmy Gardiner would not easily turn over to unelected officials what they believed to be theirs by right of status and authority. As ministers they were the true gate-keepers for huge departments; they were the ones who stayed in touch with party notables in their regions; they oversaw the letting of con-tracts of all kinds and maintained relations with important party con-tributors. Howe, to take perhaps the most obvious example from the King-St. Laurent years, bestrode some of the most important, and certainly the most patronage-laden, government departments — rail-ways and canals, marine, transportation, defence production, and trade and commerce — each one furnishing substantial opportunities which Howe would not forego. By Howe's time, the old money-before-contracts system had been reversed. It was now money-after-contracts — the contracts came first, the contributions later. Under Lambert at the Federation, the Liberal party partly financed itself by insisting that individuals or entities in receipt of a government contract make a contribution to the party based on a fixed percentage of the contract's worth, a system with which Howe and other senior ministers entirely agreed.[34]

The contract levy system extracted money — from suppliers of bridges, roads, docks, post offices and other federal buildings; from Crown corporations such as the Canadian National Railways; from firms providing defence equipment. But the implicit assumption remained that if firms refused to contribute *post facto*, they could all but forget about another contract. Through the 1920s and 1930s the Liberals had tried a variety of fund-raising campaign strategies originated by rank-and-file members and provincial associations. They had almost all failed, so that by the end of World War II, the party was still dependent upon a small number of corporations, wealthy individuals and the contract levy — a fund-raising system that laid itself open to favouritism.[35] An academic study reported that in the 1953 election, the Liberal party received fifty percent of its income from firms, forty percent from businessmen associated with particular firms, and ten percent from individuals.[36] Neither could the parties, especially the Opposition, count on these sources for sufficient funds; nor could the public be certain that favouritism was not perverting public-policy decisions. Pressures began building in the 1960s for some form of public financing for political parties, a reform finally achieved in the early 1970s. But that reform lay far down the track during Mackenzie King's years in office. The traditional methods, while not always providing as much money as he would have liked for the Liberal party, so obviously disadvantaged the Conservative Opposition — who struggled desperately for funds, especially after R.B. Bennett resigned and stopped bankrolling the party — that the thought never occurred to any Liberal to change the system.[37]

The long years of Liberal rule also saw a merger between political tactics and the techniques of Madison Avenue, a phenomenon that seemed innocent enough at the time but gradually developed into a change of profound consequence for all aspects of politics, including the durability of patronage. At first through newspapers, then through radio, and finally and most spectacularly through television, the techniques for selling toothpaste — of creating demand where none had previously existed, or at least altering perceptions of familiar products — spread through the political system. For the longest time, the new approach produced considerable unease among politicians suspicious of any talents but their own for reading the public mood and communicating political messages. Even after a well-established relationship had grown up between advertising agencies and the Liberal party, there remained politicians of an older generation, including Mackenzie King himself, who could never be fully comfortable with the new techniques. Indeed, throughout King's leadership and that of Louis St. Laurent advertising agencies remained just that: agents taking their orders from political masters and communicating with a certain professional slickness messages they received from politicians. Only in the 1960s did the advertising men, or at least some of their key players, begin shaping the substance of the message. The new style emanating from the inner councils of the Liberal party reflected the sensibility of new men who graduated from advertising to politics and therefore looked upon the political arena as a finishing school for everything they had absorbed in the pursuit of improved profits through advertising for the manufacturers of toothpaste.

The application of Madison Avenue techniques to politics produced a fundamental shift in the methods of political mobilization, a shift that took decades to become apparent and in the long run undermined public support for patronage. Certainly none of the strategists who engineered the shift and nurtured it through the early years appreciated what their efforts would bring. At first, it seemed that the grafting of advertising agencies onto politics would simply open up new areas for political patronage. And indeed, in a limited sense, that is precisely what occurred, for those who assisted the Liberal party in winning elections, in advertising as in just about everything else, received a share of the spoils of power. For advertising agencies, this meant government contracts as agencies of record, and for some executives of those agencies, appointments at the government's discretion. By the 1960s, the admen had taken up residence in the Canadian Senate; two even went to the Canadian Embassy in Washington.

The arrival of the admen in the late 1950s and early 1960s in the inner circles of the Liberal party—a parallel development occurred in the Conservative party—presaged the invasion of the pollsters. Admen and pollsters, or "market researchers" as they liked to call themselves, lived in mutual dependency in the private sector, plumbing the depths of public attitudes towards toothpaste, then designing the best techniques for selling it. Naturally, they carried their mutual dependency into politics, jointly developing arguments to persuade politicians to view issues in a certain way, or developing the road map for politicians determined to move in a certain direction. And once the admen and pollsters sat at the leader's right hand, telling him all about the public's political thoughts, the leader had less need of those networks of mini-patrons out there in the country or beside him in the cabinet acting as his political antenna. With the admen and pollsters to advise him, and television eager to provide the means, the leader could communicate directly and subtly to a mass audience, inviting political participation not by the offer of tangible preferments or the hope of same, but by the ideas and the persona of the leader himself.

Not surprisingly, the first admen who did more than execute instructions evinced skepticism and sometimes demonstrated acute hostility to patronage, although that did not stop them from accepting patronage appointments for themselves or family. Comfortable with the techniques of communicating with a mass audience, they could not understand the profound localism of patronage, the intense personal links it created, the important economic benefits it bestowed on people of modest means, since the admen all came from or worked in Toronto or Montreal, where the attractions of patronage, if they existed at all, appealed largely to the psyche rather than the pocketbook. It was not without significance that of all the representatives of this new breed—Bob Kidd, Bill Munro, Richard O'Hagan, George Elliott, Keith Davey, Jerry Grafstein for the Liberals; Allister Grossart, Dalton Camp, Finlay MacDonald, Norman Atkins for the Conservatives—Camp emerged as the most articulate defender of the importance of patronage for political mobilization, not merely because his firm so manifestly benefited from the patronage of various Conservative governments, but because as a native of New Brunswick and a veteran of political wars throughout the Maritimes, he appreciated the enduring importance of patronage in the daily lives of citizens in less economically favoured regions of the country.[38]

Whether cause or effect, the rise of the admen to prominence paralleled the decline in the strength of the links between newspaper editors and politicians, and therefore the decline in patronage bestowed by governments on friendly papers. Politicians or parties no longer owned major newspapers outright by the Mackenzie King era. Leading politicians continued to consult favoured editors—King corresponded extensively with John Dafoe of *The Winnipeg Free Press* and Joe Atkinson of *The Toronto Star*—and the political slant of most newspapers was daily apparent, since many leading cities boasted at least two papers, one Liberal and the other Conservative. But the ties of patronage, ownership and friendship were weakening, and the subsequent grip of radio and television on the attention spans of voters turned politicians away from newspapers as prime means of political communication. They needed editors less than experts who could advise them on the exigencies of the electronic media.

The bonds between the Liberal party and advertising agencies were formalized in the 1940s, but the dalliances had begun in the 1930s when Cockfield, Brown placed radio advertisements for the party and assisted in organizing a special dinner commemorating the twentieth anniversary of Mackenzie King's leadership.[39] By the 1940 campaign, Cockfield, Brown had become the chief Liberal ad agency, and from that connection received the bulk of government advertising business after the election. This designation proved extremely lucrative for Cockfield, Brown because the war years expanded government advertising through the War Savings Campaign, and because the strong personal relationship between agency executive Bob Kidd and the powerful Liberal minister Brooke Claxton gave Cockfield, Brown a reliable friend at court. The agency, confident of government business after elections, often reduced its commissions for electoral work, provided special services to particular ministers, or provided services free of charge. For the 1953 campaign, Bill Munro of Cockfield, Brown set up shop in the Chateau Laurier; his hotel bill and expenses were paid for by the Liberal party and his time and salary were "donated" to the Liberal cause by Cockfield, Brown. Cozy enough, but the relationship soon became even cozier, and more politically exposed. Munro also began representing Trans-Canada Pipelines, opening an easy avenue for attack to Conservatives during the bitter 1956 pipeline debate, when they charged, with reason, that Munro was simultaneously working for the Government of Canada, the Liberal party and Trans-Canada Pipelines. Nor was this the first time the interests of Cockfield, Brown and the Liberal party became entwined in the same person. Bob Kidd became secretary of the National Liberal Federation in 1948 while continuing to work as an executive for Cockfield, Brown, whose accounts included the Canadian Banker's Association. The agency provided research assistance for ministerial speeches, wrote some of them entirely, organized free-time political broadcasts, and in the 1945 campaign collected money from companies which—by contributing to the Liberal party through Cockfield, Brown—wrote off the costs as a business expense.[40]

The 1957 election swept the Liberals out of office, Louis St. Laurent out of politics, and Cockfield, Brown from its favoured position. So stunning was the defeat of 1957 and so complete the electoral debacle that followed in 1958, that a new wave of Liberals, many based in Toronto, stepped in to pick up the pieces. Contemptuous of the old ways, including patronage, the new arrivals analysed Cockfield, Brown's performance and found it decidedly wanting. By the 1962 and 1963 elections, Cockfield, Brown had been pushed aside and replaced by MacLaren's which had contributed Richard O'Hagan full time for the 1958 campaign. MacLaren's had always done some party work and received a slice of government advertising in return. By the 1950s, MacLaren's often did more government advertising than Cockfield, Brown, although that agency raked in more work from Crown corporations.[41] O'Hagan later joined Prime Minister Lester Pearson's staff as public relations adviser, and MacLaren's executive Jim Moore became publicity director for the National Liberal Federation. Another MacLaren's man organized the Liberal candidates' college before the 1962 election; still another MacLaren's executive provided detailed sociological information on every riding in Canada. By 1965, the Liberals having returned to office in 1963, MacLaren's was receiving about half of all government advertising contracts.[42]

The advertising men, such a fixture of contemporary federal and provincial parties, represented part of the long, slow drift towards new forms of political mobilization that no one foresaw when Mackenzie King was prime minister and that few understood even when Louis St. Laurent passed from the scene. For nearly four decades, with one minor interruption (1926) and one major one (1930-1935), the Liberals established themselves as the natural governing party of Canada. The mixing of the old style of patronage politics, played out at the local level through regional chieftains, with some new structures and attitudes relating to patronage marked the entire period. The *Civil Service Act* of 1918 had done its work by the late 1930s, so that the great bulk of full-time civil service positions had been rendered immune from patronage. Certain contractors profited handsomely during World War II, but their profit-taking was nothing like the rush for spoils that characterized the government's approach to equipping the armed forces and prosecuting the war effort during World War I. The strength the senior mandarinate displayed in conducting the economy during the war and in overseeing the acceptance of Keynesian economic policy after the war testified eloquently to the consequences of the *Civil Service Act*.

What remained open to patronage after the Act were positions at the top — and these expanded as new government agencies appeared — and positions at the bottom, the ones still allocated by ministers acting on advice from the committees of Liberal MPs, defeated candidates or party organizers. Finance minister Douglas Abbott wrote to his colleagues in 1949 that "the Liberal members for the ridings in Toronto and the Yorks have called on me to discuss a method for handling patronage in their ridings, both for members and defeated candidates." By then the system required referring all matters to the secretaries for the patronage committees of MPs and defeated candidates.[43] Such committees existed across the country, as did lists of favoured suppliers for contracts not subject to tender. Gradually, however, the protections afforded by the Act spread to an increasing number of civil service positions, and public-sector unions sought to enlist as many civil servants as possible. The patronage of jobs began slowly diminishing, and with it one of the oldest methods of securing political loyalty. The clamour for jobs and preferments from the party faithful continued, but politicians, by the end of the King–St. Laurent period, could do much less for their supplicants than they might have liked or their supplicants demanded.

Canadian politics stood on the brink of a new era, which would present challenges only hinted at in the King–St.Laurent years. In the new era, both the practice of patronage and public attitudes to patronage would dramatically change, although a full understanding of those changes escaped almost every federal politician forced to grapple with them. And those same changes were reflected in the politics of patronage at the provincial level of government where patronage had always been as deeply entrenched as at the federal.

PART II

PROVINCIAL PATRONAGE

CHAPTER 6

NEWFOUNDLAND

"To the victor goes the spiles."
Defeated Liberal candidate, 1972 provincial election.

NEWFOUNDLAND, perhaps more starkly than any part of Canada, provides a poignant and comprehensive case study of the infusion of patronage, porkbarrelling and corruption into every aspect of political life. Other Canadian provinces certainly demonstrate the durability of these forms of political behaviour. But for base political morality, pervasive patronage, persistent venality and even sheer thievery, Newfoundland's rogues' gallery of politicians until recently set the province apart.

After almost four decades within Confederation, Newfoundland's political mores now resemble those in other economically disadvantaged regions of Canada, although fortunately the irrepressible cut-and-thrust of Newfoundland's political life still thrives. Bureaucratization, expanded education, wider economic opportunities and improved communications have pulled Newfoundland up from the semi-feudal economic and political condition in which it existed for hundreds of years. But in the early decades of this century, political corruption so undermined the faith of Newfoundlanders in the efficacy of democratic institutions that "when it was decided to turn over the reins of government to an appointed Commission and so temporarily extinguish democracy on the island, scarcely a whisper of protest was to be heard."[1]

The seven-member Commission Government, appointed by the

British government in 1934, followed a royal commission investigation into the state of Newfoundland's economy, politics and society after eighty years as a self-governing dominion and four years of the Great Depression. The royal commission found Newfoundland destitute and bankrupt, paying sixty-five percent of its budget in debt-service charges. The value of cod exports had fallen from $40 million to $26.5 million from 1929 to 1931. The public debt had jumped from $43 million in 1920 to $100 million in 1933. Clearly, the underlying reasons for Newfoundland's bankruptcy were economic: the decline in revenues from the fishery compounded by the world-wide economic slump. But the British royal commissioners, undoubtedly reflecting a certain imperial arrogance, nonetheless expressed shock at the pervasiveness of political cupidity and venality on the island:

> "It is not too much to say that the present generation of Newfoundlanders have never known enlightened government. The process of deterioration, once started, could not be controlled. The simple-minded electorate were visited every few years by rival politicians, who, in the desire to secure election, were accustomed to make the wildest promises involving increased expenditures in the constituency and the satisfaction of all the cherished desires of the inhabitants. The latter, as was not unnatural, chose the candidate who promised them most. This might be said of other countries, but in Newfoundland this cajoling of the electorate was carried to such lengths that, until the recent crisis brought them to their senses, the electors in many cases preferred to vote for a candidate who was known to possess an aptitude for promoting his own interests at the public expense rather than for a man who disdained to adopt such a course. They argued that, if a man had proved himself capable of using his political opportunities to his personal advantage, he would be the better equipped to promote the advantage of his constituents; an honest man would only preach to them."[2]

The commission analysed the oppressive paternalism in the Newfoundland economy which bound outport fishermen to the merchant aristocracy of St. John's for credit, supplies and prices. It also noted that "the spoils system has for years been in full force in Newfoundland. Given the conception that it is quite fair, whilst one's party is in power, to make what one can for oneself and one's friends, it is natural, that in the minds of many people politics should be regarded simply as job farming."

The clean sweep of civil servants after each change in government hindered efficiency. "The civil service," reported the commission, "with no security of tenure, is left at the mercy of the politician. Constant changes have led to a low standard of efficiency. Departments function as individuals rather than as a team; there is no cohesion, no continuity of policy and no incentive to take responsibility." Newfoundland required, suggested these British gentlemen, a "rest from politics" and the firm smack of sensible administration. So, for the only time in the history of the British Empire, a self-governing dominion yielded up democratic political institutions and placed its affairs in the hands of an appointed committee. There political life remained until Newfoundland plunged into a lacerating post-war debate which ended in 1949 when the former dominion joined Canada, whereupon the new premier, Joseph Smallwood, built a political empire by the marriage of federal money and time-honoured practices of pre-Commission Newfoundland.

Newfoundland writers have argued with rip-snorting intensity about whether the royal commissioners exaggerated the political reasons for Newfoundland's debilitated economic and ethical state in the early 1930s. But when those writers stood back from that debate, they independently acknowledged the decisive influence of patronage, pork-barrelling and corruption. A few samples will illustrate the point. "Much of her political history reads like a travesty of acceptable political practice."[3] "The notion that 'to the victor the spoils' was generally accepted as right and just by people and politicians alike."[4] "Many . . . came with the conviction that the government would be as it had always been in Newfoundland, a spare-time pursuit and an open sesame for spoils."[5] "The large-scale use of patronage had characterized the Newfoundland political system from its inception."[6] "Newfoundland and politics became what has been called the 'politics of self-interest.' "[7]

What other conclusions commended themselves? The catechism of Opposition politicians had always been "Clean Government," but what they preached bore no relation to what they delivered. Sir Richard Squires campaigned successfully in 1919 on a campaign slogan, "Rid Newfoundland of her Grafters." Four years later the Squires government was rocked by a series of scandals. It turned out that the party's "patronage secretary," Agriculture and Mines Minister Alex Campbell, defrauded the treasury, falsely charged political expenses to government accounts, and distributed government supplies free of charge to political friends. Campbell's corruption did not bring down the government, but rumours of the premier's own personal corruption did. A subsequent inquiry by Thomas Hollis Walker, the recorder of Derby appointed by the British government, unearthed a spectacular network of corruption.

The department of the liquor controller, Hollis Walker wrote, was "little more than a front for a large-scale bootlegging operation directed by a friend of the premier's."[8] Squires himself indirectly benefited from

$20,000 received from the Newfoundland liquor commission. The premier also received $48,000 from mining companies negotiating with the government.[9] The inquiry fully indicted Campbell for all the offences alleged by the Opposition, and added one more — that he had sent gifts to officials in the auditor-general's office who were reviewing the accounts of his department. Hollis Walker concluded, "A practice under which a minister distributes among his staff at his own discretion presents from the public funds and adds a similar gift to the only person whose duty it is to check his actions seems to be fraught with mischievous possibilities and not to be in accordance with the law of the land."[10]

Squires, arrested and charged with larceny, managed to talk himself down to a fine for income tax evasion. That apparent disgrace did not end his political career. Squires, whom Joseph Smallwood always admired, returned in 1928 to preside over the last chaotic years of self-government before the commission assumed responsiblity for Newfoundland's affairs.

The Squires administration's replacements mouthed the same sanctimony. Premier Walter Monroe and his associates piously promised to end corruption and to prosecute vigorously the findings of the Hollis Walker inquiry. Monroe pledged "to clean up, to keep clean, and to give stable government." Instead, the members of this government, dominated by fish merchants, continued to reward themselves with "fees" for government work. Places on the liquor commission were awarded to friends of the government and, in one case, to a member of the executive council. The Munroe government's first budget raised tariffs on cigarettes, tobacco, rope, fishing nets, butter and margarine. The prime minister held a major interest in a tobacco company and in the country's only manufacturer of fishing net and rope. Sir John Crosbie, the minister of finance, quickly invested in a margarine factory after raising the tariffs on that product. "Less than a year after taking power, he (Monroe) and his ministry stood revealed as another merchant junta, zealously dedicated to their own financial self-interest and the interests of their class."[11]

Nothing changed when Squires returned to office after the scandals of the Monroe government. The use of public funds for personal or political gain continued. So pervasive was the maladministration, so putrid the morality of the government and so desperate the economic plight of the unemployed that mobs attacked the Government Building in St. John's, forcing Squires to flee. Years later, William J. Browne, minister in the Diefenbaker government and a sworn enemy of Smallwood, recalled the benefits of campaigning as a Squires candidate. "Squires had advised us that provision had been made for $50,000;

and we were entitled to recommend to Public Works, either for roads or wharves or bridges, up to that amount." Browne, running for the first time, envied the political savvy of his fellow candidate in the two-member constituency. "Billy Walsh, as he was known to everybody, was a professional politician. He planned his campaign carefully and had communities well organized. He had learned about the $50,000 we had to allocate, so he craftily got word of it to the communities we were visiting, although he said that we had $100,000. In that way people could plan what they wanted and how much they wanted, and he would get a lot of praise."[12]

The turbulent years preceding the denouement of representative government in Newfoundland reflected the unhappy confluence of diverse strains in the dominion's economy and political life. From the time of the first settlements, the majority of Newfoundlanders had been beholden to the decisions and whims of a handful of patrons. For several hundred years, these patrons were the representatives of foreign authorities: merchants of Bristol, Dartmouth, Poole or London; courtiers of the French king; military commanders, sea captains or pirates. Once Newfoundland became more than a servicing centre for the fishing fleet and the Royal Navy, the British government accepted the need for formal governmental structures. These, however, would be dominated by the Crown's representatives in the colony and the indigenous merchant class, whose sway extended from Water Street in St. John's around the outports huddled against the island's forbidding coast.

Representative government, won in 1855, was followed a decade later by the divisive debate over joining the Canadian Confederation. When Newfoundland declined the Canadian offer, political life settled into the pattern that culminated in the collapse of the 1930s, a pattern in which a feudal economic structure, denominational rivalries, extreme poverty, poor communications, and centralized political institutions assigned patronage a role of lasting importance. When Newfoundland emerged from the hiatus of Commission government, World War II and the Confederation debate, the old pattern re-emerged in the career of Joey Smallwood. He became the last of the one-man dispensers of patronage in Canada, a kind of political sun king who, like John A. Macdonald, Wilfrid Laurier and many pre-World War II provincial premiers, personally directed the administration of all the patronage. Only when new elites challenged and subsequently toppled Smallwood did Newfoundland's politics change sufficiently so that in matters of patronage abuse no discernible differences existed between the island and other economically disadvantaged regions of Canada.

Nowhere else in the British dominions of North America had isolation and poverty so markedly shaped the local character. On the eve of joining Canada, two-thirds of Newfoundland's population lived in settlements with fewer than one thousand residents. (Roughly one-third of the province's population still lives in communities of this size, and sixty percent live in communities of fewer than five thousand people.[13]) There were about thirteen hundred hamlets scattered along the six thousand-mile Newfoundland and Labrador coasts. Apart from those who fished near Labrador, few residents of Newfoundland ever experienced anything more foreign than the tip of their bay or the shelter of a neighbouring coastal settlement. In the days before radio, the log book in the telegraph office recorded the day's major "news" and provided the only link between outport and civilization.[14] Roads, of course, were primitive at best, impassable at worst.

Profound parochialism, a breeding ground for the politics of patronage, thus characterized Newfoundland society. Anchored by geography and fate at the margin of Britain's consciousness, Newfoundland reciprocated British indifference with the most passionate commitment to everything British, as if the link to Britain, or at least to an idealized notion of Britain, made up for the difficulties of daily existence and the sordidness of political life.

Anyone with money or authority was automatically classed with the elite in a poor, rural and scattered society. What distinguished Newfoundland, apart from the degree of isolation and poverty, was the structure of its economy. King Cod ruled in fickle majesty, tying thousands of fishermen to the yearly rituals of its lonely chase. Although thousands fished, a handful of merchants centred in St. John's enjoyed King Cod's commercial bounty. The merchants set the price for the fisherman's catch, offered him credit for next season's supplies, ran the stores at which the fisherman's family shopped, and generally organized the economic life of the dominion to their exclusive advantage. True, the system obliged merchants to keep extending further credit or to tide over fishermen experiencing especially disastrous years, for bankruptcy offered no protection either to fishermen or merchants. But the balance of economic benefit had always run strongly in the merchants' favour, so that at the time of Newfoundland's entry into Confederation, a small oligarchy lived comfortably amid a society in which the average family income was one-third of what would have been considered the "poverty line" in Canada.[15]

This economic feudalism produced the quintessential political ground for the full flowering of the patron–client relationship. Forced into virtual serfdom in the pursuit of their livelihood, the fishermen and their families displayed profound deference to everyone in authority. They were classic clients, willing to offer what they could, namely votes, in return for the patron's efforts, or at least his promises, to improve their lot. Sometimes, of course, merchant and politician were one and the same, but if not the fisherman transferred some clientelist assumptions from his economic patron to his politician.

Even William Coaker broke their hearts. This stunning orator swept down from the northern outports, preaching self-reliance and economic reform, lifting the eyes of those inclined to deference, promising to fight for the ordinary fishermen amid the seductions of St. John's. Coaker did just that in his own way, although he had to make political compromises because his movement could never capture a majority in the assembly. His Fishermen's Protective Union campaigned, among other things, for democratic local governments to replace the system of centrally controlled patronage which, Coaker said, "tends to rewards and punishments for partisan reasons and is therefore essentially corrupt." Brave and threatening at the beginning, Coaker gradually tasted life's gentler pleasures. The merchants of Water Street placated him, the Queen knighted him, and Coaker himself learned how to turn the Union's cash stores into credit outlets, from which he could siphon off money for himself. Coaker defrauded his companies, broke the people's trust, and wound up living on an estate in Jamaica. "The country knows little," he later wrote, "of the methods practised by unprincipled men to lead clean men into pitfalls and practical corruption."[16]

Politicians spoke often of principle, but understood little of which they spoke. Ideology was a stranger to Newfoundland politics. Parties represented shifting coalitions of individuals who bore few loyalties other than to themselves. Between 1904 and 1932, ten different coalitions governed, but all the major politicians in them remained precisely the same. In one eleven-month period in 1923-24, five cabinets were formed and re-formed. Getting elected meant delivering tangible benefits to the suffering electorate, regardless of the cost to the country's treasury. Members of the government were often the merchants who ran the economy, so that the greed inherent in their economic domination was also inherent in their governments. Politicians often enriched themselves at the public expense, a practice regarded with equanimity by voters who assumed that politics was made for this and who did not complain, provided some largesse flowed their way.

The Newfoundland railway, an economic folly finally scrapped in 1988, upped the ante for graft and corruption, just as railways did everywhere they were built in Canada. In 1893 the Newfoundland minister of finance resigned when it was revealed that he had been the solicitor for Montreal railway magnate Sir Robert Gillespie Reid, who proposed and built the railway. The minister, it seems, was being paid a yearly retainer of $5,000 by the Reid interests while he negotiated the contract and advocated its acceptance in the legislature, and it later came out that the minister's own firm received contracts for supplying uniforms to railway employees.[17] In 1900 Edward Morris, leading the improbably named People's party and gleefully attacking the government in a bid for power, called the finance minister "Reid's tailor" and the "Minister for Graft and Corruption." But voted into office, Morris and his "new men" quickly forgot their steamy rhetoric in the rush to get rich on the railway. As premier he presided over a government of typical improvidence and gross corruption, and he defended authorizing railway branch lines without tenders or preliminary surveys. "What do I care for the Audit Act when there are people in need of bread? It is all very well to preach political economy when you have a good dinner inside of you."[18] As one writer has said about the Morris years, "Newfoundland governments had rarely, if ever, been paragons of financial probity, but by 1909 there were opportunities for corruption on a scale hitherto undreamed of. And the 'new men' were not the sort to let the opportunity slip."[19]

The lack of any municipal government outside the city of St. John's merely augmented the power of the member of Parliament, since there was no local elite to challenge him.[20] Desperately dependent upon whatever benefits St. John's could bestow, communities judged their MPs, not for Burkean discussion of the commonweal, but on what money the constituency received. The commissioners investigating the state of Newfoundland in 1933 easily discerned the consequences:

> "The Government was looked upon as the universal provider, and it was thought to be the duty of the Member for the constituency to see that there was an ever-increasing flow of public money . . . As there was no local Government, he was expected to fulfill the functions of a mayor and of every department of public authority. In addition, he was the guardian of local interests, the counsellor and friend of every voter in the constituency and the mouthpiece of the district in the Legislature of the country . . . Under the peculiar system of administration adopted in Newfoundland, he was not only the liason between the people and the Government but the channel through which the money voted by the Legislature for public purposes within his constituency was allocated and spent."[21]

Districts voting against the winning party naturally suffered the consequences of reduced patronage and government spending. But some inducements were necessary, if only to offer voters a taste of the grander benefits they were missing and of what largesse might come their way should they display the wisdom of altering their voting habits. Thus, the defeated candidate or the government member for an adjoining district assumed responsibility for recommending grants, subsidies, contracts, concessions and appointments. "Whatever the party situation, at the local level, politics and patronage were virtually synonymous."[22]

To these characteristics of Newfoundland politics was added the critical yeast of religion. The churches — Roman Catholic, Protestant and evangelical sects — gave the outports the only institutions of secondary support. The prevailing settlement pattern of Newfoundland had left Catholics in a majority on the Avalon peninsula and Protestants dominating most of the rest of the island. They fought, of course, in St. John's and elsewhere, usually with words, ocasionally with fists. Party politics tended to be organized on religious lines, at least until the mid-1860s when the Conservatives, a Protestant party dominated by the merchant aristocracy, reached out "to give a generous share of the spoils to Catholic politicians."[23] By protecting their favoured economic position in this manner, the merchants had begun a practice that crystallized into a Newfoundland convention. "Denominationalism," or religious representation, thereafter dictated the construction of cabinets, appointments to the civil service, and the allocation of patronage. To this day, in the administration of patronage, considerations of religious faith weigh more heavily in Newfoundland than anywhere else in Canada save perhaps Prince Edward Island.

The Commission Government, which interrupted political life in 1933, temporarily ended patronage and corruption. The commissioners did indeed give Newfoundland a "rest from politics," although their secrecy, condescension and insistent stupidity (one of the commissioners, convinced that Newfoundland's salvation lay in farming, pushed various doomed and costly agricultural projects) gradually frittered away such public support as the commission had enjoyed at its inception. The war, with its influx of Allied soldiers and ships, gave Newfoundland a sniff of prosperity. When the troops departed, Newfoundland was again alone with its past: a romantic pride, the wreck of democratic institutions, a feeble economic base. The merchants and the old families of the Avalon led the fight to entice Newfoundlanders with potted tales of past glories, to keep Newfoundland from being devoured by the "Canadian wolf." In the outports, however, the people heard a different voice — at first by radio from the referendum assembly in St. John's, then increasingly in person. The voice belonged to Joey Smallwood, beckoning them to cast off the St. John's oligarchy and to fill their pockets with money supplied from Ottawa as a right of Canadian citizenship in the form of old age pensions and family allowances.

Smallwood personified the reappearance of pre-Commission

political mores, except that the monies to be distributed vastly exceeded anything the island had ever known. Smallwood did much more than persuade a bare majority of his fellow citizens to embrace the "Canadian wolf"; he also oversaw negotiations leading to the Terms of Union, won the first election, and linked his political formation in Newfoundland to the national Liberal party, then at the apogee of its political might. Nomination meetings were unknown because Premier Smallwood hand-picked Liberal candidates, federal and provincial. Those who received government appointments did so because Premier Smallwood approved their selection. Everyone in the party, everyone who received some slice of government largesse was beholden directly to him, or indirectly through one of his agents.

No Newfoundlander laboured under any illusion about Smallwood's power and his willingness to use it. Not only did he promise to reward his friends — four senatorships were "sold" to Smallwood friends for $25,000 contributions to the Liberal party[24] — but he had no qualms about porkbarrelling, the impersonal extension of the patron-client relationship. Campaigning in Ferryland in the 1949 federal election, Smallwood warned the voters about the consequences of a vote against his candidate, Greg Power. "If you do not vote for Greg Power, not one cent will you get from the government during the next four years. Mark it down. I mean every word of it." Just in case his point was lost, Smallwood repeated it. "I don't need you. I've been elected. But you need me. I'm sitting on top of the public chest, and not one cent will come out of it for Ferryland unless Greg Power is elected. Unless you vote for my man, you'll be out in the cold for five years. . . . Those settlements which vote against Greg Power will get nothing — absolutely nothing."[25] Ferryland, with its overwhelmingly Catholic majority, spurned the premier's advice, showing that a few voters could still resist Smallwood's suasion. Greg Power quickly recovered from the embarrassment of defeat. Smallwood appointed him chairman of the liquor board.

"I have smashed the spoils system . . . there was never a cleaner government in the history of Newfoundland," declared Smallwood. Sadly, this declaration proved as fatuous as all the similar ones made by previous Newfoundland political leaders. Smallwood did not enrich himself, as had so many of his predecessors, but he was still tainted by scandal. After his defeat, the new Conservative government established a royal commission to investigate allegations into the leasing practices of the Newfoundland liquor commission. The commission found that a company with which Smallwood was associated and which had been established by two close friends, Oliver Vardy and Arthur Lundrigan, held seven leases at "excessive" rents with the liquor commission. The company, argued the royal commission, had artificially "puffed up" the costs of its premises. It concluded: "Messrs. Vardy and Lundrigan used Mr. Smallwood's position for their own advantages; they were consistent in the pursuit of their own economic interests. Mr. Smallwood, of course, should not have been involved in the transactions."[26]

Still, by Newfoundland standards, this wrongdoing qualified as a misdemeanor. Smallwood did not leave politics a wealthy man, although he turned a blind eye to some of his colleagues who "not to put too fine a point on it were virtually plundering the public treasury."[27] Vardy, a long-time Smallwood crony, was part-owner of a company providing supplies to the St. John's Housing Corporation, of which Vardy was chairman. Dr. Alfred Valdamis, one of the economic wonderboys Smallwood imported to rescue Newfoundland, pleaded guilty to defrauding the provincial government of $200,000 and served four years in prison. John Sheehan and John C. Doyle were entrepreneurs who won Smallwood's blessing and absconded with Newfoundland money, leaving projects unfinished.

Public works contracts were issued without tender. Leaseback arrangements for public buildings allowed politicians and contractors to take slices of the action. Old friends got plum jobs as useless "liquor agents." Others were rewarded with positions on the liquor commission, the civil service commission and dozens of other provincial and federal bodies. In the intimate confines of Newfoundland politics, little had changed since the days before the Commission Government's purge of corrupt practices. Under Smallwood "the notion of 'to the victor the spoils' was generally accepted as right and just by people and politicians alike."[28]

Poor, barren Newfoundland had never known anything like the infusion of money that poured into the province after 1949, just as Smallwood had promised during the referendum campaign. Unfamiliar with Canadian ways or with substantial government cheques arriving monthly in the mail, Newfoundlanders ascribed their good fortune to Smallwood. The premier, who answered his own phone and had established through radio and personal visits an almost mystical link with outport Newfoundlanders, "became a kind of super patron, distributing government resources to individual clients and client communities which awarded him their votes."[29] All the deferential sentiments outport Newfoundlanders had been used to showing merchants or assembly representatives, the dispensers of patronage in earlier times, they now directed towards Smallwood. Even the assemblymen had lost their importance as patrons, since they were entirely beholden to Smallwood for their positions. "To oppose Smallwood in public was to risk financial retribution. The entire economy rested upon government spending, and this, whether federal or provincial, Smallwood controlled. He used the power of the purse with little restraint. Friends were rewarded and enemies persecuted. If Newfoundlanders feared Smallwood, they did so with good reason."[30]

Smallwood, keenly aware of the importance of continuing infusions of federal cash, needed a friend at Ottawa's court. He found one in Jack Pickersgill, the most powerful backroom operator in the capital. Pickersgill had befriended Smallwood when the lonely Newfoundlander first came to Ottawa to drum up support for Newfoundland joining Canada. Smallwood paved the way for Pickersgill to win election to the House of Commons from Bonavista-Twillingate, although Pickersgill had never set foot in Newfoundland before the campaign.

No matter. The deal was mutually fortuitous. Pickersgill glided into the House of Commons; Smallwood got his friend at court. What a friend Pickersgill turned out to be. No minister ever delivered more: post offices throughout the island, fourteen million dollars in improvements to ferry terminals on both sides of the Cabot Strait, subsidies to bail out Eastern Provincial Airlines, assumption of the debt of St. John's harbour by the National Harbours Board, ninety percent of the cost of completing the Trans-Canada Highway, fisheries aid schemes, thirty million in ferries and docks, seven million for a paved "access" road, a hundred and fifty million for the Atlantic Development Fund. Newfoundland had quite simply never seen the kind of porkbarrelling the Smallwood-Pickersgill team delivered. And Smallwood wanted every last voter to understand the reciprocal obligation for this spending. To the electors of Stephenville he wrote in 1966 in the same vein as he had spoken to the electors of Ferryland in 1949. "The minute [the U.S. Air Force base] left, it became my job to save that part of Newfoundland from unemployment, destitution, dole, despair, and finally the disappearance of much of its population. . . . Will you help me to do it? Or do you want to send me a message saying 'Stop. We don't need your help.' . . . That will be the answer you will give me if you elect the Tory candidate, or the Independent Liberal candidate. If you want to send me a message saying: 'Yes, Joe, we want you to keep on working hard for this District and the people in it,' the only way you can send me that message is to elect the Liberal party's candidate."[31]

Newfoundland's sun king could not let go. He asked for and received what he described as his final mandate in 1969, a brilliant last hurrah for twenty years as premier and a promise to retire before the next election. The promise seemed genuine at the time. He selected a crop of younger candidates; any one of five or six, including John Crosbie, might plausibly have been regarded as a capable successor. Yet within a year the tensions between the old man and some of the young turks became so palpable, and then so venemous, that the Liberal party began tearing itself apart. Crosbie and Clyde Wells resigned over the financial arrangements for the Come-By-Chance oil refinery and sat as Independent Liberals. When Crosbie challenged Smallwood's leadership, the younger man's loss disguised only for a time what had really happened. The Liberal party was fractured, and remained beset by the worst sorts of cliquishness, back-stabbing and rivalries for more than fifteen years, through seven leaders and a series of electoral defeats.

Crosbie's defection to the Conservatives symbolized the mobilization of anti-Smallwood forces into a credible political alternative which in 1972 ousted the old man from power. Still he could not let go. Replaced as leader, Smallwood led his own party — the Reform Liberals — in the 1974 election, effectively splitting the Liberal vote and allowing the Conservatives to consolidate their grip on power. Yet for all the political vicissitudes of that period, and all the Conservative promises of a new era in Newfoundland affairs, some things did not change, notably the attitudes towards political patronage. Here was a party, after all, that had not merely been out of power for awhile; it had never been in office. True, some of the Conservatives, especially the younger ones who had emerged from Memorial University, were determined to erase elements of the Smallwood legacy — the ill-fated, grandiose economic diversification projects; the dictatorial methods of running the provincial administration. In a fit of reform, Attorney-General William Marshall pushed through the *Public Tender Act* in 1974, but events subsequently revealed that the government's heart was never in the Act.

In his 1976 annual report, the auditor-general castigated the department of public works and services, a castigation that provoked stormy legislative debates and eventually the creation of a commission of enquiry under Judge John W. Mahoney of the Supreme Court of Newfoundland. His report, published in 1981 and based on forty-two hundred pages of evidence, laid bare the workings and assumptions of Conservative politicians in the 1974-1977 period, when they effectively consolidated their grip on power. Painstaking investigation led Judge Mahoney to a sad conclusion: "I believe it was hoped that the Act would somehow 'disappear' and that the old system would continue as it always had." That "old system"—Smallwood's system, that which had existed for decades before the Commission Government—Judge Mahoney described as one "whereby political backers received patronage from the Government of the day, a system which was virtually an accepted fact of life. When the new Administration took over, the ministers in question were subjected to the same sort of pressure by their supporters to 'go and do likewise' so as to remedy the drought which they had been facing for the twenty-three years during the reign of the previous administration."[32] That system included a preferred list of government contractors, which "had always existed, in one form or another, even before the change of government in 1972" and which was completely changed after the Conservatives took office.[33] As a consequence, "there was a well-defined pecking order, with the lion's share of the work being awarded to party supporters." Nor were the changes the exclusive work of the ministers responsible for the department; they represented policy articulated at the highest levels of the party. "The premier of the province, Honourable Frank Moores, testified that, although he had never given specific instructions to the Ministers as to who should be placed on such a list, he had indicated that he wanted to make sure that contractors who had not received work when the previous administration was in power, were not given an opportunity to get work. This answer, of course, does not explain why known supporters of the previous government were *removed* from the lists."[34]

Since contracts below fifteen thousand dollars in value did not require tendering, large projects were split into several or many small parcels so that ministers could reward their friends without conforming to the requirements of the Act, a practice, it should be said, common in other provinces. Judge Mahoney cited instances of ministers cancelling work because the contractors had Liberal connections, of ministers interfering in other ways in the administration of contracts, of contractors giving small gifts to ministers and departmental staff (liquor, ham, turkeys), and of contractors donating money to the Conservative party in return for their "fair share" of government work. Whatever the laudable intentions of the minister who introduced the Act, Judge Mahoney concluded, "the plain fact of the matter is that the good intentions of the government, expressed in the policy of the legislation, became sidetracked, almost immediately after the enactment of the Act. . . . I find it reprehensible that the very government which supported the introduction of the Act and voted for it then proceeded to ignore it for the next three years."[35]

Frank Moores left Newfoundland politics, eventually winding up in Ottawa where he formed Government Consultants Limited to cash in on his friendship with Prime Minister Brian Mulroney. Moores' patronage legacy to Newfoundland consisted largely in changing the cast of characters who received benefits. And in more recent times, it frequently appeared under Premier Brian Peckford that the same practices prevailed. Conservative contractors received favourable consideration; former ministers went to rewards on boards, agencies and commissions; government spending disproportionately favoured Conservative constituencies; and the whole edifice of favouritism was cloaked in the premier's fiery rhetoric—usually against the federal government—and his fiesty style, which increasingly wore thin. Unionization, in particular, chipped away at patronage. Even the fishermen, dependent for so long, unionized themselves; the bulk of the civil service formed a militant brigade of opponents to the Peckford government. And the Liberal party emerged from years of internecine warfare to elect a new breed of leader, a lawyer with a clinical mind and cool demeanour, Clyde Wells, who, like his contemporary Frank McKenna of New Brunswick, appreciated that the days of the old-style patronage were over, although patronage itself would remain in an attenuated form in the body politic of Newfoundland.

CHAPTER 7

PRINCE EDWARD ISLAND

"If it moves, give it a pension, if not pave it."
Local description of Conservative party politics,
circa 1966.

PRINCE EDWARD ISLAND was conceived in patronage, and since that moment change has come grudgingly. In such a small place, where the standard of living lags behind that of other provinces, unemployment, economic deprivation, ubiquitous familiarity, and familial propinquity bring pressures for patronage on politicians who struggle not to disappoint their supplicants.

Politicians everywhere enjoin the faithful at election time to remember that "every vote counts," but in Prince Edward Island they are not kidding. From 1893 to 1963, ten percent of Island MLAs won by twenty-five votes or fewer, and thirty-seven percent by margins of fewer than one hundred votes. Eliminating acclamations, only three of nearly six hundred successful candidates in those seven decades enjoyed majorities of more than one thousand.[1] In the 1982 election, twenty-three constituencies were decided by fewer than two hundred votes; in 1986, ten constituencies turned on fewer than two hundred.

In such circumstances, the Island's electoral fray exhibited every corrupt political practice because voters in each hamlet and along each back road calculated the precise value of a vote. The price in the last century was a pint of cheap rum or five dollars, but in close elections, the law of supply and demand inflated the price to a hefty ten dollars or more. At the turn of the century Donald Farquharson, the Liberal premier, complained: "It is simply a matter now of who will buy the

161

most votes, and the man who works the hardest and is prepared to use means fair or foul will get in." More than six decades later, so little had changed that Farquharson would have understood perfectly what went on in 1966 when Prince Edward Island treated itself and the country to a political spectacle still often recounted.

The 1966 election produced an electoral rarity — the Conservatives and Liberals in a draw.[2] The political configuration of the government rested on the outcome six weeks later of a delayed election in the dual-member constituency of First Kings. With power the prize, the Conservative government of Premier Walter Shaw mobilized every available resource. Four ministers had been defeated in the election, but only one had resigned. His portfolio, that of public works and highways, Shaw promptly bestowed upon the freshman Conservative candidate in First Kings.

Road crews invaded First Kings from across the Island and "Islanders jokingly expressed wonder that the eastern tip did not sink under the weight of road building." Observers estimated that First Kings received thirty miles of fresh paving in six weeks. Critics invented a slogan for the Conservative campaign: "If it moves, give it a pension; if not, pave it." One elector, fearful for his property, erected a sign PLEASE DON'T PAVE; THIS IS MY ONLY PASTURE.

Not by paving alone did the Conservatives woo First Kings. "Those who had more specific preferences requested gifts: a new bathroom replaced the outdoor variety for some, while paved driveways were a popular addition to the residences of the more affluent," noted one observer. "The final day of the campaign drew near amidst a current of rumours throughout the province. Some residents even claimed to have witnessed long processions of trucks travelling towards Souris in the middle of the night, their cargoes composed of many cases of the finest liquor." Despite the Conservatives' best efforts, the Liberals took both seats — and the government — proving either that the road builders did not work fast enough or that by porkbarrelling alone Islanders will not always be swayed.

Nothing that happened in First Kings, nor anything else in the political life of Prince Edward Island, discouraged Islanders from their intense interest in politics. Their participation in the struggle for patronage and government favours attests, in part, to the Island's enormous dependence upon government and to the elbow-rubbing proximity of legislator and voter. It may also have something to do with the history of an island born in imperial patronage — the granting of large parcels of land to absentee landlords in Britain. The fight to regain land from absentee owners dominated the Island's first hundred years. A string of incompetent governors either sided with the landlords' interests or allied themselves with the local oligarchy to resist popular demands for representative institutions.

Responsible government was finally achieved in 1851 after a protracted struggle between the governor and reformers who, like all Prince Edward Island politicians since, immediately felt the hot breath of those clamouring for positions and public works. Before the Island's politics had shaken down into Liberal and Conservative parties, the railway craze struck. Having observed the mania grip other parts of British North America, Islanders were determined not to be bypassed. So the railway came to P.E.I., or at least the idea of one did. With dispatch and euphoria, the assembly voted for a railway from coast to coast, from Aberdeen to Georgetown. Before long, every corner of the Island demanded branch lines, and the original railway plans buckled under the pressure. The lieutenant-governor noted confidentially, "The carrying out of the *Railway Act* of the last session has caused an unusual flow of money and patronage."[3] A cabinet minister arranged for a station to be built on property he owned. An MLA admitted he had been offered a thousand dollars by one Caleb Carleton of Souris to vote for a branch line to the town. Summoned to the House, Carleton happily acknowledged the offer and named other "parties to the eastward that would contribute pretty liberally, and help to shove along the branches."[4]

The Liberals in Opposition greeted skeptically these demands for additional branch lines; once in office they succumbed to the same pressures. A Liberal backbencher explained the change of heart: "Four members were pledged to go for the party that would go for the branch lines and without whom it was impossible to form a government, so that we either had to promise to construct the branches or allow the Honourable Leader of the Opposition to form a government with these four members."[5] The railway—"built to carry votes not passengers"—plunged P.E.I. into bankruptcy, a crisis that forced the population to reconsider Confederation, a project Islanders had resisted in 1867.

The railway, however, did not mark the last transportation pork-barrel in P.E.I. politics. Automobiles frightened Islanders who worried that the backfiring and belching of these mechanical monsters would wreck the tranquility of their Eden. In 1908, the assembly banned automobiles on the Island, one of those noble, hopeless gestures of defiance eventually superseded by the undeniable attractions of the new machine. In 1913, the assembly grudgingly allowed automobiles on certain highways under strict conditions, and then only for three days a week. Those restrictions, too, eventually collapsed in the face of the machine's popularity. Islanders fully embraced the automobile age, thus plopping road construction into the porkbarrel hopper, where it still remains.

Politicians quickly appreciated the political potential of road-work, and no election campaign in Prince Edward Island since the machines' appearance has ever been devoid of promises to pave, pave and pave again. J.P. "Big Jim Bill" McIntyre, a Liberal public works minister, was the first to capitalize on the government's road-paving record. Big Jim Bill authorized the Island's first asphalt highway, a two-mile stretch that bore his name. McIntyre bragged about being the "father of good roads in this province," a boast that lasted until the highway began to crack a short time after construction.[6]

Once politicians got the hang of promising road-building and paving, nothing could stop them. Roads could provide jobs for the unemployed and underemployed, contracts for friends, vote-attracting work for communities, and repayment of political obligations. Prince Edward Island, at the beginning of the 1980s, had the highest percentage of its total acreage paved of any province and the largest amount of paved road per square mile in Canada — hefty figures considering the province also had the lowest per capita percentage of car registrations in the country. An academic study, using admittedly rough calculations, concluded that political favouritism had consistently coloured road construction and paving decisions, a conclusion that would not surprise a single Islander.[7]

Occasionally, someone on the Island cried foul, or worried about the partisanship and attendant waste in road-building. Premier John H. Bell once warned that the department of public works had to be "above board" with tenders "because if the federal government got any suspicion of irregular or crooked work, then our chances of getting subsidy from that source would be imperilled." Bell need not have worried; federal politicians were overwhelmingly rational with partisanship in the awarding of their own contracts. But the premier did note ruefully that the number of applications for work on the new car ferry to the mainland was "sufficient to man the British Navy."[8]

The premier's concern about possible federal reaction, no matter how unnecessary, underscored Prince Edward Island's overwhelming dependence upon federal money. Islanders know better than any other voters in Canada who butters their bread, because until recently every change of party in Ottawa presaged a similar shift in Charlottetown. Not for Islanders the pattern elsewhere, where voters set up political counterweights between their provincial capital and Ottawa. Islanders prefer both governments to be disposed kindly towards them, a shrewd recognition of the province's dependence. At federal-provincial conferences, P.E.I. governments always stand firm on the majesty of their sovereignty, no matter how faintly ridiculous such posturing strikes other Canadians. By demanding a full measure of whatever Ottawa offers other provinces, Prince Edward Island finds itself disproportionately favoured, an assertion that might make Islanders' blood boil.

After all, politics worked that way on the Island, where each corner demands no less—and preferably more—than what the other corners receive. No issues of substance consistently distinguish Liberals from Conservatives. Occasionally, the parties fall out over this or that; sometimes, one party seems more attractive to a particular religious group. But the kind of brokerage politics acted out at the national level defines the politics of Prince Edward Island. And no party denies—or could deny — the indispensable role of patronage in keeping groups and individuals satisfied. After all, the constitution of the Liberal party declared: "The Patronage Committee shall keep records of service and contributions of party supporters and shall make recommendations for patronage benefits."[9] The Conservatives, occasionally more subtle, were no different. While Premier Angus MacLean pontificated in 1979 about victory having vindicated his commitment to wise statesmanship, one of his ministers defined matters differently. After thirteen years of Liberal rule, said the minister, "his people get their turn."[10]

Prince Edward Island is still one of the few places in Canada where religion counts in politics. The whole machinery of patronage on the Island, whether federal or provincial, considers it: Every Catholic appointment must be offset by a Protestant nomination, and vice versa. The "turn," as it is called, is one of those unwritten, often unspoken, rules that Island politicians try not to ignore. The "turn's" application, when combined with partisanship, can reduce the number of persons conceivably eligible for a given position to one in four.

Before 1962, government discretion determined most civil service jobs. Not every change of government precipitated the mass firings of 1935, when Liberals swept aside long-serving Conservatives on "Bloody Thursday." But each change did produce a sizeable turnover in Charlottetown and, of course, wholesale changes in the part-time and contract positions across the province. Liberal leader Joe Ghiz, campaigning in 1986, pledged to eliminate the patronage of part-time employees. He failed, or more precisely, he did not try after becoming premier. In the first winter following Ghiz's election, Liberals drove the plows while Conservatives searched for alternative employment. A few people — obnoxious academics and spiteful journalists mostly — ungraciously pointed out the discrepancies between Ghiz's promises and deeds. The bulk of the population shrugged. The wheels of political justice would turn some day, and the outs would be in.

Bloody Thursday created such a stink, even in a province accustomed to a reapportionment of the spoils after an electoral change, that the government of Premier Thane Campbell passed the *Public Service Act* of 1937. This weak reed of a statute appeared to offer civil servants protection, but it left the government's discretionary power largely intact. Two and a half decades later, in 1962, Prince Edward Island belatedly cleansed some of the patronage from its civil service and eliminated some of the oddities in its election laws. The province was the last in Canada to get a *Civil Service Act*, with a civil service commission, a classification system, and the merit principle. But even the Act removed only two-thirds of civil service posts from partisan control.

Prince Edward Island elections were as corrupt as those anywhere in Canada and, for many years, less regulated. Only in 1963 did the province modernize its election laws, creating a chief electoral officer and an impartial electoral list. Simultaneously, property qualifications were abolished. These had been introduced in the mid-nineteenth century when, in another of the Island's unique political twists, the assembly and council were fused into one institution with two categories of members: assemblymen elected by a democratic franchise; councillors chosen only by those with sufficient property. A voter who owned property in more than one location could cast more than one ballot, an invitation to the confusion of election day, on which political organizers counted to fix as many results as possible. No one knew what constituted "property" so that "gravel pits, cranberry bogs, blueberry patches, fishing shacks or duck blinds assumed the same importance as farms, businesses and summer cottages on election day. One ingenious voter attempted to claim the property vote in a constituency where he had purchased a graveyard plot."[11] With two tiers of members, multiple-member constituencies, tiny numbers of voters in each riding, short parliamentary sessions, yet all the panoply of a sovereign government, the Prince Edward Island legislature for decades looked like a satirist's dream.

The electors knew better. Their forefathers had fought for this assembly, and in such a tiny place, the chances were excellent that citizens personally knew at least their own MLA, and perhaps several more. That proximity of voter and legislator in an economically depressed corner of Canada entrenched a patronage system for rewarding individuals and a porkbarrel style of governing for their communities, a system to lift them from idleness or poverty, or to make existence temporarily easier, in exchange for their allegiance to a political party or a politician, a renewable deal at each election. The costs in inefficiency and waste were less consequential than the overwhelming and apparently unshakeable assumption that it is best to "let the government do it" and grab whatever piece of the action comes along.[12]

Last among Canadian provinces, perhaps, Prince Edward Island witnessed the old system grating against the bureaucratization of contemporary government, the impact of mass communications, the upheaval of settled patterns of rural existence. But the patron-client relationship between politicians and voters will for simple reasons of geography and demography likely remain more intimate and durable in Prince Edward Island than anywhere in Canada.

CHAPTER 8

NOVA SCOTIA

"Elections should not be fought on issues"
Premier John Buchanan, 1984 Election.

THE CONSERVATIVES OF NOVA SCOTIA had been out of power for eight years before winning the 1978 election. For half of that period, Don Cameron knew what it felt like to shiver on the cold benches of the Opposition. Cameron, a handsome and soft-spoken dairy farmer, had bucked the Liberal tide in 1974 and won the riding of Pictou East, but because his party lost the election, no one, including members of his Conservative association, paid any attention to his heretical views on political patronage.[1]

Cameron quietly informed his association — and such voters who inquired in 1974 — that he did not favour the time-honoured ways and views of political patronage in Nova Scotia.[2] If the Conservatives won, Cameron explained, there would be no mass firings of gravel-haulers, truckers, small contractors, snow-plow operators and other part-time government workers in Pictou East. True, Cameron would have the power, as a government MLA, to steer business to political friends. But that was not his way nor his vision of how the game of politics should be played. Yes, Cameron said, if two candidates of equal merit presented themselves — one Conservative, the other Liberal — he would choose the Conservative. No, he explained, mass firings and new contractors would not immediately follow a Conservative victory.

The Liberals' 1974 victory under Gerald Regan rendered Cameron's views academic. As an Opposition MLA, Cameron dispensed none of the patronage in Pictou East. The defeated Liberal candidate, the president of the Liberal riding association and, perhaps, Liberal MLAs from nearby ridings would handle hirings, firings and the minor contracts. They would administer the spoils of power, because the system of the party in power caring for its supporters had always thrived in Nova Scotia, nowhere more persistently than in Pictou, Guysborough, Antigonish and other places along the south shore of the Northumberland Strait.

After four years in Opposition, Don Cameron not only found himself in power but named minister of fisheries when the Conservatives under John Buchanan won the September 1978 election. Cameron had just settled into his Halifax ministerial offices in early November when he received a call from the president of the Pictou East Conservative Association. Would Cameron, the president asked, be willing to attend a meeting in the constituency on the forthcoming Saturday morning? Some members of the executive had a few matters they wished to discuss with him.

On Saturday morning, Cameron arrived at a church hall not far from his farm to find the room packed with angry Conservatives. Why had Cameron not immediately fired all the Liberal gravel-haulers, they demanded to know? Why were Conservatives not being given the jobs still occupied by Liberals? Didn't Cameron understand that Conservatives had been waiting eight years for those jobs? Why was a Liberal still allowed to do this? Why couldn't a faithful Conservative get the contract for that?

Cameron knew immediately what he was up against, not only from his own political career but from an appreciation of the history of patronage in those parts. After all, Allan J. MacEachen, the federal MP whose riding of Cape Breton Highlands-Canso partly overlapped with Cameron's was pastmaster of political patronage and porkbarrelling. If anyone doubted Allan J.'s clout, he need only have considered the make-work projects that had left cemetery fences and churches glistening with new paint throughout his riding; or the marine academy and heavy-water plant at Port Hawkesbury; or the new wharves sprinkled throughout the constituency; or the federal government's philatelic centre at Antigonish. Allan J. was heir to a long tradition. In the last century, supplicants beseiged federal and provincial politicians for whatever jobs and benefits might change hands after an election. John Thompson, one of John A. Macdonald's successors as prime minister, had represented part of Cameron's political territory. Thompson had felt obliged to play the game of patronage, but not to heed the importuning of supplicants. Their greed, desperation and insistence made him angry. "I revolt against Antigonish the more I think of it," he wrote his wife.*

Liberal or Conservative, it did not matter. Colin MacIsaac, Liberal MLA in Antigonish in the late 1880s and early 1890s, received dozens of letters from job-seekers. In 1921, when MacIsaac stood successfully in Antigonish-Guysborough for the Liberals, the letters poured in, some plaintive, some desperate, some threatening, all demanding. "I polled for the Liberals and I look to them for help," wrote one correspondent. "I hope the party won't forget their [sic] friends, those who worked for them so faithfully," warned another. "I am informed that Mr. Tom Dugan at the post office is going to lose his job. I am going to try to see if I will get it," wrote an erstwhile supporter, "I done [sic] all in my little power for you Mr. MacIsaac. I can prove that I got two more votes for you besides my woman and myself. . . . I am out of work with a family to support and if you see your way clear to help me, I will never forget you."[3]

The people of Pictou East had known nothing more, and demanded nothing less, than a full measure of patronage from their politicians. They had always hounded their elected officials, and even drove some politicians to despise their greed. But no politician, whatever his private thoughts, had ever challenged what the voters took to be the ordained order of politics. Like some of his predecessors, Don Cameron hated blatant patronage; like none of them, he remained true to his convictions. Confronting the hostility of his own supporters, Cameron recoiled but did not yield. He had explained his views on patronage in the 1974 and 1978 campaigns. Yes, several Conservatives replied, but that was idle chatter. The party now possessed the spoils of power. Conservatives needed work. They deserved it in return for their political support. The Conservative way was the Liberal way: no quarter for the outs, no stinting for the ins. Maybe, Cameron insisted, but that wasn't his way, either as MLA or as minister. The more Cameron defended himself, the more agitated the crowd became, until in a fit of exasperation and anger, Cameron stomped out of the hall, thus provoking a bitter internecine struggle within the Pictou East Conservative Association. Not until the 1984 association election did Cameron's friends achieve a clear majority on the executive, but by then

---

*Thompson would certainly have concurred in the sentiments expressed in a letter from a friend in Port Musgrave: "Antigonish is not worthy of you. If the wealth of Golconda was scattered amongst them, and all the favours which the government could bestow were given them it would not avail. They would cry for more. They cannot be kept bought, deception is too much in their nature. . . ." (Peter Waite, see notes for chapter 8.)

the internal strife had taken its toll. Cameron left the cabinet in 1980, and has since remained on the fringes of the Conservative caucus, a renegade against the prevailing political assumptions of his party, and of politics Nova Scotia style.

Cameron, surprisingly, was not alone in his heresy. Pat Hunt, another Conservative MLA sent to Halifax in the 1978 victory, also tried to buck the system with predictably depressing results. He failed to win renomination, and subsequently left the province. Two months after the election, Hunt returned to face the annual meeting of the East Hants Conservative Association where party workers denounced him because he would not fire two highway workers.[4] As one speaker put it, there were plenty of "good Tories" to fill those jobs. When Highways minister Tom McInnis, special guest at the annual meeting, explained that the Conservatives intended to fire fewer workers than had the Liberals in 1970, the local newspaper reported an "overwhelmingly negative" response. When McInnis announced that the Conservatives had thus far fired only twenty-one percent of the highway workers, people in the crowd shouted "not enough." For his part, Hunt said, he would not fire any men "if they are doing their jobs properly."

The dispute still simmered a year later. Hunt, badly in need of allies, brought Don Cameron to the 1979 annual meeting. Cameron's message "to lay down your weapons and reflect on what we're doing to the party" confirmed the Conservatives' anger. Rather than lay down any weapons, the East Hants Conservative Association got rid of Pat Hunt as their MLA. Before leaving politics, Hunt stated his obituary in a newspaper interview: "I would rather be a politician for four years and do what I think is right than be there for twenty years doing what gets me re-elected."[5]

Don Cameron and Pat Hunt are like rocks temporarily impeding the strong current of political patronage that runs through the history of Nova Scotia. An occasional Conservative or Liberal MLA, the odd union leader or crusading journalist and, in more recent years, the New Democrats have questioned the practices and assumptions of patronage. In one celebrated court case from the Gerald Regan era, the courts exposed systematic tollgating, a practice long condoned but seldom exposed.

The patterns of patronage in Nova Scotia politics were set long before Confederation, in the patronage wielded by colonial governors and their supporters and, subsequently, by the popularly elected men and women who exercised power under responsible government. Even the greatest Nova Scotian, Joseph Howe, campaigned against the abuses of patronage only when it served his political purpose: to break the power of the governors' cliques. Howe, seldom financially secure, several times sought an appointment for himself, and he capped his career by serving as Nova Scotia's lieutenant-governor, an appointment from John A. Macdonald. Reservations that Howe expressed after responsible government had been won were contradicted by his own deeds and those of Reformers who followed him in office. He belatedly embraced Confederation partly because Macdonald gave him major powers of patronage in Nova Scotia, powers Howe wielded with compelling effect to persuade other resenters and doubters in the province to accept entry into Canada.[6] Joining Canada did not change Nova Scotian attitudes towards patronage; if anything, it whetted appetites for more, since membership in a larger country expanded the number of public positions and government spending.

Confederation, which so sorely divided Nova Scotians, did inject into the province's political affairs a *cause célèbre* that would dominate debate for nearly a decade thereafter and resurface periodically in demands for repeal or revision of the dirty deed of 1867. The Confederation issue aberrated Nova Scotia's political traditions, whereby the two parties had always bent every effort to exaggerate their differences, but could scarcely be told apart on any matter of principle or philosophy. It had always been expected that one party would accuse the other of abusing the public trust, contravening every ethical standard of good behaviour, flouting the electoral laws and raiding the public treasury to reward supporters. But it was understood that the rascals who wanted in would do the very same if only the voters would throw the other bunch out. This was already the *status quo* by 1862 when the lieutenant-governor, noting the effect of self-rule, cabled home to Britain: "There is now no question which divides them, and which should keep them in perpetual antagonism to one another. The matter in dispute is now simply one of men, not measures."[7]

In the time between the capture of responsible government and the spectre of Confederation, Nova Scotians had indeed developed a pattern of political life wherein men counted far more than measures, a political culture framed by personalities and material rewards.

Nova Scotia's unperturbable political tradition was personified for late-twentieth century observers by Premier John Buchanan, whose summit of intellectual excitement consisted in identifying the Conservative faithful at Thursday night bingo. When during his victorious 1984 campaign he declared that "elections should not be fought on issues," he embodied that deep-seated Nova Scotian aversion to anything that might raise large and disturbing questions. Buchanan's remark showed that in the 1980s Nova Scotia's political culture was fundamentally the same as in the 1860s when, to borrow words from the province's leading historian, "the most suitable designations for the administration and its opposition had become the Ins and Outs; the struggle between the two was for place, power and the spoils of office."[8]

The Confederation debates temporarily intruded substance into the election process. In 1867 the Anti-Confederates formed the government, but they soon realized their cause was being eroded by federal patronage and seemed helpless against it. In 1871 they passed legislation denying federal office-holders the right to exercise their franchise in provincial elections, hoping by this expedience to reduce the size of the pro-Confederation vote. It did not work. Rebuffed by Britain, their ranks thinned by seductions from Ottawa, in 1875 the Anti-Confederates threw in their lot with those other Conservative-haters, the Liberals, who swallowed the old campaigner's name and later outdid them in expediency. The Liberals held power until 1878, when Simon Holmes became Nova Scotia's first Conservative premier and turned Nova Scotia politics back to the basics.

Once the debates were over and the Anti-Confederate party disappeared, the old "men, not measures" pattern resurfaced. (It was to withstand even the entry of a new third party, the New Democrats, whose objections would prove to be both infrequent and entirely inconsequential.)

It had taken Nova Scotia Conservatives eleven long years — from 1867 to 1878 — to rid themselves of the opprobrium engendered by their pro-Confederation stand, but during that time their want for patronage did not go entirely unsatisfied. A politically useful aspect of federalism is the distinct possibility that a party defeated at one level of government will find itself in office at the other. So the patronage of federal cousins assuaged the pain of provincial Opposition. From 1874 to 1878, while the federal Conservatives also languished in Opposition, the Anti-Confederates had moved modestly to improve electoral practices: by requiring that controverted election cases be heard by the Supreme Court rather than a parliamentary committee, and by providing secret balloting. Despite these reforms, the Conservative press still charged the government with corruption in the administration of Crown lands, and with paying unauthorized sums to its friends. *The Halifax Herald*, a Conservative bullhorn, alleged that a fund voted by the legislature for the settling of immigrants had "found its way into the pockets of members and supporters of the local government."[9] Premier Holmes, having railed in Opposition against government patronage, established the ground rules for future changes of government. "Office-holders who had worked electorally for the Liberals received short shrift."[10]

The Liberals, however, returned to power with a vengeance in 1882, winning over sixty-three percent of the popular vote and twenty-four of thirty-eight seats in the legislature. This election marked the beginning of the longest unbroken spell in office of any political party in Canadian history — forty-three years, twenty-seven of them under Premier George Murray. In this period of one-party dominance, Liberal patronage ran riot, although one Liberal premier, William S. Fielding, tried to show some restraint. Faced with the usual avalanche of requests for positions, Fielding chagrined his supporters by the moderation of his views. "We should aim at permanency in our public offices," he wrote. "The mere fact that a man holding [office] has been of the other political party is hardly a sufficient ground for his removal."[11] Fielding, who later filled prominent cabinet posts in Sir Wilfrid Laurier's national government, provided a classic statement of the acceptable use of patronage (echoed later by the likes of Don Cameron and Pat Hunt): "One of the principles of party politics is that 'to the victors belong the spoils,' that is, providing we can agree as to what the 'spoils' are. There are some persons who would clear out every Tory who holds office under the government. I do not agree with that, but I hold that vacancies as they occur, and patronage within limited bounds, should be given by the government to its friends and supporters, and I am prepared to give such patronage every day in the week provided the person who receives it does a dollar's worth of work for every dollar he gets."[12]

Patronage, then, would not disappear; Fielding would willingly use it for political purposes. But patronage did not require him to fire people of the other political persuasion. Fielding's views on appropriate limits to patronage certainly did not mean circumscribing government spending to favour Liberal constituencies. Road construction and repair always animated political debates in Nova Scotia, and the allocations of the highways budget always pinpointed the upcoming whereabouts of government favouritism in a province where geography made internal land communications difficult. Fielding, like all successful Nova Scotia premiers, knew that the promise of more roads curried support more surely than the notion of public-sector restraint. Prior to the 1882 election, for example, the Conservatives made a fatal political decision. They reduced the highways budget, a policy the Liberals immediately attacked with devastatingly effective results. Under Fielding, the Liberals undertook a massive road-building and maintenance program. The Conservatives labelled it a massive slush fund for winning elections.

About seventy years later, a Conservative Opposition leader, Robert Stanfield, applied Fielding's wisdom when campaigning against the fading Liberals—he too promised a massive road program. Like Fielding, Stanfield never forgot that the safest journey to political success lay along freshly paved roads. And the tradition continued. When the

Mulroney government granted Nova Scotia money for offshore energy development, the Buchanan government used some of the money to construct a road through a park nowhere near the onshore installations servicing the exploration and development.

In 1925 the Liberal hegemony collapsed around the head of Premier Ernest Armstrong, who must have sensed the coming defeat. In 1922 he had written Prime Minister Mackenzie King, looking for a position on the Supreme Court of Nova Scotia but was rebuffed. Later, after being offered a mere judgeship in Lunenburg, Armstrong poured his frustrations into a letter to a consoling friend: "I have done little else through my political life, except to use my influence, such as I had, on behalf of others."[13]

The demands for place and vengeance engulfed the new government of Premier Edgar N. Rhodes. The Conservatives had spent nearly half a century in the wilderness. Nowhere else in Canada had a major party been deprived of power for so long, and the occasional largesse of their federal cousins had merely enlarged their appetite.

Elected on June 25, 1925, a beleaguered Premier Rhodes found himself by August dictating dozens of letters with variations on the following plaintive sentence: "It was estimated by my stenographer that when I took office, I had a pile of nearly two thousand unanswered letters and telegrams to be attended to."[14] Like a true Conservative, Rhodes struggled to achieve economies in government, a struggle that merely exacerbated his patronage-supply problem. "I am sorry there will be no opportunities on the liquor commission," he wrote to one applicant, "as we have dismissed the whole board, having the work performed by the inside staff. By doing this we will be able to save to [sic] to the treasury of the province $12,000."[15]

Rhodes referred most of the applications for part-time or local work to the appropriate members of the legislature from his party. This was fine in theory but difficult, even dangerous, in practice when the representatives fell out, each one pushing to satisfy the ambitions of personal supporters. As the premier explained to one angry Conservative who assumed that the president of the local Conservative association would automatically receive a government job, "It has been the policy of the government without exception to accept the judgment of its supporters as expressed through their chosen representatives. . . . Unfortunately there has not been agreement on their part upon this subject which makes it extremely difficult, if not impossible, for the government to act."[16] Letters from personal friends, or at least old political comrades, brought special pain. "Your father was always a personal friend of mine and I always had a warm feeling for him from my earliest childhood days and I regret exceedingly to learn of his death. . . . You will appreciate [that] . . . we are in receipt of a great many applications for positions in the public service, many more applications than could possibly be met."[17]

The pressures from the rank and file were implacable and quite often uncomprehending. "I am writing you to see if there is any possible chance of your giving me some kind of permanent position this year. There are seven Tory votes in my family, and we have always been good Tories, not people who have turned their coats at every election like some of our Torys in this town whenever they wanted a job. And it is pretty hard on a young fellow to be supporting a government that can't do anything for him."[18] In a province with more than its share of unemployed and poor residents, Rhodes received dozens of letters from people wanting help to tide them over. "I am a poor widow of ninety years of age. I am writing to ask you if you would be kind enough to send me a nice little check to last me through the long, cold winter. I have supported your government in the past."[19]

Then, as always, part-time road work made the difference between a winter of discomfort and one of marginal comfort. Intense lobbying therefore surrounded the hunt for jobs as gravel-haulers, maintenance workers, truckers, snow-plow operators. "I now sit down to write to drop you a line to congratulate you on your new seats," explained a Conservative in great need of a job. "Hoping you will make some changes for us as we got nothing before. As I would like to have some share in the work. I would like to have a job looking after the gravel pit or the road plow. There is a Liberal in here now and he just hires who he likes." And, of course, the premier heard from Conservative clients who threatened to desert their local patrons if the party did not deliver. From Dartmouth came a typical letter nearly a year after the election: "As this is 5 June, 1926, I've written your government asking for work and got no satisfaction. This is the last letter I intend writing. Now there are six voters in my home. We all worked and voted for the Conservatives at the last election . . . but I didn't work for thanks. I want something for my husband, and if I don't hear of anything from you by the end of next week, I intend to work and vote for some other party that will give us work."[20]

The government possessed enormous patronage powers in the period before a civil service commission was established. A sampling of the jobs requested of Rhodes gives a sense of the types available: liquor inspector, inspector of rural telephones, game warden, jail-keeper, sheriff, superintendant of education, mines superintendent, registrar, inspector of schools, secretary, inspector of automobiles, board of vendor commissioners, liquor commission, chairman of the highway board, stenographer, stipendary magistrate, provincial police force, compensation board, board of censors, forest ranger. In addition, each constituency or county organization in a major city provided the prerequisite "list" of firms whose political inclinations made them fit recipients of government contracts. These lists contained hundreds of firms providing products and services of every imaginable kind, a small fraction of which included: architects, asbestos, auto springs, bicycles, leather belts, blinds, blacksmiths, boots, bricks, buoys, cameras, carpets, chains, clocks, coal, cutlery, draperies, glasses, fruit, furs, grain, gravel, ice, ink, keys, locks, lumber, mattresses, milk, musical instruments, oil, paint, pianos, potatoes, rags, rugs, sand, taxis, tents, typewriters.[21]

Rhodes' Conservatives, among other affronts to their partisanship, had to reckon with the massive Liberal majority in the upper house, the legislative council. Upon taking office, the Conservatives found only one of their own in the council. During forty-three years of governing, the Liberal party had used the council the way federal governments used the Senate — as a comfortable reward for political services rendered. From 1896 to 1925, twenty-one of the Liberals' thirty-three appointees had contested federal or provincial elections. "The remaining twelve appointees had performed yeoman service for the party on a lesser scale."[22] The Conservatives tried to pension off existing Liberal councillors and appointed two of their own, but still they found their legislative initiatives blocked, including two bills to abolish the council. In fury and frustration, the Conservatives taunted Liberal councillors, by repeating the pledges many of them had once made to vote for the council's abolition. After a protracted struggle, the Rhodes government seized upon a favourable ruling from the judicial committee of the Privy Council and abolished the upper house.[23]

The council had especially irritated Rhodes' Conservatives by refusing twice to pass the Tenure of Office Bill, a measure to convert the tenure of every office in the provincial government to pleasure. Whatever the cooked-up defences for the bill, a government spokesman let slip the underlying rationale: "Every official of the late government seemed to think it natural that Nova Scotia would never have anything else but a Liberal government. . . . There were officials who got the happy idea that they could go on as they liked and certain of these we deem necessary to discipline." Blocked by the council, the Rhodes government did amend some specific statutes in 1928 to remove certain officials. The mass firing at Christmas, 1928, was called the "grand slaughter of the innocents" by the slaughtered and their friends. The Liberals, upon later returning to office, charged that the Conservatives had dismissed six hundred and one employees; the Conservatives countercharged that the Liberals had dismissed five hundred.[24]

The victory of the federal Conservatives in 1930 compounded the already complicated patronage problems being experienced by the Rhodes Conservatives. The local Conservative organizations were then besieged by job-seekers who saw two treasure troves, and the insistence with which they pressed their demands, made more acute by the world-wide Depression, produced conflicts, rivalries and confusion. As usual, Antigonish clearly illustrated the problems. There, the unsuccessful provincial Conservative candidate, J.F. MacLellan, took out this adver-tisement in *The Antigonish Casket*:

> "NOTICE: To the Conservative Committees — Mr. Rice, Canso, has the federal patronage in Antigonish and Guysboro County. Mr. Rice has appointed me to look after the patronage in Antigonish County. I request the Conservative committees in each district of the county to send me their recommendations for all appointments in their dis-trict, such as old age pensions, mothers' allowances, changes in offi-cials, road foremen, or any recommendations that are to be made. If the applicant applies through any other source it will be referred back to the local committee."

At the Conservatives' annual meeting in Halifax in 1931, members complained that "one group had apportioned all the available patron-age according to their own preference or judgment without regard to what others might think." A former president charged that party mem-bers had been "double-crossed or subjected to wire-pulling and treach-ery in the ranks of our own executive."[25]

Wracked by internal squabbles, their popularity eroded by the ravages of the Depression, the Conservatives searched desperately for ways of heading off the looming defeat. They gerrymandered the elec-toral map. They passed the *Electoral Franchise Act* of 1931, a bill with the superficially innocent intent of basing provincial voting lists on municipal ones. These lists would then be reviewed for accuracy by registrars appointed by returning officers. Since the governing party named all the returning officers, it was soon apparent what the Con-servatives had in mind. The lists were rigged, then posted in places where only the most resolute could find them. Sometimes they disap-peared altogether:

> "In an apparent effort to prevent Liberals from discovering that their names had not been included, the lists were posted after dark, often in unusual places, the location of which the registrars refused to reveal. In Kings County, *The Halifax Chronicle* reported that the lists for one area were posted on a dyke where the people would have to wade ankle-deep in mud to read them. There were also other reports of lists posted on the top of telephone poles or covered with

dark varnish. The most common complaint was that they tended to disappear altogether. Even when the lists were accessible, it was still not easy for a voter to check his name since they [sic] were not arranged in alphabetical order."[26]

The Chronicle, a Liberal paper, called the Franchise Bill "Nova Scotia's disgrace," a "Frankenstein," "enough to make Howe, the great emancipator, turn in his grave." Alerted to the trickery, the Liberals fought back. They won a court order giving them access to preliminary lists and authorizing the appointment of more than one registrar per district. Liberals shadowed the registrars who posted the lists, copying the names with the aid of a flashlight, and sending letters to known supporters warning them to ensure that the lists included their names.[27] The *Electoral Franchise Act* completely boomeranged. It mobilized the Liberals and discredited the Conservatives, not just for the approaching election. "In the years to follow, the Conservative party would be associated in the minds of many Nova Scotians with bitter memories of the Depression, an unusually flagrant partisanship in dispensing patronage, and a blatant attempt to 'rig' an election."[28]

The Conservatives were banished to Opposition in 1933 for yet another long spell — twenty-three years until rescued by Robert Stanfield. The malodorous Conservative hijinks of their dying years seemed to call for a response, and the Liberals delivered one longer on form than substance: the *Civil Service Act* of 1935. This Act, which purported to remove partisan considerations from the bulk of full-time appointments, contained as many loopholes as restrictions. Examinations, for example, would be held only when "practical and necessary." The commissioners were part-time, poorly paid, and often unskilled labourers. Twelve years after its enactment, the eminent political scientist R. MacGregor Dawson studied the result and concluded: "So long as the *Civil Service Act* is applied and interpreted as it is today, there is no reason to expect anything but an outburst of dismissals following a change of government."[29]

The Act, however, did allow some men of merit to make a lifelong career in the public service. Stanfield, for example, insists that when he became premier, he found a civil service of surprisingly high quality for a small province.[30] Quality may have arrived in spite of the *Civil Service Act*, rather than from it, because patronage during the more than two decades of Liberal rule carried on much as before. The part-time jobs and many of the full-time ones went to political friends. The highways budget continued to be used, in part, to influence political behaviour with crews especially busy before and during election campaigns. Government purchasing continued to be directed to firms

approved by the party and kickbacks to the party were an expected
recompense for receiving government business. Politics enveloped the
entire liquor trade and treating remained a common (although declining) feature of elections. The restless, ceaseless demand for favours and
places continued from the Liberal grassroots in a province where political discretion, rather than bureaucratic norms, largely dictated how
many positions would be available and how public funds would be
spent.

Competition for places and public money was further characterized by rivalry between the mainland and Cape Breton—a rivalry that
Premier Angus L. Macdonald understood well. It was the constant
belief of mainlanders that the provincial economy was being drained
by the unruly Highland Scots, with their troubled industrial base and
ceaseless claims upon the public purse. It was the equally constant belief
of the Cape Bretoners that too much government money was being
lavished on the mainland. As a Cape Bretoner, the premier was kept
awash in the current of demands from across the Straight of Canso.
Perhaps patronage was always a half-shade more congenial to Cape
Bretoners, whose clannish traditions and relatively greater economic
deprivation schooled them for the patron-client system.[31] In any case,
whatever the justice of their mutual distrust, islanders and mainlanders
agreed on patronage as an essential of life, and they both poured on
the pressure.

The same attitudes towards patronage were still firm when the
Conservative party under Robert Stanfield ousted the Liberals in 1956.
There were the same calls for mass firings that always attended a change
of government in Nova Scotia, the same insistence on re-allocating the
highways budget, the same demands for places and contracts. The
claims on the Stanfield government bore especially hard on a party
whose members were more accustomed to Opposition than to power.
But Stanfield was prepared for the pressures and reacted differently
than Rhodes. Unlike his Conservative predecessor in the 1920s, Premier Stanfield circumscribed certain of the government's patronage
powers, and because of his undoubted personal integrity he had the
authority to make his views stick despite internal party grumbling.[32]
The Standfield governments were largely untouched by corruption not
because he abolished patronage, but because he reined it in.

Stanfield respected the jurisdiction of the civil service commission,
and he forbade kickbacks, although Nova Scotia companies in receipt
of government contracts understood that contributions to the Conservative party were probably a prerequisite for remaining on the lists
of approved government suppliers. Six months after winning the election, Stanfield bluntly told the annual party meeting, "I do not intend

to allow the claims of any individual seeking reward to jeopardize the future of the Conservative government or the Conservative party of Nova Scotia." Shortly thereafter, Premier Stanfield delivered the keynote speech at the party's national leadership convention and further outlined his views: "Some may say to me, 'The important thing is to keep the Conservatives happy, so that we will have an energetic party when the next election comes.' Some will say, 'Don't forget friends.' Now, let's face the future frankly. If you want to consider this subject in terms of party advantage only, there are not enough Conservatives in Nova Scotia to elect a Conservative government. We will be re-elected next time with the support of the independent voter. . . Without the support of these people, we are lost. We will not retain that support if we are vindictive or self-seeking."

Wholesale dismissals, as in 1925 and 1933, did not happen, to the consternation of many Conservatives. Even the government's purchasing agent, Eric Lewis, whom many Conservatives considered an unregenerate Grit, was interviewed by Stanfield and allowed to keep his post. Stanfield also abolished the notorious "bottle exchange" whereby beer drinkers could return their empties only to agents appointed by the party in power — a time-honoured reward for party hacks — rather than to government beer stores. These agents were expected to kick back a percentage of their profits to their political friends. Having campaigned against the "bottle exchange," Stanfield made good on his promise.

Stanfied curbed patronage, but he manifestly did not eliminate it. Nor did he even try. He was too intelligent, too aware of the mores of Nova Scotia's political culture to tempt fate. Those people in positions dealing with confidential government information and those who had taken a partisan role in the campaign were changed. So were many order-in-council appointees. Firms acceptable to the party wound up on approved lists for tendering on government contracts. The lists assumed special importance, since contracts were often not publicly advertised; instead, the government invited listed firms to tender. By these means, the government could insist it respected the principle of awarding contracts to the lowest bidder, secure in the knowledge that the vast majority of the firms were favourable to the Conservative cause. The government fired more than a thousand Liberal supporters from part-time highway jobs and replaced them with Conservative supporters. Stanfield, like other successful Nova Scotia premiers, understood the importance of roads. In the 1956 campaign, the incumbent Liberals had promised a $100 million road construction program. Stanfield had topped that by promising "hard-surfacing without delay all roads in the province that are now ready or near-ready for paving," plus an improvement in secondary roads.

Peter Aucoin nicely summed up Stanfield's patronage record: "Once he had succeeded in wresting the reins of power from the Liberals, he had attained the means of strengthening the position of his party through the spoils of government, something his Conservative predecessors had difficulty doing. . . . Everything about him permitted him to project an image of integrity and honesty devoid of any suspicion of mishandling the public trust. While not neglecting the interests of the Conservative party or its followers, he was able to escape criticism for abuse of patronage, a phenomenon that attests to his successful and seemingly fair allocation of public rewards."

The return of the Liberals to power in 1970 under Gerald Regan brought the familiar round of firings in the highways crews, changes in the lists of approved suppliers, selection arrangements for contractors and lawyers, and the replacement of Conservatives on boards, agencies and commissions. Occasionally, a brief flurry of protest accompanied these manifestations of patronage. Truckers in different parts of the province threatened to go on strike because so much work was transferred from Conservatives to Liberals. The president of the Pictou County Truckers' Association asked plaintively, "Why on election day should your family's survival depend on what happened in the voting booth?" He continued: "At election time, you wouldn't believe the tension in the village. It puts neighbour against neighbour, and relative against relative. Four years of income totally depends on how you vote."[33] These feeble contrapuntal notes were soon eclipsed in a province where the rush for spoils drowned out isolated expressions of dissent.

Fund-raising, especially in the television age, always imposed heavy burdens on a party in so small a province, since the costs of modern communications easily overwhelmed the savings from reduced treating and bribery. Party members within the province offered their share; wealthy party members living elsewhere gave at fund-raising dinners in Toronto. But more was needed, and happily for the historical record a Royal Canadian Mounted Police investigation laid bare a source. Less satisfactorily, the investigation and subsequent spectacular trial reinforced the scarcely sustainable, but nonetheless legally compelling, notion that political leaders remained in saintly ignorance of the illegal practices of their subalterns. John A. Macdonald, in organizing his constituency elections, had blazed the trail for all who followed, including provincial leaders.

In the autumn of 1978, the RCMP began investigating tollgating of liquor companies in some provinces. Elsewhere, the investigations fizzled for lack of documentary evidence, but in Nova Scotia the RCMP uncovered a bonanza of documents in a raid on the records of the Liberal party's finance committee, members of which had meticulously —if foolishly, as things turned out—recorded nearly a decade of illegal transactions. The seeds of trouble had been sown in 1968, two years before the Liberals took power, when the Nova Scotia Liberal Association established a finance committee to raise money. Senator Irvine Barrow, a stalwart in Liberal circles, chaired the committee; other members included Charles MacFadden and James Simpson. The finance committee opened two bank accounts and kept detailed records of deposits and withdrawals. One account was disingenuously called Cambridge Investments. Between December 1970 and May 1979, nearly $3.8 million passed through the accounts, siphoned from liquor companies which kicked back a fixed percentage of sales to the Liberal party as coin for their products' display in government liquor stores.

The RCMP laid charges against Barrow, MacFadden and Simpson for conspiring together and with various officials of the government and "with another person or persons unknown" to accept "rewards, advantages or benefits as consideration for co-operation, assistance, and exercise of influence" contrary to the *Criminal Code*.[34] During the trial, liquor company executives testified that their companies had paid money for years to the party in power in exchange for the listing of products at Nova Scotia liquor-commission outlets. Their testimoney confirmed that these practices had flourished under Conservative and Liberal governments; the Liberals had simply been unlucky enough to get caught. Fifty cents a case was the normal payment to the party in power. Executives of Jordan Wine, for example, testified that the company increased payments after Simpson warned that the party did not consider Jordan to be a "member of the club." Company executives insisted that their products might be blacklisted without such kickbacks. The president of Schenley told the court his company had been nicked for more than $45,000 between 1971 and 1978; he considered these payments a guarantee that Schenley could continue doing business in Nova Scotia. The company made additional payments during election campaigns.

A similar kickback scheme touched other industries. An executive from Norman Wade, a construction company, testified that he had been referred to Simpson when he inquired why his company had not received any government work. The Liberal bagman informed the executive that Norman Wade needed to show good faith. The company duly produced a $1,000 cheque and thereafter paid the governing party three percent on volume of sales. Testimony from representatives of Acres Consulting Services, intimately involved in the Canso Superport project, revealed that the company had been required to pay three to five percent of the value of all contracts received to the Liberal party. The company, in fact, kicked back four percent.

Simpson pleaded guilty four days before the preliminary inquiry and received a $75,000 fine. MacFadden and Barrow both stood trial and were found guilty. MacFadden decided not to appeal and was fined $25,000; Barrow lost his appeal before the Supreme Court of Nova Scotia, then launched a further appeal to the Supreme Court of Canada. He was granted a new trial because the trial judge had questioned potential jury members out of earshot of Barrow and his lawyer.

The trial revealed blatant corruption—patronage that spilled into illegality—of a kind many observers of Nova Scotia politics had long suspected but never publicly documented. True, a dissident charged in 1980 that kickbacks had been a way of life during his years as a Liberal MLA. Walton Cook described kickbacks involving highway contractors, gravel-haulers, suppliers at provincial hospitals, undertakers, gasoline station operators.[35] But the Barrow-MacFadden-Simpson trial so thoroughly exposed the corrupt underbelly of Nova Scotia politics that no one could deny its existence. No one, that is, but party leaders who could insist, as Premier Regan did at the influence-peddling trial, that systematic tollgating, kickbacks and other illegal fund-raising methods exceeded instructions and offended all sense of political propriety. Regan later admitted that he had received $142,000 during his years as party leader from a trust fund established with party money, $6,000 a year as Opposition leader, $10,000 a year as premier.

Conservative Premier John Buchanan's arrival in office changed nothing. As Don Cameron and Pat Hunt discovered, the grassroots still demanded their share. When the opposition Liberals caught the Conservatives red-handed with letters authorizing the hiring of only Conservatives in Liberal ridings, Buchanan's transport minister shrugged: "There is nothing new about this. It's been the system for years." In John Buchanan, Nova Scotia observed the classic parish-pump politician, most at ease discussing the fine points of political manoeuvering, arranging for the satisfaction of every local desire, administering patronage and injecting partisanship into the most routine matters. The more exacting and tiresome matters of policy deliberation bored him; partisan politics animated his spirits, and patronage helped to sustain his government and unify his party. The opportunities for patronage had been whittled back in Nova Scotia over the years, but in the Buchanan government, it seemed the intensity of interest on the part of patron and the client alike had not declined a whit.

CHAPTER 9

NEW BRUNSWICK

"Patronage is a way of life in New Brunswick. I
refuse to be hypocritical about something which has
been around for a hundred years and in some form or
another will be around for another hundred."
Liberal leader Frank McKenna, 1987 campaign.

THE DIPLOMAT MOTEL, hard by the Saint John River on the outskirts
of Fredericton, boasts a swimming pool but nothing else of distinction.
There are better establishments at which to stay or eat in the toy-town
capital of New Brunswick, but for many years Conservative politicians
and aides favoured the Diplomat with their business. Only July 18,
1972, thirteen Conservative fund-raisers and ministers gathered at the
Diplomat for a meeting, the purpose of which later became the stuff
of differing accounts, intermittent amnesia, political controversy, legal
proceedings and a spectacular trial. Premier Richard Hatfield dropped
in for awhile, delivered a brief speech, then departed, little knowing
that almost eight years later he would appear on the witness stand to
testify, in part, about why he had attended, what he had said, and why
he had left so early. In the course of that testimony, Hatfield said it had
been terribly hot that July day and he wished to get "away early for
the weekend or for whatever. . . ." That seemed an odd explanation,
the day in question having been a Tuesday, but no one asked any more
questions, because when the judge inquired of the prosecuting attorney
whether he wished to cross-examine the premier, the attorney replied,
"With regret, My Lord, we have no questions to ask of this witness."[1]
He did not elaborate.

One member of the party's finance committee, Francis Atkinson
of Fredericton, took notes at the meeting. They recorded various fund–

raisers telling ministers about the problems of organizing effective money-raising efforts, the need for better communications between fund-raisers and ministers, and, in particular, the requirement for government purchases to be held up until members of the finance committee could chase down the recipients of contracts for contributions to the Conservative party. Atkinson's notes summarized one intervention by Lawrence Machum, the finance committee chairman from Saint John, "We can't find out what is going on in purchasing until read in newspapers, must have access first, Minister should hold up until arrangements made."

Atkinson, a lawyer, had a distinguished Conservative pedigree. He lived on an eleven-acre estate in Fredericton where his father, Ewart, had been the leading Conservative bagman, organizer and MLA for York County. All his life, Francis Atkinson later testified, meticulous note-taking and record-keeping figured prominently in his daily routine. He even jotted things down before going to bed, or upon awakening in the middle of the night. So when the Royal Canadian Mounted Police swooped into his home and office looking for information about party fund-raising tactics, they hit pay dirt. In Atkinson's files lay memoranda, letters, notes, bank accounts, cheques, telephone messages — in short, the whole documentary record of what is commonly known as tollgating: the return to the party in power of a fixed percentage of contracts awarded by the government.[2]

There was also evidence—and this formed the basis for Atkinson's subsequent conviction—that the Conservative party had planted one of its own in the department of public works, paid part of the employee's salary, and in return received advance information about the awarding of government contracts to assist the finance committee in squeezing money from the contractors. Was Francis Atkinson acting alone? Lawrence Machum, the finance committee chairman, had charges against him thrown out at the stage of preliminary inquiry. The Conservative plant in the department of public works (and later in supply and services) — Allan Woodworth, or "Chowder" to his friends — never faced a trial. Only Francis Atkinson went to trial and was found guilty of corruption.

Richard Hatfield established the finance committee, chaired by Machum and on which Atkinson represented Fredericton. From the beginning, the members of the committee expressed frustration, to themselves and to ministers, about inadequate information flowing to them from the government. They also complained that some contractors grumbled about having already been approached by ministers for money. From this confusion and lack of information sprang the scheme to place Chowder Woodworth as a "buyer trainee" inside the department of public works. Woodworth, as he freely conceded, learned little and did less for the taxpayers of New Brunswick. He never bought anything for the department, never advised on purchases, just funnelled information to the Conservative finance committee. Judge Paul Barry interjected at one point, "You must have had a hard time putting in your day." Woodworth replied, "I did sometimes. It was a long day." Yet for fourteen months, from December 1971 to January 1973, he remained at his station, receiving $616 a month in civil service salary and $384 a month from the Conservative party, until the Opposition got wind of his existence in the department and raised a stink about it in the legislature, at which point the Conservatives withdrew Woodworth.

On the eve of Woodworth's employment, Francis Atkinson wrote Premier Hatfield that the "recommendation of your Finance Committee on the appointment of a Co-ordinator in Purchasing has been finally carried out and this should solve a lot of our problems." Atkinson marked the letter "Personal and Confidential," but at trial Hatfield denied ever having received it. He also said he must have corresponded with Machum and Atkinson, "but I don't exactly remember correspondence with anyone in particular." Asked whether he could remember receiving the original of Atkinson's "Personal and Confidential" letter, Hatfield replied, "No, I do not." He said he was unaware that the deputy minister in his office, Conservative strategist Lowell Murray (later a national Conservative campaign chairman, senator and minister of state for federal-provincial relations in the Mulroney government) was being paid between fifteen and thirty thousand a year by the Conservative party. Shown a typed memorandum purportedly summarizing a 1971 meeting of the Greater Fredericton Progressive Conservative Association at which Hatfield was recorded as saying he had told the chairman of the liquor commission to provide suppliers' lists to the finance committee, Hatfield testified, "I can assure you that that is not an account of what I said. . . . A lot of statements in there I did not make. . . . I am certainly not responsible for some of the comments made there attributed to me. I find them offensive." As for the meeting at the Diplomat Hotel, bringing the ministers and fund-raisers together, Hatfield said, "I for one only stayed a short time. I had met all the people who were working for the party who said they hadn't met the ministers . . . I recall it as sort of a pep talk, if you will, and then I left. . . . I really didn't attach any significance or importance to the meeting as such. It was one of those things that in politics you have to do."

The committee Hatfield established was a standard appendage for political parties in the decades before elections were partially funded by the public and tax-deductible political contributions. In poorer provinces, leaders or their agents could try to raise money in Toronto or Montreal at fundraising dinners, or appeal to sister parties elsewhere for help. But they inevitably had to look within their own provinces for the bulk of the funds to run their party, and that search inevitably drove fundraisers and ministers to scrutinize lists of those doing business with the government. By general agreement, everything revealed in the Atkinson trial, except perhaps the planting of a party agent in the civil service, had been bread and butter to all previous New Brunswick governments, including that of Hatfield's predecessor, Liberal Premier Louis Robichaud. The Liberal system undoubtedly differed at the margin from the Conservative one; in essence, they were the same. Anyone doing business with the government was fair game for contributions based on a formula agreed upon mutually or imposed by the party. The money defrayed the normal expenses of running a party and organizing an election campaign; but in some cases it also topped up the salaries of politicians, tided them over financial difficulties, provided other sorts of benefits, or simply lined their pockets.

Hatfield himself admitted receiving money from the party after becoming leader, although in 1980 he paid back $15,000. (In Nova Scotia, Premier Gerald Regan admitted to having received $174,000 from a trust fund during his years as Liberal leader.) According to Chowder Woodworth, "quite a few of them [ministers and MLAs] had received assistance," including Jean-Maurice Simard, Lawrence Garvie and John Baxter. Joseph McGuigan, minister of education from 1970 to 1974 and later the recipient of a patronage job as registrar-general of vital statistics, admitted he received one payment while a minister "to tide one over a short difficult period financially." He also said that after the 1974 election, the party paid the costs of a southern holiday for his campaign manager.

At the core of Conservative tollgating lay a list of companies doing business with the government. This list was kept and updated in Saint John under the supervision of Lawrence Machum, who corresponded frequently with Francis Atkinson in Fredericton. Other regional bagmen in, say, Moncton also sent in information. Each fall, when the Conservative fund-raisers made their rounds, they filled out a standard form about the company, its government contracts and level of contribution. As soon as the company received a piece of government business — or indeed even before — it was contacted by a member of the finance committee to negotiate the contribution. Often the scale of the contribution was known in advance, since future percentages were based on established practice. Thus, Atkinson could write Wood

Motors in 1971 with information on the percentages "on all government and related business:

Leasing—party donation $5.00 per month per vehicle

Buses—To be quoted at list price less 7%; party donation 5%

Trucks—To be quoted at list price less 7%; party donation 5%

Cars—To be quoted at list price less 7%; party donation 5%."

Another memo, this one to Brunswick Office Equipment, set forth
a different set of percentages: desks and other office furniture 2%;
office machines and equipment 10%; all other supplies 8%. Companies
were made aware that in framing their bids, provision should be made
for a contribution to the party. In a memo regarding four companies
bidding for work at the New Brunswick Electric Power Commission,
Atkinson wrote: "It must be completely understood that all four parties
above named allow 2% when making their tenders; otherwise, the
system will collapse." The finance committee also contacted out-of-
province firms doing work in New Brunswick. In a letter to the president of Thomas Bonna Co. of Montreal, Atkinson politely introduced
himself as a member of the finance committee, then suggested that "I
believe there is additional business available to your company in New
Brunswick. . . . It would be appreciated if you would advise when you
will next be in New Brunswick so that a meeting can be arranged."

It can be plausibly presumed, these sorts of practices having gone
on for years, that ministers were well aware of the essence of the fund-
raising system, if not of every detail. Indeed, Atkinson's notes of the
meeting at the Diplomat Hotel confirm that its purpose was precisely
to inform ministers of what was going on and to suggest improvements
in co-ordination between them and the members of the finance committee. And yet on the witness stand at the Atkinson trial, a parade of
ministers insisted either that the meeting was merely a social occasion
or that they could not remember much about it. One minister, Carl
Mooers, failed so frequently to recall facts that Judge Barry blurted
out, "Your evidence is incredible, just incredible." Judge Barry became
sufficiently frustrated by Mooers' answers that he recommended the
justice department investigate laying perjury charges. As for Machum
and James McMurray, another member of the committee, Judge Barry
concluded, "I am satisfied that both Machum and McMurray knew
much more than they told the court." Barry, it should be noted, had
more than a passing knowledge of politics in New Brunswick. He had
been a Liberal fund-raiser before being elevated to the bench.

Judge Barry also could not understand why others had not been
charged. "There can be little or no doubt but that several members of
the government were fully aware of the scheme, or should have been,
in view of the attendance of members of the cabinet at the so-called

Diplomat meeting," Judge Barry wrote. "There can be little or no doubt but that the accused would have found it impossible to arrange the hiring of Woodworth without active or passive co-operation of some cabinet members. . . . I stated several times during this trial that I could not understand why only the accused was being tried. I have not received any explanation." He wrote later in his judgment, "Many others were necessarily involved in the scheme and the payment of the money to Woodworth. . . . *Prima facie* at least, I can see little or no difference between the conduct of the accused and many others." The judge summed up his thoughts, "The defence appeared to endeavour to establish that if the accused was corrupt, so were many others. The defence succeeded to a substantial degree but that does not excuse the accused."[3]

After finding Atkinson guilty, Barry delayed sentencing for three days to ponder the prosecution's demand for the maximum two years in prison for Atkinson. Upon returning to court, however, he stunned everyone. He said he would consider giving Atkinson an absolute discharge if he would co-operate with the RCMP in further investigations of others Barry presumed were involved in the fund–raising scheme. The offer also required the Crown, that is the department of justice, to grant Atkinson immunity from prosecution on all other outstanding charges. The Crown prosecutor, after conferring with the provincial justice minister, declined the offer, presumably because the last thing the Hatfield government wanted was further investigations. His offer rebuffed by the Crown, Judge Barry then gave Atkinson an absolute discharge anyway. And later, the government dropped further prosecutions of Atkinson.

The Conservative party had found its scapegoat and emerged remarkably unscathed from whole sordid affair. In 1978, after a series of stormy sessions of the legislature in which the Opposition attacked the Conservatives' fund-raising methods, the Hatfield government introduced the *Political Process Financing Act*, an impressive piece of legislation providing for spending limits on contributions and election spending, and partial public funding for political parties. It was, at the time, among the most advanced election-financing legislation in Canada, and it made the methods of the Conservative finance committee irrelevant. But the Atkinson affair served a long-term political purpose by exposing the corruption in New Brunswick politics—similar to that found in some other Canadian provinces. It also contributed, however marginally, to a sense of uneasiness about Premier Richard Hatfield and his party, a sense that grew as the years went on and culminated in Hatfield's Gotterdammerung of 1987, when the Liberals under Premier Frank McKenna won all 58 seats in the New Brunswick legislature. On election night 1987, the voters of New Brunswick gave Francis Atkinson his revenge.

The fund-raising tactics revealed in the trial represented only one of many toxins from patronage that had seeped into the political groundwater of New Brunswick. Although Liberals and Conservatives might differ, perhaps strongly, over this or that particular policy, they shared the same broad perspectives on economic and political development. As the leading academic student of New Brunswick politics concluded, "Politics at the provincial level is largely a battle of the ins versus the outs for patronage plums."[4] The plums came in all sizes, and even the smallest was desirable in an economically disadvantaged province, where a little bit of government money made a lot of the difference between a hard winter and a forbidding one. So, too, the seasonal nature of commercial fishing and forestry made supplicants exceedingly eager for a bit of work in the off-season.

Back in the 1920s, the full-time provincial civil service consisted of seven hundred employees, about eighty percent of whom were dismissed when the Liberals replaced the Conservatives. More valuable still as patronage opportunities were the legions of "casual," or part-time, employees: revisers, justices of the peace, coroners, constables, registrars, schoolbook vendors, game wardens, road supervisors.[5] In the early 1970s there were as many casual employees of the provincial government hired at the discretion of the party in power as there were full-time civil servants. Even in 1987, when Frank McKenna became premier, the province employed fourteen thousand people on a casual basis.

These jobs had always been a treasure trove of patronage, although for political patrons their dispensation involved the usual headaches. Early in the century politicians created committees, with party representatives from across the constituency, to handle the vexing subtleties of patronage. In Saint John, with its large Irish-Catholic population and a municipal ward system, politicians frequently needed more than one patronage committee.[6] As one prominent Saint John politician wrote to the chairman of his patronage committee in 1912, "I am afraid from what I hear that there is a good deal of trouble in regard to the patronage committee. I am told that several of the members will not attend the meetings and that the committee is divided up into cliques who help each other to carry their men, irrespective of what is right and that trouble is being created with those who think they are not being treated properly."[7] Until Hatfield changed the system, New Brunswick elections featured multi-member constituencies which naturally required the MLAs to co-ordinate their patronage activities. Gordon Fairweather, a long-time federal MP who began in provincial politics, remembers that in his first election he shared a constituency with two other Conservatives, a doctor and a farmer. As a lawyer, Fairweather allocated the judges of probate, sheriffs, and magistrates; the other MLAs took the rest. Fairweather also recalled that shrewd Conservative supporters could play off the MLAs against each other in their hunt for patronage.[8]

In Acadia, of course, pressure for jobs was especially intense because that French-speaking area of New Brunswick traditionally lagged far behind in economic opportunities. Similarly, Acadians were usually underrepresented in the provincial government.[9] Faced with a business community and civil service dominated by English-speaking New Brunswickers, Acadians looked to political parties, especially the Liberal party—at least until Richard Hatfield's tenure as Conservative leader — to deliver economic rewards they could not attain through other means. Hatfield's major legacy, to his party and the province, consisted in having made the Conservatives acceptable to Acadians, a task he achieved through legislative changes (notably making New Brunswick officially bilingual) and ensuring that Acadians received their fair share of government positions and spending.

Not by jobs alone could elections be won. Until recent decades elections featured the usual practices of treating, the going price being five dollars a vote or a pint of rum.[10] Politicians frequently grumbled about the cost, but they dared not arrive with empty pockets lest their opponents' pockets be full. Particularly crafty voters-for-hire sometimes hung around the polls until just before closing time, knowing that the parties' willingness to grease palms increased as the day progressed. As well, politicians freely used the porkbarrel to influence voters. That kind of spending certainly did not distinguish New Brunswick from other provinces, and it still existed even to the dying years of the Hatfield government, when, for example, the Conservatives directed half of the ninety-four grants under the Small Industry Financial Assistance Program to nine Conservative ridings, six represented by Conservative ministers.

Before the age of television, profound parochialism characterized New Brunswick politics. Not only did Acadians and English-speakers seldom mix, but even within those two communities the concerns of a town, valley or small city more surely preoccupied the bulk of the citizenry than issues of province-wide, let alone national, importance. Politicians were frequently judged by what tangible public benefits they could secure for their constituents. The stakes electors held in those benefits engendered an intense interest in things political, but also a deep skepticism about politicians, especially the ones who were also the leading businessmen; all were perceived to be feathering their own nests or at least taking political decisions to favour their own economic interests. The electorate's dependence on politicians mirrored the province's economic structure wherein a handful of merchant families controlled the commanding heights.

Occasionally, political scandals involving gross patronage outraged the body politic. In 1912, Premier James Kidd Flemming (the father of Hugh John, a Conservative premier in the 1950s) was found to have condoned the payment of "bonuses" to the Conservative party by businessmen in receipt of timber leases. He also was accused of seeking a $100,000 kickback from railroad contractors building a line from Saint John to Quebec City. In the early days of World War I, the New Brunswick legislature, in a fit of patriotic fervour, decided to contribute forty thousand barrels of potatoes to the war effort.[11] Soon, leading Conservative politicians began receiving letters from the party faithful offering to supply the spuds. "I want to say that we do not let a Liberal supply one barrel. Want a chance to supply my share when it comes." The government added $75,000 to a similar amount it had already allocated for the potatoes, making the contract doubly enticing. Offers arrived from those willing to donate potatoes, or at least to supply them at cost. But the government opted instead to buy three-quarters of the potatoes from one B. Frank Smith, the most powerful Conservative in Carleton County. When some of the potatoes arrived rotten, the government had the scandal of the "Patriotic Potato Gift" on its hands.

These sorts of scandals — and the more routine ones involving minor kickbacks — temporarily soured New Brunswickers on the perpetrators, but left no lasting impression. Premier Flemming, for example, faced not disgrace after the timber affair but election to the House of Commons. Everybody knew about, and many participated in, the pervasive patronage of New Brunswick. In such a parochial place, traditions died hard. Families passed on their political loyalties from generation to generation, and the practices of fathers were assumed by their sons. Francis Atkinson never believed, for example, that he had done anything wrong, in part because he simply carried on the traditions and beliefs of his Conservative father, Ewart. Indeed, the entire political history of New Brunswick is littered with famous families involved in politics generation after generation.[12] The oligarchic structure of the province's politics closely resembled its economic structure: a small network of interlocking elites. And at the local level, generations of New Brunswickers implicitly accepted—and frequently overtly demanded — the traditional forms of patronage, either because they had known no other, or because they desperately needed the benefits.

When the first challenges to the *status quo* surfaced, in the form of unionized government employees, the custodians of the tradition rose up in alarm. In 1970, for example, when the Conservatives under Hatfield took office, they had to deal with the rights guaranteed to the Canadian Union of Public Employees (CUPE), which had made headway among permanent and even casual employees. These rights had been granted under Liberal Premier Louis Robichaud, but some Conservatives could not reconcile themselves to the new reality and demanded wholesale firings. After all, had Louis Robichaud's Liberals not wielded a sharp axe, firing 271 permanent civil servants in the first six months in office, and replacing all kinds of casual employees?[13] DeCosta Young, a Conservative MLA who championed the cause of local Conservatives infuriated by their inability to get jobs protected by CUPE, defended the traditional practices. "Doing away with the patronage system — where those who work for you are favoured by you when in power—wouldn't that be doing away with the democratic system?" he said.[14] Conservatives across New Brunswick, if not necessarily those championed by DeCosta, got their patronage eventually — through the expansion of government activities, or the change of personnel after the expiration of contracts for casual employees. But for awhile in the first years of the Conservative government, the grassroots smouldered with resentment.

So, too, the McKenna government immediately faced a firestorm from its own supporters, especially in rural areas, when the Liberals decided to honour a memorandum of understanding offering protection for casual employees similar to that in the collective agreement with full-time employees. But patronage for the party elites never changed. Partisans filled almost every board, agency and commission; lawyers, admen, and insurance agents with the proper political credentials got government work.

Despite the election-financing reforms of 1978 and the greater job security offered government employees, patronage remained a major force in New Brunswick politics until recently. Its strength had been somewhat attenuated, to be sure, by factors not unique to the province, such as better education, mass communications, bureaucratization, and urbanization.[15] Those factors would weigh in the patronage decisions of Premier Frank McKenna, who while promising to end the abuses of patronage was realistic or honest enough to recognize at the beginning of his successful election campaign that "patronage is a way of life in New Brunswick."

CHAPTER 10

QUEBEC

"It is all very well to have these young men in, but they
are mostly filled with ambition and eager to get along
to the extent that they cause us a great deal of trouble.
I prefer to have these older men who are quite satisfied
with things, provided that we allow them to enjoy the
patronage in their constituencies, and the honours and
prestige which go with being members of the legislature. They are not unduly ambitious, and so cause us
no great difficulty."
Senator "Chubby" Power, quoting Quebec's Premier
Louis-Alexandre Taschereau.

IN DECEMBER 1985, Robert Bourassa returned from ten years in political exile to resume the office of premier of Quebec, a wiser, more
reflective man, one who had come to terms with the changes that had
swept over Quebec society during the decade of government by Premier
René Lévesque and the Parti Québécois (PQ). Quebec remained, as it
had been before the PQ took office in 1976, part of Canada; but the
PQ, in addition to forcing Quebeckers to ask existential questions
about their society, systematically altered many of the political traditions of Quebec, including patronage. Whatever future generations
may conclude about the PQ's approach to sovereignty-association, language reform, constitutional negotiation or fiscal policies, the PQ did
fundamentally change historic practices of patronage in Quebec. Like
the United Farmers and Social Credit in Alberta and the Co-operative
Commonwealth Federation in Saskatchewan, the Parti Québécois considered itself to be something more than a political party: a movement
with a self-imbued mission. A secular messianism about independence
for Quebec, but also about changing traditional aspects of Quebec's
political culture, informed both the party leadership and the rank and
file. Nowhere was this secular messianism more palpably evident than
in the political career of Premier René Lévesque.

Lévesque, passionate on all subjects, reserved a special fury for
the political favouritism that had characterized fund-raising in Quebec

under the Union Nationale and the Liberals. As premier, he fairly spat out the words "slush funds" and "*chantage*" (blackmail), both of which he had condemned first as a journalist, then as a minister in Premier Jean Lesage's Liberal government. His party arrived in office after six years of allegations that patronage, nepotism and corruption had permeated the Liberal government of Premier Robert Bourassa. The cynicism and disillusionment of those years, more than a desire for Quebec independence, put the PQ in office. To Lévesque's own personal commitment to reform, then, was joined the idealism of PQ supporters, an idealism fired by visions not just of an independent Quebec, but of a thoroughly modern, technocratic state.

Not surprisingly, therefore, the PQ's first major reform overhauled Quebec's election-financing legislation. It eliminated corporate contributions, thus severing the link between corporate wealth and political performance woven through the political history of Quebec.[1] The Parti Québécois, comforted by its own sense of moral superiority, blithely assumed the bill would seriously handicap Liberal fund-raising. Instead, the Liberals soon emulated the PQ by attracting money from a multitude of individual contributors.

Nonetheless, Lévesque's initiative had important consequences. At a stroke, Quebec moved from the rear to the vanguard of Canadian provinces in eliminating an obvious invitation for political patronage. More generally, through the PQ's comportment in office — the lack of serious scandals, reforms in areas such as government purchasing, the proselytizing by Lévesque and his senior ministers — Quebeckers' tolerance for political patronage and Quebec politicians' willingness to dispense it underwent one of the most startling transformations in the history of Canada. True, the PQ built upon some changes made during the previous fifteen years in Quebec provincial politics. The emergence of new elites, the growth of mass communications, the enfeeblement of the Catholic Church, the burgeoning of bureaucratic norms and of state control over economic and social policies — these changes had been transforming Quebec society, including its political culture, for several decades before the PQ victory. But the PQ accelerated the move away from the old ideas about patronage; and by its legislation and performance, the PQ contributed to new attitudes and practices.

The PQ gave full voice to the feeble refrain of those Quebeckers who had been lamenting the sorry state of the province's political mores. A few social critics, nationalist groups, even a smattering of idealistic politicians, had decried the political practices of Quebec — the influence of money on politics, the manipulation of the civil service for political purposes, the steering of contracts to friends and, most obviously, the pervasiveness of electoral corruption. But these lonely voices cried out to an indifferent or hostile population. The criticisms counted only when they buttressed other arguments for keeping the state's hands off various aspects of Quebec society lest the incubus of patronage spread.[2]

English Canadians elsewhere, and many of those inside Quebec, frequently asserted, with varying degrees of diplomacy but unfailing sanctimony, that French Canadians were different: Their Latin blood, Catholic Church, feudal past — something — made French Canadians more receptive to patronage. English Canadians seldom ascribed to French Canadians the more righteous standards of morality and honesty they did ascribe to themselves. Such assertions represented cant at best, racism at worst. Certain distinctly French-Canadian factors did colour patronage in Quebec, but no one who seriously examined the political culture of some predominately English-speaking provinces could credibly insist that patronage in Quebec eclipsed that found elsewhere. Indeed, an academic named Pierre Trudeau captured English–Canadian hypocrisy when he wrote that French Canadians had never wanted democracy for themselves, but English Canadians had never wanted it for others.[3] Trudeau, whatever the justice of his rebuke of French Canadians, underlined how English governors had intervened to pervert election results before the province won responsible government, and how the English-speaking business elite in Quebec had manipulated Quebec politics. That elite sanctioned the prevailing political mores, indeed encouraged them, because those were the mores that allowed the elite's economic power to remain intact.

French Canadians' inability to penetrate the business world, except as tokens, contributed materially to the pervasiveness of patronage. LaFontaine, after all, had turned French Canadians from the dreams of the *patriotes* by the promise of patronage. He had delivered political patronage for the French-Canadian bourgeoisie, the men of the liberal professions who had been diverted from commerce by the grip of the English and the teachings of the Catholic Church, and had come to depend on political patronage to enhance their status and income. If English Canadians occupied the commanding heights of the economy, then French Canadians could use their demographic weight to control the provincial government and their political clout to influence the federal. So patronage, no more prevalent a phenomenon in Quebec than, say, in the Maritime provinces, took on a special utility as a tool for French-speaking Quebeckers to advance their interests and for English-speaking Quebeckers to protect theirs.

Economic deprivation, to say nothing of poverty, added a further dimension. Not only was Quebec economically disadvantaged in comparison with Ontario—the only province, then as now, that even mar-

ginally impinged on the consciousness of Quebeckers—but a high birth
rate threw onto the labour market thousands who, facing discouraging
prospects at home, emigrated to the United States. How to slow down
or prevent this exodus dominated political debates in Quebec for decades after Confederation.[4] In such circumstances, using the patronage
of small jobs and big contracts to keep as many French Canadians as
possible in Quebec represented not just a political inducement but
almost a patriotic duty.

Nowhere did the feverish interest in things political that so struck
foreigners about nineteenth-century Canada manifest itself more evi-
dently than in Quebec. So much depended, at least for the members of
the French-Canadian bourgeoisie, upon the outcome of political
debates and elections that they poured themselves into politics with
abandon. In a predominately rural society, still heavily under the influence of the Catholic Church, politics became a fierce competition
between networks of political elites, with little mass involvement save
on election day. The social and economic conditions were ripe for
entrenched patron-client relationships within which politicians offered
state benefits either to individual clients or to whole communities in
exchange for their continued political support. Church teachings about
respect for those in authority contributed to shaping this culture. So
did one-party dominance — by the Conservative party in the twenty
years following Confederation, and by the Liberal party for the first
three decades of the twentieth century.

In the Quebec national assembly, legislators were valued for what
tangible benefits they could procure for their constituents. As a historian of the early years of Quebec politics has written: "In the assembly,
the member was above all the dispenser of 'patronage'."[5] That role,
certainly not unique to Quebec legislators, prevailed for decades. The
party belonged to them—and to their colleagues in Ottawa. The links
between federal and provincial parties, later to be severed more spectacularly in Quebec than anywhere else in Canada, remained a fixture
of political life. Quebec Conservatives benefited enormously from their
party's federal power and patronage after Confederation, just as they
suffered grievously from the federal Conservatives' secular sin of hanging Louis Riel.

Elections displayed the whole gamut of political chicanery, including bribery, intimidation, impersonation, and "telegraphing," the
sophisticated technique whereby hired workers substituted improperly
doctored ballots for blank ones.[6] Public works contracts provided jobs
during the campaign, the civil service more permanent employment.
Elections cost large amounts of money, even in the era before mass
pamphleteering, since so many voters demanded payment. Politicians

often complained of these costs, and Laurier once commented: "That public opinion does not exist is a fact apparent enough; that corruption pervades every tissue of our society is also apparent. The English population in that respect is hardly better than our own."[7] Banks and railway companies in particular looked for government favours and in return contributed money to individual members or parties.

Occasionally, a full-blown scandal temporarily inflamed public opinion. The Tanneries affair, which involved shady dealings by members of the ministry in an exchange of Montreal properties, startled even a tolerant public in 1875. But most of the key players in that affair remained in politics and advanced to higher positions in later years, as John A. Macdonald did after the Pacific Scandal. The lesson from the Tanneries affair appeared to be: Don't get caught.

The lesson certainly applied in the scandal of the Baie des Chaleurs Railway which engulfed and humbled the first Liberal premier and fiery nationalist, Honoré Mercier.[8] That railway executives and politicians moved in the same circles seemed obvious, since in the 1882 federal election, for example, five federal politicians from Quebec had interests in railways, including the minister of railways himself. At the height of his popularity in Quebec, Mercier learned of disquieting revelations emanating from a Senate committee. Charles Armstrong, a railway promoter, admitted under sharp questioning that he had paid $100,000 to Ernest Pacaud, a prominent Quebec Liberal and close associate of the premier's, and that this money had been used partly to pay off campaign debts and to underwrite a Mercier trip to Europe. A preliminary report from two of three royal commissioners — the one most favourable to Mercier fell ill — declared the transaction "fraudulent, against public order . . . an audacious exploitation of the provincial treasury." The commissioners added, "It is not proven that Mr. Mercier knew of the existence of the market between Armstrong and Pacaud." No matter. The lieutenant-governor, a political foe of the premier, dismissed Mercier and asked the Conservatives to form a government. That government promptly set about changing civil servants and investigating practices of the Mercier government.

The resulting revelations did Mercier in: payments to him and Pacaud for contracts, puffed-up prices for government purchases, letters of credit without sufficient funds. The obviously partisan nature of the investigations counted for little in the subsequent election: Mercier's troops were slaughtered. When Mercier returned to Quebec City, crowds gathered beneath his balcony shouting *"À bas les voleurs"* (Down with the thieves). The nationalists lost a hero (although one resuscitated later by sympathetic historians) and the Liberals a leader.

Quebeckers demonstrated that their own wide tolerance for patronage, and even political corruption, knew limits.

Mercier's humiliation seems slightly unfair in retrospect. He got caught, but the practices that led to his political undoing were not exclusive to him.

Throughout the nineteenth century, and well on into the twentieth, parties financed themselves in Quebec either by dipping directly into the province's treasury for political purposes, or by a sophisticated system of kickbacks, or "*ristournes*." The first forty years of Quebec politics were marked by an endless exchange of charges and counter-charges, each party accusing the other of having abused the public trust. Changes in government produced startling revelations against the previous government, yet nothing fundamentally altered the questionable political practices. Periodically, a well-publicized embarrassment galvanized a government into reform, especially in election-spending. But the pattern for these forty years remained constant: Each reform soon dissolved into the *status quo ante* because politicians, whatever their stripe, could not resist the conveniences of the old ways.

In 1875, for example, a new law required all candidates to make payments only through an authorized agent, who was obligated to report all expenses. An incorrect report produced a fine of five hundred dollars. This law was not only honoured in the breach, but an 1892 amendment eliminated the need for a detailed expense report. "Thus a return to unbridled corruption began," in the words of a royal commission report, "especially as the courts, in cases of election contestations, showed themselves indulgent."[9] An 1895 law, flowing in part from the reaction against the Baie des Chaleurs payoffs fixed limits on campaign spending and again required agents to supply detailed reports on election expenses. It was one of the most advanced pieces of legislation of its kind in the world, but it too dissolved through noncompliance and was subsequently amended to permit a return to standard procedures.

In 1897 the Liberals returned to office and remained there until 1936. Thus for another thirty-nine years the political culture of Quebec was defined by a host of seldom-challenged assumptions. The Liberal party's dominance rolled smoothly on, undisturbed by periodic revelations of gross misconduct. In one celebrated instance, the owner of *The Montreal Herald* hired a private detective to set up a dummy company and ask J.O. Mousseau, chairman of the private bills committee, to sponsor a bill granting privileges to the company in exchange for $1,500. The detective kept a record of the payment and recorded conversations with Mousseau on a hidden Dictograph. Not only did Mousseau accept the money, he freely described other members who could be similarly bought. After the story broke, the committee investigating the incident agreed that Mousseau had accepted the money. He resigned, but received immunity from prosecution. Nothing changed the system whereby individual members could propose bills for corporate interests, an open invitation to graft.[10]

One-party dominance encouraged the patronage system to flourish. The provincial Conservatives remained crippled by the reputation of their federal cousins, a reputation worsened by the conscription crisis of World War I. Anyone desiring favours from the government knew from which party they flowed. Never did the Liberal party consider updating the electoral map, which gave hugely disproportionate voting strength to rural regions because the party did so well in those ridings. The province's economic growth, predominantly in the large cities, provided new revenues for the government to plow back into the rural ridings through programs and patronage, thus sealing both the allegiance of those ridings and the government's own determination to defend the existing electoral map. From this disproportionate representation of the rural population arose a classic government defence of patronage—that it redistributed income for the benefit of the needy. And of course the rural ridings, with their economic deprivation and more stable social structure, encouraged the maintenance of the patron-client networks.

The civil service, as social reformers kept properly insisting, resembled an arm of the Liberal party. Quebec had created a civil service board as early as 1868 to set job requirements, minimum qualifications and entrance standards. The board, whose members were all political appointees, never seriously impeded the use of the civil service as an institution of ubiquitous patronage. Still, the Taschereau government abolished it in 1926, removing even the pretence that merit counted in the civil service. Despite the complaints of social reformers who worried about the likely spread of patronage, Liberal governments did expand the state's activities in such areas as dairy inspection, public hygiene, labour regulation, building inspection, forest-fire prevention, utilities regulation. Similarly, the government incorporated into the civil service a number of positions previously considered outside it, such as sheriffs and revenue collectors.[11] This enlargement of the civil service expanded the opportunities for rewarding party supporters.

Elections were rife with fraudulent tactics, and substantial efforts were made to buy the loyalty of individual voters through patronage or whole communities through porkbarrelling. The manipulation of voting lists figured prominently in each campaign. The Conservatives in 1896 had handed the task of preparing and modifying the lists in Montreal to a three-member board of revisers, two of whom were appointed by the government. This system was later extended to most of Quebec's largest cities. In the early 1930s, the Taschereau government tried to consolidate its position by abolishing the boards and handing the task entirely to provincially appointed personnel. L.P. Geoffrion, the chief returning officer, described in his report on the 1931 election what transpired. "The lists of electors," he wrote, "are not prepared as they should be . . . and thus on polling day, persons with all the required qualifications to be electors are deprived of the right to vote. . . . The legislator has never thought of charging anyone with the carrying out of the *Election Act*, particularly as regards the preparation of the lists; he left this to the interested parties, and, unfortunately, we are not in the heroic ages."[12]

Bribery and telegraphing also remained election fixtures. A *Le Devoir* article during the 1935 election described what it called a "poll on wheels" in which a fleet of ten taxis, each carrying six "telegraphers," visited various polling stations, there to vote illegally following the instructions of a "telegrapher-in-chief." *Le Devoir* also reported extensively after the election about instances of telegraphers overpowering the personnel in the polling stations and stuffing the boxes with fifty or sixy ballots.[13] The government in 1932 actually invited more electoral fraud by no longer making candidates responsible for the actions of their agents, refusing to annul elections if the candidates were found guilty of only small offences, and preventing anyone who worked in the polling station from providing information on the conduct of electors in the station. *Le Devoir*, the paper Bourassa founded, was the only beacon of independent journalism in Quebec; the other major papers were house organs for the established parties, their loyalty secured by printing contracts, government advertising and tradition.

The Conservatives screamed fraud after every election; the Liberal press denounced their complaints as slurs against the good name of Quebec. The Liberal party shrugged and, in 1931, passed the *Dillon Act*, a brazen manoeuvre conceived in arrogance and sanctioned by the Liberal majority. Convinced of widespread electoral fraud against them, sixty-three defeated Conservative candidates decided to contest the election results before the courts. Party leader Camillien Houde— no prince of political virtue, as his municipal career revealed—offered to supply personally the deposit of a thousand dollars per petition, an offer the courts upheld on appeal despite the government's objections. Undaunted by this ruling, the government pushed through the *Dillon Act*, retroactively requiring that all petitioners raise the deposit themselves. A chronicler of this chicanery has written, "As a result, the courts duly invalidated the petitions before them on procedural grounds, leaving no possibility—because of an existing four months' time limit and a rule forbidding the initiation of election contestations within eight days of the beginning and end of a legislative session—that they might be reinstated."[14] The Liberals perversely justified their action on the grounds of the good name of Quebec; it was not to be sullied by frivolous election contestations. For good measure, they added that the political turbulence caused by contested elections offered succor "to the communism that raises its head amongst us." Further amendments to the *Elections Act* in 1932 and 1936 expanded opportunities for electoral corruption.

A cozy, even incestuous, relationship between corporate executives and leading politicians continued throughout the Liberal period. The rules for exploitation of Quebec's natural resources, already sold for bargain-basement prices, were made even less onerous by the Taschereau government. In 1933, for example, the government began issuing timber-cutting rights in perpetuity, scrapping the system of annual renewals. No wonder the corporate-political relationship seemed so cozy. Senior ministers held directorships in prominent companies, and Premier Taschereau himself sat on the boards of North American Life, Barclay's Bank, Royal Trust, Sun Life Assurance, Title Guarantee and Trust Corporation, Royal Liverpool Insurance Group, Canadian Investment Funds, and Metropolitan Life. Taschereau denied any conflict of interest because the provincial government did not regulate these companies. Besides, membership allowed him to promote the interests of French Canadians in the English-speaking business community. Less defensible was Taschereau's support for Quebec Power against threats of take-over by the municipal government of Quebec City, since several family members, including his brother, were associated with the firm.[15] Reformers pointed to the example of Ontario Hydro, but Quebec Liberal governments preserved private ownership of the province's hydroelectric resources. In exchange for such preferential treatment from the government, businessmen accepted the traditional system of "*ristournes*" to the Liberal party and periodic *ex gratia* payments to individual members or ministers.

The sale of liquor, that most intoxicating of political temptations, fell into the government's hands when the Taschereau government established the liquor commission. The Conservatives immediately denounced the commission as a fresh source of patronage for the Liberal party, which is precisely what the Liberals intended it to be. Unfortunately for them, the Liberals selected as chairman Georges Simard, a man with another idea, namely political impartiality. Simard struggled for his principles against Liberal organizers' complaints about a lack of "co-operation" from the chairman. In this unequal fight, principles lost, Simard left, and liquor became a lubricant for political fundraising, with money squeezed from brewers and distillers, and from tavern owners in need of permits.

The challenges to the political culture that flourished under the Liberals came mainly from nationalists, who argued that the traditional party system bred patronage and corruption.[16] In this, they reflected the criticisms of third parties or non-partisan groups in other Canadian provinces, but they added a particularly French-Canadian perspective to the standard litany of party evils. Corrupt politics, cried the nationalists, debased the name of French Canada, allowed English-Canadian capitalists to exercise excessive influence in Quebec, and led French-Canadian politicians into grubby compromises which jeopardized the economic development and cultural security of French Canada. Wilfrid Laurier, at the federal level, became their favourite target, but the Liberal premiers of Quebec—Simon-Napoléon Parent, Jean-Lomer Gouin and Taschereau—joined Laurier in the pantheon of nationalist villains. Henri Bourassa spoke for many: ". . . the energies of patriotism cannot be bathed in the filthy waters of small and corrupt politics, deprived of all morality and idealism. A band of crooked and short-sighted politicians cannot be transformed in a day into an army of champions of national causes."[17] It broke Bourassa's heart to hear the contemptuous superiority English Canadians expressed towards French Canadians, a contempt rooted in hypocrisy, even racism, but nevertheless reflective of the lamentable state of political mores in French Canada. If the province were ever to achieve equality within Canada, if the French language were to flourish outside Quebec, then Bourassa believed French Canadians must prove themselves to English Canadians by demonstrating good government in Quebec and maintaining high standards of political integrity in Ottawa.

A mixture, then, of laments about the nefarious influence of party on French Canada and on democratic institutions in general fuelled Bourassa's critique, although he offered nothing coherent by way of an alternative. Henry Wise Wood's ideas about "group government," which inspired the United Farmers of Alberta, held a transitory fascination for him; electoral reforms such as a fixed term of office or redrafting the electoral map to give even more disproportionate weight to rural regions occasionally intrigued him. But Henri Bourassa was more social critic than political organizer. The *Ligue Nationaliste* which he helped inspire certainly added spice to Quebec politics after its formation in 1903, but it never loosened the grip of the established parties. Distrustful of parties, the founders of the League never formed one themselves, and instead thrashed about at the political margins searching unsuccessfully for a formula for "parliamentary government without parties."[18] Nor did, *La Ligue d'Assainissement* (The Purity League) an outgrowth of Bourassa's campaign for "purity in politics," achieve anything apart from confirming the already disaffected in their disaffection.

Bourassa, and even the odd politician in the established parties, voiced shame and repugnance for the political culture of Quebec. And from this seed of criticism sprouted periodic appeals to keep out of politics what in other jurisdictions had already entered the government realm. Perhaps most obvious was the education system, which remained the exclusive prerogative of the Catholic Church. Clearly, the social influence and political might of the church had much to do with the divorce of education from government. But partly animating, or at least justifying, this divorce was the argument that turning the education system over to the politicians meant, inevitably, tainting its organization and administration with the malodorous standards of politics. Premier Taschereau liked to justify control of education by *les Conseils de l'Instruction Publique* rather than by the state, because they included "leading laymen and clerics in search of no personal favour or party advantage,"[19] although no compelling evidence existed that such favours corrupted the school systems in other provinces.

Borrowing an example from the United States, municipal reformers in Montreal attempted at the turn of the century to divorce government from politics by creating a "non–political" board of control.[20] And social reformers regularly argued that new government initiatives should not be administered by the state, but by quasi-independent agencies or private-sector groups removed from the long reach of political patronage. By the 1920s and 1930s, many leading observers of the Quebec scene had accepted a kind of corporatist model for organizing collective activities, that is, removing from the state's direct control the administration or application of government policies.[21] They directed their suspicions not so much at the state as at partisan control of the state bureacracy; and only years later—when the public service moved out from under the thumb of political patrons—could the social reform they sought be confidently entrusted to the provincial government, which had finally exchanged excessive cronyism, partisanship and incompetence for expertise and the merit principle. It took the collapse of the Union Nationale and the advent of the Quiet Revolution to engender that confidence.

The Liberals' nationalist critics, however, could not shake the prevailing political culture; only a brilliantly veiled hypocrisy could do that. Hypocrisy, as we have noted, has frequently been the handmaiden of politicians pledging to reform or eliminate political patronage. And in the mid-1930s, a spectacular example turned up in the imposing figure of Maurice Duplessis, who slowly fused the Conservatives and a group of dissident Liberals into a new formation called the Union Nationale.[22] Duplessis' vigorous leadership, the ossification of the Liberals, and the ravages of the Depression caught up with the Liberals in the 1935 election. They won all right, but for the first time in decades they confronted an enlarged and effective Opposition led by Duplessis.

The Union Nationale leader immediately turned the public accounts committee into a vehicle for launching withering assaults on the Liberals, in session after session raising examples of financial laxity and patronage abuses. A definitive picture gradually emerged: government members who commited public funds to pet projects without authorization; the brother of the prime minister, a provincial civil servant, who banked the interest on public funds placed in his care; defeated Liberal candidates with little to do put on the public payroll; a whole range of "administrative allocations" spent by ministers and members to favour friends or constituents. Particularly popular were the revelations that the minister of colonization, Irenée Vautrin, had run up unexplained travel expenses of eleven thousand dollars, and had even charged the government for a pair of trousers he wore on a field-inspection trip. "*Les culottes de M. Vautrin*" quickly became in the clever hands of Mr. Duplessis a devastatingly effective brickbat thrown at the Liberals.[23]

Premier Taschereau, old and reeling from the damaging revelations of the public accounts committee, resigned. His replacement, Joseph-Adélard Godbout, immediately sensed the political weakness of the Liberal party. He began promising wholesale social and economic reforms, and a royal commission to investigate the revelations of the public accounts committee. This deathbed repentance was overshadowed by Duplessis' relentless attacks on Liberal corruption and patronage. In the 1936 election Duplessis thundered, "Can you have confidence in a regime that refuses to punish those who steal elections by favouring dishonest electoral laws? When a regime refuses even to protect the source of democracy, we cannot have confidence in it."[24] Graft and corruption would be eliminated, government money would no longer be squandered, and honesty would return to provincial affairs, Duplessis promised. His strongly nationalist party would protect Quebec from federal incursions into provincial affairs and shatter the cozy links between the government and English-speaking capitalists.

Fine words they were. Impressive promises too. Yet, as the years unfolded, they disappeared like scratchings in the sand. Far from reshaping the political culture of Quebec, Duplessis reconfirmed it, beginning with his first term from 1936 to 1939, then more dramatically when his party returned to office in 1944 where it remained until 1960.

It has become commonplace to speak of Maurice Duplessis' Union Nationale as the incarnation of a political machine built on a foundation of patronage. Perhaps because memories are short, or because *Le Chef* so bestrode the province, or simply because the Union Nationale so perfected the patronage system, we tend to forget that he simply carried forward well-established practices. He added new chapters, if you like, to the book already written by a string of Liberal premiers, especially his immediate predecessor Louis-Alexandre Taschereau. And the mist of time has clouded memories that Duplessis, who perhaps more than any politician in the twentieth century is remembered for patronage and abuse of power, swept into office as a fiery reformer, committed to eradicating the very practices he subsequently incarnated.

In fairness, Duplessis' first term did bring reforms preventing cabinet ministers from holding directorships in corporate concerns, and the government did trim some positions from the civil service in the name of economy, although this also allowed the party to weed out Liberal sympathizers.

With the UN's return to power in 1944 Quebec entered what critics called "*la grande noirceur*," the great darkness, a graphic and gloomy era during which the UN maintained systematic control over many aspects of life in Quebec. The party's pervasive use of patronage did not integrate new groups; rather, it consolidated the support it had already achieved. The cornerstone of the party's control lay in accommodating, on its own terms, other potentially competing institutions — the church and the corporate sector — and in relentlessly attacking those institutions that refused to be accommodated, such as the trade unions, universities, hostile newspapers and, of course, the Liberal party. The UN's long fingers coiled around individuals and whole communities; and an enormous war–chest served to tighten its grip. The core elements of patronage — reciprocal obligations, dependence and discretion—figured prominently in the UN's elaborate system of political control. The arguments the UN employed to justify its style of politics did not vary from those used by the Taschereau government; indeed they were the same arguments used by all the governments of the old-line parties in Quebec since Confederation.

The key to the UN's style of governing lay in expanding opportunities for political spending. Each year, for example, the government's budget was inflated by large estimates based not on statutory spending requirements but on the minister's discretion. In addition, neither ministers nor senior civil servants felt compelled to live within the estimates, especially during an election year. The tactic provided the government with a huge reserve of money to spend for whatever purposes it deemed necessary, mainly to foster economic dependency and political reciprocity.

Money flowed to individuals, companies or communities whose loyalty could be bought or made more durable. Schools, hospitals, municipalities, chambers of commerce, parish organizations, cultural groups, newspapers, colleges, universities — a whole range of institutions, few capable of raising large sums themselves, depended on government grants; and these grants, in turn, depended on the political loyalty, or at least quiesence, of the institutions and the people who ran them. Communities, too, found themselves at the mercy of political discretion, since Duplessis and his ministers made clear the indissoluble links between public benefits and votes. "I warned you in 1948 not to vote for the Liberal candidate," Duplessis told the electors of one riding. "You did not listen to me. Unfortunately, your riding has not obtained subsidies, grants that would have made you happy. I hope that you will have learned a lesson and that you will vote against the Liberal candidate this time."[25] On another occasion, Duplessis said, "If you want help to build the bridge, then all you have to do is vote for Gaston Hardy [the UN candidate], because if Mr. Hardy asks for help, he will get it. If, on the other hand, you vote for the Liberal candidate, René Hamel, then the government will respect your opinions."[26]

Duplessis succeeded in wresting the rural vote from the Liberals, and his government always assiduously courted farmers. This bastion of support removed all incentives for changing the electoral map, which grew increasingly imbalanced each year. The map suited the UN's patronage politics, since economic dependence and respect for figures of authority figured more prominently in small communities than in large cities. The UN carefully cultivated the goodwill of local notables, showered preferments upon them, and expected them to influence their fellow citizens.

The UN perfected an anti-bureaucratic, anti-statist rhetoric to justify political discretion. Bearing its rural support in mind, the party fabricated one of those marvellous distinctions that politicians sometimes find useful in persuading themselves, if not others, of the purity of their intentions. "*Le gros patronage*" — that was Liberal patronage: favours to trust companies, banks, the corporate sector; "*le petit patronage*" — that was the UN's patronage: favours for the humble, dispossessed, struggling, in short, for all who legitimately needed government help.[27] A further twist to the argument distinguished between "*le bon patronage*" and "*le mauvais patronage*," good patronage being whatever favours assisted those in need without injuring the public interest through excessive cost, bad patronage being whatever favours helped the already powerful and depleted the public treasury.

These distinctions, whatever their superficial attraction, dissolved when anyone carefully examined the UN's record with the business community, especially in fund-raising. Like Taschereau, Duplessis handed enormous concessions to the largely English-speaking business community. Resources continued to be sold for a pittance, and mining companies received lucrative concessions to open up northern Quebec. In exchange for these concessions, the party gathered up substantial contributions. In addition, it nicked companies, large and small, for "*ristournes*" to the party treasury. Any company winning a contract from the Quebec government was expected to kick back a percentage, secure in the knowledge that failure to play the game meant no more contracts. Companies dependent upon government permits to do business knew that renewal of the permit required a contribution. Tavern owners were easy targets for "*le chantage*," since the liquor commission was made an arm of the party, so the owners could seldom argue about the size of their tithe with UN agents.

Similar practices marked the operation of the civil service. Godbout, alarmed by the political repercussions from evidence against the Taschereau government, created a civil service commission. Duplessis neutered it. The civil service remained completely partisan. Government purchases went to friends of the party. So did appointments to agencies and commissions. A massive porkbarrel operation preceded every voting day, especially road construction. It became the stuff of legend, largely because it reflected the truth, that stretches of highway in front of the houses of UN supporters got their asphalt, whereas sections fronting houses of political foes remained dirt.* In one celebrated case, the Roads department gave cheques to children between the ages of five and twelve; in other instances, the Health department paid hospital bills of party friends from funds purportedly set aside for indigent cases.[28]

Since the party did not publish accounts of its revenues and expenditures, no one knew the size of the UN's treasury. No one doubted that the sums were substantial, because evidence of consid-

---

*In the annals of Canadian investigative journalism, few efforts can compare with Pierre Laporte's series in *Le Devoir* in October and November, 1956, describing in minute detail the UN's methods to influence election results. *Le Devoir*'s editors aptly chose Israel Tarte's phrase for the headline over each article: "*Les élections ne se font pas avec des prières*" (Elections aren't won with prayers).

erable spending permeated the province during elections. The party is reckoned to have spent nearly three million dollars in the 1952 campaign and a staggering ten million in 1956, effectively swamping the Liberals' spending. When Duplessis died, the party's *caisse* contained about eighteen million dollars.[29]

Election campaigns ran the gamut of corrupt methods—outright thuggery, treating, bribery, massive tampering with the voting lists, a procedure made easier by the notorious Bill 34 of 1953 which opened doors to electoral manipulation.[30] That bill, among other changes, eliminated the practice of selecting two enumerators, one from each party, to prepare the voting lists. Instead, only one enumerator, hired by the government, prepared the lists; and a further change gave all the enumerators immunity from prosecution. The enumerators made telegraphing a cinch for party professionals, since the voting lists contained names of the deceased or those who had moved. Another change put election appeals in the hands of the provincially appointed magistrates' court instead of the federally appointed Superior Court of Quebec.

The Union Nationale government resembled a massive spider web with the premier playing black widow and each layer of the web drawing in ministers, members, local notables, civil servants and dependent voters. Ministers had their discretionry accounts; members disbursed funds in their constituencies; party agents spent money on pliable individuals. The province's social conditions—the influence of the church, the lack of business opportunities for French Canadians in the private sector, the continuing dependence of the middle class professionals upon government favours — contributed to the durability of the Duplessis system. The history of parliamentary democracy in Quebec running back to LaFontaine — with its assumption that democracy meant political control of everything—buttressed the system. And the simple, observable fact that the system enormously benefited the party in power steeled the UN against change. Only when the economic and social conditions of Quebec altered, giving rise to new elites and scope for thwarted ambitions, did the system crack.

The Jean Lesage government, from 1960 to 1966, and the Union Nationale interregnum for three years thereafter can be seen as a time of upheaval for Quebec's political culture, during which old ideas about patronage ground against new attitudes. That grinding of the old against the new continued through Robert Bourassa's first government. It effectively ended in 1976 with the victory of the Parti Québécois, whose legacy to contemporary Quebec was government as free of patronage abuses as in the least afflicted provinces of Canada.

Revolutions may resemble spontaneous combustion but the

proper conditions must mix for a revolution to begin. The Quiet Revolution, a vast awakening of political consciousness in Quebec, started with the election of Jean Lesage's Liberals, a brittle band, as events later proved, with numerous shadings of political opinion bound by aversion to the Union Nationale. Duplessis' death had been quickly followed by that of his respected successor Paul Sauvé, and these deaths together with new conditions opened an extraordinary opportunity for the Liberals.

Economic conditions had changed, expanding the cities, strengthening the trade union movement, highlighting the absurd inequities of the electoral map. Television, patronage's mortal foe, opened Quebeckers' eyes and forced them to compare Quebec with other jurisdictions. Post-war prosperity, although less robust than in neighbouring Ontario, nevertheless brought Quebec unprecedented wealth, reducing deprivation, lessening dependence, throwing up restless elites in search of new roles to play, feeding doubts about church doctrines. The postwar boom and the media equipped people with the means to achieve their ambitions or to question those structures of Quebec society that frustrated them.[31]

These pressures had been building before the Liberal victory, which partly explains why the Duplessis machine worked overtime and spent so lavishly in the 1956 campaign to secure what turned out to be its final victory. Lesage's triumph reflected these pressures and also created new ones when taboos suddenly fell, promising even more dramatic possibilities. Lesage soon found himself struggling to restrain runaway horses within his own party, and in society at large, who wished to go faster and farther than he did in such areas as federal-provincial relations and the expansion of state activities.[32] And, in the end, the party split. René Lévesque walked into what then appeared to be the separatist wilderness, only to reappear a few years later with an enlarged band of followers who posed a far more dangerous threat to the Liberals than the expiring Union Nationale.

While they remained together, however, the Lesage Liberals swept away parts, but by no means all, of the patronage system bequeathed Quebec. Lesage based part of the 1960 election campaign on a commitment to eliminate electoral fraud and patronage, and to produce a politically neutral civil service such as those at Ottawa and in the other provinces. These promises reflected the general pressures for change in Quebec and capitalized on negative publicity given some UN ministers who had purchased shares in a natural gas company to which a public distribution system had been sold. By placing the then-respected Bernard Pinard in charge of the department of roads and highways and by making the political neophyte René Lévesque minister of public works, Lesage sent a clear signal that change was at hand. Very soon, reforms shook up established institutions. School boards were instructed to deal directly with the government rather than through local MLAs. Departments were told that public tenders would be required for contracts. A highly respected lawyer was placed in charge of the civil service commission, previously an arm of the Union Nationale.

The Liberals also launched an extended morality play, a royal commission into the purchasing policies of the Union Nationale government. The commission, under the leadership of Judge Elie Salvas, commanded widespread media attention as it plowed through seventy-two public sessions, heard three hundred witnesses, accumulated six thousand pages of evidence and two hundred and forty-two exhibits.[33] It documented case after case of companies in receipt of government contracts paying money to "intermediaries" appointed by the UN. The appointees took their cut and paid the rest of the money to the government, the way "bottle exchangers" raked off a percentage on empty beer bottles being returned to government stores in provinces such as Nova Scotia. The system was organized by ministers, executed by Alfred Hardy, the director of the purchasing commission, and participated in by a wide range of MLAs and party officials.[34] The commission could not determine precisely how much these practices had cost the government — it guessed at nearly two million dollars — but its wider concern was the impact on public morality.

The most robust defence of the previous regime came from Gérald Martineau, a senior Duplessis cabinet minister. "Yes, I engaged in patronage. I did it all the time," he tesitified. "I don't hide it and I don't defend myself. For as long as there is misery to alleviate and family problems to resolve, I will not hesitate to reduce the profits of companies to distribute them to hundreds and hundreds of people. Those who received funds should not be ashamed. They are honest people." The commissioners rejected Martineau's defence of patronage as a kind of redistributive welfare system, saying they were "repelled by the sense of honesty and justice, in all their forms, that inspire the citizens, in general, of this province. One of the unfortunate effects has been to corrupt the moral sense of a part of the population."

While the Salvas commission hearings directed public attention towards what it called the "immoral, scandalous, humiliating and disquieting" practices of the previous regime, the Liberal caucus confronted demands for a continuation of all those practices from their own supporters. Office-seekers arrived in great number; heaps of letters landed on the desks of members of the new government.[35] At the first caucus meeting, some newly elected Liberal MLAs complained that the campaign against patronage was fine in theory, but executing it would leave them with little to do in their constituencies and without answers for importuning fellow Liberals. If the civil service were suddenly to become "neutral," as their leader had promised during the campaign, that in effect would consolidate the position of *unioniste* sympathizers throughout the service. Lesage stood firm, or so it seemed. He appeared on television after the caucus meeting, inviting the public to join his "battle of patronage."[36]

That "battle of patronage" between the previous assumptions and new ideas, between the established and emerging methods of political mobilization, raged on throughout the Lesage years, occasionally even spilling into the public domain at annual meetings of the Liberal party. One former Lesage cabinet minister, who still did not wish to be identified twenty-five years later, insisted that the turbulent caucus meeting which supported an election in 1962 spent more time arguing about patronage than agreeing to the nationalization of hydroelectricity. New policies curbing patronage emerged: in 1960 the introduction of competitive entrance examinations for the civil service; in 1963, ceilings placed on party spending during campaigns; in 1964 and 1965 the granting of the right to strike to public-sector employees, a recognition that the civil service should not be an emanation of the party in power. Election practices improved considerably. Many of the grossest abuses of the Union Nationale were seldom, if ever, practised by the Liberals. Yet these salutary changes were balanced by the record of 1960-61, when many civil servants lost their jobs for their political views, and by the custom continued through the entire Lesage period of not including 'extraordinary expenses' in the budget.[37] Similarly, whatever Lesage preached, "a large number of prominent Liberals received remunerative appointments as legal counsel, judges, and members of government bodies, and even as civil servants."[38]

A crucial change in attitudes, however, began working its way through Quebec during the Lesage period. For decades, many Quebeckers, including social critics, had worried about the extension of state activities. Some of these worries stemmed from ideological conviction, others from church influences, still others from the extension of political influence into state activities which, in Quebec's political culture, meant a larger field for patronage and corruption. The reform wing of the Liberal party, exerting its influence on the government and on public opinion, slowly began demonstrating that the old fears could be addressed, if never fully eliminated. Quebec Hydro provided one example of a state agency removed from patronage and corruption. State control of education, the other overwhelming reform of the Lesage period, offered another. So did the rapid extension of state-sponsored social welfare, pension, health and hospitalization programs, run by an army of clerks and bureaucrats following impersonal regulations rather than by a legion of politicized bureaucrats administering programs giving widespread and systematic discretion to politicians or their agents. The new technocrats had met their heroes, namely themselves; marrying their ambitions to the state, they wrapped themselves in the cloth of Quebec nationalism, altering its posture from one of defence against federal incursions to one of assertive expansion of Quebec's constitutional territory.

The triumph of the technocrats followed a long march interspersed with periodic setbacks, rather than a particular moment of glory. The Union Nationale's last gasp, its victory of 1966, reflected the snarly reaction of rural Quebec to the technocrats' ambitions. Nobody much minded Premier Daniel Johnson's view of federalism as a Cheshire cat wherein nothing would remain but the smile. Johnson's constitutional assertiveness, although bolder, fell into the UN tradition of Duplessis and that of the Tremblay commission *Le Chef* had established to provide intellectual elegance and justification for his own view of federalism as a loose confederation of provincial baronies. Johnson did not win on constitutional issues; he won because the Liberals had moved too fast, kicked too much sand in the face of traditions, unleashed too many ambitions of those contemptuous of the old ways.

Union Nationale members, not unreasonably, expected a return to the salad days. The UN's win immediately set off a scramble for jobs, contracts, and preferments of all kinds. "Three days after the victory," recalled Jérôme Proulx, a UN backbencher, "I was summoned to the office of the old-timers, who paternally dictated to me the line of conduct they were to have me follow: 'We're going to set you up in an office with a secretary who will take care of three ridings. . . . You will go to the marriages, the receptions, the cocktail parties and so on. We will take care of the rest.' "[39] Contractors offered free vacations or cash payments; even funeral-parlour directors lobbied the police for bodies. After the Liberal defeat, wrote Proulx, "our people, those who had waited for six years, those who had lost their jobs in 1960, those who had been swept aside and put on the street, young people who dreamed of making a 'quick buck' as their elders had done, those who had worked for the Union Nationale for twenty years and asked for something 'for the first time,' Liberals who had supposedly voted for us, all these people came to see us. . . . For most of them, it was simply a question of turning the page. The nightmare had finally disappeared and we were going back to the good old habits of yesterday."

The UN did lift the page off the book but did not turn it. Too much had happened in the Lesage years: the unionization of the public service, new contracting procedures in key departments, improvements in electoral conduct; in short, the opportunities for a return to the old, Duplessis style of patronage had eroded. Some still remained: the part-time local jobs and the full-time big ones on agencies and commissions; covert deals on small contracts sealed with a "*ristourne*," implicitly assumed if not overtly demanded; money raised from the business community, if not in return for specific favours, then to remain in good odour with the party in power; and, of course, the treasury with its discretionary spending. The written press, unfettered now by party links, kept a skeptical eye out for dubious practices. Television, regulated from Ottawa, remained beholden to nothing except the mass market. Competing elites, mostly hostile to the UN, no longer required patronage and disdained politicians claiming to need it for others. So the old ways and new assumptions ground against each other through the Union Nationale's final term in office.

It is, in retrospect, a bit surprising that the supreme technocrat who defeated the Union Nationale should himself have been so tarnished by allegations of patronage, including nepotism. Robert Bourassa's first spell in office was marred by accusations, frequently well-founded, that his party systematically favoured its friends, including the friends and family of the premier. Within three weeks of the 1970 election, Liberal MLAs received a letter asking them to recommend contractors in their ridings. These names were compiled in a patronage list from which the public works department issued contracts in cases not requiring tenders. Some bidding was conducted by invitation only, and all the invitees turned out to have strong Liberal connections. The PQ Opposition got its hands on the list of Liberal lawyers who received all legal work. Lottery agents were also handed out to party faithful. The Provincial Inquiry into Organized Crime uncovered evidence that Pierre Laporte, the Bourassa minister murdered by the *Front de Libération du Québec*, had had extensive contacts with the underworld and that a Liberal parliamentary secretary had had "inexplicable contacts" with members of the mafia. A company partly owned by the premier's wife and brother-in-law had received contracts from six government departments.

The pinpricks of these and other affairs slowly took their toll. Bourassa, under sharp questioning in the assembly, defended his administration, saying these patronage practices had always been prevalent in Quebec. "Give me a single case," he demanded of those who alleged wrongdoing. He used the line so often, and with such wounded pride, that he quickly became a parody of himself. The more he defended himself, the more the public sensed that the Liberals did have something to hide. The technocrat soon looked like a grubby politician, supported by a huge electoral *caisse*, tolerant of some of the old practices, including the Union Nationale trick of pouring money into carefully selected public works during election campaigns.

But Bourassa learned from his mistakes. Given a second chance to govern, after a period of personal exile, he imposed much stricter standards on ministers. In part, he had no choice. The Parti Québecois had both changed certain laws to make patronage more difficult and, by its conduct in office, helped to shape public expectations. Only the occasional accusation of blatant favouritism marred the PQ's record, and these charges were often no more serious than that the party expanded ministerial staffs or pumped money into nationalist festivals or organizations run by leading *independantistes*. Bourassa did pay off many Liberal debts through his appointments, but in contracting, fundraising, electoral practices, relations with the media, and even government spending, his government had caught up with public expectations, so that the whole issue of political patronage barely disturbed his second time in office. He had changed but, more important, Quebec's political culture had changed, especially in the domain of patronage.

CHAPTER 11

ONTARIO

"Everything else being equal, no administration was in
the habit of preferring their opponents to their friends."
Oliver Mowat, Liberal Premier of Ontario.
May 4, 1894.

"Patronage has always existed. It's part of our way of
life, part of the democratic process."
Charles McNaughton,
Conservative Transportation Minister.
April 22, 1971.

IT WAS HARD, and perhaps of only historical interest, for Ontarians to
remember, when they awoke after the electoral rebuke they handed the
Conservative party in the 1985 election, that they were slowly returning
Ontario to where it had begun: as a Liberal bastion. For nearly forty-
two years, from 1943 to 1985, the Conservatives had governed Ontario
like basset hounds, ears alert to every whisper of change in public
opinion, noses alive to the smells of danger and political opportunity,
barking at the federal government when necessary, licking Ottawa's
hand when required, an essentially cautious party, yet capable of surprising reversals or bold ventures, a pragmatic party grown homely, so
familiar in every corner of the province that it seemed as companionable
and trustworthy as a favourite dog. It also had possessed the uncommon good sense to change leaders about every decade, just before
sclerosis threatened and the Opposition parties' taunt "Time for a
Change" really told.

Yet when the time familiar for renewal presented itself with
Premier William Davis' resignation, the Conservatives' instincts for
survival suddenly vanished. They selected Frank Miller, an affable
throwback from Muskoka, whose plaid jackets and right-wing views
may have delighted the Bracebridge Rotary Club but played badly in
urban Ontario. The grassroots Conservative delegates from small-
town and rural Ontario found their man, and he turned out to be almost

exclusively theirs. Into the vacuum created by Miller's selection, and subsequently into the premier's chair, stepped Liberal leader David Peterson, known to only a minority of the electorate on the eve of the campaign. Yet political men sometimes rise to occasions: Peterson, by running an exceptionally shrewd campaign, emerged with sufficient seats to form a two-year pact of convenience with the New Democrats that allowed him to become premier, a tactical masterstroke he parlayed into an electoral majority in 1987.[1]

Peterson's arrival coincided with dispiriting times for federal Liberals, thrashed in the 1984 election by Brian Mulroney's Conservatives. For the first time since Mitchell Hepburn defeated the provincial Conservatives in 1934, Liberals looked to Toronto rather than Ottawa for the spoils of power. But the Hepburn example misled, because the Liberals-in-Toronto/Conservatives-in-Ottawa scenario lasted only about a year, until Prime Minister R.B. Bennett's defeat in 1935. Only the last century provided a fair yardstick of comparison: Oliver Mowat's Liberals in power at Queen's Park; a Conservative dynasty ruling in Ottawa. And those decades established one of the fiercest political rivalries in Canadian history, a rivalry within which patronage played a cardinal role.

In one sense, Peterson faced fewer patronage pressures than might have been expected for the leader of a party more than four decades in Opposition. The federal Liberals had so thoroughly cared for their own that many of the important party members in Ontario had long since received their rewards. Still, there were plenty of supporters who had toiled for the provincial party over the years, and perhaps a few for the federal party, who had received nothing. It was their turn now, and they demanded action, especially in small towns and rural areas. But Peterson had hammered the Ontario Conservatives so relentlessly over patronage that unless he was prepared to risk appearing as hypocritical as Brian Mulroney, he could not exercise his power of patronage as blatantly as he might otherwise have desired. Peterson was shrewd enough to have learned from Brian Mulroney's mistakes, or rather from the public outcry that greeted Mulroney's early use of patronage. Like Trudeau, Premier Miller had made a bevy of order-in-council appointments before leaving office in 1985 — three hundred and thirty-three from May 8 to June 6, including one hundred and twenty-nine in his last week in power.[2] These appointments smacked of the kind of old-style politics which Peterson, who presented himself as a thoroughly modern man in tune with contemporary Ontario, had severely attacked. Peterson was also constrained by his pact with the NDP. He understood, as Prime Minister Joe Clark had not, that his was a minority mandate, and that his government arose from fortuitous circumstances which an excess of partisan zeal might easily shatter.

Partisan patronage power in Ontario consisted partly of 4,750 order-in-council appointments, traditionally divided into the premier's list and the ministers' lists. About a thousand were considered the premier's personal prerogative. Peterson put his sister-in-law, Heather, and Gordon Ashworth, a former national director of the federal Liberal party, in charge of the appointments process. Theirs was a three-part credo: quietly reward friends; use the power of appointment to widen the Liberals' political base; appear to be reforming the system.[3]

Reform meant placing some three thousand employees of the liquor control board and the land registry offices under the control of Ontario's civil service commission. It meant publishing every six weeks black loose-leaf binders identifying the positions coming vacant on boards, agencies and commissions for members of the legislature to examine. It also meant retaining, at least for the duration of the minority government, Conservative appointees in the province's offices overseas. The appearance of reform, or at least of a changed attitude towards patronage appointments, led the Liberals to name some prominent New Democrats and even Conservatives to high-profile order-in-council positions. Widening the party's political base — a classic and proper function of patronage — meant scouring ethnic communities for candidates and a constant search for eligible women. In the first eighteen months of the Liberal government, thirty-seven percent of government appointees were women, and thirty-one percent were from ethnic or Francophone communities.[4] Rewarding friends meant just that: The Conservatives identified one hundred and nine Liberals appointed in the first year, with twenty-five more suspected of Liberal connections. Newspaper accounts added several dozen more, and one prominent newspaper columnist noted, albeit stretching the point somewhat, that "the little red machine with which Peterson came into office is growing to rival the notorious old Big Blue Machine."[5] What the Liberals would not accept were some key recommendations from a legislature committee, including mandatory committee-scrutiny of many order-in-council appointments.

The Mulroney Conservatives, regularly scorched for their handling of patronage, watched with intense frustration as the Peterson Liberals implanted their own throughout the province with only the feeblest peeps of protest from the media and the Opposition. To the Mulroney team, Peterson benefited from a double standard, confirming in some Tory minds an intense anti-Conservative bias in the media.

After all, ran the Conservative complaint, did we not also appoint some supporters of the Opposition parties to important positions? Did

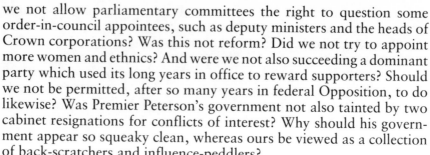

we not allow parliamentary committees the right to question some order-in-council appointees, such as deputy ministers and the heads of Crown corporations? Was this not reform? Did we not try to appoint more women and ethnics? And were we not also succeeding a dominant party which used its long years in office to reward supporters? Should we not be permitted, after so many years in federal Opposition, to do likewise? Was Premier Peterson's government not also tainted by two cabinet resignations for conflicts of interest? Why should his government appear so squeaky clean, whereas ours be viewed as a collection of back-scratchers and influence-peddlers?

They were all legitimate questions, yet the Conservatives overlooked the clues that might have answered them. A mild double standard was applied, not because of an intense anti-Conservative bias among the media, but because of Brian Mulroney's excessively pious and profoundly hypocritical declarations during his election campaign. He set a standard he never intended to match, and was judged accordingly once the game was uncovered. Then there was the matter of cronyism, of long-standing personal friends of the prime minister receiving their rewards, so that the opprobrium of patronage stuck personally to the leader rather than being more diffusely linked to the party. There was also a question of degree: the rush for spoils among federal Conservatives had been so brazen, the dispensing of them so obvious, the political camouflage so transparent. And impropriety, or at least questionable conduct, seemed to take longer to produce action from Mulroney in the first half of his mandate than from Peterson. In short, the provincial Liberals had used their power with greater subtlety and finesse.

That had frequently been the Ontario way with patronage. The provincial political culture was no less shot through with patronage than others, but a certain subtlety and discretion often accompanied its use. Perhaps it related to the long stretches of one-party rule and consequent infrequency of post-election purges prevalent elsewhere. Perhaps it also related to the essentially managerial style of Ontario politics wherein leaders tended to be — there were certainly some exceptions — rather colourless individuals. Perhaps it also had something to do with the province's relative affluence. Pockets of deprivation dotted the landscape, and northern Ontario always lagged behind the south in economic development, but in the main, the province was comfortably well-off. Economic security reduced the demand for part-time jobs which, in less economically-favoured areas of Canada, spelled the difference between the ignominy of the dole and the marginal dignity of underemployment and poor pay. There was more patronage driven by the demands of status than of economic circumstance.

Urbanization, too, played a role, since Ontario contained more large and medium-sized cities than any other province, thus rendering less personal the intimate networks of patronage that bound parties together in smaller, more rural provinces. But these factors coloured Ontario patronage in pale shades; they did not whitewash a province where politicians have always paid attention to patronage, beginning with Premier Oliver Mowat, the first of a Liberal dynasty.

John A. Macdonald called Mowat "that little tyrant who had attempted to control public opinion by getting hold of every little office."[6] The prime minister knew whereof he spoke, recognizing in Mowat's political approach precisely what he himself had always attempted to practise in Ottawa. The two men had known each other for years — Mowat articled in Macdonald's Kingston law firm — and they did not like what they knew, although they were forced on occasion to acknowledge each other's political acumen. They fought on matters of high principle and base politics, and in a paradoxical way, they were locked together by their irreconcilable differences. As federal leader, Macdonald was thoroughly preoccupied with Ontario — Quebec, the Maritimes and the West he could leave to subalterns — and it continuously galled him to find himself and Mowat practicising on their home turf the same tactics and strategies of patronage. His scorn for the Ontario premier, frequently manifested in private correspondence and conversations, often spilled into the open. "Mr Mowat," Macdonald said in 1882, "with his little soul rattling like a dried pea in a too large pod — what does he care if he wrecks Confederation and interferes with the development of Canada so long as he can enjoy his little salary as Attorney-General. . . ?"[7]

Different conceptions of federalism fired their animosity. Macdonald never doubted that the federal government should eclipse provincial governments in constitutional authority and powers of taxation. Nation-building required that the federal government direct economic development, harmonize provincial policies where necessary, and occupy contested constitutional fields. Mowat, "the father of the provincial-rights movement in Canada," viewed the two levels of government as equals, each sovereign in its own fields. He fought Macdonald on the use of the federal power of disallowance and that of the lieutenant-governor. He played an important role in convening the first interprovincial conference of premiers, a meeting Macdonald scorned. The compact theory of Confederation, which explained the grand scheme of 1867 as an agreement among the provinces, received Mowat's enthusiastic support. The premier also launched legal challenges to stop the expansion of federal powers, and found support from a sympathetic judicial committee of the Privy Council. The premier fought the prime minister for control of what is now northwestern Ontario. The Privy Council eventually upheld Ontario's claim, although Macdonald continued to assert federal control over timber and minerals in the area, an assertion that Mowat subsequently and successfully contested in the courts. More than any premier Mowat ensured that the provinces would not become the glorified municipalities some Fathers of Confederation had envisaged.[8] Governing Canada's most powerful province, Mowat had the political and financial clout to do battle with Ottawa, even to complain when Macdonald seemed ready to accede to demands from less favoured provinces for "better terms." It was Mowat's vision that the Ontario government, not the federal, would direct the province's economic development; Queen's Park, not Parliament Hill, would be the venue for private interests to bargain for support.

Different conceptions of federalism, then, drove Macdonald and Mowat into conflict. But naked political rivalry could not be divorced from — indeed, often produced — those conflicts. Two great political machines, each directed by an excellent tactician, clashed throughout Ontario, neither giving any quarter, both dispensing patronage to secure advantage. The sharpness of their rivalry owed much to the similarity in their thinking in the matter of the role and size of government. Certainly Mowat was never the object of John Alexander Macdonald's contempt on that score, as was Ontario's first premier, John Sandfield Macdonald (1867-1871). The latter, sneered the prime minister, had run a "thrifty and penurious" administration instead of using available revenues to increase the number of departments and appointments.[9] Premier Mowat shucked off Ontario's Grit tradition of thrift and limited government. Development in Ontario was what the Mowat administration supported, and as a corollary, certain mild reforms in the interests of the province's work force. Pursuing that agenda from 1872 to 1896, he expanded the provincial civil service, pushing his government into new areas of economic activity — and into inevitable jurisdictional conflicts with the prime minister and the federal civil service, as well stocked with Macdonald Conservatives as Ontario's was with Mowat Liberals.

Mowat always insisted that the Liberals he appointed have adequate qualifications as a prerequisite and display technical efficiency on the job. And those who have studied the record concede that he did not burden the province with too much dead wood. Nor did he burden it with Conservatives. Like Macdonald, Mowat defended the patronage of partisan appointments. "No administration was in the habit of preferring their opponents to their friends in making appointments," Mowat asserted. Moreover, "he only had confidence in those who had confidence in him."[10] A smattering of voices complained about the existence of patronage — Conservatives decried their lack of it — but Mowat frankly acknowledged and clinically assessed the utility of the practice. "While our opponents pretend in provincial politics to object to patronage as giving a government too much power," he told the Young Men's Liberal Club of Toronto in 1894, "some reformers would favour its being withdrawn from the provincial government because it appears to them to be a source of weakness rather than a source of strength, inasmuch as several friends are disappointed whenever an appointment is made. I cannot say that patronage is on the whole a weakness; but it is the prestige which belongs to the right of patronage that gives to it its chief advantage to the party in power."[11]

Sir John Willison, one of the leading journalists of the period and a confidant of Liberal politicians, described Mowat's attitude towards patronage: "Under Sir Oliver Mowat, there was also an extension of patronage over the minor courts and a rigid exercise of patronage in appointments to provincial institutions. For nearly a generation no Conservative was admitted to the public service in Ontario. Although fitness in appointments was seldom disregarded, the civil service was an essential portion of the organized political machinery of the Mowat administration. Sir Oliver Mowat was neither unctuous nor hypocritical. He bluntly defended patronage."[12]

The Macdonald-Mowat struggle for turf and patronage power could perhaps best be seen in the decade-long fight over control of liquor. In 1850, the power to grant licences for the sale of liquor had been transferred to the municipal governments. Twelve years later, the power shifted to boards of police commissioners, which included mayors, recorders and police magistrates. In 1876, however, the Mowat government handed the jurisdiction to a provincially appointed board of licence commissioners. The "Crooks Act," as the legislation was called, responded to growing public demands for more stringent liquor laws by limiting the number of licences per municipality and increasing the fee for licenses. It also gave the Liberal government an array of positions to fill, especially the liquor inspectors who would fan out across the province. The provincial Conservatives immediately sniffed partisan advantage; they charged that the Act handed the Liberals boundless patronage opportunities. Macdonald thought so too, and launched an unsuccessful constitutional challenge against the legislation. His government even adopted the *Dominion Liquor Licence Act*, the so-called McCarthy Act, which established a federal licensing system for the sale of beer and liquor and called for a network of federal commissioners and inspectors.[13]

The dispute led in 1884 to the famous Privy Council decision in

Hodge vs the Queen, which upheld provincial control of licensing and supervision of the liquor trade, a decision pregnant with political consequences, including the linking of provincial governments to the liquor industry. From that decision flowed, in Ontario as in other provinces: massive funds for provincial parties, raised by legal and corrupt means from liquor companies; provincial party control of the awarding of liquor licenses; and government-operated liquor stores, which provided countless part- and full-time jobs for supporters of the party in power.

Mowat was a partisan terrier all right, but his partisanship stopped short of blatant gestures of patronage that smacked of base immorality. His patronage was obvious, forthrightly admitted but not abusive. Through twenty-four years in office, Mowat's governments remained untouched by the kind of scandals that periodically afflicted Macdonald's. Macdonald avowedly gerrymandered the federal electoral map — "hiving the Grits," he called it; Mowat fairly redrew the provincial electoral map in 1874 and 1885. The Conservatives naturally cried foul, but they actually profited from the changes of 1874. Mowat insisted throughout that partisan considerations had not affected the changes, and the balance of the argument lay with him.[14] There was about Mowat, as about Peterson, a certain deftness in administering patronage, and an understanding that a powerful tool, if used to excess, can injure rather than assist the user.

When Mowat left the provincial scene in 1896 to join Wilfrid Laurier's federal cabinet the core of Liberal support in Ontario had declined. The Liberals' rural bastion had shrunk apace with relentless urbanization. And the two Liberal premiers who succeeded Mowat did not possess his combination of personal qualities and intellectual gifts. Arthur Hardy had neither the taste nor the physical stamina for leadership; he lasted only three years in office, won one election, then yielded to George Ross. Premier Ross was able enough, but nothing could disguise that the Liberal party had grown long in the tooth. With Mowat's stern presence only a memory, the party's political mores began to slip. The Liberals also faced an impressive Conservative leader in James Whitney, who had rejuvenated his party and impressed the province with his sense of honesty and integrity. The election of May, 1902, gave the Liberals fifty-one seats, the Conservatives forty-seven. But the methods of victory sowed the seeds for the Liberals' eventual demise.

Desperate to hold off the Conservatives, the Liberals resorted to widespread ballot-box stuffing, payoffs to voters, intimidation and personation. In the celebrated *Minnie M* affair, the Liberals and the Lake Superior Corporation (forerunner of the Algoma Steel Company) conspired in a 1903 by-election — itself necessitated by a successful Conservative appeal against the results in the Sault Ste. Marie riding in the 1902 election — to send the company steamship, the *Minnie M*, to Sault Ste. Marie, Michigan.[15] There, the steamship picked up twenty American citizens and brought them to the Canadian side. A special train took them to an isolated voting location, where they duly voted for the Liberal candidate under the names of absent or deceased miners. That duty completed, they proceeded to another polling station, voted again, accepted their payments, and returned home. The Conservatives, tipped off to the ruse, appealed the election result. The verdict from the notorious trial implicated company officials who, in turn, revealed the participation of prominent Liberal officials. The publicity the trial received damaged the Liberals and gave birth to a ballad, "The Cruise of the Minnie M", the last two verses of which went:

> The company is grateful, too,
> To all its merry men.
> It sends them each a souvenir,
> A five, or maybe ten.

> And when elections come again
> — An anxious time for them —
> They'll give us, perhaps, another trip
> Upon the Minnie M.

More damaging and spectacular was the Gamey affair.[16] Nine months after the election, Conservative MLA Robert Gamey, as unpredictable a character as ever graced the Ontario legislature, shocked his party by announcing that he would support the Ross government. On the second day of the legislative session following his announcement, Gamey stunned the Liberals. He told an astonished legislature that shortly after the election he had been approached by the Liberals, who offered him money and patronage privileges if he would support them. He further claimed that he had received the first instalment of the payments from the Liberal provincial secretary, James Stratton. He published documents which purportedly substantiated his charges, and he produced a package containing nine fifty-dollar bills, two twenties and a ten. An investigation by two judges revealed that Gamey had received control over some patronage. But Gamey's conduct and testimony were sufficiently erratic to lead the judges to accuse him of "systematic duplicity." The charges against Stratton were "disproved." The judges' report touched off a province-wide debate about the inquiry. Suspicions that it had not been entirely fair — one judge had three sons in the employ of the provincial government and had received money from the Liberals for work unrelated to his judicial position — cast a pall over the Ross government.

James Whitney, who drove the Liberals from office in the 1905 election, had made attacking electoral corruption and excessive patronage a staple of his political career. The rather dour new premier always found distasteful electoral chicanery and the partisan clamour for appointments. He never promised to eliminate patronage — after all, the Conservatives had been thirty-four years in the wilderness — but he did insist he would curb its excesses.

The day after the election, the office-seekers began their assault, descending on Whitney's home in Morrisburg. And the pressure for spoils never relented. Whitney wrote in despair to a friend: "It is impossible to describe the rush for office. . . . I am bound to say that half the satisfaction which I have taken in the splendid record we have been able to make has been taken away by my realization of the craze which has taken possession of our people on this subject."[17] Whitney's correspondence from Conservative officials and organizers also reflected the demand for spoils or retribution. "I am going to have some trouble over the patronage as our fellows are all after a job," wrote MLA C.A. Brower, "but hope we can make arrangements so as to satisfy the most of them."[18] The Conservative MLA from Brockville wrote, "I am overrun with applicants for positions, and am replying to them by saying, that I do not know what your intentions are. . . . I am sure I am quite within the bounds when I write you that seventy-five per cent of the Ontario officials in this Brockville Riding are the most enthusiastic, fighting kind of partisans, and in our last election they were out upon the streets buying votes openly, and driving at race-neck speed to get voters to the Polling booths to vote against me."[19] From the president of the Ottawa Conservative Association came a letter detailing which court officials should be fired and which retained. The president urged "reasonable discretion" and defended some of the officials. Others, he claimed, "have been particularly offensive in their political actions and in order to satisfy party demands they should be removed from office."[20]

The demands for patronage and retribution drove Whitney to anger. When one Conservative MLA came to the premier's office with a list of people he wanted fired and their replacements, Whitney thundered: "Get to hell out of my office. Never come to me with such a proposal again."[21]

Some of the local demands he could delegate to Conservative MLAs, defeated candidates and riding association presidents. "Applications for the position of Licence Inspector in any County should be recommended by the Member for the constituency, or our candidate," he wrote an office-seeker.[22] These licence inspectors, the offspring of Mowat's successful battle with Ottawa for control of liquor regulation, remained a prized patronage tool. The inspectors received only five hundred dollars a year, but that was alluring money to hopefuls scratching out a more meagre existence. Whitney may have insisted that "no licence should be granted and no licence refused for political reasons," but partisanship and the liquor trade's regulators refused to be divorced. The Conservatives changed all the licence inspectors, a move Whitney defended with an argument many political leaders used before and would use again: "The Government will be held responsible for the acts of these officials. Therefore, it must be expected that the Government will appoint men in whom it has confidence."[23]

So widespread patronage continued to be a partisan instrument in the hands of the Ontario government, but Whitney used it as discreetly as possible and tried to curb its excesses. His government passed legislation tightening the definitions of electoral corruption. He even denounced the practice of porkbarrelling, daring to inform a Hamilton audience in the 1908 campaign: "I am not here to promise anything to the City of Hamilton. Whatever will be said of me after I leave office, it will not be said that I stood up and did not disdain to bribe a constituency."[24] He left office a respected premier whose administration had tempered patronage, without ever dreaming of ending it, and whose personal integrity remained unsullied. "Ontario does not think I am a great man. It does think I am honest. And honest I must be."[25] A fitting epitaph.

Through the Whitney years, Ontario retained the traditional two-party system. No marked ideological difference divided the Liberals and Conservatives, although shades of policy difference clearly did. Whitney left six weeks after the outbreak of World War I, to be replaced by William Hearst, but the old man's departure removed a steadying moral influence from the Conservative party. Powerful business interests were lining up to exploit the province's natural resources, and in George Howard Ferguson, minister of lands, forests and mines, the companies found a willing ally. There was nothing new in the companies' attitudes; Ontario's mining, timber and private hydroelectric interests had tried since the nineteenth century to squeeze whatever concessions they could from the provincial government.[26] Ferguson promoted quite specific ideas about opening up northern Ontario. As his biographer noted, "his primary responsibility, he believed, was to further the economic growth of the province and in pursuit of this objective the regulations of the department were there to *guide* but not to *restrict* him."[27] Ferguson, eager to stimulate economic activity, gave

companies important concessions, often without tendering or competition. They, in turn, offered financial assistance to the Conservative
party. But it took a new political party, one whose genesis and electoral
victory represented a last gasp rather than a fresh beginning, to cast
Ferguson's methods in a darker light, and even then the impact on
voters was ephemeral rather than lasting.

Ferguson's encouragement of the corporations was only one man-
ifestation of Ontario's fast-paced industrialization and urbanization.
Pressured by these two historical forces the farm economy faltered and
the small towns and modest cities that lived therefrom could not retain
their population, political clout or social cohesion. At the turn of the
century, the ratio of rural to urban dwellers had been 57 to 43; by
1921, the ratio was 42 to 58.[28] The war, too, tore up communities
everywhere, but the dislocations and losses were probably felt more
severely in small towns and rural areas, till then untouched by the
anomie of urban life. From their sense of declining power arose a determination to resist, even arrest, the forces causing the decline, and it
embodied itself in the United Farmers of Ontario (UFO). Founded in
1914 as a business co-operative, the organization was transformed into
a political movement, especially by the federal government's decision
to conscript farmers' sons. Like its sister in Alberta, the UFO purported
to be above party politics and to scorn the ways of the old-line politics.[29]

In 1919, the UFO executive committee drafted an election platform that included a resolution to abolish patronage. At the same time,
the Independent Labour Party (ILP), a new formation in the cities,
denounced the evils of the old parties, including political corruption.
In the 1919 election, when the electoral maps still favoured rural areas,
many candidates ran as joint representatives of the UFO and the ILP.
To the astonishment and consternation of both Conservatives and Liberals, enough of his new breed won to make Ernest Charles Drury, the
UFO leader, Ontario's premier. For the first and only time in the province's history, the Conservatives and Liberals were both beaten. The
UFO party, however, did not cut a new political mould, as occurred
in Alberta. Its win represented a political fluke, rural Ontario's last
hurrah, a flickering and ineffectual rebellion by the forces of anti-
partyism.

A sense of moral superiority, the steady companion of the critics
of patronage everywhere, pervaded the UFO. Considering themselves
good citizens first and politicians second, its members felt ready to
bring the virtues of honesty and integrity to the sordid arena of politics.
They scorned, even feared, corporate power which in their eyes had
perverted the economic and social priorities of the province at the
expense of the agricultural community. They distrusted the links
between business and the old-line parties, especially the Conservatives,

believing that such links led directly to political corruption. A campaigning Drury had promised clean government and the end of patronage.

Once elected, Drury was often true to his word. He kept on civil servants from the previous regime; in his own constituency he even appointed a returning officer with no partisan credentials, a decision foreign to the political culture of Ontario. The UFO leadership may have rested comfortably with its political purity; the rank and file did not always share their comfort. UFO clubs were sometimes angry that candidates for local offices lacked UFO credentials.[30]

The Drury government, convinced that political corruption flowed from the cozy relations between politicians and the corporate sector, pursued allegations agsint Ferguson. A commission charged with investigating "maladministration and irregularities in departmental policy and procedure" found that in awarding licences Ferguson had been guilty of irregular and illegal private arrangements benefiting timber companies.[31] He had routinely granted rights, below the going rate and without public tender, to companies he thought likely to push development forward as rapidly as possible. In 1917, for example, he sold a limit at $6.26 per thousand feet when the price could have been $17. In 1919, he sold two limits for $9.50 per thousand when the price could have been $20.

Ferguson justified preferential rates on the grounds that the company intended to introduce innovative and beneficial forestry techniques. Indeed, he stoutly defended all his actions, before the commission and wherever the occasion arose: "I was superior to the regulations," he insisted, "where I thought it was in the interests of the province. . . . no regulation should hold up the development of the country. . . ." Procedures and regulations were fine in their place, so long as they did not unnecessarily impede development. "The first priority of government," he proclaimed, "is to provide businessmen with every reasonable assistance in creating large-scale, efficient industrial enterprises."

Plenty of evidence emerged that Ferguson, while not personally remunerated for these arrangements, had certainly given financial advantage to the companies he favoured. Yet the best defence, in politics as in sports, is often a relentless offence, and Ferguson executed the strategy to perfection.

Ferguson accused the commissioners of partiality. His UFO tormentors, he charged, were also letting contracts without public notice or tender — a charge fully justified in two cases involving the minister of public works, F.C. Biggs.[32] He insisted that however irregular his own actions, the best interests of the province had always animated them, and he also revealed that the Drury government's counsel to the commission held a retainer from a competitor to one of the timber companies under investigation. Stumping the province with cries of "witch hunt" and "hypocrisy," he succeeded in turning what could have been a fatal blow against his political career into a mild rebuke, easily shrugged off by him and quickly forgotten by a healthy slice of the electorate. So effective were his charges against the commission that they furthered the already growing notion that UFO ministers were amateurs in office, and not terribly gifted ones at that.

Many were the reasons for the unravelling of the Drury government — and they are beyond the scope of this essay to chronicle — but when the end came in the 1923 election, Drury himself was defeated, his movement in tatters, his own future uncertain. He ran again unsuccessfully in 1926, then began a dispiriting hunt for a patronage appointment of his own. He wrote to Prime Minister Mackenzie King — "his original political benefactor," for Drury had once been a Liberal — asking for "some sort of public service to restore his situation . . . in short, a job."[33] He wanted the chairmanship of the international waterways commission, but neither that nor any other position came his way. He ran as a Liberal-Progressive candidate in the 1930 federal election, lost, and suffered the humiliation of a newspaper story that the company for which he worked had received $80,000 to store liquor in its Toronto warehouse, a sore embarrassment to a lifelong crusader for temperance. In 1934, the Liberal win in Ontario encouraged Drury to try again for a position. He dashed off a letter to Premier Mitchell Hepburn, then appealed personally to the Liberal leader for "some position which I could fill with a certain amount of dignity and where the salary would enable me to carry on."[34] Drury subsequently received the combined position of sheriff, county clerk and local registrar of the Supreme Court of the County of Simcoe. Apparently not once during all these entreaties did Drury see any contradiction between his previous denunciation of office-seeking and his own actions, but then the allure of patronage often does turn men's heads.

Happily for Premier Howard Ferguson, elected in 1923, the UFO government had left many occupants of civil service positions unchanged, so that no purge (such as the one that was to attend the Liberal victory in 1934) was necessary. The Conservatives pushed aside a few UFO appointees, but the UFO interregnum had not fundamentally undermined the Conservative party's power in the province. As one writer has noted of early twentieth-century Ontario:

> "This was a close-knit structure of social, economic and political power. In centre after centre across the province, Conservatives occu-

pied most of the positions of influence on school boards, in municipal government, in minor appointive offices, and in areas of community leadership and prestige generally. In one sense this was what a machine was all about, but it was equally true that Tory political hegemony was so firmly established, despite the accident of 1919, that a machine was almost superfluous. Being a Liberal in Toronto in the twenties . . . was a little like being a Communist at a later date."[35]

In his seven years as premier, Ferguson grew in stature, in the eyes of his supporters, even into something resembling a statesman. But he always remained a scrappy and, when necessary, ruthless partisan. His critics labelled his methods those of Tammany Hall, but that may have just been a pejorative description of the way politics was played in Ontario. Ferguson put his private secretary in charge of ensuring that "friendly papers" received government advertising, something every Conservative and Liberal government had always done. The civil service, especially at the lower levels, was stocked with Conservatives, as were the boards and agencies at the government's command. Occasionally, somebody raised a fuss about the partisanship. Mrs. Adam Shortt, vice-chairman of the mother's allowance commission, resigned in 1927 charging that political influence, not the decisions of the civil service commission, dictated appointments. But David Jamieson, president of the commission, blandly stated the conventional view when he acknowledged his own Conservative credentials and said that like-minded partisans would continue to receive appointments, provided they demonstrated sufficient talent.[36]

Oliver Mowat's fight with John A. Macdonald had been the first of many post-Confederation struggles in Ontario over the state's role in the sale of liquor. Whatever the liquor trade did for consumers, it provided a ready supply of funds and patronage for governments. Back and forth in early twentieth-century Ontario went the arguments over temperance. A plebiscite in 1924 gave supporters of the *Ontario Temperance Act* a narrow majority (35,000 votes). But other provinces were raking in revenues from liquor, and Ontario was running a deficit. Ingenious inhabitants manufactured all manner of spirits and near-beer; smugglers brought the brew from across the border. The rural areas remained largely opposed to legalized liquor, but their weight was declining. Slowly, the majority shifted in favour of scrapping the *Ontario Temperance Act*. Just to be sure, the Ferguson government " 'hived' the dries, transforming nine mainly rural seats that had supported prohibition into ten tinged with urbanity that were more likely to be wet."[37]

In 1926, Ferguson campaigned for controlled sale of liquor with the slogan "Booze or Bankruptcy," and won handily. Four months later, the Ferguson government created the liquor control board (LCBO), which immediately became one of Ontario's prime repositories of patronage. No sooner had the legislation been passed than Conservatives scrambled for the jobs at the top and, more important, in the outlets that sprang up across the province. For decades thereafter, LCBO outlets provided political patrons with useful places to put job-seekers of the proper political persuasion.

The Conservative dynasty, interrupted only briefly by the UFO, seemed set to continue when Ferguson took his leave from politics in 1930 and accepted a prime patronage plum from R.B. Bennett's federal government, that of Canadian high commissioner in London. George Henry, Ferguson's successor, had been in the legislature since 1913, a sober, wealthy man with all the right business connections and the experience of senior portfolios in the Ontario government. It was, however, his misfortune to become premier just as that political leveller, the Great Depression, settled on Ontario. The Depression blighted everything it touched, including the increasingly helpless Henry government. While the government thrashed about, the new leader of the Liberal party gathered up the resentments of a hurting population and made them his own.

Mitch Hepburn was quite unlike any politician Ontario had ever seen. Fiery and implacable, he blitzed Ontario with a torrent of rhetoric, lashing out against the "interests," pillorying the Conservatives for excessive spending and lavish ways. He could fairly be described as a populist who knew what he opposed more clearly than what he favoured. It took some years for the whole province to know that he could be mercurial, even wildly unpredictable, characteristics those who knew him well had understood all along. But in those years of dislocation and pain, Hepburn's voice offered hope for better times and revenge against those — namely the complacent Conservatives — who rode in their limousines and dined in fancy restaurants while Ontario writhed.

The Liberals had wandered in the political wilderness for nearly three decades before Hepburn swept them into office in 1934. Thus were they inordinately hungry for the spoils of power, and Hepburn had frankly told Ontario that the civil service would take a lashing once he settled into the premier's office. Symbolic changes quickly followed the election: Ontario House in London, England, was closed, and government limousines were auctioned in a theatrical coup at Toronto's Varsity Stadium; all civil servants hired since October, 1933, were fired; government boards and agencies were amalgamated or abolished.[38]

Those gestures were among Hepburn's promised economies. Elsewhere, the purging of Conservatives and rewarding of Liberals proceeded apace. Soon after the swearing-in, the cabinet passed an order-in-council scrapping the May, 1933, list of newspapers approved for government advertising. A substitute list of sympathetic Liberal papers was ready in February, 1935, based on recommendations from Liberal MPs, sought in a private letter to them from Hepburn's principal secretary.[39] The new list, a staple of Ontario politics, would be periodically updated, depending upon the editorial behaviour of the newspapers. To give just one example, the president of the Toronto Men's Liberal Association wrote Premier Hepburn in April, 1936, that "owing to the fact that the two newspapers in my riding, *The Riverdale Gazette* and *The East Ender*, have criticized the present provincial administration recently, I would ask that they be discontinued from any further participation in provincial government advertising. . . ."[40] The request was duly approved.

Across the province, Liberal associations geared themselves up for patronage and, where necessary, prodded Hepburn to wield his axe quickly. Sometimes the appointments came so fast that the local Liberal organizations felt slighted. In Leeds the new MLA made four appointments, apparently in haste, and the president wrote to Hepburn warning that "local patronage and appointments . . . should be done with great caution and care, and only after recommendation by the local organization, otherwise trouble is ahead. Considerable grief has already arisen."[41] From every constituency came long lists of approved suppliers, replacing the previous Conservative lists.[42] These lists, the backbone of government purchasing, were circulated to all departments.

Road contractors, accounting firms, snow-plow operators — all the part-time employees of the Ontario government were changed. Letters poured in soliciting employment. Some were heartbreaking, many were blunt. A Liberal from Hepburn's Elgin riding wrote: "I have taken a lot of persecution from Conservatives and never asked a favour. . . . Now that we have them on the run, which I am sure we will keep on doing, I think a few of the spoils of war are in order. And as a taxpayer and supporter of the cause of Liberalism, I am asking you as a personal friend to do what you can for me personally."[43] Even the premier, exercising the power of patronage in his own constituency, was not held to be above reproach. Two early appointments went down poorly, and the president of the St. Thomas Liberal executive felt compelled to write Hepburn a "Dear friend" letter; the Liberals, the letter complained, "are very dissatisfied with the way appointments are being made."[44]

So, too, that invaluable source of political patronage — the government liquor outlets — witnessed wholesale changes in personnel. A good chunk of a 1936 memorandum from the deputy chief commissioner of the liquor control board to the board's chief commissioner is worth recording for the light it sheds on how the system worked.

> "In September 1934 I held a Meeting with all the Toronto Liberal Members and Defeated Candidates from the Toronto Ridings and it was mutually agreed, and according to the Toronto Members likewise agreed with the Honourable Prime Minister that the sixteen stores operated by the Liquor Control Board in the City of Toronto should be treated as one unit and that the matter of promotions or location of the various employees would be left entirely to the discretion of the Board.
>
> After holding many meetings with the representatives of the nineteen ridings and after they had gone over the list of all employees very carefully, I was finally notified through Mr. Kirby who acted as Chairman the desires of the nineteen representatives and as a result, certain dismissals were made.
>
> Since July 1934 there have been 49 men appointed to positions in the liquor stores in Toronto and of these five were former employees who were dismissed and later re-instated so that actually only 44 new men have been appointed. . . . In addition to the above, there have been five appointments made which were not directly on behalf of any Riding, but were agreed to all the ridings on behalf of Toronto Men's Liberal Organization.
>
> If in need of an employee for any of our stores, the procedure I have followed is to get in touch with Mr. Harold Kirby who calls the Members of the various Ridings together and when it is agreed which riding is to make the appointment, that particular riding notifies Mr. Kirby of their choice and he in turn notifies me. . . ."[45]

Wholesale firings occurred throughout the province, justified on grounds of economy, although most of the positions were refilled. On one Saturday in January, 1935, the government fired ten employees in Toronto, five in Belleville, two in Simcoe, and one in Peterborough.[46] Everywhere in the civil service jobs were at risk — from well-paying posts at the workmen's compensation board, Ontario Hydro and the liquor control board to the smaller positions of issuers of motor vehicle licences, coroners, registrars of deeds, sheriffs. As quickly as possible and with resolute determination, Hepburn placed a Liberal stamp on the Ontario public service and on all those positions within the scope of the Ontario government. He accepted patronage as a political way of life and used it for his party's political purposes.

George McCullagh, publisher of *The Globe and Mail* and a Hepburn confidant until their falling out, appealed to the premier: "I do believe Mitch that if you took one of your characteristic fearless stands and told the public that you were sufficiently unconventional to throw aside partisanship if necessary, and openly state that the patronage system was through as far as you were concerned . . . you could, by your example, create a much needed reform right across Canada, and I say Mitch with profound sincerity that you would go down in history as the greatest man this country has ever known."[47] Here was an entreaty from a businessman (later to found the Leadership League) reflecting the periodic concern of his ilk that patronage led to waste, inefficiencies and higher taxes. It had been the lament of critics of patronage throughout Canada's history. Hepburn was deaf to such idealistic proposals. He was operating in the cauldron of partisan politics, and having done something about trimming the size of the public service as promised, he was bound to leaven the smaller cake with Liberal worthies, accordingly placing them in some of the remaining positions.

Mitchell Hepburn began his political career in the House of Commons, winning a seat in 1925. His relations with Prime Minister Mackenzie King, therefore, predated his election as Ontario Liberal leader in 1930, an election King attempted to block. They were such different characters, playing to different audiences: Their antipathy to one another having been sealed in the events of the 1930 convention, it was perhaps inevitable that the two should fall out, and the tale of their mutual distaste has been frequently told. Soon after the 1935 federal election, the story goes, Hepburn suggested that a friend, Arthur Slaight, be made a cabinet minister. When King said no and told Hepburn to stick to provincial matters, the fight was on. The animosity between the two men spilled over into all kinds of federal-provincial disputes, public recriminations, acid references in King's diaries, a squabble over Hepburn's sale of the residence of the Ontario Lieutenant-governor, the premier's belief that King had slighted him during a Royal tour; and more important for our purposes, it thoroughly soured relations between the federal and provincial wings of the Liberal party in all areas of common concern, including patronage.

When making patronage appointments, it had been long customary, although not always essential, for prime ministers to solicit the advice of provincial premiers, and even provincial leaders in Opposition. Sometimes, because of Liberal unpopularity at one level of government, the political exigencies of the moment drove the party at the other level to keep its distance from its cousins. But the provincial and federal Liberal governments shared a common core of supporters, if not always a common cause, and the use of patronage by one could have an effect for good or ill upon the other. Yet so vituperative did relations become between the King and Hepburn camps that communications on patronage all but broke down. Even tentative attempts to circumvent the principal disputants by consulting their emissaries were conducted with extreme delicacy and overriding defensiveness. In 1936, King's government unilaterally cut back grants to the provinces without notifying any of the premiers. Infuriated, Hepburn instructed provincial organizers not to give money to the federal party and began separating the provincial and federal parties, a separation officially announced in June, 1937.

The public conflict was accompanied by a private one involving patronage duties.[48] Neither King nor Hepburn would consult the other about appointments. "I regret that I cannot comply with your request that I recommend your appointment as Judge to the Minister of Justice at Ottawa," Hepburn wrote a friend. "As I carefully explained to you some while ago, the relationship between the Ottawa government and myself is not the best and I have religiously refrained from making any recommendations."[49] To Frank Ahearn, a Liberal MP who wrote suggesting the name of a fellow Liberal for a judgeship, Hepburn instructed his secretary to reply: "Mr. Hepburn has always made it a practice not to interfere with federal appointments and they likewise do not make recommendations to this government."[50] Nothing is absolute in politics; Hepburn did make or acknowledge the occasional representation from federal Liberals, but it gave him pain to do it. "I have consistently refrained from making any recommendation to any minister of the federal government, but in this case I am making an exception."[51]

Relations between the two men worsened as the years went by. They got so bad that the Ontario legislature passed a resolution criticizing the King government's prosecution of the war effort. King sent an emissary, Minister of Agriculture James Gardiner, offering Hepburn a voice in selecting Ontario senators and one cabinet minister. The premier spurned the offer, claiming he would have nothing to do with federal Liberal politics as long as King led the party. The premier even urged voters to support the Conservatives, a statement that bewildered and angered Liberals throughout the province. But Hepburn remained his own man, bitter at King to the end, refusing to allow any federal Liberal to walk in the provincial garden. He had been idiosyncratic, irascible, unreasonable, and successful. His record, though, obscured the impending demise of the Liberal party, because "by his autocratic domination over the party machinery [despite numerous requests no annual meeting had been held since 1932], his dictatorial control of the cabinet, his tight-fisted handling of patronage, Mitch Hepburn had virtually been the Liberal party."[52] When he resigned, Ontario's Liberal party expired as a political threat for four decades.

The Conservative ascendancy that began in 1943 rolled on for forty-two seemingly endless years. George Drew got the new era started, but Leslie Frost best summarized its ethos. "The good old province of Ontario," the premier repeated ad nauseam.[53] Nothing could have been blander; nothing could have been more appropriate. The Conservatives took the province by storm, to protect the polity not from the Liberals, but from the red menace of the Co-operative Commonwealth Federation, which did surprisingly well in the 1943 election. But the red menace soon subsided, the war ended, prosperity returned, and the Conservatives outfitted themselves, as they had in the early decades of the century, as the guardians of prosperous, smug Ontario. Gradually, Conservative patronage extended everywhere, at times obtrusively, more often subtly. Premiers George Drew and Leslie Frost attended to many patronage matters themselves. The style of Premier John Robarts was more laid back; he delegated much authority to his unpaid political organizer and lifelong friend Ernie Jackson.[54]

If patronage brought Conservative dominance, it also brought scandals. In 1955, George Doucette resigned his post as Frost's minister of highways after three construction companies and six employees of the ministry were jailed for conspiracy to defraud the government. In 1958, three ministers resigned upon discovery that they had purchased stock in Northern Ontario Natural Gas Limited before general public sales began.[55] All the boards, agencies and commissions, which proliferated in the 1960s and 1970s, were staffed largely by Conservatives, especially former MLAs and cabinet ministers. MLAs could recommend the part-time workers, the employees of government beer and liquor outlets, the motor vehicle licence vendors, the lottery concessionaires. Occasionally, little puffs of protest blew up in the legislature, usually following a newspaper story, but the Conservatives easily dismissed them. The revelation in a *Globe and Mail* story in 1971 that most of the agents selling licence plates had ties to the Conservative party brought this candid response from Charles McNaughton, the minister of highways in the Robarts cabinet: "Patronage has always existed. It's part of our way of life, part of the democratic process. It is ludicrous to me, however, to suggest that patronage exists with one party and not with all the others."[56]

Ernie Jackson used to sort out patronage problems in the Westbury Hotel or over a late-night drink in John Robarts' office. William Davis' team met for breakfast in the Park Plaza or the private cabinet dining room in the basement of Queen's Park. Officially known as the "pre-

mier's appointments advisory committee," it was better known around
Queen's Park as the "patronage committee."[57] Ed Stewart, the premier's
chief-of-staff, chaired the meeting also attended by a cross-section of
Conservatives representing all shadings of opinion within the party.
Occasionally, the committee recommended a Liberal or a New Dem-
ocrat, but the overwhelming majority of nominees were Conservatives.
By the 1970s, in Ontario as elsewhere, patronage had largely become
a matter of allocating hundreds of appointments at the government's
disposal. Former ministers and long-serving backbenchers were almost
automatically guaranteed something upon their departure from politics
if they so desired. A study for three newspapers revealed that by 1984,
nearly one-third of the Conservative candidates under Davis' leadership
had received appointments.[58] Scouring the boards, agencies and commissions of the Ontario government, the newspapers found two
hundred and fifty-one positions occupied by persons with Conservative
credentials. *The Globe and Mail* reported in 1985 that many of the
major distributors for the Ontario Lottery Corporation also had party
ties. Ontario's offices abroad were staffed by Conservatives. And, of
course, the party had its lists of friendly lawyers, accountants, architects and advertising executives who received their share of government
business. Most obvious was the money directed to Camp Associates,
headed by Norman Atkins, chief political adviser and campaign chairman for Premier Davis.

For the most part, the whole patronage operation was miraculously smooth, as if providence had ordained it right and fitting that
Conservatives reward themselves. Sometimes, however, the seamier
side of patronage, or at least accusations of patronage abuses, rocked
the government. In the first Davis government (1971-1975), a minister
found himelf embroiled in controversy over land he and two contractors purchased within an area designated for rapid growth, and a minister resigned for inadvertently approving a subdivision in which his
family held a financial interest. Fidinam (Ontario) Limited donated
$50,000 to the Conservative party a month after winning a contract
to build new headquarters for the workmens' compensation board. An
investigation by the attorney-general's office cleared the donation of
criminal implications, but left observers dissatisfied with its report.
Gerhard Moog, a close personal friend of Davis, won the contract to
build new offices for Ontario Hydro. A legislative inquiry cleared Davis
of wrongdoing, but revealed that Moog had dropped the premier's
name in lobbying for the contract, and condemned the way Hydro
awarded the contract.

These blemishes hurt the Davis Government sufficiently that
minority governments followed, and from them emerged a new *Elec-*

tion Finances Reform Act limiting contributions to $4,000, requiring disclosure of names of contributors above $100, and partially reimbursing candidates for their election expenses. But the Act did not interrupt or change the party's approach to patronage appointments. The assumptions of all the premiers during the Conservative hegemony were the same as Frank Miller's, who acted more decisively in matters of patronage than in any other matter during his brief, unhappy leadership, and who opened the bolted door for the Liberals.

CHAPTER 12

MANITOBA

"I am sure that I am expressing the sentiments of every
reasonable-thinking person when I say that this is no
time when the welfare of a political party should be
allowed to interfere with the administration of public
affairs."
Premier John Bracken.

THE CRUCIBLE OF MANITOBA POLITICS has tested some of the most
searing issues in Canadian history—language rights, education for ethnic and religious minorities, tariff policy, equalization, transportation
rates, the power of the federal government to disallow provincial legislation, the rights of organized labour, public ownership of natural
resources. The Riel Rebellion, the Manitoba Schools Question, the
Winnipeg General Strike, the Progressive party, the Supreme Court
ruling on *The Manitoba Act* all divided the people and drew national
attention to the province. Add to the mix tensions between the metrop-
olis and countryside, the two official language groups, natives and
whites, and the welter of ethnic groups implanted throughout the province, and Manitoba has all the ingredients for intense politics.

Yet, with rare exceptions, the style of Manitoba politics in most
of this century has been marked by cautious, incremental leadership.
A few firebrands blazed across the political landscape, but many of
Manitoba's leading politicians have been, well, dull. Earnestness seems
to go with Manitoba's political territory. If Newfoundland and British
Columbia politicians stand at one stylistic extreme of provincial politics, Manitoba policians stand at the other.

Just why has the province's political culture produced so many
earnest, colourless premiers, especially since World War I? Perhaps the
very ethnic mix of Manitobans forced politicians to search for com-

240

promise, since the alternative could have been the inflaming of religious or ethnic passions. Perhaps the quelling of sharp class conflict in the 1920s, followed by the grip of the Depression and the political style of the long-serving Premier John Bracken, produced a desire for moderate politics. Perhaps the yeoman farm population contributed to what the province's leading historian called Manitoba's "steady ways."[1] Perhaps Manitoba's settlement pattern—a large influx of farmers from Ontario — and its geographic location at the centre of Canada have made it a Western province, indeed, but one less fervently attached to the attitudes of Western Canadian alienation than, say, Alberta. Perhaps the lack of oil, natural gas, uranium, potash—the natural resource flashpoints in disputes between Ottawa and other Western provinces—has meant that those resentments so frequently manifested in Alberta and to a lesser extent in Saskatchewan have not embroiled Manitoba. Perhaps, too, the extended period of essentially managerial government under various forms of coalition and co-operation among political parties, an outgrowth of a deep suspicion about the evils of traditional partyism, imbued the expectation that government should be far more about tidy, efficient management than partisan cock-fighting.

Although other Canadian provinces experimented with coalitions, none carried the experiment of inter-party co-operation further than Manitoba. For more than three decades, provincial political partisanship lost its cutting edge in Manitoba, and thus contributed, more than any other factor, to the dilution of political patronage in the province. Those three decades may have put many electors to sleep, too. Voter turn-outs, for example, declined from seventy-three percent in 1932 to sixty-six percent in 1936, fifty percent in 1941, fifty-six percent in 1945, and fifty-four percent in 1949, the last three percentages being exceedingly low by Canadian standards.[2]

Coalitions elsewhere — at Ottawa and in British Columbia and Saskatchewan, for example—produced some diminution of partisanship without removing either party supporters' demand for spoils or the obligation of the party leaders in the coalition to carve up the spoils according to inter-party understandings. These coalitions, or political understandings, reduced partisanship without eliminating it. But in Manitoba, the very notion of partisanship was held in bad odour; worse, to it were attributed many government ills, including lax morality, inefficiencies and waste. Reducing costs, an abiding preoccupation of Manitoba governments for three decades, meant squeezing partisanship. It also meant keeping government small, which in turn reduced the opportunities for the patronage of appointments and contracts. Much the same sentiment pervaded the United Farmers of Alberta, who governed under the theory of "group government," but the Alberta experience did not last as long, was driven by the grievances of farmers, and contained a strong dose of secular messianism foreign to the coalitions of Manitoba.

The long period of coalition government in Manitoba represented an extended hiatus between the politics of the nineteenth and early twentieth centuries, and the re-establishment of conventional party struggles in the 1950s which brought Manitoba some of the modern, well-known forms of political patronage. The hiatus began in 1915 with the scandal surrounding the construction of the Legislative Buildings in Winnipeg, bringing the Conservative party in particular, and the old line parties in general, into disrepute. It ended with the re-establishment of the Conservative party under Duff Roblin as a competitive force in Manitoba politics. The Legislative Buildings scandal brought down a government, exposed the corrupt underbelly of Manitoba political life, and, when blended with other social and economic reform currents, produced a new set of expectations about political behaviour. It also revived some of the criticisms of partyism that had flickered through Manitoba after the province joined Confederation in 1870.

The first short-lived Manitoba governments after Confederation were completely non-partisan, although in federal elections individual members undoubtedly supported one party or the other. Party discipline was unknown. Ministries ensconced themselves by balancing religious and ethnic factions and by ensuring that individual MLAs received sufficient patronage to keep them in line and their supporters happy.[3] Even Premier John Norquay, who led the sixth government and became known as a Conservative, originally opposed the introduction of parties. His argument — one that recurred throughout the early political history of all three prairie provinces—was that the needs of fledgling provinces could best be pressed on Ottawa by a united front at home. But government without party in the presence of diverse ethnicities—the French-speaking element, Métis or white, represented about a third of the electorate — proved unstable, just as it had in the Canadas and New Brunswick before Confederation.

Gradually, external forces reshaped provincial politics. Settlers from Ontario brought the partisan identifications of their native province. The national parties, organized for federal purposes, desired the creation of provincial parties. And federal government decisions, notably the disallowance of provincial railway charters designed to provide competition for the Canadian Pacific Railway, forced provincial politicians to take sides. By the early 1880s, Norquay had aligned himself with the federal Conservatives, betting that through partisan co-operation he could change Sir John A. Macdonald's disallowance policy.

The Liberals, dominated by Ontario settlers raised on Oliver Mowat's cry of "provincial rights," naturally disagreed, so that the first sharp partisan cleavages began running through Manitoba policies.[4] Under Thomas Greenway, a transplanted Ontarian and former MP for South Huron, the Liberals formed a united front. They hammered the Conservatives for being in cahoots with Macdonald's policy of disallowance and Macdonald for his protection of the CPR's monopoly clause, his denial of higher subsidies to Manitoba, and his refusal to give Manitoba control of Crown lands. Norquay, a grudging Conservative never on intimate terms with Macdonald, tried to change federal policy while accepting money for electoral purposes from the CPR bagman, the CPR having already established itself elsewhere as the "Conservative party on wheels."[5]

With the 1886 election partisan politics were established in Manitoba, and Norquay scarcely survived their arrival. His government, assisted by the federal Conservatives in the election but at the same time fighting their unpopularity, barely clung to power. In such circumstances, and now out of patience with Macdonald, Norquay proceeded to authorize construction of a rail line in the southern Red River Valley. The government believed it had had verbal assurance from John A. that federal grants would be forthcoming to defray the costs. When Macdonald denied making any such promise and disallowed the provincial legislation, the province attempted to float bonds to finance construction. Without sufficient collateral, the bond issue failed.[6] To that considerable humiliation were added substantiated charges that financial irregularities had marked relations between the premier and his provincial treasurer and the Hudson Bay Railway. Both resigned, Norquay's successor's proposed cabinet ministers were defeated in by-elections, and the Liberals under Greenway took power.[7] Now Manitoba politics took on the more sharply partisan colouration of provincial politics elsewhere in Canada: a fight between the "ins" and the "outs" for spoils, and elections featuring all sorts of illegal and dubious tricks.

No sooner did Greenway become premier than he resorted to that familiar and tempting tactic: redistribution. The 1888 redrawing of the electoral boundaries was a gerrymander, "hiving the Tories," to turn Macdonald's phrase on its ear. Greenway naturally insisted a gerrymander was the furthest tactic from his mind, but "there were all kinds of details of riding boundaries that benefited his party."[8] Norquay had ensured that most civil service jobs went to Conservatives—Macdonald was using the federal civil service for the same purpose — so Greenway pushed through legislation disenfranchising those federal and provincial employees earning more than three hundred dollars a year. Another redistribution in 1891 represented another stab at gerry-mandering the electoral map. And Greenway's attorney-general, Clifford Sifton, presented amendments to the *Election Act* absolving candidates of charges arising from any illegal activities by their supporters during an election, thereby providing candidates with the classic plea of ignorance as a defence against charges of electoral chicanery.

Sifton defended the amendments by insisting that honest candidates should not be brought low by supporters' excessive zeal. Opposition papers regarded the amendments as an invitation to widespread electoral skulduggery and howled with outrage. As Sifton's biographer wrote, "So obvious was the virtue of the legislation that the government assumed it required no debate. The chairman of the law amendments committee secured a favourable report on it by adjourning the committee, and later the same day, reconvened it without notifying the Opposition members. Two days later, Sifton had the House reconvened after dinner at 7:30 p.m. instead of the usual hour of 8:00. Unaccountably, someone again neglected to inform the Opposition, and the bill passed without a dissenting word or amendment."[9]

The whole nation later to came to know Sifton's views about patronage and political tactics after he joined Laurier's cabinet as minister of the interior in the 1896 "Ministry of all the Talents," but Manitobans knew him well before that as the dominant member of Greenway's cabinet. It was said of Sifton that he had a mind like a steel trap, the memory of an elephant and the hide of a rhinoceros, three formidable attributes in the fiercely partisan fray of late nineteenth-century Manitoba politics. To him, politics was war by peaceful, if questionable, means. He offered no quarter to political adversaries, and expected none in return. In one instance, Sifton even hired a spy to infiltrate the Conservatives' organization, so that if they brought charges against him or other Liberals, he could produce evidence against them.[10]

In those decades, in Manitoba as elsewhere, railwaymen and politicians were bound together in either mutual support or lacerating enmity. The CPR had tied Manitoba to the rest of Canada, but the tie that bound made farmers resentful of the CPR's freight rates and its refusal to countenance competition. As the population grew, so did demands for new branch and main lines, demands upon which the Liberals capitalized to oust the Conservatives. What Macdonald, facing ceaseless agitation from Manitoba, had reluctantly been prepared to concede to Norquay's Conservative successor, he granted to Greenway — the right to foster competition by sanctioning new lines. New lines produced lower rates, but none of the new companies could match the CPR in money and political clout, a practical conclusion drawn by Sifton. As the years passed, Sifton slowly guided the Greenway government into a closer relationship with the CPR. By the end of the Greenway years, the CPR had become an important source of financial support for the Liberal party and an ally that could sometimes be counted on in pre-electoral periods to place a branch line where the dictates of Liberal politics demanded. CPR employees, once captives of the Conservatives, became useful supporters of the Liberals.

Greenway himself was tarnished by allegations of scandal when the *Manitoba Free Press* accused him of having accepted bribes to give a lease to the Northern Pacific Railway instead of the Manitoba Central. A disagreement in the grand jury prevented the issue from being brought before the courts. A Liberal-appointed royal commission exonerated Greenway and cabinet minister Joseph Martin (also a director of the Northern Pacific), but the allegations hung in the political air. Whether Greenway did accept bribes is now considered an "unanswered" question, although everyone acknowledged at the time that railways financed parties and politicians.[11] Apart from souring the political atmosphere, the bribery charges drove Rodmond Roblin out of the party towards a way-station that would eventually lead him to the leadership of the Conservative party and the premiership of Manitoba.[12] Years later, he would fall in a spectacular scandal.

Roblin's departure and subsequent work for the Conservative party was brilliantly timed. The Greenway government, having lost Sifton and Joseph Martin, quickly ran out of steam. The premier himself was a second-rate politician. His railway policy had embroiled the government in difficulty, his famous compromise over schools with Laurier irritated disaffected groups, and his own performance paled beside the campaigning skills of Rodmond Roblin and the man for whom he stepped aside in the 1899 campaign, Hugh John Macdonald, son and heir of Sir John A. The Conservatives won the 1899 election, but the next year Hugh John Macdonald resigned to contest a federal seat and turned the leadership over to Roblin.

Roblin led the Conservatives to four electoral triumphs, and materially assisted the federal Conservatives in the campaigns of 1908 and 1911, thus earning himself a knighthood. He was a big man physically and an expansive one emotionally, capable of making just about every group feel he shared its concerns. He could feign interest beautifully. If ever Manitoba witnessed the working of a political machine, it was under Roblin who, with his minister of public works Robert Rogers, built an organization to rival anything the Liberals, including the federal Liberals under Sifton, could produce. Their tactics were those familiar elsewhere in Canada: reserving the civil service for partisans, engaging in every available trick at election time, dunning contractors for contributions. To take just one example, the firm that won the contract for construction of the Manitoba Agricultural College had to contribute $22,500 to the Conservative party.[13] Roblin's stout resistance to temperance brought him the services and generous support of the liquor and hotel interests. Voting lists were an irresistible temptation for tampering; all those ethnic names could be easily misrepresented and frequently were.[14] Provincial land inspectors, the Conservatives' answer to "Sifton's army" of homestead inspectors, helped fiddle the lists and secure voters' loyalty. Friendly newspapers received the bulk of government advertising. *The Emerson Journal* in 1914 nicely captured the customary pre-election mood:

> "Three weeks ago, the Roblin government kindly donated or inflicted on us a party of surveyors and this week they sent a party of telephone men. The telephone service has been on the hummer here for at least two years that we know of and it's as if the powers that be have just found out about it. Elections are undoubtedly coming soon if present indications mean anything. It seems too bad that the Roblin government let the elevators go, for if they had them now they could have sent up a party of forty or so to paint them. Has anyone heard when the road gang would arrive?"[15]

Three bruising by-elections in 1912 and 1913 — one federal and two provincial — typified the fierce clash between the Conservatives' provincial machine and that of their Liberal opponents. The losing Liberal candidate in the Gimli by-elections charged — the Conservatives matched his charges in kind—that "public moneys were improperly and corruptly employed," that "bribery was extensively practised and corrupt treating was carried on," that "liquor was freely dispensed," that "intimidation was largely practised and that employees of the Manitoba government and officers of the law were personally guilty of intimidation, bribery and distribution of liquor."[16]

The Roblin machine won seven by-elections between 1910 and 1914, but its electoral tactics and overt use of the spoils of power for partisan purposes drew unflattering notices, especially when the Liberal party began pulling itself together after 1910. Cries of "machine politics" filled the Liberal press, cries predictably dimissed by Conservative organs. More important, the Roblin government's attitude contrasted with the pious promises to reform patronage emanating from the federal Conservatives under Robert Borden. Most significant of all, however, were the various social and economic reform movements springing up in Manitoba for which "machine" politics epitomized the dead hand of entrenched control by a male-dominated, British oligarchy.

Supporters of direct legislation (an idea imported from the United

States via Ontario), women's suffrage (led by Nellie McClung), temperance (the cause of many churches), and a better deal for farmers all agitated for political change. Roblin's government, conservative at heart, took passing note of these demands, adopting legislation for workmen's compensation and establishing a public utilities commission. (It had previously created Manitoba Telephone in 1905.) But it was the Liberal party which most clearly identified itself with the broad current of reform, promising in the 1914 campaign a host of important changes. In that election, the Liberals received support from the Methodist and Presbyterian conferences, Baptist ministers, the Social Service Council, the Orangemen, the Political Equality League, *The Manitoba Free Press*, *The Winnipeg Tribune*, *The Grain Growers Guide*.[17] The Roblin machine hung on in 1914, courtesy of ethnic votes, but in that campaign first appeared the charges that eventually produced the greatest scandal in the political history of Manitoba.

For more than four decades, Manitoba's legislators had conducted the public's business in a variety of ill-equipped buildings. In 1913, the Roblin government decided that Manitoba should have its own, proud Legislative Building, a splendid neo-classical structure facing north in homage to the province's northern riches, with the British tie symbolized by a statue of Queen Victoria seated on a throne. The government duly awarded the contract to a friendly company, Thomas Kelly and Sons of Winnipeg, at an estimated cost of $2,859,700. What had plagued the construction of the Canadian Parliament Buildings now repeated itself. Design changes, or so they were called, soon pushed up the estimate by $700,000. Further changes, recommended by the provincial architect and approved by a Conservative-dominated legislative committee, increased the cost to $4,500,000.

These escalating costs convinced Liberals that something serious had gone awry. In the 1914 campaign, furious debates and fierce partisanship broke out in riding after riding. The Liberals even hired the Thiel Detective Agency to watch the Conservatives. The firm's bill included charges for such work as "cultivating the mixing with politicians, crooks and grafters," and "shadowing R. Rogers," the former minister of public works who had become a member of Borden's federal cabinet.[18] The Liberals also filed petitions alleging that funds for the Legislative Buildings had been siphoned into Conservative coffers. After the election, the Liberals resumed their attacks using the public accounts committee to pursue their investigation. That the Conservatives did indeed have something to hide seemed evident when the government conspired to keep a key witness, the government inspector for the project, out of the country throughout the hearings.[19]

The Conservative majority produced a suitably whitewashed

report the Liberals immediately denounced. They claimed that the province had been defrauded of $800,000 and that monies from the contract had freely flowed to the Conservative party. They petitioned Lieutenant-Governor Douglas Cameron, a former MLA from Ontario and an ardent Liberal appointed by the Laurier government. Cameron immediately made life thoroughly miserable for Premier Roblin. The premier demanded prorogation of the legislature. Cameron refused, unless the premier granted the Liberals' demand for a judicial commission of inquiry into their allegations. Roblin admitted to the lieutenant-governor that $250,000 had gone astray, but he denied corruption. Faced with the lieutenant-governor's intransigence, however, Roblin consented to a commission led by T. G. Mathers, chief justice of the Court of King's Bench.

It did not take the Mathers commission long to corroborate the Liberals' case. So damaging was early testimony that six weeks into the commission's hearings Roblin, premier for nearly fifteen years, agreed to resign and make way for a Liberal government under Premier Tobias C. Norris. "There is no doubt," said Roblin, "that Mr. A. B. Hudson [the Liberal MLA who made the allegations] had substantial justification for his statements regarding overpayments etc. in connection with the erection of the new Parliament buildings." Unfortunately for Roblin, whatever understandings he thought he had secured about ending the commission's work fell apart. Mathers, the lieutenant-governor, and the new government were anxious that the commission should drive a few additional nails into the coffin of the Conservative party. This the commission proceeded to do, hearing more evidence and concluding that the charges were "fully proven." The commission found that Roblin, one of his senior ministers and Kelly had entered into a fraudulent conspiracy even before the contract for the Legislative Buildings had been signed. The deal was sweet and simple; the contractors would kick back to the Conservative party the amount by which the contracts had been padded.

The scandal of the Legislative Buildings — a classic of its genre in Canadian political history—was the most compelling, but by no means the only, target of Liberal charges against the Conservatives. The Liberals had also alleged fraud in the construction of the new court-house. Again, Chief Justice Mathers was summoned for an investigation, but he found nothing improper. Another Liberal charge, this one about misuse of highway funds by Conservatives in the 1914 election, did produce a judicial finding against senior members of the Conservative party who had misappropriated funds and engaged in forgery and fraud. Still another investigation — into the construction of the Agricultural College — found that Kelly's firm had been overpaid by

$302,789 and that three Conservatives, including the former minister of public works Robert Rogers, had bought the site at $179 an acre, then sold it to the government for $350 an acre. Rogers, now a federal minister, immediately ordered another commission to review these findings, and this commission exonerated him and his colleagues.

Whatever the sordid details, whatever the allegations and denials, the entire period soured Manitobans on politics in general and parties in particular. True, the Conservatives had been found out, but strong suspicions abounded that, if given half a chance, the Liberals would have done likewise. When Kelly's firm was hauled off the Legislative Buildings project, the Norris government hired a contractor sympathetic to the Liberals, although no kickbacks sullied the deal. The whole political world stood besmirched. Politics meant parties, parties became machines, machines turned to corruption and patronage, corruption and patronage brought waste and inefficiency, waste and inefficiency heaped unnecessary burdens on the taxpayers. To struggling farmers and cost-conscious businessmen, this extended equation discredited political parties and entailed the apparently inescapable evils associated with them. That there must be politics seemed self-evident, since a democracy required the making of public choices. But there the extended equation ended, because if parties could be abolished and replaced by some other organization, then government would become a matter of administration.

Corruption, patronage and scandals were not unique to Manitoba. Nor was the kind of political behaviour revealed by the Conservative and Liberal parties. And yet in Manitoba and Alberta, the enduring antipathy towards the conventional party system took root as nowhere else in the country. Alberta, under the United Farmers of Alberta and their theory of "group government," opted for one alternative; Manitoba opted for another.

It took half a decade for Manitoba's alternative to crystallize. The Norris government, true to its reformist promises, put Manitoba in the Canadian vanguard by giving women the right to vote. It adopted prohibition which cut the links between government and the liquor and hotel interests. It introduced the *Initiative and Referendum Act* inspired by the American example, but the Canadian courts found this legislation unconstitutional, an abrogation of the Crown's supremacy in Parliament. Of special potential consequence for patronage, the legislature adopted the *Civil Service Act* of 1918, providing for a civil service commissioner. Wholesale changes in the outside service had followed the political changes of 1888, 1899 and 1915. Agitation for civil service reform had begun about 1910, reflecting pressures from social and economic reform groups inspired by the example of American reformers. The *Civil Service Act* spoke to these reformist demands, but none too effectively. The single commissioner was proscribed from dealing with classifications and promotions. He became, in the words of one student, a "glorified interviewer."[20]

The Norris government, earnestly pressing these reforms after a smashing victory in 1915, struggled to free itself from the opprobrium attached to party politics in Manitoba. It achieved a modest success, for at least the Liberal party survived to remain a factor in Manitoba politics for decades to come. But in the eyes of many voters party politics remained tarnished. Businessmen blamed it for extravagance, trade unionists equated it with class rule, single-interest groups viewed it as forcing grubby compromises. Most important, farmers increasingly looked upon parties as inadequate vehicles for addressing their own needs.

The farmers of Manitoba, or at least some of them, had first organized under the Farmers' Protective Union in 1883. Their demands resonated through the subsequent history of Western Canada: provincial control of public lands, tariff changes, an end to monopolies by railways and elevator companies. Implicit in these first complaints was the unwillingness of traditional parties, dominated by central Canadian interests, to heed the special needs of farmers in particular and Western Canada in general. Other farm organizations picked up the same refrains: the Grange, the Farmers' Alliance, the Patrons of Industry.[21] The United Farmers of Manitoba (UFM) was the most effective and durable of these organizations. It shared farmers' goals, articulated their grievances, and manifested the traditional mistrust of parties. In 1914, at the height of Liberal-Conservative partisanship, the UFM president denounced ". . . partyism gone mad, partyism that cannot see any fault in its own party, and cannot see any good in the opposition . . . partyism that puts a premium on dishonesty and . . . condones acts which, if a man or a party of men practised in other business, would mean that they would at once be frowned out of a decent society. My candid opinion . . . is that such partyism . . . is the great curse of present-day politics, inasmuch as it opens the way to all manner of corruption."[22]

The revolt against partyism took on new life following the election of the United Farmers of Ontario in 1919, the emerging strength of the United Farmers of Alberta, the scandals of Manitoba politics, the economic downturn following the war, and the persistent refusal of national parties to deal adequately with farmers' complaints. (Laurier had disappointed them; Borden annoyed them.) The farmers decided to enter politics — but in their own fashion. They would run candidates, but there would be no leader and the party platform specifically rejected partisan politics. In the 1920 provincial election, the UFM elected twelve members in a fifty-five seat legislature. The UFM, insisting on its opposition to party government, refused to move into what is conventionally called "the Opposition"; instead, it co-operated with the government on mutually acceptable legislation. The 1921 federal election saw sixty-five Progressives, the federal expression of the farm revolt, elected to the House of Commons. In Manitoba, the Progressives captured twelve of fifteen federal seats. In 1922, without a leader, a province-wide organization, or any other trappings of a conventional party, the UFM won the largest number of seats in the Manitoba legislature. The election, in the words of an eminent historian, "marked the culmination of the effort to get rid of 'politics'."[23]

The UFM members' first challenge was to decide who would lead them, since British parliamentary practice demanded a First Minister. They looked among themselves, found no one suitable or willing, and so turned to John Bracken, the principal of the Manitoba Agricultural College, a man who had not been a candidate or even voted in the 1922 election. Bracken did, however, enjoy an exemplary reputation in the province, and his attitudes towards government precisely reflected those of the UFM. Bracken's view — "Brackenism," as it became known — was that party politics led to frivolity, extravagance and corruption. Instead, the province required business-like, non-party government dedicated to keeping costs down and ears open to all elements of society. Critics called "Brackenism" a kind of sterile Conservatism; farmers, businessmen and plenty of other Manitobans accepted it as the proper vision for government. Ten years into his premiership, Bracken's views had not changed. "I have no sense of party politics. The only political platform I have is whatever is best for Manitoba . . . for all the people without respect of class or creed.[24]

The consequences of Brackenism for political patronage were profound and durable, since he remained in office for two decades. The aversion to partyism meant Bracken frequently reached out to other political formations for support, which in turn required abandoning the old notion of politics as a struggle between the "ins" and "outs." Bracken commanded clear majorities after the elections of 1922 and 1927, but he did not govern in the traditional manner. He listened to what other parties suggested. He abolished many of the unsavoury practices of politics. After 1927, he put out serious feelers to the Liberals to join his group in a coalition government, feelers welcomed by Prime Minister Mackenzie King. King believed Manitoba Liberals should join the Progressives — Bracken's group took that name after the UFM withdrew from the political field — to foil any resurgence of the Conservative party. The provincial Liberal leader agreed for awhile to support Bracken on a case-by-case basis, but the Liberals ruptured that understanding in 1929. Two years later, King bought off the Liberal leader with a judgeship, paving the way for a new leader favourable to coalition. After the 1932 election, a coalition of Progressives and Liberals began governing Manitoba, a result eminently satisfying to Bracken and intensely frustrating to Conservatives.

So snugly did coalitions fit with Brackenism that in 1940 the premier used the war and the alleged need for a common front to press for acceptance of the Rowell-Sirois commission recommendations as excuses to lure the other parties into a coalition. He threatened them with a general election if they balked, and their fear of Bracken's political stature and likely landslide victory made them accept his offer. Manitoba was then ruled by a coalition of five parties: Progressive, Liberals, Conservatives, CCF and Social Credit.[25]

Coalitions reduced the need for patronage by the "ins" to fortify their position against the "outs." A government that purported to represent all Manitobans and to disdain partisanship clearly had less need for patronage than did conventional parties. So, too, the economic philosophy of the Manitoba Progressives limited the field for patronage. The group's driving determination always seemed to be to reduce costs, to provide the cheapest government possible. This predilection largely explained why businessmen, who might otherwise have felt little affinity for a farmer-based political group, supported Bracken. In Manitoba in the Depression years, Keynes remained a stranger, the Labour Party existed as a marginal group, and Social Credit monetary doctrine barely received a hearing. Bracken repeatedly pressed Ottawa for funds to alleviate unemployment. His government launched a few public works projects, but cutbacks and retrenchment were his preferred prescriptions, even to the point of reducing the daily bread ration of patients in provincial mental hospitals.

And yet, alone among Canadian governments, Bracken's survived the Depression, a testament to his leadership and the degree to which it reflected popular sentiments in Manitoba. Clearly, a government so determined to reduce costs and trim bureaucracy was not about to preside over a proliferation of boards, agencies and commissions that elsewhere provided new ways of rewarding supporters. Nor could there be much porkbarrelling, since the government kept so little in the barrel. Manitoba roads, for example, remained in a rudimentary state compared with those of many other provinces until the 1950s. "Any modern state," said Bracken at the depths of the Depression, "has the option of paying its way or having deficits. We have chosen to pay our way. No responsible administration would decide otherwise.[26] Naturally, when confronted with an appointment, the government selected someone of like mind, but there were few appointments to go around. With the possible exception of Alberta, then, patronage played a less prominent role in Manitoba politics under Brackenism than in any Canadian province under any leader or ideology.

One scandal did mar the Bracken years, although it left the premier personally untouched. The decision to grant the Winnipeg Electric Company (WEC) rights for thirty years at the Seven Sisters hydroelectric site sparked a bitter debate between the advocates of private and of public ownership. Even some of those favourable to private development believed the government had settled for an inadequate deal.[27] Moreover, the Conservative leader charged that WEC had received the rights in exchange for a $50,000 contribution to Bracken's group. The subsequent royal commission never traced the $50,000 since the company did not keep records, although the bulk of the evidence suggested the accusation was false. But two cabinet ministers, including the one in charge of hydro development, were found to have purchased WEC stock while negotiations proceeded with the company. That ministers and MLAs should be stockholders in large private concerns doing business with the government was not unknown; indeed, two prominent Conservatives were in the same position. And the ministers denied they had profited financially from the deal; in fact, they lost money on their investments. But the Opposition managed to raise a sufficient uproar that Bracken dismissed both ministers, although he later brought them back into the cabinet in less senior portfolios.

Brackenism proved so successful in Manitoba, and Bracken so popular, that the federal Conservative party beckoned him to Ottawa as its leader, changing its name at his insistence to Progressive-Conservative. His departure, however, did nothing to alter the basic governing style in Manitoba. Only the balance of power within the Progressive-Liberal coalition shifted. His two successors, Premiers Stuart Garson and Douglas Campbell, were high-minded and dry Liberals who thoroughly embraced the tenets of Brackenism. They called their governments Coalition, in the best Manitoba tradition.

Manitoba emerged into what we might call the modern period of politics with the election as Conservative leader of Duff Roblin. Grandson of the premier who fell in the scandal of the Legislative Buildings, Roblin had energy and ideas, a sharp departure from the sterile negativism of previous Conservative party leaders. He offered expansive visions for Manitoba, especially the upgrading of its infrastructure and government services by public borrowing. He also had an inkling of what the future held in politics. In tandem with Roblin came the advertising agencies, campaign strategists and pollsters. Dalton Camp helped in the 1958 election, and from that point on the notion of politics as mere administration faded in Manitoba. Politics returned to a partisan mould, especially when the NDP emerged as the alternative to the Conservatives.

From Roblin until the 1988 election, Manitoba politics evolved into a two-party system with the Liberals relegated to the margin of political life. All the modern but limited manifestations of patronage emerged. Friendly advertising agencies got government business. Legal, architectural and consulting work went to firms supporting the government. The expansion of government boards, agencies and commissions, begun under Roblin, produced new opportunities for rewarding those of like political mind. Where possible, contracts were awarded to supportive firms. But, as in Saskatchewan, these manifestations of patronage took on a new justification.

In Saskatchewan, which elected the first CCF government, politicians of the socialist or social democratic persuasion tried to reconcile their commitment to the merit system with their conviction that a social democracy could not be faithfully executed by those who accepted the capitalist system. This meant appointing like-minded people to senior positions, then justifying those appointments by the philosophical affinity of the appointees for the ideals of the government. The classic defence of patronage—that the new "ins" deserved their chance—was given an additional dimension. Not just the party label of appointees counted; their broad philosophical views also became critical, since the CCF–NDP believed its high mission transcended the mere replacement of one party in power with another.

Ever since Manitoba's first NDP government, that of Premier Edward Schreyer, the political patronage of Manitoba has evolved into the model first moulded by Saskatchewan and imitated later by British Columbia. In this model, the bulk of the civil service is out of bounds for patronage, since the employees' rights are covered by statute and collective bargaining. But order-in-council appointments are persistently used to reward party supporters, or to lure to the province fellow-travellers in the socialist or free-enterprise cause, and these appointments multiply with activist governments of the Duff Roblin or Schreyer variety. The more changes one government makes, the more likely a government of another stripe will dig deeper in making changes, because the party out of power believes the whole edifice of government has been infiltrated with those philosophically at loggerheads with its ideas. Thus when the Conservatives under Premier Sterling Lyon replaced the Schreyer government, there was a sweep of order-in-council appointments as thorough as Liberal Premier Ross Thatcher's when his Liberals defeated the NDP in Saskatchewan, and as Grant Devine's when his Conservatives defeated the NDP in 1981. Upon the NDP's return to office in Manitoba under Premier Howard Pawley, the same process occurred, with the additional twist that New Democrats pushed out of Saskatchewan moved across the border into the now-friendly territory of Manitoba.

New Democrats, long removed from the messianic days of the early CCF, nowadays are as adept as their opponents in using such political discretion as remains in Manitoba to reward their friends, although they are somewhat more sanctimonious about it, usually denying that they are as spiteful as their adversaries. In the last years of the Pawley government, for example, defeated NDP ministers were given government contracts, and Elijah Harper, northern affairs minister, admitted giving jobs to three people with solid NDP links without the usual civil service competitions.[28] Government programs such as Community Plans funnelled disproportionate sums to NDP ridings, but the government typically denied that political favouritism entered the calculation.[29] And, of course, government boards, agencies and commissions were stocked with NDP supporters, most of whom retained their posts in the months of uncertainty following the Conservatives minority triumph of 1988.

New Democrats, then, turned out to be efficient users of modern political patronage, with the notable exception that favours passing between business and government have been decidedly fewer than in Liberal and Conservative regimes, for the sufficient reason that business-NDP links are tenuous. The patronage of Manitoba remains at the margin of politics, a far cry from the centrality of patronage up to the 1920s, but more evident than in the long dry years under Bracken, whose cautious, colourless, pragmatic style of governing is still the model for Manitoba politics today.

CHAPTER 13

SASKATCHEWAN

"We have abolished political patronage in
Saskatchewan."
Premier Tommy Douglas, 1945.

SASKATCHEWAN has been a kind of laboratory in which politicians of
every stripe have applied their practices of political patronage. For
nearly two and a half decades, the voters of Saskatchewan turned to
one of the most formidable political machines Canada has ever known.
Shifting sands then produced fifteen years of rule by various formations, one of which tried inconclusively to alter the traditional patterns
of patronage. Then for more than two decades the province turned to
a party that claimed to have eliminated patronage. More recently the
province has witnessed a strong two-party system with all the manifestations of contemporary political patronage. The sheer variety of
political movements and parties added yeast to Saskatchewan politics.
The province gave birth to the Co-operative Commonwealth Federation (CCF), the predecessor of the New Democratic Party, and the
Liberal and Conservative parties have never been absent from the field.
But Saskatchewan also had more than its share of other movements or
parties that jostled for a grip on public opinion: Non-Partisans, the
No-Party League, the Farmer-Labour Party, Progressives, Independ-
ents, Comrades of Equity, the Direct Legislation League, the Provincial
Rights Party, Social Credit.[1]

It is a curiosity of Saskatchewan history that before the province
entered Confederation in 1905 a non-partisan tradition prevailed, as
it did in Alberta. Yet the opponents of party politics and all the evils

associated with partisanship never made much headway in Saskatchewan even while they flourished in neighbouring Alberta. Certainly the critics of partyism in Saskatchewan did not lack for outlets. The Patrons of Industry, the first farm organization in the West, claimed as early as 1885 that partisans "won't deviate from the old party lines. With them 'The King party can do no wrong.' Principles are often sacrificed that party may exist. They are partisans, and aim to promote the interests of party. Many of them are seeking lucrative offices as a reward for their allegiance.[2] A variety of ginger groups carried the nonpartisan message through Saskatchewan after 1905. The Progressives took runs at elected office; proponents of Henry Wise Wood's theories of "group government" got their hearing; Premier William Aberhart carried Social Credit's banner across the Alberta border into Saskatchewan; but all these efforts came to nought. Even the CCF, which claimed to be something more than a party, soon turned into a powerful political party, albeit with a few wrinkles that delineated it from the Liberals and Conservatives. Once the hand of party politics grabbed Saskatchewan in 1905, its grip continued to tighten.

The Liberals, as they showed simultaneously in Alberta, were not about to let slip an early opportunity to turn the new provinces to their political advantage. Partisan politics developed as soon as the North-West Territory was granted seats in Parliament in 1886, but non-partisanship prevailed in the territorial council. The members of this body, and presumably the electors who sent them there, believed that nonpartisanship maximized the territory's leverage with Ottawa.[3] And that view died hard, because even after Saskatchewan gained provincial status in 1905, one of the two formations in the political battle called itself the Provincial Rights party. Indeed, the leader of that party, F.W.G. Haultain, harboured a plausible hope that he might be named Saskatchewan's first premier. Haultain, a man with a wide following and great experience, had been premier of the North-West Territory. Even Laurier supported Haultain's ambitions because the Liberal party stood in theory for the non-interference of the federal government in provincial affairs.[4] But Haultain, a federal Conservative, ruined his chances by scathing attacks on the autonomy bills granting provincial status to Saskatchewan and by campaigning in two Ontario by-elections for the Conservatives. That campaigning, wrote Laurier, "left us no alternative, but to accept the declaration of war."[5] The lieutenant-governor, himself a party stalwart, followed not the dictates of prerogative but the imperatives of party and selected Walter Scott as Saskatchewan's first premier, leaving Haultain to fume that "we want governments which are quite independent of Ottawa. We want men who when Western interests are involved will work with a single eye to those interests without regard to party interest or convenience."

Scott's nomination bestowed enormous political advantages on the Liberal party, for the Liberals now added provincial patronage to the federal patronage they already controlled. In the first election, which Scott described as "the hottest kind of scrimmage," the Liberals won sixteen of twenty-five seats. Many were the reasons for this triumph, but as a student of that campaign wrote, "the combination [of federal and provincial patronage] probably gave the Liberals in Saskatchewan a decisive advantage."[7]

Through their next twenty-four years in power, the Liberals never forgot what a decisive advantage patronage could be. They built what has fairly been called a "machine" based on an extensive network of individuals reaching into the smallest hamlets of the province. Four premiers oversaw the machine — Walter Scott (1905–1916), William M. Martin (1916–1922), Charles A. Dunning (1922–1926), and James G. Gardiner (1926–1929). They ran it in different ways. Scott delegated enormous responsibility to James A. Calder, who was a kind of political boss for the Liberal party. Martin drew the provincial party some distance away from its federal cousins. Dunning turned the operation of the machine over to Gardiner, his minister of highways. Gardiner, as premier, ran the machine himself and re-forged the close links between the provincial and federal Liberal parties.

The Liberal party in Saskatchewan was especially successful in integrating ethnic groups into the party and, through it, into Saskatchewan society.[8] The Liberals tried, as their political opponents frequently did not, to make immigrants feel welcome in Saskatchewan. To this, of course, they ascribed political benefits. Although buffeted by attacks from Conservatives and even by the Ku Klux Klan against their relations with the immigrant communities, the Liberals always maintained those links.[9] Federally appointed homestead agents spread the Liberal gospel among the ethnic communities in rural areas, and their message about the virtues of Liberalism applied equally to the provincial government. The Liberals paid special attention to friendly newspapers, including small ethnic ones. A revealing memo in Premier Martin's papers lists every newspaper in Saskatchewan and categorizes each according to its political persuasion.[10] Naturally, those of the proper persuasion received the usual benefits of government patronage: advertising, printing contracts, and subscriptions. Premiers everywhere paid close attention to such matters, but the need for friendly newspapers was especially acute in Saskatchewan with its scattered population and babel of linguistic groups. "Will you please advise me as to whether or not *The Milestone Mail* supported you in the recent election?" Martin wrote a Liberal MLA.[11] That was the level of detail to which premiers, or their principal designates, attended. Spreading the largesse around required careful attention, since papers checked up on how much government patronage other papers received. When representatives of *The Saskatoon Phoenix* complained to Premier Scott about government advertising appearing in *The Regina Leader*, Scott replied, "I am obliged to confess that a very important part of the reason for the expenditure was the desire to aid the institution. . . . We have no stronger desire to aid the Liberal press in the southern part of the province than we have to do the same thing in the northern part of the province."[12]

The Liberals also maintained the closest possible links to the farm movement, wisely bringing leaders of farm organizations into the government. Whereas in Alberta, Manitoba, and Ontario farmers bolted the Liberal party to create their own movements or political parties, the majority of Saskatchewan farmers remained true to the Liberals. That the farm organizations, with one notable exception, toyed with direct political action but usually decided against it, marked off Saskatchewan from its prairie neighbours. In fairness, this alliance between Liberals and farmers had little to do with patronage, although undoubtedly some discretion towards individual Liberal farmers accompanied the administration of some government programs. It had more to do with shrewd political leadership from the Liberal premiers. W. M. Martin, for instance, observing farmers' dissatisfaction with the federal Liberal government after World War I, moved his provincial party into a distant relationship with its federal cousin.

An independent MLA supposedly remarked in the 1925 election that if all government employees working in the campaign for the Liberals had been forced to wear a uniform, it would have appeared that Saskatchewan groaned under an occupying army.[13] Even allowing for exaggeration, the Liberals always assumed the civil service to be an extension of the party. That was how the Liberals under Laurier looked at the federal civil service, and the provincial Liberals adopted the same vision. Even the federal civil service reforms of the Borden government left the provincial Liberals of Saskatchewan unmoved. So apparent was the tie between party and bureaucracy that Calder, the party wheelhorse, even sent two deputy ministers to Alberta to work for the party in the 1909 and 1913 elections.[14] With the exception of two or three government agencies, including the Local Government Board and the Farm Loan Board, all appointments went to Liberal partisans. These appointees were expected to preach the Liberal gospel between and during campaigns, and to vote for the party at election time. They apparently did their bidding. In the 1925 federal election, for example, the provincially appointed employees of the Weyburn Mental Hospital cast one hundred and thirty-five votes for the Liberal candidate and six for other candidates, although the Liberal won about fifty-five percent of the total votes cast in the constituency. In the federal election of 1921, the employees of the provincial hospital at North Battleford cast one hundred and forty-one Liberal votes and twenty-one for other candidates in a riding where the Liberal candidate lost badly.[15] An ineffectual reform in 1913 gave Saskatchewan a civil service commission, but the power of appointment and dismissal was retained by the cabinet, and candidates for office continued to be nominated by Liberal MLAs.

Under Calder, and later under Gardiner, party organizers boasted representatives in every community. In villages or towns it was easy for the local representative to know with reasonable certainty how an individual intended to vote. This information could be supplemented by highways inspectors, homestead agents and other civil servants who, although technically not supposed to discuss politics, kept their ears open and reported news to party organizers. Through this splendid organization, patronage could be used to maximum advantage, especially in wooing the undecided and keeping Liberals in line. (Unregenerate Conservatives were left alone.)[16]

The machine also used the conventional technique of patronage lists of approved suppliers, lists compiled after suggestions from Liberal MLAs or defeated candidates. Outside workers in the civil service were "required to patronize exclusively these politically approved hotels, livery stables, hardware, lumber and general stores listed for every town, village and hamlet."[17] The governments shrewdly spread major public institutions around the province — the capital in Regina, the university in Saskatoon, the jail in Prince Albert, the mental hospitals in Weyburn and North Battleford.[18] The porkbarrel, especially the highways budget, was rolled out for every campaign. The Highways department theoretically planned the roads; Liberal constituency organizers in fact decided where they would bring the maximum political advantage. This technique, plus contracts and part-time jobs, seemed to be more important in Saskatchewan; bribery and treating, although probably condoned, were never as widely noted as in provinces further east. Preparation of the voting lists remained in the hands of agents appointed by the Liberal government who used their power for partisan purposes, including placing newly arrived and therefore ineligible immigrants on the voting lists.

Although opponents regularly fulminated against the "Scott machine," the "Scott-Calder machine," or the "Gardiner machine," they made little apparent headway until near the end of the Liberal domination of Saskatchewan politics. Above all, the critics, whatever their suspicions, could never pin anything corrupt or illegal on the premiers themselves or their closest colleagues. That a machine existed every opponent knew; that it personally benefited those at the top of the Liberal party no one ever demonstrated. On the contrary, each of the premiers commanded a reputation for personal honesty that added lustre to the party's reputation. And so accustomed had the population become to the machine's methods, including the immigrants and the arrivals from other provinces where the same practices abounded, that even those who objected to the outcome of patronage seldom questioned the system.

A notable exception to the pervasive calm occurred in 1916 when a Conservative MLA, J. E. Bradshaw, published charges of bribery, influence-peddling, fraud, and graft involving the Liberal-appointed civil service, Liberal MLAs and even some ministers.[19] These blockbuster allegations sparked a royal commission investigation which exonerated ministers but found four MLAs guilty of receiving bribes from and peddling their influence for liquor lobbyists. The commission also uncovered fraud in the Highways department. The findings touched off a predictable brouhaha, since they represented spectacular wrongdoing in a province accustomed to patronage but unfamiliar with public revelations of corruption. Martin, the new premier, acted swiftly, forcing two resignations, drumming one MLA out of the Liberal party, and moving for the expulsion of the fourth guilty MLA from the legislature. The decisive action contained the political damage. So, too, did the patronage extended to ethnic newspapers, most of which lambasted the Conservatives as plotters, "conspirators," and "wilful liars" during the Bradshaw affair.

The Liberal party rolled on through the 1920s, superficially impregnable and largely oblivious, as supremely confident parties often are, to social and economic trends gnawing at the party's base of support. Farm incomes were declining, racial prejudices surrounded the vexatious question of sectarian influence in public schools, resentments spread about the influence of non-Anglo-Saxons, the Conservatives selected a new leader who welcomed support from all those opposed to the Liberals, and the machine began showing signs of wear and tear. In the legislature, the Conservatives stepped up their attacks on the "Liberal machine," tying it to unpopular policies. And so, in 1929, the Liberal monopoly ended. The Liberals won the most votes and the largest number of seats of any party in the legislature, but they lacked a parliamentary majority. With the greatest of reluctance and after much hesitation, they turned over power to an unlikely combination of Conservatives, Progressives and Independents united by nothing more than their unalterable opposition to the continuation of Liberal rule.

Premier James T.M. Anderson could not have arrived in office at a less propitious time. Just around the corner lay the Great Depression, which was to ravage Saskatchewan with a special viciousness and sweep away governments of all stripes across the country. Moreover, the Anderson government lacked internal cohesion; it articulated more acutely what it opposed than what it wanted. There was about the government a strong aura of virtue triumphant, and if nothing creative could keep the government together, there always remained the glue of their common detestation of the Liberals. In addition, the Progressives and Independents insisted on civil service reform. So various inquiries were soon launched by the so-called Co-operative government into the allegedly dark practices of the Gardiner regime and the Liberal party in office.[20]

M. J. Coldwell, a future leader of the Farmer-Labour party, began investigating the civil service and quickly discovered the pervasiveness of patronage. It was an unspectacular revelation since Gardiner, for one, had never concealed his belief that responsible government required the ministry to appoint partisans to the civil service. Coldwell recommended, and the government accepted, the establishment of a public service commission to squeeze patronage from the civil service. This the Co-operative government earnestly attempted, to the consternation of Conservatives for whom the bending of the old ways to their partisan advantage seemed a preferable policy. True, the government admitted under Liberal probing that one hundred and two of approximately seventeen hundred civil servants had lost their jobs with the change in government. But this record, although not perfect, withstood comparisons to governments in other provinces and to what the Liberals would likely have done. Even the Saskatchewan relief commission, which the Liberals would surely have used for partisan purposes and which the Conservatives would have bent for their purposes if given a chance, remained untainted by patronage. Audits of the department of telephones and the farm loan board turned up scattered damaging evidence against the Gardiner regime, but nothing as damaging as the Co-operative government had hoped. An inquiry into certain activities of the provincial police produced a mild slap on the wrist for Gardiner, but nothing resembling a debilitating body blow.

"Liberal Ways Bring Brighter Days," an election slogan of the 1930s, did remind voters that material circumstances had been better before the Great Depression, and that perhaps they could hardly get worse if the Liberals received another chance. The Liberals indeed got another chance, and in 1934 Gardiner cruised back into office. A stout partisan, destined for bigger, if not better, things in Ottawa, he was for now confidently prepared to run Saskatchewan pretty much as he had before the aberration of the Co-operative government. John A. Macdonald had elevated partisan appointments in the civil service to a constitutional principle; Gardiner did not go quite that far, although his assumptions were similar. Governments were elected, held account-able, and therefore needed people they could trust executing decisions. Quickly, therefore, Gardiner abandoned the innovations of the Co-operative government. He disbanded the public service commis-sion, transferring its authority to the cabinet, and also abolished the practice of competitive examinations.[21] More than one-tenth of all pub-lic servants were given dismissal notices or resigned. Within a few months, the traditional patterns of political patronage returned to Saskatchewan.

Yet the restoration masked some profound changes that heralded a shift in the province's political culture, in particular, the disaffection towards the Liberals of an increasing number of farmers, many from the ethnic communities. For three decades, a variety of movements and parties had jockeyed for the pre-eminent role of battling the Liberals. The disparate parts of Anderson's Co-operative government merely reflected the continuation of this jockeying. Within the government, all factions had insisted on trying to expose the workings of the "Liberal machine." Only the Progressives and independents had pressed for fundamental reforms to curb patronage; they fell within Canadian his-tory's broad mainstream of protest groups deeply suspicious of the evils of partyism. When the Co-operative government fell apart, the ques-tion arose whether the Conservative party, committed to the virtues of party government, or another political formation suspicious of the evils of party would emerge as the Liberals' leading foe. As things turned out, the formation that emerged represented a hybrid of these two options. The Co-operative Commonwealth Federation was a political party all right, deeply anchored in constituency organizations and pre-pared to accept the conventions of parliamentary democracy. But it defined itself as more than a conventional political party, as a move-ment with a mission to educate the population that politics should bring fundamental social and economic change, not merely the periodic replacement of the "ins" by the "outs." Inevitably, this gave the CCF a self-imposed burden of moral superiority.[22]

When the New Jerusalem arrived, in the form of a smashing CCF victory in 1944, tensions soon emerged between the CCF as conven-tional party and the CCF as something more, especially in the broad realm of political patronage. The federal party's 1944 program spelled out how the CCF intended to approach patronage in the civil service:

"The CCF pledges itself to remove party patronage from the public service of Canada. While recognizing that heads of commissions, deputy ministers, etc., must be in agreement with the policy of the government and should therefore be government appointments, all other civil service appointments should be, and under a CCF government will be, placed under the control of a non-political commission."[23] What the party pledged for Canada, it delivered for Saskatchewan. A public service commission did begin administering competitive examinations and making appointments to all but a minority of senior posts. Government contracts, especially in the public works area, were given after competitive tenders, an important reform made easier by the CCF's estrangement from the business community, that traditional source of party funds. Yet by pledging itself to remove party patronage, what was the CCF to do to the civil service built by Liberal patronage?

CCF constituency associations left little doubt where they stood. The powerful Regina association demanded in a resolution that "the government remove reactionary departmental heads and put in their places people who are sympathetic to the CCF." Another resolution to the party's convention said: "Be it resolved that the government discharge all such officials coming under this class [those 'sabotaging the government'] and replace them, with loyal co-operators and efficient personnel."[24] In his early months in office, Premier Tommy Douglas heard frequent complaints from angry CCFers. "There are members all over the province that have spent time and money for the movement that deserve a job more than our opponents and are fully as much qualified as the liberals," wrote an ardent CCF supporter.[25] "I feel very badly that we should have to beg to place people as valuable, and at the same time retain people of doubtful worth, and whose record is against them from our point of view," wrote provincial CCF president Gladys Strum.[26] From another CCF enthusiast came this challenge, "I am glad that a change has been made, if for no other reason so that there may be a real house cleaning of the many political parasites that have been imposed on the people of this province for many years at great cost. . . ."[27]

These letters and resolutions certainly reflected the customary sentiments of the "outs" to get even with the "ins." But they also bore witness, in part, to the CCF's belief that the party was engaged in fundamental social and economic reforms which could not be faithfully executed by adherents of conventional political parties. They also spoke to the firm belief, whatever the practice, within the CCF that the party rank and file through convention resolutions and regular contact with cabinet ministers should direct the policies of the government. The desire for revenge joined the conviction of mission to place continuous pressure on Premier Douglas to sweep aside the Liberals nested in the civil service and replace them with CCF sympathizers.

Ministers, whatever their previous convictions, soon found the majority of civil servants useful, even indispensable, allies. None of the ministers had ever served in government before; most had been political tub-thumpers and crusaders, or people simply getting on with their jobs who entered politics and suddenly found themselves in positions of government authority. Their dependence upon the civil service annoyed the rank and file, the most impatient of whom could easily blame the civil service for impeding the instant transformation of Saskatchewan into the socialist paradise they had read about in their books and longed for in their minds. Premier Douglas, two years into the government's mandate, tried to reason with the impatient at the party's annual convention. "We know that people can't carry out a socialist program unless they believe in socialism," he said. "We want more socialists in the government service, but they must be trained and efficient. Until we have enough socialists trained for expert jobs, we must use our discretion in using civil servants who are not socialists but who are only trying to do a job."[28] To a CCF organizer pressing the claims of a supporter who wished to become a guide in the legislature, Douglas replied, "I don't know how we are going to persuade the general public that patronage is a thing of the past when one of our own employees keeps insisting that it be resurrected."[29]

Sensitive both to the party's commitments and to pressures from the rank and file, Douglas asked for regular memoranda from ministers about changes in personnel in their departments. A long memorandum to the cabinet — it is undated in the original — outlined how Douglas thought the government should proceed. It read, in part:

> "At present considerable attention is being given to the problem of overhauling the provincial civil service set-up. It is with this in mind that certain suggestions are made.
>
> "Upon delving into the record of past civil service activities it is only too obvious that the 'to the victor goes the spoils' attitude has coloured the whole fabric of civil service relationships within this province. Previous attempts of establishing a full-fledged public service system operating on a merit basis have suffered from a lack of sympathetic understanding on the part of all concerned. Civil service legislation has become in provincial activities what tariff legislation has been in the federal field, a political football.
>
> "With this in mind I would advise the government to remember in its present activities that as well as the immediate problem of setting [its] household in order, there is the long term problem of placing on the statute books legislation that will be respected and lasting. Much

of what is done now with regard to present appointments will colour the attitude of the public and the press (although the attitude of the press may be regarded as a foregone conclusion) toward any future legislation that is placed on the statute books. With this in mind, I would suggest that the present routine be held as closely as possible to the final ideal of a selection system. I realized that this may have no immediate appeal to certain 'enthusiastic' party followers but I believe that in the long run it will lead to less grief."

A memorandum from Carl Edy, the chairman of the public service commission, to Eugene Forsey, a CCF supporter in those days, outlined the extent of the early dismissals and resignations under the Douglas government. From May 1944 to April 1945, one hundred and ninety-three full-time civil servants resigned, sixty-nine retired, and eighteen were dismissed. In addition, three hundred and eighty-nine temporary employees resigned and another forty-seven were dismissed.[30]

Once the public service commission got going, after the "cleansing" operation, Premier Douglas respected its authority. But the party still insisted on having its say on appointments, an insistence that somewhat sullied the professed purity of the party leaders. The public service commission "certified" applicants for posts; that is, it selected the top three candidates. These names were then referred to the CCF members of the assembly, the defeated CCF candidate, or a party contact designated in each constituency. The results of this political checking into the political credentials of the candidate were then sent to the appropriate minister. In the words of one author, "the party checking procedure was a closely guarded process and, it appeared, was one to which some top officials in the government attached less importance than did those who operated it. Furthermore, the extent to which replies were received from the contacts varied. There is no indication of any attempt to influence certification as such, party activity being restricted to the final stage of selection."[31]

The CCF, believing itself seized of a higher mission, squirmed whenever practice conflicted with rhetoric. At least the party could always plausibly claim that nothing it did could compare with the ubiquitous patronage of the Liberals. Similarly, the CCF, possessed of a different ideology than the traditional parties, could insist that the realization of socialism could only come about if those implementing and administering CCF policies believed in them. You could not ask those civil servants wedded to the capitalist system, ran the CCF argument, to believe in CCF policies. They could not be expected, and in many cases trusted, to understand what the CCF was talking about, let alone what it precisely wished to accomplish. So from these early CCF days developed a rationale still prominent within the New Democratic Party, namely, that individuals who carry out policy decisions at the higher levels of the civil service and in all the appendages of government should preferably believe in CCF-NDP policies. Intellectual conviction, then, always provided the CCF-NDP with a handy defence for choosing its own supporters.

In the *post facto* assessments of the first CCF governments, true believers felt the party had erred in not cleaning out the senior civil servants. Seymour Martin Lipset, the distinguished American sociologist, wrote a deeply sympathetic book about the CCF experiment in which he lamented the caution, occasionally bordering on obstruction, of the senior civil servants. The Lipset analysis still commends itself to many New Democrats today, which raises the intriguing but unanswerable question: How would a national NDP government treat the public service? In Britain, the diaries of Labour minister Richard Crossman are replete with surly references to civil servants whose love of procedure and paper pulled socialist ministers away from radical policy changes towards incrementalism. British academics with left-wing credentials, such as Ralph Milliband and Colin Leys, offer the same complaints. If the Douglas and subsequent CCF-NDP governments in Saskatchewan, Manitoba and British Columbia offer any guide, a national NDP government would likely make some changes at the level of deputy minister, and perhaps even a few lower down, but the biggest changes would be in the Crown corporations, which the NDP would use to implement an interventionist economic policy.

For about two and a half decades the CCF in Saskatchewan represented the only avowedly socialist government in North America. Sociologists, journalists, trade unionists, all manner of curious observers flocked to Saskatchewan to study the unfolding of this novel political experiment. Everywhere in North America the Saskatchewan CCF gladdened the hearts of those of the socialist persuasion, some of whom quickly wrote in pursuit of a position. From England, too, the offers came. Before long, the head of the economic advisory and planning board was a member of the British Labour party; two Americans favouring socialized medicine joined the public health unit; Canadians from other provinces signed on in a variety of posts.[32] That, too, has remained a characteristic of CCF-NDP governments. Being few in number, they attract the converted from elsewhere.

The CCF leadership proudly pointed to its record in eliminating patronage from most of the civil service, but the rank and file resented it. The party executive periodically complained about inadequate consultation on appointments, an outgrowth of the members' broader insistence on tying party and government together. As late as 1962, a resolution at the party conference complained that "whereas there are too many employees in the public service that do not believe in the philosophies and policies of the government and therefore do not work to the best of their ability in the interest of the people of Saskatchewan, therefore be it resolved that the entire question of hiring public servants be referred to the incoming council."[33] Ministers took note. They promised to make no appointments of deputy ministers, chairmen of Crown corporations, or government boards without consulting members of the provincial executive.

With no ties to the business community, and no money to influence the press, the CCF, almost by definition, reduced the scope for patronage in Saskatchewan. It granted no reciprocal favours to business; it never received any from an implacably hostile press. Radio was Premier Douglas' preferred medium—at least when he could not find a soapbox — and the way he used it showed early evidence that the electronic media would be patronage's enemy because it brought voters vicariously into contact with leaders rather than through party networks and the inducements they offered.

Premier Douglas claimed to have eliminated patronage; he had actually modernized it. This modernization represented a giant step forward, given Saskatchewan's past. The CCF, with no bagmen and a lofty sense of purpose, cleaned up electoral practices which, in fairness to Saskatchewan, had been at least more salubrious than those in other provinces. The long-time CCF provincial treasurer got rich and retired from politics to Caribbean climes, but no one ever pinned corruption on him. The inside civil service was scrubbed clean by the public service commission; the activitist government of the CCF attracted some of the brightest young civil servants in Canada, not all of them socialists, some destined later for major national responsibilities. The "Saskatchewan Mafia," refugees from the provincial civil service after the Liberal victory in 1964, became pillars of the Ottawa civil service establishment. Crown corporations, boards, agencies — the appendages of expanding government — did provide opportunities for partisan CCFers, as did the order-in-council appointments inside the civil service. So, curiously, while the CCF restricted patronage in other areas of Saskatchewan political life, it opened new, although less numerous, opportunities elsewhere, a reflection in provincial politics of what happened later in federal politics.

The expansion of order-in-council appointments changed the battlefield for patronage. No longer were the coveted jobs those in the field, but those positions in the head offices of Crown corporations, on the boards of Crown agencies, and in the deputy ministers' offices of government departments. By shifting the ground for patronage, the CCF (and its successor after 1961, the NDP) created an inevitable suspicion in the other parties that if ever they came to office, the men and women in the senior reaches of the public service could not be trusted. When Ross Thatcher's Liberals finally ended CCF-NDP rule in 1964, some public servants left of their own volition, often heading for Ottawa, others got pink slips. In fairness, the majority of those civil servants who departed were not necessarily card-carrying members of the CCF-NDP. They did believe in an activist government, and the incoming government did not. By leaving, they avoided conflicts that would have been philosophical as much as partisan.[34] Their arrival in Ottawa nicely coincided with the explosion of federal programs during the 1960s, an explosion in which they were important catalysts.

The rank and file of Liberal party were less interested in vetting government appointments than in receiving them. The party executive and rank and file accepted that governing should be left to elected representatives; spoils were for those who supported them. As one writer described the Liberal attitude, "The party's duty was to propel its leaders to office. Having achieved this objective the reward was, in general, the satisfaction of victory and, in particular, the spoils of victory which the patronage system offered. Assuming that the rewards were properly dispensed, the party was content to leave administrative and legislative duties to the elected members."[35] The same transformation in a diluted form had overcome the NDP as it shed some of the secular evangelism of the early CCF years. It began increasingly to resemble a traditional party whose members looked to spoils for the faithful but left the allocation of those rewards to the elected leadership, rather than insisting, as had the CCF rank and file under Douglas, upon a continuing voice in the policies and appointments of the leadership.

Changes of government, from Thatcher on, were marked by wholesale changes in order-in-council appointments, the continuation by other means of the ongoing ideological struggle in the legislature and, during election campaigns, between the NDP and its free-enterprise alternative, the Liberals or Conservatives. The order-in-council appointments took on both a symbolic and practical importance because the boards, agencies and commissions of the Saskatchewan government were often the clearest manifestations of the NDP's commitment to activist government, and the other parties' easiest targets for allegations of socialist policies gone wrong.

A brief list from NDP Premier Allan Blakeney's years illustrates how the NDP used these boards, agencies, and commissions to give them the proper philosophical slant and to reward defeated New Democrats. Louis Lewry, who once ran against Ross Thatcher, was given a position with the Local Government Board; Jim Eaton, twice-defeated NDP candidate, wound up as director of the Saskatchewan Emergency Measures Organization; Don Keith, defeated in a 1973 by-election, became general manager of the Saskatchewan Development Fund Corporation; Don Cody, defeated in 1975, got a management job with Saskatchewan Government Insurance; Merv Johnston, defeated in the federal riding of Swift Current, got the plum job of agent-general in London; Alex Taylor, defeated in 1975, became chairman of the Workers' Compensation Board; former cabinet minister Eiling Kramer joined the Crown Investments Corporation; Frank Buck, defeated in 1972, became a corporate secretary of the Crown Investments Corporation. Other prominent Saskatchewan New Democrats who landed jobs with the NDP government in Manitoba after the party's 1982 defeat in Saskatchewan, included David Dombowski, president of the Potash Corporation of Saskatchewan; cabinet minister Jack Messer; deputy minister of agriculture Gerry Gartner; Cliff Scotton, Crown Investment Corporation's vice-president; John Sadler, president of Saskoil. Other New Democrats were sprinkled through the civil service, including the middle ranks. One Saskatchewan columnist, comparing the Blakeney years to those of Thatcher, concluded: "The NDP presence ran much deeper through the civil service, a situation that evolved over the eleven years the Blakeney government was in power. By the end, it reached a point where individuals with direct political links to the party in power were slotted into middle-management positions throughout the civil service and in Crown corporations."[36]

Whether this independent assessment exaggerated the use of patronage by the NDP or not, it did certainly reflect the beliefs of the Conservatives under Grant Devine who, for the first time since Anderson's shaky coalition, led that party to victory in 1982. What followed was political vengeance seldom seen any more in Canadian politics. Rather than waiting for positions to become available, then filling them with partisans — the pattern in federal politics and in most provinces — the Devine government began a systematic purge of order-in-council appointments and of the civil service. On the third day of the government's mandate, the government dismissed nine officials, including six deputy ministers. The bloodletting continued for months until about two hundred public servants lost their jobs.[37]

Colin Thatcher, the Liberal premier's son and Devine's minister of energy, exemplified the hard-liners within the new cabinet. "The first thing I did," he wrote, "was contact my campaign manager, Chuck Guillaume, and ask him to come to Regina as my executive assistant. I needed someone I could trust to ferret the 'reds' out of the department and the Crowns I would be in charge of. I did not want a witch-hunt, but at the same time I was not going to be sand-bagged by political appointees from the NDP arsenal of hacks. I wanted the personnel files scrutinized thoroughly and quickly and I would deal with the results."[38] Thatcher insisted he "found no joy" in dismissing people, but "it is the political way and those who go that route for employment have no right to expect clemency from the new party." Certainly, the rank and file of the Conservative party, who had never experienced their party in power, wanted revenge and spoils. "The line-up at the political trough was incredible," wrote Thatcher. "People I had never heard of were writing and phoning as though they had always been there."[39]

Soon after the change of government, the new cabinet removed the chief executive officers of eight Crown corporations. This was done, insisted the government, to assert political control over the corporations by replacing civil servants of a different philosophy with executives who shared the Conservatives' approach. In both the civil service and the Crown corporations, the Conservatives reached into the middle levels to weed out everyone suspected of NDP tendencies. Some were fired through guilt by association. For many boards, agencies and commissions there worked employees appointed by the NDP cabinet but protected by contract. Bill 16, the *Interpretation Act*, provided the means for the government to break existing contracts with all those employees they wished to fire, rather than amending statutes of each board, agency or commission. In the first year, the Devine government shelled out more than $1.5 million in severance payments. Having dismissed scores of New Democrats, the Devine government immediately rewarded its friends. George Hill, past president of the Conservative party, became president of Saskatchewan Power Corporation. Terry Leier, a long-time Conservative, became legal agent for Crown Investments Corporation. Former Saskatchewan Conservative leader Martin Pederson was appointed chairman of the Liquor Licensing Commission. And so ran the long list of Conservatives appointed to government posts, or given legal work, advertising contracts, places on the bench.

Only future changes of government will show whether Saskatchewan has now settled into a pattern more akin to the American approach to patronage than the modern Canadian approach. For now, the willingness of both New Democrats and Conservatives to make changes for partisan reasons in the public service, including the middle levels, has moved the province beyond the pattern in most other parts of Canada: that of leaving the public service largely untouched after changes of government. The deep ideological cleavage between New Democrats and their free-enterprise opponents—and the need both feel for a public service with which they can be ideologically comfortable —strongly suggests that patronage is alive and well in Saskatchewan.

CHAPTER 14

ALBERTA

"The unit of citizenship strength must be raised to an
infinitely higher degree. This can never be done
through the party system."
Henry Wise Wood,
founder of the United Farmers of Alberta.

ALBERTA, along with Saskatchewan, has witnessed a revival of political
patronage in recent years. Elsewhere, patronage has been trimmed and
re-shaped so that its pervasiveness is less evident than in previous decades, or at least no more evident. In Alberta, skepticism bordering on
antipathy to conventional political parties, indeed to "partyism," and
the messianic fervour of some of its political movements, relegated
patronage to a marginal role in the provincial political culture. So, too,
long stretches of one-party rule in Alberta, during which Opposition
parties seldom threatened the governing party, softened the intensity
of inter-party rivalry that so characterized other provinces. In Alberta,
political rivalries were so frequently those between Edmonton and
Ottawa (or Alberta as champion of the West against Central Canada,
"the East," or whatever) that all good men rallied behind the provincial
government, whatever its partisan stripe, to fight Ottawa, or at least
to show provincial solidarity in the face of some new injustice heaped
upon an already aggrieved province.

After five decades (1921–1971) of government by the United
Farmers of Alberta and Social Credit, Alberta could fairly have been
described as the Canadian province with the least political patronage.
But that reputation began changing with the arrival of Peter Lougheed,
a man who understood the use of patronage for building an entrenched
political party rooted in all quarters of Alberta society. Lougheed ruled
his Conservative party with an iron hand. He placed enormous impor-

tance on personal loyalty, rewarding many of those who had been faithful to him with appointments to the proliferating boards, agencies, commissions and overseas offices of the Alberta government. Lougheed, a thoroughly modern man, built a thoroughly modern patronage machine. Accepting that previous Alberta governments had closed off fields for patronage that lay available in other provinces, he used such that remained available to erect from the straw and sticks he inherited —sixty years of defeat and 12.7 percent of the popular vote in the 1963 election—a durable political party.

Premier Don Getty, a recipient of Lougheed patronage after temporarily departing public life, continued the Lougheed tradition when he assumed the party leadership. In the first year of his premiership, Getty favoured with government contracts or positions loyal Conservatives such as Bryce Nimmo, Ron Liepert, Joe Dutton, Ron Ghitter, Bob Dowling, George de Rappard, Tom Donnelly, Mary LeMessurier and Horst Schmid. When the Conservatives suffered stunning reversals in the 1986 election—the party fell nearly eleven percent in the popular vote and lost eighteen seats in the legislature — Getty showed classic political consideration to losing candidates. Former ministers Bill Payne, Bill Trynchy and Fred Bradley all became chairmen of government agencies.

The Conservative party under Lougheed and Getty, therefore, nudged Alberta back towards an older style of politics that characterized the province from its creation in 1905 until the arrival in office of the United Farmers of Alberta in 1921. Those initial sixteen years featured uninterrupted Liberal party rule, the first of four distinct periods in which one party consistently eclipsed the others.

That Alberta began as a Liberal bastion had much to do with patronage dispensed by the federal government under Sir Wilfrid Laurier. The North-West Territory sent members to the House of Commons elected on a partisan basis, but local politics featured universal adherence to the principle of non-partisanship. Men who turned their attention to national politics might identify themselves as Liberals or Conservatives, but back home the overriding objective of maximizing pressure on the central government made them non-partisan. The ranchers in southern Alberta, for example, usually favoured the federal Conservatives; the immigrants who streamed into the central and northern areas of the territory tended to be Liberals, their political preference a recompense of sorts for the party whose policies had beckoned them to Canada. The federal Liberals courted the new arrivals, financially supported newspapers in their languages, and assisted them in establishing homesteads.

In territorial politics, a consensus prevailed that non-partisanship made the most political sense. Alberta farm organizations, in particular, hewed to the non-partisan line, remaining aloof for many decades from active political organization. They later entered politics directly not as the supporting cast for a political party, as Saskatchewan farm organizations did in aligning themselves with the Liberals, but as a self-defined non-partisan movement capable of capturing political power. Indeed, this refusal of Alberta farm organizations to throw in their lot with a political party, or to bargain among parties, contributed significantly to the unconventional pattern of Alberta politics in which an antipathy to "partyism" seldom disappeared and often prevailed.

After agreeing to the creation of Alberta and Saskatchewan as Canadian provinces, Sir Wilfrid Laurier began imposing a partisan mould on provincial politics by selecting as lieutenant-governor for Alberta George H.V. Bulyea, a prominent Liberal from the previous territorial government. The Liberals had been supported by the North-West Territory in national elections; it therefore struck them as appropriate, even necessary, that the new provincial governments should provide a bedrock of Liberal support for the future. Bulyea, required to appoint an administration to govern until the first provincial election, asked another prominent Liberal, Alexander Rutherford, to form the province's first ministry. This initial boost gave the Liberals a leg up on their rivals. In the newly created provincial public service, Liberals of good standing found themselves in positions of authority. "I have thought," wrote one senior Liberal to Premier Rutherford, "that of all the officials we will have to appoint we should be able to raise considerable funds."[1] In other words, the Liberals would partially finance their campaign through contributions from party appointees.

The party did not lack for applicants. Civil service posts were well-paying and secure, provided the Liberals remained in office. The territory's representatives in Ottawa began lobbying for senatorships and other federal positions even before Alberta became a province, while back home Liberal supporters inundated Rutherford with requests. One letter summed up the prevailing assumptions. "I am and always have been an ardent Grit. There is no one, in northern Alberta at least, who will deny the truth of this statement. Of course, if the Conservatives or the Non-Partisans as they now call themselves, are in a majority in the new legislature, I hope for no favours."[2]

Control of the interim government materially assisted the Liberals to win the first election and cement themselves in office. That election, like those in other parts of Canada, was marked by allegations of bribery and lesser misconduct. There were also porkbarrelling promises; for example, a minister informed his audience that a Liberal vote in Edmonton would be reciprocated by the construction of a federal post office. As in Saskatchewan, control of the new government meant jobs for supporters, discretion to channel contracts towards sympathetic newspapers, and the ability to steer countless small favours towards political friends.

As the years of Liberal domination lengthened, so did Conservative frustrations. The Liberals spread patronage throughout the province, while the federal Liberals stamped their partisan imprint on Alberta. Their combined patronage network, together with an unbalanced electoral map that exaggerated the political weight of Liberal-leaning northern communities, gave the party indispensable building blocks for political success. The federal Liberals chose Edmonton as the capital, largely because they politically dominated the city, whereas Calgary preferred the Conservatives. So tightly did the Liberals bind the civil service to their party that in the 1913 campaign the Conservatives called for a "thorough and complete reformation of the laws relating to the civil service [so that] future appointments shall be made after the report of examiners upon competitive examinations."[3] The Conservatives twice polled more than forty percent of the popular vote, but in an essentially two-party system — a sprinkling of minor parties also contested elections — the party could only shake but never topple Liberal governments, even after the Alberta and Great Waterways Railway affair rocked the Rutherford government.

The Alberta and Great Waterways Railway affair of 1910 represents one of the few scandals in Alberta's political history, and it may not even have been a scandal. Allegations were made that the premier and a senior minister showed political favouritism in selling government bonds to finance the construction of the railway, and that the province therefore squandered money. Two judges on the subsequent royal commission condemned the government's deal with the railway promoters and hinted strongly at the possibility of personal advantage for the premier and his minister, but in the face of their denials of wrongdoing, the judges stopped short of a clear-cut verdict. The third judge completely exonerated the politicians. The affair dragged on for months, forced Rutherford from his job as premier (with a helping hand from Lieutenant-Governor Bulyea), shook up the Liberal ministry, and rekindled a belief that parties inevitably corrupted political men and that non-partisan government meant pure motives and clean government.[4]

The Liberals, in Alberta as in Saskatchewan, attracted the bulk of the farm vote. They were the party of free trade and immigration, the party under whose policies thousands of immigrants had flocked to the prairies. Like good political patrons, the Liberals courted farmers' votes and listened to their grievances, and the farm organizations, in turn, delivered what faithful clients must—votes. But towards the end of the

World War I, the politics of Alberta and Saskatchewan began going separate ways, until a great split opened between them, a split fostered by the return to prominence of the pre-Confederation idea that conventional parties served only the exclusive interests of their members, and that since these interests often conflicted, the resulting compromises came at the expense of good government and the specific, pressing interests of the farmers.

In Saskatchewan, the Liberals wisely co-opted the farm organizations, turning over whole ministries to members recruited directly from farm organizations; in Alberta the farmers turned to themselves. From Henry Wise Wood Alberta farmers heard the clarion call of "group government," and soon the United Farmers of Alberta, of which Wood had been a founding member, turned farmers away from the Liberal party. The election of 1921 shocked the province. The UFA, despite winning about five percent fewer votes than the Liberals, nevertheless bunched them in sufficient rural ridings to win a majority government. Wood, the UFA's most eloquent spokesman, distrusted traditional political paties, calling them mass organizations of individuals without any common purpose or ideas. "Few questions are ever settled permanently by political parties, and none that deal with primary social problems," Wood wrote.[5] The economic group, not the political party with its jostling interests, most effectively enhanced democracy by providing the clearest expression of the aspirations and demands of the members. Every interest in society required a group to press its claims, but of course in a province like Alberta the farmers' group would predominate. "Group government" would bring representatives of different organizations to the legislature where their activities could be monitored—in the farmers' case, by the UFA convention. Wood, a critic of the "reactionary forces of partyism," remained president of the UFA organization; he was never a member of the UFA government.

This strong aversion to "partyism" extended to all of the traditional practices of political parties, including patronage. In 1921, the UFA's "Declaration of Principles" included "abolition of the patronage system in the conduct of provincial business."[6] For the first time in Canadian political history, a government largely did away with patronage, although several prominent UFAers did receive appointments, including Herbert Greenfield, a UFA premier who went to London as agent-general for Alberta. Determined not to display the institutional structures of a political party or to reflect their mores, the UFA tried to abide by the righteous precepts of a higher morality. The UFA's timing could not have been better. The practices of the provincial Liberals and "the political scandals of the period in connection with the

Ross rifle, the construction of the Manitoba Parliament Buildings and the enforcement of liquor legislation in Saskatchewan, all helped to convince Alberta farmers that it was hopeless to look for reform from either political party."[7]

The Non-Partisan League, some of whose adherents had arrived in Alberta from the northern states of the American plains, influenced the political thinking of the UFA leadership. So, too, did the evangelical traditions of the Bible Belt churches spreading throughout southern Alberta. These influences, combined with Wood's messianic leadership, allowed the UFA to incorporate the farmers' grievances on commodity prices, tariffs and transportation into a movement that persuaded its members they had built a political system free from the sins of conventional partyism. Their messianism, in a province of nominally puritan personal habits, provided just the right tone for the UFA, but set the party up for a fall when the cloak of virtue fell from a UFA minister, who wound up in a messy divorce, and from Premier John Edward Brownlee, who resigned a year before the 1935 election in the wake of rumours that he had seduced his secretary.

Personal problems, however, merely accelerated the UFA's demise. By the 1930s, the movement had grown stale, and it seemed helpless to ease the anguish of the Great Depression. Nor could it offer anyone to match the charisma of William Aberhart, the leader of the nascent Social Credit movement, who incorporated the Alberta skepticism of established parties and its preference for messianism in politics into a political force that swept the province like a prairie fire. Like Henry Wise Wood and the other UFA founders, Aberhart promised always to be guided by a superior morality, one heavily influenced by biblical teachings. In this, Social Credit became the natural inheritor of a political culture profoundly shaped by the UFA. In Social Credit and the UFA, which promised and delivered governments "largely free of scandal, patronage and corruption, both at the electoral level and in the operation of the government,"[8] Alberta shattered the political mould imposed at its creation and provided the longest stretch of unconventional political behaviour in Canadian history.

With his customary fervent rhetoric, Aberhart flayed political parties as robustly as had the UFA's Henry Wise Wood. "Democracy," he told his congregation at the Bible Institute, "has merely become the arena of wire-pulling crookedness."[9] As the years rolled on, Social Credit looked more like a conventional political party than an anti-party political movement. One account, a distinctly lonely one, suggests that five hundred civil servants were fired in the first twenty months of Social Credit rule.[10] Most of the other analyses of the Social Credit era are silent on how the party handled patronage, or suggest that patronage never assumed the prominence it did in provincial parties elsewhere. A.E. Hooke, a long-time Social Credit cabinet minister, insists that with the exception of several appointments of non-partisan outsiders to the public service "all other senior appointments were made from men and women who had been in the service for many years."[11] Aberhart countenanced Social Credit MLAs making recommendations on local appointments, and he did replace some senior civil servants considered hostile to Social Credit.[12] But Social Credit never manifested the characteristics of a political machine as had the Liberal parties of Saskatchewan and Manitoba. Election-day treating, a feature of politics everywhere in Canada, never sullied UFA and Social Credit campaigns. Both parties were doggedly anti-liquor and reaped a rich harvest of votes from the Bible Belt which stretched across the southern part of the province.

Incidents such as the 1952 kerfuffle over government leases of premises owned by two Social Credit MLAs in violation of the *Legislative Assembly Act* scarcely tarnished the reputation of Aberhart's successor, Ernest Manning, although it partially accounted for the Liberals' nine-point rise in the popular vote in the 1955 election. Nor was the party seriously hurt by charges in 1967 and 1968 that two Socred MLAs—E.W. Hinman and A.E. Hooke—used their ministerial influence for personal gain. A judicial inquiry exonerated the two men, but they were chided for lack of discretion in some of their business dealings.

Peter Lougheed took over the leadership of the moribund Conservative party in March of 1965, invested it with his extraordinary energy and determination, attracted young, affluent and upwardly-mobile colleagues, and drove Social Credit from Alberta's political map. In Lougheed's victorious election of 1971, the Conservatives captured only thirty-thousand more votes than Social Credit, or fifty-three percent of all votes cast. Lougheed built such an imposing dynasty that in his last three elections, the Conservatives won two hundred and eighteen of a possible two hundred and thirty-three seats. A man fiercely loyal to his friends, Lougheed used patronage freely to reward them, especially friends who had embarked with him after 1965 on the precarious attempt to defeat an entrenched Social Credit government.

Lougheed never bothered with his predecessors' rhetorical denunciations of patronage. He was a thoroughly modern political leader, secular, technocratic, an organization man who understood the system of rewards and punishments. By the time Lougheed became premier, patronage had been all but rooted out of the Alberta government, but it reappeared in his government, in familiar modern forms: appointments to agencies, boards and commissions, government advertising contracts, and fund-raising. Firms receiving money from the Alberta government accounted for three-quarters of the Conservative party's campaign fund in the 1982 election.[13] Baker Lovick, the Alberta Conservatives' preferred advertising agency, received a substantial amount of government work without tendering, including agency-of-record work for the Heritage Savings Trust Fund and the Alberta Alcoholism and Drug Abuse Commission, two among a handful of what Alberta civil servants call "political accounts." Baker Lovick was also the exclusive agent for Alberta Government Telephones, the ninth-largest Crown corporation in Canada.

As the Lougheed party's sway over Alberta grew, so did its ability to raise money, since corporations did not wish to miss being on the winning side. In an essentially one-party province, corporations did not make equal contributions to government and Opposition parties — particularly since the Opposition party in Alberta was the NDP. They just sank increasing amounts of money into the Conservative party.

Nominally a free-marketer, Lougheed never shied from using the state to achieve economic, social or cultural objectives. Although the civil service remained largely untouched by his appointments—Lougheed did appoint some personal friends as deputy ministers — his government added to the boards, agencies and commissions set up during the Social Credit era, and these became in Alberta what they were in other provinces: the provincial equivalent of the federal Senate, sources of sinecures for retired political warhorses.

Not that it injured his government, but following the 1979 election, Premier Lougheed suffered perhaps the first sustained bout of criticism about patronage any Alberta premier had ever experienced. Even the usually supportive Alberta newspapers took skeptical note of his propensity for appointing friends when all eight cabinet ministers — Jim Foster, Roy Farran, Bert Hohol, Bob Dowling, Helen Hunley, Hugh Horner, Allan Warrack, and Don Getty — who decided not to seek re-election in 1979 received at least one patronage appointment. Later, after former Energy minister Merv Leitch retired from public life, Lougheed appointed him to the Alberta government telephone commission. The premier also appointed his press secretary, Joe Hutton, to the Alberta liquor control board, one of many appointments of friends, staff and Conservative MLAs. Lougheed picked up a trick from federal and Ontario politics. Supported by a huge caucus, many members of which had little to do, Lougheed started handing out government jobs to backbenchers to top up their incomes. Conservative cabinet ministers and fund-raisers such as Fred Peacock, James

McKibben, and Jim Seymour wound up representing the provinces overseas.

Don Getty, having observed how Peter Lougheed ran the Conservative party and the Alberta government, grafted Lougheed's ideas about the use of patronage onto his own leadership of the party. Indeed, in his first election campaign as leader he may have gone one step further. In two ridings where Opposition parties threatened, Getty reminded voters that rewards flowed to ridings that supported the government, statements so blatant that Getty back-tracked under subsequent criticism.

Getty, who took for granted the Conservative hegemony, appointed another raft of party faithful to government positions upon becoming leader. No sooner had Getty defeated Ron Ghitter for the party leadership than Ghitter received $73,000 for sixty-seven days work to find a private investor for a government hotel development. Joe Dutton, Lougheed's executive assistant, was sent to London as Alberta's director of business immigration. Bryce Nimmo, Tory campaign manager for three elections and Lougheed's tailor, wound up as director of the economic development department's Houston office. His Los Angeles counterpart was Ron Liepert, Lougheed's press secretary. Even Lougheed's private secretary, Linda Eder, was given a job setting up a southern protocol office for the government. Three other former ministers — Bill Payne, Bill Trynchy and Fred Bradley — were all named chairmen of government agencies.

Lougheed and Getty, therefore, returned patronage to its traditional place in party politics because their Conservative party, like the Liberal party from 1905 to 1921, was a coalition-building political organization. The modern Conservative party in Alberta had nothing about it of a political movement designed to combat moral evils or promote secular evangelical causes, such as farmers' rights or a new monetary theory. Lougheed, a supremely capable politician of enormous energy, built his unassailable political machine on his own personality, an economy awash with oil revenues, and a vigorous defence of provincial interests against the power of Ottawa, the East, Central Canada, Toronto, or whatever. As his years in office lengthened, Lougheed began to reward friends, to use patronage as a clearing house for political veterans so that newcomers could rise in the party, to strengthen his already considerable power as party leader, and to embed the party's roots in every sector of Alberta society. The province was basically so unfamiliar with the ways of patronage that the newspapers, in general supportive of his government, reacted to his use of patronage with neither the weary cluck-clucking or intemperate outrage that characterized editorial comment on the same phenomenon elsewhere, but with a genuine sense of disappointed astonishment. It was as if the papers had expected something nobler, or at least something different, from the province's political hero.

Indeed, so popular was Lougheed that in a province with a long history of hostility to conventional parties that no one took much notice of how effectively he used the conventional techniques of party-building, including patronage, to entrench the Conservatives in office. And, in fairness, nothing scandalous or corrupt touched his government in ways that would have drawn public attention to any gross abuses of political patronage, nothing that could bring back the echoes of the United Farmers and Socreds about the evils of party. Never having seen the Conservatives hurt by a negative public reaction to patronage, Don Getty assumed that he could carry on in the Lougheed tradition.

By the late 1980s, with the Conservatives inching towards twenty years in office, Alberta could not be distinguished from most of the other Canadian provinces in the role assigned to political patronage.

CHAPTER 15

BRITISH COLUMBIA

"Patronage is dead in B.C. government affairs."
Premier W.A.C. Bennett.

THE POLITICS OF BRITISH COLUMBIA have never failed to amuse or cause outrage. A cavalcade of colourful politicians moved through the province's history, some of them highly unconventional, a few of them comical. Broadly speaking, the political history of British Columbia can be divided into four distinct periods—individualistic politics without organized parties, the ascendancy of the two national parties in provincial politics, three parties vying for government, and the emergence of a straightforward rivalry between the Socreds and the CCF-NDP. In every period, prominent citizens raised their voices against political patronage; indeed, the province's political history is pock-marked either with pledges to eliminate political patronage or with announcements of its death. Like Mark Twain's death, however, political patronage in British Columbia kept defying predictions of its imminent demise. Patronage still figures in the province's politics, although it has certainly declined since it ran riot in the first half of this century, and the used-car-salesman spirit in the Social Credit party has produced a series of embarrassing conflicts of interest in which ministers mixed private and public business.

British Columbia has always reflected frontier characteristics, not of the "Wild West" American variety, but of a place where people constantly come to make a better life for themselves and to extract riches from the natural bounty of the territory. One writer called the

282

political culture of the province "the politics of protest," another "the rush for spoils," still another the "politics of exploitation." Behind these shorthand descriptions lies the sense of restlessness, acquisitiveness, even unpredictability that has frequently marked the politics of British Columbia. The acquisitive spirit is rooted in the nature of the province's economy. Capitalist investors exploited the timber and minerals of British Columbia. Against the power of capital, felt everywhere in the province, labour movements pitted their increasing strength, and in the last phase of the province's history, the CCF-NDP emerged as corporate capital's most feared foe. A kind of populist suspicion of corporate capital inspires even the Social Credit party, which scoops up money from a Vancouver establishment more frightened by NDP socialism than by Social Credit populism.

There is, too, in British Columbia a sense of living on the periphery of Canada and at the margin of the national political consciousness. In such circumstances, the traditional political parties — Liberal and Conservative — have been easily linked to British Columbians' suspicions about the uncaring attitudes of the rest of the country. That sense of marginality also sustained those who argued that only by abandoning the traditional framework of Liberal and Conservative could the province grab Ottawa's attention and so maximize its influence on national affairs. For nearly three decades following British Columbia's entry into Confederation, that was the principal argument for non-partisanship in provincial politics, and the argument periodically resurfaced even after parties consolidated their place in the province. Lack of tradition and periodic instability have figured prominently in the province's politics, and the personality of leaders has often dominated the merry-go-round of governments.[1]

Goldwin Smith, the acerbic Torontonian, visited British Columbia in the 1880s and delighted in recounting that a citizen of the province, upon being asked his politics, replied "government appropriations."[2] As usual, Smith caught the essence of his subject: Personal enrichment drove many politicians and almost all who attempted to influence them. British Columbia's natural resources beckoned entrepreneurs and speculators; its geography demanded major public investments in transportation, especially railways. "The business of provincial politics was business,"[3] and the majority of assembly members blatantly tried to further their own business interests through politics. The promise of a railway to the rest of Canada lured British Columbia into Confederation in 1871; the seemingly interminable wait for the last spike buttressed the conventional wisdom that only non-partisanship could maximize the province's pressure on Ottawa. From 1871 to 1902, the assembly resembled that of the early days of organized government in New Brunswick: every man for himself. Without provincial parties, coalitions came and went with dizzying frequency. Each MLA tried to extract from the treasury what he could for his constituents and, not infrequently, for himself or his business friends. Patronage and pork-barrelling ran riot. Corruption, too, figured prominently in provincial politics, especially in the relationships between the railway promoters and corporate magnates and the politicians. The province's leading historian has summed up the politics of the late nineteenth century: "A shockingly low tone pervaded politics. . . . the Canadians who were managing things were unduly interested in the spoils of office."[4]

The spoils included positions in the nascent public service, but there was nothing surprising in that. Those who had agitated for self-government and union with the rest of Canada had wanted to wrest such positions from the British governors' friends in the colonies of the mainland and Vancouver Island. Even after the union of the two colonies, the sense of exclusion persisted. British officials held the jobs that locals desired. Governor Anthony Musgrave accurately informed London that "the more prominent agitators for Confederation are a small knot of Canadians who hope that it may be possible to make fuller representative institutions and responsible government part of the new arrangements, and that they may so place themselves in positions of influence and emolument."[5] When the British yielded on all fronts, the vacuum they created was immediately filled by British Columbians who like Canadians elsewhere saw the provincial public service as a vast patronage community. Confederation confirmed their beliefs. Macdonald promptly filled all the new federal positions—post office, customs and excise offices — with Conservatives, although his habit of using British Columbia as a dumping ground for leading Conservatives from other parts of Canada ruffled provincial sensitivities.

In its first thirty-one years, fifteen administrations led by fourteen different premiers governed the province. The persistent instability inspired periodic searches for a "strong man" that found echoes even after the creation of political parties. Early on, then, the politics of personality held British Columbia in thrall. In the burlesque of the legislature, corporate interests seemed invariably to get their way, by fair means or foul. In the province's first forty-two years, the assembly granted two hundred and one railway charters, only a few of which ever produced rails on the ground.

Legislators were prized for what public benefits they could secure for their constituents, what advantages they could arrange for their corporate friends or themselves, and what positions they could offer their supporters. Here was patronage of the purest kind, direct links between individual politicians and supporters, unsullied by the demands of party, unfettered by any premier's imagination of the provincial interest or the long-term future of a party. The premier bargained with assemblymen, legislators bargained with each other, and from the swirl of private arrangements came the distribution of public benefits. This distribution served no integrative purpose; there was no binding together of disparate groups through a shared expectation of reward, no representation for ethnic groups anxious to join mainstream society through political rewards, no creation of a common sense of purpose, just an overwhelming jamboree of greed, justified paradoxically by the apparently worse evils of partyism.

Nothing became the period of individualistic politics so much as its ending. Premier Edward Gawler Prior, apprised of an imminent report critical of collusion between railway promoters and the government, fired two ministers, believing such severe action would restore credibility to his government. Alas, it soon became clear that the premier's own firm had received a government contract after he had seen informal bids submitted by other companies.[6] The lieutenant-governor demanded and got the premier's resignation in 1903, and with his departure the period of non-partisan, individualistic politics was shunted aside by public revulsion at government corruption and instability. A federal commission, investigating a 1903 labour dispute in the Canadian Pacific Railway, parenthetically noted a breakdown in political morality in British Columbia. Companies lamented that the instability of political life led to inconsistent policies, charters given and revoked, regulations passed and amended. New labour organizations wanted a political channel of their own.

The provincial election of 1903 ushered in the era of partisan politics with the national political formations, Conservative and Liberal. When parties took hold in British Columbia, the Liberals ruled in Ottawa — which partly explains why the Conservatives won. Suspicion of Ottawa has usually been front and centre in British Columbia from the earliest days of waiting for the CPR. Sir Richard McBride, the first provincial Conservative leader, understood his audience. "Better terms" he cried in that first partisan election, a cry later heard in various guises from a long series of provincial premiers, and one that still resounds throughout the province.

Parties, it was hoped, would rescue British Columbia from patronage and corruption; instead, parties channelled patronage in new ways. Rare was the Liberal or Conservative premier not dogged by at least the allegations of scandals, large and small; rare, too, were the leading politicians who spurned the opportunities afforded by control of patronage. The appearance of party may have transformed the political scene, but it could not change the economic and social structure of the province.

Once elected, the McBride Conservatives gradually asserted control over the available patronage, using funds and positions supplied by a healthy treasury. Government employees — the road superintendants and foremen, fire wardens, constables — spread the government message, reported back to their political bosses on stirrings across the province, and generally formed the advance guard for the Conservative party.[7] The press, secured by government advertising and printing contracts, furthered the party's cause. Keenly aware of the importance of partisan organs, McBride scooped up any available papers. "See Green [the party bagman] — if we can get absolute control for three thousand we will arrange," McBride told a supporter after learning of the availability of the *Trail Herald*.[8]

"The thing is to get in," said Premier McBride, "and when you're in to stay in."[9] That perfectly realistic ambition was rendered easier by the province's rapid economic growth — public works expenditures increased eight-fold between 1903 and 1913 — and by the railway mania which gripped British Columbia. Liberal critics shouted that the Conservatives were the "CPR on wheels," in British Columbia as elsewhere. The Conservatives didn't mind. They were bullish on British Columbia, and as long as the economy flourished the voters apparently did not mind the political excesses that accompanied the economic boom. McBride perfectly personified the sunny times: He smiled, delighted in chamber-of-commerce rhetoric, and insisted only naysayers stood between British Columbia and greatness. The pressures for patronage on McBride were bad enough when the federal Liberals ruled; they intensified when the federal Conservatives came to office in 1911. Local Tories not only searched for provincial rewards, they tried to enlist McBride's help for their federal ambitions. "The McBride papers during 1911 and 1912 present an irrefutable record, at times pathetic, at times amusing, of the personal and political demands made upon a powerful provincial government . . ." wrote one student of the period. "More than occasionally one finds among the patronage letters the ominous logic of the place-seeker that 'to the victor belong the spoils'."[10]

McBride, avuncular and unflappable, left the more mundane details of building a political machine to Green, the bagman, and William Bowser, the attorney-general, whose bulldog demeanour and brawling style made him a fearsome adversary. Bowser described himself as a "man of the world" and, as such, knew "that a bit of greasing sometimes has to be done."[11] The liquor trade, which Bowser regulated as attorney-general, became a spigot for Conservative party funds; the

voting lists a fit invitation for manipulation; the electoral map, disproportionately slanted to favour the Conservatives, a fixture. In the isolated towns of the interior and coast, dependency prevailed. The lure
of part-time work and government positions, handed out for partisan
reasons, confirmed political commitment. In Vancouver, the Bowser
machine overwhelmed political adversaries.

In boom times, McBride and Bowser were known as the Gold
Brick Twins; in a period of economic slump, their touch faltered. In
1913, a pause in economic activity turned into a slide, touching off
higher unemployment, a return to labour unrest, and new questions
about the government's concessions of land and rights to corporate
interests. Suddenly, the premier's sunny ways seemed ill-suited to the
prevailing economic distress, and Bowser's methods of keeping voters
in line smacked of desperate thuggery. The evils of partyism, against
which so many had inveighed in the late nineteenth century, reappeared
to explain the unfolding economic mess. McBride and Bowser "were
depicted as . . . symbols of corruption. Rumbles of discontent began
to be heard about machine politicians, the distribution of patronage,
the arrogance of 'Napoleon' Bowser and the inefficiency of the civil
service."[12] The finance minister resigned when confronted with evidence that he had purchased some livestock and horses from a government-run farm; another minister was besieged by allegations that he
had sold land to speculators for low prices; still another resigned after
it was revealed he had received $105,000 from a company whose affairs
were before the legislature. Even Bowser was charged with failing to
investigate the financial capability of the Dominion Trust Company,
whose charter he steered through the legislature although his law firm
acted for the company.

In the face of economic depression and mounting dissatisfaction,
McBride seemed incapable of doing anything but delivering pep talks
and making extended trips to Ottawa and London. Charles Hibbert
Tupper, son of the Conservative stalwart, launched a province-wide
campaign against the excesses of the McBride government. He claimed
the "real, fundamental issue between the people of British Columbia
and the government and Mr. Bowser is the question of patronage." He
told soldiers that "the least we can do is to strain every effort towards
the improvement of public conditions so that we may welcome you
home to a province cleansed of all that is evil, mean and sordid and
blessed with fine ideals and good government . . . It is not a fight of
parties, but of people against official wrong-doing."[13] Bowser, chafing
at McBride's lethargy, began agitating against him. McBride finally
quit at the end of 1915, yielding to the other Gold Brick Twin, but the
rising tide of discontent would soon sweep away Bowser.

The provincial Liberals were largely distinguished from Conservatives by not being Conservatives. No difference of ideology, no clash of vision, no dispute over important policy separated Liberals and Conservatives. They formed the classic pattern of the "ins" and "outs," political Bobbsey Twins more interested in spoils than ideas. In the first three elections contested along party lines, the Conservatives rolled over the Liberals. When the fourth election, that of 1912, wiped out the already meagre Liberal contingent in the legislature, it appeared that the Conservatives might govern forever. But economic recession, government scandals, the ferment of organized labour, clerics denouncing moral laxity in government, temperance advocates, and fissures within the Conservative ranks created the conditions for a spectacular revival of the Liberals under Harlan Carey Brewster. Sensing the public dismay with Bowser's machine politics, Brewster campaigned on integrity in government and an end to patronage. He would be the first leader to do so, but not the last to deceive.

The Liberals' victory in 1916 changed the faces on the treasury benches and offered the prospect of new attitudes towards patronage. Liberal job-seekers descended on Victoria, starved for rewards after so many years in Opposition. Brewster sent some of them away. His economic policy called for cutbacks in government spending, so that part-time workers were laid off. But the Liberals intended to play the game by traditional rules. Wholesale changes in the outside service brought Liberals to positions previously held by Conservatives. Railways minister John Oliver, defending one such switch, said simply that "the Liberals have not had a look in for fourteen years'."[14] Soon after the Liberal takeover, a commission to investigate electoral malpractices discovered that Attorney-General M.A. Macdonald had received a twenty-five thousand dollar cheque from the Canadian Northern Railway Company, a revelation that caused Brewster to demand his resignation.[15] Another inquiry, this one into the Pacific Great Eastern Railway, shed light specifically on the McBride years, but more generally on some of the political practices of the time, including the awarding of illegal contracts and channelling of corporate profits to members of the governing party.

Brewster, mindful of the clerics and reformers, introduced a Civil Service Reform Act creating a civil service commission responsible for examinations and screening of candidates. Unfortunately, the commission had powers of recommendation only; the final decision rested with the cabinet. The Act passed the legislature in May, 1917, but its application was held up pending the arrival of Liberals to positions throughout the public service. The *Civil Service Reform Act* did represent progress, even considerable progress, judged against what had gone before in British Columbia. Perhaps Brewster might have pushed reforms in other areas, but in his second year in office he died, and the party turned to John Oliver.

"Honest John" Oliver, who instructed his ministers to 'doff your broadcloth and don your overalls,' delighted in his nickname, considered himself the working man's friend, and, like his predecessor, proclaimed the death of the old ways of patronage. They were defunct, as far as he had anything to do with them, since he turned the dispensing of patronage over to his provincial secretary, who believed "it is the small matters of individual and local interest that determine the fate of governments."[16] Brewster had believed in retrenchment; Oliver favoured an aggressive program of public works, especially highways. He based almost his entire 1920 campaign on promises of new roads throughout the province. He knew that roads were needed, and that their construction would create plenty of part-time work. Farmers, of which Oliver was one, especially appreciated the part-time work of road construction. As one rural supporter wrote, "We might as well recognize this fact at once, that the average voter cares only for the party who [sic] gives him the most money for the least work."[17] Discretionary spending on public works that increased the availability of part-time work made porkbarrelling an irresistible tool for currying public favour. In 1922, for example, information on six constituencies — three Liberal and three Conservative — showed spending on roads of $1,427 per mile in Liberal constituencies and $58 per mile in Conservative constituencies.[18]

Whatever Oliver's intentions, whatever his earlier promises, as Brewster became a memory the incidence of patronage increased. The public service commission had been a noble reform, despite its obvious limitations, but it intensely irritated Liberal partisans. They complained bitterly and persistently to the premier who, in 1922, attacked the civil service commissioner for obstructing patronage appointments. "We in the innocence of our hearts," the premier told a Liberal convention, "passed over to a commission patronage rights which should have been exercised by the government and the representatives elected by the people."[19] In the Interior, where most of the jobs fell within the so-called outside service and therefore beyond even the limited purview of the civil service commission, the Liberals continued to nurture their advance guard of road foremen, game wardens, forestry officers and casual labourers. The creation of a liquor control board, after a plebiscite overthrew prohibition, offered enticing patronage opportunities. The commissioners were excellent Liberals, the distillers and brewers became important financial contributors, and discretionary granting of licences could be used to pressure tavern owners for votes and money. The Conservatives, and even a few dissident Liberals, complained of the "politico-brewery machine." The president of the Vancouver Liberal Association and a Liberal campaign manager were both implicated in a ring to sell watered-down liquor to government stores. The secretary of the provincial Liberal association sold a warehouse to the liquor control board for $150,000, although the City of Vancouver assessed its value at $58,000.[20]

Patronage, however, did not deliver undiluted blessings. There never seemed to be enough to go around; the gap between available supply and overwhelming demand taxed the party's ingenuity. Victoria Liberals complained about disproportionate favours for Vancouver; Vancouver Liberals resented public benefits for the Interior; some Vancouver Liberals resisted the control of patronage in the city by other Liberals; veterans insisted they had been insufficiently rewarded. From various quarters there arose increasingly shrill complaints about the morality of the Oliver government and the stain of partyism on the provincial body politic. Labour unions denounced the corruption of corporate-political links; organizations of returned servicemen complained they had fought to save freedom not favouritism; the social reformers, clerics, and feminists who had helped Brewster lamented the erosion of the ideals for which they had fought; a new political formation, the Provincial party, proposed to wipe away the scourge of patronage.

The Provincial party represented another example of the resistance to traditional parties sprinkled through the history of British Columbia. Its founding father, wealthy businessman Major-General Alexander McRae, reflected another strand of the reaction against partyism — that of the businessman against the sordidness of political life. McRae rallied Conservatives disgusted with Bowser, farm organizations pledged to non-partisanship, and all who were dedicated to: "Get Oliver out and not let Bowser in, the party's informal slogan ."[21] The party financed a newspaper— The Searchlight—which alleged a widespread series of scandals and boondoggles, including payments by contractors for the Pacific Great Eastern Railway to both party leaders, ubiquitous patronage appointments, and kickbacks to the major parties by firms receiving government contracts.

Presaging Social Credit rhetoric three decades later, the leaders of the Provincial party put themselves above partisan politics. They claimed to have had only the interests of the province and public virtue at heart. The party's platform for the 1924 election called for an end to "government by party," non-partisan "union government," the abolition of patronage, replacement of the "political" liquor board with a non-partisan independent commission, open tendering of government contracts, and public disclosure of campaign funds. It also pledged a reduction in taxation and government spending, and various other measures reflecting the party's orientation towards the business community. The party received 24.2 percent of the popular vote in the 1924 election, defeated both Oliver and Bowser in their ridings, but won only two seats. Soon thereafter, it disintegrated when the dissident Conservatives returned to the fold, but the Provincial party had blown on the coals of public anger at the excesses of partyism, including patronage, that had always been present in British Columbia.

The Provincial party campaign contributed to the gradual erosion of support for the Liberal party, which increasingly seemed to be held together only by a lingering public respect for Honest John Oliver. When he died of cancer in 1927, the Liberals' last political weapon disappeared. They faced a rejuvenated Conservative party under Simon Fraser Tolmie who, like so many other British Columbia politicians, pledged an end to corruption and what he called in the 1928 campaign "rampant patronage."

Tolmie boasted an unsullied personal reputation for integrity, and he apparently did find patronage distasteful. Unfortunately, the mass of his supporters did not. From his earliest days in office, Tolmie found himself caught between his own preferences and election promises on the one hand and the incessant demands for rewards and place on the other. He wrote a senator shortly after the election that "there was a tremendous fight for patronage control and it was demanded of me that I should discharge all Liberals in the civil service. This I absolutely refused to do. . . . Naturally, this did not bring satisfaction to that group of men who are interested in politics only for revenue to be derived therefrom."[22] Tolmie was technically correct; not all Liberals lost their posts, just most of them. A clean sweep pushed Liberals from the outside service, the repository of part-time jobs and positions in the field; with gathering intensity Conservative ministers removed Liberals from the inside service. The civil service commissioner was fired. The sergeant-at-arms in the legislature lost his job. Eight months after the election, The Vancouver Sun, admittedly a Liberal paper, reported that only one Liberal road-foreman remained; all the coroners, registrars, janitors, clerks, mechanics, and many senior civil servants had gotten the chop.[23] Even the staunchly Conservative Daily Province conceded a year after the election that "The Tolmie government . . . came to power determined to be the government of British Columbia, not of the Conservative party, merely, and it has had its troubles living up to its resolves and its pledges."[24]

It was discouraging enough for Tolmie to be given only lukewarm support by friendly papers for not fulfilling his commitments to end patronage; it was positively annoying to be attacked from within his own ranks. Caught between demands for patronage and the inadequate supply of preferments, he fell victim to the vented frustrations of supporters. Tensions were exacerbated by discontented Conservatives under the direction of former leader William Bowser, defeated in the 1924 election but still a force to be reckoned with in Vancouver business circles. Based in Vancouver and on Vancouver Island, these dissidents insisted that Tolmie respect what they considered the well-established rules for dispensing patronage whereby MLAs and local associations decided who got what. In the words of one student of the period, "in some constituencies relations between riding organizations and the Tolmie government became so strained over patronage that association members openly questioned whether or not to continue working for the party."[25] Here was a Conservative party squabble no robust Liberal newspaper could resist reporting. "Party rift widens as Conservatives battle over spoils," ran a *Vancouver Sun* headline a year after the Tolmie government assumed office. The *Sun* relished reporting the anguished defence of two Conservatives against charges that patronage had been too slow in arriving. "The mail is stacked two feet high with requests for positions in the gift of the government. What time have I to do work for the province?" Attorney-General R.H. Pooley demanded of Esquimault Conservatives. C.H. Dickie, the federal Conservative MP, asked for patience. "When we get into power you people will be the first considered. We will consult the Conservative associations and make them as perfect a machine as there ever has been in the country."[26]

The onslaught of the Great Depression made everything worse. The clamour for government jobs and public works projects intensified. The premier's personal standing, based largely on his ability to win elections, nosedived as the economic slump pulled the party into a vortex of public discontent. Sensing the premier's vulnerability, the Bowserites redoubled their agitation. The Bowserites, suggested *The Victoria Times*, "objected to the Tolmie government not so much because it had been unbusinesslike and extravagant as because they themselves were not among the beneficiaries of its zeal. . . . It is not the size of the patronage pot they object to but the circumstance that no place was found for them within the confine of that pot."[27]

The *Times* analysis certainly did not jibe with that of leading members of the Vancouver business community. Alarmed at the economic deterioration, businessmen under the leadership of lumber baron H.R. MacMillan demanded that Premier Tolmie allow them to analyse what had gone wrong and how to put matters right. Tolmie had campaigned on bringing business principles to bear on public administration. He had always considered himself a statesman, a politician above the grubby details of patronage and preferment. Yet here were his erstwhile allies in the Vancouver business establishment demanding that he call on their businesslike analysis and statesmanship to extricate British Columbia from turmoil. Pressed by such influential supporters, Tolmie appointed a committee under businessman George Kidd to "investigate the finances of British Columbia."[28]

The Kidd Report reflected the gospel of the Vancouver Club. It called for a massive reduction in the size of government (building no new roads, closing the university, ending compulsory education at age fourteen, halving the size of the legislature), the reduction of taxes, and a return to balanced budgets. In its political analysis, the Kidd Report spoke to the enduring suspicion of partyism that runs through the history of politics in British Columbia. It presented the businessman's assumption — or his presumption — that the elimination of politics from public administration would lead to the triumph of economic rationality and plain old-fashioned common sense. Preoccupied with excessive spending and "startling deficits," the report blamed parties for the mess. "Although excuses are, as always, futile, and while the responsibility of our present difficulties must rest with the community as a whole, which must also pay the bill, the party system has been the instrument by means of which these difficulties have been created. That system has been so long in existence and is so prevalent in all legislative assemblies that we are inclined to forget that while it originated in legitimate differences of opinion on great questions of public policy, it is today largely a struggle between one party to retain and the other to recapture the benefits of office." The report asked rhetorically, putting the words in capital letters for emphasis, "is it an exaggeration in our own case to say that a change of government has no greater significance than that the patronage list of the party in power is replaced by that of their opponents?" The report insisted "that the time has come for a complete change in the ideas, opinions, and motives which have influenced both the electors and the elected in the past. Patronage and self-interest have been allowed to control the affairs of government and the public purse has been regarded as an inexhaustible booty upon which all may prey. Our legislators and their leaders have lived so long in an atmosphere of concession, compromise and debt that it is difficult, if not impossible, for them to realize the entirely new conditions with which they are today confronted."

Conservative Tolmie may have been, suicidal he was not. He discarded the report immediately. Sufficient political problems bore down upon him without the burden of the Kidd Report hobbling him further.

Tolmie's political virtue, his only stock in trade, was becoming suspect. The Liberal newspapers had been shredding that virtue from almost his first day in office. Thomas Dufferin Pattullo, the energetic Liberal leader, was stealing the premier's mantle of statesmanship, alleging in the legislature through nearly two hundred questions that the Tolmie government had rewarded supporters with appointments. And the Bowserites, unable to take control of the Conservative party, re-entered the field as a non-partisan group denouncing the evils of partyism, including patronage.

To anyone who remembered his bruising partisanship as premier and lieutenant to Premier Richard McBride, William Bowser's conversion was certainly spectacular. Now Bowser, like a man renouncing sin, lashed out at party government, insisting that its inherent defects contributed to waste and the province's poor economic performance. "This will be the end of machine rule," he promised during the election of 1933. "I used to be a party to that system through circumstances and conditions, but I'm through with that now." His death during the campaign ended his group's prospects for an electoral breakthrough. The combined forces of economic hardship and political agitation turned the province instead towards the Liberals and their ebullient leader T.D. Pattullo.

Premier Pattullo's eight years in office represented the last gasp for the traditional two-party politics. The classic struggle between Liberals and Conservatives, between the "ins" and "outs," slowly crumbled as supporters of each old-line party took fright at a menace more ominous than defeat at the hands of the other—the prospect in office of the Co-operative Commonwealth Federation, otherwise known in British Columbia as the socialist hordes. It took several elections for the CCF to shatter the traditional party structure, but when the CCF truly threatened to take power, the threat transformed British Columbia politics into a battle between the free-enterprise "ins" against the socialist "outs." The political battle increasingly raged, not over the spoils of office, but over different conceptions of government.[29] In 1935, the CCF pledged an independent civil service, an independent highways commission, "frankness and openness in government," abolition of lobbying, and a general improvement in all aspects of political morality. These pious hopes were easily dismissed as the puffs of idealists and dreamers. When the CCF gathered electoral strength its dreams became the other parties' traditional nightmares.

The CCF threat seemed minimal, however, when Pattullo led his Liberals back into office. Despite Pattullo's attacks on the excesses of the Tolmie government, the usual patterns of patronage quickly reasserted themselves. The Vancouver Liberal machine, in limbo during the Conservative interregnum (1928-1933) swung back into action; the civil service underwent the usual changes; Liberal contractors returned to favour; the liquor trade turned its spigot on for the Liberal cause. Pattullo, a former highways minister, knew the importance of roads and bridges, especially in northern British Columbia where he had worked so hard. His own "Little New Deal" opened new opportunities for public works strategically placed for political purposes. More important, it put Pattullo in the vanguard of Liberals in Canada who embraced Keynes, economic pump-priming, and moderately progressive social policies. His periodic bouts of Ottawa-bashing found a receptive audience, except during World War II when they seemed unduly petulant; his energy convinced voters that he was at least trying to cope with the Depression. Under the trying economic circumstances, it was no mean accomplishment to be re-elected in 1937.

The next election, that of 1941, proved to be a watershed, although few recognized it as such at the time. The CCF won the largest percentage of the popular vote and formed the second-largest bloc in the provincial assembly. From that day forward, the rallying cry of all those hostile to the CCF became "Keep the socialists out," a cry that still reverberates through provincial politics. No longer could politics revolve largely around a fight for spoils. It was now heavily tinged with ideology and mission on both sides. And as in Saskatchewan, the political question became which free-enterprise — or at least non-socialist — alternative would do battle with the CCF. It took slightly more than a decade to sort out the alternative, the Social Credit party, but in the meantime the old-line parties pooled their resources in coalition the better to prosecute the war effort and keep the socialists at bay.

Pattullo's opposition to coalition, and the Liberals' loss of ten seats in the 1941 election, cost him the party leadership. A Liberal-Conservative coalition cabinet, containing five Liberals including Premier John Hart and four Conservatives, was formed shortly after the election. As the Union government in Ottawa discovered during World War I, forcing former antagonists together required, among other adjustments, sorting out the rules for patronage. Some observers hoped coalition meant the end of patronage. "For the first time in nearly four decades there will be in the offing no party organizations to satisfy, no party adherents to receive admonitions from," wrote the distinguished journalist Bruce Hutchison.[30] In fact, the careful apportionment of portfolios to Liberals and Conservatives mirrored the division of patronage within the government: Liberals used their portfolios to reward their friends; Conservatives did likewise with their portfolios. Various ministers freely conceded that they, not the public service commission, did the hiring. The government's purchasing agent told a

House committee that purchases usually followed the advice of MLAs or defeated candidates.[31] At the constituency level, however, coalition produced friction with Conservative constituency organizations which felt the Liberals were getting too many spoils.[32]

The two old-line parties worked together harmoniously enough for awhile; they even pushed through impressive reform legislation that pleased labour organizations. But by the late 1940s, the Liberals had become so powerful within the coalition that after the 1949 election they commanded a clear majority in the assembly, and some of them wondered why they still needed their Conservative partners. Terminal strains emerged within the coalition, while over on the sidelines of politics a maverick Conservative, W.A.C. Bennett, preached the virtues of fusing the two parties which, he said, were united on everything but the "disgraceful division" of spoils.[33] Here again were echoes of the nineteenth-century ideal of non-partisan politics in British Columbia, of the Provincial Party, the Kidd Report, Bowser's non-partisans in 1933. In short, it was a reaffirmation that somehow politics should be above patronage and petty divisions. The cry had taken various forms, none of which had ever shaken the fortress of the traditional parties since their establishment in provincial politics. But now with the coalition cracking and the CCF at the gates, Bennett's clarion call, delivered in that raspy, idiosyncratic voice of his, at first intrigued, then rallied an ever-larger number of British Columbians. That he was himself an outsider in the Conservative party, a self-described "man of the people," a resident of the Okanagan with no ties to the Vancouver establishment, reinforced his pretensions to be above partyism, or at least above the evils traditionally associated with the old-line parties.

How Bennett pulled off his stunning coup is beyond our purpose; suffice it to say he succeeded spectacularly.[34] The coup transformed British Columbia politics, or at least the non-socialist part of it. The Liberals kept winning about a fifth of the votes in provincial elections until in the 1970s they joined the Conservatives as political waifs. The majority of Liberals and Conservatives threw in their lot with Social Credit in provincial elections, then returned to their traditional rivalry in federal ones. In its way, this weakened the importance of patronage in British Columbia, since the lack of strong Liberal and Conservative parties at both levels of government tempered the fierce partisan allegiance characterizing the politics of many other Canadian provinces. So, too, the Vancouver business community, accustomed to chummy relations with provincial Liberal and Conservative governments, could never be fully comfortable with the unpredictable Socreds, whose battalions emerged from the Interior, where a resentment of Vancouver beat in many hearts. Social Credit governments were avowedly pro-business, but in their peculiar fashion — boosterish rhetoric, a love affair with grandiose public works such as highways, dams and hydro-electric projects, and an ever-present temptation to muck around with the workings of the free market in the name of some populist cause.

Bennett always insisted that Social Credit represented a movement, as distinct from a political party. The premier peppered his speeches with references to the Social Credit "movement," regularly insisting that Social Credit stood above all the sordidness of the traditional parties. After a decade and a half in office, Bennett regularly signed letters: Premier and Leader of the Social Credit Movement.[35] Financial contributions were made not to the party, but to the Free Enterprise Educational Fund. This was a legal nicety but a political fiction, since the fund simply financed the party. It did allow Bennett to insist that he never stooped to concern himself with the petty details of mixing government business with such party requirements as raising money. Einar Gunderson—the premier's close friend, finance minister and Social Credit bagman—supervised the fund, and its revenues were funnelled through Gunderson's private accounting firm. This certainly looked odd, since even after leaving politics Gunderson retained several government-related positions. But then the Social Credit governments of both W.A.C. Bennett and his son, Bill, were shot through with either direct conflicts of interest which caused ministerial resignations or situations that invited critics to point to the potential for conflict of interest. Yet Bennett Sr. always brushed these fears aside with that superior moral certainty of his.

Nevertheless, the problem of conflicts of interest continued periodically to dog Social Credit politicians. The conflicts seldom seemed as brazen as those regularly found in the legislature for decades after Confederation, yet they kept reappearing, a testimony perhaps to the essentially deal-making mentality of so many Socred politicians. A few of them could be called blue-bloods from the Vancouver business community; the majority hailed from the Interior or Vancouver Island, where they had been small businessmen, representatives of that acquisitive instinct never far from the surface of British Columbia political life. In their private occupations, the let's-make-a-deal-and-shake-on-it mentality tripped a few of them up over the years because they forgot, or never considered, that the procedures for getting a deal, and the public perceptions of how the deal was made, differed when the public interest rather than private gain defined the deal's utility. Boosterish almost to a person, Socreds occasionally neglected the reality that in politics, the means to an end can be as important as the end, a reality no amount of Rotary Club rhetoric could obscure. And yet, the scandals and ministerial resignations that beset Socred governments seldom sufficiently shook public confidence. For the largest number of British Columbians the political alternative to the anti-socialist party seemed more threatening to the public interest that the occasional indiscretions of individual Socred ministers.

Like a bad smell, however, the Sommers affair lingered well into the Socreds' second term, provoking endless arguments in the legislature without apparently damaging the party's political standing.[36] Robert Sommers, the minister of lands and forests in the first Bennett government, stood accused in the legislature of issuing a forestry licence to a company whose president was also lending the minister money. The tangled affair dragged on for years — through legislative debates, newspaper investigations, an RCMP report, a commission of inquiry, and eventually the courts. An RCMP report, which did not provoke immediate action from Attorney-General Robert Bonner, found a "definite indication of wrongdoing" in "Honest Bob" Sommers' relations with Wick Gray's company, Pacific Coast Services Limited. A variety of twists and turns — the disappearance of Sommers to the United States, a civil suit launched by Sommers — continued to delay the laying of charges. When the RCMP investigation eventually led to a trial, it proved to be a spectacular affair stretching over eighty-two days of testimony and one thousand and sixty exhibits. The verdict — Robert Sommers and Wick Gray were found guilty of a criminal conspiracy involving bribes. Sommers had accepted from Gray rugs, bonds and cash. Sommers was sentenced to five years in jail, and served two years and four months before being paroled. The affair, however, scarcely damaged Social Credit, which retained Sommers' seat in a by-election. To Bennett, the Sommers' affair merely proved the rectitude of the Social Credit government which would pursue wrongdoing wherever it was found.

Sommers had always been a marginal player in the Social Credit government. The same could not be said of "Flying Phil" Gaglardi, the most colourful member of the Bennett cabinets, the minister of highways who, in a party enamoured of public works, delighted in hopping about the province cutting ribbons to open yet another road. Bennett, never one to understate enthusiasms, said of his minister, "They talk about Roman roads in Europe but they don't compare to Gaglardi highways in British Columbia." Gaglardi's flamboyance had always been a red flag waved at the Opposition. In 1968, they hurled a stream of specific charges at him, including speculation by his sons on land owned by the Highways department and the use of departmental services for personal advantage. These charges were all stoutly denied by Gaglardi, but he was forced to resign when it was revealed that his daughter-in-law had taken a government jet to Texas. The government kept confidential several treasury-board investigations into Flying

Phil's administration, but they were widely assumed to have contributed to his downfall.[37]

The departures of Sommers and Gaglardi — one for criminality, the other for admitted and suspected nepotism — were dismissed as aberrations by Premier W.A.C. Bennett. Their downfall merely proved what he always insisted, namely that Social Credit would stamp out patronage in all its forms. In one 1969 speech, he called patronage a "cancer," and in a speech to Socreds in Terrace, B.C. boasted that "we are not a patronage movement, we are the opposite."[38] Certainly, by the standards of pre-Social Credit politics, Bennett could make a case that his party had been less interested in spoils than had the Liberals and Conservatives, a case that withstood comparison with the records of McBride, Brewster, Bowser, Tolmie and Pattullo. That he had never favoured friends, however, was demonstrable nonsense. His government frequently employed the porkbarrelling techniques of promising highways and dams at election time to swing constituencies. Social Credit also appointed party members to a variety of boards, agencies and commissions of the provincial government. Gunderson, for example, never could get elected to the legislature, but he nevertheless wound up as director of three provincial Crown corporations. Bennett's executive assistant, Ronald Worley, became assistant general manager of the B.C. Ferry Authority. Defeated Socred candidates often found themselves with government appointments to ease their pain.

So patronage, rather than being stamped out by W.A.C. Bennett, was largely reduced to the stuff of appointments and discretionary contracts, each round of which provoked squawks from the Opposition — by Barrett New Democratic government and by the Bennett Jr. Social Credit government — and fleeting, harmless articles in the newspapers.

Perhaps more arresting in the history of Social Credit, although not politically debilitating, were the ministerial resignations that hit the Bennett Jr. and Vander Zalm governments for real or apparent conflicts of interest. Four ministers in the Vander Zalm government resigned for alleged conflicts of interest, although two were reinstated. Patronage made little blips upon the province's political screen, but seldom lit up the province. It seemed peripheral to the driving dynamic of provincial politics — the fight between non-socialist forces and the NDP. The favouritism each party in office extended to its own supporters seemed a natural outgrowth of that battle, rather than the animating force behind it.

Patronage still lives in British Columbia, albeit in an attenuated form. Its manifestions seem less evident there than in many other Canadian provinces and perhaps, therefore, less offensive to the provincial electorate.

PART III

VELVET ROBES

CHAPTER 16

JUDGES, LAWYERS AND LIEUTENANT GOVERNORS

"There has been too much political patronage
concerned in appointments to the bench."
Prime Minister R.B. Bennett

WHETHER LAWYERS MAKE GOOD POLITICIANS is a matter for debate; that many politicians are lawyers is a fact. The vocation of politicians as lawmakers undoubtedly attracts lawyers to politics; the vocation of lawyers as interpreters of the law invites former politicians to practise law or sit on the bench. Both lawyers and politicians also play with words, fuss about procedures and institutions, work in adversarial milieus, and take themselves with great seriousness. The law and politics, then, make a natural fit, so it is not surprising that so many of our politicians have been lawyers. In the 1867 House of Commons, thirty-five percent of the members were lawyers, in 1911 forty percent, in 1945 thirty-eight percent, in 1980 twenty-seven percent, in 1984 nineteen percent. The number of lawyer MPs is dropping, but lawyers still represent one of the largest occupational groups in politics.

Not every lawyer dreams of becoming a judge, and not every judge wants the life of a Supreme Court justice. But those who so aspire know that under the Canadian (and British) tradition, they will achieve their ambitions only by appointment. In theory, they could be appointed by lot, or by their peers, or they could be elected, as are many American judges. But in our tradition they are appointed by governments—about one thousand of them by provincial or territorial governments, nearly eight hundred by the federal government. So, too, governments parcel out legal work across the country to private-sector lawyers when the government's own lawyers cannot handle a case because of its routine nature or the press of other business. And although lieutenant-governors are not practitioners of the law, strictly speaking, they can in political crises be called upon to exercise important constitutional powers which rest on convention or law.

The appointment of judges and lieutenant-governors, and the parcelling out of government legal work, require government discretion which can lead to political patronage. Indeed, legal patronage, a term of sheer convenience rather than precise meaning, has often produced some of the headaches of appointing senators, although seldom the furtive supplications of would-be contractors. In a sense, politicians who appoint judges and lieutenant-governors lose them forever. Their appointment, if patronage was involved, represents the final payoff. Senators, ambassadors, admen, contractors, businessmen — all the other recipients of government patronage can be summoned again to repay the patron's gift. Once installed, judges and lieutenant-governors cease being clients. They rise like Christian souls to another plane and bid farewell to the partisan efforts that made it all possible. They leave others to argue whether those partisan efforts represented the proper criteria for appointment, and whether years of party struggle shaped views and moulded values in ways that might colour the new kinds of judgments they must then make.

There can be little doubt how legal agents, or what the department of justice calls standing agents, are chosen. Standing agents are the lawyers, scattered in cities and hamlets across Canada, who do whatever work the department considers necessary. For a large firm, the work of standing agent is like popcorn, a nice treat of small consequence. For small firms in modest towns, government work seldom makes or breaks lawyers' careers, but it might mean the difference between an excellent year and a good one. The same can be said of legal work for the Central Mortgage and Housing Corporation, the Farm Credit Corporation, or any number of Crown corporations or agencies. These appointments are invariably political decisions based on lists of lawyers drawn up in the office of the minister of justice upon recommendations from government MPs, defeated candidates and party officials. There is nothing in the least secret about this; everybody in the legal community in perhaps all but the largest cities knows the firms and lawyers on the government's list.[1]

So this kind of political patronage is as easy to document as, say, Senate appointments before the Meech Lake constitutional accord. But because the patronage is scattered in little bits to lawyers and their firms across hundreds of Canadian communities, it goes almost unnoticed except by grateful recipients. An examination of the 1979,

1980 and 1984 lists of standing agents shows an almost complete change after each election. The Clark Conservatives wasted no time in sweeping out Liberal standing agents after the 1979 election; the Trudeau Liberals returned the compliment after returning to office in 1980; and the Mulroney Conservatives overhauled the list again after the 1984 landslide.

Consider Alberta. The Clark Conservatives made a clean sweep of standing agents in 1979, a flick of the party's revenge for having watched a handful of hardy Alberta Liberals, in the law and elsewhere, scoop up federal patronage for so many years. After 1984 the Mulroney Conservatives cleaned out almost all the Liberal standing agents, except for a few large firms in Calgary and Edmonton with lawyers of both political persuasions and those agents in one-firm towns such as Brooks, Grand Centre and Bonnyville.

The same thing happened in British Columbia. The odd firm, usually in a small community, held its place on the list. But even in the big cities, the Conservative brush swept the Liberals clean, including the Vancouver firm of former Liberal cabinet minister Ron Basford. (Not that the imposing partnership, Davis and Company, needed the work.) In Quebec, the Clark government must have scratched hard to find enough Conservative lawyers, given the lamentable state of the party there. But they worked hard at the job, and carried over only two lawyers and one firm from the Liberal list. The Mulroney Conservatives, having won fifty-eight seats in the province, kept eight lawyers in small towns on the list. In the major centres of Montreal, Quebec City, Sherbrooke and Trois-Rivières, the Conservatives did not fool around. They changed everyone. In Ontario, the Mulroney government kept on the list only fifteen of two hundred and nine lawyers from the 1980–84 Trudeau government.

The work of standing agent seldom makes a lawyer rich: a drug prosecution, perhaps a real estate transaction, a defence against small actions brought against the Crown. The occasional case might drag on and allow a lawyer to fill out his billing card. But in places like Clarenville, Newfoundland, or Salmon Arm, British Columbia, many Crown agents do little, if any, legal work. The choice of standing agents in such communities manifests petty patronage, occasionally offering worthwhile financial rewards, but usually just the prestige of having been selected. MPs, however, take seriously the responsibility of selection, because it represents one of the lingering bits of personal patronage in their hands. Gilles Bernier, a newly elected Quebec Conservative in the Mulroney government, summed up this attitude when asked about the changes in his riding, "It's one of those little privileges we have left as MPs." Bernier replied to the charge of patronage by using the old Union Nationale distinction between "good" and "bad" patronage. "It's good patronage," he said, "and there's nothing to be ashamed of."[2]

Another classic example of "psychic" patronage involves the appointment of Queen's Counsels, or QCs, by federal or provincial governments. This title is ostensibly bestowed on meritorious lawyers by disinterested governments, but the reasons are often a mixture of merit and partisanship, an obvious exception being QCs given to the government's staff lawyers. The tradition, imported from the English bar, goes back a long way in Canada. "I see you have been making QCs of some very young men," wrote E. Stonehouse of Brampton, Ontario, to John A. Macdonald. "I trust you have not quite forgotten your promise to me."[3] This sort of letter, multiplied by the thousands, poured into politicians' offices from supplicants for QCs. Federal and provincial attorneys-general, in receipt of the supplications, kept a sharp eye out for partisanship in distributing these modest prizes. Known supporters of other political parties could receive QCs, usually so that the attorney-general could defend himself against anyone who might point to all the known supporters of his own party on the annual list of QCs. Although theoretically awarded for merit, the link between the QC and proper political credentials robbed the title of any practical significance. It may have fooled a lawyer's prospective client into believing that the title implied merit, whereas all it really conferred was status, and a peculiar kind at that. The QC awards were little bits of patronage that bound lawyers to party, cost the treasury nothing, and made the recipients stand slightly taller, at least in their own minds. The Ontario and Quebec governments have now stopped awarding them; the attorneys-general of Newfoundland, New Brunswick and British Columbia take advice from a committee of the profession.

More consequential legal patronage is handed by the party in power to supporters to do work for federal corporations and agencies. Depending on the size of the corporation, the dollar value can be substantial, and the transfer of the business can hurt medium-sized firms. These choices, usually made by ministers, funnel a steady stream of business to the recipients, since agencies such as the Farm Credit Corporation turn over a large volume of work in a given year. But perhaps the most lucrative — and challenging — assignments consist of representing the federal government in major cases or acting as counsel for federal commissions. Quality counts here because the stakes are invariably high and the issues complicated, but the proper political connections help.

To take just two examples, the Trudeau Liberals used Montreal lawyer Michel Robert for critical constitutional cases heard by the

Supreme Court of Canada. He is an expert in constitutional law and a prominent Liberal who became president of the party in 1986. Michael Meighen, a former president of the Conservative party, became chief counsel to the royal commission established by the Mulroney government to examine the issue of war criminals in Canada. No one could question the legal credentials of either man, or indeed of many others given similar assignments, but only the wilfully blind could ignore their political affiliation.

Less savoury, although not unknown, are instances when important legal patronage is bestowed on an individual for no discernible reason other than partisan preferment. Sam Wakim, for example, had long been one of Prime Minister Brian Mulroney's closest buddies, or so he considered himself. They were classmates at St. Francis Xavier University, kindred spirits of intrigue in the agitation to remove Joe Clark as Conservative leader, media junkies (Wakim used to alert Mulroney every night to articles in *The Globe and Mail*'s first edition), and dreamers about how power might taste if only Mulroney led the Conservative party. Not long after Mulroney became prime minister, Sam Wakim suddenly found himself in possession of some of the legal business of the Export Development Corporation, which necessarily meant that it no longer resided in the hands of the highly respected Ottawa firm of Gowling and Henderson. Just what legal credentials Wakim possessed that exceeded those of Gowling and Henderson stumped eveyone in the legal fraternities of Ottawa and Toronto. But to Toronto and Sam Wakim the corporation's legal business went, specifically, to Weir and Foulds, the Toronto firm Wakim joined. The whole affair neither looked pretty nor smelled good, but then this sort of patronage seldom does.

If patronage permeates the government's legal business, it also effects judicial appointments, although somewhat less pervasively. From the beginning, judges have been considered too important to be appointed like senators or lieutenant-governors. They stand, after all, outside the political system, called upon to interpret laws passed by politicians. If the quality of the judiciary declines, or if judges are suspected of unvarnished partisanship, then respect for law might be jeopardized. So even the most partisan prime ministers have been prudent in appointing judges, and in more recent years a convention has developed whereby the federal government consults widely within the legal fraternity on a non-partisan basis before making senior judicial appointments.

Prime Minister John A. Macdonald, who acted as his own minister of justice from 1867 to 1873, always mixed the water of non-partisanship with the strong wine of party in making judicial appointments.

"My rule," he told one Nova Scotian, "is to consider fitness as the first prerequisite for judicial appointments and that political considerations should have little or no influence."[4] He wrote a Conservative editor who queried the appointment of a Liberal to the bench, "I have always held that the Judicial officers stand on a quite different footing from all others, that fitness with respect to the Bench must be the first consideration and that no political exigency however great would warrant the Government in appointing an unfit man to be a Judge." Macdonald was too much the partisan — he was a party leader, after all, trying to establish the Conservatives in every region — to remove political considerations entirely from the selection of judges. He did appoint prominent Conservative politicians to the bench, but his overall record in judicial appointments set the rough pattern for future prime ministers — partisanship would count but would not obliterate other qualifications.

Broadly speaking, the further down the judicial hierarchy, the more obvious the evidence of patronage. The Supreme Court of Canada, for example, is now completely devoid of patronage, or even of the tinge of partisan appointments. (What the 1986 Meech Lake accord will bring remains to be seen. It allows the federal government to appoint Supreme Court justices only from lists prepared by provinces.) Supreme Court appointments were not always so pure. A scholarly history of the Supreme Court makes clear that partisanship joined religion and region—and merit, when available—as indispensable criteria for Supreme Court appointments until the immediate post-war years. When Louis St. Laurent became prime minister in 1949, the court contained seven justices, four of whom had had extensive political ties to the Liberal party. St. Laurent himself appointed justices from a mixture of non-political and political backgrounds, the most obvious being long-time Liberal cabinet minister Douglas Abbott. But partisanship appeared to wane throughout subsequent years as prime ministers increasingly sought advice from the legal fraternity before making Supreme Court appointments.[5] Twenty-two of forty Supreme Court judges appointed before 1949 had previously been politicians; since then, only two of twenty-two justices had entered politics.[6]

That sharp decline in previous political experience of Supreme Court justices is partly — but only partly — reflected further down the hierarchy. The Canadian Bar Association said as recently as 1985 that "there is ample scope for the functioning of a political patronage system without applying it to judicial appointments."[7] The association declared itself satisfied that patronage had been rooted out of the Supreme Court, but it worried about patronage elsewhere in the judiciary, especially in the Federal Court, whose members are appointed by Ottawa. Writing after Prime Minister Pierre Trudeau sent three former ministers (Mark MacGuigan, Bud Cullen and Yvon Pinard) to the Federal Court as part of his 1984 orgy of patronage appointments, the association remarked, "at present, this court is perceived by many, rightly or wrongly, as a government-oriented court because so many former politicians and federal officials have been appointed to it." The association added, "as to appointments to the Federal Court of Canada, political favouritism has been a dominant, though not sole, consideration; many appointees have been active supporters of the party in power."

Trudeau's parting gesture also featured the appointment of two other Liberal MPs and a defeated Liberal candidate to lower courts. These appointments fitted a familiar Trudeau pattern for patronage. A professor of law before entering politics, Trudeau took considerable care in his early years in office ot temper patronage in making senior judicial appointments. This was consistent with other intermittent efforts to change traditional assumptions about patronage. But such efforts declined in intensity as his years in office wore on, so that by the end of his sixteen years as prime minister Trudeau was practising patronage as relentlesly as his predecessors.

The association also analysed federal appointments to higher courts in the provinces — so-called section 96 courts — and concluded that political favouritism still existed in Alberta, Manitoba, Newfoundland, and Ontario, and that it remained a "dominant" but not exclusive consideration in New Brunswick, Nova Scotia, Prince Edward Island, and Saskatchewan. That the three Maritime provinces appeared on the association's list was not surprising; there the traditions of political patronage have persisted longer than almost anywhere else in Canada. But Saskatchewan's inclusion might raise a few eyebrows, until one remembers that Saskatchewan was the fiefdom of Otto Lang, Trudeau's minister of justice and a former dean of the University of Saskatchewan law school.

Lang and his successor Mark MacGuigan scattered prominent or low-profile Liberals throughout the Saskatchewan judiciary, including former party leaders, MLAs, defeated candidates and loyal party workers.[8] This propensity for appointing Liberals to Saskatchewan courts led directly to a *contretemps* with the Conservative government of Premier Grant Devine. The provincial Conservatives, eager dispensers of patronage themselves, became sufficiently riled by Liberal appointments to the bench, and by Ottawa's refusal to consult the provincial government before making appointments, that they tried to restrict Liberal opportunities for patronage. In 1982 the provincial government passed an order-in-council reducing the number of judges on the Saskatchewan Court of Appeal from seven to five.

For the next two years, open warfare raged between the provincial Conservative government and the Trudeau Liberals. The provincial cabinet passed another order-in-council closing down each vacancy on the Court of Queen's Bench, so that its strength fell from thirty to twenty-four. Only the election of the Mulroney Conservatives ended the impasse. With Conservatives in Regina and Ottawa, the provincial party quickly restored the judicial positions, and filled some of them with prominent supporters such as George Hill and Irving Goldenberg, former presidents of the Saskatchewan Conservative party. The Saskatchewan experience of the 1980s mirrored that of Newfoundland in 1960 when Liberal premier Joey Smallwood, rebuffed by the federal Conservatives in his demand for control of judicial appointments, refused to proclaim legislation creating a new position on the provincial Supreme Court.

The Bar Association's 1985 review of judicial appointments gave provincial governments better marks than it gave the federal government. In five provinces — Alberta, British Columbia, Newfoundland, Quebec, and Saskatchewan — the association thought "political favouritism has played no part in appointments." In Manitoba, favouritism played "some part" in appointments, whereas in those hardy patronage perennials — New Brunswick, Prince Edward Island and Nova Scotia — the association found that "most appointees have been active supporters of the party in power."

That 1985 review, sparked by Trudeau's parting orgy of patronage and his failure to consult the bar before making Yvon Pinard's appointment, flowed from the association's decades-long campaign to squeeze patronage from the process of selecting judges. Moral suasion was about the association's only weapon for many years, although it helped the association's case when its president, R.B. Bennett, became prime minister in 1930 and tried to set a better example in selecting Supreme Court justices. But the concept of formal consultation with the legal community had to await the arrival of Trudeau as minister of justice in 1967.

Trudeau became the first minister of justice to seek an opinion of the Canadian Bar Association's National Council on the Judiciary before appointing a judge. This practice continued when John Turner became minister of justice in the first Trudeau government, and Turner is fairly credited with having improved the quality of judicial appointments across the country. In 1972, a special adviser on judicial appointments was named in the minister's office. These reforms sprang both from Trudeau's own convictions as a professor of law and from intermittent attempts to change some traditional conventions of patronage in his early years in office. In five provinces—Alberta, British Columbia, Newfoundland, Ontario, and Saskatchewan— attorneys-general now formally consult provincial judicial councils before making appointments, while in Quebec the attorney-general consults a nominating committee. British Columbia's *Provincial Court Act* even requires the cabinet to appoint only persons recommended by the judicial council.

Pressure from the bar, then, has been among those restricting the incidence of political patronage on judicial appointments. Some numbers illustrate the point. Will Klein studied federally appointed judges in Manitoba, Ontario, and Quebec from 1905 to 1970. He found that nearly ninety-five percent of former politicians appointed to Ontario courts by Liberal governments were Liberals, and eighty-one percent appointed by Conservative governments were Conservatives. But he also discovered that although forty-three percent of all Laurier's appointments had contested elections, only twenty-one percent of Trudeau's (up to 1970) had done so. Klein concluded that "political activities prior to appointment to the bench have been common to about a third of the judges appointed in Manitoba, Ontario, and Quebec between 1905 and 1970 but that . . . proportion of judges with electoral experience has diminished through these years."[9]

What Klein could not measure was the partisanship of appointees who had participated in politics other than by running in elections or serving in legislatures. It was a key omission, since many judicial appointees have been active party supporters without ever having entered electoral politics. His general conclusion that political considerations in judicial appointments have waned over this century was supported by Guy Bouthillier, who examined the careers of appointees to the Quebec Court of Appeal from 1867 to 1972. Bouthillier found that the proportion involved in politics had dropped from over seventy-eight percent between Confederation and World War I to twenty-two percent since World War II.[10] But remember that these sorts of studies undoubtedly underestimate, often considerably, the partisan factor in appointments. They trace only electoral careers, and forget that many judges with the proper political credentials never ran for office. For example, one study in the early 1950s found that in six provinces *all* the judges were supporters of the party in power at the time of their appointment. In the four other provinces, the percentage of party supporters ranged from seventy percent to eighty-seven percent. And a survey for the Association of Canadian Law Teachers in 1966 concluded, "All but a few of the judges appointed during the period were affiliated with the party in power at the time of their appointment, and most were actively engaged in politics."[11]

The practice still continues. For example, Prime Minister Joe Clark appointed five judges to the Superior Court for the Montreal district. All had Conservative credentials: Claude Gérin, who ran unsuccessfully against Liberal kingpin Marc Lalonde; Gérard Trudel, a Conservative organizer; Maurice Mercure, a former Union Nationale candidate and Conservative organizer; Bernard Flynn, who worked for Clark and his predecessor Robert Stanfield; and Claude Nolin, former president of the Conservative party in Quebec.

"Most were actively engaged in politics;" that phrase from the Association of Canadian Law Teachers certainly applies to Canada's lieutenant-governors. Next to the Senate, the office of lieutenant-governor has been the most prized patronage plum since Confederation. It is an office of prestige and status with constitutional responsibilities great in theory, infrequently exercised in practice. Like a senatorship, the office of lieutenant-governor provided a convenient nesting place for politicians whose pasts were more glorious than their futures. By appointing former ministers, prime ministers opened vacancies for younger men; by appointing party loyalists, they repaid political debts. That tradition continues today, although prime ministers now consult provincial premiers of the same party before making appointments. Mulroney, for example, sent the veteran Tory MP James McGrath to St. John's as lieutenant-governor because McGrath's path to Newfoundland's cabinet seat was blocked by the imposing figure of John Crosbie. He made Lincoln Alexander, a long-time Conservative frontbencher, lieutenant-governor of Ontario. In Alexander and in the smattering of women appointed in recent years as lieutenant-governors can be seen the same symbolic use of patronage that became intermittently apparent in the Senate, starting in the 1960s.

John A. Macdonald, for one, refused as a matter of policy to appoint lieutenant-governors to second five-year terms. After all, reasoned Macdonald, why not spread the goodies around? "If I reappointed one Lieutenant-Governor the others who are all political friends would feel slighted if the same favour was not granted them."[12] Macdonald assumed lieutenant-governors were more than figureheads, presiders over elaborate social functions; they were bulwarks of centralized control. Laurier, too, saw advantages in partisan appointments. His selection of prominent Liberals as lieutenant-governors for the new provinces of Alberta and Saskatchewan produced incumbent Liberal governments for the first province-wide elections, and incumbency materially assisted the Liberals in winning those first elections. Between them, Macdonald and Laurier appointed sixty-four lieutenant-governors, only one of whom (a Laurier choice) had no previous political experience.[13]

Partisanship, however, later became somewhat diluted. Of the seventy-six lieutenant-governors appointed between 1911 and 1955, twenty-nine had no political experience. Since 1950, only twenty-eight out of seventy-one had entered electoral politics.[14] But this figure substantially underestimates the political background of the appointees; many were fund-raisers, such as Liberal bagman John Aird of Ontario, or prominent party supporters outside of electoral politics. For those with a stomach for an endless round of socializing and ceremonial occasions, the role of lieutenant-governor has been irresistible.

CHAPTER 17

THE SENATE

"A Senate seat is a legitimate aspiration of any
Canadian."
Prime Minister Arthur Meighen

SINCE 1867 nearly eight hundred Canadians have been summoned to
the Senate. But bereft of the legitimacy of elected office and deprived
of credibility by virtue of overwhelming partisanship, most senators
have never quite known what to do with their undoubted constitutional
authority. The British government, reviewing the proposed British
North America Act, cautioned the Canadian framers that they might
rue the Senate's powers. What would stop the senators, inquired the
British, from frustrating the will of the elected House of Commons?
As things turned out, nothing in theory, almost everything in practice.
The Senate sometimes went beyond tinkering with legislation and
hurled bills back at the Commons, but more often the Senate saluted
the Commons majority, either because most senators came from the
same political tribe as the Commons majority, or because the unelected
senators knew the risks of upstaging the elected members of the Commons. (The Senate has rejected only one hundred and forty-one public
bills sent from the Commons since 1867, and none since 1940.) Then,
too, the Senate sometimes could not be bothered to be bothersome.
Some senators have always worked hard; a majority accepted the good
fortune of a sinecure with a title especially useful for parading before
Americans taught to be respectful of anyone called Senator.

The Fathers of Confederation gave the Senate three overriding
responsibilities: to protect the interests of property; to provide what

311

Sir John A. Macdonald called a "sober second thought" against the impulses of mass democracy; and to represent the interests and reflect the sentiments of the regions and minorities of Canada. The Senate never consistently met any of these responsibilities, largely because its place atop the hierarchy of political patronage in Canada fatally compromised its credibility. For twelve decades, no other place in the Canadian political system was so coveted by so many. Unlike judgeships and diplomatic postings, Senate membership demanded no specialized training; unlike the British House of Lords, membership provided reasonable pay; unlike most other jobs, a place in the Senate required no work, only occasional attendance. Docility was a senator's simplest requirement, activity a risk.

The Senate's ability to assist a prime minister's tasks as party leader eclipsed the responsibilities assigned to it by the Fathers of Confederation, who had devoted six of the fourteen days of the Quebec Conference to the problem of the second chamber.[1] The Senate's hardy band of defenders insisted that long political experience, the usual condition for appointment, would enable senators to discharge the institution's responsibilities. With experience came discernment, even wisdom, and perhaps a certain statesmanship. It soon became clear that mass democracy would not assault the interests of property, and the Senate's primary responsibilities became those of providing a sober second thought and representing the regional flavour of the country. Unfortunately, partisan appointments proved the enemy of both responsibilities. A minority of senators could transcend their roots; most could not easily lay aside a lifetime of political attachment. Any discernment, wisdom and statesmanship acquired along the way proved either incidental or secondary to an abiding partisanship. And people in the regions knew that partisanship, including membership in the national caucus and other manifestations of party discipline, usually neutered the senators' role as champions of regional interests. Senators were good Manitobans or Quebeckers or whatever, but the vast majority were also loyalists who, weighing the balance between party discipline and regional dissidence, usually opted for public silence.

In the Senate's early decades, deference to property and a limited franchise made the red chamber seem less anachronistic than it later became. But even in the early years, provincial premiers quickly decided that they best articulated regional interests, as Premier Oliver Mowat of Ontario and Premier Honoré Mercier of Quebec demonstrated in 1887 at the first interprovincial premiers' conference. Years later, premiers such as McBride, Pattullo and W.A.C. Bennett of British Columbia; Aberhart and Lougheed of Alberta; Martin, Douglas, Thatcher and Blakeney of Saskatchewan; Hepburn, Drew and Robarts of

Ontario; Duplessis, Lesage and Lévesque of Quebec; Fielding of Nova Scotia; indeed premiers across the country replaced senators as insistent and eloquent spokesmen for regional interests. The drift away from John A. Macdonald's original intentions for Canada as a highly centralized federation curtailed the Senate's effectiveness for reflecting regional perspectives. As federalism in the period after the Second World War developed into a system of competing bureaucracies and endless federal-provincial conferences — a system conveniently called "executive federalism" — senators became interested but largely irrelevant bystanders, summoned to pass *post facto* and *pro forma* judgment on irreversible decisions taken elsewhere.

The clairvoyance of hindsight was not available to the framers of the Senate. They thought the Senate would matter in ways that it did not, and that it would not matter much in ways that events proved it did. The framers, especially those from Central Canada, had experienced the shifting coalitions and chronic instability of governments before Confederation. Governments had come and gone with such merry abandon that few could have foreseen how, after Confederation, Canadian politics would evolve into extended periods of one-party rule.

Once partisanship became the overriding criterion for Senate appointments, one-party dominance produced a long series of senators from the governing party. This development in turn frequently gave the Senate lop-sided majorities that persisted regardless of any changes in the Commons. When the Liberals won in 1896, they confronted a Conservative majority in the Senate of sixty; in 1911 the incoming Conservatives faced a Liberal majority in the Senate of forty; when the Conservatives won in 1957, the Liberal Senate majority was seventy-one. The Senate majority, through no fault of its own, sometimes found itself completely out of step with the prevailing mood of the country, which merely exacerbated the inherent tension between a body with specified constitutional authority and no political credibility.

Long stretches of one-party dominance, however, meant that the Senate infrequently found itself out of sorts with the Commons majority. The possibility of a Commons and Senate displaying different partisan majorities had worried the British. When they were asked to comment on the *British North America Act*, they foresaw endless stalemates between upper and lower houses. That seldom happened in Canada, because one-party dominance gave the party in power ample opportunity to re-make the Senate in its own partisan image. In the early decades after Confederation, the Senate flexed its muscles: Even Conservatives were not above giving their friends in the Commons a difficult time. But when the franchise expanded to include every eligible Canadian over twenty-one, male and female, the notion of an unelected body blocking the will of the elected chamber became too offensive for senators to try their luck. Nevertheless, during the Mulroney government the Liberal-dominated Senate caused major difficulties for the governing Conservatives by delaying passage of bills, suggesting a series of major amendments, or being persistently ornery about government legislation.

It was considered part of the natural order of parliamentary government that there should be a second chamber. British practice commended it; federalism required it. Before Confederation, the colonies all had second chambers, either appointed or elected. In 1855, the assembly of the Canadas voted for an elected council to replace the appointed one. The next year, forty-eight councillors were elected for eight-year terms, although the terms were staggered so that one-quarter of the councillors would be up for election every two years. John A. Macdonald had been among those favouring an elected upper house, but he conceded the system had not worked "as we had expected." The sheer size of the constituencies, the labour and money required to get elected — these factors discouraged "men of the first standing" from preferring the council to the assembly. "All the young men, the active politicians, those who have resolved to embrace the life of a statesman, have sought entrance to the House of Assembly," said Macdonald.[2] (Prince Edward Island pressed hardest for an *elected* Senate, even urging *equal* representation for *every* province—foreshadowing the cry of the 1980s for a Triple E Senate, elected, effective and equal.)

John A. predicted that since the upper house would protect regional interests, "it will become the interest of each section to be represented by its very best men." Of course, it didn't work out that way, nor did the Senate fulfil in practice George Brown's expectation that "not a single appointment could be made, with regard to which the Government would not be open to censure, and which the representatives of the people, in this House, would not have an opportunity of condemning."[3] Defenders of an appointed Senate implicitly recognized that after the first selection appointments would be partisan, but they glossed over the consequences. The alternatives seemed worse: An elected upper house could produce deadlock by blocking initiatives of the Commons; Canada was too young a country for an upper house based on heredity.

Opponents, though, accurately predicted the future. At the Quebec conference David Reesor argued, "We know what the tendency is in England, and what it was in this country when the Government had the appointment of the members of the Legislative Council—the effect will be to find a place in this House for men distinguished for the aid they have given at elections to certain members of parties, and not as a reward of true merit or legislative ability."[4] Christopher Dunkin, an opponent of Confederation, argued that "the federal battle that must be fought will have to be fought in the House of Commons and in the Executive Council, very much more than in the Legislative Council."[5]

Article Fourteen of the Quebec Resolutions stipulated that the first Senate be nominated by provincial governments demonstrating "due regard" for the "claims of the Members of the Legislative Council of the Opposition in each Province, so that all political parties may, as nearly as possible, be fairly represented." That gentlemanly agreement over Senate appointments did not long survive Confederation. The spirit of the agreement did persist sufficiently for the victorious Macdonald to replace a Liberal senator who had died just after Confederation with another Liberal. For the rest of his life, Macdonald appointed only five non-Conservatives, just two of whom came without strings attached. He gave a Senate seat in 1887 to a long-time friend, John Macdonald, Liberal MP for Toronto Centre, and another to Thomas McInnis of British Columbia, who had been an MP from 1878 to 1881, but declared himself "thoroughly independent in politics."[6] Macdonald sent three other lucky Liberals to the red chamber, but each suited the Prime Minister's own partisan designs. Two Nova Scotians — Archibald Woodbury and Jeremiah Northrup — had been anti-Confederate Liberals in the 1867 election. As part of his broad strategy of wooing the anti-Confederates, Macdonald handed Joseph Howe significant patronage powers in the province and appointed a variety of anti-Confederates to federal positions. He wooed them with promises of "better terms" for Nova Scotia and the reality of patronage, which explains how Woodbury and Northrup became senators despite their Liberal credentials.[7]

The case of John O'Donoghue, an Irishman from Toronto and president of the Ontario Catholic League, is equally instructive. Here was a Liberal all right, elected but unseated in 1874 (a frequent occurrence in those days). From the Senate's inception ethnic or religious minorities always considered it a place for their interests to be represented, since representation by population in the Commons frequently denied what these minorities believed their just due. The Catholics of Ontario, and particularly the Irish Catholics, insistently pressed their claims. The appointment of O'Donoghue stilled the clamour, and served another of John A.'s purposes: sowing dismay in Liberal ranks because the good Senator had pronounced himself in favour of Macdonald's National Policy.

But the complexities of Senate appointments can frequently test the mettle and patience of even the most skilled party leader. To the requirements of religion were frequently added those of geography.

J.H. Whelan wrote Macdonald, a year after the Torontonian O'Don-
oghue's appointment, that "a large number of my co-religionists in
Eastern Ontario are deeply interested in the appointment of an Irish
Roman Catholic to the Senate."[8] As Whelan himself recognized, such
an appointment could be a tricky business since it would displease the
Orangemen. In 1885, Macdonald ran that risk by appointing another
Irish Roman Catholic, Dr. Michael Sullivan of Kingston, a defeated
Conservative candidate in 1882. Acadians, too, badgered Macdonald
— and all his successors — for their just share of the New Brunswick
appointments. Macdonald's selection of Pascal Poirier, author of a
book about the Acadians, established a precedent for future prime
ministers.

Catholics and Francophones in Ontario, Francophones in New
Brunswick and the West, Protestants in Quebec — these were the
obvious minorities demanding representation. Early on, their claims
for appointments added symbolism to the existing criterion of party
service. As the decades wore on, symbolism and service more frequently
became indistinguishable as prime ministers searched for both qualities
in the same candidate, until in more recent years symbolism eclipsed
longevity of service as the major criterion for some Senate appointments. But, of course, if some minorities were to receive representation,
then why not every minority? "If I claim to have been the first German
who openly spoke and worked in our cause in this part of the country,"
wrote Otto Klotz of Preston to Macdonald about a Senate seat, "[the
first] who first appeared as an educator in politics among his country-
man, who brought up the first contingent of Germans to our rank, and
who year after year by successive teaching increases that number; if,
in short, I claim to be politically the father of the German Conservatives, I claim that which justly belongs to me."[9] Klotz failed, as did the
bulk of those who applied for a position in the Senate, for nowhere
than in the search for Senate seats did the gap between demand for
patronage and available supply yawn more widely. J.A. Grant spoke,
if a trifle more prosaically, for many disappointed supplicants when he
wrote Macdonald," I think I have just cause for complaint. I cannot
think one I loved and respected would thus give me the cold shoulder.
If I am now left out, I shall take no further part in political life, but
retire into the quiet shades, under such treatment as even now I cannot
even credit or contemplate."[10]

Of course, Macdonald took care to consult his cabinet colleagues
and party luminaries across the country when making certain appointments. He knew the whole party better than any of them; they might
know pieces of it better than he did. But, ultimately, Senate appointments were the prime minister's personal prerogative, his very own

patronage, to be used as he saw fit in the interests of the party. The prime minister was, after all, the chief manager for the party — the influence of party staff, the coterie of unelected advisers, admen and pollsters lay decades down the road — and the Senate quickly proved an important tool for party management. It enabled a prime minister to remove political deadwood from his Commons contingent, to create openings, to weaken opponents, in short, to sharpen his party's fighting form. The Senate enhanced the party's finances, too. Senate seats did not carry a precise price tag, as House of Lords seats did in Britain, but senators did contribute handsomely to the party's ongoing expenses. Since so many senators were themselves wealthy businessmen — railway promoters, brewers, publishers, shipbuilders, lumber barons — appointment sealed their financial commitment to the party. Then, too, the Senate was supposed to defend the interests of the propertied — that is why Senate seats carried a property qualification — and who better to defend those interests than the propertied themselves? Macdonald's party rejoiced in being the party of business, especially in Central Canada. The Conservative party was the party of "progress," the National Policy, railways, public–works projects, free enterprise with the helping hand of government, so a Senate full of Conservative businessmen seemed perfectly natural and highly desirable.

Sir Wilfrid Laurier followed the pattern Macdonald had established. When British Columbia and Manitoba joined Confederation, Macdonald had appointed Conservative senators (with one exception); Laurier used the granting of provincial status to Saskatchewan and Alberta to name Liberals. (Prince Edward Island represented a special case. The Island had spurned Confederation after the Charlottetown and Quebec Conferences, but when it joined, the apportionment of senators was deemed to fit within the original Confederation rules — thus, two Conservatives and two Liberals). Prime Minister Alexander Mackenzie (who, dismayed by the Conservative majority in the Senate asked the British in vain to increase the number of senators) appointed only Liberals. So did Laurier, beginning with his first appointment in 1896 — Alfred Thibaudeau, whose father had given up Quebec-Est for Laurier after his defeat in Drummond-Arthabaska. It presumably never crossed Laurier's mind that Senate appointments could be otherwise. "When I have to come to the moment of selection," he told the Commons in 1906, "if I have to select between a Tory and a Liberal, I feel I can serve the country better by appointing a Liberal than a Conservative, and I am very much afraid that any man who occupies the position I occupy today will feel the same way, and that so long as the appointing is as it is today, in the hands practically of the First Minister, I am afraid we stand little chance of reform."[11]

Laurier made slightly over one hundred Senate appointments, roughly the same number as Macdonald and his four Conservative successors between 1891 and 1896. The exclusively partisan nature of Laurier's appointments transformed a Conservative majority of sixty when he became prime minister into a Liberal majority of forty when he left. The only difference between the two great prime ministers lay in Laurier's slightly greater propensity to reward political warriors. About a quarter of Macdonald's appointments had never entered elected politics at the federal or provincial level; only a handful of Laurier's appointments fell into the same category. Nor did Laurier appoint as many business magnates, perhaps because links between the Liberal party and the business community were not as solid as those between businessmen and the Macdonald Conservatives, especially in the early years of Laurier's governments.

Laurier did reward the usual smattering of friendly newspaper publishers and editors, but he largely used the Senate as a place for weary MPs and ministers, or defeated Liberal standardbearers in federal or provincial elections. The tireless Liberal frontbencher Richard Cartwright ended his political career there; Laurier lured Ontario Premier Oliver Mowat with a Senate seat into the 1896 cabinet as minister of justice. Raoul Dandurand got his reward, too, a harbinger of similar appointments. Dandurand, a prominent Montreal businessman (president of the Montreal City and District Savings Bank, among other positions) organized four elections for the Liberal party in the city. In the days before parties could afford full-time staff, Dandurand functioned as an unpaid organizer for the Liberal party in that critically important city, a kind of Keith Davey without pay but with the same enthusiasm. Dandurand's appointment was the first of a whole string of Liberal party organizers, national secretaries and national presidents who, by virtue of their service to the party, wound up in the Senate. The Conservatives, for their part, started using the Senate as a similar reward for their organizers in the late 1950s, so that the Senate became, in part, a convenient resting place for some of both parties' best organizers, with the taxpayer footing the bill.

World War I, which brought on the conscription crisis and the formation of the Union Government under Sir Robert Borden, temporarily modified the relentlessly partisan nature of Senate appointments. The subject of spoils naturally arose in the negotiations between Borden's Conservatives and breakaway Liberals, and both sides agreed to divide them in as gentlemanly a fashion as possible. Borden, when governing with only Conservative support, had followed the now-familiar path—he appointed only Conservatives, with one exception. In 1917, anxious to woo labour support for his government and the war effort, the prime minister named to the Senate Gideon Robertson, president of the Order of Railroad Telegraphers. (Robertson became minister of labour in 1918.) By 1917, the war had pushed an election beyond the five-year parliamentary limit. Knowing the inevitable could not be indefinitely delayed, Borden plugged the Senate vacancies with Conservatives — twenty-six of them in one year, a practice that commended itself to some of his successors, including Mackenzie King, R.B. Bennett and Pierre Trudeau. But the Union Government required the sharing of the spoils of power. So four Liberals entered the Senate under a Conservative prime minister: William Harmer of Alberta, a deputy minister in the provincial government; Michael O'Brien of Ontario, a mining magnate; William Proudfoot of Ontario, a former member of the Ontario legislature; and John Turiff of Saskatchewan, a pillar of Clifford Sifton's machine, commissioner of Dominion lands, and MP for fourteen years.

Arthur Meighen, Borden's successor, would soon meet his political doom, but not before he squeezed in eighteen Senate appointments, a tidy performance for a prime minister in office only fifteen months. Meighen, who would himself be called to the Senate in 1932 by Prime Minister R.B. Bennett, devoted a large amount of his correspondence in 1920–1921 to the headaches of Senate appointments. "Please think of . . . myself when you come to appoint a new Senator," wrote one with a sense of humour. "I am still on my feet, you know."[12] Meighen's labours drove him to conclude, "The task I am at is one I will never envy another when he undertakes it in the future."[13] The bipartisan tradition continued: Meighen's government was officially called Liberal-Unionist and Conservative, and that meant a continued sharing of Senate spoils. Meighen appointed one independent and two Liberals — Sanford Crowe of British Columbia, a contractor, alderman and Liberal-Unionist MP; and Jimmy Calder, the godfather of the Saskatchewan Liberal machine, one of the Union government's most important Liberal catches and Meighen's minister of immigration. Somehow, it seemed fitting that Calder, one of the supreme practitioners of political patronage, was to end his political career in patronage heaven.

Mackenzie King replaced Meighen and, although no one except perhaps King himself could have guessed it at the time, remained longer in office than any Canadian prime minister. King, the supreme tactician and party manager, naturally understood the tremendous political utility of the Senate. After Meighen's defeat, Canadian politics returned to strictly partisan lines, leavened by the arrival after 1921 of the 65-member contingent of Progressives. King would in time enfold them within the Liberal party — "Liberals in a hurry," he called them — but first there was the matter of reinforcing the still precarious position of the Liberal party. In that crusade, King never doubted how the Senate should be used. All through the 1920s, he publicly worried what the "Tory Senate" might do to his government's legislation. Not until 1929 could King secure a Liberal majority in the Senate. He appointed more Senators than any prime minister, of whom precisely one was not a Liberal. In 1929, King sent Robert Forke to the Senate as part of a package deal that brought T.A. Crerar, the country's leading Progressive, into the cabinet. Forke had ridden the Progressive wave to Parliament in 1921, served as house leader for the Progressives after 1922, then joined King's cabinet in 1926. The Progressives had petered out before Forke arrived in the Senate; his arrival was part of their symbolic last rites.

King may have chased spirits but he seldom harboured illusions. The Liberals had been denied rewards from 1911 to 1917, and received only a share befitting a junior partner in the governments of 1917–1921. The majority of Liberals, therefore, were hungry for spoils, especially those who dreamed of a place in the red chamber. A year after taking office, King wrote to an Ontario Liberal who had suggested reforming the Senate, "Judging from the volume of my correspondence in the last couple of weeks, I am inclined to think that the people of this Province at least are as anxious for the perpetuation of the Senate as are the members of that body itself."[14] Three years into the prime minister's job, King could write, "The filling of these positions is perhaps the most difficult of all questions with which the administration has to deal."[15] The letters poured in, pleading, demanding, informing, cautioning, threatening, asking for themselves or for others; they came from bagmen, MPs, defeated candidates, "tireless workers," "lifelong Liberals," sons of Liberal warriors, bearers of great Liberal names. The Liberal leader in Ontario wrote, "Do you not think that I would be of greater service to the cause of Liberal principles in another sphere of activity? If so there is a present and most opportune opening in the Senate . . . Why not let this one go to a live Liberal leader from Ontario?"[16] The Liberal premier of New Brunswick suggested that "consideration, when an appointment is being made, might be given to my qualifications, together with my services to the Party."[17] From a Liberal MP came a plea on another's behalf, "I hope the government will see its way clear to fill it by appointing the old Liberal war-horse who has fought no fewer than twelve elections on behalf of his party, sometimes winning, sometimes losing, but always faithful, even in 1917."[18]

Self-serving ingenuity apparently knew no limits. "I have a message which I promised to convey to you from one of our most distinguished and influential Acadian clergymen in reference to the present vacancy in the Senate," wrote Onésiphore Turgeon, a successful supplicant. "This priest is Rev. A.D. Cormier . . . who wishes me to tell you that my appointment to the Senate will meet the hearty approval of all the leading Acadians irrespective of political affiliation."[19] Letter-writing campaigns, often initiated by the supplicant himself, sometimes attended bids for Senate seats. The practice, which continued up to the Mulroney years, was particularly widespread in Atlantic Canada and Quebec, but such a campaign could crop up anywhere. W.O. Sealey of Hamilton, for example, reckoned he should be a senator. He wrote to his Liberal friends, asking them in turn to write King. If they were too busy, Sealey suggested sending along to the prime minister a letter he had drafted and enclosed for them to sign. It read, in part, "having known Mr. Sealey for many years as a consistent and enthusiastic Liberal, I take pleasure, as a member of the Liberal Party, in giving Mr. Sealey my support, and I respectfully ask for your consideration." Unfortunately, a friend of Sealey's, upon receiving his form letter intended for the prime minister, wrote King enclosing an unsigned copy of the letter and recommending another Senate aspirant from Hamilton.[20] In the final days before appointments, with rumours swirling, the last supplications arrived. "Trust self with you regarding Senatorship," cabled Arthur Hardy from the Bahamas.[21] Three days later, Hardy received his reward, and fired off a letter so fawning that it might be thought laughable were it not typical of others sent by many happy recipients of Senate seats. "There are no words for me to thank you for the news which your cable brought," wrote Hardy. "I don't expect to distinguish myself, but where I can help, I want you to command me."[22]

Like Macdonald, King confronted demands from ethnic groups searching for symbolic senatorial appointments. "For some time our people have felt that we should have a seat in that body," wrote MP S.W. Jacob on behalf of the Jewish community. "I am sure you will agree that numerically, financially and otherwise, our people are not asking too much when they request consideration from the Government for one of their own."[23] (Jews waited until 1955 for their first senator, David Croll of Windsor.) Women, too, lobbied the new prime minister, with special pressure coming from Montreal, Edmonton and Vancouver. The pressure began in 1922, but King only moved in 1930 when he appointed Cairine Wilson of Ottawa, the honorary president of the National Federation of Liberal Women of Canada. Even that long-overdue appointment did not please all women. "Allow me to express to you how deeply you have grieved a great many women of this Province," wrote Azilda Dumais of the Canadian Alliance for the Quebec Women's Vote, "by choosing for your first senatrix [sic] in Canada, a woman from Ontario!"[24] King, having bowed to the demands of symbolism, never appointed another woman.

There was nothing symbolic about party organizers. King, first among prime ministers, sanctioned a party office removed from his own, although his super-sensitive personality produced an endless series of conflicts with those running the party office. Vincent Massey, of course, got his fondest desire — High Commissioner to London. Andrew Haydon, general secretary of the National Liberal Organizing Committee, went to the Senate in 1924, following in the tradition of Raoul Dandurand. Others followed: Norman Lambert, director of the National Liberal Federation; J.A. Lesage, chief Liberal organizer of eastern Quebec; Jacob Nicol, chief Liberal organizer for Quebec. Politicians, too made obvious senators: In King's last nineteen years in office, he sent thirty-four MPs and fifteen ministers to the red chamber.[25] Here was the classic reward for long service, or to suit the political needs of the Liberal party. P.L. Hatfield of Nova Scotia, for example, was elevated to the Senate to make room for Col. J.L. Ralston's entry into the Commons. That left poor George Kyte fuming. King had promised him the seat verbally and in writing. Kyte came to Ottawa to claim his prize, only to be kept waiting six weeks for a negative answer.[26] As always, the claims of sub-regions within small regions had to be considered. On Prince Edward Island, where the lobbying for Senate seats often takes on the trappings of a full-scale campaign, the apportioning of the precious four seats among counties and between Protestants and Catholics could try a prime minister's patience. "Prince County is taking a very firm stand that the appointment must go to a Prince County man . . . the party here takes the ground [sic] that I, as a Federal Member, have the strongest claim under these circumstances," wrote A.E. MacLean, to no avail, as things turned out.[27] Convention held in New Brunswick, at least since Poirier's appointment by Macdonald, that the French-speakers should share Senate seats with English-speakers. Fine, but what about the Irish? "They feel it keenly that in the distribution of political honours and preferments their representations are passed by," complained sixteen co-authors of a letter; "the Irish citizens of this Province . . . have a grievance . . . that is, they have no representation in the Senate."[28]

The correspondence flowed on and on, hundreds of pages of it, each letter demanding the prime minister's attention. True, King consulted his cabinet colleagues, but the appointments were ultimately his. King conveniently replied to these requests for Senate consideration explaining that "there is a collective responsibility on the part of the

Cabinet as a whole." Indeed there was, but as a practical matter of politics the cabinet acted as a rubber stamp, if the prime minister even deemed it necessary to consult the cabinet at all. His explanation about the cabinet's collective responsibility, repeated hundreds of times in his correspondence, provided a kind of shield against the anger of the disappointed. King knew the flimsiness of the shield. After the Senate had balked at a bill, King wrote in 1930 to the president of *The Globe* that the Liberal senators "owe their positions in no small measure to a final word of my own."[29] Shrewd and unctuous, King often replied to the successful, "You have only yourself to thank for the appointment."[30]

Impending elections invariably produced a flurry of appointments, lest after the voting any plums fall into unfriendly hands. King made eleven appointments just before the 1925 election; five just before the 1930 election; fourteen in the two months before the 1940 election; and fourteen before the 1945 election, including twelve on one day just before the writs were issued. Borden had done likewise; Pierre Trudeau would too, with Prime Minister John Turner's help, before the 1984 campaign. Nor did the dissolution of Parliament stop prime ministers. Mackenzie Bowell appointed one senator between dissolution and voting day, Laurier four in 1904, Borden five in 1917, Meighen six in 1921, and King three in 1925, one in 1930 and fourteen in 1940. About half of all King's appointments went to MPs or ministers, some of whom had also been members of provincial legislatures. A sprinkling of defeated candidates dotted the list. About a quarter of his appointments had never entered elected politics, but they either boasted impeccable Liberal credentials or had displayed a politically useful friendship. The president of the New Brunswick Liberal Association, the president of the Ontario Liberal Association, the president of the Toronto Men's Liberal Association, the president of the National Liberal Federation—these were the kind of party stalwarts King rewarded. Those who had displayed useful friendships included the author of a flattering biography, a Liberal-oriented parliamentary correspondent, the publishers or presidents of Liberal newspapers: *The Kingston Whig*, The *Kitchener-Waterloo Record* and *La Presse*. King had no time for weak partisanship. Premier John Hart, a Liberal premier of British Columbia leading a coalition government which included Conservatives, came to Ottawa and asked for a Senate seat, but found himself rejected for inadequate partisan commitment.[31]

Sandwiched in the King years was Conservative Prime Minister R.B. Bennett's unhappy government, buffeted by economic forces it neither understood nor could control. Bennett governed from 1930 to 1935, and amassed in less than five full years nearly eleven thousand pages of correspondence about Senate positions![32] The one Alberta

vacancy he filled generated nearly two thousand pages of correspondence, the nine Quebec vacancies slightly more than three thousand
pages. And Bennett attended to them all, with varying degrees of attention, for as a student who examined the papers concluded, "in his
Senate appointments, perhaps it could be said that R.B. Bennett lived
up to his reputation for running a one-man government."[33] In fairness,
petitions supporting one candidate or another explain part of the bulk;
even leaving the petitions aside, the remaining volume attests to the
Conservatives' desperate hunger after nearly a decade of King. Bennett
made thirty-three appointments, all to Conservatives. Like King, he
rushed to fill all vacancies before an election — seventeen of them in
the six weeks prior to the 1935 election, three to ministers and eleven
to MPs anxious to flee a badly listing ship. Political debts were naturally
paid: John A. Macdonald, who had resigned his seat to allow Nova
Scotia Premier E.N. Rhodes to join the Bennett cabinet, received a
Senate seat. So did the usual assortment of party officials, Conservative
businessmen and newspaper publishers (for example, W.H. Dennis of
The Calgary Herald). There was even a woman senator, a Conservative
token to match the Liberal one — Iva Campbell Fallis, a farmer's wife
from Peterborough and a long-time party worker.

The fall of Bennett's government sent the Senate back on a twenty-
two year Liberal course. On the eve of John Diefenbaker's Conservative
government of 1957 this Senate contained the following line-up: Liberal, seventy-eight, Conservative, five, independents, two. When Newfoundland joined Canada in 1949, the Liberals chose only their own,
as the Liberals had done in 1905 for Saskatchewan and Alberta, and
as the Conservatives had when British Columbia and Manitoba joined
Confederation. As a condition of their appointment, however, the
Newfoundland Liberal senators were expected to contribute $25,000
to the party. Unfortunately, one of them died before taking his seat.
The party nevertheless sent a bagman down to extract a contribution
post mortem from the poor man's widow. She told him loudly and
indelicately to get lost.

Then, as now, the Senate provided endless material for satire but
few politically feasible demands for reform. The Co-operative Commonwealth Federation pledged to abolish the Senate; various social
critics demanded this or that change. But the two major parties found
the Senate entirely too convenient to pay any attention to these chirping
criticisms. The provinces had not yet started demanding the wholesale
rearrangement of the Canadian constitution, so that although many
premiers complained loudly about federal policies, they did not yet
fancy themselves national statesmen. Senate reform, then, remained at
the margin of political debate in Canada.

What did change when Prime Minister Louis St. Laurent replaced King was a slight diminution of Liberal partisanship. St. Laurent actually appointed one Conservative and four independents, each a friend of his, but nonetheless nominal independents. Of his fifty-five appointments, only twenty-two went to former ministers or MPs. Twenty-one appointees, or thirty-nine percent, had no elected political experience, a much higher percentage than any of his predecessors' appointees.[34] Uncle Louis was a staunch Liberal all right, but not a fierce partisan. Nor did many Liberals fear for their political futures, even before the fateful 1957 election. They expected the Liberal ship to keep plowing through calm waters; the need to jump to the Senate did not occur to them, as it obviously did to Conservative MPs before the 1935 election and to Liberal MPs before the Conservative storm of 1984. St. Laurent never felt his predecessors' urgency to fill seats before an election, presumably because the prospect of defeat seldom troubled his mind. King filled all eighteen vacancies before the 1945 election; St. Laurent left eight seats open before the 1949 election, thirteen before the 1953 election and fourteen before the 1957 election, an inadvertent gift gratefully received by the incoming Conservatives. Apart from the low percentage of elected politicians, St. Laurent's appointments fits the familiar pattern: rewards for party service sprinkled with a few for symbolic purposes.

Prime Minister John Diefenbaker confronted such a lopsided Senate that nobody, including the Liberals, expected anything other than what happened — he appointed only Conservatives. He did follow a familiar path in nominating Allister Grossart, his campaign manager and vice-president of McKim Advertising in Toronto, one of the earliest exemplars of the influence of advertising executives on political leaders. But all that really distinguished Diefenbaker's use of senatorial patronage was the somewhat greater importance he placed on symbolic appointments. He sent two women to the Senate—Josie Quart of Quebec and Olive Irvine of Manitoba, both presidents of Conservative women's organizations. He appointed the first native senator—James Gladstone, president of the Indian Association of Alberta. And he named two Ukrainians, one with no previous political experience (Professor Paul Yuzyk of Winnipeg). Five symbolic appointments from minority groups was not an imposing use of the symbolic potential of senatorial patronage, but it did offer a hint of future developments. With a few exceptions, Diefenbaker's Senate appointments were an uninspiring lot, especially his Quebec choices, but then he never did display a feel for Quebec. Rather than trying to intrigue or interest Quebeckers in his party by attracting fresh faces to the Conservatives' cause through the Senate, he insisted on warhorses and nonentities.

They fitted right in, their insignificance as senators matched only by their anonymity in Quebec.

Prime Minister Lester Pearson's appointments were, if anything, even less creative than Diefenbaker's. Diefenbaker, an outsider and an ethnic Canadian, had at least gone slightly outside the traditional hunting grounds for senators; Pearson, an establishment figure, stayed within conventional territory. Pearson also presided over only minority governments. He could ill afford to lose MPs, so he usually waited until just before an election before pensioning them off. This he did to thirteen MPs — eight from Quebec — as part of his attempt to bring along new candidates for the House of Commons and to make the federal government more attractive to Quebeckers. Pearson's list groaned with Liberal bagmen and financial contributors, and with provincial Liberals dispirited by defeat (Ontario leader Andrew Thompson, Nova Scotia leader Earl Urquhart, Alberta leader Harper Prowse, Saskatchewan Liberal Association president Herbert Sparrow, Alberta Liberal Association president Earl Hastings, Newfoundland Liberal Association president Eric Cook), or federal officials (campaign organizer Keith Davey, and national presidents John Nichol and Richard Stanbury). He appointed no ethnic Canadians and only one woman, Mary Kinnear, president of the national Liberal women's organization, of whom former cabinet minister Judy Lamarsh wrote in her memoirs, "her appointment was met with loud pained silence, and from that time to this writing [1968] she has made no contribution, either in or out of the Senate." Lamarsh also confirmed that although Senate appointments are theoretically made by cabinet, in practice they are the prime minister's decision alone.[35] "In the last year or so of his [Pearson's] administration, he never even bothered to tell Cabinet whom he planned to appoint," she wrote. Not for Pearson, then, the symbolic use of patronage in Senate appointments; just reward for service or, in the case of former CCF leader Hazen Argue, for changed political stripes.

After Trudeaumania in 1968, Prime Minister Pierre Trudeau may initially have carried the hopes of political renewal on his shoulders but his early use of the Senate dispelled any illusions that renewal might sweep through that institution. Trudeau's first appointment went to his fund-raiser in the 1968 leadership campaign, Louis (Bob) Giguère.[36] Other early appointments followed the familiar pattern of reward for service: Paul Lafond, for twenty-two years executive secretary of the National Liberal Federation; Gildas Molgat, provincial Liberal leader in Manitoba. Throughout Trudeau's sixteen years in office, the Senate proved to be a useful place for retiring the tired, luring the disaffected of other parties, recompensing the faithful, and rewarding personal friends of the prime minister. The essential characteristic of the Senate remained unchanged; the modest reform of forcing newly appointed senators to retire at age seventy-five mildly accelerated the availability of openings and restricted the number of the senile or physically incapacitated. Trudeau did, however, add one new wrinkle. Embarrassed by the lop-sided Liberal majority, he offered to replace retiring or deceased Conservative senators with other Conservatives, after consultation with the leader of the Opposition. This magnanimity allowed Conservative leader Robert Stanfield to recommend his long-time Nova Scotia ministerial colleague and successor as premier, G.I. Smith, and Conservative leader Joe Clark to pay off a debt to Ontario Premier William Davis by recommending William Kelly, one of Davis' principal bagmen.

These changes were cosmetic, however, beside a more important development: Trudeau's increasing use of the Senate for symbolic purposes. Throughout the Trudeau years there was tension between the traditional assumptions of Canadian politics and the search for new forms of political participation and mobilization. (See the following chapter.) The lion's share of Trudeau's appointments went to friends and party stalwarts, all right, but he appointed more women, ethnics, native Canadians and independents than any previous prime minister, a mild testament to the emergence in politics in the 1960s and 1970s of new interest groups demanding a fuller recognition of their contribution to Canadian society. True, all but the independents were Liberals — and even one of those, former Privy Council clerk Michael Pitfield, might just as well have been a Liberal senator—but the pattern of appointments did show a party trying to use the symbolism of Senate appointments to make itself more attractive to groups in society which defined themselves, not by partisanship, but by occupation, sex, ethnicity, colour. (Trudeau's most inspired Senate choice, that of constitutional expert Eugene Forsey, simply improved the calibre of the institution at a stroke without providing any useful political symbolism.) Liberal insiders gagged, for example, at the appointment of Anne Cools, a two-time candidate who in their eyes had not yet provided enough party service to warrant elevation to the Senate. But Cools was talented, young and, more important, black, a recognition of the growing number of her colour in Toronto. Pietro Rizzuto of Montreal became the first Italian senator, albeit by inadvertence. Trudeau had been advised that the party's enormous popularity among Italians deserved the recognition of a Senate appointment. He told his Toronto ministers and MPs to provide a name. When they fell out among themselves, Trudeau went ahead and appointed Rizzuto, a wealthy Liberal fund–raiser from Montreal. Trudeau later appointed Peter Boza of

Toronto to mollify Italian Liberals in that city. The Jewish community, another bastion of Liberal support, deserved further recognition, so wealthy businessmen Leo Kolber got the reward on the recommendation of Trudeau's Quebec lieutenant Marc Lalonde.

Trudeau, who did not know the party well outside Quebec, usually asked for advice from ministerial colleagues in English Canada before making an appointment; in Quebec, he kept important appointments for himself, except in cases involving ethnic communities or intricate political machinations. The Liberals' attempt to free up Créditiste seats in the 1970s provided one example of these machinations. In that decade, only the Créditistes impeded the Liberals' bid for total federal hegemony in Quebec. To weaken the Créditistes, Trudeau instructed cabinet minister André Ouellet to lure various Créditiste MPs with federal appointments. Ouellet was authorized to offer a Senate seat to Adrien Lambert, the enormously popular MP for Bellechasse, and to float the possibility of Senate seats by other Créditiste MPs.[37] The Liberals used the same tactics with the few Quebec Conservatives. Heward Grafftey, Tory MP for Brome-Missisquoi, was offered a Senate seat. Claude Wagner, desperately unhappy at Joe Clark's side after losing the Conservative leadership, accepted a Senate seat, thus opening St. Hyacinthe for a victorious Liberal candidate in a by-election.[38] Other Quebec senatorial appointments broke down almost evenly between party stalwarts and Trudeau's personal friends.[39]

The Senate, stuffed with Liberals, only occasionally bared its constitutional claws, a notable case being the complete rewriting of the legislation creating the civilian spy agency. For the most part, the Senate tinkered, sometimes creatively, with bills. But the partisan stripe of the Senate, combined with its reluctance to defy the lower house, usually neutered the institution. Instead, senators, or at least the minority who were active, created work for themselves and some knowledge for the public by launching a series of studies into subjects as varied as the role of women in Canadian society, the mass media, relations with the United States and the Caribbean, aspects of defence policy, and poverty. Even these projects, however worthy, did not improve the Senate's standing in the country. It remained, as the critics of Confederation had predicted, a body so dominated by partisanship and so deprived of credibility by patronage that cosmetic reforms could not rescue its reputation.

It took the Meech Lake accord of 1987, one hundred and twelve years after the first cry by Prime Minister Alexander Mackenzie for Senate reform, to set in motion a fundamental change in the Senate. A few voices, mostly on the political left, had always called for abolition of the Senate. After all, the five provinces that once had upper houses abolished them either for reasons of economy or low prestige: Manitoba in 1876, New Brunswick in 1892, Prince Edward Island in 1893, Nova Scotia in 1928, and Quebec in 1968.[40] Far more numerous were a dizzying variety of schemes to reform the Senate. The demand from Western Canada for an elected Senate had begun in British Columbia in the 1970s and spread in the mid-1980s to Alberta. To some western Canadians, an elected Senate giving even more weight to less populous provinces might counter the strength of Ontario and Quebec in the Commons. An assortment of academic studies and a report by a joint Commons-Senate committee added further impetus to the demand for change. Trudeau himself had proffered several reform ideas, including one that would have given legislatures the right to nominate senators on the basis of the percentage of the popular vote in the previous provincial election. Finally, Prime Minister Brian Mulroney gave away this traditional treasure trove of patronage.

Mulroney had begun in the traditional way by appointing Conservative faithful, although he soon understood the potential for symbolism in Senate appointments. In his last three unfettered appointments, he discarded the advice from party notables in Newfoundland, Manitoba and Prince Edward Island. When they provided lists of male party worthies, he insisted they return with women nominees. He then appointed three women, to the consternation of the worthies, one of whom in Prince Edward Island wanted the job so badly he phoned the prime minister's office to press his claim even as the flag was being lowered to half-mast in deference to the death of the senator he wished to replace. Mulroney, scorched in his first two years for his handling of patronage, might well have continued using the Senate for symbolic purposes had not the Meech Lake negotiations intervened.

A Gordian knot developed in the run-up to those constitutional negotiations. Three demands seemed mutually exclusive: a veto for Quebec over constitutional changes involving federal institutions, a veto for all provinces, and the smoothest possible move towards Senate reform. A short time before the First Ministers' Conference, the Canada West Foundation, a persistent supporter of an elected Senate, suggested that Alberta should demand Ottawa not make any more appointments until full Senate reform. Federal officials pointed out to Alberta officials the constitutional difficulties with this approach, but the two sides continued exploring ways of breaking the log-jam. On the night before the Meech Lake negotiations, Alberta circulated a proposal giving the provinces the power to appoint senators until everyone could agree on an elected Senate. Ottawa countered with a proposal for fifty percent by the provinces, fifty percent by Ottawa. At the very end of the Meech

Lake negotiations, as the last item on the agenda, Premier Brian Peckford of Newfoundland suggested that the formula for Supreme Court nominees—provincial nominations, federal approval—be adopted for the Senate pending the second round of constitutional talks leading to an elected Senate. This kept Quebec's veto intact, gave all provinces a veto, and left Alberta content that Ottawa's commitment to Senate reform would no longer be impeded by the attraction of Senate patronage. No one knew whether Alberta had bought a pig-in-a-poke, since the unanimity rule might make an elected Senate difficult to achieve, if not impossible. But in a swoop, just before midnight and almost as an afterthought, a federal prime minister yielded up, for the purposes of a constitutional reform package, the most enduring and personal patronage power prime ministers of Canada had ever possessed. The Senate would remain, as Arthur Meighen once said, a "legitimate aspiration of any Canadian," but the route there would henceforth be different.

PART IV

THE NEW FACE OF PATRONAGE

CHAPTER 18

TRUDEAU
RETURN TO GRIT HEAVEN

"Patronage is incompatible with modern government."
Prime Minister Pierre Trudeau, October 26, 1968.

THOSE WERE HEADY DAYS, in the fall of 1968, with our new prime minister and his intriguing ideas. He seemed so clever, so worldly, so effortlessly bilingual, so unconventional, a politician *pas comme les autres*, beckoning us we knew not precisely where, but surely to new and arresting ways of confronting old and intractable problems. His clothes, his gesticulations, his aphorisms, his smile, his cool — everything about the man reeked of modernity. He was the man many Canadians dreamed of becoming, and like all men whom we assume to be larger than life, he never ceased to intrigue us, for when we came to know him better, his weaknesses seemed as awesome as his strengths. He created a kaleidoscope of emotions in the country towards himself, so that all but his most implacable critics could not deny certain virtues and all but his blind admirers could not ignore certain limitations. We respected and feared him, we adored and reviled him, we elevated and kicked him, we believed and distrusted him, but we could never ignore him, not just because he served as prime minister, but because as no other politician in our lifetime he left so few Canadians personally unmoved by the fact of his presence, the force of his ideas, and the challenge of his performance. After leaving politics, he was asked what had been his most important accomplishment. "I survived," he replied. His critics would say that to have survived him was the country's greatest accomplishment.

Pierre Trudeau came to Liberal politics from social criticism, legal teaching, brilliant pamphleteering, and a flirtation with the CCF. A commitment to party had never been part of his personal history or intellectual development. He was too independent, even iconoclastic, for that; indeed he joined the federal Liberal party as the best available vehicle to fight separatism and nationalism in Quebec, rather than because of any wider commitment to the party. He had sharply criticized the Liberal party, especially over defence policy, just a few years before joining. Of Quebec Liberals Trudeau had written, "The shameful incompetence of the average Liberal MP from Quebec was a welcome asset to [an English-Canadian dominated] government that needed little more than a herd of donkeys to file in when the division bells rang. The party strategists had but to find an acceptable stable master—Laurier, Lapointe, St. Laurent—and the trained donkeys sitting in the back benches could be trusted to behave."[1]

A classic outsider and loner, Trudeau led the Liberal party by example, not fraternity. The ways of the party were foreign to him, and although he proved an adept learner of its traditional practices, his whole leadership can be viewed as a halting attempt to change those practices, or at least to modify them. In terms of patronage, he can be seen as a transitional figure, accepting many of the traditional practices while groping towards new forms of political mobilization. And he can also be viewed as one of those prime ministers prepared to use the tools of patronage and porkbarrelling to secure the loyalty of a disaffected region, his native province of Quebec, in much the same way that John A. Macdonald had weaned Nova Scotia from its hostility to Confederation slightly more than one hundred years before.

Soon after entering the Liberal leadership race, Trudeau began preaching the virtues of what he called "participatory democracy." No one was ever sure what "participatory democracy" would mean in practice, but the phrase implied that the traditional party structure could no longer suffice for encouraging widespread political participation. In his first speech to a party gathering after the 1968 election, Trudeau told the Nova Scotia Liberal Association that the party had to become much more open to new ideas. He said that parties could no longer be mere vote-getting machines at election time and distributors of jobs and contracts for the faithful between elections. It was "only right," he conceded in a province steeped in patronage, for the "hard core" of the party faithful to expect rewards, but politics was no longer a private affair among parties. "Patronage is incompatible with modern government," he said, adding that "appointments must go to the very best qualified people, and the work to the lowest and best qualified bidders." He insisted that "open and free" communications between politicians and the people represented the greatest challenge for modern parties. If parties did not enter into this dialogue, "it will be the end of parliamentary democracy and the beginning of something cold — of mass democracy and mob rule."[2]

From his first months in office Trudeau articulated a sense of discontent with formal Liberal party structures and dearly held assumptions, a discontent that had begun to emerge during the leadership of Lester Pearson. At first, the discontent lay not so much with the party's inability to reflect social and economic changes as with its internal organization. Keith Davey, the Liberal party's organizer in the wake of its shattering defeat at the hands of John Diefenbaker in 1957 and 1958, reckoned that the decentralized structure of the party had prevented coherent planning and organization. Davey, cabinet minister Walter Gordon and the other members of the so-called Cell 13 who had taken over the Toronto Liberal organization after Lester Pearson became leader believed that the Liberal party depended excessively on powerful regional cabinet ministers and provincial party organizers, most of whom did not understand the new techniques of advertising, polling and mobilizing votes through the media.

In particular, they considered patronage an outmoded method of mobilization, a throwback to an earlier method of encouraging political participation.[3] The organization they wished to build would be tied by committees to the political wing of the party, but it would stand organically alone. There would be a federal campaign chairman and a four-member federal campaign committee in each province to assume the political work of regional ministers. This new system had the merit of organizational neatness, but it failed to account for deeply-entrenched regional sensitivities. In the Maritimes and the West (especially in Alberta and Saskatchewan), prominent Liberals distrusted the influence of Ontario at Liberal headquarters. What worked for Cell 13 members in Toronto, they argued, would flop where the old traditions, including patronage, died hard.

Provincial Liberal associations resented the assumption that they could not properly organize campaigns, especially when they observed the failure of the Davey-Gordon group to engineer a national Liberal majority in the election of 1965. Saskatchewan Liberals under Premier Ross Thatcher were particularly resentful, feeling themselves in no need of political lessons. To placate them, the federal party even divided the campaign committee into sections, including one for patronage, and allowed Thatcher to name the members. After all, Liberals had done so poorly in provincial elections on the prairies that the only patronage they ever received flowed from Ottawa. Deprived of power themselves, the least they expected was control of federal patronage. Policy differences exacerbated these organizational squabbles, especially in Western Canada where the mildly nationalist, left-of-centre policy preferences of Davey and Gordon grated on provincial Liberals. A bit like the tensions that beset the Conservatives in the decade 1910–1920, the intra-party Liberal fights of the 1960s reflected the pressures between new and old methods of organization and mobilization.

The arrival of Trudeau as party leader and Richard Stanbury as party president in 1968 ushered in the rhetoric of "participatory democracy." Stanbury preached the cause as fervently as Trudeau. He kept warning Liberals that their party — all parties, for that matter — no longer adequately reflected social, cultural and economic trends. Interest groups, rather than parties, had become the chosen vehicles for political expression and mobilization, and unless parties opened new lines of communications ("feedback" was the jargon) to individuals and groups, they risked becoming increasing irrelevant.[4] To the earlier Davey-Gordon concerns about internal party organization were now added the more prosaic, but nonetheless compelling, assertions of the new leader and party president that the old ways of organizing parties and mobilizing participation would no longer suffice.

Stanbury was nothing if not ambitious. The party executive organized a "thinkers" conference at Harrison Hot Springs in 1969, sent the ideas of that conference to riding associations for the development of resolutions, then brought Liberals together at a huge policy convention in 1970 that spawned hundreds of resolutions, all designed to chart a future path for liberalism and to demonstrate that Canadians could have an impact on policy through the Liberal party. While the party rank and file engaged in "participatory democracy," the prime minister tried new devices of his own. A political cabinet, formed of the most important regional ministers, met regularly with party officials. Party affairs in each province were handed to a three-person committee: a senior minister, an MP and a representative of the provincial party's membership. So-called "regional desks" staffed by officials in the Prime Minister's Office, would stay in touch with party and non-party people across the country.

Implicit in all this was what Trudeau had made explicit in Nova Scotia: Systematic patronage could no longer be relied upon to mobilize support. People would only give their loyalty for the psychological rewards of being consulted, participating in policy development, and seeing the consequences of their labours enshrined in government decisions. It all seemed so neat and tidy on paper, a rational man's model, an innocent's dream, an impressive plan and bold enterprise that lacked nothing save a sober recognition of reality. It smacked of a scheme of the scientist in the Sinclair Lewis novel *Arrowsmith*, who built temples to humanity, then kicked out all the humans. Still, there was a nobility of purpose about the whole exercise, and, at the very least, a groping recognition that the Canadian political culture was changing and that the old ways of mobilizing participation would no longer suffice.

Yet the old ways could not be discarded. Across the country, Liberals still demanded rewards. The troika committees soon bogged down in lengthy squabbles over appointments and preferments. The regional desks infuriated Liberal MPs who reckoned that they understood their regions, and the people who counted in them, better than did some minions in the Prime Minister's Office. The prime minister himself, with no talent for small talk, no interest in the seamless web of personal contacts that bind a political tribe together, and no network of friends rooted in all regions of the country, could not understand why people counted on the "psychic patronage" (the phrase belongs to Senator John Nichol) of the friendly word or the materialistic benefits of political preferment. He did not need either; why should anyone else? Perhaps he could have justified his attitude, or at least made it marginally palatable, if the government had acted on the eruption of resolutions that poured from the Liberal party's policy conference. Instead, the government disregarded most of them, paid lip service to the rest, and glided into the 1972 campaign on a slogan memorable for its banality, "The Land Is Strong."

While all this shuffling, huffing and restructuring went on inside the Liberal party, the prime minister continued to use his patronage powers in the traditional Liberal way. At one level, the party tried to encourage new forms of citizen participation in politics. The leader, the party president (himself a senator) and new ministers such as Otto Lang kept insisting that the traditional methods no longer sufficed, but while they preached these sermons they practised something quite different. Trudeau's first Senate appointment, for example, went to Louis (Bob) Giguère, his bagman in the 1968 leadership race. Ministers who left the first Trudeau cabinet landed patronage appointments: Hédard Robichaud became lieutenant-governor of New Brunswick, Leo Cadieux ambassador to France, Paul Martin and Jean-Pierre Côté senators, Edgar Benson chairman of the Canadian Transport Commission. Indeed, of the twenty-five members of Trudeau's first cabinet, only five remained in politics throughout the Trudeau years and two died not long after leaving politics. Of the remaining eighteen, fifteen received patronage positions. A sprinkling of early Trudeau appointments went to non-Liberals: Alberta Socred leader Ernest Manning to the Senate, former Conservative minister Michael Starr to the citizenship courts. But these were isolated exceptions to the Liberal floodtide that covered all the positions at the government's discretion. In that Halifax speech of October, 1968, after all, Trudeau had added to his strictures against the old ways of political mobilization, "Of course, I'm not against helping a friend of the Liberal party when I get the chance." He meant what he had said.

As part of the new government's determination to provide fresh analyses of old problems, it established a task force to examine how the government could better communicate with the public.[5] From the task force sprang the idea for the infamous Information Canada, but the government ignored a series of the task force's recommendations for breaking the patronage links between the party in power and friendly advertising agencies. The task force examined the effectiveness of government advertising, found it wanting, then asked sixty-one agencies if they agreed with the existing procedures. By a majority of four to one, they did not. The task force reported that in the United States an outside voluntary group selected agencies and that "agencies and the media co-operate with the U.S. administration on a non-partisan basis, and politics stay out of advertising." In Britain, an advisory council of distinguished businessmen assisted the Central Office of Information in selecting agencies. The American and British examples commended themselves to the task force, which suggested that "an independent advisory committee or board" recommend the selection of advertising agencies, a suggestion put forward eight years before by the Glassco royal commission on government organization. The task force concluded, "The question facing the government is whether it should now make a clean break and apply principles to ensure that efficiency and the public interest will guide the use of public spending on advertising as part of a total program of communication. The answer given in this study is: Yes."

The Trudeau government's answer was no. The Liberal party under Mackenzie King had begun the marriage of Madison Avenue and government by linking the party to several friendly firms, rewarding them with government business after a successful election. This was patronage, neat and brazen. It had served the party and its agency friends too well, and its natural and enduring convenience proved no match for the mere scratchings of a task force.

One important patronage reform, largely unheralded at the time, did mark the first Trudeau government — Postmaster-General Eric Kierans placed the appointment of postmasters under the public service commission.[6] Kierans, a minister who believed in applying the principles of business efficiency to the post office, eliminated at a stroke one of the federal government's oldest bastions of local patronage, one that had served and bedevilled ministers since Confederation. This move, following the unionization of post office workers, illustrates how the dual forces of professionalization and unionization can squeeze out patronage. The pattern had crept through federal and provincial governments for decades; Kierans' decision represented the triumph of these forces in the post office.

Defeated in the post office, patronage nevertheless found new outlets. Starting with the Pearson government, and continuing through most of the Trudeau years, the size and complexity of the federal government grew by leaps and bounds. Dozens of new boards, agencies and commissions sprang up to deliver services or administer government regulations. Each provided irresistible opportunities for Liberals to reward the faithful. There were some notable exceptions — the National Council of Welfare springs to mind — but Liberal partisans received the vast majority of positions on these boards, agencies and commissions.[7]

To take just one example, the immigration appeal board expanded in 1973 to clear up a backlog of immigration cases. Immigration minister Robert Andras filled the new positions with Liberals, and sometimes used his appointment power to winkle concessions from other ministers for his part of the country, Northern Ontario. Ministers such as Otto Lang of Saskatchewan and John Munro of Hamilton relentlessly pursued positions for Liberals and friends from their areas.

The growth in government spawned demands for new services, including those of consultants who attached themselves like barnacles to the ship of state, their staying power partly dictated by partisan considerations. In addition, judicial posts, ambassadorships, citizenship court judgeships, lieutenant-governorships, Senate seats were routinely and overwhelmingly handed to Liberals. There was nothing in the least unconventional about any of this; Canadian parties had always rewarded the faithful. But the whole vast apparatus of patronage rested uneasily with the brave promises of "participatory democracy" and the halting search for new methods of political mobilization that Trudeau, Stanbury and the others had preached. And, of course, the disappointing performance of the first Trudeau government, coupled with its near defeat of 1972, disabused Trudeau of any thought he might have entertained about his superior political touch. Chastened by near defeat, he signed up for political finishing school run by the old pros in the Liberal party, graduated with honours and led the party to victory in the 1974 election.

The mid-1970s were times of economic stress as Canada, like other western industrial democracies, grappled with the consequences of sharp increases in oil prices. But for Trudeau the most compelling issue remained national unity, an issue thrown into sharp relief by the 1976 election of the Parti Québécois. The fight against both Quebec nationalism and English-Canadian intolerance had always animated Trudeau the writer, professor and politician. He had written more extensively and thought more deeply about the place of French Canadians than about any other subject.

In the 1950s, Trudeau and other social critics in Quebec lambasted the corrupt electoral practices, administrative chicanery, malodorous fund-raising tactics and patronage of Maurice Duplessis' Union Nationale government. Trudeau insisted that these abuses, and the defensive nationalism of the Union Nationale, had fostered an excessive reliance on so-called collective rights instead of individual liberties. They had also skewed Quebeckers' attitude towards democracy and federalism. In a bristling attack on attitudes towards democracy in Quebec, Trudeau wrote, "For the mass of the people the words Tory and Grit, Conservative and Liberal, referred neither to political ideals nor to administrative techniques. They were regarded only as meaningless labels, affixed to alternatives which permitted the auctioneering of one's support. . . . In such a mental climate, sound democratic politics could hardly be expected to prevail, even in strictly provincial or local affairs where racial issues were not involved. Through historical necessity, and as a means of survival, French Canadians had felt justified in finessing the parliamentary game; and as a result the whole game of politics was swept outside the pale of morality."[8]

The combination of government institutions imposed by the conquerors and the resistance of the Catholic Church to the expansion of state activities created political superstition and social conservatism. French Canadians, Trudeau wrote, never understood that state services could be theirs by right rather than by the discretion of those in authority. "Electoral processes for the mass of the people remained mysterious rituals of foreign origin, of little value beyond that for which the individual can barter his vote: a receipted grocery bill, a bottle of whiskey, a workman's compensation, a contract to build a bridge, a school grant, a community hospital," he wrote. "For it is noteworthy that in Quebec, a school or a hospital is not expected by the citizens as of right, being their due from an obedient government and for which they pay, but as a reward for having returned a member to the government benches."[9]

Only by cleansing the state of corruption and favouritism could Quebeckers be persuaded that the state might honourably and fairly serve society's purposes. And the state represented an indispensable, although not exclusive, instrument for dragging Quebec out of *la grande noirceur* to face the challenges of social reform, economic growth, protecting civil liberties, modernizing Quebec's institutions, and federalism. Trudeau wrote extensively and with barbed eloquence about the lamentable state of democratic institutions and political mores in Quebec. Yet he was silent on the patronage of political appointments, perhaps because the apparatus of the Quebec state remained minimal under Duplessis. Certainly, Trudeau insisted on the separation of political considerations from appointments to the civil service, but the great growth of agencies, boards and commissions, the nesting place for partisan appointments, was yet to come. Most of the appointments were of the small-fry variety, so that in comparison with other stains on the Quebec body politic the patronage of appointments seemed a minor blemish.

Trudeau's criticisms were those of an intellectual rather than a political participant. His motto was Reason Over Passion, his intellectual inspirations the French *philosophes* and the English liberals of the nineteenth century, his principles for defending liberties the balancing of arbitrary or exclusive power, his federalist convictions an outgrowth of his belief in balance and reason. His whole intellectual make-up screamed against the discretionary, back-scratching, favour-imploring and–dispensing, secretive, untidy and highly personal ways of operating a state on the time-honoured methods of rewarding friends and penalizing adversaries. A man of strict self-discipline, he was undoubtedly offended to observe the inherent or derivative weaknesses afflicting so many of both patrons and clients, that is, the politicians and voters of Quebec.

The English, he argued, had never truly wanted democracy for others. They had grudgingly granted it to French Canadians while reserving for themselves a disproportionate degree of influence in Quebec and Ottawa.[10] Trudeau remarked bitterly on the general ineffectiveness of French-Canadian politicians in the federal capital, most of whom at the pinnacle of their careers filled portfolios whose impressive titles masked a lack of political clout. French Canadians routinely received portfolios such as justice, solicitor-general, and public works, a ministry that the English-Canadian establishment in both major parties considered a proper match for French Canadians' interest in patronage. Unless Francophones could make a greater mark in federal affairs, French-speaking Quebeckers would turn increasingly toward their own government and, perhaps ultimately, toward creating their own sovereign state.

The first Trudeau government, following the recommendations of the royal commission on bilingualism and biculturalism, made it an important point of policy to appoint Francophones to high-profile positions in the civil service and at the top of boards, agencies and commissions. This utterly defensible policy, which nonetheless provoked a backlash among some English Canadians, flowed naturally from Trudeau's convictions that French Canadians must be shown that the national government reflected their needs and personality. Trudeau's own decision to seek federal office, which amazed so many of his friends, tangibly demonstrated that conviction. Not only did he appoint Francophones to the public service, he named Francophones to senior ministerial portfolios, so that by the end of his career the last barriers had fallen and Francophones had occupied the ministries of finance, energy and treasury board. Their presence fortified his first government's broad reforms to the official languages policy.

Trudeau's insistence on using his patronage powers to increase the Francophone presence in the federal government followed a tradition begun by John A. Macdonald. In the years following Confederation, Macdonald used his patronage powers to lure dissident Nova Scotians from their hostility to Confederation. Macdonald offered the province "better terms," which in a sense is what "French Power" was for French Canadians—better terms for them within Confederation. Macdonald also dispensed federal patronage lavishly in Nova Scotia, bringing the anti-Confederate clarion Joseph Howe into his cabinet, appointing anti-Confederates to the Senate, and allowing his new allies in Nova Scotia a full measure of federal patronage. This same use of patronage and porkbarrelling for the purposes of national integration animated Trudeau's policy towards Quebec. And just as John A. hoped for political benefits to the Conservative party in his use of patronage for national integration, so Trudeau and his Cabinet colleagues from Quebec could never deny the partisan political advantages that patronage might bring the Liberal party in Quebec.

As a French-Canadian prime minister from Quebec, Trudeau obviously did not need a "Quebec lieutenant," à la Ernest Lapointe for Mackenzie King. He would reserve for himself those dossiers relating to Quebec's place in Canada: language rights, constitutional reform, federal-provincial relations. But he needed help, as any prime minister would, with his own province's myriad of party matters, routine policy and administrative questions. So he appointed Jean Marchand, his long-time friend and fellow "wise man," minister responsible for Quebec, the role Guy Favreau had played for awhile under Prime Minister Lester Pearson. Marchand was responsible for staying in touch with the Quebec caucus and other ministers, organizing at the local and regional levels, providing advice on the Quebec angle of national dossiers, and deciding on appointments and discretionary contracts for Quebeckers and their firms. In Marchand's office, the bulk of decisions were made about the appointment of Quebec advertising agencies, architects, and consultants. Within the Prime Minister's Office, Trudeau established an appointments secretariat—first under Francis Fox (later a minister), then under Marie-Hélène Fox (Francis' sister) and Florence Ievers—to scrutinize the lists of all order-in-council appointments prepared by the Privy Council Office and to suggest names for filling them, canvassing ministers and party officials across the country. The names, of course, were overwhelmingly those of Liberals, qualified or otherwise, for the hundreds of jobs on government boards, agencies and commissions.

The system of making appointments in Quebec changed with the arrival of Marc Lalonde in Trudeau's cabinet. Lalonde, one of Trudeau's two or three most trusted confidants, replaced Marchand as political minister for Quebec. Although everyone in the Quebec caucus respected Lalonde's intellect and knew that he spoke with the endorsement of the prime minister, his self-assurance frightened Liberal backbenchers. Lalonde therefore had the good sense to enlarge and institutionalize the consultations before making appointments or awarding contracts. Almost every Thursday morning, Quebec ministers met for breakfast under Lalonde's chairmanship, usually in the New Zealand room adjacent to the parliamentary dining room. The last portion of each meeting dealt with appointments and contracts. A senior member of Lalonde's staff—for example Michel Drapeau, the son of Montreal's mayor, or Richard Lafontaine, subsequently an executive with Lavalin — would have prepared a list of forthcoming appointments and contracts. Quebec ministers were responsible for regions surrounding or near their constituencies. For example, Pierre De Bané from Matane was responsible for the Gaspé; Yvon Pinard from Drummondville for the Eastern Townships and the ridings south of the St. Lawrence River; Pierre Bussières from Charlesbourg for the Quebec City area, and so on. Jean Chrétien from Shawinigan was responsible for Trois-Rivières-La Mauricie, but being on bad terms with Lalonde and believing himself to have an independent standing in the party by virtue of his personal popularity, he seldom attended these Thursday morning meetings. Only Liberals received consideration for appointments. None of the ministers believed that occasional newspaper articles about patronage or shrieks of outrage from assorted groups ever harmed the Liberal party. Moreover, the Liberals were so utterly dominant in Quebec — winning seventy-four of seventy-five seats at the apogee of the party's domination — that most of those ambitious federalists seeking appointments were Liberals anyway.

The patronage of appointments blended perfectly with the extraordinary burst of federal spending that occurred in Quebec, first with the creation of the Department of Regional and Economic Expansion, then with a host of public works projects and job-creation programs that followed the Parti Québécois' victory in November, 1976.

The PQ victory exacerbated the long-term economic difficulties of Montreal and the province of Quebec. Capital flowed out of the province, and Quebec became a less attractive place to invest, so that Quebec's share of private capital investment in Canada dropped from about twenty-six percent in 1976 to about eighteen percent in the early 1980s. Federal ministers, observing this decline, worried that it might bolster the Parti Québécois' appeal, since if membership in Confederation did not bring economic benefits, Quebeckers might ask why they should remain partners.

Ottawa's spending, therefore, had two aims: to enhance the federal government's profile in Quebec and to create more buoyant economic conditions for the vote on sovereignty-association. The analysis may have been correct. A study for the Macdonald royal commission in 1986 found that Quebeckers displayed the weakest attachment to the idea of Canada, but the strongest attachment to the federal government.[11] Federal spending also responded to a sector of the political culture of contemporary Quebec that wishes governments, federal and provincial, to promote directly economic enterprise. The laissez-faire of many English–Canadian businessmen and commentators has had little appeal in Quebec since the early 1960s.

Consider the example provided by the expansion of DREE grants into Montreal. As originally conceived by minister Jean Marchand and deputy minister Tom Kent, regional development programs were to provide assistance only to the least advantaged regions of Canada. After the election of the Parti Québécois, pressure grew within the Quebec Liberal caucus and among Quebec ministers to designate Montreal under DREE's incentives program. Ministers from other parts of Canada, especially the Atlantic provinces, resisted, fearing a dilution of money for their areas. Ministers from other major cities asked: if Montreal, why not our cities? But DREE minister Marcel Lessard, with solid support from Quebec ministers, changed departmental policy to designate for DREE purposes discretionary centres for high-growth manufacturing industries in the Montreal area.

A series of other programs and public works projects provided opportunities for porkbarrelling and patronage. The LaPrade affair offers a case in point. Having promised a heavy–water plant at LaPrade on the St. Lawrence River in 1974, Ottawa backed out of the deal in mid-1978 after further studies revealed that no market existed for the product. The federal Liberals proposed an indemnity of $200 million in exchange for Quebec abandoning its rights under previously signed federal-provincial agreements concerning LaPrade. This money was to be spent on energy-related and high-technology projects identified in conjunction with the Quebec government. Returned to office in 1980, the Trudeau Liberals decided as a matter of general policy to stop co-operating with the *péquiste* government and to spend money directly in Quebec. As a result, Energy minister Jean Chrétien decided to spend $75 million from *les fonds LaPrade* in seven ridings within a large radius of the intended site at LaPrade. Liberal MPs were encouraged to identify projects and spend the money largely at their own discretion, whether or not the projects had anything to do with high technology or energy. In the seven ridings, forty-five projects were financed, most of which involved new recreation facilities, improvements to airports or ports, industrial parks, and various municipal projects. In Chrétien's own riding, Ottawa built one of the few high-technology projects: an $8 million institute for research into metals. The whole LaPrade affair, which came to light during the 1984 election campaign, smacked of a political slush fund of the most blatant kind.[12]

The renovation of the old port at Quebec City provided another classic case of porkbarrelling and patronage. The project grew exponentially in scope and cost; its budget swelled from $42 million to $115 million in five years. A *Le Devoir* inquiry revealed that half of the contractors had contributed to the Liberal party, although that probably reflected only the general understanding that firms should contribute *post facto* to political parties, especially the one in power, and that most of the construction and contracting firms of any size in Quebec contributed as a matter of course and prudence to the Liberal party.

Much more revealing was the discovery that nearly all senior officers of the corporation established to oversee the port project had close ties with the Liberal party, including the president, vice-president, treasurer, and most of the members of the board of directors. Almost every one had contributed financially to the party, occupied positions within the party or worked directly for Pierre Bussières, the minister responsible for the Quebec City region. Bussières also succeeded in by-passing the normal procedures of the public service commission in hiring summer students. He and local Liberal MPs were able to hand out jobs at the old port, and the sons and daughters of many senior managers found summer employment on the site. Although the contractors entered the competitive tendering process, the engineers, architects and consultants were all selected without tenders by the board of directors and management.

The same practice prevailed throughout Quebec, and it represented one of the largest sources of patronage in the hands of Quebec ministers. At the Thursday morning meetings, ministers could allocate architectural, consulting, auditing and other service contracts for major public works projects. Regional ministers chose the firms in their areas, subject to approval from the meeting of Quebec ministers. Of course, in areas such as Abitibi there were neither ministers nor a network of firms, so André Ouellet chose the firms. For large contracts, such as Place Guy Favreau in Montreal, improvements to Dorval airport, and the construction of Mirabel airport, the contracts were worth tens of millions of dollars. The jockeying among ministers to award contracts could be fierce. One Quebec MP said privately after the 1984 election, "If as much energy had gone into formulating policy as had gone into choosing architectural and engineering firms, we'd still be in power. You'd have been astonished to see the absolute in-fighting, the back-stabbing that went on." But participants at those meetings agreed; in the event of deadlock, Marc Lalonde decided.

The same ministerial discretion applied, of course, to legal work. André Ouellet, the Liberals' chief organizer in Quebec, had special responsibility for advertising contracts which he directed to several Liberal-oriented firms in Montreal, including BCP and B.B. Advertising Ltd. B.B., to give just one example, was awarded without tender the contract for advertising the Olympic coins for the 1976 Games. B.B. was owned by Communications Group Ltd., whose president, Jacques Bouchard, directed the Liberals' advertising campaign in Quebec in 1972. Ouellet, a great personal friend of Bouchard's, awarded the contract. Ed Prévost, BCP's president, was close to Lalonde. Similarly, small public works projects below the financial limits set by the department of public works could be awarded without tender. These decisions were usually made by the minister for each region, sometimes after consultation with local MPs.

Ouellet, it should be noted in passing, assumed special responsibility for placating Quebec's dairy farmers, one of the most effective pressure groups in Canadian politics. In the early 1970s, the dairy farmers grew increasingly angry at Liberal governments in Ottawa and Quebec City. They displayed their anger in striking ways: painting anti-provincial government slogans on barn roofs and dumping a large can of milk over the head of federal Agriculture minister Eugene Whelan. Ouellet and Whelan were assigned the task of designing a dairy policy. The result bought political peace at the cost of one of Canada's most lavish subsidy programs.

Ministers also recommended judgeships. Since most of the province's lawyers — and the Quebec Liberal ministers — came from Montreal, a group recommendation on judges usually emerged for the minister of justice. Legal competence was required; Liberal credentials helped. Later on in the Trudeau years, the government consulted the Canadian Bar Association before making appointments, although in the rush to appoint Privy Council president Yvon Pinard to the Federal

Court in Trudeau's last crush of appointments, the Liberals conveniently "forgot" about consultation.

Trudeau did worry about the visibility of Quebec MPs. It remained an abiding practice to credit the local MP with any federal spending or good deed. A piece of 1984 campaign literature from André Ouellet nicely illustrated the point. It showed only a series of buildings fully or partially financed by the federal government in Ouellet's riding of Papineau. The pamphlet listed federal monies spent in Papineau—including *pensions and family allowances*!—as if somehow Ouellet had been responsible for bringing these benefits to the residents of Papineau. The large federal spending programs—LIP, Opportunities for Youth, Canada Works, Special Recovery Capital Works Program, Canada Community Development Projects—all allowed MPs to recommend and, in some cases, all but choose who would get the money. These became prized porkbarrelling opportunities which, of course, the Liberals justified by the need to persuade Quebeckers to remain in Canada.

Here are just a few examples. In 1980 Trudeau unilaterally ended a job–creation program which had been negotiated and administered by Ottawa and Quebec. He insisted that Ottawa had received insufficient recognition for spending federal money in Quebec. Later job–creation programs established by Ottawa included local programs which MPs could fund at their discretion. Churches were encouraged to apply. Many did and wound up with freshly painted exteriors or basements. All they had to do in return was place a sign on the property indicating that Ottawa provided the money. The same applied for the Special Recovery Capital Works Program designed to "fast-track" construction projects. MPs had a large say in which projects should proceed in their constituencies. When a parliamentary brouhaha forced the government to reveal the list of projects funded, it became clear that the money had been spent in grossly disproportionate amounts in Liberal ridings across Canada. Quebec received a larger share than could be justified by its share of either national population or national unemployment. Similarly, within the renamed department of regional industrial expansion, special funds were allocated to Quebec projects. Finally, special Canada Works funds were assigned to Liberal MPs, who could recommend small projects in their ridings.

A classic instance of porkbarrelling came to light in the auditor-general's 1986 report. In August, 1983, the department of employment and immigration agreed to finance three-quarters of the $1.5 million cost of an arena in a Quebec Liberal MP's riding. When the remaining one-quarter of the cost could not be raised in the community, the minister agreed to alter the original terms of the agreement so that Ottawa paid the entire cost. Changed plans and unexpected costs drove up the final price tag to $4.9 million. According to the auditor-general, "The member of Parliament for the riding and members of his family played an active role in initiating and running the projects. After leaving public life, the former MP was appointed president of the corporation and now administers the sports centre."[13]

To what degree the patronage and discretionary spending of the federal Liberals turned back the tide of Quebec independence can never be precisely known. Certainly, the *péquistes* in defeat ascribed to federal money a determining influence, as if they had not themselves used the provincial treasury in the same political battle. In the late 1970s and early 1980s only the blind could have failed to see ubiquitous evidence of federal spending. Projects fairly dotted the Quebec landscape, and when the Special Recovery Capital Works Program got rolling, a forest of large red signs bearing maple leaves graced urban areas of Quebec, especially in suburban Montreal. John A. Macdonald would probably have justified every penny, if not to the accountants, then loudly to the country in the name of national unity and softly to his partisans in the name of the Conservative party. Trudeau, too, never once showed the slightest defensiveness. Retaining Quebec within Canada was his life's work, his generation of Quebeckers' most lacerating battle. History cannot measure the influence of Liberal patronage and porkbarrelling in Quebec, but history does record the result of the referendum and the overwhelming loyalty of Quebeckers to the Liberals in every election under Trudeau's leadership. To say that he bought Quebec would grossly distort his appeal; to ignore his use of patronage and porkbarrelling would be to dream.

In retrospect, of course, many who observe the nation's politics fell victim to a seductive myth: that of the impregnable Liberal organization in Quebec, a machine rooted in the constituencies, branching into every elite group (excepting perhaps the unions), topped by French power in Ottawa. But when Trudeau retired from politics, provoking some of the leading French-Canadian Liberals to leave as well, the Liberal party stood exposed as an organization with inadequate leadership and withered roots. In the 1984 campaign, no amount of pre-election spending, no litany of previously financed projects could instill sufficient gratitude in the Quebec electorate. Challenged by the Mulroney Conservatives, the Liberals toppled like trees in a fierce storm. Quebeckers undoubtedly voted for a winner and a native son, and also for the highest bidder, for Mulroney papered the province with promises to do even more for Quebec. It was a bidding game bound to produce disillusionment, since if 1984 had proven anything it was that spending does not secure enduring loyalty; it just prevents, and then only temporarily, the levying of political penalties.

Mulroney discovered, as Trudeau had, that substantial discretion- ary spending in Quebec can fuel jealousies elsewhere, although to be fair to Quebec, the same regional or provincial jealousies can be fuelled by spending almost anywhere in Canada. The sense of let-down or resentment in one region over spending in another must be assuaged, or so federal politicians come to feel. Call it envy or greed, call it a proper sense of injustice, call it a laudable demand for regional equity, the federal government's discretionary spending is sure to evoke minute examination or fiery demands in other regions, which, given Canadian history, means almost the entire country.

Where a party is weak, the temptation to use discretionary federal spending commends itself, for lack of a better policy. The Liberals, for example, racked their brains to figure out how to improve their lot in Western Canada and found themselves inevitably driven back on fed- erally financed projects. In British Columbia, for example, the Trudeau government spent huge sums on infrastructure projects, but it did them no political good whatsoever. In Manitoba, federal minister Lloyd Axworthy became the closest modern-day equivalent to Mackenzie King's minister of agriculture Jimmy Gardiner. He funnelled vast sums into Winnipeg, organized an extensive patronage network of Liberals throughout the province, assembled an enormous personal staff as minister of employment and immigration and minister of transport, and often used as justification for this mini-empire that since Quebec received so much, the West deserved its fair share. As the only elected Liberal minister west of Ontario in the last Trudeau government, Axworthy insisted that his office be the funnel for all federal initiatives. The release of Special Recovery Capital Works Program figures showed that nearly three-quarters of all money allocated to Manitoba went to Axworthy's riding (one of the two or three wealthiest in the province) and that of the province's only other Liberal MP. Neither ingenuity nor bluster could mask the blatantly partisan method of allocating the monies. This was politics practised in the old style by one who, like Trudeau himself, had been an early and eager campaigner for "parti- cipatory democracy."

But what choice, Axworthy would ask, did the Liberal party have? The West distrusted the party, feeling it was dominated by the Toronto- Montreal-Ottawa elites. Westerners smarted under the National Energy Policy and other Liberal assaults on perceived western interests, resented the unshakeable economic grip of Ontario and the political clout of Quebec, and could only be persuaded that Confederation might be rendered more equitable and the Liberal party more attractive if the government used what lay at its fingertips: discretionary spending and the power of appointments. The political temptation, then, to scatter these seed-corns on fallow ground can seem like compelling strategy to the politically desperate.

The political climate encouraging western Liberals to demand federal patronage had not changed since the rebellion against the Davey-Gordon changes of the early 1960s. Ross Thatcher's Liberal government in Saskatchewan provided western Liberals with their last look at provincial power. Only Liberal greybeards could remember provincial Liberal governments in Manitoba, Alberta and British Columbia, although in the west–coast province many federal Liberals remained on the good side of the provincial Socreds. With feeble provincial parties, western Liberals could look realistically only to Ottawa for rewards. There, they found ministers such as Axworthy and Lang anxious to use their power of patronage to reward long-sufferers and at least to keep alive the interest in participating in Liberal party affairs. Unfortunately, they used patronage defensively, merely to reward the faithful rather than to induce the uncommitted. And the patronage they could offer illustrated one of the distinguishing characteristics of modern patronage almost everywhere in Canada, a characteristic that has contributed to the eroding of public support of patronage.

In Jimmy Gardiner's day, patronage could be for everyone with the proper political credentials. The party elite got patronage (senatorships, judgeships, presidencies of Crown agencies, etc.), and the rank and file received their rewards (postmasterships, inspectorships, etc.). Big companies could get on the government's patronage list for major projects; little companies could supply everything from cutlery to coal. As the years wore on, spreading bureaucratization both eliminated much of the small patronage for the party rank and file and expanded patronage opportunities for the elite. Eric Kierans' placing of postmasters under the public service commission symbolized and furthered the shift from patronage to bureaucracy.

True, part-time jobs as census-takers, enumerators and some summer-student positions could be filled by the time-honoured methods, but these lay at the margin of federal government employment. A job in the penitentiary, harbour commission, customs house or any other government installation now depended on regulations, procedures, norms, standards, perhaps even exams, with political influence again relegated to the margin. Both the rank and file of the party in power, and that of the other parties, increasingly appreciated that the patronage their fathers had known, or counted upon, was no longer available. The "psychic" satisfaction of participation had supplanted the tangible inducement of patronage, and that fundamental shift carried with it enormous consequences for political mobilization.[14]

Yet for the elite, patronage remained in the burgeoning boards,

agencies and commissions, in the existing troves of the Senate, judgeships and lieutenant-governorships, in Canadian embassies abroad, in
advertising agencies, polling firms, lobbying companies, in contractors
with the right connections. In the Trudeau years, a period of transition
in patronage, the age-old phenomenon of patronage became almost
exclusively by, for, and of the political elites. A huge gap thus developed
between the commitment to the patronage system of the party elites
and of the rank and file, and more broadly between the political elites
and the general population. The elites periodically seemed dimly aware
of the gap, and cast about for new ways of encouraging participation,
or tried to camouflage the old ways with a smattering of appointments
to supporters of other parties.

Within the Liberal party, you could see the resentment swell up in
1982 when at a party convention aggressive delegates pushed through
a resolution condemning the influence of "polls, propaganda and
patronage orchestrated by a small elite." You could sense it in the communications strategies of the entire Liberal period when Trudeau, as
he reminded the party in his final speech, tried to "appeal over the
heads" of premiers, interest groups and multinational corporations to
the population at large. You could even see it in Trudeau's Charter of
Rights and Freedoms, which bade individuals and groups to press their
claims not through the traditional conventions of party and Parliament
but through the courts. For all the rhetoric, though, the enduring pull
of the old ways tugged at the ministers and the prime minister. So Lang
and Axworthy, with Trudeau's blessing, for he neither knew nor understood the West, doled out the patronage for the party elite, which
merely exacerbated the Liberal party's problems, since the patronage
went to a minority of members of an already minority party.

Important reforms to party financing marked the Trudeau years.
These lessened the importance of patronage by weakening the link
between financial contributions and political influence, forcing parties
to develop new methods of raising money, and shedding light on what
had been for decades one of the dark corners of Canadian political
life.[15] In 1974, the government introduced the *Canada Elections Act*
which subsequently made candidates less dependent on contributions
from large corporations and wealthy individuals. The link between
party contributions and government favours had been central to many
of the best-known scandals in Canadian history, including the Canadian Pacific Scandal, the McGreevy affair, and the Beauharnois affair.
But the Trudeau election-financing reforms considerably sanitized
political fund-raising and the patronage that sometimes accompanied
it. This vital reform of 1974 represented Trudeau's last sustained
attempt to reform any part of the patronage system. Another change

— it wasn't really a reform — consisted of using the symbolic aspects of patronage by appointing more women and ethnics. After placing himself, circa 1972, in the hands of the Liberal party's political pros who helped him win a majority in 1974, Trudeau contented himself with only sporadic rhetorical attempts and the occasional policy conference to go back to those early gropings for new ways of mobilizing political participation. The old pros did not bring back the old ways, which had never disappeared; they just stopped the search for anything new.

Yet while Trudeau relentlessly used his patronage powers — to have served him almost guaranteed a patronage post if one was desired — the utility of patronage except for internal party management kept declining. Of profound importance in this decline was the influence of television, the medium Trudeau used so effectively.

Television searches restlessly for a faceless mass audience. Its reach is stupendous, an observation confirmed by the statistics on the ownership of television sets, the number of daily hours of viewing per household, the penetration of cable (higher in Canada than anywhere in the world), the shift from newspapers to television as the prime source of information for the majority of the population. The influence of television on politics began to become evident in the late 1950s, but Diefenbaker and Pearson never felt comfortable with the medium. Nor had the factors that made television of such crucial importance fully emerged until the 1960s. Trudeau, wonderfully telegenic, provided in his physical demeanour and speaking style the almost ideal television performer. But more than this, television fitted snugly with his philosophical views. He saw society as an agglomeration of individuals who best achieved their potential and exercised their liberties divorced from community constraints or notions of collective rights. In political philosophy, he believed the crucial link to be that between the individual and the government — and the television age enables the government through its leader to speak directly to citizens.

Another crucial dimension of television is its inability, as a visual medium, to deal intelligently with issues other than by personalizing them. Put simply, television prefers, wherever possible, to find spokesmen for each side of an issue and to put them on the screen, rather than attempting the more challenging feat of explaining an issue on its substance and merits alone. Political leaders have always been the principal spokesmen for their parties, and their reputation could never be discounted when assessing the popularity of the party. But television magnifies the leader's importance, by constantly thrusting his persona into the living rooms, and by allowing citizens everywhere to believe they vicariously know all about him. Television profoundly strengthens the link between leader and citizen, almost to the exclusion of every other contact between party and voter, with consequences for all aspects of politics, including patronage.

Patronage has always been an intensely personal phenomenon, for patrons and clients alike. It is characterized by personal contacts between patrons and clients, between politicians and their supporters through correspondence, conversations, shared trials and battles, the loyalties of tribe. Even if the leader could not personally know his legions of supporters, his ministers or local notables acted as mini-patrons with the leader's blessing, partly binding supporters to party by the distribution or expectation of rewards. These mini-patrons were the regional or local kingpins so prevalent in Canadian cabinets, the prime agents for the party's patronage networks, and some of them even lingered in the Trudeau period — Otto Lang, Lloyd Axworthy, Allan MacEachen, Don Jamieson. But television is among the enemies of the traditional kingpins, the powerful mini-patrons, if you like. The medium, preferring simplicity, focuses its attention not on a multiplicity of faces, but on one, that of the leader. The medium's national scope, vividly displayed on the evening news broadcasts — the most important vehicle of political communication in the age of telepolitics — diminishes the importance of merely regional figures.

In addition to diminishing the regional kingpins, television introduces a new kind of facelessness into politics. Before television, only a tiny fraction of voters ever saw, let alone personally knew, the party leaders. People relied for their knowledge on friends, newspapers (frequently party bullhorns) and local party officials. Even radio, with its nation-wide reach, conveyed only limited dimensions of a leader's character. Television allowed everyone to believe that they knew the leader, and they were largely correct in that belief. For television's one brilliant capacity is to convey over time a rounded and penetrating picture of the leader's persona, especially his attitudes and values. But the audience is utterly faceless, a collection of viewers the leader cannot see. The medium provides vicarious intimacy in one direction, and facelessness in the other. When this phenomenon of one-way intimacy is combined with television's brilliant capacity to convey the leader's attitudes and values — the extension of the medium's preference for personalizing issues — then these attitudes and values colour almost every aspect of the public reaction to what the leader says, how he runs the government, and substantive issues of the day. And if those attitudes and values are discordant with those of the public, the leader can find himself in enormous, almost irredeemable, difficulty with the public.

Facelessness is patronage's sworn enemy, since it rips personal relations out of politics. Modern cities do this by creating constituencies within which only a tiny fraction of the voters will ever come in contact with party representatives, including members of Parliament. Bureaucracy does its part by squeezing political discretion from the delivery of government services. Better education and greater affluence contribute, too, by making fewer people dependent on government for the necessities of life. Television plays its role by creating a faceless political audience, the appeal to which depends on an approach completely foreign to the traditional ways of the patronage system. All these factors contribute to a society in which the daily experiences of increasing numbers of citizens revolve around practices and assumptions, values and attitudes, hostile to those of traditional patronage. No wonder, then, that such a gap yawned throughout the Trudeau years between public attitudes and party practices, with the party periodically struggling to catch and reflect the new public attitudes without, for internal party purposes, being able to discard the old ways of rewarding friends.

It was therefore entirely fitting that the Liberal party should fall headlong into this gap upon the transfer of power in 1984 from Pierre Trudeau to John Turner. After Trudeau's walk-in-the-snow, he began winding up his leadership like a man clearing out his desk and finding envelopes full of IOUs. From May 31 to June 29, the cabinet approved two hundred and twenty-five order-in-council appointments, most of them to Liberals. Firms with connections to the Liberal party received new government advertising contracts. And in one stunning swoop, eighteen high-profile Liberals, including seventeen MPs, scooped up full-time patronage jobs. Some appointments had been promised to the recipients as an inducement to run in the 1980 election. The same round of appointments had happened in the months before the 1979 election; eleven high-profile Liberals took their shares of the spoils of power in the Senate, the diplomatic corps, and various boards, agencies and commissions. Two opposition MPs received positions because the Liberals had targeted their seats in the upcoming election. But in 1984, the sheer effrontery of a retiring prime minister rewarding loyalists with no chance for the public to pass judgment on him seemed to symbolize the arrogance of the man and the party. One by one, Trudeau dealt with the supplicants, asking them what he could do for them like a turbaned sultan offering up his jewels. He canvassed, too, offering first Marc Lalonde, then Jean Chrétien the vacant Senate seat in Quebec. When they declined, he gave it to a grateful former minister, Pierre De Bané. It was all done with such haste that the government did not consult the Canadian Bar Association about naming Privy Council president Yvon Pinard a Federal Court judge, nor float the name of Liberal warhorse Bryce Mackasey by the Portuguese government, as is the diplomatic custom, before appointing him ambassador to Portugal.

Liberals expecting rewards and contemplating the next election never dreamed of the public storm ahead. For them, this last orgy of appointments represented the vintage Trudeau: bold, breathtaking, clever, dismissive. Naturally, some supplicants worried that they might be overlooked or abandoned, but they could have rested easily. Trudeau looked after them all. He entered his last Liberal caucus meeting and said he had secured an agreement in writing from Turner — the need for a letter testified to Trudeau's distrust of Turner—that the new prime minister would make every last appointment on the list. At a luncheon with Liberal leadership candidates early in the campaign, Trudeau had informed them he intended to pay off some debts. When he asked whether he should do so during the leadership campaign, the candidates all said no. When Turner was elected, therefore, there could have been no surprise that Trudeau intended to make a last round of appointments. The sheer size of the list did surprise, even disgust, Turner.

Turner demonstrated a full range of confused emotions leading in those early days and weeks to bizarre decisions. He swore a lot when shown Trudeau's list, fulminated about his predecessor's arrogance, listened to conflicting advice, added a few names of his own to the list, and explained that he had no option. Why? Because the Privy Council had warned him that if Trudeau made the appointments, as the departing prime minister suggested, the Liberals would lose their parliamentary majority. A Liberal minority in the Commons might in turn lead Governor-General Jeanne Sauvé to refuse Turner's request for dissolution and to ask Conservative leader Brian Mulroney to form a government. This explanation was so tortuous and so demonstrably dubious in constitutional practice (Eugene Forsey, among other experts, tore it to shreds; Trudeau's staff told him it was bunk) that only the most blindly Grit partisan could possibly have believed it. Trudeau, in a brief appearance late in the election campaign, defended his appointments, claiming that all whom he rewarded were well qualified. But it fell to Turner to carry the bell around his neck throughout the campaign, and every time it tinkled "I had no option," the plaintive sound merely furthered the impression of his weakness, since a leader worth his salt always has an option, however unpalatable.

The end of the Trudeau years, then, seemed long removed in time and spirit from those heady days of the young prime minister and his new-fangled ideas about "participatory democracy," the sterility of existing party structures, and the need to engage the commitment of those turned off by political parties. The final, defiant patronage orgy mocked all the brave experiments, some nobly inspired, of the Trudeau years, and testified again to the difficulty of modern political parties bringing their internal practices and the demands of governing into line with a changed political culture that required new ways of capturing the public's attention, currying its favour, mobilizing its commitment, encouraging its participation. The gap between expectation and performance into which the Liberals plunged could only be sidestepped by those with the discernment to understand how the country had changed and the commitment to seek ways of closing that gap. Unfortunately, the victorious Brian Mulroney assumed no change had occurred, and so tumbled headlong into the very gap between expectation and performance he had so brilliantly exploited in the 1984 campaign.

CHAPTER 19

MULRONEY 1988
POWER DESPOILED

"I'm not trying to hang onto patronage. I think it's a
pain in the neck. I mean to have to go and appoint an
unemployment insurance commissioner in North Bay
and then you find out that his sister happened to be
married to the brother of someone who was a Conservative candidate in the provincial election, and all of a
sudden it's Question Period time. We need that like a
hole in the head."
Prime Minister Brian Mulroney.

LIBERAL SENATOR PIERRE DE BANÉ attended Laval University law
school with Brian Mulroney when new ideologies and fresh intepre-
tations of old ones were swirling through the intellectual air of Quebec.
The law school, De Bané recalled, featured students of every stripe:
nationalist, federalist, separatist, Liberal, Conservative, Union
Nationale, socialist, capitalist. Into this swirl of ideas and factions
strode Brian Mulroney, friends with everyone in his first year and, upon
graduation, still friends with everyone. All through law school Mulroney made every group believe that he supported its ideas. Almost
every student fits into a pigeonhole; Mulroney fitted into them all, or
so his classmates believed. It was, concluded De Bané, an astonishing
performance.

This desire to be liked by everyone runs deep in Brian Mulroney's
character. So does a willingness to act according to the demands of the
moment, whether pleasing everyone at Laval, or stroking people as he
moved upwards through Quebec society, or reassuring Conservatives
in the 1983 leadership campaign that he would never support free trade
with the United States, or insisting privately that the Conservatives
should drop the intellectual precursor of the Meech Lake constitutional
accord — Joe Clark's "community of communities" — or promising
Conservatives free drinks at the patronage bar. An almost morbid fascination with what others, especially the media, think of him represents

the flip side of this intense desire to please. Mannerisms also reflect this desire to make a good impression: the darting eyes scanning a room; the smoothing or adjusting of his impeccable, conventional clothes; the ham performances; the blarney; the unctuous phrases. His Irish background is often advanced to explain these affectations. An abiding insecurity provides a better explanation.

While most of his politically-minded classmates at Laval embraced the Liberal party or the *indépendantiste* movement, Mulroney became a Conservative, a decision, whether through accident or design, that displayed courage. He admired Union Nationale Premier Daniel Johnson, the last of Quebec's old-style *patroneux*, but by the time Mulroney began immersing himself in politics, the Union Nationale was heading towards extinction, a fate with which federal Conservatives in Quebec had periodically flirted.

Nowhere in Canada did conspiratorial politics rage more virulently than among Quebec Conservatives. After the Union Nationale breathed its last, pathetic sighs, the *bleus* of Quebec held nothing but their memories and their resentments, which they often took out upon each other. The deaths of Premier Maurice Duplessis, his successor Paul Sauvé and then Daniel Johnson robbed them of their *chefs*; the defeat of Prime Minister John Diefenbaker deprived them of an erstwhile ally. By the late 1960s, the *bleus* of Quebec were leaderless and dispirited, a rabble army without a cause. Those dedicated to provincial politics chose other options; those interested in federal politics could join the Liberals, encourage the Social Credit, or suffer with the Conservatives.

A Conservative political rally in the 1970s or early 1980s combined low farce with pathos. On the seats, or at least those that were filled, sat the blue-rinse set bused from miles around, bribed with an offer of a free meal or a break in their daily routine. Around the periphery of the hall stood the organizers and hangers-on, men in shiny suits with bulging ambitions but few accomplishments, men invariably scratching for action in their own communities, peripheral players in the political game, quick-buck artists in the economic. A few preliminary speakers tried to whip up enthusiasm, usually with excessively histrionic performances, before the colossal let-down of a Robert Stanfield or Joe Clark speech delivered in earnest, mangled French. Having endured this agony, the crowd filed towards the buses for the long rides home and the organizers retired to a nearby watering hole to stiffen their pretensions with liquor. The media hustled to the phones to deal yet another blow to the Conservatives' already dismal prospects by reporting accurately just what a prefabricated fiasco the whole affair had really been.

Here and there, in the private clubs and hotel bars where Quebec's political players cut deals and swapped stories, the odd Conservative swam in the Liberal sea. A few lingered from the Duplessis-Johnson years; others had joined the apparently forlorn cause later on. The *bleus* of Quebec business and law had the cheques to keep the tattered Tory flag flying, pay the lost deposits, grease the proper palms, but they deliberately kept a low profile in the party and the province. They played politics in the shadows, their kinship apparently forged by the shared fate of being political "outs." A sense of Quebec nationalism seemed to provide an additional cement, for many of them rejected what they believed to be the astringent, centralizing federalism of Pierre Trudeau. Mulroney, however, insisted to his listeners at the Mount Royal Club and the downstairs bar at the Ritz Hotel that the Conservatives should stop playing footsie with Quebec nationalists, forget about "deux nations" or "community of communities," or any other sop to nationalist politics, and get on with replacing the Liberals as the defenders of a strong central government.

It is almost an iron law of politics that the more marginal the party, the greater the factionalism. The Conservatives of Quebec provided a splendid example of this iron law at work. Deprived through repeated defeat of the opportunity to run anything substantial, they squabbled furiously over the right to direct something inconsequential, namely themselves. In 1976, the intrigues and bitterness between the Claude Wagner and Brian Mulroney camps at the Conservative leadership campaign was the stuff, if not of legends, then of lingering and profound recriminations. Wagner's death left Mulroney as Quebec's only indigenous pretender to the Conservative leadership, although by dint of hard work and pluck Joe Clark gained a respectable toehold among Quebec Conservatives, a toehold he expanded into a bridgehead. In 1981, while professing undying fidelity to Clark's leadership, Mulroney agitated quietly for the stab in the back. At the convention to test Clark's leadership, the anti-Clark forces from Quebec whom Mulroney had helped to organize gathered in a Hull motel. They stayed clear of the convention until the hour of voting, when they slipped into the hall, cast their ballots for a leadership review, then retired furtively into the night, their mission almost accomplished.

Once Mulroney declared his candidacy — after Clark's second unsuccessful attempt to rally more than two-thirds of the party to his side — trench warfare erupted again in Quebec. Tales of instant delegates from the Old Brewery Mission in Montreal, payoffs, appeals against delegates' credentials punctuated the 1983 leadership campaign. As if all this did not adversely colour Mulroney's triumph, misty stories followed about offshore contributions to Mulroney from financier Walter Wolf.

Mulroney emerged from this conspiratorial, almost brutal, world of Quebec Conservative politics to lead the national party. Years of intrigue had taught him the value of loyalty, a loyalty that he required for his own political purposes and that his personality seemed to demand. Mulroney understood acutely from his Quebec Conservative background the pain of permanent exclusion from power; worse, the silent scorn of all the movers and shakers of the establishment. And he also appreciated, for he had witnessed this in Quebec, the factionalism of the Conservative party. Its failure to understand the discipline of power had stamped too many party supporters with the mentality of the "outs" whereby doubts ate at confidence, suspicions bred distrust, and convictions hardened into impractical, impossible positions the urgency of which bore an inverse relationship to their likelihood of ever being implemented.

Intrigue among Quebec Conservatives was never driven by ideology or intellectual conviction, but by personal rivalries and relationships sealed in telephone calls and secret meetings. In the politics of the shadows, networks of personal contacts counted for almost everything, and at this Mulroney excelled, for his capacity to reward friendship is matched by his intolerance of slights. More at home with a telephone than a book, more comfortable with conversation than briefing-papers, more attuned to the psyche of personalities than to the stimulation of ideas, Mulroney became a superb network politician, reaching out to stroke his interlocutors with just the right words and the hint or promise of a desired reward.

When Mulroney stepped onto the national stage, he could not shake the habits of politics in the shadows. These habits, combined with the special needs of the Conservative party across Canada, perfectly suited the old-style politics of patronage, which depended upon a network of intense personal relationships, a commitment to personalities rather than ideas, and the need to expand political coalitions and mobilize participation by the expectation or receipt of rewards. Mulroney thus spoke from a mixture of conviction and expediency when in the 1983 leadership campaign he promised Conservatives an extended spell at the patronage trough. Genuine sympathy for a fellow political warrior, as well as the love of a good phrase, produced Mulroney's "there's no whore like an old whore" crack about Bryce Mackasey. It was entirely fitting, although supremely hypocritical, for Mulroney to quietly select the chairmen of the Conservative patronage committees (PACs) across the country, during an election campaign in which he excoriated Liberals for patronage excesses and pummelled a hapless John Turner — "You had an option, sir" — in their television debate. It was therefore not in the least surprising that upon becoming prime minister Mulroney should have approached patronage in the traditional way. Nor was it surprising that the country, increasingly skeptical of patronage before Mulroney, then grossly misled during the campaign about his intentions, hoisted him on the petard of his own rhetoric and so forced the halting retreat from the traditional politics of patronage that marked the latter part of his mandate.

In a broad historical sense, Mulroney and Trudeau, prime ministers during the transitional stage of the politics of patronage through which the country is still moving, were polar opposites. Trudeau arrived in office seeing the inadequacies of traditional patronage for mobilizing support and encouraging participation, and he tried through his early years as prime minister to temper or even eliminate some traditional manifestations of patronage. But Trudeau abandoned those efforts in his later years, then ended his career with an outlandish display that inflamed the country's reduced tolerance for patronage. Mulroney, conversely, entered 24 Sussex Drive without sensing how the country's tolerance had changed, let alone how he had accentuated that change, and so began practising the traditional politics of patronage, only to realize later, as Trudeau had at the beginning, that the old ways would no longer suffice. They were both stuck with a power their parties demanded be used, the use of which, without suitable and convincing explanations, simply irritated the country and widened the gap between the political elites and the rest of the population. Neither could summon the courage to explain forthrightly why patronage, properly and sensibly used, could assist the better functioning of parties and parliamentary democracy.

The Conservatives' provincial and national advisory committees on patronage took awhile to click into action. The PAC chairman met in Ottawa the day before the swearing-in of the Mulroney cabinet. The PAC chairmen had to find suitable Conservatives to fill their committees, and ministers needed time to settle into their portfolios. (For a list of the members of the PAC committees, see Appendix.) But by December, 1984, the PAC system was fully operational, and the first wave of appointments began. They were preceded, however, by a bit of political camouflage which pleased Mulroney greatly, since he proudly informed his staff that the appointment of former Ontario NDP leader Stephen Lewis as ambassador to the United Nations would blunt any criticism of the forthcoming Conservative wave. So would the appointment of former Commons Speaker Lloyd Francis, a Liberal, as ambassador to Portugal.

When the Conservative wave began breaking, followed by another and another and another, newspapers quickly reminded readers of the previous Mulroney hyperbole. "There's not a Grit left in town. They've all gone to Grit heaven" (July 9, 1984). "They [Trudeau and Turner] have dishonoured the system . . . and it shall never happen again with a Conservative government" (July 12, 1984). "Every morning that every citizen in the Sept-Iles region gets up and goes to work, remember that every tax dollar you pay to the end of your days will go to pay for the golden retirement of tired Liberals. It's a deceit and a sham. It has to be corrected by dramatic gestures and I propose to take them" (July 14, 1984). "They [the Liberal appointments] confirm the old boys' network is back in town — that the boys are back and that the Liberal party doesn't want change" (July 25, 1984). And, of course, there was Mulroney's justifiably famous line from the televised debate: "You had an option, sir. You could have said 'I am not going to do it. I'm not going to ask Canadians to pay the price.' You had an option to say no and you chose to say yes to the old stories of the Liberal party. . . . You could have done better" (July 25, 1984).

Mulroney's "better" way consisted of replacing Liberals with Conservatives or filling vacancies with Conservatives. This began with twenty appointments on December 4, most to Mulroney's personal friends or Conservative organizers. To the Citizenship Court, a favoured Liberal repository of patronage, went Helga Paide, for many years chief financial officer of the Conservative party of Ontario, and Huguette Pageau, the widow of Rodrique Pageau, one of Mulroney's *bleu* mentors in Quebec, who died of cancer shortly after the election. Two Conservatives from Sept-Iles, site of a Mulroney denunciation of Liberal patronage, received positions. On the last Friday before Christmas, the timing designed to minimize publicity, another long list of Conservatives appeared; it replaced eleven Liberals with Conservatives on the board of directors of Petro-Canada.

Three months later, Mulroney disbursed one of Ottawa's prized patronage plums: positions on the board of directors of Air Canada with their accompanying free passes. The appointments caused immediate political trouble, inside the Conservative party and beyond. Like all Opposition politicians, Mulroney had pledged to appoint only men and women of superior ability. And yet here was Gayle Christie, a perfectly competent municipal politician in Toronto and a Conservative, replying to a question about her qualifications by saying that she knew how to drive a car. And here were thirteen Conservatives, only two of whom had any demonstrable experience in areas related to travel. Worse still from the party's perspective, four of the new board members were PAC chairmen. Nine out of ten PAC chairmen had quickly received patronage posts — four on the Air Canada board, two on the Petro-Canada board, one on the Bank of Canada board, one on the bench, and one as commission counsel to a royal commission. The grumbling of the rank and file grew everywhere, because it justifiably appeared that the mini-patrons, the PAC chairmen, cared for themselves first, and only thought later of supporters or political clients.

Trouble, too, was brewing in the multicultural communities. A Carol Goar column in *The Toronto Star* praised the prime minister for appointing women and Francophones but noted the paucity of so-called ethnic appointments. The column caught Mulroney's eye—what didn't, in the media? — because he had given instructions that multicultural appointments should be a priority; he liked to recall that in the smashing triumph of 1984 only among Mediterranean Catholics had the Conservatives failed to win a majority of the votes. Historically, the Conservatives had done poorly among many ethnic groups, and Mulroney, like Trudeau, sought to employ the symbolism of patronage to appoint leading members of the ethnic communities. Yet the first spate of Conservative nominees reflected the traditional Anglo-Saxon and new-found French elements in the party. Peter White, in charge of the appointments system in the Prime Minister's Office, therefore created a multicultural advisory board in Ontario to assist that province's PAC.

That helped somewhat, but Conservative MPs in Toronto remained unhappy with the party's approach to the multicultural communities. In a draft report of a Metro caucus sub-committee, dated September, 1986, the members recommended a series of changes, including improved relations with the ethnic press. "High standards should be maintained for the news packages supplied to media outlets, a process the effectiveness of which can be maximized by 'spoonfeeding' the media. It is imperative that unfavourable news be displaced quickly from the headlines." The report reflected the traditional hostility of MPs towards any non-elected official dispensing or advising on patronage. "PAC and NAC should be replaced by regional caucus and MPs." Money, of course, provided the surest means to political exposure. "MPs may improve their visibility among ethnic groups by presenting grant cheques at events as often as possible." Money should be directed to politically favourable groups. "Liberal funding patterns among ethnic groups should not be retained, especially if they prove to be stumbling-blocks to the implementation of politically effectual PC funding." The lack of insufficient ethnic appointments rankled. "Increasing the number of ethno-cultural appointments should be recognized as an immediate priority, as appointments continue to be predominantly Anglo. Effective communication of multiculturalism policy and ethnic appointments must be seen to be as important as the policy and appointments themselves."

While Conservative appointments to boards, agencies and commissions — the new motherlodes of political patronage — continued apace, Mulroney wisely resisted the counsel of certain advisers to recast the civil service in a Conservative mould. Some Conservatives, searching for scapegoats other than themselves, fingered the civil service for having contributed to the Joe Clark debacle. They wanted heads to roll, just as Mulroney had promised in the Conservative leadership campaign. During planning for the transition of power, frontbencher Don Mazankowski (later the deputy prime minister) had recommended placing near the top of every civil service department a partisan assistant deputy minister to ensure that the civil servants followed the government's political priorities. This insidious scheme quickly evaporated when subjected to withering scrutiny by other members of Mulroney's transition team who correctly asserted that the civil service would follow proper ministerial direction. But pockets of deep hostility towards the civil service remained, even within the prime minister's entourage. Peter White, the appointments secretary who left after two years to work for business tycoon Conrad Black, was among the hard men of the Conservative party agitating for significant changes. White's imperious, dismissive attitude struck his more moderate successor Marjory LeBreton as so distasteful that she shredded some of White's memoranda.

Only two notable cases of political vengeance marred an otherwise commendable record. The Conservatives fired Edmund Clark from the Energy department because they considered him the author of the Liberals' detested National Energy Program. Robert Rabinovitch, who had served Clark with distinction in the Privy Council Office, was nevertheless viewed by Conservatives as a protégé of former Privy Council clerk Michael Pitfield. Rabinovitch, too, was fired in an act of senseless vengeance. But some Mulroney appointments—Montreal lawyer Stanley Hart as deputy minister of finance, Montreal economist Judith Maxwell as chairman of the Economic Council of Canada, Frank Iacobucci from the University of Toronto law school as deputy minister of justice — reflected a refreshing desire to leaven the civil service with top-quality, non-partisan talent, and not to use it as a playpen for Conservative worthies.

The same could not be said for Mulroney's approach to the diplomatic service. The temptation to use the diplomatic service for party purposes had been present from 1926 when Canada began sending its own diplomats overseas without prior approval of the British government. Indeed, even before that Canadian governments had sent as High

Commissioners to London men with links to the party in power —
Charles Tupper, one of John A. Macdonald's closest political associates, was Canada's first High Commissioner to London. Prime Minister
Mackenzie King made eighteen partisan appointments over twenty-
two years in a service a fraction of the size of today's diplomatic corps.
Prime Minister R.B. Bennett appointed two partisans in five years;
Prime Minister Louis St. Laurent four in eight years; Prime Minister
John Diefenbaker four in six years; Prime Minister Lester Pearson three
in five years. Prime Minister Pierre Trudeau revived King's habit by
appointing eighteen Liberal partisans over sixteen years, including four
members of his personal staff and seven former cabinet ministers.

Three weeks after taking office, Mulroney wrote to the Professional Association of Foreign Service Officers (PAFSO), "The Canadian
diplomatic corps is to be commended for the high esteem in which it
is held by the international community. I can assure you the standard
of professionalism so characteristic of our foreign service will be maintained by my government and reflected in the diplomatic appointments
we will be making." This echoed his colleague John Crosbie's laments
during the election campaign that "the diplomatic corps, once the pride
of Canada and of the world . . . is being penetrated by a new kind of
termite, the Liberal politician." The presumption, when combined with
Mulroney's campaign promises, was therefore inescapable that the
Conservatives would not use the diplomatic service for patronage.
Instead, within the first fifteen months, nine Conservatives or friends
of Mulroney received diplomatic posts. These appointments were all
engineered by Mulroney himself, sometimes over the objections of Secretary of State for External Affairs Joe Clark. In one case, the department had decided to close the consul-general's office in Philadelphia as
an economy measure. But Mulroney instructed the post be kept open
for a friend, Pierrette Lucas. When the office eventually did close, Lucas
became consul-general in Boston.

When Mulroney staffer Patrick MacAdam received a position in
London already designated for a foreign service officer, PAFSO predictably cried foul. They sought to prove that Mulroney had more
severely damaged morale within the service than had any previous
prime minister. Although Mulroney had certainly used the diplomatic
service for partisan purposes, PAFSO exaggerated the impact. Montreal mayor Jean Drapeau's appointment as ambassador to the United
Nations Educational, Scientific and Cultural Organization in Paris was
undoubtedly a poor one — Drapeau was too infirm to continue as
mayor of Montreal — but not a patronage one, although elements of
the media and Opposition parties so described it. Drapeau had never
rendered service to the Conservative party, nor would he in recompense

for the Paris post. The appointment of Mulroney's friend Lucien Bouchard, a lawyer from Chicoutimi and a former member of the Parti
Québécois, proved to be inspired. Bouchard, although a diplomatic
neophyte, adeptly negotiated the minefields of French politics, especially in organizing the first summits of La Francophonie. He became
Secretary of State, then won a by-election in the early summer of 1988.

Bouchard's appointment reflected part of Mulroney's approach to
building the Conservative party in Quebec. Mulroney delivered spectacularly on his solemn promise to the Conservative party. They won
fifty-eight seats in that formerly hostile province, but everyone associated with that remarkable triumph understood that the party
remained rootless in Quebec. A particular set of circumstances gave
Mulroney the opportunity he brilliantly exploited — the departure of
Trudeau, the factionalism of the Liberal party without his cementing
presence, Mulroney's clear victory over Turner in the French-language
television debate, a well-heeled and organized Conservative campaign,
the recruitment of some excellent Conservative candidates, the willingness of Parti Québécois supporters to participate in federal politics
after the defeat of the referendum on sovereignty-association, the
knowledge seeping through Quebec that a Conservative band wagon
was rolling in the rest of Canada, and a desire for change. But his 1984
Quebec coalition, which included many provincial Liberals and
péquistes, represented a dalliance rather than a political marriage. The
Conservatives' overriding political priority therefore became to cement
their standing in Quebec, for without a respectable number of Quebec
seats, the Conservatives would continue to be Canada's minority party.
For this cause, then, Mulroney deployed the instruments of patronage,
sometimes in a heavy-handed and politically injurious manner, but with
that overriding priority always in mind. There was, too, the prime
minister's belief that the process of reconciling the former supporters
of sovereignty-association with their Canadian future could be accelerated if a few of them received federal appointments. Within three
years, former péquistes found themselves as the Canadian ambassador
to France, a senior executive of Via Rail, an officer of Telefilm Canada,
and a member of the board of governors of the Bank of Canada.

The Quebec PAC committee reviewed appointments from that
province Thursday nights at the Ritz Hotel. Members would gather
before the meeting in the main-floor bar, where various supplicants
and would-be contractors hung about hoping for a word with Fernand
Roberge and the other members of the committee. There was nothing
terribly secretive about these meetings. It seemed as if le tout Montréal
knew about them, and the notice board in the Ritz lobby indicated the
where and when of the meeting upstairs.

The 1984 Conservative triumph in Quebec brought to Ottawa the widest possible range of MPs. The vast majority of newly elected Quebec MPs had never been actively involved in politics. They had often been recruited by Bernard Roy, Mulroney's close friend and Conservative organizer who all but dropped his solid legal practice for a year prior to the election to beat the bushes in Quebec for candidates. Some of these men and women were intellectually impressive and philosophically progressive. Person for person, the Quebec Conservative caucus could match in talent any provincial group within the national party caucus, a considerable testimonial for so green a group.

Yet at the margin of this inexperienced caucus, a handful of MPs and two ministers still thought politics could be played the old way, and their presumptions and activities got the Conservatives into serious trouble. To this group, the game of politics still revolved around spoils for supporters. The Conservatives could count themselves fortunate that although rumours flew throughout Quebec about kickbacks, *ristournes*, and stern messages to contractors that without political contributions they could forget about further business, no newspaper could ever lay its hands upon a smoking gun.

Roch LaSalle, the last of the old style *patroneux*, never hid his commitment to patronage for securing allegiance and rewarding friends. As a minister in Joe Clark's government, LaSalle said that Conservatives in Quebec "can look forward to being on the receiving end of government work and service contracts," because "patronage is a fact of life at all levels. Obviously, it was a tool that was used by the Liberals during their tenure in office, and I don't intend to pass up our opportunity. As you know, we haven't done very well in attracting Francophone votes, so this way we will at least be able to make some inroads with them."

Although the Conservatives won fifty-eight of seventy-five seats in Quebec, that left seventeen seats in Liberal hands, seventeen seats where local contractors and Conservatives might not know where to turn for advice. So LaSalle instituted a "Godfather" system in certain parts of Quebec, whereby Conservative MPs were assigned Liberal ridings in which to maintain political contacts. There was nothing startling about this development; parties had been covering seats held by Opposition parties for patronage and contract recommendations since John A. Macdonald's day. Michel Gravel, MP for the Montreal riding of Gamelin, took the responsibility for the Liberal riding of Hull where, among other projects, the federal government was funding the massive Museum of Civilization. On May 15, 1986, Gravel was charged with ten counts of bribery or attempted bribery, thirty-two of defrauding the government, and eight of breach of trust. The charges alleged that Mr. Gravel peddled influence "in Montreal, Hull and

Ottawa and elsewhere in Canada between December 1, 1984 and February 1, 1986." Gravel's lawyer, however, had prevented the charges from going further than the arraignment stage, until Quebec's attorney-general, utilising a seldom-invoked procedure, ordered Gravel to stand trial.

The Oerlikon affair, which broke in January, 1986, brought the immediate dismissal of a cabinet minister, André Bissonnette. It involved land flips of property near Saint-Jean-sur-Richelieu selected by the Oerlikon company after it received a $600 million contract to build Canada's low-level air-defence system. In eleven days the property changed hands and soared in value from $800,000 to nearly $3 million. An ashen-faced Mulroney told the press he had demanded Bissonnette's resignation and asked the RCMP to conduct a complete investigation. That investigation produced charges of conspiracy, fraud and breach of trust against Bissonnette and his top political organizer, Normand Ouellette. Bissonnette was found innocent, Ouellette guilty.

There were, too, pinprick stories which, when added together, furthered the impression of a party eager to use the spoils of power for dubious purposes. The assistant to MP Marcel Tremblay sent a "personal and confidential letter" to contractors in his Québec-Est riding informing them that the department of public works gave more than a billion dollars in contracts of which less than $30,000 went without competitive bidding. The letter said Québec-Est should gear up for a share of this money. The letter discussed preparation of a list of suitable companies, suitability being defined, among other criteria, by "subscribers to the 1984 campaign," and "members of the Club Brian Mulroney." Tremblay said the letter had been a mistake and apologized publicly for this "erroneous information."

Pierre Blouin, a Conservative advance–man in the 1984 campaign, pleaded guilty to accepting or demanding $70,000 to use his influence in the awarding of a contract for the renting of space at a Canada Employment and Immigration Commission centre in Drummondville. He was fined $3,000.

More serious by far was the resignation of Michel Coté, a minister from Quebec City whose political star fell further, faster than any other in the Conservative cabinet. The reason for his dismissal was failure to report, as the conflict-of-interest guidelines required, a loan secured from a personal friend. But the whole Coté affair was tinged with sadness, since the break-up of his marriage and failure to handle the pressure of Ottawa placed financial and psychological burdens on Coté. He had become the poodle of some prominent Quebec Conservatives of the old style, and his downfall cast the public eye, however briefly, on a part of the Conservative party in Quebec that knew nothing but the politics of the shadows.

The winning of contracts and the granting of permits had always brought businessmen, lawyers and middlemen to Ottawa eager by fair means or foul to win a slice of government work. In the nineteenth century, when Ottawa was a rough-hewn lumber town masquerading as a capital city, the contractors and lobbyists frequented the same hotels as the politicians, drank in the same bars, and wandered freely through the corridors of the Parliament Buildings searching for the right political shoulder to tap. Until well into the twentieth century, prominent politicians held directorships, collected legal fees or received personal campaign contributions from firms doing business with the government. A variety of embarrassing scandals, conflict-of-interest guidelines, more rigorous tendering procedures and new election-financing legislation had shredded many of the direct links between politicians and contractors, but the sheer volume of government work on offer made the pursuit of influence and information an abiding preoccupation of some corporate concerns.

In the Trudeau years a new breed of firms therefore took root in Ottawa, staffed by men with experience in government and the right political connections who then sold both to companies for handsome fees. The appellation "lobbyist" pained almost everyone to whom it was applied, for the word connoted a series of unsavoury practices they vehemently denied. By the waning Trudeau years, these firms had multiplied in number and expanded in size. The two largest — Executive Consultants Limited and Public Affairs International — took special umbrage with the appellation "lobbyist," since they insisted they supplied only information about government activities without ever seeking directly to influence a government decision on behalf of a client. They provided only advice so that clients could present a more effective case to the government. Or so ran the firms' credo. Staffed by former civil servants and political aides, the firms quickly amassed an impressive list of corporate clients.

The arrival of the Mulroney government sent these firms, heavily stocked with Liberals, hustling to recruit Conservatives. For example, William Neville, former chief of staff to Joe Clark, signed on as president of Public Affairs International, a position he left for personal reasons in 1987. But the most dramatic change occurred with the creation of Government Consultants Incorporated, a high-powered firm established by Mulroney's buddy Frank Moores, former premier of Newfoundland; Gerry Doucet, the brother of a senior Mulroney staffer; and Gary Ouellet, a long-time Mulroney friend from Quebec City. Despite occasional protestations of political innocence, GCI clearly capitalized handsomely on its Conservative connections. Moores, after all, had been among the leading schemers trying to engineer Clark's defeat by Mulroney. One day Moores would tell a columnist at lunch he had no special entrée to the Prime Minister's Office; the next day he would be seen dining with Ian Anderson, the prime minister's deputy principal secretary. He claimed he had no special contacts with the prime minister, but still spent New Year's Eve 1987 at Mulroney's home. He claimed he did not lobby — the word ostensibly pained him — but his firm did precisely that for a variety of corporate clients, even on one occasion charging money to set up a meeting with a minister. His firm threw a big party for Deputy Prime Minister Don Mazankowski upon his receipt of an honorary degree from the Technical University of Nova Scotia. Moores and his colleagues—and the smaller firms established by former Conservatives aides such as Harry Near and William Fox—epitomized this new style of influence in Mulroney's Ottawa: pervasive, expensive and clearly based on the right political credentials. The test of that assertion was a simple one. Would these men have plied their trade with such success had a Liberal or NDP government been in office? The answer could only be a resounding no.

The ethics of these politico-corporate operators sparked periodic debates in Ottawa and the media, especially since some of them had jumped directly from government or political service into lobbying. And the ethical principles of Moores himself became the subject of debate when it was revealed that he had accepted a patronage position on the board of Air Canada, although his firm represented two of Air Canada's competitors: Wardair and Nordair. A row in Parliament and prominent newspaper stories forced Moores to resign his Air Canada directorship.

The swirl of Mulroney's friends trying to peddle their political connections around Ottawa gave rise to the charge of "cronyism" around the prime minister. This charge bore some weight, but not too much. Certainly, almost every friend and political associate of Mulroney got his reward within the first eighteen months of the government. But that sort of behaviour was hardly new in Canadian affairs, since those who had served Macdonald, Laurier, King and other prime ministers had invariably received their rewards. To have served Pierre Trudeau was a ticket to an appointment, if one were so desired. What gave the charge its heft was not that the prime minister surrounded himself with some friends and rewarded others, but that many of these people lacked the talents and judgment their positions demanded. Within a year, it became abundantly clear that many of those who had assisted Mulroney in winning the Conservative leadership were political liabilities, whereas those who had supported Joe Clark — the

Establishment of the Conservative party — held the government together. Only when Mulroney rid himself of his friends and brought experienced and talented people to his side did the fortunes of his government improve.

The lobbyists thus joined the pollsters and admen, long since arrived in federal politics, to form the new triumvirate of clients at the top of the political patronage system, with the important twist that the pollsters and admen got their patronage directly while the lobbyists received theirs indirectly through retainers and percentages from clients. Predictably enough, the Conservatives moved quickly to give the government's advertising business to friendly firms, although not as quickly as they might have liked. The Liberals, who since the days of Mackenzie King had considered advertising a tidy reward for their own friends in the business, had left few hostages to fortune. Sensing the *fin du regime*, the Trudeau cabinet gave $26.4 million worth of advertising contracts to friendly firms during its last eight months in power. The Conservatives immediately fired the three Liberal admen in the Supply and Services department, put there by a special Treasury Board ruling that waived the normal practices for public–sector hiring, and installed two of their own. From there, the entire panoply of advertising patronage opened out to Conservative firms whenever contracts became available.

First to go, predictably enough, was the tourism account. It went to Camp Advertising, whose president happened to be Norman Atkins, Conservative campaign chairman. Another early winner turned out to be Lawson Murray Ltd. for placing advertisements for government bonds. The bonds program, of course, is the responsibility of the Finance department, and the Opposition immediately cried personal favouritism when they discovered that Lawson Murray's principal was none other than Finance Minister Michael Wilson's brother-in-law. But then, family ties did seem to carry weight with Conservative ministers. Joe Clark's brother-in-law was named legal counsel for all federal government work associated with the Calgary Olympics.

These sorts of patronage earned the prerequisite howls from the Opposition and headlines in the media. Although each incident was quickly forgotten, the cumulative impression of rampant favouritism stuck like a barnacle to the Mulroney government. Then the Sinclair Stevens affair attracted intermittent headlines from May, 1986 to February, 1987, and made another splash when a judicial inquiry under Judge William Parker found that Stevens had been in repeated conflicts of interest as a senior member of the Mulroney cabinet.

Sinclair Stevens was an odd duck in the Conservative party and, as such, considerably misunderstood. He acquired the nickname "Slasher" in the Clark government for his attempt to reduce the size of the civil service. The media depicted him as a right-winger in the party; in fact, he was nothing more than a pragmatist. Making deals, rather than propounding ideological nostrums, made Stevens happy. He often got angry with bureaucrats, red tape, even ministerial colleagues who questioned the deals he made as Minister of Regional Industrial Expansion. He professed to distrust big government, but he delighted in using government as a spur to economic growth or a partner with private concerns. An MP from an affluent riding north of Toronto, he developed a deep interest in Cape Breton, one of the country's most depressed economic areas.

Stevens, who smiled easily and had about him a certain bonhomie, nevertheless remained a loner in the Conservative party. Although a frontbencher in Clark's government, he was never close to the prime minister, and when the Conservatives lost power in 1980, he quietly joined the anti-Clark group within the party. In 1983, Stevens was the only prominent frontbencher from the Clark government who actively supported Brian Mulroney. He wished to be named finance minister, but his poor reputation on Bay Street—a holdover from his days with the ill-fated Western Bank — destroyed that possibility. He settled instead for what Mulroney offered, and quickly began making deals.

Unfortunately, as the Parker Inquiry report documented in numbing detail, while making deals for the government he also dealt with private interests on behalf of the York Centre group of companies he headed. On fourteen occasions, Judge Parker found, Stevens violated conflict-of-interest guidelines.

In the long sweep of Canadian history, Sinclair Stevens' conflicts of interest might well be considered almost the norm. Until well on into this century, leading politicians routinely carried on their business dealings while cabinet ministers, and the question of conflict of interest came to be asked only when their ministerial decisions clearly produced private advantage. They had to earn their bread elsewhere because politics was a part-time, poorly paid occupation. Prime ministers accepted trust funds, premiers sat on boards of directors, cabinet ministers carried on legal practices, senators openly pressed business interests. But by the 1960s, especially in the wake of the mini-scandals that buffeted the Pearson government, a new attitude took hold: The law of Caesar's wife applied to politicians. Conflict-of-interest guidelines arrived under Pierre Trudeau, but they remained just that: guidelines instructing ministers how to arrange their personal affairs to avoid the reality or appearance of a conflict of interest. A major study under former Liberal cabinet minister Mitchell Sharp and former Conservative minister Michael Starr examined the issue again and recommended a commissioner of ethics to whom ministers could turn for advice. Then

Mulroney introduced a conflict-of-interest code. All of these guidelines, studies and codes stopped short of mandatory full disclosure, on the theory that a balance should be struck between protecting the public interest and the private affairs of ministers.

Judge Parker, however, rejected the balance, recommending instead full disclosure and, if necessary, divestiture of assets. He also fully sanctioned an approach to conflict of interest whereby the potential of an appearance of a conflict of interest sufficed to place a minister in an unacceptable position. It was no longer enough, argued the judge, for conflicts to be real or even apparent; that a situation had the potential for creating real or apparent conflicts would condemn a minister to a conflict of interest. This exceptionally wide approach, which until recently would have been beyond the comprehension of most politicians, received almost universal acclaim in the media, reflecting inadequate analysis and the kind of rigid moralism adopted by those outside politics.

A Gallup poll in October, 1986, with the Stevens affair fresh in the public mind, showed that forty-nine per cent of respondents believed "favouritism and corruption" were increasing in Ottawa, compared with thirteen percent who thought it was in decline. However, previous polls—in 1974 and 1966—had also found many more people who believed favouritism and corruption were rising rather than declining. If these numbers showed anything, it was not so much that the Mulroney government had soured people on the integrity of the political process, but that for several decades confidence in the integrity of politicians, and politics generally, had been on the wane. Although the disappointments of the Mulroney government undoubtedly contributed to this erosion, the sapping of public faith in politicians and their institutions—Parliament and the political parties—had been growing apace for decades. In response to this decline, and to the poor image of his government, Mulroney introduced conflict-of-interest legislation which fortunately stopped short of full disclosure. It envisaged a commission of ethics responsible to Parliament to which members would be forced to report their personal affairs. If necessary, the commission could then decide to make public such affairs as it deemed appropriate.

The decline of commitment to political parties holds profound consequences for all aspects of political life, including the practice of patronage. As government has grown, the influence of parties on the government they purport to run has shrunk. Quasi-judicial or largely independent agencies, over which the cabinet has limited review powers, hold sway in crucial areas of economic activity: communications, transportation, regional development, international trade. A minister in a sprawling department such as Transport must acknowledge, if

honesty counts for anything, that with all his other ministerial responsibilities and the plethora of cabinet committee meetings requiring his
attendance, he can only immerse himself in a handful of departmental
dossiers. Further and further down the bureaucratic hierarchy are
found the pressure points for the special interests and the trade associations or lobbyists who represent them. In the post-Charter of Rights
era, even the courts beckon citizens or groups to press their claims in
the legal rather than the political arena.

The atomization of politics breaks down the coalition-building
functions of parties, because an increasing number of individuals participate through single-interest groups. Parties, by definition, force
compromises upon their members; single-interest groups try to play
for all or nothing. The proliferation of these groups may have increased
democratic participation, but the participation lies outside political
parties. They seek the achievement of their aims by influencing key
bureaucrats, public opinion through the media, the courts through
legal arguments, government tribunals through representations—and
political parties not by joining but by often relentless letter-writing,
personal contacts, confrontational meetings, position papers, conferences and whatever other means they have the wit to devise.

Paradoxically, the parties have unwittingly assisted in their own
decline by offering massive amounts of state funding to all manner of
interest groups, a development that exploded in the early Trudeau years
when "participatory democracy" was much in vogue. The consequence
for natives, women's groups, linguistic minorities—to name just a few
examples — was that members channelled their energies and offered
their allegiance not to the government that funded them, and the parties
vying for control of that government, but to the organizations themselves. Even large corporations, in the era after reforms to the *Elections
Act*, often spent more money on trade associations, the Business Council on National Issues, or lobbying firms than they did on contributing
to the non-socialist political parties. For them political contributions
are a kind of civic duty, whereas the money spent on lobbyists and the
like can directly reward self-interest.

In such circumstances, the old political patronage of material or
honorific rewards seemed an increasingly feeble inducement to participation. Patronage worked best as a mobilizer when governing was
largely about accommodating elites, brokering interests, winning the
loyalty of key players who held sway over large number of followers.
But as elite accommodation faltered in face of the pursuit of self-interest
through single-issue groups, the massive, intermittent but utterly vicarious participation of television viewers, and the burgeoning bureaucratization of government, the mobilizing capabilities of patronage

diminished. Even worse, patronage came to be viewed as a vestigial remnant of a political culture that only some of the political actors themselves seemed to think still existed.

The gap between demand for place and supply of positions, a gap that had tormented every Canadian political leader and driven a few of them to rage and despair, remained, and a new gap opened. The political elites insisted on using patronage for themselves. The rest of the population, finding they could no longer dream of receiving any material benefit or preferential treatment through the exercise of political discretion, were attracted by other inducements for political participation. This new gap so terrified politicians that none of them dared explain that political patronage, sensibly and moderately used, could still be justified. None of them dared argue that the very explosion of government made political control more problematic, and that therefore men and women who shared the broad philosophy and specific goals of the winning party might help further the democratically expressed desire for new approaches. Nor would they dare say that patronage often advanced the cause of minorities more rapidly than any other political tool, that an appointment could more quickly offer opportunities for participation in public life than the vagaries of electoral politics, and that an abiding purpose of national parties in such a diverse country lay in their integrative function, a function assisted by patronage. Nor would they dare insist that the satisfaction of a reward held the feet of some men and women to the political fire, and by so doing sustained their commitment to the public life of their country.

In Opposition no politicians would dare do anything but feed the public outrage about patronage, an outrage which they would then confront themselves if given a chance to govern. Instead, modern-day politicians treated patronage as a matter of raw justice and even retribution. They refused in Opposition to explain honestly how they proposed to handle patronage; in government they therefore could not compellingly defend what they had previously lambasted. So patronage remained, like pornography, a subject closed to rational discourse, obscured by perfervid rhetoric, clouded by an enveloping hypocrisy, the peep show of politics.

The decline of patronage in the face of urbanization, modernization, better education, television, an aroused public opinion, among other factors, left parties in a terrible predicament. Many of their supporters continued to demand it, but the more politicians acceded to these demands, the more they risked alienating an unsympathetic public. If they curtailed patronage, then they would have to search for other means of securing participation and mobilizing commitment and these means proved elusive. It was easy to decry patronage and certainly possible to limit it. But what would take its place, and prove as effective as patronage had once been in cementing loyalties and encouraging participation? The answer seemed to be, as Mulroney belatedly discovered, participation driven by an intellectual or emotional commitment to a set of vigorously-pursued, clearly-articulated policies. Indeed, his experience and that of Trudeau in the current transitional stage of Canadian politics seemed to suggest that the "psychic patronage" of ideas had replaced material or honorific patronage as the great mobilizer of public participation.

Similarly, the time-honoured practices of political porkbarrelling seemed to be paying fewer political dividends. With the explosion in government activity, battles for private needs got carried into the political arena, and with the arrival of persistent deficit financing came a massive increase in the political temptation to spend vast sums of public money. This temptation had always been central to the Canadian political experience. The promise of a railway branch line, the construction of a new canal or bridge, the paving of a road, the opening of a post office — these were the stuff of local political debates in Canada, and few politicians ignored the political possibilities of such promises or projects. In the modern era all that changed was the scale and scope of government spending, but the change represented a quantum leap from what had gone on before. Although programs carried the prerequisite regulations and bureaucratic norms, by either adjusting these norms or simply overriding them with an act of political discretion, politicians could try to turn these programs to their political advantage. In this, the Mulroney government differed not a whit from its Liberal predecessors.

The tip-off that nothing had changed came early. Six months after the election, Domtar threatened to close its mill at Windsor, Quebec, unless it received money from Ottawa to finance a modernization. Domtar, whose biggest shareholders were agencies of the Quebec government, was turning a profit, yet it threatened seven hundred jobs. Sinclair Stevens, then minister for Regional Industrial Expansion, looked at Domtar's balance sheet, heard complaints from other pulp and paper producers, and correctly said no. But the political pressure from Quebec intensified, for a succession of Liberal governments had not accustomed the province to hearing no. So the prime minister got involved in the dossier, rejected Domtar's grab for a federal grant, and settled instead for an interest-free loan.

The Domtar decision signalled that political pressure — not economic reasoning — would sway this supposedly market-oriented government. Thereafter, the government littered the landscape with government assistance packages to industries and individual firms that had succeeded in generating the prerequisite political heat. An initial $1-billion payment to grain farmers was followed by another dollop the next year; there was assistance for Cominco's modernization of a smelter at Trail. Re-opening the old Cyprus Anvil Mine in the Yukon; keeping Sysco afloat in Sydney; handing the oil patch $350 million; helping Algoma Steel at Sault Ste. Marie; offering money to General Motors, the world's largest corporation, for its plant at Ste. Thérèse, Quebec — each of these decisions and many others like them served merely to tighten the political squeeze on the Mulroney government. Assistance to one region immediately set off a chain reaction from other regions for similar treatment, a reaction made more insistent by the uneven pattern of economic growth across the country.

The awarding of the CF-18 maintenance contract provided a classic illustration of the inflationary consequences of political bribery. A panel of seventy-five government experts analysed bids from a Halifax consortium, Bristol Aerospace of Winnipeg, and Canadair of Montreal. They soon dismissed the Halifax bid as technically inadequate, but after an exhaustive analysis awarded Bristol 926 out of a possible 1,000 points for technical merit, compared with only 843 for Canadair. They also found that for the core element of the contract — "systems engineering" — Bristol's bid was thirteen percent lower, and three percent lower over all in the first three and a half years of the contract. Despite the experts' clear verdict, the prime minister and other Quebec ministers steered the contract to Canadair, devising a rationale about technology transfer to camouflage a purely political decision. Manitoba, having been defeated by Quebec's superior clout, then received the consolation prizes of the maintenance contract for the older CF-5 aircraft and a Health Sciences project proudly announced by Manitoba's senior minister, Jake Epp.

The policy of assisting first this company or region, then another, seldom brings a discernible political benefit and often lands the government in the unwinnable game of meeting exaggerated expectations everywhere. The game continues, however, because refusal to act may produce penalties even though the decision to act does not automatically bring advantages. A fear of what may happen if discretion is not exercised, rather than the certainty of benefit if discretion is applied, drags politicians into the vortex of exaggerated expectations. In the CF-18 case, no immediate political gratitude greeted the decision in Montreal; outrage, however, persisted in Winnipeg.

By the early months of 1987, the Mulroney government had been rocked by so many allegations, ministerial resignations, screaming headlines about political patronage and other damaging assaults that its popularity had sunk to depths that made recovery seem improbable, if not impossible. When Mulroney entered 24 Sussex Drive, he spoke enviously of what he called U.S. President Ronald Reagan's "comfort zone" with the American people: the broad acceptance of the president's values and the widespread approval of his personality that encouraged Americans to forgive policy mistakes or presidential blunders. Americans liked their president, even though they did not always agree with him. Mulroney's search to establish his own "comfort zone" with the Canadian people produced completely the opposite result. Many Canadians felt uncomfortable with his values, distrusted his integrity, remained confused about where he wished to lead the country, so that every error, allegation and damaging incident stuck to him. Instead of creating a "comfort zone" with the Canadian people, Mulroney became the flypaper Prime Minister.

And yet, very slowly and quite painfully, Mulroney was learning about the changed political culture with its reduced tolerance for political favouritism and its intense focus on the attitudes and values of the political leader. The classic network politician, the man who loved to spend hours on the telephone rapping with friends or simply touching base with those whom he thought might be helpful, increasingly understood that brokerage politics in the modern age was more difficult than he had imagined. He began a searching re-examination of what had gone wrong, and began listening to those who recommend remedial action. He completely overhauled the personnel in his office, and the new advisers were seasoned professionals: Dalton Camp and Marjory LeBreton from the Conservative party, Derek Burney from External Affairs. A weekly tactics meeting chaired by Deputy Prime Minister Don Mazankowski improved the government's performance in the Commons. Mulroney began distancing himself from secondary issues, concentrating instead on major dossiers brought to a successful conclusion: the Meech Lake constitutional accord and a trade agreement with the United States. He curbed his blarney, as best he could.

Still plagued by the allegations of favouritism and patronage, the government launched a multi-faceted series of reforms. It perservered with an earlier change allowing Commons committees the right to hear testimony from order-in-council appointments. It sent a white paper on lobbying to a parliamentary committee, which recommended the registration of lobbyists. It responded to the Parker Inquiry with an ethics-in-government package that tried yet again to define how ministers should avoid conflicts of interest. As part of the Meech Lake accord, Mulroney yielded up most of the prime minister's historic powers of appointing senators. And the party wound up the provincial advisory committees, and so bade farewell to another in a long series of efforts winding through the political history of Canada to balance the conflicting demands of political patrons and clients.

The PACs had been central to the Conservatives' attempts to involve the extra-parliamentary party in patronage. They had created a series of mini-patrons, the PAC chairmen, beholden to the prime minister, the ultimate political patron, but possessed of considerable powers themselves to act as mini-patrons. The PACs had never been popular with MPs who resented extra-parliamentary interference in what they considered the prerogatives of elected officials. Too many grassroots Conservatives disliked the closed appearance of the PACs which seemed to be recommending appointments largely for friends of the members. Ministers found the PACs cumbersome and sometimes inadequate in recruiting the most suitable candidates. The prime minister and his new senior staff, aware of the damage that the government's use of patronage had done to the Conservative cause and the Mulroney image, believed the PACs persisted in recommending Conservatives for a partisanship unblemished by special qualifications. In December, 1987, cabinet decided to abolish the PACs; on February 1, 1988, a majority of the PAC chairmen learned in a telephone call from LeBreton that the responsibilities they had been secretly given during the election campaign of 1984 were ended.

The wheel of politics brought the Conservatives full circle. They replaced the PACs with a system almost identical to the Trudeau system: A political minister, the caucus chairman, and the campaign director would recommend the patronage in each province. John A. Macdonald, who ran the patronage himself and through senior ministers, would have smiled.

The new system pleased the parliamentary party. Whether it would produce better-qualified candidates, and whether it could contribute to using patronage is a less politically injurious way remained open questions. Indeed, after four years of Mulroney, the future of political patronage in Canada remained uncertain. That patronage could never be abolished—indeed, should not be abolished—seemed clear, since the exercise of political discretion would always be central to democratic politics. The question remained, however, how governments would use the tool of patronage.

Provincial governments provided, roughly speaking, three models, at least for the patronage of appointments. In the western provinces, the political fight had evolved into a struggle between social democrats and free-enterprisers. Each change in government brought considerable shifts in personnel justified by the need to staff departments, boards, agencies and commissions with those philosophically, even ideologically, attuned to the government of the day. In Ontario and Quebec, a more managerial politics prevailed; new governments moved cautiously, albeit methodically, to reward supporters and left the civil service largely intact. In Atlantic Canada, the old-style politics of patronage was slowly dying, but with economic dependence still a regrettable fact of life, the scope and demand for patronage remained greater there than anywhere else in Canada.

As Mulroney himself admitted several times, his government would pay for having misled the public in the 1984 campaign and having misread the changed political tolerance towards patronage in Canada. How much the government had paid could only be sorted out by pollsters and academic specialists who picked over the voters' reasons for judgment. In a historical sense, it was perhaps fitting that political patronage, which drove nineteenth-century reformers into demanding responsible government and helped to glue Canada's nation-wide parties together after Confederation, should even in the latter part of the twentieth century still be enticing and tormenting the practitioners of Canadian politics. The centrality of patronage in Canadian political life had disappeared, but the practice of patronage remained, challenging all those charged with exercising political discretion and currying democratic support to practise craftily and judiciously this most demanding of the political arts.

NOTES

INTRODUCTION

1. Richard Simeon and David Elkins, "Regional political cultures," *Canadian Journal of Political Science* (CJPS), vii (1974), p. 3.

2. See Donald Carty, "Three Canadian party systems: An interpretation of the development of national parties," in George Perlin (ed.), *Party Democracy in Canada* (Toronto, 1987); and David Smith, "Party government, representation and national integration in Canada," in Peter Aucoin (ed.), *Party Government and Regional Representation* (Toronto, 1985).

3. For example, "Patronage is the process by which governments award employment or contracts on the basis of partisan support rather than on merit." Definition by Kenneth Gibbons, "The Study of Political Corruption," in Gibbons and Donald Rowat (eds.), *Political Corruption in Canada* (Toronto, 1976), p. 9.

4. James Q. Wilson, the distinguished American political scientist, uses this definition: "Patronage is customarily used to refer to all forms of material benefits which politicians may distribute to party workers and supporters," in "The Economy of Patronage," *The Journal of Political Economy*, 69, August, 1961, footnote p. 370.

5. S.J.R. Noel, a leading Canadian student of patronage, defines the practice as "bestowal of material rewards or advantages, security, or access to opportunities on the part of the patron, in return for his client's reciprocal bestowal of loyalty or service, not abstractly but in some specific context where these constitute exchangeable goods, or in politics, where they take the form of political support — voting, persuading, campaigning, organizing for the patron or the patron's client," in "Leadership and Clientelism," in David Bellamy et al., (eds.), *The Provincial Political System* (Toronto, 1976), p. 197. Frank Sorauf, a leading American scholar, also opts for a broad definition: "appointive positions in government awarded either for past political services or in expectation of future work" but also other rewards "which one may call preferments . . . which are grants of extraordinary treatment by government," in *Political Parties in the American System* (Boston, 1964), pp. 82–83. Sorauf's insights into the diminishing importance of patronage are also found in "The Silent

Revolution in Patronage," *Public Administration Review*, 20, 1960, no. 1, pp. 28–34, and "Patronage and Party," *Midwest Journal of Political Science*, 3, 1959, no. 2, pp. 115–126.

6. For a full discussion of controverted elections, bribery and procedures for dealing with electoral fraud, see Norman Ward, "Electoral Corruption and Controverted Elections," *Canadian Journal of Economics and Political Science (CJEPS)*, 15, 1949, 1, pp. 74–86.

7. See Carl Friedrich, *The Pathology of Politics* (New York, 1972), p. 128. Friedrich writes, "The pattern of corruption may therefore be said to exist whenever a power-holder who is charged with doing certain things, that is a responsible functionary or office-holder, is by monetary or other rewards, such as the expectation of a job in the future, induced to take actions which favour whoever provides the reward and thereby damages the group or organization to which the functionary belongs, more specifically the government."

8. James C. Scott, "Corruption, Machine Politics and Political Change," *American Political Science Review*, 63, 1969, 73, p. 1144. Scott writes: "Given its principal concern for retaining office, the machine was a responsive, informal context within which bargaining based on reciprocity relationships was facilitated."

9. Some writers do insist, however, that corruption necessarily involves the breaking of laws. See Michael Johnston, *Political Corruption and Public Policy in America* (Monterey, 1982), p. 8. "Corruption," he writes, "*is abuse of a public role for private benefit in such a way as to break the law* (or formal administrative regulations, which I will call 'laws' for brevity's sake). Italics his.

10. Scott, op. cit., p. 1146. Also S.J.R. Noel, op. cit.

11. Samuel Huntington, "Modernization and Corruption," in Arnold Heidenheimer, (ed.) *Political Corruption* (New York, 1970), pp. 499–500.

12. Martin and Susan Tolchin, *To the Victor . . . .* (New York, 1971), p. 320.

13. An impressive body of literature, theoretical and descriptive, exists on the nature of patron-client relationships. The most useful is by Canada's leading student of patronage, Vincent Lemieux, *Le Patronage Politique* (Quebec, 1977). Others include, Vincent Lemieux and Raymond Hudon, *Patronage et Politique au Québec, 1945–1972* (Boréal, 1975), especially ch. 2; S.E. Eisenstadt and René Lemarchand (eds.), *Political Clientelism, Patronage and Development* (Sage Publications, 1981), especially Lemarchand's essay "Comparative Political Clientelism," and Mario Caciaglo and Frank Belloni, "The 'New' Clientelism in Southern Italy: The Christian Democratic Party in Calabria"; various essays in Arnold Heidenheimer (ed.), op. cit.; and Robert Paine, "A Theory of Patronage and Brokerage," in Robert Paine (ed.), *Patrons and Brokers in the East Arctic* (St. John's, 1971).

14. R. MacGregor Dawson defines porkbarrelling as "a kind of patronage and bribery offered to a community in hope of winning support, an appeal to what President Cleveland called 'the cohesive power of public plunder'." *The Government of Canada*, 4th edition (Toronto, 1963), p. 517.

15. The categories are Johnston's, op. cit., pp. 12–16. He is writing only about corruption.

16. The inflationary consequences of patronage are described in Caciagli and Belloni, op. cit., pp. 36–42.

17. Walter Lippmann, "A Theory About Corruption," in Heidenheimer, op. cit., p. 295.

CHAPTER 2   RESPONSIBLE GOVT.

1. Lewis Namier, *The Structure of Politics at the Accession of George III* (London, 1929) and *England in the Age of the American Revolution* (London, 1930);

J.H. Plumb, *The Growth of Political Stability in England, 1675–1725* (London, 1967); Gordon Stewart, *The Origins of Canadian Politics* (Vancouver, 1986), pp. 9–20; Samuel Finer, "Patronage and the Public Service: Jeffersonian Bureaucracy and the British Tradition," in Arnold Heidenheimer, op. cit. (1970), pp. 106–129.

    2. Hilda Blair Neatby, *Quebec, The Revolutionary Age, 1760–1791* (Toronto, 1966).

    3. Fernand Ouellet, *Lower Canada, 1791–1840, Social Change and Nationalism* (Toronto, 1980), p. 40. Gilles Paquet and Jean-Pierre Wallot write in *Patronage et Pouvoir Dans Le Bas-Canada, 1794–1812* (Quebec, 1973), p. 38: "L'ancienne élite seigneuriale canadienne . . . quémande sans cesse des places, avec un étalage indiscret de flatteries, de malheurs domestiques, parfois de délation afin de se gagner les faveurs du pouvoir."

    4. Paquet and Wallot, op. cit., p. 44.

    5. Ibid., p. 42, footnote 20. Between 1792 and 1812, for example, half the surveyors were English-speakers, English-speakers got nineteen of twenty-one places in the department of Indian affairs, established in 1796. By 1804, English-speakers outnumbered French-speakers among justices of the peace, customs officers and government commissioners.

    6. Stewart, op. cit., p. 28.

    7. Paquet and Wallot, op. cit., p. 191.

    8. Ibid., p. 123.

    9. Ouellet, op. cit., 109.

    10. Ibid., p. 213.

    11. For a full and lively description of the uses, abuses and origins of the term, see Graeme Patterson, "The myths of Responsible Government and the Family Compact" in *Journal of Canadian Studies*, vol. 12, no. 2, 1977, pp. 3–16.

    12. Gerald Craig, *Upper Canada, the Formative Years, 1784–1841* (Toronto, 1963), p. 265.

    13. Aileen Dunham, *Political Unrest in Upper Canada, 1815–1836* (Toronto, 1963), pp. 36–37.

    14. Ibid., p. 40.

    15. Craig, op. cit., p. 223. Also William Kilbourn, *Firebrand* (Toronto, 1964).

    16. Ouellet, op. cit., pp. 223–224.

    17. Gerald Craig (ed.), *Lord Durham's Report* (Toronto, 1963), p. 142. Subsequent quotations, pp. 79–80 and 54–55.

    18. Wayne MacKinnon, *The Life of the Party, A History of the Liberal Party in Prince Edward Island* (Summerside, 1973), p. 7.

    19. Frank MacKinnon, *The Government of Prince Edward Island* (Toronto, 1951), pp. 30–31.

    20. Frank MacKinnon, "Prince Edward Island" in Martin Robin (ed.), *Canadian Provincial Politics* (Toronto, 1972), p. 241.

    21. Frank MacKinnon, *The Government of Prince Edward Island*, op. cit., pp. 83–85.

    22. Margaret Ells, "Governor Wentworth's patronage," in G.A. Rawlyk (ed.), *Historical Essays on the Atlantic Provinces* (Toronto, 1967), 69.

    23. Ells, op. cit., p. 71.

    24. J. Murray Beck, *Joseph Howe, Conservative Reformer* (McGill-Queens, 1982), vol. 2, p. 37. See also pp. 38–39.

    25. Ibid., p. 92.

    26. Ibid., p. 26.

    27. Howe's first letter to Lord John Russell, as quoted in Rawlyk, *Historical Essays*, op. cit., p. 55.

    28. Ibid., p. 61.

29. J. Murray Beck, *The Government of Nova Scotia*, op. cit., p. 95.

30. Ibid., p. 98.

31. Ibid., p. 111.

32. For more detail on the timber trade, see W.S. MacNutt, "The Politics of the timber trade in colonial New Brunswick, 1825–1840," *Canadian Historical Review*, vol. 30, 1949, pp. 47–65.

33. MacNutt, a giant among Canadian historians both for his prodigious research and a rare felicity of phrase, has amply documented the assembly's practices, briefly sketched in this section. See his *New Brunswick, A History: 1784–1867*. (Toronto, 1976), pp. 104–105, 226–227, 257–258, 274–276, 291. See also his "The coming of responsible government to New Brunswick," *Canadian Historical Review*, vol. 33, no. 2, 1952, pp. 111–128, and *The Atlantic Provinces* (Toronto, 1965), pp. 193, 196–198, 261.

34. MacNutt, "New Brunswick's age of harmony: the administration of Sir John Harvey," *Canadian Historical Review*, vol. XXXII, no. 2, 1951, p. 111.

35. MacNutt, *A History*, op. cit., p. 340. For an analysis of Head's career, see D.G.G. Kerr, *Sir Edmund Head, a Scholarly Governor* (Toronto, 1954).

36. MacNutt, ibid., p. 385.

37. J.M.S. Careless, *The Union of the Canadas, 1841–1857* (Toronto, 1967), p. 76.

38. Carol Wilton-Siegel, "The transformation of Upper Canadian politics in the 1840s," unpublished Phd. dissertation, University of Toronto, 1984, p. 275. Some of the analysis in the text relating to the patronage assumptions and practices of the Upper Canadian reformers is drawn from this excellent thesis.

39. Careless, op. cit., p. 45.

40. Stewart, op. cit., p. 52; Careless, op. cit., p. 41.

41. Careless, op. cit., p. 44.

42. John Garner, *The Franchise and Politics in British North America, 1755–1867* (Toronto, 1969), p. 197.

43. Ibid., p. 202.

44. Ibid., p. 206.

45. Stewart, op. cit., p. 48.

46. The events of this crisis have been extensively analysed in the following works: Careless, op. cit.; Stewart, op. cit.; W.G. Ormsby, *The Emergence of the Federal Concept in Canada, 1839–1845* (Toronto, 1969); J.C. Dent's still-enjoyable *The Last Forty Years: Canada Since the Union of 1841*, vol. 1 (Toronto, 1881); G.E. Wilson, *The Life of Robert Baldwin* (Toronto, 1933); Wilton-Siegel, op. cit.; and (in magnificent and insightful prose) Jacques Monet, *The Last Cannon Shot* (Toronto, 1969).

47. Monet, op. cit., p. 116.

48. Careless, op. cit., p. 83.

49. Ibid., p. 101.

50. Ibid., p. 116.

51. Ibid., p. 119.

52. Monet, op. cit., p. 279.

CHAPTER 3   SIR JOHN A. MACDONALD

1. J.K. Johnson, "John A. Macdonald," in J.M.S. Careless (ed.), *The Pre-Confederation Premiers; Ontario Government Leaders, 1841–1867* (Toronto, 1980), p. 201.

2. George Stevenson to Macdonald, Macdonald papers, Public Archives of Canada (PAC), vol. 339.

3. This aspect of Macdonald's life was given comparatively short shift in Donald Creighton's magisterial and adoring two-volume biography of Macdonald, *The Young Politician* and *The Old Chieftain* (Toronto, 1965). Much of the detail about Macdonald's business career comes from J.K. Johnson, "John A. Macdonald, the young non-politician," *Canadian Historical Association Papers*, 1971, and the same author's "John A. Macdonald and the Kingston Business Community," in Gerald Tulchinsky (ed.) '*To Preserve and Defend, Essays on Kingston in the Nineteenth Century*' (Montreal, 1976) . . . See also Johnson's article in Careless, *The Pre-Confederation Premiers*, op. cit., pp. 200–206.

4. Michael Bliss, *Northern Enterprise: Five Centuries of Canadian Business* (Toronto, 1987), p. 187.

5. Sir Joseph Pope, *Memoirs of the Right Honorable John Alexander Macdonald*, vol. 1 (Ottawa, 1894), p. 303.

6. Ibid., vol. 2, p. 69.

7. This point is excellently developed by Gordon Stewart, "John A. Macdonald's greatest triumph," *Canadian Historical Review* (CHR), vol. 63, 1982, pp. 3–33.

8. J.K. Johnson, *The Letters of Sir John A. Macdonald*, vol. 2, PAC, 1969, p. 75.

9. Ibid., p. 303.

10. C.W. deKiewiet and F.H. Underhill (eds.), *Dufferin-Carnarvon Correspondence, 1874–1878*, Toronto, The Champlain Society, 1955, p. 7.

11. J. Murray Beck, "The Party System in Nova Scotia," *CHR*, vol. 20, 1954, p. 516.

12. J. Murray Beck, *Joseph Howe, Conservative Reformer*, vol. 2 (McGill-Queen's, 1982), p. 172.

13. Ibid., p. 245.

14. Ibid., p. 245.

15. Ibid., p. 256.

16. E.B. Biggar, *An Anecdotal Life of Sir John Macdonald* (Toronto, 1891), p. 197.

17. Pope, op. cit., vol. 2, p. 3.

18. Ibid., p. 12.

19. Quoted in J.K. Johnson's article in J.M.S. Careless (ed.) *Pre-Confederation*, op. cit., p. 215.

20. Edward Clarke to Macdonald, Macdonald papers, PAC, vol. 331, part I.

21. Norman Ward, "Responsible Government: An Introduction," *Journal of Canadian Studies* (JCS), vol. 14, 1979, p. 3.

22. House of Commons Debates, May 14, 1868, p. 700.

23. Sandra Gwyn, *The Private Capital* (Toronto, 1984) p. 91.

24. Richard Cartwright, *Reminiscences* (Toronto, 1912), p. 129.

25. Commission to Inquire into the Present State and Probable Requirements of the Civil Service (1868–1870); Report of Select Committee appointed to inquire into the Present Condition of the Civil Service, 1877, appendix to *Journals*, vol. 2; First Report of the Civil Service Commission, sessional papers, no. 113, 1881; Report of Royal Commission into Civil Service of Canada, sessional papers, vol. 25, 1892.

26. Ari Hoogenboom, *Outlawing the Spoils, A History of the Civil Service Reform Movement, 1865–1883* (Urbana, 1961).

27. The following account is based on the summary of the judge's decision in *Reports of Election Cases, 1874* (Toronto: Carswell and Co.). See also Thomas Brady, "Sinners and Publicans: Sir John A. Macdonald's Trial under the Controverted Elections Act, 1874" in *Ontario History*, vol. 76, March 1984, pp. 65–87.

28. James Eadie, "The federal election in Lennox riding and its aftermath: a glimpse of Victorian political morality," *Ontario History*, vol. 66, no. 4, December 1984, p. 369.

29. Norman Ward, "Electoral corruption and controverted elections," *Canadian Journal of Economics and Political Science (CJEPS)*, vol. 15, 1949, p. 77.

30. Ibid., p. 80.

31. For more details than are here provided, see James Eadie, op. cit., pp. 354–372.

32. Ibid., p. 366.

33. See Gordon Stewart, "Macdonald's greatest triumph," *CHR*, vol. 63, 1982, pp. 3–33.

34. Ben Forster, Malcolm Davidson and R. Craig Brown, "The franchise, personators, and dead men: an inquiry into the voters' lists and the election of 1891," *CHR*, vol. 62, 1986, p. 20. See also Norman Ward, *The Canadian House of Commons* (Toronto, 1950).

35. Forster et al., op. cit., p. 31.

36. Robert Hill, "A note on newspaper patronage in Canada during the late 1850s and early 1860s," *CHR*, vol. 69, March 1968, p. 44.

37. Figures taken from an excellent survey by Brian Beavan, "Partisanship, Patronage, and the Press in Ontario, 1880–1914: Myths and Realities," *CHR*, vol. 64, no. 3, 1983, p. 322.

38. See Gwyn, op. cit., pp. 389–430 for a wonderful description of the Ottawa years of O.M. Hammond, the young parliamentary correspondent for the Liberal organ *The Globe*.

39. Norman Ward, "The press and the patronage: an exploratory operation," in *The Political Process in Canada, Essays in Honour of R. MacGregor Dawson* (Toronto, 1963), p. 9.

40. F.G. Neelin to Macdonald, Macdonald papers, PAC, vol. 434.

41. W. Carey to Macdonald, Macdonald papers, PAC, vol. 388.

42. Lewis Shannon to Macdonald, Macdonald papers, PAC, vol. 455.

43. William Marsh, *Red Line: The Chronicle-Herald and The Mail Star, 1875–1954* (Halifax, 1986), Appendix I, p. 393.

44. Norman Ward, op. cit., p. 9. In 1883-84, for example, *The Mail* received $3,623 in government advertising, compared to $56 for *The Globe*.

45. For a description of this interconnectedness, see Michael Bliss, *A Living Profit: Studies in the Social History of Canadian Business, 1884–1911* (Toronto, 1974), and the early chapters of *Northern Enterprise*, op. cit.

46. The details of the scandal of the Parliament Buildings are recounted in J.E. Hodgetts, *Pioneer Public Service, An Administrative History of the United Canadas, 1841–1867* (Toronto, 1955), pp. 198–200; and in Douglas Owram, *Building for Canadians: A History of the Department of Public Works, 1840–1940* (Ottawa, 1979), pp. 82–87.

47. For information on Langevin's career and his demise, see Barbara Fraser, "The Political Career of Sir Hector Louis Langevin," *CHR*, vol. 62, no. 2, June 1961, pp. 93–132. See also Owram, op. cit., pp. 158–163.

48. Quoted in Owram, op. cit., p. 159.

49. Tarte's mercurial career is dissected in Laurier Lapierre "The political career of Joseph Israel Tarte"; Ph. D. thesis, University of Toronto, 1962. Tarte's role in breaking the scandal is summarized in Lapierre's "Joseph Israel Tarte and the McGreevy-Langevin scandal" *Canadian Historical Association Report*, (1961), pp. 47–57.

50. Fraser, op. cit., p. 129.

51. P. Baskerville, "J.C. Rykert and the Conservative Party, 1882–92: Study of a Scandal," *CHR*, vol. 52, no. 2, June 1971, pp. 144–164. When Rykert was finally manoeuvred out of his seat, Macdonald found a Conservative candidate with railway interests and told him: "I think it would be in your interest as connected with railway interests to have a seat in Parliament." Baskerville writes: "Macdonald's attitude could not be clearer: Rykert had been punished, not because he indulged, but because he was caught."

52. *Report of Royal Commission in reference to certain charges made against Hon. Sir A.P. Caron*, Queen's Printer, 1893.

53. Lowell Clark, "The Conservative Party in the 1890s," *CHA* Papers, 1961.

54. The story of the Pacific Scandal has been recounted by, among others Donald Creighton in *The Old Chieftain*, op. cit., ch. 4, pp. 129–180, and Pierre Berton, who has told the story popularly and well in *The National Dream* (Toronto, 1970), pp. 76–90. See also Sir Joseph Pope, op. cit., ch. 23.

55. Pope, ibid., p. 184.

56. Ibid., p. 187.

57. P.B. Waite in *Hamelin*, The Political Ideas of the Prime Minister of Canada (Ottawa, 1969), p. 58.

58. Quoted in Frank Underhill, "National political parties in Canada, *CHR*, vol. 16, 1935, p. 382. Op. cit., p. 381.

59. Ibid., p. 380–381.

60. The phrase, "*la noblesse professionelle*" belongs to J.C. Faraldeau, cited in Stewart, "Political patronage under Macdonald and Laurier, 1878–1911," *The American Review of Canadian Studies*, vol. 10, no. 1, spring, 1980, p. 17.

61. Cartwright, op. cit., pp. 48, 305.

62. Gordon Stewart, "Political patronage . . . ," op. cit., p. 69.

63. Goldwin Smith in *The Week*, April 10, 1884, quoted in Frank Underhill, "National political parties in Canada," op. cit., p. 382.

CHAPTER 4   LAURIER

1. These and subsequent quotations are taken from André Siegfried, *The Race Question in Canada* (London, 1907), pp. 142–143, 173.

2. Norman Ward, *The Public Purse: A Study in Canadian Democracy* (Toronto, 1962), pp. 103–104.

3. Hilda Blair Neatby, *Laurier and a Liberal Quebec* (Toronto, 1973).

4. O.D. Skelton, *Life and Letters of Sir Wilfrid Laurier*, vol. 2 (Toronto, 1921), p. 270.

5. Sir John Willison, *Sir Wilfrid Laurier* (Toronto, 1926), p. 468.

6. Quoted in Frank Underhill, "The development of national political parties in Canada," *CHR*, vol. 16, no. 4, 1935, p. 384.

7. Ibid., p. 383.

8. Quoted in T.A. Burke, "Mackenzie and His Cabinet, 1873–1878," *CHR*, vol. 41, June 1960, p. 128.

9. P.B. Waite, *Arduous Destiny* (Toronto, 1971), p. 19. Waite notes that Leonard Tilley's appointment as lieutenant-governor of New Brunswick Mackenzie found impossible to cancel.

10. Quoted in William Buckingham and George Ross, *The Honourable Alexander Mackenzie, His Life and Times* (Toronto, 1892), p. 525.

11. Dale Thomson, *Alexander Mackenzie: Clear Grit* (Toronto, 1960), p. 174.

12. Ibid., p. 179.

13. Ibid., p. 219.

14. Underhill, op. cit., p. 385.

15. Mackenzie to Brown, October 8, 1874, PAC, call no. M-197.

16. Thomson, op. cit., pp. 232–233.

17. Norman Ward, "Money and Politics: The Costs of Democracy in Canada," *CJPS*, vol. 5, no. 3, September 1972, p. 335. See also Ward, "Electoral Corruption and Controverted Elections," *CJEPS*, vol. 40, 1949, pp. 79–80.

18. Buckingham and Ross, op. cit., pp. 525–526.

19. Albert Malouin to Laurier, November 24, 1896, PAC file 850.

20. Mulock to Laurier, May 12, 1898, PAC file 850.

21. Laurier to Willison, November 10, 1896, quoted in A.H.U. Colquhoun, *Laurier* (Toronto, 1935), p. 59.

22. Laurier to Edouard Nadeau, June 28, 1898, PAC file 850.

23. Laurier to A.S. Hardy, July 23, 1898, call no. C-758.

24. The fascinating story of how Quebec changed is beyond the scope of this book, and anyway the story has been captured by Neatby, in *Laurier*, op. cit., and by the early volumes of Robert Rumilly's massive *Histoire de la Province de Québec*. Rumilly, of course, offered only grudging admiration for Laurier, preferring his heroes to be nationalist politicians.

25. F. Landon, "A Canadian Cabinet Episode, 1897," in *Transactions of the Royal Society of Canada*, 1938, p. 52, quoted in Neatby, *Laurier*, op. cit., p. 125. See also Paul Stevens, "Wilfrid Laurier, Politician," in Marcel Hamelin (ed.), *The Political Ideas of the Prime Ministers of Canada* (Ottawa, 1969).

26. The handling of Dansereau is recounted in Neatby, op. cit., p. 128.

27. Laurier Lapierre, "Politics, Race and Religion in French Canada: Joseph Israel Tarte," Ph.D. Thesis, University of Toronto, 1962, p. 357.

28. House of Commons debates, March 28, 1899.

29. Lapierre, op. cit., pp. 523–524.

30. Laurier to E. Pacaud, December 13, 1900, quoted in Neatby, op. cit., p. 136.

31. Laurier to S. Springer, January 22, 1900, file 873.

32. Paul Stevens, "Laurier and the Liberal Party in Ontario, 1887–1911," Ph.D. Thesis, University of Toronto, 1966, p. 308.

33. Quoted in Stevens, "Wilfrid Laurier, Politician," op. cit., p. 80.

34. D.J. Hall, *Clifford Sifton, The Young Napoleon*, vol. 1 (Vancouver, 1981), p. 57.

35. Skelton, op. cit., p. 269.

36. Hall, op. cit., p. 133.

37. Hall, vol. 2., op. cit., p. 150.

38. Hall, vol. 1, op. cit., pp. 125–126.

39. Hall, vol. 2, op. cit., p. 3.

40. Quoted in Hall, vol. 2, op. cit., p. 129.

41. Ibid., p. 141.

42. Quoted in P.G. Shea, "Electoral Practices in the Province of Quebec, 1861–1882," M.A. Thesis, McGill University, 1968, p. 196.

43. J.A.A. Lovink, "The politics of Quebec: provincial political parties, 1897–1936," Ph.D. Thesis, Duke University, pp. 158–159.

44. Norman Ward, "The press and the patronage: an exploratory operation," in J.H. Atkinson (ed.), *The Political Process in Canada* (Toronto, 1963), p. 9.

45. These figures are supplied by R. MacGregor Dawson, *The Civil Service of Canada* (London, 1929), p. 72.

46. Quoted in Hall, vol. 2., op. cit., p. 86.

47. Sir John Willison, op. cit., p. 468.

48. See Carl Berger, *A Sense of Power: Studies in the Ideas of Canadian Imperialism, 1867–1914* (Toronto, 1971), especially chapter 8. Berger quotes critics of political chicanery as disparate as Goldwin Smith, Henri Bourassa and Sir Sandford Fleming. A less likely trio with a common interest can scarcely be imagined.

49. Hall, vol. 2, op. cit., p. 189.

50. Ward, *A Public Purse*, op. cit., pp. 130–133.

51. These and subsequent quotations are taken from *Royal Commission into the Civil Service Commission*, 1908, sessional papers 29a.

52. See J.E. Hodgetts et al., *The Biography of an Institution: The Civil Service Commission of Canada, 1908–1967* (Montreal, 1972), ch. 2.

53. Years later, this shift still dismayed some Ontario Liberals of the Grit tradition. See Underhill, op. cit., pp. 384–386.

54. Gordon Stewart, "Political Patronage under Macdonald and Laurier," *The American Review of Canadian Studies*, vol. 10, no. 1, pp. 12–14.

55. Quoted in Berger, op. cit., p. 203.

CHAPTER 5   BORDEN, KING AND ST. LAURENT

1. Desmond Morton, *Ministers and Generals* (Toronto, 1970), Appendix A, p. 201.

2. This theme runs through Morton's fascinating book, ibid.

3. John English, *The Decline of the Politics: The Conservatives and the Party System*, (Toronto, 1977), p. 96. This a wonderfully nuanced account of the shifting sands of politics under Borden.

4. See Norman Ward, "The Bristol papers, a note on patronage," *CJEPS*, vol. 12, 1946, p. 85.

5. Quoted in English, op. cit., p. 95.

6. Ibid., p. 101.

7. For Borden's own account, see Robert Laird Borden, *Memoirs of Sir Robert Borden*, vol. 1 (London, 1968).

8. For the background to Borden's promises, see R. Craig Brown, *Robert Laird Borden*, vol. 1, chapters 10–12 (Toronto, 1975).

9. English, op. cit., p. 70. See also Brown, ibid.

10. Borden papers, PAC, call no. MG26Hi(a), vol. 37, p. 15597, undated.

11. English, op. cit., p. 63.

12. Quoted in J.E. Hodgetts, William McCloskey, Reginald Whitaker, V. Seymour Wilson, *The Biography of an Institution: The Civil Service Commission of Canada, 1908–1967* (Montreal, 1972), p. 47.

13. English, op. cit., p. 73

14. Hodgetts et al., at pp. 13-14, carefully refuted R. MacGregor Dawson's charge to the contrary in *The Civil Service of Canada* (London, 1929). Borden, in retirement, was furious with Dawson's conclusions and said so in letters and public statements

15. English, op. cit., p. 162.

16. See Hodgetts et al., pp. 50–56 for a detailed description of the Act.

17. English, op. cit., p. 225.

18. Borden memoirs, vol. 2, op. cit., p. 977.

19. Thick, impressive volumes chronicle the King years and the man himself, although none pay more than passing attention to King's use of patronage, including: Jack Pickersgill, *The Mackenzie King Record*, vols. 1–4 (Toronto, 1960);

R. MacGregor Dawson, *William Lyon Mackenzie King* (Toronto, 1958); and Blair Neatby, *William Lyon Mackenzie King: The Lonely Heights* (Toronto, 1963).

20. See Jack Granatstein's two fine portrayals of this development in *The Ottawa Men: The Civil Service Mandarins, 1935–57* (Toronto, 1982), and *A Man of Influence: Norman A. Robertson and Canadian Statecraft, 1929–1968* (Ottawa, 1981).

21. Norman Ward, "The politics of patronage: James Gardiner and federal appointments in the West," *CHR*, vol. 58, no. 3, September 1977, pp. 294–310.

22. Ibid., p. 296.

23. Ibid., p. 298.

24. Ibid., p. 306.

25. See Reginald Whitaker, *The Government Party; Organizing and Financing the Liberal Party of Canada, 1930–1958* (Toronto, 1977), p. 276.

26. Norman Ward (ed.), *A Party Politician, The Memoirs of Chubby Power* (Toronto, 1966), ch. 21.

27. Recounted by Professor Fred Gibson of Queen's, who knew Power.

28. The evolution of the extra-parliamentary structure of the Liberal party lies far beyond the scope of this book. It has been meticulously and definitively recounted by Whitaker, op. cit.

29. Neatby, op. cit., p. 330.

30. See *Canadian Annual Review*, 1931, pp. 64–71, for a summary of the parliamentary inquiry and debate into the Beauharnois affair. See also Neatby, op. cit., pp. 369–390, and various references in Whitaker, op. cit. The House and Senate debates on the scandals also make fascinating reading.

31. Quoted in Neatby, op.cit., p. 376.

32. Whitaker, op. cit., p. 18.

33. Joseph Wearing, *The L-Shaped Party: The Liberal Party of Canada, 1958–1980* (Toronto, 1981), pp. 10–11.

34. Robert Bothwell and William Kilbourn, *C.D. Howe* (Toronto, 1979) p. 81. See also Whitaker, op. cit., pp. 102–111. Historian Michael Bliss wrote of Howe, "He revelled in face-to-face negotiation, sought and gave favours, enjoyed flattery, promoted friends and lashed back at enemies. . . . He unashamedly and personally dunned government contractors for contributions to the Liberal party, serving as a political bagman and often handling large amounts of cash in bags and safety deposit boxes. Young men who worked under Howe in Ottawa became his 'boys,' their careers advancing nicely on the minister's patronage." See Bliss, *Northern Enterprise: Five Centuries of Canadian Business* (Toronto, 1987), pp. 470–471.

35. Khayyam Z. Paltiel and Jean Brown Van Loon, "Financing the Liberal Party, 1865–1965," in *Committee on Election Expenses, Studies in Canadian Party Finance* (Ottawa, 1966), pp. 166–193.

36. Cited in the Barbeau commission's *Report of Committee on Election Expenses* (Ottawa, 1966), p. 237.

37. The Conservatives' relentless problems of raising money are detailed in Jack Granatstein's *The Politics of Survival: The Conservative Party of Canada, 1939–1945* (Toronto, 1967), and in his "Conservative Party finances, 1939–1945," *Committee on Election Expenses* (Ottawa, 1966).

38. See periodic references in the early chapters of Dalton Camp's *Gentlemen, Players and Politicians* (Toronto, 1970).

39. Whitaker, op. cit., p. 221. Chapter 6 provides a wealth of detail about the relationship between the Liberals and their agencies.

40. Ibid., pp. 238–239.

41. Ibid. See Table on p. 257.

42. Brian McFadzen, "The Liberal Party and MacLaren Advertising Company Ltd., 1957, 1965," M.A. Thesis, Queen's University, p. 150.

43. Memo from Abbott to St. Laurent, Dec. 7, 1949, St. Laurent papers, PAC, vol. 131, P-15-5.

CHAPTER 6   NEWFOUNDLAND

1. Terry Campbell and G.A. Rawlyk, "The Historical Framework of Newfoundland and Confederation," in *The Atlantic Provinces and the Problems of Confederation* (Portugal Cove, Nfld., 1979), p. 66.

2. *Report of Royal Commission on the Economic State and Prospects of Newfoundland and Labrador* (Queen's Printer, 1933), p. 82.

3. Ralph Matthews, "Perspectives on recent Newfoundland politics," *Journal of Canadian Studies*, vol. 9, no. 2, 1974, p. 21.

4. S.J.R. Noel, *Politics in Newfoundland* (Toronto, 1971), p. 274.

5. Richard Gwyn, *Smallwood, The Unlikely Revolutionary* (Toronto, 1972), p. 135.

6. Peter Neary, *The Political Economy of Newfoundland. 1929–1972* (Toronto, 1973).

7. Campbell and Rawlyk, op. cit., pp. 66–67.

8. Noel, op. cit., p. 159.

9. Noel, ibid., p. 165. See also Valerie Summers, "The Politics of Underdevelopment: Regime Change in Newfoundland," chapter 3, Ph.D. Thesis, Memorial University, 1986.

10. Noel, op. cit., p. 169.

11. Noel, op. cit., p. 182.

12. William J. Browne, *Eighty-Four Years a Newfoundlander*, vol. 1 (St. John's, 1981), p. 99.

13. Royal Commission on Employment and Unemployment (Queen's Printer, 1986), summary report, p. 32.

14. George Perlin, "Patronage and Paternalism: Politics in Newfoundland," in D.I. Davies and Kathleen Herman, *Social Space: Canadian Perspectives* (Toronto, 1971), p. 191.

15. Perlin, ibid., p. 191.

16. Gwyn, op. cit., p. 24.

17. Noel, op. cit., p. 28.

18. Ibid., p. 106.

19. Ibid., p. 104.

20. John Crosbie, "Local Government in Newfoundland," *CJEPS*, vol. 22, no. 3, 1956, pp. 332–347.

21. *Royal Commission*, op. cit., section 220, p. 82.

22. Noel, op. cit., 21.

23. Noel, ibid., p. 20.

24. Gwyn, op. cit., p. 21, 99.

25. Gwyn, ibid., pp. 99–100; Browne, op. cit., p. 359.

26. *Royal Commission to Enquire into the Leasing of Premises for the Use of the Newfoundland Liquor Commission* (St. John's, 1972), Part 2, pp. 44–45.

27. Gwyn, op. cit., p. 136.

28. Noel, op. cit., 274.

29. Perlin, op. cit., p. 193.

30. Gwyn, op. cit., p. 236.

31. Gwyn, op. cit., p. 239.

32. *Report of the Commission of Enquiry into the Purchasing Procedures of the Department of Public Works and Services* (St. John's, 1981), pp. 288–289.

33. Ibid., pp. 128–129.

34. Ibid., p. 131.

35. Ibid., p. 35.

CHAPTER 7   PRINCE EDWARD ISLAND

1. Marlene Russell-Clark, "Island Politics" in Francis Bolger (ed.), *Canada's Smallest Province* (Charlottetown, 1973), p. 305.

2. Ibid., p. 315.

3. Wayne MacKinnon, *The Life of the Party, A History of the Liberal Party in Prince Edward Island* (Summerside, 1973), p. 50.

4. Ibid., p. 50.

5. Ibid., p. 50.

6. Ibid., p. 96.

7. Albert Francis MacDonald, "The Politics of Acquisition, a Study of Corruption in Prince Edward Island," M.A. Thesis, Queen's University, 1979.

8. Wayne MacKinnon, op. cit., p. 86.

9. Frank MacKinnon, "Prince Edward Island" in Martin Robin (ed.) *Canadian Provincial Politics* (Toronto, 1972), p. 255.

10. David Milne, "Politics in a Beleaguered Garden," in Smitheram et al., *The Garden Transformed, P.E.I., 1945–1980* (Charlottetown, 1982), p. 61.

11. Marlene Russell-Clark, op. cit., p. 301.

12. Frank MacKinnon in Robin, op. cit., p. 247.

CHAPTER 8   NOVA SCOTIA

1. This and subsequent information comes from interviews with Cameron.

2. P.B. Waite, *The Man from Halifax: Sir John Thompson, Prime Minister* (Toronto, 1985), p. 176.

3. I am grateful to Professor Ray MacLean of St. Francis Xavier University for samples of MacIsaac's correspondence. MacIsaac, like all politicians, probably disappointed more supporters than he pleased. In addition to letters of supplication and thanks, he received some such as this one from a disappointed supporter turned down by MacIsaac's friend, Will Chisolm: "When I asked Will Chisolm for the position you promised me, he practically laughed me out of court," wrote the erstwhile supporter. "I am much obliged to you for the almost desperate position you have placed me and my family. No man can do this to me and escape, even if I have to smash him in the dirt beneath my feet. Will Chisolm and his party will need my friends in the future and I will meet you before long."

4. *Hants Journal*, November 29, 1978.

5. *Hants Journal*, January 23, 1980.

6. For more details about Howe's view of responsible government and patronage, see chapter three of his book.

7. J. Murray Beck, *The Government of Nova Scotia*, Volume I (Toronto, 1957), p. 111.

8. J. Murray Beck, "Nova Scotia, the party system in Nova Scotia: tradition and conservatism" in Martin Robin (ed.), *Canadian Provincial Politics* (Toronto, 1972), p. 172. See also Beck, *The Government of Nova Scotia*, p. 111.

9. Robert Dickey, "Party Government in Nova Scotia, 1867–1879," M.A. Thesis, Dalhousie University, 1941, pp. 10–12.

10. Beck, *The Politics of Nova Scotia*, op. cit., p. 206.

11. Ibid., p. 236.

12. Beck, *The Government of Nova Scotia*, vol. 1 (Toronto, 1985), p. 220.

13. Allan Jeffrey Wright, "The Hapless Armstrong, Premier of Nova Scotia, 1923–1925," Honours B.A. Thesis, Dalhousie University, 1974.

14. Rhodes papers, Nova Scotia Archives (NSA), no. 12507.

15. Ibid., no. 12512.

16. Ibid., no. 32588.

17. Ibid., no. 12542.

18. Ibid., no. 32635.

19. Ibid., no. 33115.

20. Ibid., no. 11981.

21. Ibid., no. 50798.

22. Beck, *The Government of Nova Scotia*, op. cit., p. 238.

23. Beck, Ibid., p. 250.

24. Beck, Ibid., p. 221.

25. Ernest Forbes, "The rise and fall of the Conservative party in the provincial politics of Nova Scotia, 1922–33," M.A. Thesis, Dalhousie University, 1967, pp. 178–180.

26. Ibid., p. 187.

27. Ernest and Fulton Logan, "Personality as issue in Nova Scotia politics," M.A. Thesis, Dalhousie University, 1970, p. 57.

28. Forbes, Ibid., p. 196. See also John Hawkins, *The Life and Times of Angus L.* (Windsor, 1969), pp. 157–164.

29. Beck, *The Government of Nova Scotia*, op. cit., pp. 222–224. Unfortunately, the papers of Premier Angus L. MacDonald are still in the family's possession and not available for scrutiny.

30. Interview with author.

31. See D. Campbell and R.A. MacLean, *Beyond the Atlantic Roar, A Study of Nova Scotia Scots* (Toronto, 1974), especially pp. 240–254.

32. The following comes from an interview with Stanfield, and from Geoffrey Stevens, *Stanfield* (Toronto, 1973), and Peter Aucoin, "The Stanfield Era: A Political Analysis," *Dalhousie Review*, autumn, 1967.

33. *The Globe and Mail*, "N.S. truckers ready to strike over political patronage," May 10, 1974.

34. The following information is found in factums and accompanying material submitted by lawyers for the Crown and for Senator Irvine Barrow, whose appeal before the Supreme Court of Canada was heard March 25, 1987.

35. *The Toronto Star*, "Ex-Liberal tells all on N.S. kickbacks," March 23, 1980.

CHAPTER 9   NEW BRUNSWICK

1. All quotations relating to the Francis Atkinson trial are taken from the transcript of proceedings heard in the trial division of the Court of Queen's Bench of New Brunswick under Judge Paul Barry, May 5, 6, 7, 8, 12, June 24, 25, 26 and July 28, 1980. Quotations are also taken from Judge Barry's reasons for judgment, deposited with the clerk July 28, 1980.

2. I am grateful to Francis Atkinson, for whom this entire affair has been terribly painful, for permission to review all his files, only some of which were introduced in evidence against him. He never asked what I might conclude from or write about the information.

3. These quotes are taken from the judge's ruling. Other details of the Atkinson affair are found in Richard Starr, *Richard Hatfield, The Seventeen-Year Saga* (Halifax, 1987), especially ch. 9.

4. Hugh G. Thorburn, *Politics in New Brunswick* (Toronto, 1961), p. 163. This is the general thesis of P.J. Fitzpatrick, "New Brunswick, The Politics of Pragmatism," in Martin Robin, *Canadian Provincial Politics: The Party Systems of the Ten Provinces* (Toronto, 1972).

5. Arthur Doyle, *Front Benches and Back Rooms* (Fredericton, 1976), p. 142.

6. The papers of J.D. Hazen, minister of marine and fisheries in Robert Borden's government, clearly show Hazen preoccupied with satisfying both Protestants and Catholics. Hazen papers, Archives of New Brunswick (ANB), MG H13.

7. Hazen to Fred Macneill, Hazen papers, Nov. 29, 1912, ANB MG H13.

8. Interview with author.

9. See Peter Leslie, "The role of political parties in promoting the interests of ethnic minorities," *CJPS*, vol. 11, no. 4, pp. 419–433.

10. Thorburn, op. cit., is especially good at describing an election day in New Brunswick.

11. For a full description of this hilarious tale, see Doyle, op. cit., ch. 4.

12. This may account, in part, for the astonishing paucity of political writing about New Brunswick provincial politics, which do not lack for colour, only supporting documents. The provincial archives, for example, are nearly bereft of papers of provincial premiers, an exception being those of Premier Hugh John Flemming. But even these have been carefully culled to remove potentially controversial material. In some cases, the papers do not exist; in others, family members still involved in public life prefer for their own reasons to keep the papers of their forebears private.

13. Della M.M. Stanley, *Louis Robichaud, A Decade in Power* (Saint John, 1984), p. 55.

14. Quoted in "We've waited ten years for these jobs;" *Saint John Telegraph-Journal*, March 30, 1971.

15. Some of these influences are analysed in Mark Pedersen, "The transition from patronage to media politics and its impact on New Brunswick political parties," M.A. Thesis, Queen's University, 1982.

CHAPTER 10   QUEBEC

1. Graham Fraser, *René Lévesque and the Parti Québecois in Power* (Toronto, 1985), pp. 114–116.

2. Ralph Heintzman cites four areas—education, colonization, municipal affairs and welfare, and the vogue for corporatism—in which some Quebec politicians and commentators defended the state's inactivity because they feared the possible spread of political patronage. See his seminal article, "The political culture of Quebec, 1840–1960," *CJPS*, vol. 16, no. 1. pp. 3–59. Heintzman's insights, as discerning readers will observe, influence parts of this chapter.

3. Pierre Trudeau, "Some obstacles to democracy in Quebec," in Mason Wade (ed.), *Canadian Dualism/La Dualité Canadienne* (Toronto, 1960).

4. Marcel Hamelin, *Les premieres anneés du parlementarisme québecois, 1867–1878* (Quebec, 1974).

5. Ibid., p. 353.

6. P.G. Shea, "Electoral practices in Quebec, 1861–1882," M.A. Thesis, McGill University, 1968, p. 240.

7. Quoted in ibid., p. 36.

8. For details of the scandal, and a sympathetic portrait of Mercier, see Robert Rumilly, *Honoré Mercier et son temps*, vol. 2 (Montreal, 1975), pp. 238–280.

9. Barbeau commission, *Report of the Committee on Election Expenses* (Queen's Printer, 1966). See ch. 7.

10. Joseph Levitt, *Henri Bourassa and the Golden Calf, The Social Program of the Nationalists of Quebec, 1900–1914* (Ottawa, 1969), pp. 69–70.

11. J.I. Gow, "One hundred years of Quebec administrative history, 1867–1970, *Canadian Public Administration*, vol. 28, no. 2, p. 254.

12. J.A.A. Lovink, "The politics of Quebec: provincial political parties, 1897–1936," Ph.D. Thesis, Duke University, 1967, p. 181.

13. Ibid., p. 183.

14. Ibid., p. 321.

15. Bernard Vigod, *Quebec before Duplessis: The Political Career of Louis-Alexandre Taschereau* (Montreal, 1968), p. 191.

16. M.P. O'Connell, "The ideas of Henri Bourassa," *CJEPS* vol. 19, no. 3, pp. 368–369.

17. Levitt, op. cit., p. 72.

18. Ibid., p. 72.

19. Heintzman, op. cit., p. 25.

20. For a description of efforts to clean up the municipal politics of Montreal, see Michel Gauvin, "The reformer and the machine: Montreal civic politics from Raymond Préfontaine to Médéric Martin," *JCS*, vol. 13, no. 2, pp. 16–27.

21. Ibid., pp. 29–31.

22. For two deeply sympathetic analyses of the Duplessis years, see Robert Rumilly's two-volume *Maurice Duplessis et son Temps* (Montreal, 1973); and Conrad Black's *Duplessis* (Toronto, 1977).

23. Lovink, op. cit., pp. 313–315. See also Herbert Quinn, *The Union Nationale* (Toronto, 1963), pp. 66–68.

24. Quinn, ibid., p. 70.

25. Ibid., p. 137.

26. Ibid., p. 137.

27. These distinctions emerged in interviews with former UN ministers and members as reported by Vincent Lemieux and Raymond Hudon, *Patronage et Politique au Québec, 1944–1972* (Montréal, 1975); Raymond Hudon, "*Les partis politiques au Québec depuis 1944*," M.A. Thesis, Laval University, 1973, p. 79. See also Hudon's paper, "*Le patronage des partis politiques au Québec depuis 1944: une analyse politique*," delivered at the Canadian Political Science Association congress, 1973.

28. Quinn, op. cit., p. 135.

29. Black, op. cit., p. 302.

30. Quinn, op. cit., pp. 146–151.

31. Heintzman, op. cit., pp. 37–39.

32. Lesage's difficulties are explained in the second half of Dale Thomson's, *Jean Lesage and the Quiet Revolution* (Toronto, 1984).

33. Commission d'enquête sur les méthodes d'achat utilisés au Départment de la colonisation et au Service des achats du gouvernement. (Québec, 1963).

34. Hardy's splenetic reply is contained in his memoires, *Patronage et Patroneux* (Montreal, 1973). Hardy, director of the Service from 1937 to 1959, claimed that he had simply followed orders, that after each election the party gave him a list of accredited suppliers, and that those around the premiers harassed him during elections to place orders. "After elections," he wrote, "the first who were recommended to me

were the contributors to the electoral *caisse*, whatever the regime," p. 37. The commission, however, described Hardy as a *"mauvais serviteur de la province."*

35. Georges-Émile Lapalme, a former party leader and minister of justice, recounts some of those pressures in volume three of his *Le paradis du Pouvoir* (Montreal, 1973). Lapalme claims that although he had authority over the liquor commission, he never knew who authorized the wholesale staff changes that occurred immediately after the election. p. 33.

36. Thomson, op. cit., p. 92.

37. J.I. Gow, op. cit., p. 258 provides a useful summary of the reforms and counter-reforms in Quebec's public administration. His Table wonderfully summarizes the painfully slow climb to bureaucratic modernity.

38. Ibid., p. 92.

39. Jérôme Proulx, *Le Panier de Crabes* (Montreal, 1971), ch. 1.

CHAPTER 11 ONTARIO

1. These events are meticulously recorded in Rosemary Speirs', *Out Of The Blue: The Fall of the Tory Dynasty in Ontario* (Toronto, 1986).

2. "Miller aides' appointments rapped," *Ottawa Citizen*, June 14, 1985.

3. Information from interviews with staff members in Peterson's office.

4. "Ontario Grits build network with patronage," *The Globe and Mail*, January 2, 1987.

5. Rosemary Speirs, "Ontario Liberals discovering the joys of patronage," *The Toronto Star*, July 23, 1986. See also her column, "Ontario Liberals' patronage machine in gear," *The Toronto Star*, March 28, 1987.

6. Margaret Evans, "Oliver Mowat and Ontario, 1872–1896: A Study in Political Success," Ph.D. Thesis, University of Toronto, 1967, p. 315.

7. Macdonald speech, September 14, 1882, cited in Margaret Evans, "Nineteenth-century Ontario Liberal," in Donald Swainson (ed.), *Oliver Mowat's Ontario* (Toronto, 1972), pp. 40–41.

8. Christopher Armstrong, "The Mowat Heritage in Federal-Provincial Relations," in Swainson, Ibid., p. 93.

9. Gordon Stewart, *The Origins of Canadian Federalism* (Vancouver, 1986), p. 69.

10. Evans Thesis, op. cit., p. 311.

11. Quoted in Sir John Willison, *Reminiscences: Political and Personal* (Toronto, 1919), p. 96.

12. Willison, Ibid., p. 95.

13. C.R.W. Biggar, *Sir Oliver Mowat: A Biographical Sketch* (Toronto, 1905), pp. 264–267; Adam Shortt and Arthur G. Dougherty (eds.), *Canada and its Provinces* (Toronto, 1914), pp. 150–160; Evans Thesis, op. cit., p. 306.

14. Graham White's thorough analysis of the 1874 redistribution concludes: "On balance, then, the manner in which the boundaries were drawn was decidedly fair, particularly for the 1870s." See White, " 'Christian Humility and Partisan Ingenuity': Sir Oliver Mowat's Redistribution of 1874," *Ontario History* (OH), vol. 73, December 1981, pp. 219–238.

15. Brian Tennyson, "The Cruise of the Minnie M," *OH*, vol. 49, no. 2, 1967, pp. 125–128.

16. Charles Humphries, "The Gamey Affair," *OH*, vol. 49, 1967, pp. 101–109.

17. Quoted in Charles Humphries, *"Honest Enough to be Bold," The Life and Times of Sir James Pliny Whitney* (Toronto, 1985), p. 119.

18. Brower to Whitney, Whitney papers, Archives of Ontario (AO) MU3115.

19. Whitney papers, op. cit.

20. W.D. Hogg to Whitney, Whitney papers, op. cit.

21. Humphries, *Whitney*, op. cit., p. 119.

22. Whitney to J.A. Morrison, Whitney papers, op. cit.

23. Humphries, *Whitney*, op. cit., pp. 117–118.

24. Ibid., pp. 170–171.

25. Quoted in Willison, op. cit., p. 330.

26. The public policy and private ambitions of Ontario's resource exploitation are superbly analysed in H.V. Nelles, *The Politics of Development: Forest, Mines and Hydroelectric Power in Ontario, 1849–1941* (Toronto, 1974). At p. 47, Nelles writes: "The maintenance of the old, imperial habit of authority into the industrial age stemmed primarily from the interaction of interest groups and moderately conservative ideology, within an agriculturally barren environment. The lumberman, the shield, the threat of direct taxation sanctioned a set of resource laws that preserved the germ of an earlier, collectivist conception of the state."

27. Peter Oliver, *G. Howard Ferguson: Ontario Tory* (Toronto, 1977), p. 68.

28. Joseph Schull, *Ontario Since 1867* (Toronto, 1978), p. 187.

29. Charles M. Johnston, *E.C. Drury: Agrarian Idealist* (Toronto, 1986).

30. Ibid., p. 80.

31. The background to the timber scandal is recorded in Peter Oliver, *Public and Private Persons: The Ontario Political Culture, 1914–1934* (Toronto, 1975), pp. 40–63; Nelles, op. cit., pp. 386–394; Johnston, op. cit., pp. 171–173; Oliver, *G. Howard Ferguson*, op. cit., 96–97.

32. Johnston, op. cit., p. 108.

33. Ibid., p. 217.

34. Ibid., p. 232.

35. Oliver, *G. Howard Ferguson*, op. cit., p. 268.

36. Ibid., p. 360.

37. Schull, op. cit., p. 277.

38. Neil McKenty, *Mitch Hepburn* (Toronto, 1967), p. 61.

39. Hepburn papers, AO RG3, Box 285. Also Elmhirst to ministers, AO RG3, Box 229.

40. Major H.P. Snelgrove to R.H. Elmhirst, April 26, 1936, Hepburn papers, AO RG3, Box 254.

41. J.R. Maclaren to Hepburn, July 24, 1935, AO RG3, Box 229.

42. See, for example, the list supplied by Percy Wilson, a lawyer with Honeywell, Wilson and McDougall, at the request of the Ottawa West Liberal Association. The "confidential preferred list" names ninety firms or individuals. Wilson to Hepburn, July 24, 1934, AO RG3, Box 229.

43. Bert Woods to Hepburn, July 11, 1934, AO RG3, Box 223.

44. E.W. Brown to Hepburn, October 23, 1934, AO RG3, Box 223.

45. Arnold Smith to E.G. Odette, Hepburn papers, March 9, 1936, AO RG3, Box 259.

46. *The Toronto Telegram*, January 7, 1935.

47. McCullagh to Hepburn, October 7, 1937, AO RG3, Box 270. McCullagh later formed the Leadership League.

48. McKenty, op. cit., p. 127.

49. Hepburn to R.S. Colter, December 14, 1937, AO RG3, Box 270.

50. Elmhirst to Ahearn, June 22, 1936, AO RG3, Box 253.

51. Hepburn to Ian Mackenzie, September 10, 1936, AO RG3, Box 253.

52. Richard Alway, "Mitchell F. Hepburn and the Liberal Party in the Province of Ontario: 1937-1943," M.A. Thesis, University of Toronto, 1965, pp. 215–216.

53. A great and somewhat myster.ous gap in writing about Ontario history yawns across the Conservative dynasty. This has something to do with the lack of access to the Drew papers and lack of a biography of Leslie Frost. It may also be that the Ontario Tories have largely put the academic community to sleep, just as they did to much of the population.

54. A.K. McDougall, *John P. Robarts: His Life and Government* (Toronto, 1985), p. 78.

55. Jonathan Manthorpe, *The Power and The Tories: Ontario Politics 1943 to the Present* (Toronto, 1974), p. 51.

56. *The Globe and Mail*, April 22, 1971.

57. Claire Hoy, *Bill Davis* (Toronto, 1985), ch. 13.

58. A joint study by *The Windsor Star*, *The Hamilton Spectator* and *The Ottawa Citizen*, reported in *The Windsor Star*, October 12, 1984.

CHAPTER 12   MANITOBA

1. W.L. Morton, *Manitoba, A History* (Toronto, 1957), p. viii.

2. T. Peterson, "Ethnic and class politics in Manitoba," in Martin Robin, *Canadian Provincial Politics: The Party Systems of the Ten Provinces* (Toronto, 1972), p. 95.

3. John Holmes, "Factors affecting politics in Manitoba: A study of the provincial elections, 1870–1899," M.A. Thesis, University of Manitoba, 1936, p. 8.

4. Ibid., p. 120.

5. Joseph Hilts, "The political career of Thomas Greenway," Ph.D. Thesis, University of Manitoba, 1974, pp. 71–72.

6. James Jackson, *The Centennial History of Manitoba* (Toronto, 1970), pp. 127–129.

7. Morton, op. cit., p. 221.

8. Hilts, op. cit., pp. 122–123.

9. D.J. Hall, *Clifford Sifton, The Young Napoleon* (Vancouver, 1981), p. 57.

10. Ibid., p. 5.

11. Hilts, op. cit., p. 151.

12. Morton, op. cit., p. 236.

13. Lionel Orlikow, "The Reform movement in Manitoba 1910–1915," in Donald Swainson, *Historical Essays of the Prairie Provinces* (Toronto, 1970), p. 225.

14. See Peterson, op. cit., p. 74.

15. Orlikow, op. cit., p. 225.

16. M.S. Donnelly, *The Government of Manitoba* (Toronto, 1963), p. 50.

17. Orlikow, op. cit., p. 224.

18. Alexander Inglis, "Some factors in the demise of the Roblin government, 1915," M.A. Thesis, University of Manitoba, 1968, p. 69.

19. The details of the Legislative Buildings scandal have been extensively analysed by Morton, op. cit., pp. 341–347; Jackson, op. cit., pp. 186–195; and especially by Inglis, op. cit.

20. Donnelly, op. cit., p. 123.

21. See Brian McCutcheon, "The Patrons of Industry in Manitoba, 1890–1898," in Swainson, op. cit.

22. John Kendle, *John Bracken: A Political Biography* (Toronto, 1979), p. 63.

23. Morton, op. cit., p. 379.

24. Kendle, op. cit., p. 125.

25. The CCF faced the most difficult decision before joining the coalition, as Nelson Wiseman describes in "The CCF and the Manitoba 'Non-partisan' Government of 1940," *CHR*, vol. 54, no. a, June 1973.

26. Ibid., p. 124.

27. The labyrinthine Seven Sisters affair is detailed in Kendle, chapters 6 and 7.

28. *The Winnipeg Free Press*, May 2, 1987.

29. *The Winnipeg Free Press*, November 6, 1987.

CHAPTER 13   SASKATCHEWAN

1. D.S. Spafford provides an interesting description of the groups that rejected conventional party politics in "Independent politics in Saskatchewan before the Non-Partisan League," *Saskatchewan History (SH)*, vol. 18, no. 1, 1965.

2. Ibid., p. 1.

3. For a detailed description of politics before 1905, see C.C.Lingard, *Territorial Government in Canada: The Autonomy Question in the Old North-West Territories* (Toronto, 1946), and J. William Brennan, "A political history of Saskatchewan, 1905–1929," Ph.D. Thesis, University of Alberta, 1976, pp. 1–55.

4. John Saywell, "Liberal politics, federal politics, and the lieutenant-governor: Saskatchewan and Alberta, 1905," *SH*, vol. 8, no. 3, 1955, p. 84.

5. Quoted in Saywell, ibid., p. 85.

6. Quoted in Brennan, op. cit., p. 54.

7. D.H. Bocking, "Saskatchewan's first provincial election," *SH*, vol. 17, no. 2, 1964, p. 44.

8. David Smith insists on the word "machine," too, albeit with several qualifications. See his *Prairie Liberalism: The Liberal Party in Saskatchewan 1905–1971* (Toronto, 1975), pp. 26–28. Anyone writing about the political history of Saskatchewan must acknowledge freely an enormous debt to Smith's work, including *The Regional Decline of a National Party: Liberals on the Prairies* (Toronto, 1981).

9. The fascinating and disturbing story of the Ku Klux Klan in Saskatchewan is beyond the purview of this essay. See, however, Patrick Kyba, "Ballots and burning crosses," in Norman Ward and D.S. Spafford (eds.), *Politics in Saskatchewan* (Toronto, 1968). The Klan capitalized after the war on complaints by ex-servicemen that the bribery of immigrants with jobs and other favours discriminated against those who had served in the war. See Smith, op. cit., p. 125.

10. Martin papers, Archives of Saskatchewan (AS), document 35068.

11. Martin papers, AS, document 35047.

12. Scott papers, AS, document 50378.

13. Quoted in J. William Brennan, "C.A. Dunning and the challenge of the Progressives, 1922–1925," in D.H. Bocking (ed.), *Pages from the Past, Essays on Saskatchewan History* (Saskatoon, 1979), p. 208.

14. Smith, *Prairie Liberalism*, op. cit., p. 34. Smith writes on p. 32 "Any man or woman who benefited from government largesse was expected to work for the party when requested. . . .

15. Figures taken from Escott Reid, "The Saskatchewan Liberal machine before 1929," in Ward and Spafford, op. cit., p. 102.

16. Reid's article, a classic in the literature of Canadian patronage, describes in detail the organization's meticulous work.

17. Evelyn Eager, *Saskatchewan Government: Politics and Pragmatism* (Saskatoon, 1980), p. 68.

18. Smith, op. cit., p. 45.

19. The following account follows Smith, op. cit., pp. 51–52.

20. These are chronicled in Smith, op. cit., ch. 6; and in Norman Ward, "Oppositions and coalitions: James Gardiner and Saskatchewan provincial politics, 1929–1934," *Canadian Historical Association papers*, 1979.

21. Eager, op. cit., p. 161.

22. A cornucopia of literature analysed the rise of the CCF, including Seymour Martin Lipset, *Agrarian Socialism* (New York, 1968).

23. Cited in Lipset, op. cit., p. 313.

24. Ibid., p. 307.

25. Alfred Larsen to Douglas, Douglas papers, AS, June 29, 1944.

26. Gladys Strum to Douglas, Douglas papers, AS, September 19, 1944.

27. Thomas Hewitt to Douglas, Douglas papers, AS, June 30, 1944.

28. Lipset, op. cit., p. 322.

29. Douglas to T.J. Bentley, Douglas papers, AS, September 23, 1947.

30. Memorandum requested by Douglas from Carl Edy to Eugene Forsey, Douglas papers, April 17, 1947.

31. Eager, op. cit., p. 165.

32. Lipset, op. cit., pp. 322–323.

33. Eager, op. cit., p. 166.

34. C.E.S. Franks, "The legislature and responsible government," in Norman Ward and D.S. Spafford, *Politics in Saskatchewan* (Toronto, 1968), p. 37.

35. Eager, op. cit., p. 168.

36. Dale Eisler column, *Regina Leader-Post*, May 26, 1984.

37. For a thorough and balanced examination of the Devine government's attitudes towards the public service, see Hans J. Michelman and Jeffrey S. Steeves, "The 1982 transition in power in Saskatchewan," *CPA*, vol. 28, no. 1, pp. 1–23. The figure of "about two hundred" is the authors' best estimate, p. 10.

38. Colin Thatcher, *Backrooms* (Saskatoon, 1985), p. 187.

39. Ibid., p. 191.

CHAPTER 14   ALBERTA

1. L.G. Thomas, *The Liberal Party in Alberta, A History of Politics in the Province of Alberta, 1905–1921* (Toronto, 1959), p. 29.

2. Ibid., p. 30.

3. Quoted in Ibid., p. 140.

4. J.A. Long and F.Q. Quo, "Alberta, One-Party Dominance" in Martin Robin, *Canadian Provincial Politics*, op. cit., p. 5. The thesis that the seeds of non-partisanship were planted before Alberta entered Confederation and sprouted thereafter is outlined in C.B. Macpherson, *Democracy in Alberta* (Toronto, 1953), p. 41.

5. Macpherson, op. cit., p. 41.

6. United Farmers of Alberta Provincial Platform, 1921.

7. William Kirby Rolph, *Henry Wise Wood of Alberta* (Toronto, 1950), p. 36.

8. Rand Dyck, Provincial Politics in Canada (Toronto, 1986), p. 454.

9. Quoted in J.A. Irving, *Social Credit in Alberta* (Toronto, 1959), p. 136.

10. Fred Kennedy, *Alberta Was My Beat* (Calgary, 1975), p. 265.

11. Correspondence with author.

12. L.G. Thomas (ed.), *William Aberhart and Social Credit in Alberta*, (Toronto, 1977), p. 142.

13. *The Globe and Mail*, Nov. 20, 1984.

14. *The Edmonton Journal*, Oct. 19, 1982.

CHAPTER 15   BRITISH COLUMBIA

1. For an excellent description of the frontier aspects of B.C. politics and the lack of political tradition, see Ed Black, "British Columbia: The politics of exploitation," in Hugh G. Thorburn (ed.), *Party Politics in Canada*, 4th edition (Toronto, 1979).

2. Quoted in Frank Underhill, "The development of national political parties in Canada," *CHR*, vol. 16, no. 4, p. 380. Also quoted in Martin Robin, *The Rush for Spoils: The Company Province, 1871–1933* (Toronto, 1972), p. 11.

3. Donald Blake et al., *Two Political Worlds: Parties and Voting in British Columbia* (Vancouver, 1985), p. 12.

4. Margaret Ormsby, *British Columbia: A History* (Toronto, 1958), p. 256.

5. Ibid., p. 242.

6. Ibid., p. 335. See also Robin, op. cit., p. 84.

7. Blake et al., p. 15.

8. Quoted in Brian Smith, "Sir Richard McBride: A Study in the Conservative party of British Columbia, 1903–1916," M.A. Thesis, Queen's University, 1959, p. 208.

9. Quoted in Robin, op. cit., p. 129.

10. Ibid., p. 189.

11. Ibid., p. 132. Chapter 5 of *The Rush for Spoils* colourfully portrays, from a relentlessly left-wing perspective, the McBride-Bowser approach to patronage — no holds barred.

12. Ormsby, op. cit., p. 363.

13. Ibid., p. 393.

14. Robin, op. cit., p. 171.

15. Ibid., p. 166, also Ormsby, op. cit., p. 395.

16. Ormsby, op. cit., p. 412.

17. Ibid., p. 412.

18. Robin, op. cit., p.211.

19. Ibid., p. 192.

20. Ibid., pp. 187–188.

21. Ibid., p. 196. For a fuller description of the provincial party see: Robin's chapter "The Shaughnessy Crusade", op. cit.; Ormsby, op. cit., pp. 420–424; Donald Alpen, "From Rule to Ruin: The Conservative Party of British Columbia, 1928–1954," Ph.D. Thesis, University of British Columbia, 1975, pp. 15–31.

22. Parker, op. cit., p. 82.

23. *The Vancouver Sun*, April 1, 1929.

24. *The Daily Province*, August 30, 1929.

25. *Alpen*, op. cit., p. 52.

26. *The Vancouver Sun*, July 8 and August 9, 1929.

27. Quoted in Alpen, op. cit., p. 53.

28. The following quotations are taken from the *Report of the Committee appointed by the Government to Investigate the Finances of British Columbia*, popularly known as the Kidd Report, executive papers (King's Printer, 1932).

29. Blake et al. remind us in *Two Political Worlds* that crude caricatures of the Social Credit and NDP often mask important assumptions shared by supporters of each party.

30. Quoted in Martin Robin, *Pillars of Profit: The Company Province, 1934–1972* (Toronto, 1973), p. 76.

31. Ibid., p. 76.

32. Donald Alpen, "The effects of coalition government on party structure: the case of the Conservative party in B.C.," *B.C. Studies*, vol. 33, spring, 1977, p. 43. Alpen quotes one Conservative, upset at not receiving enough patronage, demanding the party withdraw from the coalition. Another demanded that a joint Liberal-Conservative committee be established for dispensing patronage. I am grateful to Professor Donald Blake for bringing this to my attention.

33. Ibid., p. 91.

34. The story of how Bennett founded and nurtured Social Credit, turning it into the province's natural governing party, can be found in Robin, op. cit., who offers a highly jaundiced view; in David Mitchell, *W.A.C. Bennett and the Rise of British Columbia* (Vancouver, 1983), chapters 5 and 6; H.F. Angus, "The British Columbia election, June 1952," *CJEPS*, 18, 1952. Also David Elkins, "Politics makes strange bedfellows: The BC party system in the 1952 and 1953 provincial elections," *B.C. Studies*, 30, summer, 1976.

35. Mitchell, op. cit., p. 364.

36. The best description of the Sommers affairs is found in Mitchell, op. cit., chapter 7, "A definite indication of wrongdoing," pp. 211–254.

37. Ibid., pp. 373–374.

38. *The Vancouver Sun*, May 22, 1969.

CHAPTER 16   LAWYERS, SENATORS . . .

1. The information about standing agents in this section is based on lists for 1979, 1980 and 1984 provided to me by the access-to-information co-ordinator of the department of justice, whose efficiency and help I acknowledge.

2. Quoted in *The Montreal Gazette*, "Tories sack 500 in patronage purge," November 14, 1985.

3. Macdonald papers, E. Stonehouse to Macdonald, October 3, 1883, PAC file 26a, vol. 23.

4. I am grateful to Professor Peter Waite for his analysis of Macdonald's approach to judicial appointments in a draft copy of his essay on Macdonald for *The Dictionary of Canadian Biography*, vol. 12. This quote is taken from Waite's essay, written with his customary *élan* and wisdom.

5. James Snell and Frederick Vaughan, *The Supreme Court of Canada: History of the Institution* (Toronto, 1985).

6. Peter Russell, *The Judiciary in Canada: Third Branch of Government* (Toronto, 1987). I am grateful to Professor Russell for a draft copy of chapter 5, months before publication. It contains the most complete summary of patronage and the judiciary.

7. *Report of the Canadian Bar Association Committee on the Appointment of Judges in Canada* (Ottawa, The Canadian Bar Foundation, 1985).

8. For a list of these judges and their backgrounds, see "Political backgrounds of Saskatchewan judges listed," *Regina Leader-Post*, August 12, 1985.

9. William J. Klein, "Judicial recruitment in Manitoba, Ontario and Quebec, 1905–1970," Ph.D. Thesis, University of Toronto, 1975, p. 282.

10. Cited in Russell, op. cit., p. 114.

11. Ibid., p. 115.

12. Quoted in John Saywell, *The Office of Lieutenant-Governor* (Toronto, 1957), p. 232. This is the definitive study of the office and its occupants to 1955.

13. Ibid., p. 22.

14. This figure was compiled by me from a list of lieutenant-governors appointed since 1950.

CHAPTER 17   THE SENATE

1. Robert Mackay, *The Unreformed Senate of Canada,* revised edition (Toronto, 1963), p. 37.

2. *Parliamentary debates on subject of the Confederation of the British North American provinces* (Quebec, 1865), p. 36.

3. Ibid., p. 89.

4. Ibid., p. 331.

5. Ibid., p. 513.

6. Parliamentary guide, 1881.

7. Some of the information about individual senators in this chapter is drawn from a data base of all senators, compiled for me by a researcher, Alastair Sweeney. Anyone with a taste for the esoteric is welcome to it.

8. Macdonald papers, PAC vol. 17, 6095–6096.

9. Macdonald papers, PAC vol. 16, 5957–5959.

10. Macdonald papers, PAC vol. 16, 5804–5809.

11. House of Commons debates, 1906, p. 2304, cited in Guy Chauvin, "The Senate of Canada with particular reference to the Diefenbaker years," M.A. Thesis, Dalhousie University, 1966, p. 71. See also Mackay, op. cit., p. 143.

12. Quoted in F.A. Kunz, *The Modern Senate of Canada* (Toronto, 1965), p. 35.

13. Ibid., p. 30.

14. King to Alexander Bruce, King papers, PAC C-2243, 60324–60325. Note that all subsequent PAC files refer to the King papers.

15. King to W.H. Irvine, PAC C-2264, 86064.

16. Hartley Dewart to King, C-2244, 61463–61467.

17. W.E. Foster to King, PAC C-2252, 73050.

18. W.D. Euler to King, PAC C-2244, 61758.

19. Onésiphore Turgeon to King, PAC C-2250, 69618.

20. King's correspondence with W.O. Sealey and W.H. Whitaker, PAC C-2250, 69910–69915.

21. Arthur Hardy to King, PAC C-2245, 63006.

22. Arthur Hardy to King, PAC C-2245, 63009.

23. S.W. Jacob to King, PAC C-2245, 63595.

24. Azilda Dumais to King, PAC C-2317, 147646.

25. Kuntz, op. cit., pp. 42–43.

26. Ibid., p. 45.

27. A.E. MacLean to King, PAC C-2267, 88594.

28. William Varrily et al. to King, PAC C-2284, 107625.

29. King to W.J. Jaffray, PAC C-2318, 149580.

30. To wit, King to D.E. Riley, PAC C-2292, 116569.

31. Judith Barbara Ward, "Federal-provincial relations within the Liberal party of British Columbia," M.A. Thesis, University of British Columbia, 1966, p. 67.

32. Irene McEwen, "The Senate Appointments of R.B. Bennett: 1930–1935," M.A. Thesis, University of British Columbia, 1978, p. 1.

34. Kuntz, op. cit. See Table on p. 64. The comparison with prime ministers before King is from my own data base.

35. Judy LaMarsh, *Memoirs of a Bird in a Gilded Cage* (Toronto, 1968), p. 291.

36. Christina McCall-Newman provides a splendid list of Liberal senators in the Trudeau era, complete with calculations of pensions and the total value of the senatorship at retirement. See her *Grits, An Intimate Portrait of the Liberal Party* (Toronto, 1982), pp. 407–427.

37. One veteran *Créditiste* MP, Charles Gauthier, claimed he had been approached by the Liberals before each of his election campaigns with various offers, including a Senate seat.

38. McCall-Newman, op. cit., p. 296.

39. Friends would include Carl Goldenberg, a law professor and constitutional adviser to Trudeau; Jacques Hébert, one of Trudeau's oldest friends; Renaude Lapointe, *La Presse* editorialist who wrote glowingly of Trudeau; Jean Le Moyne, essayist, journalist and Trudeau speechwriter; Dalia Wood, president of Trudeau's riding association.

40. See William Kitchen, "The abolition of upper chambers," in Donald Rowat (ed.), *Provincial Government and Politics* (Carleton University, 1973). See also, Edmond Orban, "*La fin du bicaméralisme au Québec,*" *CJPS*, vol. 2, no. 3, September 1969.

CHAPTER 18   TRUDEAU

1. Quoted in Christina McCall-Newman, *Grits, An Intimate Portrait of the Liberal Party* (Toronto, 1982), p. 89.

2. Quotes from *The Ottawa Journal, The Ottawa Citizen, The Halifax Chronicle-Herald*, October 26, 1968.

3. The best description of this effort is found in David Smith, *The Regional Decline of a National Party, Liberals on the Prairies* (Toronto, 1981). See especially ch. 4, which analyses the tensions between the Davey/Gordon group and Liberals in Alberta, Saskatchewan and Manitoba.

4. Smith, op. cit., gives a superb description of participatory democracy in ch. 5, especially pp. 72–83. See also McCall-Newman, op. cit., pp. 120–123.

5. *To Know and Be Known, The Report of the Task Force on Government Information*, vol. 1 (Queen's Printer, 1969).

6. David Stewart-Patterson, *Post-Mortem: Why Canada's Mail Won't Move* (Toronto, 1987). See chapters 2 and 3.

7. *The Globe and Mail* undertook an extensive investigation into Trudeau patronage appointments in May and June of 1977, attempting to trace the background of several hundred defeated Liberal candidates in federal and provincial elections. The list, with one-paragraph descriptions of each person, filled one and a half pages in the newspaper. Nothing I have seen provides more sober evidence of the extent of Liberal party patronage, but even this story could not trace more than a fraction of the order-in-council appointments. See Hugh Winsor and Dorothy Lipovenko, "Patronage, The Trudeau Government Says Thanks," *The Globe and Mail*, June 13, 1977.

8. P.E. Trudeau, "Some obstacles to democracy in Quebec," in *Federalism and the French Canadians* (Toronto, 1967), p. 107.

9. Ibid., p. 109.

10. See various references in the essays of *Federalism*.

11. Richard Johnston, *Public Opinion and Public Policy in Canada*, study no. 35, Royal Commission on the Economic Union and Development Prospects for Canada. See ch. 2.

12. *Le Devoir*, August 14–16, 1984.

13. *Report of the Auditor-General of Canada, 1986*, paragraphs 6.91–6.96.

14. Important analyses of the strains in contemporary patronage are provided by Reginald Whitaker, "Between patronage and bureaucracy: democratic politics in transition," and by S.J.R. Noel, "Dividing the spoils: the old and new rules of patronage in Canadian politics," in *JCS*, vol. 22, no. 2, summer, 1987.

15. For an excellent analysis of the consequences of the Act, see W.T. Stanbury, "The mother's milk of politics: political contributions to federal parties in Canada, 1974–1984," *CJPS*, vol. xix, no. 4, December 1986, pp. 795–821. Stanbury's extensive data illustrates the substantial increase in the number of small contributors.

APPENDIX

National Advisory Committee (NAC), December, 1987

Marjory LeBreton, deputy chief-of-staff, Prime Minister's Office

Bernard Roy, principal secretary, PMO

David Angus, chairman, PC Canada Fund

Senator Norman Atkins, PC campaign director

Gerry St.-Germain, MP, PC caucus chairman

Sam Wakim, Toronto lawyer, Mulroney friend

Bill Jarvis, PC Party national president

Judith Hendin, Ottawa lawyer, PC women's commission

Jean-Carol Pelletier, PC national director

Ron Doering, chief-of-staff to Secretary of State

Elizabeth Roscoe, chief-of-staff to Minister of State, Status of Women

Provincial Advisory Committees (PACs)

Newfoundland

John Lundrigan, St. John's, chairman
Daniel Williams, St. John's

Mike Monaghan, Corner Brook
Senator William Doody
James Greene, St. John's
Morrissey Johnson, MP
John Crosbie, Minister of Transport

Prince Edward Island

Greg Deighan, Summerside
Thomas McMillan, Minister of the Environment
Any PC MP from Prince Edward Island

Nova Scotia

Joe Stewart, New Glasgow, chairman
Fred Dickson, Halifax
David Read, Halifax
Michael Power, Bridgewater
Lloyd Crouse, MP
William Mansen, Sydney River
Elmer MacKay, Minister of National Revenue

New Brunswick

Aubrey Brown, Dalhousie, chairman
Percy Mockler, Saint Leonard
David Smith, Moncton
Janice Clarke, Sussex

Ted Flemming, Rothesay
Arnold Roach, Newcastle
Fernard Lanteigne, Caraquet
Dennis Cochrane, MP
Gerald Merrithew, Minister of State
  (Forestry and Mines)

Quebec

Fernand Roberge, Montreal, chairman
Senator Michel Cogger
Marc Dorion, Quebec
Brian Gallery, Westmount
Mario Beaulieu, Montreal
Pierre-Claude Nolin, Montreal
Jean Dugré, Montreal
Gilles Bernier, MP
Louise Bertrand, Montreal
Pierre Cadieux, Minister of Labor
Marcel Masse, Minister of Energy,
  Mines and Resources

Ontario

Michael Meighen, Toronto, chairman
Ruth Grant, Toronto
Donald Guthrie, Toronto
Ian Hollingsworth, Sault Ste. Marie
Bill McAleer, Toronto
Paul Mitchell, Waterloo
Ken Binks, Ottawa
Allan Schwartz, Toronto
Peter Rekai, Toronto
Jack Ellis, MP
John McDermid, MP
Michael Wilson, Minister of Finance
John Wise, Minister of Agriculture
Paul McCrossan, MP (alternate)
David Daubney, MP (alternate)

Manitoba

Arni Thorsteinson, Winnipeg,
  chariman
Susan Hoplock, Winnipeg
Duncan Jessiman, Winnipeg
Annis Shaddy, Winnipeg
Thomas Goodman, Stonewall

Craig Stewart, Minnedosa
Robert Kozminski, Winnipeg
Leo Duguay, MP
Jake Epp, Minister of Health and
  Welfare

Saskatchewan

William Elliott, Regina, chairman
Alf Bentley, Saskatoon
Peter Lysak, Regina
Herb Pinder Jr., Saskatoon
R. Boyd Robertson, Regina
Gordon McMillan, Swift Current
Helen Swan, Saskatoon
Betty Harris, Codette
Len Gustafson, MP
William McKnight, Minister of Indian
  Affairs and Northern Development

Alberta

Peter Bawden, Calgary, chairman
Bob Dowling, Edmonton
Roy Deyell, Calgary
Susan Green, Edmonton
Cathy Fraser, Edmonton
Carol Kraychy, Calgary
Stan Schellenberger, MP
Don Mazankowski, Deputy Prime
  Minister

British Columbia

James Macaulay, Vancouver, chairman
Jacob Brouwer, Vancouver
J. Gavin Connell, Vancouver
Malcolm Wickson, Vancouver
Jim Doak, Kelowna
Michael Donison, Victoria
Lyall Knott, Vancouver
Alayne McFetridge, Prince George
Floyd Murphy, Vancouver
Ray Castelli, Vancouver
Ian Reid, Vancouver
Pat Crofton, MP
Pat Carney, Minister of International
  Trade

INDEX

Abbott, Douglas, 144,305
Aberdeen, Lord, 106
Aberhart, William, 257, 277, 312
Advertising techniques, and politics, 140–44; at federal level, 336; Manitoba, 254
Ahearn, Frank, 235
Aird, John, 310
Alberta and Great Western Railway affair, 275
Alexander, Lincoln, 309
Allan, Sir Hugh, 89, 92
Anderson, James T.M., 262–63, 267
Andras, Robert, 337
Anne, Queen, 53
Appointments: Alberta, 278–9; judicial, 300–1, 304–7; of lieutenant–governor, 309–10; Macdonald, Sir John A., and, 79; Manitoba, 254; by Mulroney, 24–26, 31, 360; Ontario, by Frank Miller, 218–19; Ontario, by William Davis, 238; Queen's Counsels (QCs), 303; Saskatchewan, 268, 270; Senate See under names of prime ministers; Trudeau's final round of, 352–53
Argue, Hazen, 326
Armour, Judge John Douglas, 84
Armstrong, Charles, 199
Armstrong, Ernest, 175
Ashworth, Gordon, 219

Ashworth, Heather, 219
Atkins, Norman, 18, 22, 142, 238, 369
Atkinson, Ewart, 186–87, 193
Atkinson, Francis, 185–86, 188–90, 193
Atkinson, Joe, 142
Aucoin, Peter, 182
Axworthy, Lloyd, 347, 349
Aylesworth, Allan, 112

Bagot, Charles, 65
Baie des Chaleurs Railway scandal, 199–200
Baillie, Thomas, 52–53
Baldwin, Robert (father), 35, 46, 50, 56–57, 60–61, 70
Baldwin, Robert (son), 46
Barrett, Dave, 299
Barrow, Senator Irvine, 183–84
Barry, Judge Paul, 187, 189–90
Basford, Ron, 302
Baxter, John, 188
Bawden, Peter, 18
Bazin, Jean, 30
Beauharnois campaign contribution scandal, 27, 92, 133, 136–38, 349
Beauregard, Elie, 135
Bell, John H., 164
Bennett, Bill, 293, 299
Bennett, R.B., 93, 140, 218, 232, 307, 319, 363; Senate appointments, 323–24

Bennett, W.A.C., 282, 286, 295–97, 312
Benson, Edgar, 335
Bernier, Gilles, 302
Biggs, F.C., 229
Bissonnette, André, 366
Black, Conrad, 362
Blackmail, in Quebec, 196, 209
Blair, Andrew, 112
Blake, Edward, 66, 99, 101, 115
Blakeney, Allan, 269, 312
Blouin, Pierre, 366
Bond Head, Sir Francis, 57
Bonner, Robert, 298
Borden, Robert, 118, 123, 125–30, 246–
47, 318–19, 323
Borden, Sir Frederick, 118
Bottle exchanges, 11, 181, 212
Bouchard, Jacques, 344
Bouchard, Lucien, 364
Bourassa, Henri, 117, 202, 204–5
Bourassa, Robert, 195–96, 210, 215–16
Bouthillier, Guy, 308
Bowell, Mackenzie, 323
Bowser, William, 386–87, 290–92, 294,
299
Boza, Peter, 327
Bracken, John, 240–41, 251–53
Bradley, Fred, 273, 280
Bradshaw, J.E., 261
Brewster, Harlan Carey, 288–90, 299
Bribery, 10, 83–84, 202, 298, 375
Broadbent, Ed, 22
Brokerage politics, 132–33
Brower, C.A., 226
Brown, George, 70, 104, 314
Browne, William J., 149–50
Brownlee, John Edward, 277
Bryce, James, 121
Buchanan, John, 169, 172, 185
Buck, Frank, 270
Buller, Charles, 46
Bulyea, George H.V., 274–75
Burney, Derek, 376
Bussières, Pierre, 341, 343

Cadieux, Leo, 335
Calder, James, 131, 258, 260, 319
Cameron, Don, 168–70, 174, 185
Cameron, Douglas, 248, 253
Camp, Dalton, 18, 142, 254, 376
Campbell, Alex, 148–49
Campbell, Alexander, 82–83
Campbell, Thane, 166
Canadian Pacific Scandal, 14, 21, 27, 69,
81, 89, 92–93, 101, 137, 199, 349
Cardin, P.J.A., 135
Carleton, Caleb, 163

Caron, Sir A.P., 91
Cartier, George–Etienne, 66, 68, 71, 78,
89, 93, 106
Carvell, Frank, 131
Cartwright, Richard, 66, 79–80, 84, 96,
110, 112, 119, 318
Cauchon, Joseph, 88–89
CF-18 contract, 375
Chantage, le. See Blackmail
Chapleau, Joseph-Adolphe, 78, 109
Chrétien, Jean, 341, 343, 352
Christie, David, 105
Christie, Gayle, 360
Civil List, 41–42, 45, 48, 53
Civil service: Alberta, 275; Borden reforms
of, 127; British Columbia, 288–89, 295;
Civil Service Act of 1917, 127–29, 131,
134; commission (Laurier), 130;
Mulroney and, 362; investigations of,
116; Laurier reforms of, 117;
Macdonald, Sir John A. and, 79;
Manitoba, 249; New Brunswick, 191,
194; Newfoundland, 147–48, 160;
Nova Scotia, 176–77, 179; Ontario,
219, 234; and patronage (1877), 80–81;
and new forms of patronage, 144–45;
Prince Edward Island, 165–66; Quebec,
201, 207, 209, 213; Saskatchewan,
259–60, 262–65, 268, 270; Sifton,
Clifford, and, 114, 116, 118
Clark, Edmund, 362
Clark, Joe, 8, 18–20, 302, 304, 309, 327–
28, 355–57, 362–63, 365, 367–69
Claxton, Brian Brooke, 133, 143
Coaker, William, 152
Cockfield, Brown (ad agency), 143–44
Cody, Don, 270
Colborne, Sir John, 43–44
Coldwell, M.J., 262
Colebrook, Sir William, 54
Conflict of interest, 370–71
Contract levy system, 140
Cook, Eric, 326
Cook, Watson, 184
Cools, Anne, 327
Corruption: definition of, 10; patronage,
compared to, 10–11
Côté, Jean-Pierre, 335
Coté, Michel, 366
Country, forces of (hereditary privilege),
37
Court, forces of (strong central authority),
37, 64
Craig, Sir James Henry, 40–42, 47, 57–58
Crerar, T.A., 320
Croll, David, 321
Crosbie, John, 20, 157, 309, 363

Crosbie, Sir John, 149
Crossman, Richard, 267
Crowe, Sanford, 319
Cullen, Bud, 306
Customs scandal of 1926, 133

Dafoe, John, 100, 115, 142
Dalhousie, Governor, 57–58
Dandurand, Raoul, 318, 322
Dansereau, Arthur "Boss", 109–10, 115
Davey, Keith, 22–23, 29, 142, 318, 326, 333–34
Davis, William, 217, 237–38, 327
Dawson, R. MacGregor, 179
De Bané, Pierre, 341, 352, 355
Dennis, W.H., 324
de Rappard, George, 273
Devine, Grant, 18, 255, 270, 306
Dickie, C.H., 292
Diefenbaker, John, 18, 149, 324, 350, 356, 363; Senate appointments by, 325–26
Dobell, R.R., 111
Dombowski, David, 270
Donnelly, Tom, 273
Dorion, Antoine-Aimé, 105
Doucet, Fred, 24
Doucet, Gerry, 367
Doucette, George, 237
Douglas, T.C. (Tommy), 256, 264–69, 312
Dowling, Bob, 273, 279
Doyle, John, C., 156
Drapeau, Jean, 8, 363
Drapeau, Michel, 341
Draper, William, 62, 72
Drew, George, 237, 312
Drury, Ernest Charles, 228–30
Dufferin, Lord, 73
Dumais, Azilda, 322
Dunham, Aileen, 44
Dunkin, Christopher, 315
Dunning, Charles A., 258
Duplessis, Maurice, 28, 206–11, 214, 313, 338–39, 356
Durham, Lord, Report of, 43–44, 46–47, 54, 56, 59
Dutton, Joe, 273, 280
Dyer, David, 26, 29, 32–33

Eaton, Jim, 269
Eder, Linda, 280
Education, politicization of in Quebec, 205
Edy, Carl, 266
Election financing. See political fund-raising

Electoral abuses: Lower Canada, 58–59; Prince Edward Island, 166; Quebec, 201–2, 210, 213; See also Telegraphing; Minnie M affair
Elgin, Lord, 62–63
Elliott, George, 142
Emmerson, Henry R., 118
Epp, Jake, 375
Executive Consultants Limited, 367
Executive federalism, 313

Fairweather, Gordon, 191–92
Fallis, Iva Campbell, 324
Family Compact, 41, 43, 47, 52, 60, 71
Farquharson, Donald, 161–62
Farran, Roy, 279
Favreau, Guy, 340
Ferguson, George Howard, 227–31
Fielding, William S., 112, 174, 313
Fisher, Sydney, 111
Flemming, Hugh John, 193
Flemming, James Kidd, 193
Fleming, Sir Sanford, 69
Flynn, Bernard, 309
Forke, Robert, 320
Forsey, Eugene, 266, 327, 353
Foster, Arthur, 126
Foster, Jim, 279
Foster, Sir George, 126
Fox, Francis, 340
Fox, Marie-Hélène, 341
Fox, William, 368
Francis, Lloyd, 359
Frost, Leslie, 237
Fulton, Davie, 18

Gaglardi, "Flying Phil", 298–99
Galt, Alexander, 68
Gamey, Robert, 225
Gardiner, James Garfield (Jimmy), 133–34, 139, 236, 258, 260, 262–63, 347–48
Garland, William, 126
Garson, Stuart, 253
Gartner, Gerry, 270
Garvie, Lawrence, 188
Geoffrion, L.P., 202
Gérin, Claude, 309
Gerrymandering, 178, 225, 243
Getty, Don, 273, 279–81
Ghitter, Ron, 273, 280
Ghiz, Joe, 165
Giguère, Louis (Bob), 326, 335
Gladstone, James, 325
Glenelg, Lord, 53
Goar, Carol, 361
Godbout, Joseph-Adélard, 206, 209

Goldenberg, Irving, 307
Goldfarb, Martin, 21
Gordon, Walter, 333–34
Gosford, Lord, 57
Gouin, Jean-Lomer, 115, 204
Government Consultants Limited, 159
Grafftey, Heward, 328
Grafstein, Jerry, 142
Grant, J. A., 316
Gravel, Michel, 365
Gray, Wick, 298
Greenfield, Herbert, 276
Greenway, Thomas, 243–45
Grey, Earl, 55, 62
Grossart, Allister, 142, 325
Gunderson, Einar, 299

Haliburton, Thomas, 50
Harder, Peter, 34
Hardy, Alfred, 212
Hardy, Arthur, 224, 321
Harmer, William, 319
Harper, Elijah, 255
Hart, John, 295, 323
Hart, Stanley, 362
Harvey, Sir John, 54
Hastings, Earl, 326
Hatfield, P.L., 322
Hatfield, Richard, 18, 138, 185–89, 192, 194
Haultain, F.W.G., 255
Haydon, Andrew, 136–37, 322
Hazen, J.D., 130
Head, Sir Edmund Walker, 54–55
Hearst, William, 227
Henry, George, 232
Hepburn, Mitchell, 133, 218, 230, 232–33, 235–37, 312
Highways. See Roads
Hill, George, 271, 307
Hincks, Francis, 68
Hinman, E.W., 278
Hohol, Bert, 279
Holmes, Simon, 173
Holton, Luther, 68, 78–79
Hooke, A.E., 278
Horner, Hugh, 279
Houde, Camillien, 202
Howe, Clarence Decatur (C.D.), 133–34, 139–40
Howe, Joseph, 48, 50, 62, 74–75, 171–72, 315, 340
Howland, W.P., 71
Hughes, Sam, 125–26
Hunley, Helen, 279
Hunt, Pat, 171, 174, 185
Hutchinson, Bruce, 295

Hutton, Joe, 279
Hyman, Charles, 118

Iacobucci, Frank, 362
Ievers, Florence, 341
Ilsley, James Lorimer, 133
Irvine, Olive, 325

Jackson, Andrew, 103
Jackson, Ernie, 237
Jacob, S.W., 321
Jamieson, David, 231
Jamieson, Don, 351
Johnson, Daniel, 214, 356
Johnston, Merv, 270
Jones, Alfred, 104

Keith, Don, 270
Kelly, Thomas, 247–49
Kelly, William, 327
Kent, Tom, 342
Kickbacks: in Nova Scotia, 183–84; Quebec (les Ristournes), 200, 203, 209, 215, 365
Kidd, Bob, 142–43
Kidd, George, 293
Kierans, Eric, 336–37, 348
King, Mackenzie, 7, 13–14, 27–28, 92, 123, 132–45, 175, 230, 251–52, 319, 336, 340, 347, 363, 368–69; Beauharnois scandal and, 137; Mitchell Hepburn, feud with, 235–37; Senate and, 320–23
Kinnear, Mary, 326
Klein, Will, 18
Klein, W., 308
Klotz, Otto, 316
Kolber, Leo, 328
Kramer, Eiling, 270
Kyte, George, 322

Lafond, Paul, 326
LaFontaine, Louis-Hippolyte, 50, 57, 60–63, 70–71, 95, 197, 210
Lafontaine, Richard, 341
Laird, David, 105
Lalonde, Marc, 29, 309, 328, 341, 344, 352
Lamarsh, Judy, 326
Lambert, Adrien, 328
Lambert, Norman, 138, 140, 322
Lang, Otto, 306, 335, 337, 348–49
Langelier, François, 109
Langevin, Hector-Louis, 78, 88–91, 110
Lapointe, Ernest, 133, 135, 332, 340
Laporte, Pierre, 209 n., 215
LaPrade affair, 342–43

Larkin, Peter, 138
LaSalle, Roch, 365
Laurier, Sir Wilfrid, 7, 13, 27, 66, 98–
  123, 127, 133, 150, 174, 204, 224,
  244–45, 248, 273–74, 309–10, 317–
  18, 332, 368; civil service reform, 116–
  19; patronage system, 107; on public
  opinion and corruption, 199; Senate
  and, 317–18
LaBreton, Marjory, 362, 376–77
Legal patronage, 301–3
Leier, Terry, 271
Leitch, Merv, 279
LeMessurier, Mary, 273
Lesage, J.A., 322
Lesage, Jean, 196, 210–11, 213
Lessard, Marcel, 342
Lévesque, René, 195–96, 211, 313
Lewis, Eric, 181
Lewis, Stephen, 359
Lewry, Louis, 269
Leys, Colin, 267
Liepert, Ron, 273, 280
Lippman, Walter, 15
Lipset, Seymour Martin, 267
Liquor: bootlegging in Newfoundland,
  148–49; British Columbia, 286, 289,
  295; kickbacks in Nova Scotia, 180,
  182–83; leasing practices in
  Newfoundland, Joey Smallwood and,
  156–57; Ontario, 219, 223–24, 227,
  231–32, 234; Quebec, 203–4;
  Saskatchewan, 261; See also Treating
Lobbyists, federal, 367–69
Logrolling, 53
Lougheed, Peter, 272–73, 278, 280, 312
Lucas, Pierrette, 363
Lundrigan, Arthur, 155
Lundrigan, John, 18, 33
Lyon, Sterling, 254

MacAdam, Patrick, 363
Macaulay, Jim, 8, 32, 34
Macdonald, Angus L., 180
MacDonald, Finlay, 18, 24–25, 29–34
Macdonald, Hugh John, 245
Macdonald, John Sandfield, 222
Macdonald, John A., 324
Macdonald, Sir John A., 7, 13, 19, 21,
  26–27, 31, 65–97, 100, 102–5, 107,
  120–21, 133, 137–38, 142, 150, 169,
  172, 199, 221, 231, 243–44, 263, 284,
  303–5, 309, 312–17, 321, 332, 340,
  346, 363, 365, 368, 377; disallowance
  policy of, 243; franchise laws and, 84–
  85; Oliver Mowat, struggle with, 220–
  24; party building by, 72–73; political

genuis of, 66; Senate and, 312–17
Macdonald, M.A., 288
MacEachen, Allan J., 169, 351
MacFadden, Charles, 183–84
MacGuigan, Mark, 306
Machum, Lawrence, 186–89
Mackasey, Bryce, 21–22, 352, 358
Mackenzie, Alexander, 13, 66–67, 99,
  101–6, 317, 328
Mackenzie, William Lyon, 45, 50
MacLaren's (ad agency), 143–44
MacLean, Angus, 165
MacMillan, H.R., 292
MacLean, A.E., 322
Maclean, A.K., 131
MacLellan, J.F., 178
MacNab, Sir Allan Napier, 68
Mahoney, Judge John W., 158–59
Maitland, Sir Peregrine, 43–44
Malouin, Albert, 106
Manitoba Legislative Buildings scandal,
  242, 247–48
Manning, Ernest, 278, 335
Marchand, Jean, 340–42
Market researchers, 141
Marshall, William, 158
Martin, Joseph, 245
Martin, Paul, 335
Martin, William M., 258–59, 261, 312
Martineau, Gérald, 212
Massey, Vincent, 138, 322
Mathers, Chief Justice T.G., 248
Matthews, Ken, 18
Maxwell, Judith, 362
Mazankowski, Don, 362, 368, 376
McBride, Sir Richard, 129, 285–88, 294,
  299, 312
McClung, Nellie, 247
McCullagh, George, 234
McDougald, W. L., 136–37
McGee, Thomas D'Arcy, 77
McGrath, James, 309
McGreevy, Robert, 90
McGreevy Scandal. See Parliament
  Buildings Scandal
McGreevy, Thomas, 88–91
McGuigan, Joseph, 188
McInnis, Tom, 171, 315
McIntyre, J.P. "Big Jim", 164
McKenna, Frank, 160, 185, 190–91, 194
McKibben, James, 279–80
McMillan, Charles, 24
McMurray, James, 189
McNaughton, Charles, 217, 237
McRae, Alexander, 290
Meighen, Arthur, 131, 312, 319, 330
Meighen, Michael, 18, 304

Mercier, Honoré, 85, 108, 199–200, 313
Mercure, Maurice, 309
Messer, Jack, 270
Metcalfe, Charles, 57, 59–62
Militia lobby, 124
Miller, Frank, 217, 239
Millibrand, Ralph, 267
Minnie M affair, 224–25
Minto, Lord, 119
Molgat, Gildas, 326
Monet, Jacques, 60
Monroe, Walter, 149
Montesquieu, Charles-Louis, 10
Mooers, Carl, 189
Moog, Gerhard, 238
Moore, Jim, 144
Moores, Frank, 159, 367–68
Morris, Edward, 153
Mousseau, J.O., 200
Mowat, Oliver, 67, 79, 112, 217–18,
   221–24, 231, 243, 312, 318
Mulock, William, 106, 109–10, 112
Mulroney, Brian, 8, 13, 16–24, 28–29,
   50, 139, 159, 175, 218–20, 302, 304,
   307, 329, 346–47, 354–78;
   appointments by, 24–26, 360; cronyism
   of, 220, 368; on Liberal appointments,
   17; network politics of, 358, 376; on
   patronage, 355; Senate appointments
   by, 329
Munro, Bill, 142–43
Munro, John, 337
Murray, Lowell, 187
Murray, Sir George, 130
Murray, George, 174
Musgrave, Anthony, 284

National advisory committee (NAC), 30,
   359, 361
National office, of political parties, 135–36
Near, Harry, 368
Newpapers: British Columbia, 286;
   patronage and, 87–88, 113, 115–16;
   142; political debate, role in, 86;
   Saskatchewan, 258
Neville, William, 367
Nicol, Jacob, 322
Nicol, John, 326, 335
Nielsen, Erik, 24, 30, 33
Nimmo, Bryce, 273, 280
Nolin, Claude, 309
Norquay, John, 242
Norris, Tobias G., 248–50
Northrup, Jeremiah, 315

O'Brien, Michael, 319
Odell, William, 52

O'Donoghue, John, 315–16
Oerlikon affair, 306
Ogilvie, William, 114
O'Hagan, Richard, 142–43
Oliver, John, 288–91
Ouellet, André, 29, 111, 328, 344–45
Ouellet, Gary, 367
Ouellette, Normand, 366

Pacaud, Ernest, 115, 199
Pacific Scandal. *See* Canadian Pacific
   Scandal
Pageau, Huguette, 360
Pageau, Rodrigue, 360
Paide, Helga, 360
Papineau, Louis-Joseph, 42, 46, 50
Paradis, Philippe, 135
Parent, Simon-Napolean, 111, 115, 204
Parker Inquiry, 369–71, 377
Parker, Judge William, 369–71
Parliament Buildings Scandal, 88–89, 110,
   349
Participatory democracy, 332, 334, 337,
   353
Patriotic Potato Gift scandal (New
   Brunswick), 193
Patterson, Walter, 47, 57
Patronage: advertising techniques and,
   140–42; civil service and, 7, 80, 116;
   contract levy system, 140; corruption,
   compared to, 10–11; criminality and, 9;
   definition of, 8; history of, 7; legal, 301;
   military and, 124–25; newspapers and,
   87–88, 113–16, 142; party control of
   (mid-1800s), 63; party discipline and,
   16; party staffs and, 136; patron-client
   relationship, 12; professionals and, 95;
   public works, 88; regional attitudes
   towards, 9; responsible government and,
   7, 35; and television, 350–51; *See also*
   Appointments; Civil service: Liquor;
   Public works contracts; Railways; Roads
Patron-client relationship: dependence, 12;
   discretion, 12–13; reciprocity, 12
Pattullo, Thomas Dufferin, 294–95, 299,
   312
Pawley, Howard, 255
Payne, Bill, 273, 280
Peacock, Fred, 279
Pearson, Lester, 37, 100, 144, 333, 337,
   340, 350, 363; Senate appointments by,
   326
Peckford, Brian, 159, 330
Pederson, Martin, 271
Peterson, David, 218, 224
Pickersgill, Jack, 157
Piggot, Jean, 20

Pinard, Bernard, 211
Pinard, Yvon, 307–7, 341, 344, 352
Pitfield, Michael, 327, 362
Plunkitt, George Washington, 17
Poirier, Pascal, 316
Political fund-raising: federal reforms of,
    348; New Brunswick, 185–88, 191;
    Nova Scotia, 182; Ontario, 238–39;
    Quebec, 195–96, 200
Political ministers, 29
Pollsters, 141–42
Pooley, R.H., 292
Pope, John Henry, 93
Pope, Sir Joseph, 65, 70, 77
Porkbarrelling, 13–14, 33, 110, 121, 332,
    340, 342, 374; Alberta, 274; British
    Columbia, 299; Newfoundland, 155,
    157; Prince Edward Island, 163–64;
    Quebec, 201, 209; Saskatchewan, 260,
    by Pierre Trudeau, 332, 345–46
Power, Senator Charles (Chubby), 135,
    195
Power, Greg, 155
Prévost, Ed, 344
Prevost, George, 42, 57
Prior, Edward Gawler, 285
Proudfoot, William, 319
Proulx, Jérôme, 214
Provincial advisory committees (PACs),
    29–34, 359, 361, 377
Prowse, Harper, 326
Psychic patronage, 335, 374
Public Affairs International, 367
Public works contracts: British Columbia,
    295; federal, 367; federal Parliament
    Buildings, 88–89; New Brunswick, 186;
    Newfoundland, 158–59; Nova Scotia,
    181; Ontario, 229–30; and patronage,
    88; Quebec, 215; Saskatchewan, 264;
    See also Tollgating
Purchasing policies, in Quebec, 212

Quart, Josie, 325
Queen's Counsels (QCs), 303

Rabinovitch, Robert, 362
Railways: Alberta, 275; British Columbia,
    283–84, 286; Grand Trunk, 68–70, 86;
    Manitoba, 242–45; New Brunswick,
    193; Newfoundland, 152–53; Prince
    Edward Island, 163; Quebec, 199
Ralston, Col. J.L., 322
Reagan, Ronald, 376
Reesor, David, 314
Regan, Gerald, 138, 168, 171, 182, 184,
    188
Reid, Sir Robert Gillespie, 152–53

Religion, and patronage: Newfoundland,
    154; Prince Edward Island, 165
Responsible government, 35, 46, 64; New
    Brunswick, 51–56; Nova Scotia, 48–51;
    Prince Edward Island, 47–48
Rhodes, Edgar N., 175–78, 180, 324
Richards, William, 82
Riel, Louis, 97, 198
Ristournes, les. See Kickbacks, in Quebec.
Rizzuto, Pietro, 327
Roads: British Columbia, 289, 295;
    Manitoba, 252; Nova Scotia, 174, 176,
    179, 181; as form of patronage, 8;
    Prince Edward Island, 162, 164;
    Quebec, 209; Saskatchewan, 260
Robarts, John, 237, 312
Roberge, Fernand, 364
Robert, Michel, 303
Robertson, Gideon, 319
Robichaud, Hédard, 335
Robichaud, Louis, 188, 194
Robinson, Chief Justice John Beverly, 44
Roblin, Duff, 253–54
Roblin, Rodmond, 129, 245–48
Rogers, Robert, 126, 131, 245, 249
Ross, George, 224–25
Ross, Jim, 18
Roy, Bernard, 18, 30, 365
Russell, Lord John, 42, 51, 57
Rutherford, Alexander, 274–75
Rykert, J.C., 91

St. Laurent, Louis, 7, 133, 138, 141, 143–
    44, 305, 332, 363; Senate appointments
    by, 325
Salvas, Judge Elie, 212
Sauvé, Paul, 211, 356
Scales, Alan, 18
Schmid, Horst, 273
Schreyer, Edward, 254
Scotton, Cliff, 270
Scott, Walter, 257–58
Sealey, W.O., 321
Senate, 311–25; appointments to, See
    under names of prime ministers
Seymour, Jim, 280
Sharp, Mitchell, 370
Shaw, Walter, 162
Sherbrooke, Sir John, 42
Siegfried, André, 98–99, 121
Sheehan, John, 156
Shortt, Mrs. Adam, 231
Sifton, Clifford, 27, 112–18, 130, 135,
    244–46, 319
Simard, Georges, 203
Simard, Jean-Maurice, 188
Simcoe, Sir John Graves, 43

Simpson, James, 183–84
Skelton, Oscar Douglas, 100, 113
Slaight, Arthur, 235
Smallwood, Joseph, 148–50, 154–57, 307
Smith, B. Frank, 193
Smith, Goldwin, 96, 101–2, 283
Smith, G.I., 327
Sommers, Robert, 298–99
Sparrow, Herbert, 326
Squires, Sir Richard, 148–49
Stanbury, Richard, 29, 326, 334, 337
Standing agents, 301–2
Stanfield, Robert, 18, 174, 179–81, 309, 327, 356
Starr, Michael, 335, 370
Steele, Sam, 114
Stephen, George, 93
Stevens, Sinclair, 369–71, 374
Stewart, Ed, 238
Stonehouse, E., 303
Stratton, James, 225
Strum, Gladys, 264
Sullivan, Dr. Michael, 316
Sweezey, Robert Oliver, 137
Sydenham, Lord, 54, 57–58

Tanneries affair (Montreal), 199
Tarte, Joseph-Israel, 90–91, 110–12, 119–20, 209 n.
Taschereau, Louis-Alexandre, 135, 195, 202–6, 209
Taylor, Alex, 270
Telegraphing, 198, 203, 210
Television, influence on patronage of, 350–52
Thatcher, Colin, 270
Thatcher, Ross, 254, 269, 312, 333, 348
Thibaudeau, Alfred, 317
Thompson, Andrew, 326
Thompson, John, 169–70
Thorsteinson, Arni, 18
Tollgating, 9, 89, 91; New Brunswick, 186, 188; Nova Scotia, 171, 182
Tolmie, Simon Fraser, 291–94, 299
Treating, 8, 82–83, 192
Tremblay, Marcel, 366
Trudeau, Pierre, 8, 23, 28–29, 76, 111, 138, 197, 302, 307, 319, 323, 329, 331–54, 357, 361, 363–64, 368, 370; appointments by, final round of, 352–

53; Charter of Rights and Freedoms, 349; judicial appointments, 306; on patronage, 331; participatory democracy, 332, 334; Senate appointments by, 326–28
Trudel, Gérard, 309
Trynchy, Bill, 273, 280
Tupper, Sir Charles, 74, 106, 363
Tupper, Sir Charles Hibbert, 287
Turgeon, Onésiphore, 321
Turiff, John, 319
Turner, John, 8, 21–23, 30, 307, 323, 352–53, 359

Urban political machines, United States, 10, 32
Urquhart, Earl, 326

Valdamis, Dr. Alfred, 156
Vander Zalm, William, 299
Van Horne, William, 93
Vardy, Oliver, 155
Vautrin, Irenée, 206
Viger, Denis-Benjamin, 62
Vote-buying, 8, 9

Wakefield, Edward, 46
Wakim, Sam, 304
Walker, Thomas Hollis, 148–49
War purchasing commission, 131
Warrack, Allan, 279
Wells, Clyde, 138, 158, 160
Wentworth, John, 36, 49
Whelan, Eugene, 344
Whelan, J.H., 316
White, Peter, 30, 361–62
Whitney, James, 129, 224, 226–27
Willison, Sir John, 100, 115, 223
Wilson, Cairine, 321
Wilson, Michael, 369
Wilson, Sir Daniel, 96
Wolf, Walter, 358
Woodbury, Archibald, 315
Wood, Henry Wise, 204, 257, 272, 277
Woodworth, Allan (Chowder), 186–88
Worley, Ronald, 299

Young, DeCosta, 194
Yuzyk, Paul, 325

12 - anomic

†5 - inflation → reprisals if say no

(q's) Que vs. Man - CF18, Alumax, red

(q) Turner's sappts - agree f weston?

2.5 - a repeat of p. 7 word-for-word

2.55 - Manitoba - NDP supporters out

346 - Que - not loyal cy v money.

347 - Axworthy - old style.

349 - gap between elites + rank + file

351-2 - TV + new ways are ending patronage

(q) - you almost seem nostalgic f good old days

(q) why is p'ge not an issue in '88?

366 - Gravel + Bussonnette dismissed in a para

(q) why didn't you do book on
scandals v Mulroney years?

371 - Parker's sweeping rem's

(q) - why do you call it triad aural + rigid
moralism?

(q) are you too worldly-wise f most ppl
on q v patronage? Is it an evil
to be obliterated or a nec'y evil?

373 - defence v p'ge.

375 - CF18.
(q) why has it died as a pol issue?
no benefit in Que?